Adekeye Adebajo is Director of the Institute for Pan-African Thought and Conversation at the University of Johannesburg, South Africa. He obtained his doctorate from the University of Oxford, where he studied as a Rhodes Scholar. Dr Adebajo has served on United Nations (UN) missions in South Africa, Western Sahara and Iraq, and is the author, co-editor and editor of numerous books including *The Eagle and the Springbok: Essays on Nigeria and South Africa* (2017) and *Thabo Mbeki: Africa's Philosopher-King* (2016).

Kudrat Virk is an independent researcher and consultant based in Cape Town, South Africa. She holds a doctorate in international relations from the University of Oxford. Dr Virk is co-editor of and contributor to several volumes, and her work has also appeared in the journals *Global Responsibility to Protect* and *International Review of the Red Cross*.

FOREIGN POLICY IN POST-APARTHEID SOUTH AFRICA

Security, Diplomacy and Trade

Edited by
ADEKEYE ADEBAJO AND KUDRAT VIRK

I.B. TAURIS
LONDON · NEW YORK

Published in association with the Centre for Conflict Resolution,
Cape Town, South Africa

Published in 2018 by
I.B.Tauris & Co. Ltd
London • New York
www.ibtauris.com

International Library of African Studies 58

ISBN: 978 1 78831 082 6 (HB)
       978 1 78831 083 3 (PB)
eISBN: 978 1 78672 332 1
ePDF: 978 1 78673 332 0

A full CIP record for this book is available from the British Library
A full CIP record is available from the Library of Congress

Library of Congress Catalog Card Number: available

Typeset in Garamond Three by OKS Prepress Services, Chennai, India
Printed and bound by TJ International Ltd. PL28 8RW

CONTENTS

LIST OF ILLUSTRATIONS

Figure

Tables

LIST OF CONTRIBUTORS

Dr Adekeye Adebajo is Director of the Institute for Pan-African Thought and Conversation at the University of Johannesburg, South Africa. Previously, he was Executive Director of the Centre for Conflict Resolution (CCR) in Cape Town. He obtained his doctorate from the University of Oxford in Britain, where he studied as a Rhodes Scholar. Dr Adebajo has served on United Nations (UN) missions in South Africa, Western Sahara and Iraq. He is the author of six books: *The Eagle and the Springbok: Essays on Nigeria and South Africa* (2017); *Thabo Mbeki: Africa's Philosopher-King* (2016); *UN Peacekeeping in Africa: From the Suez Crisis to the Sudan Conflicts* (2012); *The Curse of Berlin: Africa After the Cold War* (2010); *Liberia's Civil War (2002)*; and *Building Peace in West Africa* (2002). He is co-editor or editor of eight books, on managing global conflicts, the UN, the European Union (EU), West African security, South Africa's and Nigeria's foreign policies in Africa and Nobel peace laureates of African descent.

Mr Richard Cawood is Director of Strategy for Ernst & Young, the global professional services firm, in Melbourne, Australia. Previously, he was based in Johannesburg, where he was one of the founders of Ernst & Young's Africa strategy consulting practice in 2012. Mr Cawood works with leadership teams on issues related to growth and innovation, with a particular focus on international business strategy and scenario planning. He has worked across the African continent, including with major South African corporates and multinationals expanding their footprints in Africa. He holds an MBA from the University of Minnesota and a BA in economics and international studies from Macalester College, both in the United States (US).

Dr Devon E.A. Curtis is Senior Lecturer in the Department of Politics and International Studies at the University of Cambridge in Britain, and a Fellow of Emmanuel College. Her main research interests and publications deal with power-sharing and governance arrangements following conflict; UN peacebuilding; non-state armed movements in Africa's Great Lakes region (Burundi, Rwanda and the Democratic Republic of the Congo (DRC)); and critical perspectives on conflict, peacebuilding and development. She is the co-editor of *Peacebuilding, Power and Politics in Africa* (2012). Previously, Dr Curtis worked for the Canadian government and the United Nations Staff College. She has also worked as a consultant for the United Kingdom's (UK) Department for International Development and the Overseas Development Institute; and was a Visiting Senior Adviser at the New York-based International Peace Institute. She has held fellowships at Columbia University and Stanford University.

Ms Nicole Fritz is an independent human rights consultant based in Johannesburg, with a particular interest in the intersection between human rights law and foreign policy. She is the founder of the Johannesburg-based Southern Africa Litigation Centre (SALC) and served as its executive director for ten years. She is an Extraordinary Adjunct Lecturer at the Centre for Human Rights at the University of Pretoria, and the University of the Witwatersrand School of Law in Johannesburg. She previously taught at the Fordham University School of Law in New York. Ms Fritz clerked for Justice Richard Goldstone at South Africa's Constitutional Court. She holds an LL.B from the University of the Witwatersrand, and an LL.M in international legal studies from New York University (NYU). Ms Fritz is a Trustee of the Women's Legal Centre.

Professor Richard Gibb is an Associate of the Brenthurst Foundation in Johannesburg. Previously, he was Provost at Abu Dhabi University and Pro Vice-Chancellor at the University of Plymouth in Britain. He obtained his doctorate from the University of Oxford, before taking up a position at the University of Cape Town. Professor Gibb has an international reputation for his work on regional integration and trading blocs, with a particular focus on Southern Africa. He has published several books and numerous articles on regional trade and regional integration, most recently on the Southern African Customs Union (SACU). He has also worked on the trading regime between the EU and Southern Africa, with detailed studies on the Trade, Development and Cooperation Agreement (TDCA);

the Cotonou Partnership Agreement; and Europe's economic partnership agreements with Africa.

Professor Liu Haifang is Associate Professor in the School of International Studies; and Executive Deputy Director and Secretary-General of the Centre for African Studies, both at China's Peking University. She is also Vice-President of the Chinese Society of African Historical Studies. Previously, she worked at the Institute of West Asian and African Studies, and the Chinese Academy of Social Sciences. She was a visiting scholar at the Institute of African Studies at Carleton University in Canada, and the Institute of Social Studies in The Hague. Professor Liu has published widely, in English and Mandarin, on various aspects of China–Africa relations. She has published in the *Journal of Sustainable Development Law and Policy*, among other outlets. Her research interests include Chinese migrants in Africa; African perceptions of China and Chinese migrants; Chinese aid; Chinese business history in Africa; and African sustainable development studies.

Dr Faizel Ismail is Adjunct Professor in the School of Economics and the Faculty of Law, both at the University of Cape Town. Previously, he served as South Africa's Ambassador to the World Trade Organisation (WTO) from 2010 to 2014. He holds a doctorate in politics from the University of Manchester in Britain; a master's in development studies from the University of Sussex in Britain; and a bachelor's and an LL.B from the University of KwaZulu-Natal, South Africa. Dr Ismail is the author of *Reforming the World Trade Organisation* (2009) and *Mainstreaming Development in the WTO* (2007) and has published over 50 articles, chapters and working papers in international journals and books on issues related to economic development, trade and development. He is Associate Editor of the *Journal of World Trade* and a member of the Practitioner's Advisory Board of the journal *Global Policy*, based at the London School of Economics and Political Science (LSE).

Professor Gilbert M. Khadiagala is Jan Smuts Professor of International Relations at the University of the Witwatersrand in Johannesburg. He has previously taught comparative politics and international relations in Kenya, Canada and the United States. He obtained his doctorate in international studies from the Paul H. Nitze School of Advanced International Studies (SAIS) at the Johns Hopkins University in

Washington, DC. His research focuses on governance, security, leadership and conflict management in Eastern Africa, Southern Africa, the Horn of Africa and the Great Lakes region, and he has published widely on these issues. Professor Khadiagala is the author of *Meddlers or Mediators? African Interveners in Civil Conflicts in Eastern Africa* (2007), and co-author of *Sudan: The Elusive Quest for Peace* (2007). He has also edited or co-edited several volumes, including most recently *War and Peace in Africa's Great Lakes Region* (2017).

Professor Chris Landsberg is South African Research (SARChI) Chair of African Diplomacy and Foreign Policy and Senior Associate at the School of Leadership, both at the University of Johannesburg. Previously, he was Director of the Centre for Policy Studies (CPS) in Johannesburg, and founding Co-Director of the Centre for Africa's International Relations at the University of the Witwatersrand. He obtained his doctorate from the University of Oxford, where he studied as a Rhodes Scholar. Professor Landsberg is the author of *The Diplomacy of Transformation: South African Foreign Policy and Statecraft* (2010) and *The Quiet Diplomacy of Liberation: International Politics and South Africa's Transition* (2004). He is co-editor or editor of eleven volumes, including *Africa Rise Up! Perspectives on African Renewal* (2017); *South African Government and Politics: Coming of Age* (2017), with Suzy Graham; *From the Outside In: Civil Society and South African Foreign Policy* (2017), with Lesley Masters; *South Africa in Africa: The Post-Apartheid Era* (2007), with Adekeye Adebajo and Adebayo Adedeji; and *From Cape to Congo: Southern Africa's Evolving Security Challenges* (2003), with Mwesiga Baregu.

Dr Daniel Large is Assistant Professor at the School of Public Policy at the Central European University in Budapest, Hungary. He is also a Non-Resident Senior Fellow at the China Policy Institute at the University of Nottingham in Britain; and a Fellow of the Rift Valley Institute. His publications include *Sudan Looks East: China, India, and the Politics of Asian Alternatives* (2011), co-edited with Luke Patey; and *China Returns to Africa: A Rising Power and a Continent Embrace* (2008), co-edited with Chris Alden and Ricardo Soares de Oliveira.

Professor Eddy Maloka is Chief Executive Officer of the Secretariat of the African Peer Review Mechanism (APRM). He is also Adjunct Professor at the University of the Witwatersrand School of Governance. Previously, he was Special Adviser to South Africa's Minister of International Relations and Cooperation, Maite Nkoana-Mashabane, and served as South Africa's Special Representative to the Great Lakes Region. He has also been Special Adviser to South Africa's Deputy President, and Adviser to the Secretariat of the New Partnership for Africa's Development (NEPAD). He has served as Chief Executive Officer of the Africa Institute of South Africa (AISA). Professor Maloka obtained his doctorate from the University of Cape Town. He has published widely on aspects relating to the politics, history and development challenges of Africa.

Dr Roland Marchal is Senior Research Fellow at the National Centre for Scientific Research (CNRS), based at the Centre de la Recherches Internationales (CERI), Sciences-Po, in Paris, France. He was Chief Editor of the French academic quarterly *Politique Africaine* from 2002 to 2006. He has conducted research and published widely on the politics of, and conflicts in, the Horn of Africa and Central Africa. Dr Marchal has also worked as a consultant for several governments and international organisations including the World Bank and the European Union. His current research focuses on Somalia, the Central African Republic (CAR), Chad and the Sahel countries, and the policies of great powers in Africa.

Mr Doctor Mashabane is Chief Director: United Nations at South Africa's Department of International Relations and Cooperation (DIRCO) in Tshwane (Pretoria). He was previously South Africa's Deputy Ambassador to the UN from 2010 to 2014, and represented the country during its 2011–2012 tenure as a non-permanent member on the UN Security Council. Mr Mashabane also serves as South Africa's Focal Point for the Responsibility to Protect (R2P) and Commissioner at the African Commission on Nuclear Energy. He holds an LL.M in human rights and democracy in Africa from the University of Pretoria.

Dr Dawn Nagar is Senior Researcher at the Centre for Conflict Resolution in Cape Town, where she works on issues related to African politics; regional security; the political economy of regional integration in Africa; South Africa's foreign policy (mainly economic and security challenges); international organisations; and conflict resolution and mediation. She is co-editor of *Africa and the World: Bilateral and Multilateral International Diplomacy* (2017); *Region-Building in Africa: Political and Economic Challenges* (2016); and *Region-Building in Southern Africa: Progress, Problems and*

Prospects (2012). She holds a doctorate in international relations from the University of the Witwatersrand, and two master's degrees, from the Nelson Mandela University (formerly the University of Port Elizabeth) and the University of Cape Town.

Mr Sagaren Krishna Naidoo is Director of Defence Policy Formulation at South Africa's Department of Defence. From 2011 to 2015, he headed the Secretariat of the Defence Review Committee, which produced the South African Defence Review of 2015. Prior to that, from 2007 to 2010, he was seconded to the Military Veterans Task Team to draft the executive policy for the establishment of South Africa's Department of Military Veterans. Mr Naidoo previously worked as a researcher at the South African Institute of International Affairs (SAIIA) and the Institute for Global Dialogue (IGD), both in South Africa. He holds a master's in international studies from Rhodes University in Grahamstown, South Africa.

Ambassador Mxolisi Nkosi is the Head of Global Governance and Continental Agenda at South Africa's Department of International Relations and Cooperation. Previously, he was South Africa's Ambassador to Belgium and Luxembourg, and Head of Mission to the European Union. Prior to that, he was Head of the Africa Branch at DIRCO. Before joining government, he was a trade union leader and served as Deputy General Secretary of the South African Democratic Teachers Union (SADTU). He represented his union in the Central Executive Committee of the Congress of South African Trade Unions (COSATU). He was also a member of the Gauteng Provincial Executive Committee of the South African Communist Party (SACP). Ambassador Nkosi was a student and youth activist in Soweto, and held several leadership positions in the Azanian Students' Congress (AZASO) and in the South African Students' Congress (SASCO). Trained as a teacher, he holds a master's in international relations and diplomacy from the University of Pretoria.

Professor Georges Nzongola-Ntalaja is Professor of African Studies at the Department of African, African American and Diaspora Studies at the University of North Carolina at Chapel Hill in the United States. He was previously President of the African Studies Association (ASA) and the African Association of Political Science (AAPS). He is the author of several books and numerous articles on African politics, development and conflict issues, including *The Congo from Leopold to Kabila: A People's History* (2002);

Le Mouvement Démocratique au Zaïre, 1956–1996 (1997); *Nation-Building and State Building in Africa* (1993); and *Revolution and Counter-Revolution in Africa* (1987). Professor Nzongola-Ntalaja is the editor of *Conflict in the Horn of Africa* (1991) and *The Crisis in Zaire: Myths and Realities* (1986); and co-editor of *The State and Democracy in Africa* (1997) and *The Oxford Companion to Politics of the World* (first and second editions). He obtained his doctorate from the University of Wisconsin–Madison in the US.

Professor Lloyd M. Sachikonye is Associate Professor at the Centre for Applied Social Sciences (CASS) at the University of Zimbabwe, where he teaches courses on political science and development studies. His research focuses on South Africa–Zimbabwe relations and China–Zimbabwe relations, as well as civil society, democratisation and electoral studies. He obtained his doctorate in political studies in 1989, from the University of Leeds in Britain. Professor Sachikonye has written several books, including *Zimbabwe's Lost Decade: Politics, Development, and Society* (2012) and *Civil Society, Democracy, and the State: Social Movements in Southern Africa* (1995). He was co-editor of the 2013 African Governance Report, produced by the UN Economic Commission for Africa (UNECA). Between 2007 and 2012, he also served as a consultant to the African Union (AU) and UNECA.

Professor Chris Saunders is Emeritus Professor at the University of Cape Town, South Africa. He completed his undergraduate studies there, and his doctorate at the University of Oxford, before returning to teach at the University of Cape Town. Professor Saunders is particularly interested in the recent political history of South Africa and its neighbours, and has written widely on the history and historiography of Southern Africa. He is the author of *The Making of the South African Past* (1988); co-author of *South Africa: A Modern History* (2000); and co-editor of *Southern African Liberation Struggles: New Local, Regional, and Global Perspectives* (2013) as well as *Region-Building in Southern Africa: Progress, Problems and Prospects* (2012).

Professor Jack Spence is Professor of Diplomacy at the Department of War Studies at King's College London. He previously lectured at various universities including the University of Natal, South Africa; University College, Swansea, Wales; and the University of Leicester, England, where he was Head of Department, Pro-Vice Chancellor and Acting Vice-Chancellor between 1973 and 1991. Professor Spence was Director of Studies at the

Royal Institute of International Affairs (Chatham House) from 1991 to 1997, and also served as Academic Adviser to the Royal College of Defence Studies, both in London. Professor Spence is a former Chair of the British International Studies Association; former President of the African Studies Association of the UK; former Chair of the Advisory Board of the London-based David Davies Institute; and former Chair of the Advisory Board of the Association for the Study of Ethnicity and Nationalism at the London School of Economics and Political Science. In 2003 he was awarded an OBE in the Jubilee Honours List.

Dr Rawia Tawfik is Assistant Professor at the Faculty of Economics and Political Science at Cairo University in Egypt. She holds a doctorate in politics from the University of Oxford and a master's in politics from Cairo University. Her research interests include issues around Africa's political economy. She was a visiting research fellow at the South African Institute of International Affairs in Johannesburg, the Africa Institute of South Africa in Tshwane and the German Development Institute (DIE) in Bonn. She has published a number of research papers, book chapters and journal articles on Nile hydro-politics, regional integration in Africa, Egypt's foreign policy towards Africa and conditionality and democratisation in Africa.

Dr Brendan Vickers is Economic Adviser in the Trade, Oceans and Natural Resources Directorate at the Commonwealth Secretariat in London. Previously, he was Head of Research and Policy in the South African Department of Trade and Industry (DTI). Dr Vickers also worked in the non-governmental sector as lecturer, writer, researcher and thought leader, including positions at the Institute for Global Dialogue and the Thabo Mbeki African Leadership Institute. He obtained his doctorate from the University of London as a Commonwealth Scholar. He has published widely on issues of international economic diplomacy, and trade and development. He is the author of *A Handbook on Regional Integration in Africa: Towards Agenda 2063* (2017), and contributed to the 2015 Commonwealth report, *The Commonwealth in the Unfolding Global Trade Landscape: Prospects, Priorities and Perspectives*. Dr Vickers is Visiting Professor in African Diplomacy and Foreign Policy at the University of Johannesburg.

Dr Kudrat Virk is an independent researcher and consultant based in Cape Town, South Africa. She was previously Senior Researcher at the Centre for Conflict Resolution in Cape Town. She holds a doctorate in international relations from the University of Oxford. Most recently, Dr Virk is co-editor of *The Palgrave Handbook of Peacebuilding in Africa* (forthcoming in 2018) and *The ACP Group and the EU Development Partnership: Beyond the North-South Debate* (2017). She has contributed chapters on aspects of India's foreign policy to several volumes. Her work has also appeared in the journals *Global Responsibility to Protect* and *International Review of the Red Cross*. Dr Virk's research interests include the responsibility to protect and humanitarian intervention; international peacekeeping and the protection of civilians; issues related to human rights, peace and security; and emerging powers, in particular the BRICS countries (Brazil, Russia, India, China and South Africa).

Professor Stephen R. Weissman is an independent political scientist and policy analyst. He holds a doctorate from the University of Chicago in the US. Professor Weissman has taught and researched at Fordham University, the Université Libre du Congo, Stanford University and the University of Texas at Dallas. He subsequently served as Staff Director of the US House of Representatives Subcommittee on Africa, Senior Governance Adviser on Africa to the US Agency for International Development and Ford Foundation Education Programme Officer for South Africa and Namibia. He is the author of *A Culture of Deference: Congress's Failure of Leadership in Foreign Policy* (1995) and *American Foreign Policy in the Congo 1960–1964* (1974). Among his writings on international affairs are articles on US and international policies towards South Africa, Zimbabwe, Angola, the Democratic Republic of the Congo, Sudan and Libya.

LIST OF ABBREVIATIONS

ACIRC	African Capacity for Immediate Response to Crises
ACP	African, Caribbean, and Pacific Group of States
AEC	African Economic Community
AEOI	Atomic Energy Organisation of Iran
AfDB	African Development Bank
AFISMA	African-led International Support Mission in Mali
AFRICOM	Africa Command
AGOA	African Growth and Opportunity Act
AISA	Africa Institute of South Africa
AMEC	Afro–Middle East Centre
AMIB	African Union Mission in Burundi
AMIS II	Second African Union Mission in Sudan
AMISOM	African Union Mission in Somalia
AMU	Arab Maghreb Union
ANC	African National Congress
APLA	Azanian People's Liberation Army
APRM	African Peer Review Mechanism
ARF	African Renaissance Fund
ASF	African Standby Force
ASGISA	Accelerated and Shared Growth Initiative for South Africa
AU	African Union
AUHIP	African Union High-Level Implementation Panel for Sudan
AUHPD	African Union High-Level Panel on Darfur
AUSTF	African Union Special Task Force in Burundi

BASIC	Brazil, South Africa, India, and China
BDF	Bophuthatswana Defence Force
BEE	Black Economic Empowerment
BIC	Brazil, India, and China
BLNS	Botswana, Lesotho, Namibia, and Swaziland
BLS	Botswana, Lesotho, and Swaziland
BNC	Bi-National Commission (South Africa–China)
BRIC	Brazil, Russia, India, and China
BRICS	Brazil, Russia, India, China, and South Africa
CADFund	China–Africa Development Fund (also CADF)
CAR	Central African Republic
CARICOM	Caribbean Community
CARIFORUM	Forum of the Caribbean Group of ACP States
CBC	Congressional Black Caucus
CBS	citrus black spot
CCM	Chama Cha Mapinduzi (Tanzania)
CCR	Centre for Conflict Resolution (South Africa)
CDF	Ciskei Defence Force
CET	common external tariff
CFSP	Common Foreign and Security Policy (European Union)
CIA	Central Intelligence Agency (US)
CIAT	International Committee to Accompany the Transition
CITIC	China International Trust and Investment Corporation Group
CNDD-FDD	National Council for the Defence of Democracy – Forces for the Defence of Democracy (Burundi)
CNDP	National Congress for the Defence of the People (DRC)
CNKI	Chinese Network of Knowledge Infrastructure
COMESA	Common Market for Eastern and Southern Africa
CONSAS	Constellation of Southern African States
COP	Conference of the Parties
COSATU	Congress of South African Trade Unions
CPA	Comprehensive Peace Agreement (Sudan–South Sudan)
CPA	Cotonou Partnership Agreement
CRP	Common Revenue Pool
CSSDCA	Conference on Security, Stability, Development, and Cooperation in Africa
CTDSS	Committee on Trade and Development Special Session (WTO)

CUTS	Consumer Unit and Trust Society
DBSA	Development Bank of Southern Africa
DCI	Development Cooperation Instrument
DDR	disarmament, demobilisation, and reintegration
DFA	Department of Foreign Affairs (South Africa)
DFID	Department for International Development (Britain)
DIRCO	Department of International Relations and Cooperation (South Africa)
DOD	Department of Defence (South Africa)
DPE	Department of Public Enterprises (South Africa)
DRC	Democratic Republic of the Congo
DTI	Department of Trade and Industry (South Africa)
EAC	East African Community
EBA	Everything But Arms initiative
EC	European Commission
EC	European Community
ECCAS	Economic Community of Central African States
ECIPE	European Centre for International Political Economy
ECOSOC	Economic and Social Council (UN)
ECOSOCC	Economic, Social, and Cultural Council (AU)
ECOWAS	Economic Community of West African States
EDD	Economic Development Department (South Africa)
EDF	European Development Fund
EEAS	European External Action Service
EEC	European Economic Community
EIB	European Investment Bank
EMIA	Export Marketing and Investment Assistance initiative
EPA	economic partnership agreement
EPC	European Political Cooperation
EPG	Eminent Persons Group
EU	European Union
EUSA	European Union Studies Association
FACA	Central African Armed Forces
FARDC	Armed Forces of the DRC
FAW	First Chinese Automobile Works
FCO	Foreign and Commonwealth Office (Britain)
FDI	foreign direct investment
FDLR	Democratic Forces for the Liberation of Rwanda
FES	Friedrich Ebert Stiftung

FESPACO	Pan-African Film and Television Festival of Ouagadougou
FIB	Force Intervention Brigade
FJP	Freedom and Justice Party (Egypt)
FLN	National Liberation Front (Algeria)
FLS	Frontline States
FNI	Nationalist and Integrationist Front (DRC)
FNL	National Forces of Liberation (Burundi)
FOCAC	Forum on China–Africa Cooperation
FOMUC	Multinational Force in the Central African Republic
Frelimo	Mozambique Liberation Front
FRODEBU	Front for Democracy in Burundi
FTA	free trade agreement/area
FTSE 100	*Financial Times* Stock Exchange Index
G-4	Group of Four
G-7	Group of Seven
G-8	Group of Eight
G-20	Group of 20
G-20	Group of 20 (WTO)
G-33	Group of 33 (WTO)
G-77	Group of 77
G-90	Group of 90 (WTO)
G-110	Group of 110 (WTO)
GATT	General Agreement on Tariffs and Trade
GCHQ	Government Communications Headquarters (Britain)
GDP	gross domestic product
GEAR	Growth, Employment, and Redistribution strategy
GIA	Armed Islamic Group (Algeria)
GIA	Global and Inclusive Agreement (DRC)
GIGA	German Institute of Global and Area Studies
GIPC	Ghana Investment Promotion Centre
GNA	Government of National Accord (Libya)
GNC	General National Council (Libya)
GNI	gross national income
GNP	gross national product
GNU	Government of National Unity (Zimbabwe)
GPA	Global Political Agreement (Zimbabwe)
GTL	gas-to-liquids
HDI	Human Development Index
HSRC	Human Sciences Research Council

IAEA	International Atomic Energy Agency
IAFS	India–Africa Forum Summit
IBSA	India, Brazil, and South Africa
ICBC	Industrial and Commercial Bank of China
ICC	International Criminal Court
ICD	Inter-Congolese Dialogue
ICG	International Crisis Group
ICGLR	International Conference on the Great Lakes Region
ICT	information and communications technology
ICTR	International Criminal Tribunal for Rwanda
IDC	Industrial Development Corporation (South Africa)
IDRC	International Development Research Centre
IEC	Independent Electoral Commission (Côte d'Ivoire)
IFP	Inkatha Freedom Party (South Africa)
IFRI	Institut Français des Relations Internationales
IGAD	Intergovernmental Authority on Development
IGD	Institute for Global Dialogue
IISS	International Institute for Strategic Studies
IMC	International Marketing Council (South Africa)
IMF	International Monetary Fund
IORA	Indian Ocean Rim Association
IPAP	Industrial Policy Action Plan
IPF	IGAD Partners Forum
IPI	International Peace Institute
IPPG	Institutions and Pro-Poor Growth programme
IRIN	Integrated Regional Information Network
ISS	Institute for Security Studies
ITAC	International Trade Administration Commission (South Africa)
ITC	International Trade Centre
JAM	Joint Aid Management
JCC	Joint Cooperation Council
JIPSA	Joint Initiative on Priority Skills Acquisition
JSE	Johannesburg Stock Exchange
JVMM	Joint Verification and Monitoring Mechanism
LAPSSET	Lamu–Port Southern Sudan–Ethiopia Transport corridor
LDC	least developed country
LGBT	lesbian, gay, bisexual, and trans-sexual

LGBTI	lesbian, gay, bisexual, trans-sexual, and inter-sex
LIC	low-income country
M23	March 23 Movement (DRC)
MAP	Millennium Africa Recovery Plan
MDC	Movement for Democratic Change (Zimbabwe)
MDC-T	Movement for Democratic Change – Tsvangirai (Zimbabwe)
MDGs	Millennium Development Goals
MENA	Middle East and North Africa
MERCOSUR	Southern Common Market
MFN	most favoured nation
MICOPAX	Mission for the Consolidation of Peace in the Central African Republic
MK	Umkhonto we Sizwe (ANC)
MNC	multi-national corporation
MNE	multi-national enterprise
MOD	Ministry of Defence (Britain)
MOFCOM	Ministry of Commerce (China)
MONUC	United Nations Organisation Mission in the DRC
MONUSCO	United Nations Organisation Stabilisation Mission in the DRC
MOU	memorandum of understanding
MPLA	Popular Movement for the Liberation of Angola
MTEF	Medium-Term Expenditure Framework
MTN	Mobile Telephone Networks
NAASP	New Asia–Africa Strategic Partnership
NAM	Non-Aligned Movement
NAMA-11	Non-Agricultural Market Access group
NATO	North Atlantic Treaty Organisation
NCP	National Congress Party (Sudan)
NDB	New Development Bank
NDP	National Development Plan
NEHAWU	National Education Health and Allied Workers Union
NEPAD	New Partnership for Africa's Development
NGO	non-governmental organisation
NGP	New Growth Path
NIH	National Institutes of Health (US)
NKP	national key point
NPT	Non-Proliferation Treaty

NSG	Nuclear Suppliers Group
NTC	National Transitional Council (Libya)
NUSA	Nigeria Union in South Africa
NUTW	National Union of Textile Workers (South Africa)
OAU	Organisation of African Unity
ODA	official development assistance
ODI	Overseas Development Institute
OECD	Organisation for Economic Cooperation and Development
ONUB	United Nations Operation in Burundi
OPDS	Organ on Politics, Defence, and Security (SADC)
OPDSC	Organ on Politics, Defence, and Security Cooperation (SADC)
P-5	permanent five members (UN Security Council)
PAC	Pan-Africanist Congress
Palipehutu-FNL	Party for the Liberation of the Hutu People – National Forces of Liberation (Burundi)
PAP	Pan-African Parliament
PCRD	Post-Conflict Reconstruction and Development (AU policy)
PDCI	Democratic Party of Côte d'Ivoire
PEPFAR	President's Emergency Programme for AIDS Relief (US)
PICI	Presidential Infrastructure Championing Initiative (NEPAD)
PIDA	Programme for Infrastructure Development in Africa
PJCC	Permanent Joint Commission for Cooperation (South Africa–Ghana)
PPP	purchasing power parity
PRC	People's Republic of China
PSC	Peace and Security Council (AU)
PTA	Preferential Trade Area (predecessor to COMESA)
R2P	responsibility to protect
RDF	Revenue Distribution Formula
RDF	Rwandan Defence Forces
RDP	Reconstruction and Development Programme (South Africa)
REC	regional economic community (Africa)
Renamo	Mozambican National Resistance
RIBS	Russia, India, Brazil, and South Africa
RIC	Russia, India, and China

RISDP	Regional Indicative Strategic Development Plan (SADC)
RPF	Rwandan Patriotic Front
RPR	Rally of Republicans (Côte d'Ivoire)
RSF	Revenue Sharing Formula (SACU)
S&D	special and differential treatment
SA-IEC	South African Independent Electoral Commission
SAA	South African Airways
SAB	South African Breweries
SACBA	South Africa–China Business Association
SACP	South African Communist Party
SACU	Southern African Customs Union
SADC	Southern African Development Community
SADCC	Southern African Development Coordination Conference
SADF	South African Defence Force
SADPA	South African Development Partnership Agency
SAFPI	South African Foreign Policy Initiative
SAIIA	South African Institute of International Affairs
SALC	Southern Africa Litigation Centre
SALO	Southern African Liaison Office
SAMP	Southern African Migration Programme
SANDF	South African National Defence Force
SAPA	South African Press Association
SAPS	South African Police Service
SARB	South African Reserve Bank
SARF	Southern African Relief Fund
SARS	South African Revenue Service
SCO	Shanghai Cooperation Organisation
SDECE	French External Intelligence Service (1947–1981)
SDGs	Sustainable Development Goals
SEOM	SADC Electoral Observer Mission
SGB	General Society of Belgium
SPLA	Sudan People's Liberation Army
SPLM	Sudan People's Liberation Movement
SPS	sanitary and phytosanitary
SSM	special safeguard mechanism
SSR	security sector reform
STAP	(Infrastructure) Short-Term Action Plan (NEPAD)
SWAPO	South West Africa People's Organisation
T-FTA	Tripartite Free Trade Area (COMESA-EAC-SADC)

TCL	Tanganyika Concessions Ltd.
TDCA	Trade, Development, and Cooperation Agreement (EU–South Africa)
TDF	Transkei Defence Force
TEC	Transitional Executive Council (South Africa)
TICAD	Tokyo International Conference on African Development
Tralac	Trade Law Centre
TRIPS	Trade-Related Aspects of Intellectual Property Rights
UHMK	Mining Union of Upper Katanga
UKZN	University of KwaZulu-Natal
UN	United Nations
UNAMID	United Nations/African Union Hybrid Operation in Darfur
UNCTAD	United Nations Conference on Trade and Development
UNDP	United Nations Development Programme
UNECA	United Nations Economic Commission for Africa
UNFCCC	United Nations Framework Convention on Climate Change
UNHCR	United Nations High Commissioner for Refugees
UNISA	University of South Africa
UNITA	National Union for the Total Independence of Angola
UNMEE	United Nations Mission in Ethiopia and Eritrea
UNMIL	United Nations Mission in Liberia
UNMIN	United Nations Mission in Nepal
UNMIS	United Nations Mission in Sudan
UNOCI	United Nations Operation in Côte d'Ivoire
US	United States
USAID	United States Agency for International Development
VDF	Venda Defence Force
WEF	World Economic Forum
WHO	World Health Organisation
Wits	University of the Witwatersrand
WTO	World Trade Organisation
ZANU-PF	Zimbabwe African National Union – Patriotic Front
ZAPU	Zimbabwe African People's Union

ACKNOWLEDGEMENTS

This book emanates from a project undertaken by the Centre for Conflict Resolution (CCR) in Cape Town, South Africa, between 2013 and 2016, aimed at strengthening South Africa's foreign policy role in promoting peace and security, as well as regional integration and development in Africa. We would like, first and foremost, to thank the government of Norway for its generous support of this project, without which this endeavour would not have been possible. We would also like to thank the main funders of the Centre's Africa Programme over the past decade and a half – the governments of the Netherlands, Sweden, Denmark and Finland.

This book reflects CCR's commitment to the production of knowledge on Africa by African scholars, while simultaneously gaining the critical perspectives of academics from North America, Europe and Asia on key African issues. Since 2006, the Centre has published 20 books on diverse topics including the African Union and its institutions, the role of the United Nations in Africa, relations between China and the European Union and the continent, as well as the myriad challenges of peacebuilding and region-building in Africa. This work, in particular, builds on CCR's 2007 edited volume *South Africa in Africa: The Post-Apartheid Era*, with a view to both updating it and expanding its scope beyond Africa to cover relations with key states outside the continent, as well as with important multilateral institutions. The volume thus provides a comprehensive assessment of South Africa's contemporary foreign policy by diverse authors from within and outside the continent. It also examines critically ongoing debates on the nature, evolution and prospects of South Africa's foreign policy and leadership roles.

We owe an immense debt of gratitude to the contributing authors for their patience, perseverance and perspicacity in completing this volume.

We thank the staff at CCR who supported the production of the book. We are also grateful to Jason Cook for his meticulous copy-editing of the manuscript, as we similarly are to participants at a CCR research seminar, held in Cape Town in 2013, for their useful insights on the early drafts of many of the papers in this volume.

Finally, a special word of thanks must go to Sophie Rudland, Sara Magness, Lizzy Collier and their colleagues at I.B.Tauris in London, as well as the indexer, Nic Nicholas, and three anonymous peer reviewers who provided valuable feedback on the draft manuscript. We hope that this book will enrich discussion, provoke debate and inspire innovative thinking about the challenges and opportunities facing post-apartheid South Africa's foreign policy in the twenty-first century.

Adekeye Adebajo and Kudrat Virk
Johannesburg and Cape Town

INTRODUCTION

THE CONCENTRIC CIRCLES OF SOUTH AFRICA'S FOREIGN POLICY

Adekeye Adebajo[1]

It is an often repeated truism in foreign policy that countries can only be strong abroad if they are strong at home. Post-apartheid South Africa – Africa's ninth largest country in geographical terms – remains one of the world's most unequal societies. In a hard-hitting speech to the South African parliament in May 1998, Deputy President Thabo Mbeki had famously talked of his country as "two nations": a white population now represents ten per cent of a 55 million-strong population with a living standard of Spain, while an 80 per cent black majority has a living standard of Congo-Brazzaville. Unemployment has remained stubbornly stuck at an estimated 40 per cent (officially around 27 per cent). White-dominated South African companies are ubiquitous across the continent, sometimes creating resentment in local markets. The apartheid-era army's destabilisation of its neighbours has left a profound distrust of South African military interventionism, which remains strong in contemporary Southern Africa: an estimated one million deaths and $60 billion in damages had resulted from these actions between 1980 and 1988 alone.[2] The ghost of apartheid still haunts the sub-region even as South Africa's own economic, military and educational institutions remain stubbornly untransformed two and a half decades after the formal end of apartheid.

There is an urgent need for a comprehensive study of South Africa's post-apartheid foreign policy like this one that covers both its main themes and its geographical scope in a conceptually coherent manner. Many of the previous books on this subject are now dated. They include: a 2007 edited volume by Adekeye Adebajo, Adebayo Adedeji and Chris Landsberg, *South Africa in Africa: The Post-Apartheid Era*; James Barber's 2004 *Mandela's World: The International Dimension of South Africa's Political Revolution, 1990–99*; Chris Alden and Garth Le Pere's 2003 Adelphi paper *South Africa's Post-Apartheid Foreign Policy: From Reconciliation to Revival?*; and Elizabeth Sidiropoulos's 2004 edited volume *South Africa's Foreign Policy, 1994–2004: Apartheid Past, Renaissance Future.*[3]

The most recent books on South Africa's foreign policy with which this one might compare are the 2012 and 2015 volumes of *South African Foreign Policy Review*, edited respectively by Chris Landsberg and Jo-Ansie van Wyk; and Lesley Masters, Siphamandla Zondi, Jo-Ansie van Wyk and Chris Landsberg.[4] Though useful collections, these two books examine such broad topics as public diplomacy and branding; science and technology; global governance identity; voting behaviour at the United Nations (UN); and selected regions such as Southern Africa, the Middle East, North Africa, Latin America, Asia and the West. They are thus not as comprehensive as this volume, and almost all their authors as well as all their editors are parochially South African, denying the books the critical non-South African perspectives that this volume provides.

This book on South Africa's post-apartheid foreign policy complements – but does not compete with – two recent books on South Africa's foreign policy. Former United States (US) government analyst John Siko's *Inside South Africa's Foreign Policy* (2014) examines the processes of foreign policymaking through the government bureaucracy, political parties, the media, academia and public opinion, while Matthew Graham's *The Crisis of South African Foreign Policy: Diplomacy, Leadership and the Role of the African National Congress* (2016) – as its sub-title suggests – focuses more narrowly on the leadership role of the ruling African National Congress (ANC). Neither volume claims the historical, geographical and thematic comprehensiveness that this book does.[5]

The present volume is divided into five main parts. The first examines the domestic imperatives of South Africa's foreign policy; peacemaking; defence and security; human rights; and corporate economic expansion by South African firms into the rest of the continent. The second and third parts respectively assess South Africa's key bilateral and multilateral relations in Africa, while the fourth and fifth analyse the country's key external bilateral and multilateral relations. South Africa's post-apartheid foreign policy is thus examined in terms of four overlapping "concentric circles", with the first focusing on domestic South African drivers and constraints, the second on the Southern African sub-region, the third on the broader African continent and the fourth on relations with the rest of the world outside Africa. The concept of hegemony is also used to explain South Africa's leadership ambitions in Africa and beyond.

Post-apartheid South Africa has actively pursued ties with important countries on its own continent, the most important among which are Angola in Southern Africa; Nigeria in West Africa; the Democratic Republic of the Congo (DRC) in the Great Lakes; Tanzania in Eastern Africa; and Algeria in North Africa. Tshwane (Pretoria), though it has had strong political, economic and/or military ties with these countries, has shied away from explicitly identifying "anchor states" on the continent. It has, however, sought to use regional bodies such as the Southern African Customs Union (SACU), the Southern African Development Community (SADC) and the African Union (AU) to promote its foreign policy interests on the continent. Key external actors have included traditional partners such as the United States, Britain and France, and newer ones such as China, Brazil, Russia and India. South Africa has also been active in multilateral bodies, contributing to UN peacemaking and peacekeeping efforts; pushing for the world body to strengthen cooperation with, and the conflict management capacity of, Africa's regional bodies; seeking to transform global institutions with its allies in the Brazil, Russia, India, China and South Africa bloc (BRICS); waging trade battles in the 79-member African, Caribbean and Pacific (ACP) Group of States (with the 28-member European Union (EU)), as well as at the World Trade Organisation (WTO); and declaring the country's candidacy for a future permanent African seat on an expanded 15-member UN Security Council. South Africa is the only African country in the BRICS and the Group of 20 (G-20) major economies, and is one of only 11 global strategic partners of the EU, all of which has increased Tshwane's global prestige.

But this prestige has not translated into continental dominance, and *Pax South Africana* continues to struggle with issues of political legitimacy in Africa. SADC countries like Angola, Zimbabwe and Namibia have challenged South Africa's policies in the DRC. Many of its Southern African neighbours continue to complain of mercantilist behaviour by the government and its corporate firms that disadvantages their own domestic industries. Nigeria – with a domestic market of about 170 million that is three times the size of South Africa's – remains a major rival in Africa, with the largest economy on the continent in 2017. Tshwane's efforts to pursue economic and political interests in the Central African Republic (CAR), and its peacemaking efforts in Côte d'Ivoire and Madagascar have also been challenged by France. China further provides strong economic competition in Southern African countries like Angola, Zambia and Zimbabwe, even as South Africa continues to struggle with domestic socio-economic and security challenges.

Hegemony and *Pax South Africana*[6]

Historically, much of the Eurocentric literature in the West about Africa's international relations and security studies has often assumed that African states do not have much agency and are often acted upon by external powers such as the US, Russia and France. This was never totally accurate, even during the Cold War, when Southern African states and Nigeria played important roles in the liberation of Namibia, Zimbabwe and South Africa. The concept of "hegemony" can be used to frame South Africa's regional role. Much of the rich literature on this subject, however, focuses on cases outside Africa in North America, Europe, Latin America and Asia, and the concept thus has to be applied with great caution to the African context, where an empirical understanding of the domestic and regional dynamics of Africa's international relations is critical for any analysis.

The rather arcane and often esoteric academic debates about whether South Africa is a "hegemon", "pivot" or "middle power" can be sensibly settled by clearly defining the terms.[7] "Constructive" hegemons are able not only to articulate the rules and norms for respective regions, but also to convince other states to follow such rules.[8] A pivotal state is an *important* rather than a *dominant* state, and South Africa is a pivot in global terms and a hegemon in regional terms. The middle-power robes are also ones that are made to be worn by South Africa, since the country does seek, through multilateral organisations – the UN, the BRICS, the G-20 and the WTO – to play a leadership role in security, trade and economic issues as a respected voice of the global South.

It is important to note that "hegemony" is used here to refer only to the regional and not the global level. The term describes a state that has the *capacity* and *legitimacy* to dominate its sphere of influence with the consent of other states and seeks to provide security and prosperity as the often self-interested public goods of a hegemon.[9] South Africa is a regional hegemon wielding preponderant military and economic resources (accounting for about 60 per cent of Southern Africa's economy in 2017) relative to its neighbours, and has tried – not always successfully – to promote military security, political stability and economic integration in Southern Africa. In seeking to engage the Group of Eight (G-8) industrialised countries on behalf of the continent between 1999 and 2008, South Africa's president, Thabo Mbeki, was effectively pursuing collective goals for other African states as a regional hegemon.

South Africa, however, lacks the legitimacy and capacity of a global hegemon like the US to create viable institutions that set the rules that others can be encouraged to follow. Institutions such as the AU, the New Partnership for Africa's Development (NEPAD), the African Peer Review Mechanism (APRM) and SADC remain fragile, under-resourced and dependent on external funding. These organisations are also not yet norm-promoting bodies on which regional states can rely. In some ways, France has been more successful than South Africa at exerting its hegemony in its francophone sphere of influence in Africa, due to eight decades of colonial rule during which it entrenched cultural, political and economic dominance, particularly over the elites of francophone Africa. *Pax South Africana* has not been able to leave a lasting political and cultural influence on Angola, Zimbabwe, Burundi or the DRC in the way that France, through decades of colonialism, was able to leave its mark on all aspects of political and administrative life in its former African colonies.

Constructive hegemons often exercise "soft power" to persuade rather than coerce other states to accept their leadership through acquiescence and socialisation of elites rather than through coercion and the imposition of their will.[10] Soft power seeks to convince other states to want the same outcomes and to shape the preferences of other states through co-opting rather than coercing them. France has educated African political and military elites at its schools for over six decades. It uses regular Franco-African and Francophonie summits to build political solidarity with the 22 francophone African states, which often act as voting cattle at multilateral forums like the AU and the UN in support of French interests. Paris also uses cultural resources through an annual FESPACO (Pan-African Film and Television Festival of Ouagadougou) event in Burkina Faso.

South Africa continues to educate elites from African countries such as Zimbabwe, Botswana, Swaziland, Angola, Rwanda and Nigeria at its universities. The country has produced Nobel literature laureates in

Nadine Gordimer and John Coetzee, and Nobel peace laureates in Albert Luthuli, Desmond Tutu, Nelson Mandela and F.W. De Klerk;[11] it successfully organised Africa's first soccer World Cup in 2010; and the country is a magnet for tourists from Africa and around the world. South Africa's fast-food chains such as Nando's (with branches not just across Africa but also in Europe, the US and Asia), Steers and Spur, as well as an American-style "mall culture" exported to the rest of the continent, are also signs of the country's soft power, as is its World Cup-winning (1995 and 2007) almost lily-white rugby team, the Springboks.

But in assessing South Africa's post-apartheid foreign policy, it is always important to note the great historical damage inflicted on the country's current continental leadership ambitions by the "beggar thy neighbour" mercantilist trade policies, economic sabotage and dislocation, as well as the destructive military policies, of successive apartheid regimes between 1948 and 1990.[12] Mercantilist states have historically believed in pursuing policies such as maintaining favourable trade balances with their neighbours, establishing colonies, developing mining and industry and accumulating gold reserves: an accurate reflection of South Africa and its historical role in Africa. South Africa's past military destabilisation of Southern Africa and the domineering mercantilist economic role of its largely white entrepreneurs have left profound scars on its neighbours and a deep distrust that even a black-led ANC government will need decades to overcome.

South African scholar-diplomat Brendan Vickers and his co-author Richard Cawood examine in their chapter the controversial corporate expansion of mostly white-dominated South African companies to the rest of the continent. This has created jobs and improved services, but also caused resentment and opposition in countries like Nigeria, Kenya, Tanzania and the DRC. The two authors call for a more coordinated approach between the South African state and corporations – which they describe as "SA Inc" – that other emerging powers such as Brazil and China have pursued, in order to promote policy, profit and development more effectively. This issue of the role of South Africa's corporate sector is also covered in the five chapters that examine South Africa's bilateral relations in Southern, Central, West, Eastern and North Africa.

In a sense, post-apartheid South Africa is still haunted by past domestic, regional and external structures that continue to disturb its present. Domestically, South Africa's economy and the senior levels of key institutions such as universities, non-governmental organisations (NGOs) and the military continue to be controlled by its white minority – the major beneficiaries of apartheid. Chris Landsberg, one of South Africa's most prominent foreign policy analysts, assesses in his chapter in this book the under-studied area of domestic challenges in South Africa's foreign policy – social, economic and political – demonstrating the constraints that have prevented the country from playing a more effective role as a regional hegemon. Regionally, South Africa's control of about 60 per cent of the sub-regional economy and a large trade imbalance with its neighbours continue to spread fears of a mercantilist ogre dominating Southern Africa; and externally, much of South Africa's trade remains with Asia, Western Europe and the United States, in ties established largely when apartheid's architects believed that the country was a "Western" bulwark against communist infiltration into Africa. South Africa's leaders effectively established a *Pax Pretoriana* in Southern Africa through administering Namibia between 1919 and 1989; creating institutions such as the Southern African Customs Union through which Pretoria exerted economic influence over Botswana, Swaziland and Lesotho; and through military destabilisation policies of awesome destructiveness in countries such as Angola, Mozambique, Lesotho, Zambia and Zimbabwe.

As the late Kenyan intellectual Ali Mazrui noted, Western imperialism involved God, gold and glory,[13] with missionaries seeking to convert Africans from their "pagan" ancestor worship; with private business interests seeking mineral and agricultural resources; and with empire-builders justifying the whole enterprise as a *mission civilisatrice* of "savage barbarians".[14] (See also Adebajo in this volume.) In the South African case, could the expansion of mostly white-led businessmen and white civil society activists across the continent represent a modern-day equivalent of a bygone era? Could a post-apartheid South Africa be forced to protect the activities of its own trade pioneers such as De Beers in the DRC and Randgold in Côte d'Ivoire? Could South Africa's peacemaking efforts become linked to interventions in strategically important countries such as the Congo in which it dominates the telecommunications market, in which its companies control mines and in which its leaders have backed South African state electricity utility Eskom's plans to establish a hydropower project by the 2020s centred around Congo's Grand Inga Falls, to supply electricity to the entire continent?

A Brief History of South Africa's Foreign Policy: From Mandela to Zuma[15]

Nelson Mandela, 1994–1999

With this historical and conceptual context for understanding South Africa's post-apartheid foreign policy in mind, it is important to sketch the main contours of the country's foreign policy since 1994. Nelson Mandela, South Africa's president between 1994 and 1999 and a Nobel peace laureate, had spent 27 years in jail for the struggle to protect the rights of the black majority in South Africa, before winning his freedom in February 1990. His enormous stature as the "Founding Father" of the post-apartheid state gave the country a global moral stature that a former international pariah could never have imagined. Mandela outlined five core principles to guide his country's international relations in 1993: the centrality of human rights; the promotion of democracy; respect for international law; the pursuit of peace through non-violent mechanisms; and international cooperation to promote economic development.[16] Tshwane's foreign policy ambitions would thus prioritise pan-African positions and the reform of the international multilateral order in order to promote the interests of the global South and reverse Africa's marginalisation in the international order.

Beyond South Africa's borders, Mandela led peacemaking efforts in Burundi, Zaire (now the DRC) and Lesotho.[17] But these efforts were not always successful, as his failed mediation between Zairian strongman Mobutu Sese Seko and rebel leader Laurent Kabila in May 1997 demonstrated. During "Madiba's" (Mandela's clan name) rule, South Africa largely shunned a military role in Africa out of fear of arousing allegations of hegemonic domination – recent history had seen the apartheid army wreak destruction and havoc in neighbouring states. Post-apartheid South Africa's military intervention in Lesotho in 1998 was an exception that revived some of the memories of the destructive apartheid era. Though justified as a bid to restore order after fears of a military coup d'état, and though undertaken with military troops from Botswana, a major driving force of the South African incursion into the tiny mountain kingdom was to protect the Highlands Water Project, which supplies water to South Africa's industrial heartland of Gauteng.[18]

However, in what came to be known by some as the "Mandela Doctrine", South Africa's saintly president told his fellow leaders at the Organisation of African Unity (OAU) summit in Ouagadougou in 1998: "Africa has a right and a duty to intervene to root out tyranny . . . we must all accept that we cannot abuse the concept of national sovereignty to deny the rest of the continent the right and duty to intervene when behind those sovereign boundaries, people are being slaughtered to protect tyranny".[19] Mandela courageously championed human rights, although he was diplomatically isolated on the continent by a bruising political battle after Nigeria's autocrat, General Sani Abacha, ignored his pleas for clemency and hanged Ken Saro-Wiwa and eight Ogoni activists in November 1995.[20]

Thabo Mbeki, 1999–2008

Mandela's successor between 1999 and 2008, Thabo Mbeki, had spent two decades of exile, from 1971, working for the African National Congress in Zambia, Nigeria, Botswana and Swaziland.[21] Leaders like Mbeki were profoundly aware of their debt of gratitude to the continent, which had made great sacrifices for South Africa's liberation. The ANC's presence in the Frontline States (FLS) was nevertheless not assured. ANC operatives were arrested in Botswana. After Angola's independence in 1975 and its collapse into a 27-year civil war, Zambia's and Tanzania's support for a united front of liberation movements in Angola strained relations with the ANC, which strongly backed the ruling Popular Movement for the Liberation of Angola (MPLA). Zambia at one stage shut down the ANC's *Radio Freedom* broadcasts, while Tanzania became increasingly averse to hosting the ANC's military camps, which impelled its fighters to set up facilities in Angola.[22] Underground ANC operatives were jailed and tortured in Zimbabwe in 1982. These developments all shaped Mbeki's understanding of the potential ambivalence, shifting nature and even duplicity of pan-African diplomacy. Though a pragmatic Marxist pan-African at the time, Mbeki took to heart many of the lessons learned from these African experiences. While African governments all pledged rhetorical support to South Africa's liberation struggle, many also promoted more parochial, short-term interests, while some – above all Mozambique with the Nkomati Accord in 1984 – felt forced to bow to apartheid pressure. Mbeki therefore adopted an approach of diversifying the ANC's dependence without becoming over-reliant on African governments. A similar pragmatism guided his foreign policy once he assumed power in 1999.

At a foreign policy retreat in February 2001, Mbeki identified five key priorities for South Africa's external relations: restructuring the OAU/AU and SADC; reforming regional and international organisations such as the UN, the World Trade Organisation, the World Bank and the International

Monetary Fund (IMF); hosting major international conferences; promoting peace and security in Africa and the Middle East; and fostering ties with the Group of Eight industrialised countries, while devising a global South strategy.[23]

As president, Mbeki pursued an "African Agenda", consistently seeking multilateral solutions to regional conflicts. He was more prepared than Mandela to send peacekeepers abroad, deploying about 3,000 troops to Burundi and the DRC as well as others to Sudan's Darfur region and Ethiopia/Eritrea with the goal of ending these conflicts.[24] In her rich chapter in this volume, Canadian scholar Devon Curtis examines South Africa's peacemaking role in Lesotho, Burundi, the DRC, Zimbabwe, Madagascar, Sudan, Côte d'Ivoire and Libya. She argues that South Africa's own approach of a government of national unity has been "exported" to the rest of the continent with mixed results. In order to ensure effective implementation of the Arusha peace agreement for Burundi of August 2000, South Africa led the cash-strapped African Union Mission in Burundi (AMIB), involving 2,645 South African, Mozambican and Ethiopian peacekeepers, from February 2003. AMIB, however, struggled to keep peace in a decade-long civil war due to a lack of financial and logistical support. In May 2004, the UN Security Council established the 5,650-strong UN Operation in Burundi (ONUB), subsuming AMIB's peacekeepers into the new mission under the leadership of South African force commander Derrick Mbuyiselo Mgwebi.[25]

Under Mbeki's presidency, South African diplomacy was also instrumental in securing a peace accord in the DRC by 2002, with the country sending 1,400 troops to a strengthened UN mission in the Congo (MONUC). By December 2002, Congolese parties meeting in Tshwane under the mediation of Thabo Mbeki signed the Global and All-Inclusive Agreement on the Transition in the Democratic Republic of the Congo, calling for a two-year transition period with the establishment of a government of national unity. The accord led to the holding of the first national elections in 40 years in 2006 (supervised by the UN), and a more controversial disputed poll in 2011 (run by the DRC's electoral commission). Despite continued instability in Kivu and Orientale provinces, South Africa's role helped to promote stability in a conflict that has seen over three million deaths since 1996.[26]

Thabo Mbeki also skilfully used both a strategic partnership with Nigeria and his chair of the African Union between 2002 and 2003 to pursue his foreign policy goals on the continent. South Africa's second post-apartheid leader served as the chief mediator in Côte d'Ivoire between 2004 and 2006 in a bid to resolve the conflict. Tshwane was the host and chief architect of the African Peer Review Mechanism of 2003 – comprising 36 African states in 2017 – which involved a peer review of governance and economic performance including both government and civil society actors.[27] South Africa further hosted the AU's Pan-African Parliament (PAP) – without legislative powers in 2017 – from March 2004.

Having felt that Mandela had been set up for failure over Nigeria in 1995–1996 by powerful Western countries – chiefly the US and Britain – that quietly continued to benefit from General Sani Abacha's oil and large economy while making critical noises to assuage domestic human rights activists, Mbeki was determined not to suffer the same fate over Zimbabwe. Unlike Mandela's tough reaction to Abacha after the hanging of the Ogoni activists in 1995, Mbeki pointedly ignored calls by Western leaders to sanction Robert Mugabe, judging that such actions would not only be ineffectual, but could also result in a loss of leverage within both Zimbabwe and the broader African context. Mbeki further felt that South Africa had few alternative policies to deal with the Zimbabwe crisis, since any spill-over effects resulting from its neighbour's implosion would drive even more refugees and instability into South Africa (there were an estimated one million Zimbabweans in South Africa in 2017). He therefore sought to "contain" the situation, by bringing Zimbabwe's government and opposition together in an interim government, a policy that eventually succeeded in 2009. The riddle of Zimbabwe was that no one seemed to have a viable alternative to Mbeki's "quiet diplomacy", and the key to resolving the problem clearly lay in Harare and not in Tshwane. But by apparently legitimising flawed elections in 2002; by vociferously, but unsuccessfully, defending Zimbabwe from suspension from the Commonwealth in 2003; and by adopting a distrustful approach towards Zimbabwe's opposition Movement for Democratic Change (MDC), Mbeki was, sometimes justly, criticised for not playing a difficult hand with more diplomatic tact.

South Africa often promoted negotiations rather than punitive sanctions in dealing with autocratic or abusive regimes in Sudan and Myanmar (Burma). During its tenure on the UN Security Council in 2007–2008, its diplomats – led by its long-serving permanent representative at the UN, Dumisani Kumalo – cautioned against a militarisation of the concept of the "responsibility to protect" (R2P) and called for urgent international action and a more effective peacekeeping force in anarchic Somalia, where over

300,000 people had died since 1991.[28] Mbeki clearly had a strategic foreign policy vision and personally drove initiatives assisted by South Africa's foreign minister, Nkosazana Dlamini-Zuma, and her deputy and trusted Mbeki ally, Aziz Pahad.

One of the most important aspects of Mbeki's foreign policy was its pan-African outlook and Diasporic reach. In 2000, Mbeki travelled to the Brazilian state of Bahia to receive an honorary doctorate degree from the University of the State of Bahia in a region whose population is largely descended from African slaves. After reading from a poignant poem – "The Slave Ship" by the nineteenth-century Brazilian poet Castro Alves – South Africa's president called for the banishment forever of the nightmare of the slave ship. He then went on to tell his audience: "Brazil cannot achieve its full identity unless it celebrates, also, its historical and cultural connection with Africa", before calling for the emergence of more Afro-Brazilian scientists, economists and businesspeople.[29] Mbeki also promoted his vision of an African Renaissance at the University of Havana, Cuba, in March 2001, and visited the US several times, notably addressing an African-American audience at Martin Luther King Jr's famous Ebenezer Baptist church in Atlanta in May 2000. South Africa's "Philosopher-King" further sought to play a role on the small Caribbean island of Haiti. In January 2004, he was the only African head of state to attend the bicentenary celebrations of the country's slave revolt against France, following which it had won its independence as the first black republic in the world. The South African president provided R10 million (about $1.4 million at the time) to support these celebrations. After Haitian president Jean-Bertrand Aristide was pressured to leave Haiti in 2004, reportedly by American and French diplomats, Mbeki offered him and his family political asylum in South Africa.

Mbeki further pursued an active "global South" strategy, symbolised by the creation of the India, Brazil and South Africa Forum (IBSA) in 2003, which provided a framework for the three countries to coordinate efforts in sectors such as defence, health, education and global governance in multilateral institutions such as the UN. The three IBSA members of the BRICS effectively built on this cooperation.

Jacob Zuma, 2009–2017

Jacob Zuma, who assumed South Africa's presidency after democratic elections in April 2009, had previous wide-ranging peacemaking experience in South Africa's KwaZulu-Natal province as well as in

Burundi, as deputy president. His administration stressed the continuity of Mbeki's multilateral approach to Africa,[30] and announced its intention to become an aid donor by authorising the creation of the South African Development Partnership Agency (SADPA), which was still struggling to get off the ground in 2017. Zuma was criticised for populating the foreign service with a disproportionate pool of ideological ANC deployees, with sometimes negative effects on policy. The most important shift in South Africa's foreign policy under the Zuma administration was the adoption of Angola as a strategic ally on the continent, thus ending the frosty relationship between Mbeki and Angolan president Eduardo Dos Santos. By this time, Luanda had become Tshwane's second-largest trading partner in Africa after Nigeria. Whereas Mbeki sought leadership at the continental AU level, which he was sometimes unable to translate into leverage at the sub-regional level, Zuma – in securing strong sub-regional support – gave South Africa greater influence at the continental level, as evidenced by former South African foreign minister Nkosazana Dlamini-Zuma's controversial SADC-driven appointment as AU Commission chair in July 2012 (see Maloka in this volume).

Under Zuma, South Africa has also pursued what government officials described as a national interest-driven foreign policy,[31] and a more openly mercantilist trade policy seeking to position the country as "open for business" and as the "gateway to Africa".[32] In May 2013, Zambia's then vice-president, Guy Scott, provoked a storm of controversy in South Africa when he noted: "The South Africans are backward in terms of historical development. They really think they're the bees' knees and actually they've been the cause of so much trouble in this part of the world. I have a suspicion that the blacks model themselves on the whites now that they're in power". Scott also criticised South Africa as being "too big and too unsubtle", comparing Jacob Zuma to F.W. De Klerk in the way he engaged the rest of the region.[33] When these comments were first made, many South Africans condemned them as the drunken ramblings of a maverick politician. Much of the rest of the continent, however, understood the sentiment behind these undiplomatic musings.

Zuma would unwittingly confirm what Scott had said six months later. Though South Africa's president had lived in exile in Swaziland, Mozambique and Zambia, and has often defended African tradition and Zulu culture, he provoked a storm of controversy across the continent in October 2013 by his response to a question about introducing e-tolling on a highway in South Africa's Gauteng province: "We can't think like

Africans in Africa, generally. We are in Johannesburg. It is not some national road in Malawi".[34] Though the comments led to an official apology to the government of President Joyce Banda in Lilongwe, they also reflected the unconscious dangers of "South African exceptionalism". South Africa is often compared to America – as Guy Scott did in his 2013 comments – which also continues to insist on an "American exceptionalism" that much of the rest of the world continues to resent and reject. This has frequently taken the form of an arrogant penchant by Washington to act unilaterally, sometimes placing itself above international law in invading other countries or dispatching killer drones into theatres like Afghanistan, Pakistan, Yemen, Somalia and Mali without a UN mandate. Americans and South Africans have greater access to information than their neighbours, but both also have populations that are often more ignorant about the world and their respective continents.

In the area of human rights, South Africa refused Tibet's spiritual leader and Nobel peace laureate, the Dalai Lama, a visa to enter the country in March 2009. Many of the country's civil society activists were critical and pushed for a more human rights-centred focus in promoting South Africa's foreign policy. South African legal scholar Nicole Fritz argues in her chapter in this book that South Africa's inconsistent support for human rights in its foreign policy has been due to its support for continental positions and a bid to ensure fairer institutions of global governance, which she views as a false choice, criticising its October 2016 decision to withdraw from the Hague-based International Criminal Court (ICC).

After South Africa was heavily criticised – including by its own judiciary, which ruled that it had acted unlawfully – for not having arrested Sudanese leader Omar al-Bashir during a visit to Johannesburg to attend an AU summit in June 2015, the ruling ANC party called for the country to withdraw from the Court four months later. In October 2016, Tshwane submitted its instruments of withdrawal from the Court to the United Nations, triggering a storm of criticism from domestic and external civil society groups and many Western governments. Senior members of the ruling ANC were particularly irked by what they saw as the double standard of the US, China and Russia – none of which are members of the ICC – sitting in judgement on ICC-related matters on the UN Security Council, and being able to refer matters to the Court.[35] Most African states similarly argued that the ICC was selectively targeting African leaders in Sudan, Kenya and Côte d'Ivoire, while ignoring human rights abuses in the Middle East, Sri Lanka and the Philippines. Tshwane's decision to withdraw from the ICC was, however, later reversed by the country's high court in February 2017 due to what it saw as the unconstitutional process that had been followed.

Advocates of the school of realism such as former American secretary of state Henry Kissinger have often argued that viewing foreign policy primarily through a human rights lens is flawed, value-laden and naive.[36] Human rights and their promotion are undoubtedly important, but international politics, according to realists, does not work solely on this basis and never has. South Africa, for example, is consistently scolded by hectoring headmasters for behaving like a naughty boy by selling arms abroad, yet it is important to remember that the five veto-wielding permanent members (P-5) of the UN Security Council, responsible for promoting international peace and security – the US, Russia, China, France and Britain – sold about 70 per cent of arms worldwide in 2016.

Foreign policy, according to realists, is thus the art of the possible and not some monastic pastime for secular saints. Even the saintly Nelson Mandela insisted on remaining friends with Libya's Muammar Qaddafi and Cuba's Fidel Castro – two Western *enfants terribles* who committed human rights abuses – on the grounds that both leaders had strongly supported the fight against apartheid, while Western democracies such as the US, Britain and France were supping with the apartheid devil without the requisite long spoon. Human rights are certainly an important aspect of foreign policy, but they are often shrouded in hypocritical rhetoric – such as America's "war on terror" after 2001 – and every country mainly pursues what it believes to be its own interests while trying to observe human rights where they can. Some of South Africa's leaders have thus complained that they are being judged by different standards than the rest of the world.

Reinforcing the need for a strong domestic base in order to pursue an effective foreign policy – the first of our four concentric circles – in the area of defence, the 78,000-strong South African military lacks air defence capacity; half of the navy's ships are obsolete; the country has no maritime patrol aircraft; and long-range airlift and sealift are almost non-existent. Tshwane's military brass-hats often complain of being overstretched: conducting peacekeeping missions; patrolling South Africa's 4,471-kilometre land border; and hunting rhino poachers in Kruger National Park. Some estimates note that half of the country's defence budget goes to paying salaries. In his chapter in this book, Sagaren Naidoo, a director in South Africa's defence ministry and a scholar, exposes the mismatch between the roles and responsibilities of the South African military and the mandates and resources that have been provided to it. A low-growth economy in one of the world's most unequal societies, however, means that prioritising guns over butter is politically difficult.

This perhaps explains the decision announced by South Africa's defence minister, Nosiviwe Mapisa-Nqakula, in May 2016 – on the grounds of lack of cooperation from the Sudanese government in Khartoum in fulfilling the protection mandate of South African peacekeepers – to withdraw 757 out of the country's 797 troops from the UN mission in Darfur. Tshwane also appears to be tiring of its leadership role in the volatile eastern Congo. But the one reason that will maintain South Africa's commitment to regional peacekeeping is the future prospect that it could win a permanent African seat on a reformed UN Security Council. In order to compete with countries like Nigeria, Ethiopia and Egypt, Tshwane will need to maintain its credibility as an international peacekeeper. As Nigeria has done in Liberia and Sierra Leone, South Africa will most likely continue to insist that the UN ensure more equitable international burden-sharing in future peacekeeping missions.

The Concentric Circles of South Africa's Foreign Policy: From Theory to Praxis

The concept of "concentric circles" has often been used in relation to Nigeria's foreign policy by analysts such as scholar-diplomat Ibrahim Gambari and scholar Adekeye Adebajo.[37] In the South African context, it was used by British scholar James Barber in 1976 to describe the foreign policy of the apartheid state, and more recently by Chris Landsberg in 2006 and 2014 to assess the foreign policy of the Mbeki and Zuma administrations.[38]

According to this concept, South Africa's foreign policy can be assessed through a series of concentric circles starting with an inner circle representing the country's domestic environment; a second larger circle representing its immediate neighbours in Southern Africa; a third circle depicting the broader African environment; and a fourth, larger circle illustrating relations with the world beyond Africa. As Landsberg succinctly noted: "Concentric circles thus have different radiuses, but common epicentres".[39] South Africa's foreign policy is therefore conducted simultaneously within these four overlapping circles in a complementary manner that prioritises its domestic base, its geographical location in Southern Africa and Africa, while leveraging relations with the world beyond Africa to strengthen its position within its own sub-region and the broader continent. This book has adopted, in its structure, this idea of concentric circles with the domestic context and with bilateral and multilateral relations in Africa assessed, before examining South Africa's bilateral and multilateral relations with the world beyond Africa.

One of the unique aspects of this volume is that 12 of the 24 authors are non-South Africans offering unique pan-African, European, American and Asian "outsider" perspectives of the country's foreign policy. This is complemented by strong South African academic contributions as well as six South African scholar-diplomats who are currently working, or have worked, in the country's foreign, defence and trade ministries, thus providing "insider" perspectives of key aspects of the country's foreign policy.

Africa: Key Bilateral Ties[40]

Southern Africa: The Good, the Bad and the Ugly

As Zimbabwean scholar Lloyd M. Sachikonye argues in this volume, while South Africa's ties in Mozambique were close, and those with Zimbabwe were ambivalent and cool, there was a warming of ties with Angola only after 2009. Tshwane established a bi-national commission with Zimbabwe, and its Department of Trade and Industry (DTI) set up an office in Southern Africa's second-largest economy at the time. As earlier noted, Thabo Mbeki's "quiet diplomacy" towards Zimbabwe was widely criticised by the Western media, several Western governments and many South African analysts. However, in light of Tshwane's difficulties in rallying regional support on issues such as political initiatives in the DRC and Lesotho, and being sensitive to accusations that South Africa is a "Trojan horse" for promoting Western interests in Africa, Mbeki was careful not to become diplomatically isolated over the Zimbabwe issue.[41] Most SADC states also backed President Jacob Zuma's mediation efforts in the country after April 2009, with sub-regional leaders even criticising state intimidation and violence in Zimbabwe at a SADC security organ troika summit in Livingstone, Zambia, in March 2011. By that year, SADC economies had lost an estimated $36 billion in potential investments due to Zimbabwe's long-running crisis.[42]

Jacob Zuma's first state visit as president was to Angola in August 2009, leading a large business and ministerial delegation. Angola, a country that South Africa's apartheid army had occupied and bombed during the 1980s, was now providing lucrative opportunities for South African businesses to rebuild the very infrastructure that the apartheid army had previously destroyed. Angola's potential as a regional power is clear: this is a diamond and oil-rich state – among Africa's largest oil producers, with reserves of four billion barrels – and a strong, battle-hardened army that has intervened successfully in the DRC and Congo-Brazzaville. Angola is the only country that could become a future rival to South Africa in Southern Africa in the foreseeable future. By 2002, Tshwane had become Luanda's largest source of imports (12 per cent), and a South African–Angolan chamber of commerce was launched a year later. Thousands of Angolan students study in South African secondary schools and universities: a potential source of future pro-South African elites. Luanda further influenced Tshwane's pro-Laurent Gbagbo policy in Côte d'Ivoire in 2011, and was instrumental in mobilising support for the successful candidacy of South Africa's minister of home affairs, Nkosazana Dlamini-Zuma, to become chair of the AU Commission in July 2012.

One of South Africa's most important strategic relationships in Southern Africa is with Mozambique. A permanent joint cooperation commission was established between the two countries in July 1994, as well as a heads-of-state bilateral economic forum three years later that included cabinet ministers. In 2002, Mozambique overtook Zimbabwe to become Tshwane's largest trading partner in Africa, with 27 per cent of its imports coming from South Africa. Two years later, South Africa became the country's largest investor, helping to diversify Mozambique's agricultural economy with industrial investments: a $2.3 billion Mozal aluminum smelter was established by 2000; Sasol's $1.2 billion project built an 865-kilometre pipeline in a joint venture with Mozambique's government; Vodacom invested $567 million; and an agreement was signed for a $1.3 billion hydroelectric dam in the Zambezi valley. Many of these investments – which sought to promote technology and skills transfer – were concentrated in the Maputo Trade Corridor between Mozambique's capital and South Africa's industrial heartland of Gauteng. This could be a model to be replicated in South Africa's other strategic relations with its neighbours. Incidents like the xenophobic attacks in South Africa in May 2008 – which disproportionately targeted Mozambicans (and Zimbabweans) and led to a return home of thousands of its 60,000 migrants in South Africa – could, however, negatively affect Tshwane's bilateral relations with other states in its neighbourhood.[43]

Having assessed the first and second concentric circles of South Africa's foreign policy, focusing on domestic constraints and the Southern African sub-region, the book turns to an examination of the third concentric circle – South Africa's relations with Africa beyond Southern Africa.

The Great Lakes: Gulliver and the Lilliputians

Congolese scholar Georges Nzongola-Ntalaja focuses in his chapter on South Africa's peacemaking role in Burundi and the DRC, noting – like Devon Curtis – the limits of "exporting" the country's own peacemaking model abroad, and raising issues about the economic interests in its peacemaking role in the Congo. He also assesses the deteriorating relations with Rwanda after assassination attempts in South Africa against senior Rwandan officials who had been granted political asylum in Johannesburg.

Based on its size as Africa's geographically second-largest country (after Algeria), the Congo's strategic position at the heart of Africa, and its rich mineral resources, this Central African "Gulliver" is the most important country for the stability of a large part of Africa: one of the key reasons why South Africa pushed for the DRC's inclusion in SADC in November 1997. During the early part of the Congo crisis from 1997, differences between South Africa and its interventionist neighbours – Zimbabwe, Angola and Namibia – paralysed SADC, and the OAU (now the AU) took over mediation efforts. South Africa, which had earlier supplied military matériel to Rwanda and Uganda, urged Kigali and Kampala (Angola mostly led the process with Uganda) to withdraw their troops from the DRC. President Mbeki thus led peacemaking efforts and contributed 1,400 troops to the 20,000-strong UN mission in the Congo.

A critical part of South Africa's role in the DRC relates to its economic role, and some scholars, such as Congolese analysts Georges Nzongola-Ntalaja and Claude Kabemba, have even questioned Tshwane's motives in playing such an active mediation role, wondering whether it is mainly because of its economic interests in the Congo (see Nzongola-Ntalaja in this volume).[44] These interests involve mining, agriculture, fishery, energy, construction and communication. South Africa had become one of the DRC's largest trading partners in Africa by 2015, and its companies in the country included AngloGold Ashanti, De Beers, Anglo Vaal, BHP Billiton, JIG Mining, Meorex, Kumba Resources and Mwana Africa. But South African companies have also been accused of using dubious means to pursue their business interests. AngloGold Ashanti had to admit to paying bribes of $9,000 to Nationalist and Integrationist Front (FNI) rebels in northeastern DRC. However, in contrast, Vodacom has provided scholarships to Congolese youths to study in South Africa, and sponsored sports events in the DRC.[45] The most ambitious South African project in the DRC is, doubtless, state utility Eskom's 15-year effort to transform the Congo's Grand Inga Dam into a source of electricity for much of sub-Saharan Africa.

This section now moves from Central Africa's Gulliver to its two Lilliputians of Burundi and Rwanda. After 1999, South Africa was active in mediation efforts in Burundi through Nelson Mandela and Jacob Zuma. In further support of a regional approach to the conflicts in the Great Lakes, the UN Security Council finally heeded South African calls to take over the cash-strapped AU mission in Burundi – with South African, Mozambican and Ethiopian peacekeepers – and subsume it under a UN force. The peacekeepers experienced delays in obtaining troops, deployment was slow, and even the mission's South African backbone expressed an unwillingness to continue providing many of its specialised units to the mission.[46] Burundi's post-constitution referendum was finally adopted in February 2005, and presidential elections were held six months later, which Pierre Nkurunziza won. However, the early termination of the UN peacekeeping mission in December 2006 resulted in continued instability in Burundi.[47] By 2016, South Africa was being urged to re-engage in mediation efforts as 400 people were killed in the aftermath of a controversial third electoral victory for President Nkurunziza.

South Africa's involvement in Burundi was partly a recognition that it could not succeed in the Congo unless it adopted a regional approach to the conflicts in the Great Lakes region that prioritised peace in the DRC, Burundi and Rwanda. Its companies have invested in Rwanda, while Rwandan students have studied at South African universities at the same reduced fees as SADC citizens. Kigali, however, played an interventionist role in the Congo (also involving looting of mineral resources according to several UN reports) that sometimes adversely affected Tshwane's peace-making efforts. South Africa led the SADC force that routed the Rwandan-backed rebel March 23 Movement (M23) by December 2013. The bilateral relationship, however, deteriorated badly when Kigali was suspected of assassination attempts on two former Rwandan military officials granted political asylum in South Africa. Kayumba Nyamwasa survived three murder attempts, while Patrick Karegeya was assassinated in Johannesburg in January 2014. Both countries expelled each other's ambassadors, and most consular staff were withdrawn (see Nzongola-Ntalaja in this volume).

West Africa: God, Gold and Glory

Nigerian scholar Adekeye Adebajo, in his chapter in this volume, uses the leitmotifs of God, gold and glory to describe South Africa's relations with West Africa's three largest economies: Nigeria, Ghana and Côte d'Ivoire. "Glory" represents South Africa's rivalry with Nigeria for leadership in Africa; "gold" represents Tshwane's relationship with fellow gold producer Ghana; while "God" represents South Africa's efforts to promote peace and reconciliation in Côte d'Ivoire. Relations between South Africa and Nigeria had a difficult beginning. After the brutal hanging of activist Ken Saro-Wiwa and eight of his Ogoni campaigners by the regime of General Sani Abacha during the Commonwealth summit in Auckland in November 1995, a deeply betrayed President Nelson Mandela called for the imposition of oil sanctions on Abacha and advocated Nigeria's expulsion from the Commonwealth. South Africa's president also called on a SADC summit to take collective action against Nigeria. However, even Mandela's iconic status failed to rally a single Southern African state to take action against Nigeria. Instead, it was South Africa that was being accused by many African leaders of sowing seeds of division in Africa and undermining African solidarity. Seeking to isolate Abuja, Tshwane instead found itself isolated on the continent. This was the most painful lesson in navigating the treacherous waters of African diplomacy in the post-apartheid era. It was a watershed moment for South Africa's future engagement on the continent, and involved a determination not to be diplomatically isolated by other African states.

While the presidencies of Nigeria's Olusegun Obasanjo and South Africa's Thabo Mbeki between 1999 and 2007 are widely considered to have been the "golden age" of relations between Nigeria and South Africa, there were tensions in 2011 in the approach of both countries on the UN Security Council to tackling the conflicts in Côte d'Ivoire and Libya under the presidency of Jacob Zuma and Goodluck Jonathan. Both African powers acted at cross-purposes on both issues. The state visit by President Jacob Zuma to Nigeria in March 2016 was significant, and represented somewhat of a thaw in relations between Africa's two largest economies. Abuja had felt – under Goodluck Jonathan – that it had been replaced by Angola as South Africa's strategic partner in Africa. The fact that Zuma was the first foreign leader to have been hosted on a state visit by Nigerian president Muhammadu Buhari (in office only from May 2015) was therefore significant.

Under Mbeki and Obasanjo, bilateral trade also increased greatly, with Nigeria becoming South Africa's largest trading partner in Africa, a relationship worth R55 billion in 2015. After 1994, the South African telecommunications giants MTN (Mobile Telephone Networks) and M-Net/SuperSport blazed the trail into Africa's largest market. By 2003– 2004, MTN Nigeria's post-tax profit of R2.36 billion had surpassed MTN South Africa's R2.24 billion profit.[48] MTN's success convinced many other South African firms to invest in Nigeria. Other prestigious companies that followed included Stanbic, Rand Merchant Bank, Alexander Forbes, the Protea hotel chain, Chicken Licken, the Debonairs pizza chain and Shoprite Checkers.[49] South African-dominated malls are now ubiquitous in Nigeria's megalopolis and main commercial hub of Lagos, as well as in major cities like Ibadan. Despite these successes, many Nigerians remain deeply resentful that the relationship disproportionately favours South Africa, arguing that the South African market remains closed to Nigerian companies while over 90 per cent of its own exports to South Africa consist of oil.

During the colonial era, Ghana was known as the "Gold Coast". Like South Africa, the country was an African El Dorado. Gold still remained Ghana's main export in 2016, though oil exports are increasing, and cocoa remains important. While South Africa's relationship with Nigeria has been both political and economic, its relations with Ghana have tended to focus largely on trade. In 1999, South African state utility, Eskom, launched the Self-Help Electricity Project, which helped boost electricity supplies to Ghana's rural areas. A bi-national commission was established in 2004. While Ghana imports mostly processed and manufactured goods from South Africa, it exports agricultural and semi-processed commodities to South Africa. Companies from South Africa have become major players in Ghana's mining, telecommunications, construction, tourism and general trade sectors. In one of the most successful pan-African commercial ventures, South Africa's AngloGold acquired a 50 per cent stake in Ghana's Ashanti Goldfields in 2004. The new conglomerate, AngloGold Ashanti, was in 2016 the world's third largest gold producer, with 17 gold mines in nine countries. South African brand-names also dominate a large mall opened in Accra in 2008.

After 1994, South Africa recognised the potential of Côte d'Ivoire to become a strategic sub-regional partner due to its strong economy. A bilateral accord to promote and protect South Africa's investments was concluded in 1999, but a military coup by Ivorian general Robert Guei at the end of that year led to a thaw in growing bilateral relations. However, the country had still become South Africa's third largest bilateral trade partner in West Africa after Nigeria and Ghana by 2001, at a time when South African companies like Randgold and MTN had entered the Ivorian market. Then president Thabo Mbeki also sought to mediate Côte d'Ivoire's civil conflict between 2004 and 2006. Mbeki's mediation, however, came to be perceived by opposition parties as being biased towards President Laurent Gbagbo. West African actors also became increasingly critical, and Mbeki stepped down from his role, with both Nigeria and Senegal insisting on the leadership of the process by the Economic Community of West African States (ECOWAS).[50] Despite the country's political fragility, Côte d'Ivoire still remains the largest economy in francophone West Africa, and the third-largest market in the sub-region after Nigeria and Ghana. It also has gold mines, oil and other economic prospects in sectors that South African companies find attractive.

Eastern Africa: Building Peace and Making Money

Moving from West to Eastern Africa, Kenyan scholar Gilbert Khadiagala shows in his chapter how Tanzania and Uganda have acted as bridges for South Africa's peacemaking role in the Great Lakes region. He also assesses South Africa's peacemaking and peacebuilding roles in Sudan and South Sudan, as well as its difficult political and economic relations with Kenya, which have subsequently improved under the Jacob Zuma administration after 2009. Khadiagala recommends that Tshwane pursue its interests in this sub-region by building closer ties with multilateral institutions such as the East African Community (EAC) and the Intergovernmental Authority on Development (IGAD).

Tanzania, a SADC member, could potentially serve as a bridge between Southern and East Africa, in the same way that the DRC could bridge Southern and Central Africa. Tanzania had hosted military cadres of South Africa's ruling ANC during much of its liberation struggle, forging strong personal ties between leaders in both countries. Tshwane and Dar es Salaam also worked closely in peacemaking efforts in Burundi between 1999 and 2005. Both further formed the bulk of peace-enforcement troops deployed to the eastern Congo in 2013. By 2007, between 4,000 and 5,000 South Africans – the largest presence on the continent at the time – lived in Dar es Salaam and Arusha. Tanzania's capital came to be known as "Little Pretoria" by locals as a result of its large Boer presence (referred to as *kuburu* in the local vernacular). South Africans in Tanzania worked in sectors as diverse as banking, construction, mining, tourism, retail and telecommunications, though they have created some resentment among locals for their apparently draconian labour practices.[51] A bi-national commission was established in 2011 to coordinate political, economic and social ties between both countries, by which time South Africa had become Tanzania's largest foreign investor.

Like Tanzania, Uganda had also hosted ANC cadres (eventually about 3,000) following their departure from Angola in 1988. Tshwane involved Kampala in its peacemaking efforts in Burundi, though the Ugandan military played a more destabilising role in South Africa's peacemaking efforts in the DRC (like Rwanda, also accused of looting mineral resources in several UN reports). A South Africa–Uganda joint cooperation commission was established in 2002, with South African companies such as MTN, South African Breweries (SAB) Miller, Stanbic, Shoprite Checkers and Sanlam also investing in the country.

In stark contrast to the friendly ties with Tanzania and Uganda, South Africa's relations with Eastern Africa's economic giant – Kenya – have been difficult. As Khadiagala notes in his chapter, successive Kenyan governments had maintained commercial ties with the apartheid regime that poisoned relations with the post-apartheid government in Tshwane. There were also tensions in trade relations, with South African companies such as SABMiller, Shoprite Checkers and MTN stoking up resentment by failing to work with local partners and sometimes faltering as a result. This was corrected somewhat after 2012 when mergers were negotiated with Kenyan counterparts in areas such as banking, insurance, retail and tourism, though with mixed results. Political relations, however, warmed between Jacob Zuma and Uhuru Kenyatta, resulting in a state visit to Nairobi by the South African president in October 2016.

Sudan remains a strategically important country that could potentially serve as a bridge between Eastern Africa and North Africa if it can stabilise long-running conflicts in Darfur, Southern Kodorfan and Blue Nile.[52] South Africa was often asked by both sides to mediate the conflict in South Sudan (which gained its independence in July 2011), but declined in favour of regional actors within IGAD. Thabo Mbeki, after stepping down from power in September 2008, became the AU's key mediator in this dispute, though he remained deeply distrusted in Juba due to a perceived closeness with Sudanese leader Omar al-Bashir. Tshwane also chaired the AU Committee on Post-Conflict Reconstruction in Sudan, and provided capacity-building training to Khartoum and Juba (over 1,600 civil servants were trained by 2011) through its foreign ministry and the University of South Africa (UNISA). There were also reports of arms sales and military training to the South Sudanese army (see Khadiagala in this volume). On the economic front, South African companies such as SABMiller and MTN invested in the new state of South Sudan after 2011. Sudanese leader Omar al-Bashir first visited South Africa in August 1997, while a South African business delegation went to Sudan in July 2001. Tshwane established an embassy in Khartoum in January 2004 and a consulate in Juba in March 2007.[53]

South Africa also contributed troops to the second, and expanded, 7,000-strong African Union Mission in Sudan (AMIS II), composed mainly of soldiers from Nigeria and Rwanda, which was established in October 2004 to operate primarily in Darfur. The mission was transformed into the UN/AU Hybrid Operation in Darfur (UNAMID) by September 2008. As earlier noted, though, South Africa decided to withdraw all 797 of its troops from the UN mission in Darfur in May 2016. Tshwane has also sought to balance its ties with Khartoum and Juba, and its deputy president, Cyril Ramaphosa, was appointed as a mediator in South Sudan's civil war in 2014.

Finally, South Africa's bilateral ties with Ethiopia – a country not covered in Khadiagala's chapter – also deserves a special mention. This Eastern African giant – with a population of about 95 million in 2017 – given its military strength, growing economy and hosting of the AU Commission's headquarters, continues to be a leading power, and potential hegemon, in the region. Ethiopia was the largest contributor to UN peacekeeping in August 2017, with troops deployed largely in Abyei, Darfur and South Sudan, while Addis Ababa was also a major contributor to the AU mission in Somalia. Ethiopia, however, continues to suffer from serious internal governance issues, and declared a state of emergency in October 2016 following persistent unrest in parts of the country. Thabo Mbeki and Ethiopian prime minister Meles Zenawi were political allies, and two of Africa's Philosopher-Kings (visionary, intellectual leaders) and members of the Progressive Governance Forum. Tshwane provided capacity-building assistance to Ethiopia's public sector during this era. The University of South Africa also opened a campus in Addis Ababa in 2007 – at the request of the Ethiopian government – to strengthen the country's education sector, while Mbeki proposed Meles to chair NEPAD's implementation committee in January 2007. South Africa further built a showpiece embassy in Addis Ababa – its largest in Africa –

as a potent symbol of its leadership role in the AU, which again highlights the geo-strategic importance of Ethiopia in African diplomacy.[54]

North Africa: In the Shadow of the Afro-Arab Spring

Moving from Eastern Africa to North Africa, Egyptian scholar Rawia Tawfik assesses in her chapter how South Africa has sought to reformulate its foreign policy towards Egypt, Libya, Tunisia and Algeria in light of the "Afro-Arab Spring" of 2011 and its tendency – as noted by Curtis and Nzongola-Ntalaja – to attempt to "export" its peacemaking model to other countries. I identify here Egypt, Libya and Algeria as the three most important countries for South Africa in this sub-region. Oil and gas-rich Algeria has been prevented from assuming its role as the natural hegemon of the Maghreb due to a bloody civil war after its military brass-hats annulled democratic elections that Islamists were poised to win in 1991.[55] Algeria also continues to suffer from sporadic terrorist attacks. Nelson Mandela had famously travelled to Algeria in 1961 and been profoundly impressed with its National Liberation Front (FLN) movement. During the anti-apartheid struggle, many ANC cadres were hosted in both Algeria and Egypt. Algerian president Abdelaziz Bouteflika played an important role as foreign minister and president of the UN General Assembly, in suspending apartheid South Africa from the General Assembly in 1974. Under Mandela's government, Tshwane's hosting of the leaders of what Algiers considered the "terrorist" Armed Islamic Group (GIA) had strained bilateral ties. But Thabo Mbeki established a presidential commission with Algeria involving cabinet members, and Algiers was a reliable partner within NEPAD (with Bouteflika being one of the five members of its steering committee) and the AU.[56] Growing economic ties must, however, catch up with strong diplomatic relations. Jacob Zuma also visited Algiers in April 2015.

In contrast to Algeria's Bouteflika, Libya's mercurial Muammar Qaddafi was a thorn in South Africa's flesh under President Thabo Mbeki. The self-styled "Brother Leader" was the moving force behind the transformation of the OAU into the AU between 1999 and 2002, though his vision of a federalist "United States of Africa", an all-African army and a common monetary union, was – like the integrationist ideas of Ghana's Kwame Nkrumah in the 1960s – rejected by most African leaders, including South Africa, at the AU summit in the Ghanaian capital of Accra in July 2007.[57] Qaddafi used his oil wealth to buy influence within the African Union by hosting several important meetings, and provided $4.5 million to pay off the arrears to the OAU of several states.[58] Under Mandela's rule, bilateral relations between Tshwane and Tripoli were strong, based on the personal relationship between both leaders. This period saw South Africa brokering a deal over the Lockerbie crisis in 1999 that led to a lifting of sanctions on Libya, earning Mandela much gratitude in Tripoli. However, tensions increased under Mbeki's administration after 1999, as Qaddafi sought to move the AU inaugural summit in 2002 from the South African port city of Durban to his home-town of Sirte. Qaddafi thus tried to thwart South Africa's leadership goals within the AU. Mbeki's successor, Jacob Zuma, enjoyed much better relations with the Libyan leader, but was unsuccessful in efforts to mediate an end to the crisis that led to the toppling and assassination of the Libyan autocrat in October 2011.

Egyptian leader Hosni Mubarak was – until the battle for a UN Security Council seat with South Africa and Nigeria in 2005 – seen as detached from African affairs, rarely attending continental diplomatic meetings, despite being one of five members of the South African-driven NEPAD steering committee. Mandela visited Cairo in 1997, and bilateral relations were cordial under his rule. Tensions over the UN Security Council seat and Cairo's bid against South Africa to host the Pan-African Parliament in 2004 and the soccer World Cup in 2010, however, led to tensions under Mbeki's rule. Ruffled feathers were smoothed over somewhat by Mubarak's state visit to South Africa in August 2008, and Tshwane established a trade office in Cairo.[59]

The Afro-Arab Spring of 2011 toppled Mubarak's dictatorship and eventually led to a coup d'état by General Abdel Fattah el-Sisi in July 2013 and the country's subsequent suspension from the AU. Only after elections – of questionable legitimacy – in Egypt in May 2014 was the country allowed back into the AU fold. These events resulted in Cairo playing an even more active role in the Middle East and pursuing a less active role in Africa (though it has played a strong military role in post-Qaddafi Libya). Egypt remains the Arab world's political and cultural epicentre, and with South Africa's historical ambitions to play a mediation role in the Middle East crisis, good bilateral ties with Cairo will be critical.

The Bicycle Strategy

With this assessment of South Africa's bilateral ties in Africa as a foundation, a bicycle strategy can be used to describe the country's contemporary foreign policy on the continent. Based on the last two and a half post-apartheid decades, the five hubs in South Africa's foreign policy are Angola in Southern Africa, Nigeria in West Africa, the DRC in the Great Lakes region, Tanzania in Eastern Africa and Algeria in North Africa. In Southern Africa, the two spokes would be Mozambique and Zimbabwe. In the Great Lakes region, they would be Burundi and Rwanda; in West Africa, Ghana and Côte d'Ivoire; in Eastern Africa, Tanzania and Ethiopia; in North Africa, Egypt and Libya. It is around these five hubs and ten spokes – a total of about a quarter of the African Union's membership – that South Africa can build solid strategic bilateral relationships in Africa. Six of these strategic countries – Nigeria, Angola, Algeria, Libya, Sudan and South Sudan – produce 80 per cent of Africa's oil and possess 90 per cent of the continent's petroleum reserves.[60] Four other important countries included here – Nigeria, Algeria, Libya and Egypt – are assessed, along with South Africa, to pay 75 per cent of the AU's annual operating budget. Based on history, population, sub-regional political clout, trade and the importance of bilateral ties developed over the past two and a half decades, these are the key actors for promoting South Africa's bilateral interests in Africa.

Africa: Key Multilateral Ties

SADC and SACU

Within the second of our four concentric circles, South Africa's key multilateral ties in its sub-region are with the Southern African Customs Union and the Southern African Development Community. Many of Southern Africa's other 226 million citizens still fear today that contemporary institutions such as SADC and SACU could be used as instruments by a black-led government to fulfill the historical aims of South Africa's white leaders and big business to incorporate neighbouring "vassals" into a South African-dominated "constellation of states". These sentiments are often greatly underestimated by many ahistorical scholars of South African foreign policy, though the South African government itself tends to be more sensitive about its past.[61]

South African scholars Chris Saunders and Dawn Nagar assess in their joint chapter the political and economic aspects of South Africa's role in the 15-member SADC, noting that the country has failed to pay sufficient account to the sub-regional body. Though South Africa has played a leadership role within SADC, particularly in the area of peacemaking, it has been less successful at promoting regional integration despite accounting for about 60 per cent of the sub-regional economy. British scholar Richard Gibb then examines South Africa's role in SACU (with Botswana, Swaziland, Lesotho and Namibia), which he observes is the world's oldest existing customs union (founded in 1910). Noting that South Africa's interests have determined the nature, evolution and character of the Union, Gibbs calls on Tshwane to lead efforts to achieve deeper regional integration and better coordinated regional development in Southern Africa.

South Africa is no longer as mercantilist a power as it once was under apartheid. The country has loosened some of its protectionist policies in Southern Africa. Tshwane agreed to restructure SACU to render greater benefits to its other members, whose share of revenues increased from 2.6 per cent in 1969–1970 to 31.8 per cent in 1991–1992. In October 2002, a new SACU agreement was signed that sought to democratise the institution and introduced decision-making by consensus. Its secretariat was moved from South Africa's Department of Trade and Industry in Tshwane to the Namibian capital of Windhoek. But SACU has not created a single joint project in its over 100-year history, and there continues to be serious anger across Southern Africa at what is seen as South Africa's use of its economic muscle to block other countries' industrialisation efforts. Namibia's cement industry and Botswana's car assembly plants have been cited as examples. Zimbabwe has traditionally complained about South Africa's protectionism of its textile industry. Several SACU members have further argued that Tshwane's regulations have prevented them from protecting their infant industries from South African firms. There continues to be widespread grumbling about the dumping of cheaper South African goods to the detriment of local producers.

The OAU/AU

Moving from our second concentric circle in Southern Africa to the third of our four concentric circles focusing on relations with Africa beyond Southern Africa, South African scholar-diplomat Eddy Maloka argues that any understanding of the country's engagement with the OAU/AU must be set within the context of the relationship of the ANC – Africa's oldest liberation movement, established in 1912 – with the OAU in the post-colonial liberation struggle. He then explores Tshwane's "African Agenda" since 2008 and South Africa's contributions to building the institutions of the AU, with three key bodies – NEPAD, the APRM and the Pan-African

Parliament – hosted by South Africa. Thabo Mbeki, along with Nigeria's Olusegun Obasanjo, led efforts to transform the OAU into the AU after 1999. They challenged the OAU's inflexible adherence to absolute sovereignty and non-interference in the internal affairs of member states.[62] At the OAU summit in Algiers in 1999, both African leaders were instrumental in pushing for the ostracism of regimes that engaged in unconstitutional changes of government. The organisation subsequently barred the military regimes of Côte d'Ivoire and Comoros from attending its summit in the Togolese capital of Lomé in 2000. Mbeki also successfully convinced his colleagues that the OAU must recognise the right of other states to intervene in the internal affairs of its members in egregious cases of gross human rights abuses and to stem regional instability. These ideas were later enshrined into the AU's Constitutive Act of 2000.

Mbeki further stressed the importance of conflict resolution in Africa, pushing the AU to launch interventions into Burundi, Darfur and Somalia. South Africa and Nigeria succeeded in curbing much of Libyan leader Muammar Qaddafi's grand federalist ambitions and helped to create an African Union that would pursue more gradualist integration based on strong sub-regional pillars. However, many of the AU institutions that were established – the APRM (headed by Maloka since February 2016), NEPAD and the PAP – have remained fledgling and reliant on external funding. As earlier noted, Tshwane's successful effort to elect South Africa's former foreign minister, Nkosazana Dlamini-Zuma, as AU Commission chair in July 2012, divided the organisation, and broke the unwritten rule of no large country traditionally contesting the position. The AU has also failed to establish an African Standby Force (ASF) to undertake peacekeeping missions, resulting in interventions by France in Mali and the CAR in 2013 in contravention of late Kenyan scholar Ali Mazrui's principle of *Pax Africana*. President Jacob Zuma subsequently led efforts to set up an interim 5,000-strong African Capacity for Immediate Response to Crises (ACIRC), but even this force had not been fully established by 2017.

The World Beyond Africa: Key Bilateral Ties

Moving to the fourth of our four concentric circles involving ties with the world beyond Africa, this book's fourth part examines bilateral relations with Britain, France, the United States and China. Along with Germany, these remain among South Africa's largest trading partners.

Britain and France

Historically, the ANC's relations with the British government were difficult, with Prime Minister Margaret Thatcher (1979–1990) in particular having opposed sanctions and backed the apartheid government against what she regarded as ANC "terrorists". But relations were mostly warm under the anglophile Nelson Mandela and Thabo Mbeki. As British scholar Daniel Large argues in his chapter, the main bone of contention under the Mbeki government was over Zimbabwe, where British premier Tony Blair adopted a hard line, with Mbeki later accusing him of trying to convince Tshwane to embark on a "regime change" military adventure into the country (a claim that Blair denied). British companies also sold South Africa arms under Blair. Relations remained cordial under David Cameron and Jacob Zuma, though London's announcement of a cessation of bilateral aid in April 2013 (a decision on which the South Africans said they had not been consulted) ruffled diplomatic feathers. A large share of British exports to Africa, however, continue to go to South Africa.

This book also examines the important bilateral relationship between South Africa and France, through the trenchant chapter by French scholar Roland Marchal. He argues that the paradoxical relationship between South Africa and France has been marked by leadership rivalry and policy differences, but also cooperation in several key areas. Marchal is critical of South Africa's efforts to play a leadership role in Africa, and highlights the failures of its policies in Libya (2011) and the Central African Republic (2013). Historically, Paris had helped the apartheid government in South Africa to develop nuclear technology and traded profitably with it, including selling arms to Pretoria. Nelson Mandela and Thabo Mbeki engaged France pragmatically, expanding trade ties but being wary of too-close political cooperation. However, Mbeki particularly courted French support under the presidency of Nicolas Sarkozy (2007–2012) to make South Africa and Africa's case to the leaders of the Group of Eight industrialised countries in a bid to secure support for the continent's development and security efforts.

The acerbic, deeply prejudiced Sarkozy did not waste time in revealing his true colours on the global stage. During a speech in the Senegalese capital of Dakar in July 2007, he noted: "One cannot blame everything on colonisation – the corruption, the dictators, the genocide, that is not colonisation." He went on to note that France might have made "mistakes", but believed in its "civilising mission ... and did not exploit anybody".

The French pseudo-philosophical president then incredibly noted: "Africans have never really entered history. They have never really launched themselves into the future. In a world where nature controls everything, man has remained immobile in the middle of an unshakable order where everything is determined. There is no room either for human endeavour, nor for the idea of progress".[63] This speech was widely condemned across Africa and in some French intellectual circles. Mbeki, who had earlier been insulted in February 2005 by French president Jacques Chirac during his mediation efforts in Côte d'Ivoire, with the complaint that the South African leader did not understand "the soul and psychology of West Africans", incredibly sent Sarkozy a bizarre letter published in *Le Monde* praising parts of Sarkozy's speech, and noting: "What you have said in Dakar, Mr President, has indicated to me that we are fortunate to count you as a citizen of Africa, as a partner in the long struggle for a true African Renaissance in the context of a European Renaissance".[64] Cameroonian scholar Achille Mbembe's eloquent riposte perhaps best captures the surprise of many in Africa: "That two years before he exits power, Mbeki would tie his impeccable pan-Africanist credentials to Sarkozy is but the latest paradox in the political journey of a man who has thrived on contradictions."[65]

The greatest symbol of the contemporary rivalry between Tshwane and Paris, however, was the incident in the mineral-rich Central African Republic – a former French colony – in 2013. The French-backed president François Bozizé had come to power through force of arms in 2003, before organising flawed elections in 2005 and 2011. A 400-strong French-backed all-francophone Mission for the Consolidation of Peace in the Central African Republic (MICOPAX) had been in the CAR since 2008. France was the CAR's largest development partner and kept 320 troops in the country under a defence agreement. Disagreements between Bangui and Paris, however, emerged over Bozizé's efforts to diversify his economic ties beyond France. Bozizé granted oil exploration rights to China in 2009, and Paris considered Beijing's growing presence as damaging to its own economic interests.[66] In a bid further to reduce dependence on France, Bozizé turned to South Africa (reportedly visiting Jacob Zuma in Tshwane in March 2013) and China for increased security and technical assistance for his army. Bangui had signed a military cooperation accord with Tshwane under Thabo Mbeki in February 2007 to conduct infantry training; facilitate protection of very important persons; provide equipment and uniforms; and refurbish military bases.

This agreement had annoyed France.[67] There were 26 South African trainers in the CAR before this accord was renewed by Jacob Zuma in December 2012. South African firms also entered the country's mining sector to compete with French and other firms. As the military situation in the Central African country deteriorated, South Africa deployed another 400 soldiers in January 2013, ostensibly to continue capacity-building and reintegration efforts and to protect South African assets and troops, some of whom had been patrolling the streets of Bangui.[68] The effort, however, fell between two stools: not providing enough force to act as a credible deterrent to rebels, while encouraging Bozizé to believe that his regime would be protected.

After a power-sharing peace agreement reached in the Gabonese capital of Libreville in January 2013 collapsed, Bozizé was toppled by Séléka rebels who marched into the capital three months later. South Africa suffered a humiliating debacle as its clearly inadequate troops failed to protect the regime, and suffered 13 deaths and 27 injured when about 3,000 Séléka rebels attacked its barracks in the CAR. MICOPAX had earlier been deployed between the rebels and the capital, but failed to halt the rebel attack. South African civil society and opposition parties launched a scathing attack on the Zuma administration for this disastrous incident, with some even accusing the government of having sought to protect a dictator for private commercial interests.[69] With Chad and Congo-Brazzaville driving regional mediation efforts, Zuma announced the withdrawal of all South African troops from the CAR in April 2013.

France's role in the CAR had been to protect the airport, increasing its troops to 600 as rebels approached Bangui. However, Paris was also providing technical cooperation to MICOPAX and coordinating efforts closely with the mission's dominant force, Chad. The Gallic power had intervened in 2006 and 2007 to save Bozizé's regime, but decided not to do so this time. During the rebel invasion of March 2013, South African officials accused the French of working with Chadian troops to allow the rebels to attack their soldiers. Paris retorted that South Africa had breached the Libreville agreement that had called for a withdrawal of all foreign troops, though it was unclear whether France – with troops deployed at the airport in Bangui – considered its own soldiers as belonging to this category. Paris also noted that it had helped to treat and evacuate South African troops at the airport in Bangui.[70]

A final case in which France was felt to have frustrated South Africa's mediation efforts was in former French colony and SADC member

Madagascar following a military coup in March 2009. Tshwane led peacemaking efforts on behalf of SADC, but complained about obstruction by Paris (which was accused of covertly backing the military junta) and a feeling of continuing possessiveness in France over its former colony.

The United States and China

We next turn to South Africa's relations with the United States and China. Regarding Washington, the Congressional Black Caucus (CBC) and TransAfrica had previously had their greatest success in influencing US policy when sanctions were imposed on South Africa's apartheid regime in 1986 after two-thirds of the US Congress had overridden a reactionary veto by conservative US president Ronald Reagan. This followed years of daily protests in front of the South African embassy in Washington, DC, led by TransAfrica, and involving prominent African-American legislators and civil society leaders who had founded the Free South Africa Movement to lead the drive for sanctions against South Africa. Since the US itself had operated a racist, apartheid system until the 1960s, it was possible to rally support for this cause by comparing it to an experience with which many Americans could clearly identify.

For the post-apartheid era, American analyst Stephen Weissman demonstrates in his chapter how pragmatic this bilateral relationship has been. Presidents Nelson Mandela and Bill Clinton had good personal relations, with Mandela – as a former president – famously supporting Clinton during the Monica Lewinsky sex scandal in 1998. As president, Mandela had however publicly opposed American efforts to create a military African Response Force and dismissed the three-year American aid programme to South Africa of $600 million as "peanuts". Mandela had similarly criticised Clinton's flagship African Growth and Opportunity Act (AGOA), which mostly imported African oil to the US. George W. Bush's illegitimate war against Iraq from 2003 – launched without a UN Security Council mandate – was condemned by both Mandela, from retirement, as an attempt to act as the "world's policeman", and Mbeki, who opposed the intervention more diplomatically. Mbeki, however, was more vociferous in his opposition to Bush's 2007 proposal to establish a US Africa Command on the continent. The Bush administration, for its part, was critical of what it saw as Tshwane's accommodationist policy towards Zimbabwe's Robert Mugabe. Both countries, however, cooperated in peacemaking efforts in Burundi, the DRC and South Sudan.

Under the Jacob Zuma and Barack Obama administrations, relations remained pragmatic. The South African president acceded to President Obama's call on the UN Security Council to support the North Atlantic Treaty Organisation (NATO) intervention in Libya in 2011, but then became one of the most vocal critics of the intervention following the morphing of a humanitarian mandate to protect civilians into a "regime change" agenda that led to the assassination of Muammar Qaddafi in October 2011. Obama, himself, later described the lack of post-reconstruction planning and the resulting domestic and regional instability as one of his greatest foreign policy "regrets".[71]

Chinese scholar Liu Haifang notes in her chapter that South Africa, which had previously recognised Taiwan during the apartheid era, established diplomatic relations with mainland China only in 1998. She argues that though South African policymakers tend to talk about bilateral ties as "strategic" and often stress South-South cooperation, Beijing tends to be far more pragmatic in pursuing its bilateral diplomacy with Tshwane. Though China had become South Africa's largest trading partner by 2016 and Beijing was instrumental in bringing Tshwane into the BRICS in April 2011, this relationship is far more important to South Africa than it is to China, which also competes with South Africa for economic influence on the continent.

Diplomatic relations between the ANC-led South African government and the People's Republic of China (PRC) were established in January 1998. High-level visits have since occurred, with then South African deputy president Thabo Mbeki visiting Beijing in April 1998, and Nelson Mandela visiting in May 1999. In April 2000, Chinese president Jiang Zemin visited South Africa, with both countries pledging to build South-South cooperation and to restructure Western dominance of the global economic architecture.[72] Tshwane and Beijing established a bi-national commission in 2001 – the only one of its kind established with an African country at the time[73] – through which to coordinate their bilateral relations and to promote increased investment, trade, skills transfer and cultural exchanges. As president, Mbeki paid a state visit to China with a business delegation in December 2001. The bi-national commission met in both countries three times between 2001 and 2007, during which time a Centre for Chinese studies was established at South Africa's Stellenbosch University; a $5 billion China-Africa development fund was created, with its headquarters in Johannesburg; and a free trade agreement was planned between China and the five SACU countries.[74]

Trade between South Africa and China, enhanced by the establishment of the South Africa–China Business Association (SACBA), increased from $1.5 billion in 1997 to about $9 billion in 2006. Between 2006 and 2008, South Africa became Beijing's second-largest trading partner in Africa after Angola, with 16 per cent of total continental trade in 2008.[75] While China exports manufactured and agricultural goods, electronics and textiles to South Africa, it imports manganese, gold, copper, tobacco, aluminum, car parts and chrome ore. South African brand-names such as SABMiller, AngloGold Ashanti, Anglo-American, Standard Bank, BHP Billiton and Spur also established a presence in China.[76] Tensions in this relationship, however, have revolved around Chinese exports of garments, which led to an estimated 23,000–85,000 South African job losses, in response to which South African labour unions successfully lobbied their government to impose curbs on Chinese imports in 2006.[77] Thabo Mbeki warned in December 2006 that Africa risked entering into a "colonial relationship" with Beijing if the continent continued to export raw materials to China while importing Chinese manufactured goods. The 2007 purchase by China's Industrial and Commercial Bank (ICBC) of 20 per cent of the shares of South Africa's Standard Bank at a cost of R36.7 billion ($5.5 billion), however, represented the largest foreign direct investment in South Africa's history at the time. By 2016, China had become South Africa's largest global trade partner, with trade worth about R293 billion. If care is not taken to manage their activities in Africa, however, both *Pax South Africana* and *Pax Sinica* could come to be seen as a new breed of economic exploitation and political imperialism in Africa.

In the area of foreign policy, South Africa and China have worked together in global forums and groupings such as the Group of 77 (G-77), the Non-Aligned Movement (NAM), the WTO and the Group of 20 to seek a fairer global trading system; collaborated within the UN Security Council between 2007 and 2008 to thwart Western policies on Iran and Zimbabwe; and pushed for a restructuring of the World Bank and the IMF to give greater voice to non-Western states.

The World Beyond Africa: Key Multilateral Ties

The book concludes with an exploration of the multilateral ties of our fourth concentric circle, focusing on an examination of South Africa's multilateral ties within the UN, the BRICS, the ACP, the EU and the WTO.

The United Nations

As Doctor Mashabane, South Africa's deputy ambassador at the UN between 2010 and 2014, argues in this volume, while South Africa was on the UN Security Council between 2007 and 2008, and 2010 and 2011, it pushed forcefully for a strengthening of security cooperation between the UN Security Council and African regional bodies such as the African Union. But Tshwane also became embroiled both times in controversial decisions. During its stint on the Security Council in 2007–2008, South Africa became caught up in unnecessary spats with Western powers over Iran and Myanmar. On the world body's most powerful organ, Tshwane sometimes acted like a lightweight boxer trying to fight with heavyweights and suffering the inevitable technical knock-outs that result from such hopeless mismatches. The country could simply have abstained and hidden behind Russian and Chinese vetoes. The hypocrisy of states such as the US, which invaded Iraq in 2003 without UN authorisation, must naturally be exposed. But post-apartheid South Africa should clearly not have been making the same arguments over Myanmar as the apartheid government was making over punishing apartheid South Africa's behaviour.[78]

During South Africa's second stint on the UN Security Council in 2011–2012, the main crisis focused around Libya. President Zuma's close ties with Libyan strongman Muammar Qaddafi enabled him to serve as an AU envoy to Tripoli during the crisis of 2011. However, the Zuma administration was stung by criticisms within the ruling ANC – in which Qaddafi still enjoyed much popularity as a revolutionary leader – that South Africa's support of the UN resolution to protect civilians had opened the door to NATO's "regime change" agenda and the subsequent assassination of Qaddafi in Sirte in October 2011. Along with its BRIC (Brazil, Russia, India and China) allies on the UN Security Council, South Africa subsequently accused NATO of having abused its protection mandate in Libya, and became one of the most vociferous critics of the Libyan intervention, straining ties with powerful Western countries such as the US, Britain and France.

South Africa was also elected to serve on the UN Human Rights Council from 2006 to 2010 and between 2014 and 2018. It pushed for such measures as the right to development; anti-racism; increasing the accountability of private security companies and multinational corporations; and the justiciability of socio-economic rights. Some of the country's civil society activists, however, criticised Tshwane for what they saw as its inconsistent support for the rights of lesbian, gay, bisexual, trans-gender and inter-sex (LGBTI) people, as well as its alleged failure to consult civil society groups ahead of important meetings of the UN Human Rights Council.[79]

The BRICS, the ACP/EU and the WTO

As Indian scholar Kudrat Virk shows in her chapter, the Libyan crisis of 2011 exposed the lack of unity of the BRICS bloc to act cohesively on the UN Security Council. The incident also raised questions about whether the group really had the clout to transform the global order, and whether it consisted instead of status quo powers merely seeking to negotiate a place at the top table of the very institutions that they have claimed to want to transform. South Africa joined the group in April 2011 and hosted its annual summit in Durban in March 2013. While membership in the BRICS may have raised South Africa's international profile, the fact that Nigeria overtook South Africa as the continent's largest economy in 2014 (South Africa regained this position in 2016), may have undermined its claims to speak for African interests and advocate for the continent's development. The BRICS have created a New Development Bank and announced plans to establish a credit-rating agency. But the bank would initially be capitalised only at $50 billion, half the amount at which the African Development Bank (AfDB) was capitalised.[80] As earlier noted, BRICS members have diverged on critical political issues, and by 2016 all but India suffered from sluggish growth. In crucial institutions of global governance – the UN Security Council, the World Bank and the IMF – BRICS members have been far from acting as revisionist powers seeking to transform the global system, but have instead often acted defensively and been unable to challenge Western dominance within these institutions.

As the long-serving South African ambassador to Brussels between 2012 and 2016, Mxolisi Nkosi, notes in his chapter, South Africa joined the 79-member African, Caribbean and Pacific Group in 1997 in order to further South-South solidarity and to derive trade benefits from relations with the 28-member European Union. Tshwane played a key role in often acrimonious trade negotiations with Brussels that eventually resulted in the signing of a SADC economic partnership agreement (EPA) in 2016. Like other African countries, South Africa had feared that the heavy-handed EPAs would disrupt regional integration efforts in Southern Africa and force open trade in sensitive areas in which sub-regional actors could not compete.[81] Tshwane had earlier concluded a free trade deal with the EU in 1999 that provided generous development aid to South Africa. The country subsequently became one of only 11 strategic global partners of the EU, and embarked on a regular political dialogue with Brussels from 2007, in which issues of conflict resolution, development, trade, education, culture, climate change and international crime were discussed.

Finally, Faizel Ismail, South Africa's ambassador to the World Trade Organisation between 2010 and 2014, examines in his chapter Tshwane's role in the failed Doha round of trade negotiations between 2001 and 2015. Ismail – who was instrumentally involved in the talks he describes – argues that South Africa built an alliance of developing countries to deal with agricultural issues. He also credits Tshwane with playing a leadership role on intellectual property rights and public health, while acknowledging the country's leading role in establishing the Non-Agricultural Market Access (NAMA-11) group, which successfully opposed efforts to force developing countries to reduce their industrial tariffs. There were, however, accusations from some Southern countries that South Africa, India and Brazil were engaging in non-transparent negotiations in smoke-filled "green rooms", cutting deals with powerful countries that would have benefited these developing countries as large agricultural producers. Such critics complained that these deals contradicted the interests of weaker countries, which were insisting on concrete trade concessions from richer countries. South Africa was particularly criticised by other African delegates for acting as a self-appointed African spokesperson without necessarily promoting the continent's interests.[82]

Concluding Reflections

In concluding this introduction, it is important to return to the concept of hegemony with which we began. In the post-apartheid era, South Africa has often acted as a regional hegemon in its peacemaking efforts across Africa, but has often lacked the capacity and vision to drive economic integration even in its Southern African sub-region, in which it accounts for about 60 per cent of the economy. Its leadership claims have also sometimes been challenged by countries such as Nigeria, Angola, Libya and – outside Africa – France and China.

Linking the two main concepts of hegemony and concentric circles used in this introduction, hegemony is clearly about both leadership and followership. The related idea of concentric circles, meanwhile, is about a country being strong at home in order to be able to project influence and power in its sub-region, continent and the wider world. South Africa certainly has influence at all three levels based on its role in SADC, SACU and the AU, as well as its membership in institutions such as the G-20 and the BRICS, and its strategic partnership with the EU. But while clearly able to act as a regional hegemon, South Africa is far from being a global power with a permanent seat on the UN Security Council and commensurate weight in such institutions of global governance as the World Bank, the IMF and the WTO.

Hegemonic theory describes a "gate-keeping" role in which regional gate-keepers seek to fence off their region and keep external powers out of their issues.[83] Could South Africa formulate a future continental "Monroe Doctrine" that keeps France out of Africa? South Africa and Nigeria appear to be starting to collaborate more closely in response to continuing Gallic influence in countries such as Mali, the CAR, Côte d'Ivoire and Madagascar. They would, however, need to work with other important African states such as Algeria, Ethiopia and Angola. Algiers, in particular, shares a similar antipathy as Tshwane and Abuja to French interventionism in Africa.

Some analysts have argued that South Africa has more legitimacy than Nigeria to provide leadership in Africa,[84] though it is often unclear whether South Africa is the "great white hope" or the "great black hope" on the continent. The idea of a liberal "Leviathan on the Limpopo" spreading "Western" democratic values into the heart of darkest Africa is still very much a recurring fantasy of many Eurocentric analysts. However, such views seriously underestimate the level of continuing widespread suspicions of post-apartheid South Africa as evidenced by African reactions to the expansion into the continent of its mostly white corporate sector; the continued lack of transformation of its senior military brass-hats; and the continued dominance of whites in the leadership of many South African academic institutions and NGOs.

South Africa had an impressive 44 embassies in Africa in 2017. It served on the UN Security Council in 2007–2008 and 2011–2012. Its citizens have also held high-profile international positions: Navi Pillay served as UN High Commissioner for Human Rights between 2008 and 2014, while Phumzile Mlambo-Ngcuka has headed UN Women since 2013. However, the country's diplomatic ambitions have not always been matched by its military capacity. Though Tshwane has continued to play an active peacekeeping role in the DRC – South Africa's General Derrick Mgwebi was appointed the force commander of the UN mission in the Congo in December 2015 – and, more recently, in Lesotho and South Sudan, the killing of 13 of its soldiers in the CAR in 2013 exposed its continuing lack of regional knowledge in parts of Africa.

The ruling African National Congress still believes that South Africa should continue to play an active leadership role on the continent, but also recognises – as noted at the start of this introduction – that the country needs to get its domestic house in order before it can fulfil these ambitions. The ruling party, however, damaged its international reputation by publishing a bizarre foreign policy discussion document in September 2015 that described the 1989 Tiananmen Square protests as part of an American-backed "counter-revolution", and condemned US policies in Africa and the Middle East as having the "sole intention" of toppling democratic governments. At the party's general council a month later, the ANC – angered by widespread criticism that it had not arrested Sudanese president Omar al-Bashir during the AU summit it hosted three months earlier – announced that the country would start proceedings to leave the International Criminal Court, and Tshwane subsequently submitted its instruments to quit the ICC in October 2016 – only to be forced to revoke the decision following the South African high court's ruling against it in February 2017.

Another June 2017 document from the ANC National Executive Committee's International Relations sub-committee, titled "The ANC in An Unpredictable and Uncertain World",[85] was poorly crafted and analytically weak, devoid of a clear understanding of the world and South Africa's place in it. The document used undefined terms like "national interest" as well as woolly phrases such as "Ubuntu Diplomacy" and "progressive internationalism", as if phraseology could be a substitute for concrete strategy. It adopted a Manichean view of the world in which unnamed "progressive" forces are battling invisible "reactionary" global imperialists, patriarchy and neo-colonialism. It was disappointing that one of the world's most successful liberation movements that relied enormously on international solidarity and a sophisticated and nuanced understanding of the world – under its redoubtable president Oliver Tambo – could again produce such an analytically shallow and intellectually weak document.

Though South Africa has energetically gained membership in key institutions such as the BRICS grouping and the Group of 20, it is still too early to tell whether this role might come to constitute "representation without power", and whether *Pax South Africana* can develop the capacity, legitimacy and followership to act as an effective regional hegemon on its own continent.

Notes

1. I thank Chris Landsberg for his invaluable comments on this chapter.
2. *See* Adebayo Adedeji, "Within or Apart?", in Adebayo Adedeji (ed.), *South Africa in Africa: Within or Apart?* (London: Zed, 1996), p. 9.
3. Adekeye Adebajo, Adebayo Adedeji and Chris Landsberg (eds), *South Africa in Africa: The Post-Apartheid Era* (Scottsville: University of KwaZulu-Natal (UKZN) Press, 2007); James Barber, *Mandela's World: The International Dimension of South Africa's Political Revolution, 1990–99* (Cape Town: David Philip, 2004); Chris Alden and Garth Le Pere, *South Africa's Post-Apartheid Foreign Policy: From Reconciliation to Revival?*, Adelphi Paper no. 362 (London: Institute for Strategic Studies, 2003); Elizabeth Sidiropoulos (ed.), *South Africa's Foreign Policy, 1994–2004: Apartheid Past, Renaissance Future* (Johannesburg: South African Institute of International Affairs (SAIIA), 2004).
4. Chris Landsberg and Jo-Ansie van Wyk (eds), *South African Foreign Policy Review*, vol. 1 (Tshwane: Africa Institute of South Africa, 2012); Lesley Masters, Siphamandla Zondi, Jo-Ansie van Wyk and Chris Landsberg (eds), *South African Foreign Policy Review*, vol. 2 (Tshwane: Africa Institute of South Africa, 2015).
5. John Siko, *Inside South Africa's Foreign Policy* (London: I.B.Tauris, 2014); Matthew Graham, *The Crisis of South African Foreign Policy: Diplomacy, Leadership and The Role of the African National Congress* (London: I.B.Tauris, 2016).
6. This section builds on Adekeye Adebajo, *The Curse of Berlin: Africa After the Cold War* (London: Hurst; New York: Columbia University Press; and Scottsville: UKZN Press, 2010), pp. 101–121.
7. *See* Barber, *Mandela's World*; Chris Landsberg, *The Diplomacy of Transformation: South African Foreign Policy and Statecraft* (Johannesburg: Pan Macmillan, 2010); Adam Habib and Nthakeng Selinyane, "South Africa's Foreign Policy and a Realistic Vision of an African Century", pp. 49–60, and Jack Spence, "South Africa's Foreign Policy: Vision and Reality", pp. 35–48, both in Sidiropoulos (ed.), *South Africa's Foreign Policy, 1994–2004*; Maxi Schoeman, "South Africa as an Emerging Middle Power, 1994–2003", in John Daniel, Adam Habib and Roger Southall (eds), *The State of the Nation: South Africa 2003–2004* (Cape Town: Human Sciences Research Council (HSRC) Press, 2003), pp. 349–367.
8. *See, for example*, Adekeye Adebajo and Chris Landsberg, "South Africa and Nigeria as Regional Hegemons", in Mwesiga Baregu and Chris Landsberg (eds), *From Cape to Congo: Southern Africa's Evolving Security Challenges* (Boulder, CO: Rienner, 2003), pp. 171–203; Paul Kennedy, *The Rise and Fall of the Great Powers* (New York: Vintage, 1987), pp. 151–158; Ali A. Mazrui, "Hegemony: From Semites to Anglo-Saxons", in *Cultural Forces in World Politics* (London: Currey, 1990), pp. 29–64.

9. I have found helpful in this area research by Stephen G. Brooks, "Can We Identify a Benevolent Hegemon?", *Cambridge Review of International Affairs* 25, no. 1 (March 2012), pp. 27–38; Sandra Destradi, "Empire, Hegemony, and Leadership: Developing a Research Framework for the Study of Regional Powers", Working Paper no. 79 (Hamburg: German Institute of Global and Area Studies (GIGA), June 2008); Miriam Prys, "Hegemony, Domination, Detachment: Differences in Regional Powerhood", *International Studies Review* 12 (2010), pp. 498–499.

10. I am indebted here to the work of John G. Ikenberry and Charles A. Kupchan, "Socialization and Hegemonic Power", *International Organisation* 44, no. 3 (Summer 1990), pp. 283–315; and Joseph S. Nye Jr., *Soft Power: The Means to Success in World Politics* (New York: PublicAffairs, 2004).

11. *See, for example*, Adekeye Adebajo (ed.), *Africa's Peacemakers: Nobel Laureates of African Descent* (London: Zed, 2014).

12. *See* Sam Nolutshungu, *South Africa in Africa: A Study in Ideology and Foreign Policy* (Manchester: Manchester University Press, 1975).

13. I owe this expression to Mazrui, "Hegemony", p. 30.

14. *See, for example*, Niall Ferguson, *Empire: How Britain Made the Modern World* (London: Penguin, 2003); Mazrui, *Cultural Forces in World Politics*; James Morris, *Pax Britannica* (London: Harvest, 1968).

15. This section builds on Adebajo, *The Curse of Berlin*, pp. 101–121.

16. Nelson Mandela, "South Africa's Future Foreign Policy", *Foreign Affairs* 72, no. 5 (November/December 1993), pp. 86–97.

17. *See* Kristina Bentley and Roger Southall, *An African Peace Process: Mandela, South Africa, and Burundi* (Cape Town: HSRC Press, 2005). *See also* Alden and Le Pere, *South Africa's Post-Apartheid Foreign Policy*; Barber, *Mandela's World*; Chris Landsberg, "Promoting Democracy: The Mandela-Mbeki Doctrine", *Journal of Democracy* 11, no. 3 (July 2000), pp. 107–121.

18. *See* Khabele Matlosa, "The Lesotho Conflict: Major Causes and Management", pp. 6–10, and Roger Southall, "Is Lesotho South Africa's Tenth Province?", pp. 19–25, both in Kato Lambrechts (ed.), *Crisis in Lesotho: The Challenge of Managing Conflict in Southern Africa*, African Dialogue Series no. 2 (Johannesburg: Foundation for Global Dialogue, March 1999).

19. Quoted in Eboe Hutchful, "Understanding the African Security Crisis", in Abdel-Fatau Musah and J. Kayode Fayemi (eds), *Mercenaries: An African Security Dilemma* (London: Pluto, 2000), p. 218.

20. *See* Adekeye Adebajo, "South Africa and Nigeria: An Axis of Virtue?", in Adebajo, Adedeji, and Landsberg, *South Africa in Africa*, pp. 213–235.

21. For accounts on Thabo Mbeki's leadership and thinking, *see* Adekeye Adebajo, *Thabo Mbeki: Africa's Philosopher-King* (Johannesburg: Jacana, 2016); Mark Gevisser, *Thabo Mbeki: The Dream Deferred* (Johannesburg: Jonathan Ball, 2007); William Mervin Gumede, *Thabo Mbeki and the Battle for the Soul of the ANC* (Cape Town: Zebra, 2005); Sean Jacobs and Richard Calland (eds), *Thabo Mbeki's World: The Politics and Ideology of the South African President* (Pietermaritzburg: University of Natal Press, 2002); Ronald Suresh Roberts, *Fit to Govern: The Native Intelligence of Thabo Mbeki* (Johannesburg: STE, 2007).

22. Confidential correspondence.

23. Alden and Le Pere, *South Africa's Post-Apartheid Foreign Policy*, p. 32. *See also* Walter Carlsnaes and Philip Nel (eds), *In Full Flight: South African Foreign Policy After Apartheid* (Midrand: Institute for Global Dialogue (IGD), 2006); and Roger Southall (ed.), *South Africa's Role in Conflict Resolution and Peacemaking in Africa* (Cape Town: HSRC Press, 2006).

24. *See, for example*, Adebajo, Adedeji, and Landsberg, *South Africa in Africa*; Alden and Le Pere, *South Africa's Post-Apartheid Foreign Policy*; Landsberg, *The Diplomacy of Transformation*; Sidiropoulos, *South Africa's Foreign Policy*.

25. *See* United Nations (UN), *Report of the UN Secretary-General on Burundi*, UN Doc. S/2004/210, 16 March 2004.

26. *See, for example*, Devon Curtis, "South Africa: 'Exporting Peace' to the Great Lakes Region", in Adebajo, Adedeji, and Landsberg, *South Africa in Africa*, pp. 253–273; Gilbert M. Khadiagala, "UN Peacekeeping in the Great Lakes Region: The DRC, Rwanda, and Burundi", in Adekeye Adebajo (ed.), *From Global Apartheid to Global Village: Africa and the United Nations* (Scottsville: UKZN Press, 2009), pp. 305–322; Chris Landsberg, "South Africa", in Gilbert M. Khadiagala (ed.), *Security Dynamics in Africa's Great Lakes* (Boulder, CO: Rienner, 2006), pp. 121–140; René Lemarchand, "Region-Building in Central Africa", in Daniel H. Levine and Dawn Nagar (eds), *Region-Building in Africa: Political and Economic Challenges* (New York: Palgrave Macmillan, 2016), pp. 231–244.

27. *See* Adebayo Adedeji, "NEPAD's African Peer Review Mechanism: Progress and Prospects," in John Akokpari, Angela Ndinga-Muvumba and Tim Murithi (eds), *The African Union and Its Institutions* (Johannesburg: Jacana, 2008), pp. 241–269.

28. I am grateful for these insights to Chris Landsberg, "Pax South Africana and the Responsibility to Protect", *Global Responsibility to Protect* 2, no. 4 (2010), pp. 436–457. *See also* Festus Aboagye, "South Africa and R2P: More State Sovereignty and Regime Security Than Human Security?", in Malte Brosig (ed.), *The Responsibility to Protect: From Evasive to Reluctant Action? The Role of Global Middle Powers* (Johannesburg and Tshwane: Hanns Seidel Foundation, Konrad Adenauer Stiftung, Institute for Security Studies, and SAIIA, 2012), pp. 29–52.

29. Thabo Mbeki, *Mahube: The Dawning of the Dawn, Speeches, Lectures, and Tributes* (Braamfontein, South Africa: Skotaville Media, 2001), pp. 179–183.

30. For an assessment of South African foreign policy after Mbeki, *see* Elizabeth Sidiropoulos, "South African Foreign Policy in the Post-Mbeki Period", *South African Journal of International Affairs* 15, no. 2 (December 2008), pp. 107–120.

31. *See, for example*, South Africa's Department of International Relations and Cooperation (DIRCO), *Strategic Plan 2013–2018* (Tshwane: Department of International Relations and Cooperation, 2013).

32. *See* Chris Landsberg, "The Concentric Circles of South Africa's Foreign Policy Under Jacob Zuma", *India Quarterly* 70, no. 153 (2014), pp. 153–172.

33. *See* David Smith, "Zambian Vice-President: 'South Africans Are Backward'", *Guardian* (London), 1 May 2013, https://www.theguardian.com.

34. Quoted in Adrian Ephraim, "Zuma: Don't Think Like An African – Pay UP for E-Tolls", *Mail and Guardian* (Johannesburg), 22 October 2013, http://mg.co.za.

35. *See* Centre for Conflict Resolution (CCR), "South Africa in Africa: The Dilemmas of Foreign Policy and Human Rights", Policy Brief no. 31 (Cape Town, September 2016); CCR, "South Africa, the ICC, and the UN Human Rights Council", Policy Brief no. 30 (Cape Town, August 2016), both available at http://www.ccr.org.za.

36. *See, for example*, Henry Kissinger, *World Order* (New York: Penguin, 2014).

37. *See* Ibrahim A. Gambari, "From Balewa to Obasanjo: The Theory and Practice of Nigeria's Foreign Policy", in Adekeye Adebajo and Raufu Mustapha (eds), *Gulliver's Troubles: Nigeria's Foreign Policy After the Cold War* (Scottsville: UKZN Press, 2008), pp. 58–80.

38. James Barber, *South Africa's Foreign Policy 1945–1970* (London: Oxford University Press, 1973); Chris Landsberg, "Foreign Policy-Making and Implementation in Post-Settlement South Africa", in Albert Venter and Chris Landsberg (eds), *Government and Politics in the New South Africa*, 3rd ed. (Tshwane: Van Schaik, 2006), pp. 255–258; Landsberg, "The Concentric Circles".

39. Landsberg, "The Concentric Circles", p. 154.

40. This section builds on Adekeye Adebajo, "The Bicycle Strategy of South Africa's Bilateral Relations in Africa", *South African Journal of International Affairs* 15, no. 2 (2008), pp. 121–136.

41. *See, for example*, Merle Lipton, "Understanding South Africa's Foreign Policy: The Perplexing Case of Zimbabwe," *South African Journal of International Affairs* 16, no. 3 (December 2009), pp. 331–345.

42. International Crisis Group, "Zimbabwe's Election: The Stakes for Southern Africa", Africa Briefing (Brussels, 11 January 2002), p. 9, http://www.crisisgroup. org/~/media/files/africa/southern-africa/zimbabwe/b008%20zimbabwes%20 election%20the%20stakes%20for%20southern%20africa.pdf.

43. I have relied for the information in this paragraph on Augusta Conchiglia, "South Africa and Its Lusophone Neighbours: Angola and Mozambique", in Adebajo, Adedeji and Landsberg, *South Africa in Africa*, pp. 247–251.

44. *See* Claude Kabemba, "South Africa in the DRC: Renaissance or Neo-Imperialism?", in Sakhela Buhlungu, John Daniel, Roger Southall and Jessica Lutchman (eds), *State of the Nation South Africa 2007* (Cape Town: HSRC Press, 2007), pp. 533–551.

45. *See* Kabemba, "South Africa in the DRC"; Judi Hudson, "South Africa's Economic Expansion into Africa: Neo-Colonialism or Development?", in Adebajo, Adedeji and Landsberg, *South Africa in Africa*, pp. 128–149.

46. *See* UN, *First Report of the Secretary-General on the United Nations Operation in Burundi*, UN Doc. S/2004/682, 23 August 2004, p. 8.

47. African Union Commission, *Report of the Chairperson of the African Union Commission on Conflict Situations in Africa*, Executive Council, 7th Ordinary Session, 28 June–2 July 2005, pp. 12–14.

48. Dianna Games, "An Oil Giant Reforms: The Experience of South African Firms Doing Business in Nigeria", *Business in Africa Report* no. 3 (Johannesburg: South African Institute of International Affairs, 2004), p. 57.

49. John Daniel and Nompumelelo Bhengu, "South Africa in Africa: Still a Formidable Player", in Roger Southall and Henning Melber (eds), *A New Scramble*

for Africa? Imperialism, Investment, and Development (Scottsville: UKZN Press, 2009), p. 149.

50. *See, for example*, Adekeye Adebajo, *UN Peacekeeping in Africa: From the Suez Crisis to the Sudan Conflicts* (Boulder, CO, and London: Rienner, 2011), pp. 139–170; Abdul Rahman Lamin, "The Conflict in Côte d'Ivoire: South Africa's Diplomacy, and Prospects for Peace", Occasional Paper no. 49 (Johannesburg: Institute for Global Dialogue, August 2005).

51. John Daniel, Jessica Lutchman and Alex Comninos, "South Africa in Africa: Trends and Forecasts in a Changing African Political Economy", in Buhlungu, Daniel, Southall and Lutchman, *State of the Nation 2007*, p. 526.

52. *See, for example*, Francis Deng, *War of Visions: Conflict of Identities in the Sudan* (Washington, DC: Brookings Institution, 1995); Dunstan M. Wai, *The African-Arab Conflict in the Sudan* (New York and London: Africana, 1981); Peter Woodward, *Sudan, 1898–1989: The Unstable State* (Boulder, CO: Rienner, 1990).

53. Some of this paragraph draws information from Iqbal Jhazbhay, "South Africa's Relations with North Africa and the Horn: Bridging a Continent", in Adebajo, Adedeji and Landsberg, *South Africa in Africa*, pp. 274–292.

54. This paragraph has also benefited factually from Jhazbhay, "South Africa's Relations with North Africa and the Horn".

55. *See* Hakim Darbouche, "Algeria: Presidential 21st Century Vision of the Future", *Africa Report* no. 5 (January 2007), pp. 72–74.

56. I am again grateful for some of the information in this paragraph to Jhazbhay, "South Africa's Relations with North Africa and the Horn".

57. *See* Adekeye Adebajo, "Africa's Quest for El Dorado", *Mail and Guardian* (Johannesburg), 29 June 2007. For another view, *see* Kwesi Kwaa Prah, "Without Unity There Is No Future for Africa", *Mail and Guardian* (Johannesburg), 29 June 2007.

58. Asteris Huliaras, "Qadhafi's Comeback: Libya and Sub-Saharan Africa in the 1990s", *African Affairs* 100, no. 398 (January 2001), p. 18.

59. This paragraph draws from Jhazbhay, "South Africa's Relations with North Africa and the Horn".

60. Sharath Srinivasan, "A Marriage Less Convenient: China, Sudan, and Darfur", in Kweku Ampiah and Sanusha Naidu (eds), *Crouching Tiger, Hidden Dragon? Africa and China* (Scottsville: UKZN Press, 2008), p. 61.

61. For a general overview, *see* Adebajo, Adedeji, and Landsberg, *South Africa in Africa*; Alden and Le Pere, *South Africa's Post-Apartheid Foreign Policy*; Landsberg, "Promoting Democracy"; Sidiropoulos, *South Africa's Foreign Policy*.

62. Adekeye Adebajo and Chris Landsberg, "The Heirs of Nkrumah: Africa's New Interventionists", *Pugwash Occasional Paper* 2, no. 1 (January 2000), pp. 65–90.

63. Quoted in Achille Mbembe, "*Sacré Bleu!* Mbeki and Sarkozy?", *Mail and Guardian* (Johannesburg), 24–30 August 2007, p. 24.

64. Quoted in Mbembe, "*Sacré Bleu!*", p. 24.

65. Mbembe, "*Sacré Bleu!*", p. 24.

66. Oladiran Bello, "Resource GeoPolitics Fuelling External Rivalry in the CAR", briefing paper (Johannesburg: SAIIA, 17 April 2013).

67. Glynnis Underhill, Phillip De Wet and Mmanaledi Mataboge, "SA, France Battle for Africa", *Mail and Guardian* (Johannesburg), 12 April 2013, http://www.mg.co.za.

68. Parliamentary Monitoring Group, South Africa, "Defence Minister on Central African Republic SA Soldier Deployment", 3 April 2013, http://www.pmg.org.za.

69. *See, for example*, Stephanie Wolters, "Did Zuma Fail Africa 101?", *City Press* (Johannesburg), 7 April 2013.

70. Underhill, De Wet and Mataboge, "SA, France Battle for Africa".

71. Quoted in the interview with Thomas L. Friedman, "Obama On The World," *The New York Times*, 8 August 2014, http://www.nytimes.com.

72. See Garth Le Pere and Garth Shelton, *China, Africa, and South Africa: South-South Co-operation in a Global Era* (Midrand: IGD, 2007), pp. 160–181; Garth Shelton, "South Africa and China: A Strategic Partnership?", in Chris Alden, Daniel Large and Ricardo Soares De Oliveira (eds), *China Returns to Africa: A Rising Power and a Continent Embrace* (London: Hurst, 2008), pp. 275–294.

73. I thank Garth Le Pere for this observation.

74. This paragraph and the next build on Adebajo, *The Curse of Berlin*, pp. 191–212.

75. These figures are from China's Ministry of Commerce and are cited in a short report by a policy analyst with Britain's Department for International Development in China: Mark George, "China Africa Two-Way Trade: Recent Developments", 30 January 2009, pp. 1–2.

76. Le Pere and Shelton, *China, Africa, and South Africa*, p. 171.

77. I rely in the following two paragraphs on Sanusha Naidu, "Balancing a Strategic Partnership? South Africa–China Relations", in Ampiah and Naidu, *Crouching Tiger, Hidden Dragon?*, pp. 167–191.

78. *See, for example*, Suzanne Graham, *Democratic South Africa's Foreign Policy: Voting Behaviour in the United Nations* (London: Palgrave Macmillan, 2016).

79. *See* CCR, "South Africa, the ICC, and the UN Human Rights Council".

80. This paragraph is partly summarised from CCR, "South Africa and the BRICS: Progress, Problems, and Prospects", Seminar Report no. 50 (Cape Town, November 2014), http://www.ccr.org.za.

81. *See* Gilbert M. Khadiagala, "Africa and Europe: Ending a Dialogue of the Deaf?", pp. 217–235, and Mareike Meyn, "An Anatomy of the Economic Partnership Agreements", pp. 197–216, both in Adekeye Adebajo and Kaye Whiteman (eds), *The EU and Africa: From Eurafrique to Afro-Europa* (London: Hurst, 2012).

82. *See* Patrick Bond, *Talk Left, Walk Right: South Africa's Frustrated Global Reforms* (Scottsville: UKZN Press, 2004), pp. 51–73.

83. Prys, "Hegemony, Domination, Detachment", pp. 498–499.

84. *See, for example*, Daniel Flemes and Thorsten Wojczewski, "Contested Leadership in International Relations: Power Politics in South America, South Asia, and Sub-Saharan Africa" Working Paper no. 121 (Hamburg: GIGA, February 2010), pp. 19–25.

85. African National Congress (ANC), "The ANC in an Unpredictable and Uncertain World That Is Characterised by Increased Insecurity and the Rise of Populism: An ANC NEC International Relations Sub–Committee Discussion Document Towards the 5th National Policy Conference", Midrand, South Africa, 30 June– 5 July 2017, http://www.anc.org.za.

PART I

KEY THEMES IN SOUTH AFRICA'S FOREIGN POLICY

CHAPTER 1

THE DOMESTIC IMPERATIVES OF SOUTH AFRICA'S FOREIGN POLICY

Chris Landsberg

While an extensive body of work on post-apartheid South Africa's diplomacy has emerged since 1994, the domestic imperatives of foreign policy and diplomacy have received relatively little attention. What we have seen instead are works about domestic "actors" in South Africa's foreign policy, and actors and agents are typically – and wrongly – conflated and confused as "domestic sources", or drivers and imperatives of foreign policy. From a source-based and textual analysis perspective, there is little doubt that, during the course of the past two decades, policymakers in Tshwane (Pretoria) have implicitly and explicitly operated on the assumption that there was a clear link between domestic politics and foreign policy as they sought to consolidate constitutional democracy and to address the scourges of poverty and inequality at home, while transforming South Africa from a global pariah into a responsible global citizen and seeking to address inequalities both at home and globally between the global South and the industrialised North.

From the presidency of Nelson Mandela in 1994 to the one of Jacob Zuma since 2009, successive governments in Tshwane have worked on the assumption that foreign and domestic policies are inextricably intertwined, with the former driven by the latter. Primary sources on South Africa's foreign policy are littered with statements and verbal commitments underscoring the fact that South Africa's foreign policy is driven by domestic goals. As such, the stated and articulated domestic agenda of South Africa's foreign policy has contained political and socio-economic dimensions from the outset. In 2005, for example, the then Department of Foreign Affairs (DFA) in Tshwane – now the Department of International Relations and Cooperation (DIRCO) – explicitly argued that the domestic goal of foreign policy was to "help overcome the challenges of the second economy".[1] It was Thabo Mbeki who in May 1998 invoked the idea that South Africa was a country of "two economies" and of "two nations" – a poor and underdeveloped one, typically belonging to the majority population, and a wealthy and "First World" one in which the participants typically come from apartheid's privileged sectors.[2] In a speech in 2003, Mbeki opined:

> Our country is characterised by two parallel economies ... The First Economy is modern, produces the bulk of our country's wealth, and is integrated within the global economy. The Second Economy (or the Marginalised economy) is characterised by underdevelopment, contributes little to GDP [gross domestic product], contains a big percentage of our population, incorporates the poorest of our rural and urban poor, is structurally disconnected from both the first and global economy, and is incapable of self-generated growth and development.[3]

This is the "second economy" that Mbeki referred to and the one that the country's foreign policy was forced to seek to redress and overcome.

In line with Mbeki's "two economies/two nations" analogy, the African National Congress's (ANC) Reconstruction and Development Programme (RDP) of 1994 also noted: "Our history has been a bitter one dominated by colonialism, racism, apartheid, sexism and repressive labour policies. The result is that poverty and degradation exist side by side with modern cities and a developed mining, industrial and commercial infrastructure. Our income distribution is racially distorted and ranks as one of the most unequal in the world – lavish wealth and poverty characterise our society."[4] Like the "two nations"[5] theory, the RDP raised the notion of a schizophrenic society, deeply divided, and facing high levels of trauma, brought about by decades of white minority domination and repression. It is these features that the country's foreign policy was also expected to help overcome.

In terms of President Jacob Zuma's government, since 2009 this administration has consistently declared South Africa to be "open for business", thus again highlighting the need for the country to engage in business and commercial activities that would help it to address the huge poverty and inequality gaps left by apartheid.[6] In 2010, during state visits to India, Russia, China and Brazil, President Zuma repeatedly vowed that South Africa is "open for business, in a big way",[7] highlighting issues of investment, trade and economic diplomacy so as to build "a developmental economy that is able to serve the needs of the people of our country and be an engine of economic development for our region and the continent and beyond".[8] For Zuma too, therefore, we see a centrality of domestic economic considerations in the country's foreign policymaking, with the search for market and economic opportunities abroad, almost in "cargo-cult" fashion, supposed to translate into major dividends at home.

Tshwane's rhetoric has clearly placed domestic imperatives at the heart of South Africa's foreign policy agenda over the past two decades, begging the following questions: What are the particular domestic objectives to which South African diplomacy has sought to contribute since the transition to democracy in 1994? How have successive South African governments sought to ensure that their regional, continental and international strategies have a concrete impact on the domestic agenda? To what extent has South Africa's foreign policy been successful in this endeavour, and what are the challenges that it has faced?

The central argument of this chapter is that research investigating the link between external affairs and nation-building, democracy consolidation and economic growth in the conduct of South Africa's foreign policy has been almost totally neglected. Even less attention has been paid to the socio-economic domestic drivers of the country's foreign policy. There is thus a need to fill an important gap here, and this chapter hopes to make a contribution in this regard by unpacking the domestic socio-economic imperatives of South Africa's foreign policy.

On the Concept of Domestic Imperatives

"All politics is local", goes the aphorism coined by former Speaker of the United States (US) House of Representatives, Tip O'Neill. There is thus a symbiotic relationship between domestic and foreign policy. States pursue foreign policy strategies that are in large measure driven by domestic considerations and fundamentals. Domestic considerations are indeed the lifeblood of foreign policy. In American scholar Robert Putnam's metaphor of politics as a "two-level game", policymakers are seen as "playing politics on two boards, the domestic and international", with governments constantly under pressure to address domestic concerns.[9] As British scholar Christopher Hill further argues, foreign policy elites "must address their own constituents – the 'inside' of their own community . . . They must face the fact that policy outcomes are vulnerable to events which are primarily 'domestic' and, conversely, that foreign policy impacts upon domestic politics".[10] For Hill, the domestic dimensions of foreign policy include constitutional and regime issues, as well as constraints imposed by society, intra-elite disputes and shortage of resources.[11]

Writing in 1969, American scholar-diplomat Henry Kissinger – a bastion of twentieth-century realism – observed that, in traditional approaches to international relations, "the domestic structure is taken as a given; foreign policy begins where domestic policy ends".[12] For him, this implies that the stability and legitimacy of domestic structures provide the basis for predictability in a country's diplomacy, and that they are key to minimising the "temptations to use an adventurous foreign policy to achieve domestic cohesion".[13] With respect to the domestic context, American scholar Kal Holsti argued that "the standard purposes of security, welfare, autonomy and prestige derive from a host of historical developments, ideologies, and assumptions about the good life", for which governments are responsible, and which are based upon trade.[14] What is significant about the two preceding views by Kissinger and Holsti respectively is the inference that stability and cohesion at home allow a country to project itself more successfully abroad and to place security and welfare at the apex of the concerns of states in the international system. So, even in international dealings, domestic cohesion, security and welfare or development rank as key aims of all states.

Writing in their 2001 edited volume, *African Foreign Policies: Power and Process*, Kenya's Gilbert Khadiagala and American Terrence Lyons noted that "foreign policy makers attempt to reconcile domestic interests with external circumstances, taking account of the available means, resources, and institutions for doing so".[15] They further argued that "important to understanding foreign policy are specific domestic and external contexts and interaction between these two environments".[16] For these scholars, the local and international contexts of foreign policy are thus equally important.

In unpacking the domestic imperatives that underpin the foreign policies of African states, Khadiagala and Lyons also observed that "African foreign policy at the beginning of the twenty-first century is still dominated by overarching constraints on the survival of weak states".[17]

British scholar Christopher Clapham concurred with this point when he opined that, for African elites, foreign policy reflects the continual attempts by elites to manage threats to domestic security and insulate their decision-making from untoward external manipulation.[18] African governing elites thus value their autonomy greatly.

In short, the domestic sources of foreign policy include a range of internal dynamics and drivers that shape the conduct of a country's diplomacy. If we apply the points raised by Kissinger, Holsti and Khadiagala and Lyons to the South African context, it becomes clear that imperatives such as constitutional consolidation, socio-economic development and addressing poverty and inequality, alongside nation-building and social cohesion, rank as key domestic essentials of South Africa's foreign policy.

Constitutional and Politico-Economic Imperatives of Diplomacy

The first imperative to consider is that of preserving the hard-won, two-and-a-half-decade domestic political democratic order in South Africa. The country's peaceful, negotiated transition from apartheid to democracy yielded a national constitution in 1996 that has since become the cornerstone of Tshwane's domestic policies and international diplomacy. In particular, the country's central concern with the promotion and protection of human rights is seen by a number of commentators to derive directly from the national constitution (see Fritz in this volume). In the words of South African analyst David Monyae, for example:

> South Africa today has one of the most liberal constitutions in the world, with human rights protected in terms of Chapter 2. The Constitution is the supreme law of the Republic and there is a duty on the government to follow its provisions ... [D]omestic and foreign policy must both comply with the provisions of the Constitution and therefore it is partly in the context of the Constitution that South Africa's militancy in international human rights issues since 1994 should be understood.[19]

Even before the country's constitution was adopted in 1996 and before he was elected South Africa's first post-apartheid president in 1994, Nelson Mandela declared – in a much cited article published in the influential

American journal *Foreign Affairs* in 1993 – that Tshwane would pursue a foreign policy committed to human rights, democracy promotion, justice and international law and a belief in the peaceful settlement of disputes.[20] Given the disrespect shown by the disgraced and defeated apartheid system to liberal human rights values, this impulse espoused by one of the most notable victims of white minority rule in South Africa was understandable. Similarly, the ruling ANC stated in 1994 that "belief in and preoccupation with human rights" and "promotion of democracy worldwide" would be central to the country's post-apartheid foreign policy.[21] As British academic James Barber opined, this concern with human rights was "broadly interpreted to cover economic, social and environmental as well as political rights".[22] In light of these views, it is easy to discern how the pro-human rights values enshrined in South Africa's constitution carried over into its post-apartheid diplomacy.

According to South African analyst Garth le Pere and Canadian scholar Chris Alden, Mandela's foreign policy represented a "human rights crusade",[23] while South African analyst Anthoni van Nieuwkerk similarly observed that South Africa's foreign policy was "initially infused with notions of human rights activism".[24] Indeed, at the level of rhetoric, human rights and democracy promotion have continued to feature prominently in the foreign policy narrative of successive post-apartheid governments (see Fritz in this volume). In 2005, for example, during the Thabo Mbeki administration, the then Department of Foreign Affairs explicitly noted that "the universal values [of human rights] which South Africa strives to achieve for itself are also those to which it aspires for Africa, the South and the rest of the world".[25] Here is an explicit correlation between domestic and foreign policy, wherein stated policy clearly articulates the vision that the ANC-led government had for the country as the same one it harboured for international society.

Under President Thabo Mbeki (1999–2008), South African diplomacy played a key role in identifying the promotion and protection of human rights as an integral part of the African Union's (AU) agenda, exactly as it set out in its own strategies to promote "human rights and democracy" in its domestic and foreign policies. South Africa's role on the African continent, and in negotiating continental institutions and rules of the game, therefore reflected a domestic, constitutional imperative. In 1998, Mbeki reminded South Africans that "we would organise ourselves to unite as a people, around common national aspirations and a common identity, while we honour and respect our identity",[26] and augmented this with a statement in 1999 that "it remains for us to build on the progress we have made, in fact to build an equitable society, to banish the antagonism of the past, to build a new national identity in which all of us will draw pride and strength from the great variety of our colours, cultures, languages and religions".[27] These were emphatic statements in favour of nation-building, social cohesion and non-racialism.

The promotion and protection of human rights, so central to South Africa's constitution, is also part of the AU's agenda and is enshrined in its Constitutive Act of 2000 (see Maloka in this volume). In May 2013, then deputy minister of foreign affairs, Ebrahim Ebrahim, stated that "our message is ... consistent throughout – the importance of establishing inclusive dialogue, the importance of justice, democracy and the rule of law, and a legitimate Constitution as the basis for peaceful coexistence".[28] The idea of a rules-based society and order is one that Ebrahim and other government officials have consistently promoted as priorities for South Africa's domestic and foreign policies.

The foregoing has highlighted some of the domestic, constitutional imperatives of South Africa's foreign policy, and how the government has tried to ensure that these are reflected in diplomatic and foreign policy imperatives. It is clear that the emphasis and interests of many scholars have remained on the political and human rights aspects of the domestic dimensions of foreign policy. In contrast, Tshwane's domestic socio-economic imperatives have enjoyed rather scant attention.

Domestic Socio-Economic Imperatives

There is a clear need here to highlight and focus on not just the domestic thrust or pillar of South Africa's foreign policy, but also the socio-economic dimension in particular – that of overcoming the legacy of apartheid. Closing the apartheid-era gap between domestic and foreign policies – most notably helping to reduce poverty and inequality – has been a key tenet of post-apartheid South Africa's diplomacy, at least as far as stated policy is concerned. Yet over the past two decades, neither the best hopes nor the worst fears of South Africa's democracy have been realised, with signs on the domestic front of both progress and stagnation.

In this regard, it is important to go beyond the rhetoric and the stated and professed foreign policy of South Africa, and test it against the harsh reality of a socially combustible and highly unequal society. There is no gainsaying that South Africa has both made progress and shown signs of stagnation, poor performance and even regression in some instances. On the constitutional and policy fronts, there are clear signs of progress. But in terms of socio-economic development and implementation and operationalisation of policy, the country has clearly struggled.

In an important working paper for the Overseas Development Institute (ODI), published in 2013, Sian Herbert argued in terms of progress that, since the end of apartheid in 1989, and the first democratic elections in 1994, the South African government has pursued an inclusive national development agenda.[29] Herbert continued to argue that "[m]uch progress has been made in this short time, including the establishment of inclusive democratic institutions, a huge increase in provision of basic education, health, sanitation and housing, and around 3 million more jobs".[30] That this advancement has been made is beyond dispute. On a less sanguine note, however, Herbert also reminded us that "South Africa still faces many serious development challenges. Ten per cent of the population suffer from HIV/AIDS; homicide of women by intimate partners is six times the global average; unemployment was 25 per cent in 2012; 39 per cent of the population live under the national poverty line; and life expectancy in 2008 was 62 for women and 55 for men. The HDI [Human Development Index] ranks South Africa 121st out of 187 countries".[31]

Overcoming the debilitating political and socio-economic legacies of apartheid was a significant driver and rationale of post-apartheid South Africa's foreign policy, at the expense of stagnation on the domestic front. Since 1994, socio-economic development considerations have always underscored South Africa's foreign policy, a drive that has become more pronounced under the Zuma government, which has articulated an even more utilitarian, business-friendly foreign policy.

The African Peer Review Mechanism (APRM) report of 2007 emphasised that "contemporary South Africa remains a country of imbalances, disparities, distortions and many paradoxes".[32] The report noted that, "the legacy of apartheid continues to manifest itself in many fields of human and social endeavour".[33] "For example", continued the report, "despite the impressive gains achieved in stabilising the economy and the higher [growth] rates that have been consistently realised since 1994, the economy still manifests imbalances between the rates of savings and investment; between exports and imports, thus becoming heavily dependent on imports for consumption purposes; between economic diversification and self-reliance on the one hand and monoculturalism on the other; and between the wealth and quality of life of the people in South Africa's 'first economy' and the lack

of economic empowerment of people living in the 'second economy'".[34]
So while the South African economy gives expression to socio-economic
rights, it has not been successful in helping South Africa to overcome the
wealth-poverty gap. Apartheid has clearly left in its wake a deeply divided
society, a legacy that would take decades, if not centuries, to address.

I will next assess these issues in more detail over the three
administrations of Nelson Mandela, Thabo Mbeki and Jacob Zuma
between 1994 and 2017.

Socio-Economic Imperatives and the Mandela Government, 1994–1999

Under the Nelson Mandela government, between 1994 and 1999,
his domestic agenda sought to be transformative and to dismantle the
repressive and oppressive state edifice that it had inherited from the
apartheid regime. Towards this end, Mandela's administration
prioritised "reconstruction and development"; progressive policymaking
that tried to address the negative legacies of apartheid; and the
consolidation of the "new" democratic order. The government took its
cue from the 1996 constitution, which called for a "progressive
realisation of rights", therefore encouraging the incremental redress of
poverty and inequality.

In terms of the socio-economic imperative, the Mandela administration
argued that, "maximizing the objectives of the RDP by way of engaging
the outside world, in trade and investment particularly, [was] of overriding
importance".[35] Here a direct correlation was being drawn between
the domestically driven RDP and interaction with the international
community in a manner that would help to attract resources for
reconstruction purposes. It should be remembered that the RDP had,
"apart from the task to uplift the deprived majority socially and
economically, another dimension, namely strengthening the country as a
whole".[36] Foreign policy was thus predicated on an economic and material
rationale as much as it was on socio-economic essentials.

Closing the Material Gap and the Mbeki Government, 1999–2008

President Thabo Mbeki's government between 1999 and 2008 shared its
predecessor's concern with the strengthening and deepening of the
domestic democratic order. In addition, addressing apartheid's socio-
economic legacies of poverty and inequality, and building the capacities of

the state to deliver on its obligations to the majority of the population were major preoccupations during this era. Indeed, one of the great shifts on the part of the Mbeki government was to place a greater emphasis on the material or socio-economic dimensions of domestic and foreign policy. The government stressed economic diplomacy and placed a strong emphasis on domestic economic objectives. Strategies designed to improve the economy were seen as efforts to address first and foremost poverty, unemployment and inequality. Eradicating poverty, unemployment and inequality was in turn regarded as a way of boosting the economy. Emphasis was placed on creating a macro-economic environment that could boost growth, and create opportunities for sharing growth.

During his presidency, Mbeki placed a strong emphasis on strategies to address the challenges of the poorer "second economy".[37] At the same time, he sought to create a Keynesian macro-economic environment that could boost the country's economic growth, while attempting to bolster the capacity of the state to deliver on its domestic objectives. These goals included halving unemployment and poverty by 2014; achieving the United Nations' (UN) Millennium Development Goals (MDGs) by 2015;[38] accelerating economic growth to a minimum of 6 per cent by 2010; ensuring that the benefits of growth were more equitably distributed between the "two economies"; and improving the quality of life of all 55 million South Africans by enhancing their access to housing, water and sanitation, healthcare, education, as well as a range of social welfare services.[39]

To achieve these goals, the Medium-Term Expenditure Framework (MTEF) – a comprehensive poverty alleviation and economic growth strategy – was developed in 1999. By 2004, the notion of a "developmental state" had emerged, reflecting the logic that state intervention held the key to inclusive economic growth and development. Based on the progress achieved by then, the Mbeki government's ten-year manifesto for 2014 – released in 2004 – identified a number of key objectives, targets and measures for the first five years under the following themes: a growing economy; sustainable livelihoods; access to services; comprehensive social security; combating crime and corruption; constitutional rights and governance; and Africa and the world.[40] Subsequently, in 2005, the Accelerated and Shared Growth Initiative for South Africa (ASGISA) was launched, as a set of interventions to promote the conditions necessary for accelerated and inclusive economic growth, and to modernise the South African state. In the words of the 2007 APRM report, ASGISA was launched "to unlock some binding constraints to broad-based economic development. The expectation [was] that growth will be raised to 6 per cent per annum and above by 2010 and therefore benefit the majority of the citizenry through more employment opportunities and a reduction in poverty".[41] Here again we see an assumption that there would be some "trickle down" from foreign economic policy to the domestic arena. Within this framework, education and skills development were identified as key priorities, as reflected in the establishment in March 2006 of the Joint Initiative on Priority Skills Acquisition (JIPSA), which brought government, business, labour and civil society groups together to address South Africa's human resources challenge.

The Mbeki government's foreign policy sought to contribute to this domestic agenda, with a 2005 Department of Foreign Affairs policy paper explicitly asserting – as mentioned earlier – that the domestic goals of South Africa's foreign policy were to "help overcome the challenges of the second economy".[42] Again, for Mbeki at least, the domestic imperatives of foreign policy were clear: address and overcome the racial, economic and social legacies of apartheid and decades of white minority domination. For Mbeki, the link between the national interest, and the extension of the security, development and economic interests of the rest of the continent as part of South Africa's interests, was taken as a given. Again, the problem lay in operationalisation and tangible demonstration of these goals in practice.

The Zuma Government, 2009–2017

Contrary to the expectations of some scholars like South Africa's Adam Habib[43] and Garth le Pere and Chris Alden,[44] the domestic and foreign policies of the Jacob Zuma government since 2009 have been marked more by continuity than by change.[45] Not unlike in the Mbeki era, the stated priorities for 2009–2014 included halving poverty and unemployment; reducing inequality and ensuring a more equitable distribution of the benefits of economic growth; improving health and skills; ensuring universal access to basic services; improving public safety; and building a nation free of all forms of racism, sexism, ethnic discrimination and xenophobia. Within these priority areas, a set of strategic objectives were also identified in the 2009 Medium-Term Strategic Framework including: a commitment to more inclusive growth and sustainable livelihoods; economic and social infrastructure; rural development, food security, and land reform; access to quality education; improved healthcare; combating crime and corruption; cohesive and sustainable communities; sustainable resource management and use; and a "developmental state" including improvement of public services.

These strategic objectives and priorities were placed within the context of *Vision 2025*, a framework crafted during the Mbeki years and adopted by the new Zuma government in 2012.[46] *Vision 2025* was based on the understanding that South Africa operates in a global environment with much uncertainty and turbulence, and that the challenges the country faces have deep historical roots in its apartheid past. Furthermore, change in the social and economic structure would take a long time to achieve. In order to ensure its goals, the Zuma government believed that there was a need for a shared development agenda that enjoyed the popular support of all sectors of society, and that such an agenda had to be informed by the ideals of South Africa's 1996 constitution. The government further held that such a national agenda had to define a common and shared vision for growth and development. The Zuma administration also emphasised the need for the democratisation of policymaking but vowed to pursue an "open" and "consultative" form of foreign policy.[47] South African civil society organisations would thus have a greater role in shaping foreign policy.[48] In order to achieve its aims, *Vision 2025* contained four key elements: a democratic and legitimate state based on the values of the 1996 constitution, which would work with all sectors of society to promote human development; a people united in their diversity, fully appreciating the common interests that bind them together as a nation; the creation of conditions for the full participation of women in all critical areas of human endeavour; and the establishment of effective programmes to protect the most vulnerable in society, including youth, children, people with disabilities and the elderly.

The National Development Plan (NDP) of 2012, like its predecessor strategic frameworks such as the RDP; the Growth, Employment, and Redistribution (GEAR) macro-economic programme; ASGISA; and the New Growth Path, reflects the overwhelming preoccupation of the South African government with the elimination of poverty and the reduction of inequality, under the overarching goal of the "creation of a caring society". Within the context of growing xenophobia in South Africa, which saw the killing of 62 foreigners and displacement of 100,000 people in 2008, the NDP further asserted that the state also has responsibilities to care for those beyond its borders. The plan is based on the concept of, and need for, a capable "developmental state" premised on the involvement of people in their own development; the redressing of injustice; faster economic growth and higher investment and employment; more effective and capable government; and the need for leadership, unity, cohesion and trust (that is, the need to create a national consensus). At the same time, the NDP indicates implicit, if not explicit, recognition within the government that state capabilities are an important factor that will determine the success or failure not only of domestic growth and development, but also of performance in international relations. The plan also speaks to a key domestic imperative: nation-building and social cohesion. In this regard it seeks to define "who we are", because the identity of South Africans informs their foreign policy. It states: "We are Africans. We are an African country. We are part of a multinational region. We are an essential part of our continent." The plan further asserts: "We are a community of multiple, overlapping identities, cosmopolitan in our nationhood." The point here is clearly to highlight the need to overcome apartheid-created and apartheid-style racial divisions and to transform the country into a "non-racial democracy". These passages speak to the social cohesion and nation-building imperatives, and the commitment by the ruling ANC to construct South Africa into a non-racial, non-sexist and racially inclusive democracy.

Notably, the Zuma government made it clear that "our [South Africa's] foreign policy – our engagement with our partners all over the world – has to respond to these priorities [of unemployment, poverty and socio-economic exclusion]". In particular, the Zuma administration presented a uniting message to the world in the aftermath of the internal factionalism that had marred the ANC's Polokwane Conference in December 2007. Rhetorically, there is no doubt that foreign policy formulators in South Africa have sought for more than two decades to place domestic imperatives and priorities at the epicentre of foreign policy. But making declarations about foreign policy and diplomacy is one thing; backing them up in reality is quite another.

Assessing the Two-Decade Record from Mandela to Zuma: Rhetoric and Reality

The three administrations from Mandela to Zuma have been consistent through assertions, statements and declarations that they would have to pursue development, economic and international policies that would help them to address apartheid's deep socio-economic and political legacies. All three administrations articulated both domestic and foreign policy priorities that placed at their apex such objectives as achieving transformation and growth; addressing unemployment; and increasing investment. Again, these priorities were infused into both domestic and foreign policies. Articulated policy was thus clear and consistent.

The South African economy had grown continuously since 1999 at an average rate of just 1.9 per cent, with growth accelerating towards the end of 2006 to 5.4 per cent. During this period, foreign economic policy was identified as key to the country's attaining its stated domestic aims. All the efforts at foreign economic policy, as well as economic and commercial diplomacy, notwithstanding, there is no gainsaying that, with an economic growth rate of 5.1 per cent in 2007, there were clear limits to the impact of the economic growth trajectory, and thus the contribution of foreign economic policy. The problem was that there was little in the form of trickle down of such policies to the majority of the population. There was awareness that positive and sustained growth trends were being challenged by high levels of inequality and a lack of equitable sharing of the benefits of growth, as well as negative global economic conditions, high current-account deficits, high inflation and high interest rates. Although unemployment had decreased from 31 per cent in March 2003 to 23 per cent in September 2007, more than 12 million people continued to receive social grants, suggesting that, on a per capita basis, South Africa may have been the world's largest welfare state (about 17 million South Africans received these grants by 2017). Some critics may have even gone so far as to say that, far from reinforcing the idea that South Africa was on the verge of becoming a "developmental state", the country was displaying palpable signs of becoming a "nanny state", a state on which large pockets of society were dependent for social benefits.

In addition, life expectancy had fallen by the end of the 1990s. This was due in large part, according to some analysts, to the Mbeki government's "denialist" HIV/AIDS policies. According to Mark Heywood, for example, "by the late-1990s HIV/AIDS was beginning to be the cause of rising mortality in South Africa. As a result the inequity between the life-saving treatment that could be purchased privately by those who could afford to pay for it, and the absence of policy on treatment in the public health service became more apparent".[49] Heywood even suggested the need for a "truth commission" to probe such denialist HIV/AIDS policies.[50]

It is clear that, to a large extent, foreign policy is, for South African governments, local. But despite the stated assumption that foreign policy was underpinned by the domestic agenda, a coherent strategy that augments the broad, stated policy is clearly lacking. For example, although much work is being done in the area of economic diplomacy, the policy frameworks in this regard are yet to be concretised and implemented. The conclusion is that the impact of foreign policy is often indirect and intangible, rather than direct and explicit.

Concluding Reflections

Since 1994, South Africa's foreign policy has been based on the premise that it should help to address the country's most pressing domestic challenges. For successive post-apartheid governments – from Mandela to Zuma – the main domestic drivers of foreign policy have been the consolidation of democracy, the reduction of poverty and inequality and the achievement of accelerated and inclusive growth. Yet, after two decades, the country is mired in domestic economic woes and viewed with concern by its once-firm international supporters during the apartheid decades (for example, Britain, the United States and Germany).

The domestic context within which South Africa's foreign policy has operated has always had a complex and somewhat schizophrenic nature. On the one hand, South Africa was able to play a highly influential role in world affairs because it enjoyed a unique legitimacy derived from the nature and credibility of its negotiated settlement; global reverence for Nobel Peace laureate, Nelson Mandela; and its celebrated constitution of 1996. In this regard, there was a link between the domestic and the external. But South Africa's constitutional order has been built on somewhat shaky socio-economic foundations, based mainly on the legacies of decades of white minority domination and apartheid era oppression. These legacies include structural ills such as massive youth unemployment; lack of skilled labour; inequality; poor quality of service delivery; and violent crime, all of which have contributed to the creation of social instability at levels that could have a troubling impact on political predictability and stability for years to come.

A key challenge that South Africa's foreign policy continues to face is to show that it can make a concrete contribution to addressing critical domestic concerns through its economic, commercial, cultural and public diplomacy instruments; and through improved coordination among various government departments and agencies, as well as with non-state actors. In particular, cooperation between South Africa's Department of International Relations and Cooperation and its Department of Trade and

Industry (DTI), as well as the National Treasury, is critical to achieving the desired outcomes and impact of South Africa's increasingly economic foreign policy, one driven by its domestic socio-economic imperatives (see Vickers and Cawood in this volume). Additionally, South Africa's foreign ministry could also facilitate engagement at different levels of government, through programmes such as the twinning of South African cities and municipalities with those elsewhere, and help build the domestic capacity of the South African state. Platforms such as the IBSA Forum (India, Brazil and South Africa), the BRICS bloc (Brazil, Russia, India, China and South Africa), and the Forum on China-Africa Cooperation (FOCAC), could also be more effectively used to access training resources (see Virk, and Liu in this volume).

Two elements in particular require attention, a critical shortage in skills and human resources within government, and the absence of a domestically based foreign policy constituency. South Africa has an ambitious foreign policy agenda that needs to be supported and implemented by a meritocratic diplomatic corps with strong ideational, political, technical and organisational capacities. The professionalisation of the country's foreign service through rigorous training and development programmes, as well as the achievement of a more effective balance between career public servants and political appointments, should be a priority area for the government in Tshwane. This can provide the framework for boosting the analytical capacity of the service – a critical gap. In the meantime, policymakers would be well-advised to heed the idea that foreign policy begins at home.

Notes

1. South African Department of Foreign Affairs (DFA), "A Strategic Appraisal of South Africa's Foreign Policy in Advancing the Agenda of Africa and the South", draft discussion paper (Cape Town: Policy Research and Analysis Unit, 2005), p. 2.

2. Statement by Deputy President Thabo Mbeki at the opening of the debate in the National Assembly on "Reconciliation and Nation-Building", Cape Town, 29 May 1998.

3. Quoted in Sian Herbert, "The Future of EU Aid in Middle-Income Countries: The Case of South Africa", Working Paper no. 370 (London: Overseas Development Institute (ODI), 2013), p. 13.

4. African National Congress (ANC), Reconstruction and Development Programme (RDP), Johannesburg, 1994.

5. Statement by Thabo Mbeki at the opening of the debate in the National Assembly, 1998.

6. See Chris Landsberg, The Diplomacy of Transformation: South African Foreign Policy and Statecraft (Johannesburg: Macmillan, 2010), p. 218.

7. Cited in Landsberg, *The Diplomacy of Transformation*, p. 197.
8. Cited in Landsberg, *The Diplomacy of Transformation*, p. 198.
9. Christopher Hill, *The Changing Politics of Foreign Policy* (Basingstoke: Palgrave Macmillan, 2003), p. 221. *See also* Robert D. Putnam, "Diplomacy and Domestic Politics: The Logic of Two-Level Games", *International Organization* 42, no. 3 (1988), pp. 427–460.
10. Hill, *The Changing Politics of Foreign Policy*, p. 220.
11. Hill, *The Changing Politics of Foreign Policy*, p. 220.
12. Henry A. Kissinger, "Domestic Structure and Foreign Policy", in James N. Rosenau (ed.), *International Politics and Foreign Policy: A Reader in Research and Theory* (New York: Free Press, 1969), p. 261.
13. Kissinger, "Domestic Structure and Foreign Policy", p. 262.
14. Kal J. Holsti, *International Politics: A Framework for Analysis*, 4th ed. (Englewoods-Cliffs, NJ: Prentice Hall, 1995), pp. 253–254.
15. Gilbert M. Khadiagala and Terrence Lyons, "Foreign Policy Making in Africa: An Introduction", in Gilbert M. Khadiagala and Terrence Lyons (eds), *African Foreign Policies: Power and Process* (Boulder, CO: Lynne Rienner, 2001), p. 1.
16. Khadiagala and Lyons, "Foreign Policy Making in Africa", p. 1.
17. Khadiagala and Lyons, "Foreign Policy Making in Africa", p. 7.
18. Khadiagala and Lyons, "Foreign Policy Making in Africa", p. 7.
19. Cited in South African Presidency, *Medium-Term Strategic Framework: Together Doing More and Better – A Framework to Guide Government's Programme in Electoral Mandate Period 2009–2014* (Tshwane, August 2009), p. 146.
20. Nelson Mandela, "South Africa's Future Foreign Policy", *Foreign Affairs* 72, no. 5 (November/December 1993), pp. 86–94.
21. Cited in Gerrit Olivier and Deon Geldenhuys, "South Africa's Foreign Policy: From Idealism to Pragmatism", *Business and the Contemporary World* 9, no. 2 (1997), p. 364.
22. James Barber, "The New South Africa's Foreign Policy: Principles and Practice", *International Affairs* 81, no. 5 (2005), p. 1079.
23. Cited in Anthoni van Nieuwkerk, "A Review of South Africa's Peace Diplomacy Since 1994", in Chris Landsberg and Jo-Ansie van Wyk (eds), *South African Foreign Policy Review*, vol. 1 (Tshwane: Africa Institute of South Africa (AISA), 2012), p. 86.
24. Van Nieuwkerk, "A Review of South Africa's Peace Diplomacy Since 1994", p. 97.
25. DFA, "A Strategic Appraisal", p. 2.
26. Cited in Chris Landsberg, "Thabo Mbeki's Legacy of Transformational Diplomacy", in Daryl Glaser (ed.), *Mbeki and After: Reflections on the Legacy of Thabo Mbeki* (Johannesburg: Wits University Press, 2010), p. 222.
27. Cited in Landsberg, "Thabo Mbeki's Legacy", p. 222.
28. Deputy Minister Ebrahim Ebrahim, Budget Vote Speech by Deputy Minister of International Relations and Cooperation, National Assembly, Cape Town, 30 May 2013.
29. Herbert, "The Future of EU Aid", p. 13.
30. Herbert, "The Future of EU Aid", p. 13.
31. Herbert, "The Future of EU Aid", p. 13.

32. African Peer Review Mechanism (APRM), *Country Review Report* no. 5 (Midrand, September 2007), p. 4.

33. APRM, *Country Review Report* no. 5, p. 4.

34. APRM, *Country Review Report* no. 5, p. 4.

35. Landsberg, *The Diplomacy of Transformation*, p. 90.

36. Cited in Landsberg, *The Diplomacy of Transformation*, p. 91.

37. Statement by Thabo Mbeki at the opening of the debate in the National Assembly, 1998.

38. *See* Centre for Conflict Resolution (CCR), *Achieving the Millennium Development Goals (MDGs) in Africa*, Policy Report no. 44 (Cape Town, November 2013), http://www.ccr.org.za (accessed 5 July 2017).

39. Statement by Thabo Mbeki at the opening of the debate in the National Assembly, 1998.

40. African National Congress, "Manifesto 2004, Vision 2014: Forward to the Second Decade of Freedom", http://www.anc.org.za/elections/2004/manifesto.html (accessed 2 August 2014).

41. APRM, *Country Review Report* no. 5, p. 11.

42. DFA, "A Strategic Appraisal", p. 2.

43. *See* comments on domestic and foreign policy in Adam Habib, "Is Economic Policy Likely to Change Under Zuma?", 2009, http://www.polity.org.za (accessed 2 August 2014).

44. Garth le Pere and Chris Alden, "Strategic Posture Review of South Africa", *World Politics Review*, 19 May 2010.

45. This paragraph and the next three paragraphs in this section on the Zuma government are drawn from Landsberg, *The Diplomacy of Transformation*, chap. 10, esp. pp. 207–209.

46. South African Presidency, *Vision 2025: Revised Green Paper* (Tshwane: National Planning Commission, 2012), http://www.thepresidency.gov.za/docs/pcsa/planning/gp_nsp.pdf (accessed 2 August 2014).

47. *See, for example*, Chris Landsberg, "South African Foreign Policy-Making, 1989–2010", in Albert Venter and Chris Landsberg (eds), *Government and Politics in South Africa*, 4th ed. (Tshwane: Van Schaik, 2011), p. 246.

48. Landsberg, "South African Foreign Policy-Making", p. 246.

49. Mark Heywood, "Civil Society and Uncivil Government: The Treatment Action Campaign Versus Thabo Mbeki, 1998–2008", in Glaser, *Mbeki and After*, p. 139.

50. Heywood, "Civil Society and Uncivil Government", p. 139.

CHAPTER 2

SOUTH AFRICA'S PEACEMAKING EFFORTS IN AFRICA: IDEAS, INTERESTS AND INFLUENCE

Devon E.A. Curtis

More than 20 years after South Africa's own remarkable transition to democracy, the country is still trying to define its role in brokering and sustaining peace on the African continent and in the rest of the world. When Tshwane (Pretoria) established its post-apartheid foreign policy in 1994, it seemed appropriate that peacemaking would play an important role. After all, South Africa's successful transition had become a powerful brand for the country, and successive South African governments have since been involved in mediating and facilitating peace talks across Africa, including in Angola, Burundi, Comoros, Côte d'Ivoire, the Democratic Republic of the Congo (DRC), Kenya, Madagascar, Mozambique, Sierra Leone, Sudan and Zimbabwe.

While these efforts have had some welcome effects, I argue that South Africa's peacemaking activities largely constitute a missed opportunity to develop a coherent alternative approach to peace. In some cases such as Burundi, South African involvement helped to facilitate an end to violence or instability, often with the establishment of a government of national unity inclusive of former belligerents. However, in other cases such as the DRC, Libya and Côte d'Ivoire, it proved more difficult to reach a durable agreement, with South African mediators encountering a range of conflicting interests on the part of diverse belligerents, and among other African and international interlocutors. Even the most successful cases of peacemaking by South Africa highlighted the limits of its efforts. There are no guarantees that a signed peace agreement will inevitably lead to sustainable "peace", and the case studies in this chapter show that there was often a trade-off between short-term imperatives to end immediate violence, and longer-term institutions and attitudes that may be conducive to a more enduring peace. Consequently, in two decades of post-apartheid peacemaking, South Africa and other would-be peacemakers are no closer to finding a magic formula in their inexorable quest for continental peace.

South Africa's own transitional experience and its aftermath have, in part, provided the prism through which the country's mediators have tended to view conflicts elsewhere in Africa, along with their possible solutions. The first post-apartheid decade was marked by South African enthusiasm for peacemaking. The hallmark of Thabo Mbeki's (1999–2008) foreign policy was the emphasis on an African Renaissance. This Renaissance depended on a peaceful continent, and the South African government was keen to share the perceived lessons from its own transition with the rest of the continent. However, these extensive peacemaking ambitions were not always matched by capacity and resources and, within South Africa, there was no consistent agreement about which specific features were essential for peace. Furthermore, South African peacemaking ideas and approaches in the Nelson Mandela and Thabo Mbeki eras (1994–2008) did not always lead to their intended outcomes, when confronted with the messy local and regional realities in Africa's conflict zones. Under President Jacob Zuma (since 2009), peacemaking activities have also had mixed results. South Africa's peacemaking efforts have increasingly been linked to its more mercantilist economic interests (see Vickers and Cawood in this volume), and the moral vision and optimism that influenced South Africa's earlier post-apartheid peacemaking efforts are at risk of dissipating.

The difficulties encountered by South Africa have not been exceptional, and reflect many of the problems faced by other international peacemakers. They do, however, raise questions about the overall peacemaking enterprise and its limits, as well as the future ability of South Africa to deliver on its hope and promise of a peaceful, just and prosperous continent.

This essay begins by briefly discussing the key elements in South Africa's own transitional experience that have served as foundational pillars for Tshwane's post-apartheid peacemaking role. Second, the chapter traces several South African post-apartheid foreign policy activities focused on peacemaking, which show that the country's mediators faced a number of competing and conflicting priorities, leading to tensions, contradictions and unintended consequences. I argue that although some lessons were learned under the administrations of Mandela (1994–1999), Mbeki (1999–2008) and Zuma (since 2009), South Africa's motives for its peacemaking diplomacy have been mixed, and a continental roadmap to peace remains elusive. Success in reaching a negotiated agreement is not the same as building a lasting peace within a new normative framework. Furthermore, the domestic challenges facing the Zuma administration have made it more difficult for the government to focus on peacemaking in Africa. The chapter concludes by discussing ways in which South Africa might reclaim a continental peacemaking space, by rearticulating aspects of its own post-apartheid identity and offering distinctive global leadership mobilised around alternative readings of peace.

A South African Approach?

It is unsurprising that South Africa's emergence as a key global actor in conflict prevention, management, and resolution has been inspired by its own successful democratic transition. Key actors during South Africa's transition in 1990–1994 – including Jacob Zuma, Cyril Ramaphosa, Roelf Meyer, Ebrahim Ebrahim and Nicholas "Fink" Haysom – have remained active in mediation and facilitation in the two and a half decades since the end of apartheid. There is a widely held view that the "new" South Africa is a "rainbow nation" that has managed peacefully to overcome its racial divisions. The country has become a powerful mythic and moral symbol to the world, arguably showcasing the possibilities of accommodation and compromise. As this "new" South Africa catapulted onto the international stage in the early 1990s, the sense of optimism surrounding its own transition led to an enthusiasm for promoting peace settlements and transitions elsewhere. There was a sense among the country's leadership under Nelson Mandela that since South Africa had emerged from a seemingly intractable conflict into a robust democracy, it was now in a good position to help others achieve similar success.[1]

The South African transition, culminating in multi-party democratic elections in 1994, was the result of a complex range of factors. Yet certain elements from that experience have informed the broader South African approach to peacemaking elsewhere. These have included, first and foremost, a belief in the possibility of negotiated settlements to conflict. In other words, there is an underlying faith that it is *possible* to solve conflict through negotiation and dialogue. Second, South African-brokered negotiations have tended to be comprehensive, in terms of both issue areas and participants. Third, South African negotiators have tended to promote national unity or power-sharing governments, with representatives of the different belligerent groups granted political office on either a temporary (transitional) or permanent basis.

Of course, these three features of peacemaking are not unique to South African-brokered agreements. To the contrary, comprehensive peace negotiations to end conflict, often through a power-sharing agreement leading to a national unity government, have become part of the standard international tool-kit.[2] Since the end of the Cold War by 1990, negotiated settlements to conflicts have become much more frequent, while power-sharing agreements are much more commonplace as well, particularly in Africa.[3] This rise in popularity cannot be solely attributed to South Africa's experience, although the negotiated end to apartheid was symbolically important since it showed that a seemingly intractable conflict could, in fact, be resolved peacefully through negotiations.

Peacemaking, however, usually involves far more than brokering a power-sharing agreement between diverse belligerent groups in order to stop conflicts. For example, in the context of peace negotiations, mediators may promote certain justice provisions, the establishment of a truth and reconciliation commission and mechanisms for the protection of human rights.[4] There may be discussions about appropriate institutions for post-conflict economic governance and pathways to economic development and sustainable livelihoods.[5] There may be provisions for gender inclusivity, including quotas for the participation of women in post-conflict institutions.[6] There are often profound disagreements between various belligerents and stakeholders about when (and whether) these political, economic, social and legal issues should be addressed, and how. Even within South Africa's own transition, questions related to economic policy were (and remain) highly contentious, with some left-wing members of the African National Congress (ANC), such as former parliamentarian Ben Turok, believing that the accommodation with Western capitals had gone too far. These critics believe that the ANC abandoned its earlier social justice ideals and aspirations over the course of the transition and its aftermath.[7]

The more issues that are placed on the table in a peacemaking context, the harder it may be to reach an agreement between belligerents. The toughest peacemaking settings are the ones in which it is least likely that it will be possible to come to an agreement on a broader range of economic, political, social and legal issues. In these more contentious peacemaking environments, South Africa has often sent peacekeeping troops under a multilateral umbrella, with the South African National Defence Force (SANDF) deployed to Burundi in 2001 (re-hatted as part of an African Union (AU) force in 2003, and part of a United Nations (UN) force in 2004); the Central African Republic (CAR) in 2013; the DRC in 1999, with further deployments including the 2013 Force Intervention Brigade; Ethiopia and Eritrea from 2000 to 2008; and Sudan starting in 2004 (see Naidoo in this volume).[8] On balance, however, South Africa has tended to prefer peacemaking through negotiations, rather than more coercive peacekeeping or peace enforcement.[9]

Furthermore, while Tshwane has played a leading role on the African continent in promoting negotiated settlements to conflicts, it is not the only peacemaker in Africa. As shown in this chapter, a conflict environment typically includes many different mediators, special envoys, private actors, belligerents and other interests. South Africa's involvement in these complex environments occasionally clashed with other regional and international interests, leading to uncoordinated and fragmented responses. In addition, although the broad emphasis on negotiated settlements, consensus and power-sharing has continued to underpin many of Tshwane's peacemaking efforts, other interests and peacemaking strategies have become more prominent in recent years.

Post-Apartheid Peacemaking

The focus of South Africa's peacemaking efforts has been on the African continent. In part, this reflected the post-apartheid government's view that South Africa's future was inextricably linked to the future of the rest of Africa and that a strong, prosperous, peaceful continent was in everyone's interest. For instance, in outlining his foreign policy vision, Nelson Mandela wrote: "South Africa cannot escape its African destiny. If we do not devote our energies to the continent, we too could fall victim to the forces that have brought ruin to its various parts."[10] The focus on Africa continued in subsequent administrations. For example, in a statement to parliament in June 2004, President Mbeki said: "[L]et me emphasise the fact that we have sent troops to countries like Burundi and the DRC because we know that we will never develop and be happy forever all by ourselves while wars and poverty are prevalent in our neighbouring states."[11]

Nonetheless, South Africa's earliest forays into post-apartheid peace-making suffered from an overly optimistic assessment of its ability to broker peace. Upon becoming president, Nelson Mandela (1994–1999) focused primarily on South African domestic reconstruction and reconciliation, but he also occasionally turned his attention to conflicts elsewhere on the continent. For example, in Zaire (now the Democratic Republic of the Congo), Mandela tried to broker a deal between then-president Mobutu Sese Seko and his rival, Laurent Kabila, in 1996–1997. This was unsuccessful, and Kabila went on to fight his way to power in Zaire, with support from Rwanda and Uganda. Since then, South Africa's peacemaking efforts in various African countries have faced ambiguities and difficulties in reconciling the country's moral vision for the continent, with a wider set of interests both within and outside South Africa. As seen in later initiatives by Tshwane, these include questions about the appropriate use of force in peacemaking. I next examine eight case studies in Lesotho, Burundi, the DRC, Zimbabwe, Madagascar, Sudan/South Sudan, Côte d'Ivoire and Libya.

Lesotho

South Africa launched a peace operation into Lesotho in September 1998. Tshwane argued that this was a "preventive" action intended to avert a military coup d'état and to restore peace to Lesotho. This was the first foreign military engagement by the newly transformed South African military, SANDF. The action was said to have been taken under the framework of the Southern African Development Community (SADC), with the military support of Botswana, but did not have full sub-regional support nor a United Nations mandate, and the mission proved to be hugely controversial.[12] Securing the Lesotho Highlands Water Project – a critical water supply source for South Africa's Gauteng province – was a key element of the SANDF operation.[13]

In the aftermath of the Lesotho intervention and in response to related criticisms, South Africa issued a white paper on South African participation in international peace missions, which was adopted by its parliament in 1999.[14] This document was intended to help establish clearer guidelines for military action, and was to serve as a guide for future missions (see Naidoo in this volume).

Burundi

The difficulties in these early post-apartheid peacemaking ventures in Zaire and Lesotho meant that South Africa subsequently approached conflict situations with greater caution, although the Mbeki presidency can generally be characterised as an era of idealism vis-à-vis peacemaking in Africa. South African involvement in Burundi's peace process was the first time that the post-apartheid government would become deeply involved in conflict resolution. Burundi had experienced civil war since 1993, when its democratically elected Hutu president, Melchior Ndadaye, and several of his associates, were assassinated by members of the predominantly Tutsi army. Unlike in Lesotho, South Africa had minimal direct interests in Burundi, and initially Tshwane's involvement in the Burundian peace process was rather limited. Former Tanzanian president Julius Nyerere was the facilitator of Burundi's peace negotiations. South African involvement centred around the participation of Mandela's former chief legal adviser, Nicholas Haysom, who was the chair of the commission that facilitated negotiations between Burundian actors on constitutional issues, including power-sharing and governance arrangements. Previously, Haysom had been closely involved in the constitutional negotiations leading up to the interim and final constitutions in South Africa.

Tshwane became more heavily involved in Burundi when its then former president, Nelson Mandela, took over as facilitator of the negotiations in December 1999 after Nyerere's death two months earlier.[15] Although several of Mandela's advisors discouraged him from taking on this role, fearing that the negotiations would be more complicated than they appeared, Mandela believed that the peace talks could be wrapped up quickly with a power-sharing agreement between the different sides. With Mandela's involvement in the process, there came to be a much larger South African stake in the success of the negotiations, and the Mbeki administration increased its engagement on several levels. The Arusha agreement, with significant power-sharing provisions, was signed in August 2000 under enormous pressure from South Africa and other international and regional sponsors.

The Burundian peacemaking experience was a key event for South Africa. Through the negotiations process, it became clear to South Africa that an approach focusing on dialogue, negotiations and power-sharing was not enough to bring peace to Burundi. Two key Burundian rebel movements – the National Council for the Defence of Democracy-Forces for the Defence of Democracy (CNDD-FDD), and the Party for the Liberation of the Hutu People – National Forces of Liberation (Palipehutu-FNL) – did not join the process and continued their armed resistance. In order to ensure that the transitional institutions went ahead despite continued fighting, Tshwane sent a 700-strong military protection force to guarantee the safety of Burundian politicians who had returned from exile, so that they could take up their positions in the new government.[16] South African involvement was maintained throughout the transitional period between 2001 and 2005. Then deputy president Jacob Zuma spent considerable time and effort brokering ceasefire agreements with the rebel movements who had stayed out of the initial peace agreement. Eventually, a series of democratic elections were held in 2005, which were won by the former rebel movement, the CNDD-FDD.

Particular narratives about South Africa's own conflict resolution experience helped to shape its response to the conflict in Burundi. As facilitator, Mandela tended to view the Burundian conflict through a South African lens, which was not always appropriate in such a different context.[17] Nonetheless, without South African involvement, it is unlikely that the Burundian conflict would have ended when and how it did. The security guarantees provided by Tshwane were absolutely critical in such a volatile environment. Not only had South Africa provided an initial protection force for politicians returning from exile, but it also contributed 1,600 troops to the 2,860-strong African Union peace-keeping mission in Burundi (the first of its kind) from 2003 to 2004, along with Mozambican and Ethiopian troops. These AU troops were re-hatted in 2004 to serve in the new 5,650-strong UN peacekeeping mission. Overall, South African involvement in Burundi succeeded in helping to end large-scale violence in that country (that had killed an estimated 200,000 people), but was not able to prevent continued low-level violence, simmering insecurity and increased authoritarian tactics being deployed by the Burundian government of Pierre Nkurunziza since its election in 2005. Moreover, South Africa's incoherent response to the Burundian crisis in 2015 highlighted the limits to externally driven peacemaking and Tshwane's inability or unwillingness to guarantee the longer-term success of a peace process that it had helped to steer to success. Over 500 Burundians have died since 2015 and almost 300,000 have fled to neighbouring countries such as the DRC, Rwanda, Tanzania and Zambia, yet there was a lack of a coherent, clear response to this crisis from South Africa and regional institutions and bodies such as the

East African Community (EAC), the International Conference on the Great Lakes Region (ICGLR) and the AU.

The Democratic Republic of the Congo

In the mid-2000s, however, Burundi was largely viewed as a South African peacemaking success. The Mbeki administration used a roughly similar template in its approach to peacemaking in the Democratic Republic of the Congo, but with different consequences and obstacles. Conflict in the DRC involved a wide variety of political and economic interests, and compared with Burundi, it was even more difficult to coordinate diverse regional and international actors involved in the peace process. (See also Nzongola-Ntalaja in this volume.)

The Second Congo War, beginning in August 1998 and officially ending in July 2003, involved the armies of at least seven African countries: Rwanda, Uganda, Angola, Zimbabwe, Namibia, Chad and Burundi.[18] In July 1999, the Lusaka agreement had been signed, which provided for an inter-Congolese political dialogue among the country's factions, including representatives of the Congolese government, the armed groups, the unarmed opposition and civil society. Former Botswanan president Ketumile Masire was named facilitator of these talks, and South Africa hosted the dialogue, which began in the country's gambling casino of Sun City in February 2002.

The goal of the inter-Congolese dialogue was to bring about a new political dispensation in the DRC. Progress was slow, but as South Africa became more involved, the country became increasingly invested in the success of the talks. No comprehensive agreement was reached at the Sun City inter-Congolese dialogue, but through a combination of carrots and sticks the Mbeki administration brokered an agreement between the governments of the DRC and Rwanda in Tshwane in July 2002. This paved the way for an all-inclusive accord also signed in Tshwane later in December 2002, and the subsequent establishment of transitional institutions in the DRC in 2003.

Brokering a transitional power-sharing agreement between different Congolese belligerents did not mean an end to the violence. Many Congolese politicians signed onto the agreement and assumed political office in the transitional institutions, but continued to maintain parallel relationships with armed groups. During the transitional period between 2003 and 2006, South African president Mbeki, as well as other mediators from Africa and beyond, continued discussions with key

Congolese political figures. Democratic elections were held in July 2006, won by the incumbent, Joseph Kabila. Yet conflict in eastern Congo continued after the elections and insecurity still persisted in 2017, showing the limits to the South African-led peacemaking efforts.[19] The Congo case demonstrated that it is one thing to get belligerents and factions to sign a peace agreement, and quite another to ensure compliance and to build frameworks for a durable peace.

South Africa's focus in the DRC has changed several times in the post-apartheid era. From Mandela's emphasis on elite dialogue and his failed attempt to broker an agreement between Mobutu and Kabila in 1996–1997, to Mbeki's attempt to bring all belligerents and unarmed opposition groups together in transitional power-sharing governance structures from 2003 to 2006, and finally to Zuma's ardent promotion of South African economic interests alongside Tshwane's contribution to "robust" peacemaking in the DRC in 2013, all demonstrate the evolution of South African thinking. Tshwane's involvement has shifted from facilitator/mediator of inclusive Congolese peace agreements, to a contributor to peace enforcement operations. About 1,400 of the country's troops were deployed to the UN Organisation Mission in the DRC (MONUC) since 1999, and from 2010 in the UN Organisation Stabilisation Mission in the DRC (MONUSCO). However, South African military engagement became even more important after the adoption of UN Security Council Resolution 2098 in March 2013, which provided the mandate for a robust SADC intervention force to neutralise armed groups in the eastern Congo. South Africa was the leading troop contributor to this 3,000-strong Force Intervention Brigade with Tanzania and Malawi, demonstrating that its involvement had shifted from an emphasis on negotiated settlement and dialogue, to more coercive involvement.

Crucially, this shift from an approach privileging negotiations and power-sharing in the Congo to a more robust militarised approach occurred at a time when South Africa's economic interests in the DRC were expanding. Relations between South Africa's president, Jacob Zuma, and the Congolese president, Joseph Kabila, are close. A memorandum of understanding for a major deal was signed between South Africa and the DRC in November 2011, shortly before Congolese national elections, which were deemed to be highly flawed by Western observers, but free and fair by South African observers under the rubric of SADC.[20] The world's largest hydroelectric dam is planned to be built on the Congo River's Inga Falls. South Africa plans to buy more than half of the power produced by the dam in its first phase, the Inga 3 dam, which is scheduled to produce 4,300–4,800 megawatts for export to South Africa as well as to the mines in the Congo's Katanga province.[21] Costs for this phase are estimated to be $12 billion, including the building of power lines to South Africa.[22] Unlike in Burundi, where Tshwane's economic interests are minimal, it is difficult to untangle South Africa's economic motives in the DRC from its peacemaking priorities and approaches. Similar to Burundi, however, South Africa under Jacob Zuma has been reluctant to support the democratic institutions set up by peace processes. Tshwane was conspicuously silent regarding the political and constitutional crisis faced by the DRC in 2016, as Congolese president Joseph Kabila's term came to an end without new elections. Despite its role as an architect in the 2002 peace deal that helped establish Congolese democratic institutions, South Africa adopted a cautious wait and see approach vis-à-vis the latest political crisis.

Zimbabwe

In Zimbabwe, South African peacemaking was influenced by different sets of interests. Unlike in Burundi and the DRC, there was not a recent overt civil war in Zimbabwe, but South African officials approached the conflict between the Zimbabwean president, Robert Mugabe, and his long-time rival, Morgan Tsvangirai, through a similar framework of dialogue and negotiations leading to power-sharing between elites.

During two rounds of elections in Zimbabwe in March and June 2008, opposition members were often the targets of Mugabe's state-sponsored violence. The AU condemned the electoral violence in Zimbabwe and referred the situation to SADC in June 2008.[23] Drawing on South Africa's own transitional experience and under the endorsement of SADC, President Mbeki brokered a power-sharing arrangement in Zimbabwe, signed in September 2008, between Mugabe and his Zimbabwe African National Union – Patriotic Front (ZANU-PF) party, and both factions of the opposition Movement for Democratic Change (MDC).[24] Mbeki became the guarantor of this agreement, which came into force in February 2009, with Mugabe as president and Tsvangirai as vice-president. However, this agreement proved to be unstable and unworkable in the Zimbabwean political context. (See Sachikonye in this volume.)

As in Burundi and the DRC, South Africa's peacemaking in Zimbabwe could be said to have succeeded in a very narrow sense, in that Mbeki did persuade both sides to put their names on an agreement. After Mbeki was forced out of office by the ANC in September 2008, Jacob Zuma carried on as the main mediator for Zimbabwe, largely maintaining Mbeki's policies, though with less attention to detail.[25] The continued low-level violence and the inability of Zimbabwe's political groups to work together showed the inherent limits to this accord. In the July 2013 Zimbabwean elections, Mugabe and his ZANU-PF party re-established political dominance in the country.[26] More generally, South Africa has been criticised for its policy of "diplomatic engagement" vis-à-vis Zimbabwe, avoiding public condemnation of human rights abuses committed by the regime.[27] Zuma was more outspoken on Zimbabwe before he became South Africa's president, but became more cautious after taking office in 2009, not wanting to go against the SADC consensus, which constrained Tshwane's peacemaking activities.[28]

Madagascar

Jacob Zuma also led South Africa to become involved in Madagascar. Similar to Zimbabwe, this involvement may have helped to solve an immediate problem in Madagascar, but was unable to address some of the longer-term issues in the country. In March 2009, Madagascan president Marc Ravalomanana was unconstitutionally deposed by the country's military, which installed Andry Rajoelina as president of a High Transitional Authority. Ravalomanana went into exile in South Africa. Both the AU and SADC condemned the military coup, but there was subsequent competition between the UN, the AU and SADC over the leadership of the mediation, as well as between Tshwane and Paris, Madagascar's former colonial ruler.[29] SADC appointed former president Joaquim Chissano of Mozambique as its mediator, with South Africa playing an important role behind the scenes. During a meeting in the Mozambican capital of Maputo in August 2009, a power-sharing agreement was signed between the rival Madagascan sides, and a follow-up accord was concluded in October 2009 agreeing on the principle of an interim government leading to elections.

In June 2011, in light of the failure of previous efforts, the SADC summit approved a new revised roadmap for ending the crisis in Madagascar. The goal was to facilitate a transitional national unity government and an electoral framework leading to the establishment of a democratically elected government. In December 2012, South Africa helped to persuade Ravalomanana and Rajoelina to accept a SADC "solution" whereby neither of them would enter the presidential race.[30]

Subsequently, however, in April 2013, Ravalomanana announced that his wife, Lalao, would contest the election and, in May, Rajoelina reneged on the agreement and said he would also run. In August 2013, the Special Electoral Court in Madagascar ruled that both candidatures were invalid, since Lalao Ravalomanana had not fulfilled the six-month residency period prior to the election and Rajoelina had registered after the deadline. There is some speculation that the court responded to international pressure led by South Africa and SADC that a ruling was needed before elections took place.[31] Elections were eventually held in December 2013, which were won by Hery Rajaonarimampianina, a former finance minister and close ally of Rajoelina. The African Union lifted its suspension of Madagascar in January 2014 and international donors resumed development assistance. Nonetheless, the underlying causes and impact of the 2009 coup have not been resolved, the country remains divided and the military remains outside civilian control.[32] So, while an immediate crisis was resolved in Madagascar despite the confusion and disagreements between various mediators, the longer-term settlement remained uncertain in 2017.

Sudan and South Sudan

Disagreements and tensions between different peacemakers were also a feature in the case of Sudan. Like other regional and external actors, South Africa supported the Comprehensive Peace Agreement (CPA) in 2005, which ended the war between the National Congress Party (NCP) in the north and the Sudan People's Liberation Movement (SPLM) in the south. Both Mbeki and Zuma were involved in these CPA negotiations, and mistakenly believed that the Darfur crisis could be resolved through the framework of the CPA.[33] After leaving office in 2008, Mbeki continued his involvement in Sudan as the chair of the AU High-Level Implementation Panel for Sudan (AUHIP), which was tasked with resolving outstanding issues between Sudan and South Sudan.

Meanwhile, Tshwane has maintained close relations with the ruling SPLM in South Sudan, and South Africa's deputy president (since May 2014), Cyril Ramaphosa, has been involved in attempts to mediate between two factions of the SPLM that have been fighting a civil war since December 2013.[34] The South African government's strong ties with its South Sudanese counterpart stem from links between the liberation struggles of the ANC and the Sudan People's Liberation Army

(SPLA)/Movement, and South Africa has provided training for the SPLM to help it with governance, human resource capacity and institution-building.[35] The Intergovernmental Authority on Development (IGAD) brokered a peace agreement in 2015 leading to a transitional government of national unity, but by July 2016 this had unravelled and South Sudanese rebel leader and former vice-president Riek Machar moved to South Africa in October 2016. In Sudan and South Sudan, therefore, Tshwane has adjusted to a much more pragmatic peacemaking role, responding to the changes in the political environment in those two countries. Yet the continued fighting and tensions in Sudan and South Sudan highlight obvious peacemaking shortcomings. (See Khadiagala in this volume.)

Côte d'Ivoire

Côte d'Ivoire is yet another example of a South African peacemaking focus on elite negotiations and power-sharing, but with this approach clashing with other actors' understanding of the conflict.[36] When war broke out in Côte d'Ivoire in 2002, there was a proliferation of mediators, special envoys and organisations involved in peacemaking in the country.[37] In 2004, the AU appointed Thabo Mbeki as its mediator for Côte d'Ivoire, and between 2004 and 2006 the South African president was extensively involved in the Ivorian peace process. The country was divided between north and south, with frequent clashes. Under Mbeki's auspices there were a series of peace conferences in 2005, and the parties eventually agreed to implement earlier agreements. In 2005, South Africa also sent a military advisory and monitoring team to Côte d'Ivoire to assist in disarmament, demobilisation and reintegration (DDR) efforts.

Mbeki's appointment as mediator for Côte d'Ivoire was not uniformly accepted. The Forces Nouvelles rebels accused Mbeki of being biased towards President Laurent Gbagbo. Other West African countries, particularly Nigeria and Senegal, also became critical of South African involvement in Côte d'Ivoire, though this was in the context of other tensions between Tshwane and Abuja at the time.[38] It was felt that the South African role was undermining the efforts of the sub-regional organisation, the Economic Community of West African States (ECOWAS). Mbeki stepped down as mediator in October 2006, following renewed accusations that he was too close to President Gbagbo's government (see Adebajo in this volume).

Further continental divisions emerged in 2010 over Côte d'Ivoire. Following democratic elections held in October and November 2010, the AU again appointed Mbeki to help resolve the dispute between Laurent Gbagbo and Alassane Ouattara, who both claimed to have won the election. While the AU, ECOWAS and the UN (which largely oversaw the electoral process), along with many Western governments, recognised Ouattara as the winner over Gbagbo, Mbeki believed that power-sharing between the two rivals would have been more appropriate.[39] He submitted a report to the African Union in support of power-sharing proposals.[40] Mbeki later expressed disappointment with the international response to electoral violence in Côte d'Ivoire, arguing that there should have been an international commission to verify the election results, that the UN had abandoned its neutrality as a peacemaker and that France had used its position on the UN Security Council to play a role in determining the outcome of the election in Côte d'Ivoire.[41] While most countries, including France, the United States (US) and Nigeria, immediately recognised Ouattara as the country's president, Zuma and the South African government belatedly recognised his victory only in March 2011.

Libya

Contradictions in South Africa's approach to peacemaking also emerged over Libya. During the first two months of 2011, in response to protests and fighting in that country, President Zuma tried to convince Libyan president Muammar Qaddafi to agree to peace talks with the opposition National Transitional Council (NTC). In March 2011, the AU reaffirmed its commitment to the unity and territorial integrity of Libya and rejected foreign military intervention "whatever its form".[42] One week later, however, South Africa voted to support UN Security Council Resolution 1973 to establish a no-fly zone over Libya. President Zuma later backtracked on the vote, denouncing the North Atlantic Treaty Organisation's (NATO) air strikes and the killing of civilians. Even so, Tshwane did not recognise the National Transitional Council as the government of Libya until September 2011. Qaddafi's previous support to the ANC in its liberation struggle, as well as his contributions to the AU, undoubtedly played a role in South Africa's complicated, contradictory and shifting peacemaking positions on Libya. This flip-flopping posture reflected the diversity of views on Libya within the ANC, and shows that it is not always possible to talk of a clear, coherent, singular South African message on peacemaking.

Tensions and Contradictions

From the relative, limited, short-term success in Burundi to the contradictory approach in Libya, these examples demonstrate that, through the Mandela to the Mbeki and Zuma administrations, South Africa has had important experiences in peacemaking. Typically, South African mediators have promoted power-sharing in the form of national unity governments through comprehensive negotiations. Yet South Africa has also been pragmatic in its involvement, often acting in its economic interests and responding to changing situations on the ground, as in the cases of the DRC, Zimbabwe and Sudan. Sometimes, Tshwane has found itself at odds with other African allies, particularly when it has had difficulty articulating a coherent message, as in Libya. While there is a clear sense that peacemaking is part of South Africa's identity and an important component of its Africa policy, a precise and consistent South African approach has become more difficult to articulate, and sustain, when faced with the messy political and economic realities on the ground.

One way that Tshwane has tried to overcome these tensions is to focus on building regional and continental institutions to take on peacemaking roles. A key aspect of South Africa's peacemaking strategy has therefore been its engagement with regional, continental and international institutions.[43] Tshwane has been a strong supporter of the African Union (see Maloka in this volume), and has played an important role at the United Nations, including serving as a non-permanent member of the UN Security Council in 2007–2008 and 2011–2012 (see Mashabane in this volume).[44] South Africa also played a leading role in trying to revitalise the Southern African Development Community (see Saunders and Nagar in this volume), and has generally played a key role in the creation and strengthening of Africa's evolving peace and security architecture. However, many of these institutions – such as SADC, and the Post-Conflict Reconstruction Policy Framework of the New Partnership for Africa's Development (NEPAD) – remain weak.[45]

There is also the question as to whether South Africa's peacemaking ambitions are bigger than its capacity on the one hand, and its continental legitimacy on the other. Several African countries have not always welcomed South Africa's prominence on the global stage. For example, these tensions were on display when it came to the contest between South Africa's candidate, Nkosazana Dlamini-Zuma, and the incumbent, Gabon's Jean Ping, for the position of chair of the AU Commission. While Dlamini-

Zuma eventually won in July 2012 after four rounds of voting and amid strong opposition from Nigeria, Ethiopia, Uganda and Rwanda, this was a hard-fought battle highlighting some of the disagreements on the continent. Kenyan scholar Gilbert Khadiagala characterised South Africa as "groping for leadership" within Africa, against a backdrop of limited room and resources.[46]

More generally, South Africa's role as an African peacemaker may be in part motivated by the country's attempt to situate itself as an African power and a global internationalist leader.[47] Tshwane's position in Africa was an important component of its efforts to be recognised as a member of the BRICS bloc (Brazil, Russia, India, China and South Africa) (see Virk in this volume), and has also been a key part of its multilateral strategy. Indeed, South Africa's peacemaking role in the DRC, Burundi and South Sudan contributed to its conviction that it belonged in the BRICS club.[48] And yet, at the same time, Tshwane appears somewhat uncomfortable with its position as an African hegemon. For example, in 2009, South Africa's Department of Foreign Affairs (DFA) changed its name to the Department of International Relations and Cooperation (DIRCO). This was a deliberate move to emphasise solidarity, South-South cooperation and partnership, rather than hegemonic international relations.[49]

Thus, the enthusiasm with which the new South Africa entered the continental and international peacemaking stage two and a half decades ago has since been somewhat tempered. There are three key reasons for this. First, this is a response to the messy realities of peacemaking on the ground. Whereas South Africa has, in many cases, been able to broker power-sharing agreements between former belligerents, this has often not translated into a framework for sustainable peace. Over the past two decades, Tshwane has therefore moved from a more idealistic view of peace on the continent under the Mandela and Mbeki administrations, to a more pragmatic assessment of its interests under President Zuma. Second, South Africa has had to confront other views and perspectives from several mediators and regional groupings that do not always correspond to its own visions and interests. In other words, Tshwane is not always perceived to be the most legitimate African peacemaker in all contexts, as demonstrated by the case of Côte d'Ivoire. South Africa's significant economic interests in several of its peacemaking sites, most notably the DRC, have also led to questions about its motives. Third, there are sometimes policy disagreements within South Africa's policymaking establishment, as highlighted in the cases of Libya and Zimbabwe. As South Africa has experienced increasingly vocal internal divisions and domestic dissent under the Zuma administration, its focus on continental peacemaking may also be starting to decline. So, while peacemaking has become an important component of South African identity, this is not always compatible with the country's diverse interests and aspirations, along with those of its neighbours.

Concluding Reflections: Reclaiming the Peacemaking Space

Drafted by its Department of International Relations and Cooperation, South Africa's *Strategic Plan 2011–2014* described its vision for an "African continent which is prosperous, peaceful, democratic, non-racial, non-sexist and united, and which contributes to a world that is just and equitable".[50] It is difficult to refute this kind of normative vision and the laudable aspirations that it evokes. In order to help fulfil that vision, the South African government, and South African individuals, have embarked on a number of peacemaking initiatives over the past two decades. Faced with violence and instability on the continent, it is not surprising that South Africa would play a peacemaking role, particularly given its own history. Yet, as this chapter has shown, despite some successes in reaching agreements to end violence, these efforts have been unable to set the foundations for a longer-lasting equitable peace. There is sometimes a trade-off between short-term incentives to secure an agreement between belligerents and longer-term emancipatory alternatives.[51] These realities on the ground, in addition to divisions between various peacemakers and the presence of other interests including economic ones, have meant that South Africa has shifted from a more idealistic and universalist vision of continental peace, to a more pragmatic policy of getting involved selectively, thus reflecting self-interest and more modest ambitions.

Furthermore, a narrow focus on reaching an agreement between belligerents has meant that the debate about peacemaking has remained limited. Typically, suggestions for improvement include calls for increased coordination, increased resources for continental institutions, greater capacity for South African mediation and more capacity for the South African military to guarantee peace agreements through its peacekeeping role. Arguably, however, this kind of peacemaking contributes to the securitisation of socio-economic development and to the entrenchment of national and global inequalities.[52] Tshwane has often expressed concern with the way that powers such as the US, China, Russia, Britain and France have manipulated multilateral institutions for their parochial interests (see Weissman, Liu, Large and Marchal in this volume),[53] and has expressed a rhetorical commitment to ending national and international inequalities.[54] Nevertheless, the actual peacemaking activities conducted by South Africa have not deviated very far from dominant global scripts. At a time of immense uncertainty, with populations around the world reacting against what they see as unrepresentative elites, the reliance on previous models seems to be insufficient. In other words, Tshwane has not yet offered a distinctive way of approaching issues of war and peace. Its emphasis on comprehensive negotiations and power-sharing, and its shift to a more pragmatic approach that takes into account economic interests and more robust military measures, as highlighted by its recent involvement in the Central African Republic (see Marchal in this volume), follow logics similar to those of other outside interveners. A more far-reaching debate in South Africa that gets beyond existing peacemaking frameworks and templates could yield more equitable results.[55]

It may be possible for South Africa to reclaim the peacemaking space, and to use the international moral authority garnered through its support for regional and continental structures, as well as its own struggles and experiences, to articulate an alternative vision of peace. Interestingly, South Africa appears much more likely to forge its own path when it comes to matters outside Africa. For instance, Tshwane has been a strong supporter of the Palestinians, has maintained good relations with Cuba and has tried to serve as a bridge between Iran on the one hand, and the US and the European Union (EU) on the other, in finding a constructive solution to the country's nuclear issue.[56] Innovative and independent thinking could usefully be applied to the continental peacemaking sphere as well.

Inevitably, peace can result only from a dialogue among affected populations. However, an alternative reading of peace can be found within some aspects of South Africa's national experience. Its 2011 white paper on foreign policy, *Building a Better World: The Diplomacy of Ubuntu*, contains a long and admirable list of objectives, but without a concrete description of trade-offs and priorities.[57] Nevertheless, there are hints of what a different direction might entail. The starting point of *Ubuntu* – discovering a common humanity – and the emphasis on pan-Africanism and South-South solidarity, could offer a distinctive South African outlook. Indeed, Tshwane's efforts to forge a more inclusive identity, and the international and continental legitimacy that South Africa has garnered as a country that underwent a difficult transition from oppressive white minority rule to democratic governance, could provide a distinct vantage point from which the country could re-channel debates about peace and peacemaking. Specific ideas and institutions can be derived only from discussions within conflict-affected countries themselves, but post-apartheid South Africa is well positioned to initiate and host debates about alternative ideas for a more equitable peace and how these might be actualised. As many parts of Africa and the world confront division, hatred, injustice and fear, the need to reclaim a space for peacemaking will remain a vital priority.

Notes

1. Chris Landsberg, *"Pax South Africana* and the Responsibility to Protect", *Global Responsibility to Protect* 2, no. 4 (2010), pp. 436–457; Christopher Williams, "Peacemaking from the Inside Out: How South Africa's Negotiated Transition Influenced the Mandela Administration's Regional Conflict Resolution Strategies", *South African Journal of International Affairs*, 22, no. 3 (2015), pp. 359–380.

2. The United Nations (UN) website has a "Peacemaker database" containing more that 750 peace agreements and guidance documents. *See* http://peacemaker.un.org (accessed 20 December 2016).

3. *See* Denis M. Tull and Andreas Mehler, "The Hidden Costs of Power-Sharing: Reproducing Insurgent Violence in Africa", *African Affairs* 104, no. 416 (2005), pp. 375–398; Caroline A. Hartzell and Matthew Hoddie, *Crafting Peace: Power-Sharing Institutions and the Negotiated Settlement of Civil Wars* (University Park: Pennsylvania State University Press, 2007).

4. *See* Andrew Rigby, *Justice and Reconciliation: After the Violence* (Boulder, CO: Lynne Rienner, 2001); Chandra Sriram and Suren Pillay (eds), *Peace Versus Justice? The Dilemma of Transitional Justice in Africa* (Scottsville: University of KwaZulu-Natal (UKZN) Press; and Oxford: Currey, 2010).

5. James K. Boyce and Madalene O'Donnell (eds), *Peace and the Public Purse: Economic Policies for Postwar Statebuilding* (Boulder, CO: Lynne Rienner, 2007); Astri Suhrke, Torunn Wimpelmann and Marcia Dawes, *Peace Processes and Statebuilding: Economic and Institutional Provisions of Peace Agreements* (New York: United Nations Development Programme (UNDP) and Chr. Michelsen Institute, 2007); Susan Woodward, "Soft Intervention and the Puzzling Neglect of Economic Actors", in Matthew Hoddie and Caroline A. Hartzell (eds), *Strengthening Peace in Post–Civil War States* (Chicago: University of Chicago Press, 2010), pp. 189–218.

6. Donna Pankhurst (ed.), *Gendered Peace: Women's Struggles for Post-War Justice and Reconciliation* (New York and Abingdon: Routledge, 2007).

7. *See, for example*, Patrick Bond, "Sub-Imperialism as Lubricant of Neoliberalism: South African 'Deputy Sheriff' Duty Within BRICS", *Third World Quarterly* 34, no. 2 (2013), pp. 251–270.

8. For a statistical summary of all of South Africa's UN peacekeeping contributions by month, *see* http://www.un.org/en/peacekeeping/resources/statistics/contri butors.shtml (accessed 20 December 2016). For descriptions of the South African National Defence Force's (SANDF) international deployments and peace operations, *see* http://www.dod.mil.za/operations/international/int_op.htm (accessed 25 June 2014).

9. Laurie Nathan, "Consistency and Inconsistencies in South African Foreign Policy", *International Affairs* 81, no. 2 (2005), pp. 361–372.

10. Nelson Mandela, "South Africa's Future Foreign Policy", *Foreign Affairs* 72, no. 5 (1993), p. 87.

11. President Thabo Mbeki, State of the Nation Address, National Assembly, 23 June 2004. Quoted in Thomas Mandrup, "The South African National Defence Force: Midwives of Peace in Africa?", in Len le Roux (ed.), *South African Army Vision 2020*, vol. 2 (Tshwane: Institute for Security Studies (ISS), 2008), p. 98.

12. *See* Fako Johnson Likoti, "The 1998 Military Intervention in Lesotho: SADC Peace Mission or Resource War?", *International Peacekeeping* 14, no. 2 (2007), pp. 251–263. For a more positive analysis of South African involvement in Lesotho, *see* Roger Southall, "An Unlikely Success: South Africa and Lesotho's Election of 2002", *Journal of Modern African Studies* 41, no. 2 (June 2003), pp. 269–296. *See also* Chris Saunders, "South Africa and Africa", *Annals of the American Academy of Political and Social Science* 652 (March 2014), p. 227.

13. Francis K. Makoa, "Foreign Military Intervention in Lesotho's Elections Dispute: Whose Project?", *Strategic Review for Southern Africa* 21, no. 1 (June 1999), pp. 66–87.

14. South African Department of Foreign Affairs (DFA), "White Paper on South African Participation in International Peace Missions", adopted by parliament in October 1999.

15. For a discussion, *see* Roger Southall and Kristina A. Bentley, *An African Peace Process: Mandela, South Africa, and Burundi* (Tshwane: Human Sciences Research Council (HSRC) Press, 2005).

16. Devon Curtis and Gilbert Nibigirwe, "Complementary Approaches to Peace-keeping? The African Union and the United Nations in Burundi", in Hany Besada (ed.), *Crafting an African Security Architecture* (Farnham: Ashgate, 2010), pp. 109–128.

17. In particular, Mandela and many South Africans viewed the conflict as a contest between the minority dominant Tutsi and the majority historically oppressed Hutu, but this overlooks many of the other political divisions that existed in the country. Devon Curtis, "South Africa: 'Exporting' Peace to the Great Lakes?", in Adekeye Adebajo, Adebayo Adedeji and Chris Landsberg (eds), *South Africa in Africa: The Post-Apartheid Decade* (Scottsville: University of KwaZulu-Natal Press, 2007), pp. 253–273.

18. *See* Gérard Prunier, *Africa's World War: Congo, the Rwandan Genocide, and the Making of a Continental Catastrophe* (London: Hurst; and New York: Oxford University Press, 2009).

19. *See, for example*, Séverine Autesserre, "Dangerous Tales: Dominant Narratives on the Congo and Their Unintended Consequences", *African Affairs* 111, no. 443 (Spring

2012), pp. 202–222; Cheryl Hendricks, "South Africa's Approach to Conflict Management in Burundi and the DRC: Promoting Human Security?", *Strategic Review for Southern Africa* 37, 1 (2015), pp. 9–30.

20. "Zuma Ratifies DRC Elections Amid Protests", *Mail and Guardian*, 5 December 2011, http://mg.co.za/article/2011-12-05-zuma-ratifies-drc-elections-amid-protests (accessed 11 August 2014); Brian Latham, "South Africa, Congo Plan Pact on World's Biggest Hydropower Project", *Bloomberg News*, 10 November 2013.

21. If the project is successful, South Africa will receive 2,500 megawatts of power. Michael J. Kavanagh, "US Considers Funding Part of Congo's $12 Billion Inga Dam", *Bloomberg News*, 16 December 2013. See also "SA-DRC Pact Paves Way for Grand Inga", *AllAfrica News*, 20 May 2013, http://allafrica.com/stories/201305210073.html (accessed 11 August 2014); Mmanaledi Mataboge, "SA Squeezes Water Power Out of DRC", *Mail and Guardian*, 1 November 2013, http://mg.co.za/article/2013-10-31-sa-squeezes-water-power-out-of-drc (accessed 11 August 2014); François Misser, *La Saga d'Inga: L'Histoire des Barrages du Fleuve Congo* (Paris: L'Harmattan, 2013).

22. Michael J. Kavanagh, "Congo Confident $12 Billion Power Plant Will Proceed by 2015", *Bloomberg News*, 28 May 2013. It is estimated that the Inga project could eventually produce 50,000 megawatts of power. Franz Wild and Janice Kew, "Africa's Biggest Investor's Energy Drive to Include Shale, Inga", *Bloomberg News*, 8 April 2014.

23. The AU resolution on Zimbabwe recommended that "SADC mediation efforts should be continued in order to assist the peace and leadership of Zimbabwe to resolve the problems they are facing. In this regard SADC should establish a mechanism on the ground in order to seize the momentum for a negotiated solution". Report of the Pan African Parliament Election Observer Mission on the Presidential Run-Off Election and House of Assembly By-Elections, PAP/S/RPT/76/08, Zimbabwe, 27 June 2008, p. 19.

24. Miles Blessing Tendi and Nic Cheeseman, "Power-Sharing in Comparative Perspective: The Dynamics of Unity Government in Kenya and Zimbabwe", *Journal of Modern African Studies* 48, no. 2 (2010), pp. 203–229.

25. Saunders, "South Africa and Africa", p. 230.

26. Brian Raftopoulos, "The 2013 Elections in Zimbabwe: The End of an Era", *Journal of Southern African Studies* 39, no. 4 (2013), pp. 971–988; Miles Blessing Tendi, "Robert Mugabe's 2013 Presidential Election Campaign", *Journal of Southern African Studies* 39, no. 4 (2013), pp. 963–970.

27. South Africa has been criticised for this policy in other countries such as Myanmar and Iran as well. Hussein Solomon makes the comparison between this policy and the US policy of "constructive engagement" with apartheid South Africa in the 1980s. See Hussein Solomon, "South Africa in Africa: A Case of High Expectations for Peace", *South African Journal of International Affairs* 17, no. 2 (August 2010), p. 135.

28. Alex Vines, "South Africa's Politics of Peace and Security in Africa", *South African Journal of International Affairs* 17, no. 1 (April 2010), pp. 53–63.

29. David Zounmenou, "Madagascar's Political Crisis: What Options for the Mediation Process?", *African Security Review* 18, no. 4 (2009), pp. 72–75.

30. Saunders, "South Africa and Africa", p. 230. This had been proposed by France much earlier, in 2010; Laurie Nathan, "A Clash of Norms and Strategies in Madagascar: Mediation and the AU Policy on Unconstitutional Change of Government", Mediation Argument no. 4 (Tshwane: University of Pretoria, April 2013), p. 7.

31. International Crisis Group (ICG), "A Cosmetic End to Madagascar's Crisis?", Africa Report no. 218, 19 May 2014, p. 4.

32. ICG, "A Cosmetic End to Madagascar's Crisis?".

33. Laurie Nathan, "Interests, Ideas, and Ideology: South Africa's Policy on Darfur", *African Affairs* 110, no. 438 (2011), p. 60.

34. Mmanaledi Matoboge, "ANC: Ramaphosa to Mediate in S Sudan", *Mail and Guardian*, 6 February 2014, http://mg.co.za/article/2014-02-06-anc-ramaphosa-to-mediate-in-s-sudan-to-strengthen-relations (accessed 11 August 2014).

35. Cheryl Hendricks and Amanda Lucey, "South Africa and South Sudan: Lessons for Post-Conflict Development and Peacebuilding Partnerships", Policy Brief no. 49 (Tshwane: Institute for Security Studies, December 2013).

36. However, Abu Bakarr Bah claims that all international actors relied on traditional peace formulas that failed in part because they ignored the central question of citizenship disputes. Abu Bakarr Bah, "Democracy and Civil War: Citizenship and Peacemaking in Côte d'Ivoire", *African Affairs* 109, no. 437 (2010), pp. 597–615.

37. Adekeye Adebajo, *UN Peacekeeping in Africa: From the Suez Crisis to the Sudan Conflicts* (Boulder, CO, and London: Lynne Rienner, 2011).

38. Adebajo, *UN Peacekeeping in Africa*, p. 156.

39. Giulia Piccolino, "David Against Goliath in Côte d'Ivoire? Laurent Gbagbo's War Against Global Governance", *African Affairs* 111, no. 442 (2012), pp. 1–23.

40. This report, dated 7 December 2010, was leaked in January 2011. "Mbeki: Côte d'Ivoire Rivals Must Talk to End Crisis", *Mail and Guardian*, 24 January 2011, http://mg.co.za/article/2011-01-24-mbeki-cocircte-divoire-rivals-must-talk-to-end-crisis (accessed 26 September 2014).

41. Thabo Mbeki, "What the World Got Wrong in Côte d'Ivoire", *Foreign Policy*, 29 April 2011.

42. Cited in Eduard Jordaan, "South Africa, Multilateralism, and the Global Politics of Development", *European Journal of Development Research* 24, no. 2 (2012), p. 292.

43. Maxi Schoeman, "South Africa in Africa: Behemoth, Hegemon, Partner, or 'Just Another Kid on the Block'?", in Adebajo, Adedeji and Landsberg, *South Africa in Africa*, pp. 92–104.

44. Centre for Conflict Resolution (CCR), *Africa, South Africa, and the United Nations' Security Architecture*, Seminar Report no. 42 (Western Cape, South Africa, June 2013).

45. *See* Gilbert M. Khadiagala, "The Role of the African Union, New Partnership for Africa's Development, and African Development Bank in Postconflict Reconstruction and Peacebuilding", in Devon Curtis and Gwinyayi A. Dzinesa (eds), *Peacebuilding, Power, and Politics in Africa* (Athens: Ohio University Press, 2012), pp. 107–120; Medhane Tadesse, *The African Union and Security Sector*

Reform: A Review of the Post-Conflict Reconstruction and Development (PCRD) Policy (Addis Ababa: Friedrich Ebert Stiftung (FES), 2010).

46. Gilbert M. Khadiagala, "South Africa in Africa: Groping for Leadership and Muddling Through", in Devan Pillay, Gilbert M. Khadiagala, Prishani Naidoo and Roger Southall (eds), *New South African Review 4: A Fragile Democracy Twenty Years On* (Johannesburg: Wits University Press, March 2014), pp. 275–289.

47. Chris Alden and Maxi Schoeman, "South Africa in the Company of Giants: The Search for Leadership in a Transforming Global Order", *International Affairs* 89, no. 1 (2013), pp. 111–129.

48. Alden and Schoeman, "South Africa in the Company of Giants", p. 118.

49. *See* "Statement by Minister Maite Nkoana-Mashabane on the Name Change to Department of International Relations and Co-operation (DIRCO)", 19 May 2009, http://www.dirco.gov.za/docs/speeches/2009/mash0514.html (accessed 18 May 2014); Chris Landsberg, "The Foreign Policy of the Zuma Government: Pursuing the 'National Interest'?", *South African Journal of International Affairs* 17, no. 3 (December 2010), p. 277. *See also* Adekeye Adebajo, *The Curse of Berlin: Africa After the Cold War* (London: Hurst, 2010).

50. South African Department of International Relations and Cooperation (DIRCO), *Strategic Plan 2011–2014*, p. 8.

51. For a general discussion of this long-term and short-term trade-off, *see* Anna Jarstad and Timothy Sisk (eds), *From War to Democracy: Dilemmas of Peacebuilding* (Cambridge: Cambridge University Press, 2008).

52. *See, for example*, Mark Duffield, *Development, Security, and Unending War* (Cambridge: Polity, 2007); Devon Curtis, "Introduction: The Contested Politics of Peacebuilding", in Curtis and Dzinesa, *Peacebuilding, Politics, and Power in Africa*, pp. 1–28.

53. Adam Habib, "South Africa's Foreign Policy: Hegemonic Aspirations, Neoliberal Orientations, and Global Transformation", *South African Journal of International Affairs* 16, no. 2 (August 2009), p. 144.

54. *See, for example*, the address of then foreign minister Nkosazana Dlamini-Zuma to the United Nations General Assembly, New York, 29 September 2008, http://www.dfa.gov.za/docs/speeches/2008/dzum0929.html (accessed 15 June 2014).

55. *See, for example*, Funmi Olonisakin, "A Human Security Approach to Peacemaking in Africa", *Strategic Review for Southern Africa* 31, no. 1 (2015), pp. 3–8.

56. Leaked United States (US) diplomatic cables refer to South Africa (along with India, Brazil, Egypt and Pakistan) as a country that routinely opposes the US in multilateral debates at the UN, despite its strong bilateral ties with the US. WikiLeaks cable no. 66945, cited in Matthew J. Stephen, "Rising Regional Powers and International Institutions: The Foreign Policy Orientations of India, Brazil, and South Africa", *Global Society* 26, no. 3 (July 2012), p. 307, n. 98.

57. South Africa, *Building a Better World: The Diplomacy of Ubuntu*, White Paper on South Africa's Foreign Policy, 13 May 2011, http://www.safpi.org/sites/default/files/publications/white_paper_on_sa_foreign_policy-building_a_better_world_20110513.pdf (accessed 9 August 2014).

CHAPTER 3

SOUTH AFRICA'S DEFENCE AND SECURITY ROLE: UNRAVELLING THE DEFENCE PREDICAMENT

Sagaren Krishna Naidoo[1]

Under apartheid, the racially structured South African Defence Force (SADF) executed tasks of internal suppression against the liberation of the country's black majority, as well as the destabilisation of neighbouring states. Constituted largely by white male conscripts, the then SADF was also pivotal in the illegal occupation of Namibia, which escalated into insurgent and conventional warfare in Angola.[2] Military attacks in Southern Africa by the SADF resulted in an estimated one million deaths and $60 billion of damages in the 1980s alone.[3] After the 1994 elections, the reconstruction and reconfiguration of state institutions was critical for the consolidation of a non-racial and democratic state in South Africa. The country's defence forces, which had been used domestically as well as beyond South Africa's borders to bolster the security of a white minority regime, were among those most profoundly affected. Following the transition to democracy, a 1996 white paper on defence and the subsequent defence review of 1998 laid out the priorities and goals of the armed forces, focusing in particular on integration in terms of their internal structure and on normalisation in terms of their external security role.[4] At the same time, post-apartheid South Africa's defence establishment also had to grapple with the additional challenge of balancing new domestic defence obligations with its external security responsibilities.

I argue in this chapter that, since the political transition to multi-racial democracy ended in 1994, the new South African National Defence Force (SANDF) has endured a constant mismatch between the roles and responsibilities prescribed for it by the 1996 white paper and the 1998 defence review, and the operations that it has been called on to undertake in an unpredictable security environment. As a consequence, the SANDF has often lacked the capabilities to respond more effectively to the demands that have been placed on it by the country's political response to its external security challenges.

Unsurprisingly, this defence predicament – the imbalance between functions and capabilities – has generated a wider debate over the domestic and foreign policy goals of successive post-apartheid South African governments. This situation has also led to suggestions that South Africa has taken on more obligations than it has the capacity to deliver; and that the country should rationalise its foreign policy aims for achieving its security goals (see also Landsberg in this volume).[5]

I argue, however, that the nature of the post-apartheid state has not allowed for the appropriate restructuring and consolidation of the SANDF in the manner required for it to undertake its varied post-apartheid responsibilities more effectively. Furthermore, the ideal balance between the two main tenets of South Africa's defence policy – national defence and foreign security responsibilities – has been unattainable, mainly due to the unforeseeable insecurity that has characterised the country's geo-strategic environment since 1994. This chapter assesses the current policy formulation process, with a view to providing a long-term policy prescription for addressing the recurring imbalance between defence functions and capabilities. Any such discussion must necessarily be grounded in an assessment of the SANDF's domestic operational experience, as provided for by South Africa's 1996 constitution and relevant defence legislation such as the Defence Act of 2002, as well as the country's external operational experiences, as shaped by the demands of South Africa's national security interests and foreign policies. This essay is also informed by my first-hand experiences as Director of Defence Policy Formulation in South Africa's Department of Defence (DOD).

Domestic Obligations

Following the advent of democracy, South Africa's defence forces were singularly focused on the need to transform into an integrated multi-racial institution, with policymakers also keen to re-orient the military away from its apartheid-era focus on internal and external regime security. As Catherine Pringle explained, "the emphasis under the Mandela administration was exclusively on transforming the military. In this regard, structural, organisational and ethos changes were the order of the day".[6] Predicated also on a demand to minimise defence spending, the new government ensured a fairly smooth integration of once opposing armed forces – the SADF and the African National Congress's (ANC) Umkhonto we Sizwe (MK) – while establishing a Department of Defence with an organisational structure that was designed to ensure robust civil-military relations. The other armed forces in South Africa that were integrated into the new SANDF were the Azanian People's Liberation Army (APLA), the Transkei Defence Force (TDF), the Ciskei Defence Force (CDF), the Venda Defence Force (VDF) and the Bophuthatswana Defence Force (BDF). The integration of armed forces into the SANDF began in 1993 and was concluded in 2002.

The immediate post-apartheid years were thus characterised by a predominantly introverted approach to defence that prioritised force transformation and re-organisation. In Pringle's words: "The focus was primarily on creating a military representative of South African society and on crafting policy documents that could successfully guide the country's new military".[7] Little emphasis was placed on the new defence force being fully capacitated with all military capabilities for South Africa's post-apartheid security requirements that necessitated operations beyond its borders. The transformative focus became even more crucial with the submission to President Nelson Mandela in February 1998 of the controversial Meiring Report, which attempted to frustrate the transition process with allegations of a seizure of power through a coup.[8]

Strategically, the newly formed SANDF had a defensive posture in a security environment devoid of any foreseeable conventional military attack in the short to medium term. Given the constitutional basis of this defence mandate,[9] the consolidation of a conventional force design for the SANDF has since remained a pre-occupation within South Africa's defence department. In this respect, the peacetime environment has been opportune for the consolidation of the SANDF. In other words, without the immediate possibility of a conventional war, the defence department has enjoyed "considerable space [in its attempt] to rationalise, redesign and 'rightsize' the SANDF".[10] Of particular significance was the creation of constitutional mechanisms that ensured the transparency and account-ability of the SANDF to a democratically elected political authority. This resulted in the establishment of a civilian defence secretariat as well as parliamentary oversight committees. The military structure and its force design were also overhauled. While the SADF had been racially structured as an offensive armed force that was designed to serve a counter-insurgency function with extensive covert military capabilities, the SANDF was established as a demographically representative armed force structured to be defensive, with the termination of counter-insurgency units like the infamous 32 Battalion.

In the absence of an external military attack, South Africa's national defence role has been relegated to the undertaking of non-conventional domestic tasks that have either emanated from the government's programme of action or been a response to the country's threat assessment. Put differently, in the absence of a need militarily to defend the country's territorial integrity and sovereignty against external aggression, the SANDF has been deployed in non-conventional operations that mainly use its "collateral capabilities". A collateral capability refers to military personnel and equipment that can be utilised for non-military tasks; for example, army engineers have a range of skills and equipment that would be useful to help small rural communities to address problems such as damaged bridges, broken borehole pumps and washed-away sections of roads. Similarly, South African Military Health Service personnel are able to provide medical services in especially remote rural communities.

The SANDF's new mandate for supporting the South African Police Service (SAPS) was a significant re-orientation of the defence function of the post-apartheid democratic state's armed forces as articulated in the 1996 white paper on defence. It was assumed that the SAPS would be capable of adequately combating crime and driving down the high levels of violence in the country. However, the SANDF was compelled, from the outset of its formation, to increase its support to the police in the execution of non-military tasks such as fighting crime, and eventually border protection – a more conventional function – for the prevention of illicit cross-border activity from 1994 onwards.

The SANDF's domestic obligations, as enumerated in the 1998 defence review, are undoubtedly directed towards the defence of

South Africa and its 55 million citizens. Accordingly, the SANDF can provide support to civil authorities and other government departments if a situation or emergency beyond their capabilities arises. Typical tasks that the armed forces could carry out in support of civil authorities include the augmentation of vital services during strikes; support to special and major national events; and the provision of relief after man-made and natural disasters. Other possible tasks for which the SANDF could provide support include anti-narcotics operations; the combating of terrorism; arms control; restoration of law and order; and protection of life and state property, including "national key points" (NKPs) such as the Union Buildings (the offices of the Presidency). In this respect, it is worth noting that the functions and assets related to the National Key Points Protection Act of 1980 were transferred from the minister of defence and military veterans to the minister of police in 2004. In times of heightened threat, however, the SANDF will assist the SAPS in ensuring security in accordance with the NKP protection plan.

Table 3.1, listing internal operations that have involved both the SANDF and SAPS, illustrates the range of non-traditional military tasks that South Africa's armed forces have undertaken and are expected to execute in the future, as ordered by the government.

Support provided by the SANDF for purposes of crowd control during civil unrest has been, and is likely to remain, controversial. This function dates back to the SANDF's deployment in 1994 in Operation Protectoa, which was undertaken to support the South African police in restoring peace and stability in Johannesburg's volatile East Rand. However, as Christopher McMichael has argued "the deployment of the SANDF to quell internal protest not only bears disturbing continuities with the apartheid government's practices but it is also paralleled by efforts to re-militarise the SAPS".[11] Even though such tasks have been, and are likely to be, carried out in exceptional circumstances, the SANDF itself does not favour such tasks and prefers to focus on more conventional military operations. At the same time, it is not unforeseeable that growing public dissatisfaction with poor or inadequate service delivery at the local government level, as well as attempts to coordinate such protests nationally, will continue to cause instability and violence. Between 2005 and 2008, there were about 26,500 peaceful and "unrest-related" demonstrations in South Africa.[12] In post-apartheid South Africa, the SANDF is required to

Table 3.1   Internal Operations Involving the SANDF and the SAPS as of 1994

Operation	Duration	Mandate
Arabella	1994–present (ongoing as required by government; remains a standing task for the SANDF)	Search-and-rescue tasks country-wide as ordered
Intexo	1994–2009	Borderline control, South Africa–Zimbabwe
Prosper	2007–present (ongoing and standing task for the SANDF)	Crime prevention operations country-wide
Carona	2009–present (ongoing and standing task for the SANDF)	Border safeguarding operations country-wide
Kgwele	January–October 2010	Security for Confederations Football World Cup of 2010
Chariot	2011–2012	Disaster support and humanitarian assistance country-wide

be impartial and apolitical. Unfettered military responses to social unrest could constitute not only an erosion of such principles, but also, more detrimentally, a re-militarisation of society reminiscent of the apartheid era.

Any juxtaposition of the SANDF's domestic obligations against its participation in foreign missions does not necessarily indicate a need for contestation between the two functions. The state must, after all, ensure that it has the ability both to provide domestic security and to carry out its foreign policy objectives. Nonetheless, at times, the domestic security functions of the SANDF have significant implications for South Africa's foreign relations. Social unrest in the country has, on occasion, been characterised by a xenophobic dynamic, such as the attacks on largely Mozambican and Zimbabwean nationals in Johannesburg in May 2008 in which 62 people were killed and about 100,000 displaced. Similarly, when undertaking border protection duties, the SANDF will likely have to deal with large numbers of legal and illegal migrants, mainly emigrating due to socio-economic factors but also including criminal elements. To manage such situations, effective cross-border cooperation with neighbouring defence forces – especially within the Southern African Development Community (SADC) sub-region – will be vital (for example, the cross-border cooperation that exists between Lesotho and South Africa, especially over stock-theft).

Even if the SANDF's participation in foreign missions, particularly within peace support operations, were to be diminished, over-reliance on the SANDF's "collateral capabilities" domestically has risky implications in terms of the availability of key conventional elements for undertaking its constitutional obligations. Put differently, South Africa's maritime security (which forms a critical part of the SANDF's defence of the country's territorial integrity), for example, cannot be provided with just a riverine capability (river boats). It requires conventional elements such as frigates, corvettes and submarines.

External Responsibilities

In the foreign policy sphere, the South African National Defence Force's engagements have centred mainly on peace support operations and post-conflict security sector reform (SSR) in Africa. The SANDF's role during President Thabo Mbeki's administration (1999–2008) to become the "midwives of peace" in his government's quest to stabilise conflict-ridden parts of the continent such as the Democratic Republic of the Congo (DRC), Burundi and Sudan's Darfur region, has earned much praise (see also Curtis in this volume).[13] Such views have been predicated on the realisation that the SANDF constitutes an important tool to achieve foreign policy and security objectives of creating peace and stability for development in Africa.[14] Embedded within this approach, and central to it, is the ruling African National Congress party's "political project for the peaceful resolution of disputes", which translates into the SANDF being deployed as the last option to monitor successful diplomatic and political efforts.[15]

In addition to foreign policy goals and political objectives, geographical proximity and military capacity are other key determinants in understanding South Africa's use of the SANDF beyond its borders. In recent times, for example, the defence force has come to be deployed in multinational maritime operations to safeguard sea traffic in the Indian Ocean. Generally speaking, littoral states in Southern Africa lack the capacity to monitor maritime traffic along their coastlines. Consequently, piracy and the smuggling of weapons, contraband, people and goods have emerged as prominent security threats. South Africa's participation in operations to combat these threats, and to protect regional maritime trade and resources including fisheries, seabed minerals, as well as energy deposits, will likely continue into the future.

After apartheid, the SANDF's earliest external deployment was probably also its most controversial. This mission involved South Africa leading a regional intervention into neighbouring Lesotho in September 1998. Touted as a pre-emptive tool, the SANDF was deployed, alongside forces from Botswana, to intervene militarily in Lesotho following an escalation in post-election unrest and violence in the country, and to forestall a "creeping" military coup that threatened to undermine peace, stability and infrastructure in the country.[16] Code-named Operation Boleas, the 1998 intervention defied expectations of being a quick and simple military operation. Its objectives were neither met with the allocated capacity, nor achieved within the predicted timeframe. Operation Boleas, which lasted between September and November 1998, entailed the deployment of 600 SANDF troops within a mechanised battalion, and an airborne company in reserve that consisted of six Oryx transport helicopters, two Alouette III helicopter gunships, two Alouette III helicopters (in a command role) and a Cessna Caravan.[17] The violence that ensued claimed casualties on both sides, destroying homes, property and businesses. An important aspect of this intervention was to secure the Lesotho Highlands Water Project, which supplies much of South Africa's industrial heartland of Gauteng with water. A modicum of stability was eventually restored, allowing negotiations to be concluded between Prime Minister Pakalitha Mosisili and the country's opposition parties.[18]

The casualties for the SANDF during the Lesotho intervention were eight dead and 17 wounded, while the operational cost was more than R24 million (these costs included more than R6.2 million for personnel allowances, R13 million for civilian transportation, and R2.7 million for air support services). It was eventually revealed that the total expenses of the operation amounted to R36 million.[19]

The fatalities incurred during the Lesotho intervention raised questions about the SANDF's preparedness for such missions. As Danish analyst Thomas Mandrup noted, the intervention raised concerns that if South Africa could not handle a relatively small problem like Lesotho, it could not serve as the sub-region's police force. The Lesotho operation suggested that the SANDF was not adequately trained and equipped for a peacekeeping operation that rapidly changed to a peace-enforcement mission. Lack of focus on peacekeeping training along with a preoccupation with conventional war-fighting probably lay at the root of the problem.

Mandrup further noted that the badly managed intervention raised doubts internationally about South Africa's military competence.[20]

The concerns generated by the Lesotho operation were not confined to South Africa's military capacity. The country's foreign policy and state institutions also came under the spotlight in a search for clarification about the international auspices under which the SANDF had been deployed. As South African scholar Garth Shelton noted: "It was perceived that the decision to respond militarily was essentially a South African undertaking that only enjoyed the political support of a few countries from the sub-region and as such was made without explicit SADC authorisation."[21]

Yet, despite the problems encountered in the Lesotho operation, the SANDF has subsequently increased its involvement in similar missions on the continent. This can be attributed to the foreign policy goals of the Thabo Mbeki government at the time. (See Introduction in this volume.) By way of testimony to the argument presented here, there were three deployments in 2001 alone. In April 2001, a technical support force of 150 South Africans was deployed to participate in the United Nations Organisation Mission in the Democratic Republic of the Congo (MONUC). This was followed in October 2001 by the dispatch of almost 700 troops to Burundi in support of the Arusha peace agreement, which entailed provision of protection to returning leaders participating in the transitional government. Then, in December 2001, a four-person observer team was sent to the Comoros to assess the conditions for providing the election process there with logistical support.

Since the inception of the ANC government, the African continent has remained at the centre of South Africa's foreign policy, and the growth and success of the South African economy are dependent on enduring peace, stability, economic development and deepened democracy on the continent. For example, the SANDF mission code-named Operation Espresso was undertaken in December 2000 after the former Organisation of African Unity (OAU), now the African Union (AU), had brokered a cessation of hostilities between Eritrea and Ethiopia.[22]

Nosiviwe Mapisa-Nqakula, South Africa's minister of defence and military veterans, reflected on the peacekeeping and post-conflict reconstruction efforts undertaken by the SANDF in April 2014. She made reference to the extensive involvement of the post-1994 SANDF in peacekeeping operations under United Nations (UN) and African Union commands in mainly African countries, such as the United Nations Mission in Sudan (UNMIS), the United Nations Operation in Burundi

(ONUB) and the United Nations Organisation Stabilisation Mission in the DRC (MONUSCO). Most notable of the deployments is South Africa's commitment of troops (code-named Operation Mistral) to the United Nations Force Intervention Brigade, a 3,000-strong force authorised by the UN Security Council in March 2013 and specifically tasked to carry out offensive operations against armed rebel groups operating in the eastern DRC.[23] In this context, it is worth noting that *South Africa's Contribution to Peace in Africa* is a belatedly publicised examination by Thabang Makwetla, former deputy minister of defence and military veterans, of the peacekeeping operations undertaken by the SANDF.[24] It provides a detailed tabulation of the SANDF's array of external operations and an assessment of their nature and duration.

These external SANDF missions (see Table 3.2), undertaken in support of the South African government's foreign policy, sought to further peace and stability by supporting conflict resolution mechanisms and contributing to the building of post-conflict security sector capacity, mainly on the continent. The SANDF will have to continue conducting similar peacekeeping and peacebuilding roles in future. Promoting peace and security on its continent is therefore both a requirement and an obligation for post-apartheid South Africa, which has a relatively more developed military capacity than most states on the continent. It is also a strategic imperative for Tshwane to manage conflicts that affect its own national security interests. A significant development in the SANDF's external deployments has been the termination of South Africa's contribution to the UN/AU Hybrid Operation in Dafur, Sudan (UNAMID). The withdrawal of South Africa's 797 troops from UNAMID was announced in May 2016. This raised questions about the scale of future deployments.

The Defence Predicament

The SANDF has received both praise for its external deployments – particularly given its lack of previous experience in peace support operations – and criticism for its occasional poor performance. While the SANDF's involvement in these missions has gained both African and international respect for its efforts, acts of misconduct – including sexual offences – placed a stigma against its professionalism and discipline.[25] Moreover, it became apparent that "the increasing commitment to peace operations led to the critical problem of operational over-commitment".[26] Over the past two and a half decades, the "state of

Table 3.2 The SANDF's External Missions and Operations Since 1999

Operation	Duration	Country/Location	Mandate
Mistral	September 1999–present	Democratic Republic of the Congo	Peacekeeping under UN mandate
Espresso	November 2000–August 2008	Eritrea and Ethiopia	Deployment of military observers to UN Mission in Ethiopia and Eritrea (UNMEE)
Fibre	October 2001–December 2006	Burundi	Assistance with protection of Burundian leaders in line with Arusha peace agreement
Triton	November 2001–July 2007	Comoros	Assistance to AU Military Observer Mission to Comoros with 371 SANDF members
Amphibian	August 2002–June 2004	Democratic Republic of the Congo	Assistance to third-party verification mechanism
Sunray	June–September 2003	Democratic Republic of the Congo	Assistance to European Union Interim Emergency Multinational Force
Montego	October 2003–January 2005	Liberia	Assistance to United Nations Mission in Liberia (UNMIL)
Cordite	July 2004–2016	Sudan	Assistance to AU and UN missions in Sudan, and to UN/AU Hybrid Operation in Darfur (UNAMID)
Teutonic	January 2005–present	Democratic Republic of the Congo	Security sector reform assisting with integration and training of the Armed Forces of the Democratic Republic of the Congo (FARDC)
Pristine	July 2005–December 2006	Côte d'Ivoire	Support of peace process

Table 3.2   *Continued*

Operation	Duration	Country/Location	Mandate
Curriculum	January 2007–December 2009	Burundi	Assistance to African Union Special Task Force in Burundi (AUSTF)
Induli	April 2007–July 2009	Nepal	Assistance to United Nations Mission in Nepal (UNMIN)
Vimbezela	March 2007–June 2013	Central African Republic	Security sector reform assistance
Bongane	June 2007–July 2009	Northern Uganda and Southern Sudan	Troop assistance to peace process

readiness" of the SANDF has been strained to maintain core capabilities, and this has compromised the ability of the defence force to become a fully equipped and operational conventional force.

The SANDF has exhibited a growing list of inadequacies that have been widely publicised, as well as presented to defence oversight structures, in particular the Parliamentary Portfolio Committee on Defence. For example, John Stupart has noted that "the cutting of flight hours for fighter pilots and the heavy reliance on charter strategic airlift are flashy reminders of this ... [while at the same time] the Army ... [has] a basket of needs ranging from the replacement of 50-year old trucks to the constant need for training exercises to keep troops at a professional level" of preparedness.[27]

In order to regain the strength that it will likely require to respond to its future security environment, it is critical that there is greater investment in training the SANDF and ensuring that it attains required capabilities. Army reservists, for example, had not been sent on training exercises since 1996. Similarly, military equipment had gravitated towards disrepair as the SANDF experienced a gradual "blanket obsolescence of several major weapon systems".[28]

As early as 2009, Lindiwe Sisulu, minister of defence and military veterans at the time, "highlighted the most important Defence challenges facing the Zuma administration as: the country's increasing international role in peacekeeping, the deteriorating military infrastructure, the outflow of qualified personnel and the lack of up-to-date policy documents".[29]

In other words, there was a lack of appreciation for the non-traditional roles that South Africa's armed forces were increasingly required to execute.[30] Indeed, as Catherine Pringle noted, "defence functions such as participation in peace missions, support to the police, participation in regional security missions and humanitarian assistance are to be executed with the collateral utility (the spare capacity) of the SANDF".[31] However, as explained by General Siphiwe Nyanda, a former chief (and the first black general) of the SANDF, "the provision [in policy] that the defence force may be employed for [such functions] does not imply that the defence force must be designed or exist for this reason". Rather, because of the SANDF's "inherent capabilities", the armed forces can be utilised to perform non-conventional tasks.[32] In other words, Nyanda agreed that "the SANDF should be designed to fulfil its strategic purpose and must provide other services [to the state] through its collateral utility".[33]

At the same time, the reality of South Africa's strategic environment has compelled acceptance that the requirement for "collateral capabilities" will dominate the operational landscape of the SANDF into the future. South Africa's democratic state was born into a tumultuous global environment characterised by insecurity from the Cold War era in countries like Angola, Mozambique and Somalia, and has been challenged by conflicts in its own Southern African neighbourhood, distinguished by their scale and resulting loss of life such as in the DRC (ongoing) and Angola (before 2002). It is fortunate that the SANDF has been spared, relatively speaking, from being required to perform much more intensive and extensive operations.

The defence predicament that South Africa faces is not the result of overextending its armed forces. Rather, it stems from an inability adequately to consolidate and capacitate the defence institutions of the state in an environment characterised by the "twin pressures of late state making" and by the need to respond to a multitude of unforeseen functions between war and peace.[34] The late advent of democracy in South Africa meant that, in 1994, the new government of Nelson Mandela had, first and foremost, to prioritise and expend national resources on rectifying apartheid's socio-economic discrimination against the majority-black population. At the same time, the euphoria that greeted the demise of racial supremacy was also accompanied by disdain for a security apparatus that had been responsible not only for destabilising the regional neighbourhood, but also for the internal suppression of South Africans. As such, the Mandela government's focus on the armed forces was restricted to the transformation aspects "of ensuring robust and stable civil-military relations in a democracy, almost as a first principle, rather than adopting as its departure point an appraisal of the strategic environment within which South African defence found itself situated".[35]

In this context, which was compounded by a general post-Cold War trend towards reduced defence spending (as a percentage of gross domestic product (GDP)), the SANDF was neither adequately funded nor appropriately structured from the outset. The decision to strengthen the SANDF's war-fighting capabilities to fight a future conventional war, through the strategic defence packages of 1999, proved to have limited usage for operations in a persistently insecure environment engulfed by non-traditional and non-conventional threats such as illegal migration.[36] Equally, the infancy of the democratic state, and its concomitant emphasis on transformation, prevented a comprehensive and congruent formulation of foreign policy, a national security strategy, and a statement of national interests, to provide strategic direction to the building of South

Africa's post-apartheid security architecture. These policy tools have since been developed, but the absence of an integrated effort between security and foreign policies to create harmony with one another at the outset has resulted in unilateralism in defence planning that remains parochially focused on internal transformation, and the construction of a conventional armed force that is limited in confronting contemporary and foreseeable security challenges.

This defence predicament has not been left unaddressed. Accepting that "the policy directives" of South Africa's first defence review of 1998 were less relevant and less applicable since the SANDF continued to prioritise collateral activities, a review (as opposed to rewrite) of existing defence policy was undertaken by the defence department in 2004.[37] However, the resulting defence update was not approved by the government due to the unaffordable costs of the force design that were proposed for the SANDF. A subsequent attempt in 2009, that took the form of a defence strategy for 2010 through 2030, similarly did not see the light of day.

Successive governments made a conscious effort to address this inertia in the defence policy review process. In 2011, then minister of defence Lindiwe Sisulu established an independent Defence Review Committee with a mandate to review previous attempts to update national defence policy, and thereafter to engage in a comprehensive public consultation process with key stakeholders, interested parties and civil society across South Africa to seek consensus on the role of the SANDF. More specifically, the committee's mandate was to validate and confirm the defence mandate as prescribed in South Africa's national constitution and other statutes; provide a defence policy that was supportive of the government's strategic intent; determine the complete spectrum of its defence responsibility; indicate a strategic defence concept, broad capability requirements, and high-level defence doctrine; posit the level of defence effort that should be funded by the government; provide policy guidance for the development of a blueprint to structure the country's defence institutions; and provide a high-level discussion on funding principles for defence.

The draft version of the new defence review of 2012 contains a steadfast understanding that South Africa's military capability must be commensurate with the country's international status, its overall strategic posture and its continental leadership role. As such, the SANDF is viewed in the document as a vital and unique tool that complements the South African government's diplomatic efforts and helps to enhance its influence on the international stage. The SANDF should therefore be required, and be able, to conduct a wide range of multi-dimensional military operations across a spectrum of complex conflicts, characterised by a wide variety of highly lethal and fluid threats. Accordingly, South Africa's 2012 defence review stresses that the country's armed forces must be maintained as a balanced, modern and flexible force that employs advanced technologies appropriate to operations in the African security environment; that their defence capability must be robust and flexible, and be able to project and sustain joint land, air, maritime, special forces and military health capabilities over extended distances for protracted periods; and that the SANDF must, therefore, be appropriately equipped, resourced and trained to operate successfully across the spectrum of potential conflict.[38]

There is a clear and inseparable link between national security, foreign policy and defence operations. To this end, the defence review aimed to be a comprehensive national-level policy document that translates the South African government's security and foreign policies into an overall orientation and set of tasks for the SANDF. The document must, though, also obtain consensual high-level support for restructuring the country's armed forces in a coherent manner, and with the appropriate set of capabilities required to achieve the array of operational objectives.[39]

Concluding Reflections

At the conclusion of South Africa's two and a half decades of freedom from apartheid, reflections on the country's defence and security role can point to the fulfilment of key domestic obligations and foreign responsibilities. However, in carrying out these functions, South Africa's defence institutions, in particular the SANDF, have had to endure a mismatch between their capacity and the expanding array of roles and tasks with which they have been entrusted. This defence predicament is largely a consequence of the transitional nature of the post-apartheid state. At the same time, overextended armed forces have also increasingly become a reality for developing countries, in general, in an overall context of geo-strategic insecurity generated by non-conventional threats – for example, domestic maritime security issues such as illegal fishing and acts of piracy. In an attempt to address these challenges, South Africa has sought to re-orient and to undertake a functional review of its defence policy, alongside other critical and relevant national security policy frameworks.

Informed by the country's national security strategy, national interests and foreign policy objectives, the new defence review was formulated with specified strategic goals and tasks for the South African National Defence Force with a view to helping the force fulfil its constitutional mandate, as well as South Africa's strategic security and foreign policy goals and priorities.

Notes

1. I was seconded to head the Defence Review Secretariat. My permanent position is Director of Defence Policy Formulation, South Africa's Department of Defence. I write here in my personal capacity.

2. Jacklyn Cock and Laurie Nathan (eds), *War and Society: The Militarisation of South Africa* (Cape Town: David Philip, 1989), p. 7; Phyllis Johnson and David Martin, *Apartheid Terrorism: The Destabilization Report* (London: Currey), pp. 1–12.

3. Adebayo Adedeji, "Within or Apart?", in Adebayo Adedeji (ed.), *South Africa in Africa: Within or Apart?* (London: Zed, 1996), p. 9.

4. Government of South Africa, "Defence in a Democracy: White Paper on National Defence for the Republic of South Africa", 1996; Government of South Africa, "South African Defence Review", 1998. *See also* Centre for Conflict Resolution (CCR), *The South African Defence Review of 2012: Problems, Progress, and Prospects*, Policy Brief no. 11 (Cape Town, 3 May 2012), http://www.ccr.org.za/images/pdfs/CCRPB11_defence_review_1jun2012.pdf (accessed 10 March 2014).

5. Catherine Pringle, "South Africa's Military: A Case of 'Biting Off More Than It Can Chew'?" *Consultancy Africa Intelligence*, 8 December 2010, http://www.polity.org.za/article/south-africas-military-a-case-of-biting-off-more-than-it-can-chew-2010-12-08 (accessed 18 September 2016).

6. Pringle, "South Africa's Military".

7. Pringle, "South Africa's Military".

8. Rocky Williams, "Integration or Absorption? The Creation of the South African National Defence Force, 1993–1999", *African Security Review* 11, no. 2 (2002), p. 22.

9. Constitution of the Republic of South Africa, Act 108 of 1996, chap. 11, art. 200 (2): "The primary object of the defence force is to defend and protect the Republic, its territorial integrity and its people in accordance with the Constitution and principles of international law regulating the use of force".

10. Garth Shelton, "The South African National Defence Force (SANDF) and President Mbeki's Peace and Security Agenda: New Roles and Mission", Occasional Paper no. 42 (Tshwane: Institute for Global Dialogue (IGD), 2004).

11. Christopher McMichael, "South Africa: State of Emergency 2.0", *Pambazuka News* no. 567 (26 January 2012), http://www.pambazuka.org (accessed 18 September 2016).

12. Jane Duncan, "Thabo Mbeki and Dissent", in Daryl Glaser (ed.), *Mbeki and After: Reflections on the Legacy of Thabo Mbeki* (Johannesburg: Wits University Press, 2010), p. 110.

13. Thomas Mandrup, "The South African National Defence Force: Midwives of Peace in Africa? An Evaluation of SANDF Involvement in Peace Support Operations", in Len le Roux (ed.), *South African Army Vision 2020*, vol. 2, *The South African Army Relevant and Ready for Future Security Challenges in Africa* (Tshwane: Institute for Security Studies (ISS), 2008), pp. 11, 99.

14. Mandrup, "The South African National Defence Force", pp. 102, 109.

15. Mandrup, "The South African National Defence Force", p. 112.

16. Shelton, "The South African National Defence Force".

17. Theo Neethling, "Conditions for Successful Entry and Exit: An Assessment of SADC Allied Operations in Lesotho", http://www.operationspaix.net/DATA/DOCUMENT/6069~v ~ Conditions_for_Successful_Entry_and_Exit_An_Assessment_of_SADC_Allied_Operations_in_Lesotho.pdf (accessed 16 January 2017).

18. Shelton, "The South African National Defence Force".

19. Neethling, "Conditions for Successful Entry and Exit".

20. Mandrup, "The South African National Defence Force", pp. 109–111.

21. Shelton, "The South African National Defence Force". At a meeting on 21 September 1998, the South African minister of safety and security, Sydney Mufamadi, and representatives from Botswana, Mozambique and Zimbabwe, reportedly confirmed that the Southern African Development Community (SADC) had authorised a possible military intervention in the event of a coup in Lesotho. The status of the intervention as a SADC mission, however, remains contested.

22. "African Peacekeeping Deployments Show What the SANDF Can Do", 1 April 2014, http://www.defenceweb.co.za/index:sa-defence (accessed 8 June 2014).

23. "African Peacekeeping Deployments".

24. Thabang Makwetla, "South Africa's Contribution to Peace in Africa", *SA Army Journal* no. 5 (2012), pp. 24–32.

25. Pringle, "South Africa's Military".

26. Pringle, "South Africa's Military".

27. John Stupart, "Military Scrabbling for Petrol Money", *African Defence Review*, 4 March 2014, https://www.africandefence.net/sas-military-scrabbling-for-petrol-money (accessed 16 September 2016).

28. Mandrup, "The South African National Defence Force", p. 110.

29. Pringle, "South Africa's Military".

30. Rocklyn Williams, "How Primary Is the Primary Function? Configuring the SANDF for African Realities", *African Security Review* 8, no. 6 (1999), pp. 70–83.

31. Pringle, "South Africa's Military".

32. Siphiwe Nyanda, "Restructuring the SA Military: Between Domestic Imperatives and External Obligations", *South African Journal of International Affairs* 8, no. 2 (2001), p. 47.

33. Nyanda, "Restructuring the SA Military", p. 47.

34. Mohammed Ayoob, *The Third World Security Predicament: State Making, Regional Conflict, and the International System* (London: Rienner, 1995), p. 13.

35. Williams, "Integration or Absorption?", p. 20.

36. Shelton, "The South African National Defence Force".

37. Shelton, "The South African National Defence Force".

38. Paraphrased from draft versions of South Africa's new defence review. *See* Government of South Africa, *South African Defence Review 2014*, http://www.gov.za/sites/www.gov.za/files/dfencereview_2014.pdf (accessed 16 September 2016).

39. *See* CCR, *The South African Defence Review of 2012.*

CHAPTER 4

HUMAN RIGHTS IN SOUTH AFRICA'S FOREIGN POLICY: A LIGHT OR A LIABILITY?

Nicole Fritz

Assessments of the role of human rights in post-apartheid South Africa's foreign policy since the inauguration of democracy in 1994 have run between two extremes. Early on, there was acclaim for the ostensible aim of making human rights the lodestar of South African diplomacy, fuelled by an article written by Nelson Mandela in the influential international relations journal *Foreign Affairs* declaring that human rights would be the "light that guides our foreign affairs".[1] Inevitably, there was disappointment as Tshwane (Pretoria) appeared to fall short of this mark, with several assessments in the aftermath of the financial crisis of 2008–2009 decrying the absence of principled leadership from emerging powers in the global South and singling South Africa out for particular criticism.[2]

However, South Africa's foreign policy merits a more measured assessment. Over a span of two and a half decades of constitutional democracy, the country's apparent failure to uphold human rights in a number of its international dealings does not register as a single, coherent narrative. I suggest in this chapter that South Africa's disappointing support for human rights has come about generally in two sets of circumstances: either when it has felt compelled to adopt regional or continental positions at odds with its own normative stance; or when Tshwane has believed that its posture might advance its principled objective of building a fairer, more equitable and more representative global governance architecture. Admittedly, these two factors – regional or continental consensus; and a desire for a fairer international order – are often difficult to distinguish from each other, with both serving on occasion to inform similar outcomes. In recent years, South Africa's equivocal stance in relation to the International Criminal Court (ICC) – culminating in October 2016 in a bid (since halted by the South African High Court in March 2017 due to the process followed) to withdraw from the Rome Statute for the ICC and a far cry from its initial enthusiastic support for the institution – appears to be driven both by the enmity felt by several African states for the ICC, and by its concern that the Court is selective in its prosecutions, exempting leaders of the world's most powerful states. However, at times, South Africa has had, and will continue to need, to make the hard choice between abiding with regional consensus and supporting human rights. Furthermore, in pitting the pursuit of fairer representation in global governance against the promotion of human rights, South Africa has often not appreciated that this might represent a false choice.

This chapter also seeks to show that a fuller assessment of South Africa's foreign policy posture vis-à-vis human rights must go beyond an exclusive focus on positions adopted by the executive branch. South Africa's constitutional democracy reserves specific roles for its judiciary and legislature in upholding human rights, and this responsibility inevitably impacts the formulation and conduct of the country's foreign policy. South African courts, in particular, have become increasingly cognisant of their responsibility to protect and promote human rights, and have not stepped back from rendering judgements with explicit foreign policy implications.

Human Rights vs Collective Consensus

Within the global community, certain states are identified as rights-promoting, not only domestically but also at the international level. American scholar Alison Brysk has called these states "global good Samaritans".[3] For some states this tradition is long established, while for others it is more recent – the product of the wave of constitutionalism that happened at the end of the twentieth century. These global good Samaritans tend to be "small to medium sized and highly dependent on interaction, which fosters consensus and proposes a purposeful form of niche foreign policy".[4] They appreciate that a principled foreign policy can be leveraged for global influence – projected as a form of what American scholar Joseph Nye described as "soft power".[5]

In some circles, South Africa might be seen as an exemplar of just this type of state. Yet Tshwane often lacks what Brysk identifies as a compelling influence for the formulation of principled foreign policy: communal pressure. By way of example, it would be exceedingly difficult "for a European state to consistently abuse human rights and still be deemed to belong to contemporary 'Europe'".[6] South Africa, however, does not inhabit such a neighbourhood.

Instead it is located in a region in which its maturity as a constitutional democracy and "good Samaritanism"[7] place it in a minority. Yet Tshwane cannot afford to antagonise its neighbours: security and economic justifications compel South Africa's assumption of an "African" identity. Historically, there is the debt that is owed to the continent for the solidarity offered by African states (evidenced by the policies of individual states and collective positions adopted within the Organisation of African Unity in opposition to the apartheid regime). Looking to future advantage South Africa is often granted an elevated profile on the international stage on the basis that it can deliver the African "bloc".[8] South Africa's fluctuating positions vis-à-vis two different international tribunals – the International Criminal Court and the Southern African Development Community (SADC) Tribunal, both of which hold potential for significant human rights promotion – are indicative of the inconsistencies that arise in attempting to uphold human rights principles alongside consensual regional and continental positions.

The International Criminal Court

The International Criminal Court, although not an institution concerned per se with establishing individual rights against state rights, is an important extension of the post-1945 global human rights architecture that has been tasked with securing the accountability of those most responsible for the world's worst atrocities: genocide, crimes against humanity and war crimes.[9] The perpetrators of such crimes are generally those clothed in state or state-like power. Impetus for the creation of the ICC was provided both by the obvious horrors perpetrated during the Rwandan genocide and the Balkan Wars in the early 1990s,[10] and by the unprecedented opportunity for international cooperation created by the end of the Cold War by 1990.

South Africa had ample reason to recognise the need for an institution such as the ICC, since its own transition was conditioned, in part, on the agonising determination to allow those responsible for apartheid's crimes to escape civil and criminal liability.[11] Just four years after its transition to democracy in 1994, South Africa seized the opportunity to play a leadership role in negotiations for the Rome Statute of 1998, which established the ICC in 2002.[12] Under its then minister of justice, Dullah Omar, and his adviser, Medard Rwelamira, South Africa was instrumental in achieving the necessary consensus among a critical mass of states to resist the attempts of other states, such as the United States (US), that were intent on creating a less-independent court beholden to the United Nations (UN) Security Council. In keeping with this position, in 2003, Tshwane refused to enter into a bilateral impunity agreement with Washington, choosing to suffer a withdrawal of American bilateral aid rather than undermine the Rome Statute. This was an executive decision taken collectively and unanimously.[13]

South Africa demonstrated further commitment to the ICC when it enacted domestic legislation to enforce the obligations that it had taken under the Rome Statute. This legislation – the Implementation of the Rome Statute of the International Criminal Court Act of 2002[14] – has served as a model for domesticating ICC commitments into national legislation for several other states (for example, Mauritius and Kenya). Yet, despite making so substantial an intellectual investment in the development of international criminal law and its architecture, South Africa has since stepped back from this investment, and even undermined it grievously on occasion, notwithstanding its potential to elevate South Africa's voice in the field of human rights.

That is not to say that the direction of, and developments within, the ICC have not given South Africa real cause for concern. Nine of the ten situations under investigation or prosecution before the ICC are in Africa (the Central African Republic (two), Côte d'Ivoire, Darfur (Sudan), the Democratic Republic of the Congo, Kenya, Libya, Mali and Uganda).[15] Furthermore, the conduct of the Court's first prosecutor, Argentina's Luis Moreno-Ocampo, did little to indicate that those within the ICC appreciated that an exclusively African focus for an institution intended to have global reach was problematic, and that it could be used to discredit the Court. Unsurprisingly, this was exactly what Sudanese president Omar al-Bashir did after earning ICC indictments in 2009 for crimes against humanity and war crimes and, a year later, for genocide.

The African Union (AU) has, at various summits since 2009, issued communiqués expressing its opposition to the indictment of al-Bashir and resolving not to cooperate with the ICC over the matter. Another battleground opened up between the AU and the ICC over the summonses issued by the Court to Kenya's sitting president, Uhuru Kenyatta, and his deputy, William Ruto, in March 2011. South Africa has been party to the AU communiqués, notwithstanding the example of recorded dissent provided by Botswana. At the domestic level, this has meant substantial and embarrassing back-pedalling on the part of South Africa. For example, after President Jacob Zuma returned from the AU summit in Sirte, Libya, in 2009, at which it was resolved that the African Union would withhold cooperation from the ICC in the case of al-Bashir, South Africa's justice department – in an unprecedented move and in the face of substantial civil society pressure – announced that Tshwane remained cognisant of its ICC obligations, and that it had in fact secured a domestic arrest warrant for al-Bashir in order to meet these obligations, when it appeared that the Sudanese president might attend Zuma's inauguration in 2009. South Africa was also party to the decision emanating from the October 2013 AU Summit, which, while not urging mass African withdrawal from the Court as had been threatened in the lead-up to the summit, nonetheless amounted to an endorsement of impunity: demanding that no international criminal charges be pressed against any serving AU head of state or government and that the trials of Kenyatta and Ruto be suspended.

Worse perhaps than these confused and conflicting positions have been the proposals fashioned by South Africa in its attempt to address the AU's opposition to the Sudanese and Kenyan indictments. South Africa has been in the lead in calling for the UN Security Council to defer the ICC's investigation and prosecution of al-Bashir, Kenyatta and Ruto under Article 16 of the Rome Statute of 1998, which permits such a deferral by the Security Council for a renewable period of 12 months.[16] (The cases against Kenyatta and Ruto had been dropped by the Court by 2016.) Any serious consideration of this proposal, however, allows for an appreciation of the perverse incentives it would generate in clear violation of the principles that the ICC is intended to uphold. Al-Bashir would only be mollified by an Article 16 deferral if he were to be assured that it could be obtained in perpetuity. The only guarantee of such an outcome would be for al-Bashir to remain in power or to ensure that his successors were sufficiently like-minded to guarantee him the political power necessary to make annual renewals by the UN Security Council feasible.

Given South Africa's historic role in the establishment of the ICC, it was well placed to play a facilitating role in rebuilding the relationship between the Court and Africa, pushing back against the crude anti-ICC discourse that appeared in the aftermath of the al-Bashir indictment, while publicly and forthrightly warning the Court of a continuing loss of credibility should it continue to focus its docket only on African cases. In so doing, South Africa might have preserved and safeguarded its substantial investment in the processes of international criminal accountability, while maintaining widespread continental and regional support. Specifically, Tshwane could publicly push for the UN Security Council to bear the costs of its ICC referrals, as the decision-making body is obliged to do in terms of the Rome Statute and which it has thus far failed to do.[17]

Far from playing the role of moderator, however, and in a surprising turn of events, South Africa announced in October 2016 that it was to withdraw from the Rome Statute of the ICC. A visit by al-Bashir to South Africa's shores in June 2015 to attend an African Union summit had sparked an urgent court bid to have al-Bashir arrested and surrendered to the ICC. Despite assurances to the court by the South African government that al-Bashir was still in the country when the court considered the matter, it later transpired that he had, in fact, fled the country leaving the court's order that all reasonable steps be taken to arrest him impossible to execute.[18]

Despite the fact that there seemed very little chance of a repeat of circumstances requiring the government to enforce the order, it sought to appeal the judgment, leading to a decision by the Supreme Court of Appeal in March 2016 that not only confirmed the earlier court ruling but also underlined, in the most authoritative terms, the nature of South Africa's obligations towards the ICC. Specifically, in the face of the Zuma administration's insistence that it was obliged under international law to respect head of state immunity, the Supreme Court ruled that South Africa's domestic law clearly demanded that it not recognise head of state immunity and that, through its domestic law, South Africa "was taking a step many other nations have not yet. If that puts this country in the vanguard of attempts to prevent international crimes and when they occur cause the perpetrators to be prosecuted, that seems to me a matter for national pride rather than concern. It is wholly consistent with our commitment to human rights both at a national and an international level."[19]

Faced with the prospect that the Constitutional Court – South Africa's highest court on all constitutional matters – would likely only make this pronouncement more eminent by virtue of its agreement when it was slated to hear the matter in November 2016, the government announced that it would withdraw from the ICC and also withdraw its appeal to the country's Constitutional Court on the basis that there was now no law requiring interpretation. It publicly sought to defend its position by arguing that its ICC obligations impeded its ability to play the role of peacemaker on the continent effectively (see Curtis in this volume) and that it was challenging the double standards that characterise so much of global governance. Neither of these positions withstands critical scrutiny,[20] but this overlapping of ostensible concern for its role in, and obligations towards, the continent and the desire to champion the global underdog is very much a hallmark of those foreign policy positions in which South Africa is said to have departed from its human rights commitments.

The SADC Tribunal

The suspension of the Southern African Development Community Tribunal, and South Africa's role therein, has received scant attention in discussions about the place of human rights in the country's foreign policy. Established in 1992 to allow for the peaceful settlement of disputes arising from the SADC Treaty (revised in 2001) and its protocols (see Saunders and Nagar in this volume on SADC), the Tribunal was the most critical SADC institution in terms of conditioning compliance with the rule of law in the Southern African sub-region. Its 15 member states, as well as legal and natural persons, were entitled to approach the Tribunal for adjudication, and the Tribunal understood itself to have a significant human rights protection mandate under the SADC Treaty.

However, following a series of successful challenges to Zimbabwe's land expropriations process before the Tribunal in 2007 and 2008, Harare not only refused to adhere to the body's rulings, but also impugned the legality of the Tribunal's establishment. The SADC Committee of Ministers of Justice/Attorneys-General was tasked with responding to Zimbabwe's objections. The committee recommended that a review of the role, functions and terms of reference of the SADC Tribunal be undertaken. This was subsequently authorised by the SADC heads of state summit in August 2010. While the review itself was not necessarily threatening to the rule of law, the SADC summit also elected to couple the process with an effective suspension of the Tribunal by depriving it of the quorum necessary to hear cases, and by ordering it not to adjudicate any new cases. In May

2011, the SADC summit mandated its Committee of Ministers of Justice to draft proposals for amendment of the Tribunal, indicating that the August 2012 summit meeting would make a definitive determination as to the judicial body's future. The 2011 summit also extended the suspension of the SADC Tribunal, ordering that no cases – including those already before the Tribunal – be heard by it.

The SADC Committee of Ministers of Justice recommended that the Tribunal should be revived. The committee also recommended that individual access to it ought to be preserved, but that the Tribunal's human rights mandate be curtailed. This, in and of itself, would have been a setback for the rule of law in the sub-region. In any event, despite these recommendations, the 32nd summit of SADC heads of state and government resolved in August 2012 that an entirely new protocol for the Tribunal would have to be negotiated. Sub-regional leaders further agreed that the mandate of the new Tribunal would be confined to "interpretation of the SADC Treaty and Protocols relating to disputes between Member States".[21] SADC thus determined to lock out individuals from any future Tribunal, denying them access to justice in cases where domestic legal systems offered no redress, and ensuring that the future Tribunal would be a court in name only.

The SADC Summit's August 2012 decision on the Tribunal represented the violation of a raft of rule-of-law principles, specifically of the right of SADC's 281 million citizens to access justice and obtain remedies; of judicial independence; of institutional accountability; and of administrative justice principles requiring that decisions not be unlawful, arbitrary and unreasonable. South Africa's president, Jacob Zuma, was not present at the time the Tribunal decision was made. However, a spokesperson from the country's Department of International Relations and Cooperation (DIRCO) explained – in a surprisingly frank manner – that Tshwane's position on the Tribunal was "neither here nor there", and that the country was obliged to uphold the collective decision of the SADC Summit.

Certainly, all the information gleaned by those groups (for example, the International Commission of Jurists and the Southern Africa Litigation Centre)[22] working for the restoration of the SADC Tribunal suggests that, if anything, South Africa is among those states most supportive of a fully restored Tribunal. At the same time, Tshwane does not believe the issue to be sufficiently critical to its own interests, and so its officials have not been prepared to expend political capital across the sub-region on securing the Tribunal's restoration.[23] Yet there is little doubt that, were South Africa so inclined, it could compel the body's full restoration, using its role as the primary member state funder of SADC as leverage.[24] It is not entirely speculative to suggest that the debts owed by South Africa in other political campaigns, such as that which secured Nkosazana Dlamini-Zuma the AU Commission chair in July 2012 (see Maloka in this volume), have been repaid in part by Tshwane acquiescing in the demise of the SADC Tribunal.[25]

Even if South Africa's role in the Tribunal's demise has not been one of chief proponent, but more that of quiet opportunist, the potential negative repercussions of the SADC decision are likely to be felt most acutely by Tshwane within the world of international diplomacy. At the domestic level, the rule of law is well entrenched in South Africa. Additionally, Tshwane well understands the rhetorical and strategic value of this principle at the international level, too. As a middle power,[26] South Africa stands to benefit from, and is less vulnerable in, an international order regulated by uniformly applied norms and laws. At the same time, as a middle power that aspires to a leadership role and has been granted entry to collectives of more powerful states (such as the BRICS bloc (Brazil, Russia, India, China and South Africa) in 2010 and the Group of 20 (G-20) in 2009) (on the BRICS bloc, see Virk in this volume), South Africa's domestically burnished reputation for the rule of law can be projected on the international level as a form of "soft power"– enabling it to accrue respect and influence by its example of principled conduct. Both practically and rhetorically, the rule of law principle thus protects and promotes South Africa internationally. However, it is hard to see how the role sought by Tshwane – as consensus-builder on different aspects of the rule of law – will not be seriously impaired by its participation in the decision to dismantle the SADC Tribunal, when it is regarded by many within the international community (such as the European Union (EU) and the United Nations) to have sufficient regional clout to ensure that its views predominate in such matters (see Nkosi, and Mashabane in this volume).

For example, South Africa will find it especially hard to reconcile the SADC Tribunal decision with the importance that it attaches to the rule of law in securing gender equality and women's empowerment, both regionally and internationally.[27] In 2012, the annual opening of the UN General Assembly was supplemented for the first time with a high-level meeting on national and international rule of law. South Africa astutely sought to profile itself at this high-level meeting, sponsoring two of the nine side-events at the gathering. One of the two side-events, which

Tshwane hosted alongside Finland and UN Women, focused on the access of women to justice. Yet even as South Africa sought to position itself as an international champion of women's access to justice, in its own sub-region, it had acted in a way that undermined such access by acquiescing in the demise of the SADC Tribunal. SADC's 2008 Protocol on Gender and Development commits its member states to a host of laws and policies intended to ameliorate and advance the condition of women in the sub-region. The only provision in the protocol ensuring that these commitments are achieved, and do not remain illusory, is the one requiring that any dispute arising from the application, interpretation and implementation of the protocol should be referred to the SADC Tribunal for adjudication. However, that Tribunal is now dead, with the SADC Protocol on Gender and Development consequently rendered as part of the collateral damage.

Maintaining the Balance

There can be no gainsaying the role that South Africa has sought as a valued and respected member of regional and continental institutions. As its former president Thabo Mbeki (1999–2008) remarked in 2002: "I don't think you can have sustainable and successful development in this country if the rest of the continent is in flames."[28] This reputation of the country as regional anchor and heavyweight, and its comparative economic strength, yield a national interest in stabilising poorly governed neighbouring states that may become regional aggressors or generate spill-over of refugees and social deterioration through poor governance. However, the approach that it follows is one that emphasises conflict resolution, and not necessarily democracy or human rights promotion. It also encourages a regional rather than a global focus. The more these two foreign policy objectives – human rights promotion, and regional peace and security – pull in different directions, the less possible it becomes for South Africa to inhabit both identities – principled protagonist on human rights, and responsible regional peacemaker – with integrity, forcing hard choices on policymakers in Tshwane.

Human Rights vs Fairer Representation

South Africa has made no secret of its ambitions for greater representation and an enhanced profile within multilateral institutions that constitute the organs of global governance. One of Tshwane's key objectives at the United

Nations is to realise reform of the 15-member UN Security Council with a view to securing a permanent seat on the body for itself in future.[29] While failing so far to achieve this specific objective, South Africa has nonetheless gained a considerably greater say in the international sphere through its participation in new global formations such as the G-20 and the BRICS bloc, as well as two near-consecutive turns as a non-permanent member of the UN Security Council in 2007–2008 and 2011–2012 respectively (see Mashabane in this volume).

There can be no principled counter to South Africa's protest at the inequality and unrepresentative nature of many global institutions. Indeed, the country's persistent use of international forums to draw attention to this "democratic deficit", as well as the distortions and double standards it produces, has earned South Africa the moniker "mouth of the South".[30] However, in choosing to draw attention to the duplicity and double standards within the current international system, South Africa has sometimes been seen to oppose human rights protection in order to thwart the agenda of major powers. More specifically, it has sought to ensure equal treatment for all countries by opposing censure of human rights violations in the developing world, thereby seeming to take the position that a single standard of no censure is preferable to the selective application of censure. In so doing, the protection and promotion of human rights has sometimes been set up as a principle in conflict with the goal of achieving a fairer and more representative international order.

South Africa's vote in the UN Security Council in 2007 against a draft resolution censuring Myanmar's military junta for human rights violations provides a clear illustration of this point (see Mashabane in this volume). Tshwane earned much criticism for this vote,[31] but what made this discussion extraordinary was not so much South Africa's unwillingness to censure Myanmar, as the process behind it. The Myanmar resolution was defeated by two vetoes, cast by China and Russia. Tshwane would have been aware that these vetoes would be cast, and that the resolution would be defeated without its participation, rendering its opposition nugatory. Indonesia, for example, recognised this likely outcome and chose simply to abstain on the draft resolution. In this context, South Africa's negative vote indicates that it wanted to be seen to oppose the resolution's proponents – to protest the use of what it maintained was the incorrect forum (that is, the UN Security Council) for the proposed measure, but more importantly, to oppose the selective censure of human rights violations by the US and Western Europe.

However, in taking this action, South Africa downplayed its own history of a hard-won human rights struggle, forfeiting the legitimating discourse of human rights to more powerful states, and also ceding a potentially important source of "soft power" for itself.

There are other, more innovative ways through which states such as South Africa, which are less powerful than the veto-wielding permanent five members (P-5) of the Security Council – the US, China, Russia, Britain and France – can counteract obvious inconsistencies in the Council's actions. For example, they could propose to initiate the referral of a human rights-violating state to the ICC through a request to the Security Council. Although such a request would not necessarily lead to a vote, nor pass if voted upon, in showing up a lack of response it would shine a more glaring light upon the UN Security Council's double standards, making the political costs of such inconsistency at least more onerous.

Small and/or less powerful states could also seek consensus with the P-5 on a different approach to adopting resolutions and using the veto. France, for example, proposed in 2013 that the UN Security Council should refrain from using the veto to block action aimed at ending genocide, war crimes and crimes against humanity. This would not mean that votes on action could not be defeated, as the majority vote would have to prevail, but only that the proposed measure could not be defeated by use of the veto. Interestingly, South Africa has aligned itself with this position, thereby backing not only structural reform of the UN, but also normative reform of its processes. Yet Tshwane has not sought to earn any capital from its stance, doing little to publicise its support for the French proposal.

This is surprising, considering that if South Africa is serious about leading the reform of multilateral institutions and securing more equitable representation in them, it will have to build constituencies not only among like-minded states, but also among the populations of those powers most likely to resist such efforts: powerful Western countries in Europe and North America. In countries such as the US and France, the people who are most likely to care about greater equality in institutions such as the United Nations and the World Trade Organisation (WTO) (see Ismail in this volume) are exactly those people who are also most likely to care about human rights violations and about more principled use of the veto.

Similarly, much of the criticism South Africa has earned regarding the wavering human rights orientation of its foreign policy has emanated from international non-governmental organisations (NGOs) such as Human Rights Watch and Amnesty International bewildered at the often chilly reception, and sometimes non-reception, that they have received from the South African government in seeking access to it. Here, too, Tshwane has forfeited a potential opportunity. South Africa could cajole international NGOs to take up the issue of fairer representation within multilateral institutions more vigorously. These organisations could be potentially invaluable allies in the country's quest for institutional reform.[32]

A Disaggregated Foreign Policy: Place for the Courts

Foreign policy is typically thought of as the exclusive preserve of the executive. In many traditionally Westphalian jurisdictions, courts tend to extend generous deference to the executive when legal issues involving foreign policy considerations are put before them. In the United States, for example, the political-question doctrine seeks to distinguish fundamentally political issues from those that are essentially legal. If a US court finds that a question brought before it is fundamentally political, it will typically refuse to hear the case, and claim that the courts do not have jurisdiction, leaving the issue to the political process to settle. Issues involving foreign policy often must be held to be archetypal political questions.

However, in South Africa, the constitution mandates a different approach, requiring that all public power be exercised in accordance with the rule of law, that it be rational, and that relevant considerations be taken into account and given appropriate weight to ensure informed and accountable decision-making. For example, in 2012, Sri Lanka proposed sending General Shavendra Silva to South Africa as its deputy ambassador. General Silva has been implicated in the mass killings of civilians during the Sri Lankan civil war (1983–2009), with UN reports linking him to the commission of crimes against humanity and war crimes in that country.[33] Civil society groups in South Africa (including the Tamil Federation of Gauteng and the South African Tamil Federation) alerted the Presidency in Tshwane to these allegations, and provided it with a legal opinion examining the president's powers to receive and recognise foreign representatives, and the necessary corollary power to refuse to recognise such persons.[34] The opinion pointed to the international conventions regulating diplomatic immunities and privileges to buttress the submission that certain persons are ineligible for diplomatic recognition, and also made reference to the South African foreign ministry's own policy documents with respect to the purpose of diplomatic immunities and privileges. While the civil society groups hoped that the Presidency would exercise its discretion and refuse to recognise General Silva, they reserved the right to launch legal proceedings to review the president's powers to recognise the Sri Lankan nominee in case Zuma did not do so. In the event, Sri Lankan authorities were discreetly informed that General Silva would not be welcome in the country, and no legal action was necessary.

However, if the Sri Lankan issue spoke to the potential of South African courts to make pronouncements with overtly foreign policy repercussions, a 2013 case before the country's Constitutional Court actually realised that potential. At first glance, the case of *Government of Zimbabwe v Fick and Others*[35] seemed to concern the rather technical and politically uncontroversial issue of the enforcement of costs orders issued by the SADC Tribunal – a regional court to which South Africa was party. However, the fact that the government of Zimbabwe was party to the proceedings gave a clue to the political sensitivities involved. The case arose from a series of cases brought before the SADC Tribunal by Zimbabwean farmers who had been dispossessed of their farms as part of the Zimbabwean land reform process. The Tribunal had found in their favour, issuing a costs order for the legal expenses incurred. The applicants had sought unsuccessfully to have this order enforced in Zimbabwean courts and then turned to South Africa, seeking execution of the orders against several commercial properties owned by Zimbabwe in South Africa. From the point of view of South African foreign policy, more interesting than the facts was the reasoning of the country's Constitutional Court once the case reached it. In justifying its extension of the common law to recognise the enforceability of the SADC Tribunal's rulings, the Court placed much emphasis on the concept of comity. However, comity is traditionally understood to be the deference extended by one state to another. In this case, the Court extended deference to a regional institution at the cost of a neighbouring state. Furthermore, the Court also held that its decision to extend the common law in this manner was supported by the fact that the applicants could not avail themselves of the right to access justice within their own domestic jurisdiction, namely Zimbabwe.[36] It in effect ruled on the conduct of a state – a matter that had not explicitly been put before it. In reaching the decision, the Court did not suggest that it was doing anything extraordinary. Yet the judges cannot have been unaware of the fierce resistance that the judgement would trigger from the Zimbabwean government of President Robert Mugabe, and the potentially negative implications this ruling would have for Zimbabwe–South Africa relations (see Sachikonye in this volume).

Indeed, *Zimbabwe v Fick* has not been an isolated instance, and South African courts have addressed cases with foreign policy implications on several occasions. For example, in 2012, a South African High Court ruled that the government was obliged to investigate torture committed in the build-up to the 2008 elections in Zimbabwe. Torture is a crime against humanity under the 1998 Rome Statute of the International Criminal Court, and South Africa's international crime legislation obliges the country to investigate these crimes irrespective of where they have been committed and by whom. This case did not involve prosecution though, but instead was a judicial review in which the High Court was asked to decide whether South Africa had acted in accordance with its international legal obligations. Importantly, in its ruling on an issue that involved political sensitivities vis-à-vis Zimbabwe, the court ruled: "At that stage [the stage leading to a decision to embark on an investigation] it was not their [South Africa's National Prosecuting Authority and its police] obligation to take political and policy considerations into account",[37] suggesting that such considerations might be proper at a later stage.

Hence, while South African courts have not held back from issuing judgements that have discernible foreign policy implications, particularly in cases where a court believes that its ruling will advance human rights and therefore promote the constitution, it would be erroneous – indeed damaging – to imply that South African courts are unappreciative of the limits of judicial intervention. Rather, the suggestion here is that they recognise the constitutional import of human rights-rooted limitations constraining even the most coveted of executive powers.

It is widely recognised that globalisation has made for a disaggregated state at the international level. States are no longer represented in the world solely by executive leaders and their diplomats. Increasingly, regulators, parliamentarians and judges engage across national lines and speak on behalf of their respective countries. However, while judges participate in international exchanges and conferences in the same way as other national representatives do, they also have a unique ability to engage in international discussion and debate through the citation and examination of other countries' court decisions in their own judgements. Through such citation and examination, influence is spread and values are promoted. In this way, courts and judges become leaders of international thought.

There can be no doubt that South Africa's courts, particularly its Constitutional Court, are just such leaders. Since its inception, the Constitutional Court has demonstrated an absence of intellectual timidity, engaging robustly with judgements from other jurisdictions in a bid to fashion a uniquely South African approach. More telling in terms of influence and respect is the extent to which South African judgements and South Africa's Constitution are cited authoritatively and approvingly by foreign courts, and studied by foreign legal academics.[38] In this context, South Africa plays a powerful role clearly disproportionate to its size, standing head and shoulders above any of the other BRICS countries, bar India, or any of the other influential rising democracies. Brazilian jurisprudence is not examined or cited in international law journals with the same frequency as are South African court decisions. Academic courses in law schools around the world are not devoted to the study of Turkey's constitution and the judgements of its courts in the same way that they are to South Africa's. Of course, it is not the intellectual rigour of South Africa's judges that alone accounts for the influence of its court decisions. Rather, the interest is generated by the country's constitution itself.

Concluding Reflections

In the two decades since the transition to democracy, South Africa's foreign policy has not always appeared to place human rights front and centre. In fact, on several occasions it has appeared to disregard such considerations entirely. Still, in the formulation and conduct of its foreign policy, South Africa is not the deviant some of its sternest critics — disappointed by its failure to make real Nelson Mandela's promise of 1993 — would have us think. Sometimes the compromise as regards human rights comes about as a result of genuinely hard choices: it would be unrealistic to expect South Africa easily, or even strategically, to ignore the regional and continental pressures that often compete with human rights norms. That said, South Africa has on too many occasions been seen to adopt positions that run counter to human rights for no apparent strategic foreign policy gain — risking too easily the perception that it is a dog in the manger. And in its defensiveness at criticism of its foreign policy's compliance with human rights, the South African government appears to forget why — given its history — observers might justifiably expect more. In needlessly squandering that legacy at times, it appears blind to how its hard-won history, leveraged for global influence, might secure future advantage and power.

Notes

1. Nelson Mandela, "South Africa's Future Foreign Policy", *Foreign Affairs* 72, no. 5 (November/December 1993), pp. 86–97.
2. *See, for example*, Jorge G. Castañeda, "Not Ready for Prime Time: Why Including Emerging Powers at the Helm Would Hurt Global Governance", *Foreign Affairs* 89, no. 5 (September/October 2010), pp. 109–122; "The See-No-Evil Foreign Policy", *The Economist*, 13 November 2008, http://www.economist.com/node/12607346 (accessed 25 January 2014).
3. Alison Brysk, *Global Good Samaritans: Human Rights as Foreign Policy* (Oxford: Oxford University Press, 2009).
4. Brysk, *Global Good Samaritans*, p. 34.
5. Joseph S. Nye, Jr., *Soft Power: The Means to Success in World Politics* (New York: PublicAffairs, 2004).
6. Brysk, *Global Good Samaritans*, p. 34.
7. *See* Brysk, *Global Good Samaritans*.
8. Part of the justification for South Africa's inclusion in the BRIC grouping (Brazil, Russia, India and China) – all countries of which far exceeded South Africa's economic power – was its so-called representation for Africa.
9. *Rome Statute of the International Criminal Court*, 17 July 1998, UN Doc. A/CONF.183/9.
10. The internecine civil war in the Balkans, which involved ethnic cleansing and mass killings, and the genocide in Rwanda, are the most obvious examples, both of which put the United Nations' (UN) capacity and willingness for peacekeeping to shame.
11. *See* Yasmin Sooka, "Race and Reconciliation: *E Pluribus Unum?*", in Adekeye Adebajo, Adebayo Adedeji and Chris Landsberg (eds), *South Africa in Africa: The Post-Apartheid Era* (Scottsville: University of KwaZulu-Natal Press, 2007), pp. 78–91.
12. A parallel regional initiative by South Africa was the inclusion of Article 4(h) in the African Union's (AU) Constitutive Act, providing the organisation with a right to intervene in a member state in cases of war crimes, genocide and crimes against humanity.
13. *See* Brysk, *Global Good Samaritans*, p. 172.
14. *See* Implementation of the Rome Statute of the International Criminal Court Act (27) of 2002.
15. In January 2016, the Prosecutor of the International Criminal Court (ICC) was authorised to commence an investigation into crimes committed in the state of Georgia.
16. With respect to the International Criminal Court, the UN Security Council's deferral power is the reverse of its referral power. It allows the Security Council to suspend an ICC investigation or prosecution for one year.

17. *See* Article 115, "Funds of the Court and of the Assembly of States Parties", of the Rome Statute of 1998. *See also* R. Michael Reisman, "On Paying the Piper: Financial Responsibility for Security Council Referrals to the International Criminal Court", *American Society of International Law* 99, no. 3 (2005), pp. 615–618.

18. *Southern Africa Litigation Centre v Minister of Justice and Constitutional Development and Others* 2015 (9) BCLR 1108 (GP) (24 June 2015).

19. *Southern Africa Litigation Centre v Minister of Justice and Constitutional Development and Others*, para. 103.

20. *See* Nicole Fritz, "By Withdrawing from the ICC South Africa Loses Much More Than Just the Argument", *Daily Maverick*, 27 October 2016.

21. Final Communiqué of the 32nd Summit of SADC Heads of State and Government, Maputo, 18 August 2012, http://www.afdb.org/fileadmin/uploads/afdb/Docum ents/Generic-Documents/Communique_32nd_Summit_of_Heads_of_States.pdf (accessed 25 January 2014).

22. I was the executive director of the Southern Africa Litigation Centre (SALC).

23. In interviews conducted by SALC with South African officials, South Africa's support for the Southern African Development Community (SADC) Tribunal was emphasised.

24. South Africa contributed 20 per cent of the 2012/2013 SADC budget (R70 million) and was assessed at R138 million for the 2013/2014 financial year. Andisiwe Makinana and Mmanaledi Mataboge, "South Africa's Moneyed Diplomacy", *Mail and Guardian*, 30 May 2013, http://mg.co.za/article/2013-05-30-00-south-africas-moneyed-diplomacy (accessed 25 January 2014).

25. Negotiation around Nkosazana Dlamini-Zuma's election and the fate of the SADC Tribunal, involving many of the same states, would have been almost concurrent. Dlamini-Zuma's nomination was fiercely contested by several African states, particularly those of francophone Africa, and South Africa would have needed the support of SADC states to secure Dlamini-Zuma's election.

26. Maxi Schoeman, "South Africa as an Emerging Middle Power, 1994–2003", in John Daniel, Adam Habib and Roger Southall (eds), *State of the Nation: South Africa 2003–2004* (Pretoria: Human Sciences Research Council (HSRC) Press, 2004); Janis van der Westhuizen, "South Africa's Emergence as a Middle Power", *Third World Quarterly* 19, no. 3 (1998), pp. 435–455.

27. *See* Elizabeth Otitodun and Antonia Porter, "Gender and Peace-Building", in Chris Saunders, Gwinyayi A. Dzinesa and Dawn Nagar (eds), *Region-Building in Southern Africa: Progress, Problems and Prospects* (London: Zed, 2012), pp. 107–127.

28. Rachel Swarns, "Awe and Unease As South Africa Stretches Out", *New York Times*, 17 February 2002, http://www.nytimes.com/2002/02/17/world/awe-and-unease-as-south-africa-stretches-out.html?pagewanted=all&src = pm (accessed 25 January 2014).

29. *See* Adekeye Adebajo (ed.), *From Global Apartheid to Global Village: Africa and the United Nations* (Scottsville: University of KwaZulu-Natal Press, 2009).

30. Brysk, *Global Good Samaritans*, p. 174.

31. "South Africa's Decision on Burma Questioned", *Mail and Guardian*, 15 January 2007, http://mg.co.za/article/2007-01-15-sa-decision-on-burma-questioned

(accessed 25 January 2014); "South Africa and the World: The See-No-Evil Foreign Policy", *The Economist*, 13 November 2008, http://www.economist.com/node/12607346 (accessed 25 January 2014).

32. For example, ahead of a UN Security Council debate on the ICC in October 2012, Human Rights Watch observed: "[C]ouncil selectivity and double standards in making – and failing to make – referrals undercuts the appearance of the court's impartiality and independence especially in relation to the role of the United States, Russia and China, which are permanent Security Council members but are not subject to the Court's authority. The Security Council has on key occasions failed to act in situations where there was strong evidence of widespread and serious international crimes and little prospect of local accountability." Human Rights Watch, "UN Security Council: Address Inconsistency in ICC Referrals", 16 October 2012, http://www.hrw.org/news/2012/10/16/un-security-council-address-inconsistency-icc-referrals-0 (accessed 25 January 2014).

33. United Nations, *Report of the Secretary-General's Panel of Experts on Accountability in Sri Lanka*, 31 March 2011, http://www.un.org/News/dh/infocus/Sri_Lanka/POE_Report_Full.pdf (accessed 25 January 2014).

34. "Legal Opinion Provided to the South African Government by the Southern Africa Litigation Centre and Others", December 2012, http://www.southernafricalitigationcentre.org/1/wp-content/uploads/2012/12/SALC-Briefing-Paper-Shavendra-Silva-Sri-Lanka-061212.pdf (accessed 25 January 2014).

35. *Government of Zimbabwe v Fick and Others* (CCT 101/12) [2013] ZACC 22; 2013 (5) SA 325 (CC); 2013 (10) BCLR 1103 (CC) (27 June 2013).

36. The need to extend common law so as to recognise the SADC Tribunal's judgements was particularly pronounced in the case, since Zimbabwe's constitution denied the aggrieved farmers access to the domestic courts and compensation for their expropriated land. It was also important that a further resort to the Tribunal had been necessitated by Zimbabwe's refusal to comply with the decision of the Tribunal. *Government of Zimbabwe v Fick and Others*, para. 68.

37. *Southern African Litigation Centre and Another v National Director of Public Prosecutions and Others* (77150/09) [2012] ZAGPPHC 61; 2012 (10) BCLR 1089 (GNP); [2012] 3 All SA 198 (GNP) (8 May 2012).

38. *See, for example*, comments by US Supreme Court Justice Ruth Bader Ginsberg in 2012, suggesting that Egyptians, contemplating constitutional change, look to the South African constitution as a model in favour of the US constitution. Rowan Philip, "In Love with SA's Constitution", *Mail and Guardian*, 24 February 2012, http://mg.co.za/article/2012-02-24-in-love-with-sas-constitution (accessed 25 January 2014); Nicole Fritz, "Sending Mixed Signals on the Judiciary", *The Star*, 6 March 2014, http://www.iol.co.za/the-star/sending-mixed-signals-on-judiciary-1.1249533 (accessed 25 January 2014). *See also* David S. Law and Mila Versteeg, "The Declining Influence of the United States Constitution", *New York University Law Review* 87, no. 3 (2012), pp. 762–858; the authors of the preceding article examine several countries' constitutions, concluding that the only one that appeared to be growing in stature and influence was the South African constitution.

CHAPTER 5

SOUTH AFRICA'S CORPORATE EXPANSION: TOWARDS AN "SA INC." APPROACH IN AFRICA

Brendan Vickers and Richard Cawood

Following decades of apartheid-induced economic isolation, South Africa's democratisation in April 1994 opened a heady new era for the internationalisation of South African capital and the global expansion of its corporations. The demise of apartheid had coincided with the ostensible "end of history"[1] that symbolised the triumphalism of Western capitalism and its core policies of liberalisation, privatisation and deregulation. These ideas underpinned the high noon of globalisation in the 1990s.[2] This domestic and external context provided propitious enabling conditions for South African corporations to expand internationally, especially into the rest of Africa where many firms appeared to have a locational advantage. More recently, Africa's vastly improved economic prospects as the world economy's "last frontier"[3] have also opened up new commercial opportunities, albeit not without growing competition from other public and private operators from outside the continent.[4] Today, South African state-owned companies and corporations are heavily invested in the African continent and elsewhere, while seven multinational enterprises (MNEs) are ranked among the top 100 non-financial trans-national corporations from developing and transition economies.[5]

The rapid outward expansion of South African capital has not been without controversy. The presence of heavily invested South African firms in the rest of Africa has led some analysts to depict South African firms as "new exploiters", "hegemons" or "neo-colonialists" that displace or crowd out local businesses, while others have argued more optimistically that these same firms are the "industry shapers" and "market leaders" that increase competition in underdeveloped markets and contribute to the vision of a renascent Africa.[6] These crude characterisations, however, do little to advance our understanding of the roles, interests and impact of South African corporations, or their individual outward investment strategies and operations in the post-apartheid era. In contrast to South Africa's largely private sector-led approach to investment in Africa, there is also a valuable lesson to be drawn from the state-led and supported approach to African markets by emerging economy operators from outside the continent, especially Brazil, China and India.[7] This is in addition to the aid, trade, and investment commitments of industrialised economies such as the United States (US), the European Union (EU) and Japan, which help to create new economic opportunities for their national firms to expand into the African continent. There is certainly scope for greater synergies between the state and business to contest more strategically the African market and to maintain or grow South Africa's commercial footprint in it.

This chapter proposes the need for a more coordinated "SA Inc." approach between the state and business for engaging the rest of Africa, particularly as this relates to improved competitiveness and outward foreign direct investment (FDI) by South African firms. This closer alignment of interests and strategies may assist the state and business better to advance and achieve their respective policy and profit objectives on the continent more effectively, and collectively to contribute to achieving Africa's development agenda as outlined in the African Union's (AU) *Agenda 2063* (see Maloka in this volume). The chapter begins by outlining the extent of the internationalisation of South African capital at the dawn of democracy in 1994; then reviews South Africa's corporate expansion over the first two and a half decades of democracy; next looks to the third decade of democracy and proposes the concept of "SA Inc." as a pragmatic framework for the future; and offers recommendations for a programme of action, drawing on our professional experiences of working for the South African government on matters of economic diplomacy (Vickers), and advising South African and other multinational companies on strategies to expand across Africa (Cawood).

The First Phase of Corporate Expansion: Apartheid South Africa Before 1994

Due to the effects of international isolation, economic sanctions and stringent exchange controls, South Africa's corporate landscape at the dawn of democracy in 1994 was highly concentrated and dominated by a few diversified conglomerates. The withdrawal of foreign investment since the 1980s and the sale of local assets by foreign firms provided opportunities for cash-endowed South African corporations to build their bases quite cheaply through the acquisition of other South African companies and their former subsidiaries.[8] The constraints of the protected domestic market and the need for greater organic growth and profitability led several of the larger companies to invest abroad and operate internationally – at least since the 1970s – although on a limited scale. These included companies like South African Breweries (SAB), Sappi, Barloworld and Gencor (forerunner to BHP Billiton). Depending on the prevailing economic and political climate of the time, these companies used various strategies to expand internationally, establishing international investment arms and holdings in countries such as the Netherlands, Luxembourg, Switzerland and Britain, while using transfer pricing mechanisms to fund their operations.[9]

SABMiller (previously SAB) is a good case in point, operating breweries in the 1970s in Swaziland, Botswana and Lesotho, where local markets were unsophisticated but familiar with South African brands. By the early 1980s, SAB had also negotiated small acquisitions overseas, including in the US, in some cases disguising their South African origins. Following the lifting of international sanctions in the 1990s, SAB began aggressively pursuing global operations, acquiring stakes in Hungary in 1993 and China in 1994.[10] This would set the stage for its strategic acquisitions and other joint ventures across both emerging and established markets, using its strong performance management capability to turn around failing, previously state-owned breweries in Africa, China and Central Europe.[11] Through visionary leadership and management, SABMiller would become the world's second-largest brewer, operating in more than 80 countries as of 2014.[12] In 2016, Anheuser-Busch InBev acquired SABMiller for more than $100 billion, creating a truly global brewer.

The SAB experience highlights the new opportunities occasioned by the lifting of sanctions and opening up of the South African economy by the early 1990s. In this changed environment, many South African conglomerates unbundled their non-core assets and restructured their domestic operations before embarking on significant international acquisitions. They used the proceeds from their unbundling and, importantly, their firm-specific advantages developed through home market dominance, to expand internationally, even before any global competitive pressures existed. To facilitate the raising of hard currencies to finance these acquisitions, several multinational firms such as Anglo-American, Billiton, and SAB would shift their primary stock market listings and head offices to London during a "new wave" of internationalisation after 1994, as discussed later.

The Second Phase of Corporate Expansion: Democratic South Africa After 1994

Since the political transition in 1994, South African corporations, supported by the post-apartheid state and its macro-economic policies, have internationalised and expanded their global presence in two ways: through re-domiciling abroad, and through significant trade and outward foreign direct investment, especially into the rest of Africa.

South Africa's Émigré Corporations[13]

In the late 1990s, a number of established South African multinationals re-domiciled abroad by shifting their primary stock market listings and head offices to the financial centre of London, in order to finance their international acquisitions. These initial émigré corporations included Anglo-American, Billiton, Liberty Life, Old Mutual and SAB. By listing in London, these entities acquired membership in the prestigious *Financial Times* Stock Exchange Index (FTSE 100), an international rating, and thus access to cheaper capital. In so doing, these companies were able to accelerate their already rapid international expansion and become global corporations.[14]

The re-domiciling of these companies resulted in their existing South African operations being reclassified as foreign-owned in South Africa's international investment position. Over time, shareholdings in these non-resident multinationals have become much more international as a result of their primary stock exchange listings in London, especially in the case of BHP Billiton and SABMiller. Their international mergers and acquisitions have also resulted in more geographically diverse operations for these companies. These former South African "champions" have become important international investors in the South African economy, in terms of their ownership of existing operations and subsequent investments in the country.

Whereas the post-apartheid state under President Thabo Mbeki had sanctioned the re-domiciling of South African capital from 1999, even enacting legislation to allow the free transfer of assets and shares to other companies,[15] by the early 2000s, the state had tightened these rules. Today, the state prohibits such re-domiciling, partly due to the risks to South Africa's tax base. So, for example, Investec, Mondi and Bidvest were permitted secondary listings in London only in 2002, 2007 and 2014 respectively. Overall, the re-domiciling of South African corporations has been scant and accounted for by only a dozen or so émigré corporations. Outward foreign direct investment from South Africa is a much larger and more diverse phenomenon. This has been the other defining characteristic of the second phase of corporate expansion: South Africa's rapidly growing trade and investment links with the rest of Africa.

Trade and Investment Relations with Africa

Drawing on their locational and other firm-specific advantages, South African firms, franchises and brands dominate the African trade and investment landscape today. South Africa's trade in goods and services with the rest of Africa has grown rapidly during the last two and a half decades. In 2016, South Africa's total goods trade with Africa exceeded R437 billion, representing about 20 per cent of the country's total merchandise trade with the world. About 30 per cent of South Africa's goods exports are now destined for the rest of Africa (R317 billion in 2016), while imports from the continent lag at 11 per cent (R120 billion in 2016).[16]

As Table 5.1 demonstrates, the bulk of South Africa's trade and outward foreign direct investment take place predictably within the century-old Southern African Customs Union (SACU) and the Southern African Development Community (SADC) – (see Gibb, and Saunders and Nagar in this volume) – where a free trade agreement (FTA) among 13 of the 15 members underpins trade.[17] South African firms also have some corporate footprint in the three larger economies of the East African Community (EAC): Kenya, Uganda and Tanzania (see Khadiagala in this volume). While the locational advantages and knowledge of the immediate neighbourhood may provide a strategic advantage to South African firms, there are untapped investment opportunities in the growing economies of

Table 5.1   South Africa's Top Ten Trading Partners in the Rest of Africa, 2016

		Value (million rand)
1.	Botswana	60,632
2.	Namibia	58,039
3.	Mozambique	43,428
4.	Nigeria	36,874
5.	Zimbabwe	35,124
6.	Zambia	33,313
7.	Swaziland	32,387
8.	Angola	26,968
9.	Lesotho	21,049
10.	Democratic Republic of the Congo	12,883

Source: South African Department of Trade and Industry (DTI).

Central and East Africa, and especially West Africa, where South African corporations have largely limited their exposure to Nigeria and Ghana (see Adebajo in this volume). In this regard, more strategic coordination between the state and business through an "SA Inc." approach could play a key facilitating role for other firms to expand successfully into these new markets.

There are two major challenges facing South Africa's growing trade with the rest of the continent. The first relates to the structure of bilateral trade. Whereas South Africa's export profile to the rest of the world is dominated by minerals and commodities, its exports to the rest of Africa are mainly value-added manufactured goods. The latter includes machinery; mechanical appliances and electrical equipment; vehicles and aircraft; iron and steel products; chemicals; prepared foodstuffs; and plastic and rubber goods. An important determinant of the advantage of South African manufacturing firms on the continent is their proximity to African markets, as well as the fact that they provide services related to the assembly, maintenance and repair of goods and facilities. In return, South Africa's imports from its African trading partners are mainly mineral fuels (especially from Nigeria and Angola), raw materials and other commodities.

Second, although the share of sub-Saharan Africa in South Africa's imports has more than doubled over the last decade, South Africa still runs a trade surplus with the rest of Africa (R197 billion in 2016). This reflects structural factors such as South Africa's relative size, level of development and productive and supply capabilities. It also reflects historical trade relationships that naturally cast the region in a "hub-and-spoke" relationship with South Africa. The South African government appears to be sensitive to this challenge in particular, and is seeking to address this trade imbalance and build a more sustainable trade partnership by promoting "developmental regionalism" in Africa.[18] This approach is based on the contention that the barriers to intra-regional trade in developing countries, and Africa in particular, have more to do with underdeveloped production structures and inadequate infrastructure than tariffs or regulatory barriers. Developmental regionalism therefore prioritises industrial development and infrastructure, especially transport links connecting goods and services markets, to overcome the real-economy constraints to higher levels of diversified intra-African trade. This approach is now being pursued in SACU and SADC, as well as in the tripartite free trade agreement spanning Eastern and Southern Africa, which was launched in June 2015.[19]

It is a significant achievement that South African state-owned companies and private enterprises have established themselves among the top investors in Africa in a wide range of sectors covering manufacturing; natural resources, mining and agriculture; services (from telecommunications and construction, to financial services and tourism and leisure); and wholesale and retail trade (see Table 5.2). According to a 2012 study, South African direct investment in the rest of Africa has increased at four times the rate of overall South African FDI since 1994. Total South African direct investment in the rest of the continent has also increased from R3.8 billion in 1994 to R115.7 billion in 2009, or by 31 times. The study further showed that 76 per cent of all South African investment in the rest of Africa was direct investment.[20] Anecdotal evidence suggests that South African firms invest on the continent for a variety of reasons, with "push factors" such as domestic market saturation, policy uncertainty, stagnant growth and labour market rigidity, and "pull factors" that include geographic proximity, cultural similarity, profit potential and risk diversification. The relative influence of these push and pull factors for outward foreign direct investment from South Africa varies according to industries and firms, as Table 5.2 illustrates.

Many international investors also regard South Africa as a "gateway" or "springboard" into Southern Africa and beyond for their operations, owing to the country's sound financial markets, regulatory regime and relatively advanced infrastructure. So, for example, foreign-owned multinationals, such as Kraft Foods, Kimberly-Clark, Lafarge and Wal-Mart (following its acquisition of Massmart), also leverage their South African bases as means to unlock wider regional opportunities.[21] However, there is some debate in South Africa about the country's continuing "gateway" status and value proposition as a regional business hub.[22] Today, multinationals increasingly enter the African market from jurisdictions more suited to the nature of their operations, whether mining, manufacturing or services. Countries such as Angola, Egypt, Ethiopia, Ghana, Kenya, Nigeria and Rwanda increasingly operate as "gateways" into their respective sub-regions too. South Africa's geographic distance from some of Africa's major markets, as well as increased policy uncertainty during the Jacob Zuma presidency since 2009, may have led to the decisions of General Electric, Coca-Cola, Nestlé and Heineken to establish their regional headquarters for sub-Saharan Africa in Nairobi.[23]

The South African government has purposefully designed an incentive structure to encourage and promote outward foreign direct investment into the rest of Africa, which in 2014 was valued at over R200 billion and hosted 37 per cent of all such investment, largely in Southern Africa (see Table 5.3 and Figure 5.1). South Africa's exchange controls, for example, have been liberalised since the 2000s to support outward investment in SADC and the wider African continent. By 2014, Tshwane had also eliminated restrictions on investments "passing through" South Africa to the rest of the continent through specific tax and exchange control rules that apply to qualifying international headquarter companies. This increases South Africa's attractiveness as a location for regional headquarters, especially when part of a "gateway" or branding strategy for the country.

As noted earlier, the rapid outward expansion of South African franchises and brands, and the predominance of South African capital in the regional market during this second phase, have not been without controversy. So, for example:

By 2003, South African companies ran Cameroon's national railroad, Tanzania's national electricity company, and managed the airports of seven African countries. In the same period, Shoprite's 72 shops in the rest of Africa sourced South African products worth R429 million rather than buying some of these products in their host countries.

Table 5.2 Drivers of Outward FDI by South African Firms

Industry	Enterprise	Drivers of Outward FDI
State enterprises		
State-owned companies	Airports Company of South Africa Eskom Industrial Development Corporation PetroSA South African Airways (SAA) Transnet	Government policy supporting regional cooperation and infrastructure development; investment opportunities; privatisation in host countries; regional network of operations
Private enterprises		
Manufacturing	DPI Plastics Illovo Sugar Mondi PPC Sappi Sasol Spanjaard Steinhoff Universal Footwear	Access to markets and growth; sourcing of materials; diversification; trade support
Natural resources, mining and agriculture	AngloGold Ashanti Illovo Sugar Metorex Sappi	Access to natural resources; investment opportunities from privatisation; control value chains; access new markets; lower cost of production
Services	Anglo-American City Lodge Datatec Dimension Data First Rand Group Five MTN Murray and Roberts Nedbank Old Mutual Standard Bank	Access to markets and growth; investment opportunities from privatisations; strengthen market position; build regional networks; profit/risk diversification motives; raising capital

Table 5.2   *Continued*

Industry	Enterprise	Drivers of Outward FDI
	Tsogo Sun	
Wholesale and	Barloworld	Access to markets and growth;
retail trade	Bidvest	investment opportunities from
	Famous Brands	privatisations;
	Pick n Pay	strengthen market position;
	Shoprite Holdings	build regional networks;
	PEP	profit/risk diversification motives
	Woolworths	

Local resentment has swelled in places like Kenya, Tanzania and Nigeria to what some saw as efforts to export apartheid labour practices and destroy infant industries.[24]

Rather than generalising about the impact of South African multinationals during this second phase of corporate expansion, there is a need for more specific sector, industry or firm-level studies to determine whether South

Table 5.3   Outward FDI by South African Firms to SADC and Africa, 2001–2013

	SADC	Africa	Total (billion rand)
2001	4.4	19.5	23.9
2002	4.1	1.3	5.4
2003	5.5	3.9	9.4
2004	1.4	0.3	1.7
2005	2.8	3.0	5.8
2006	4.8	17.8	22.6
2007	8.7	3.9	12.6
2008	13.8	8.2	22.0
2009	9.7	6.4	16.1
2010	9.8	4.3	14.1
2011	9.6	5.4	15.0
2012	19.4	4.9	24.3
2013	24.5	7.8	32.3
Total			205.2

Source: South African Reserve Bank (SARB) Excon approvals.

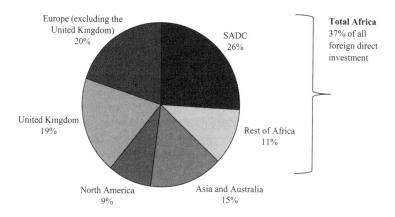

Figure 5.1   Total Outward FDI by South African Firms to the World, 2014.
Source: South African National Treasury.

African capital is indeed overly competitive to local disadvantage, or broadly complementary to national development plans of host countries.[25] Many of the concerns expressed may be due to a perception deficit about the role and impact of South African investment in the rest of Africa. Certainly, there may be challenges related to local pricing, labour practices or local supplier development in particular sectors, especially wholesale and retail trade. Overall, however, there may be many developmental dividends associated with South African operators investing in the rest of Africa. These include employment creation; upgrading of existing and building new infrastructure, including investment in network services such as finance, transport and telecommunications; technology transfer through human resource development; increased tax revenues for the state; increased consumer choice; exporting of strong corporate governance practices; improved national competitiveness; and boosting of general investor confidence in host countries.[26] To address negative perceptions about South Africa's corporate expansion, and to promote more socially responsible behaviour and investment into the rest of Africa, in July 2016, the South African government released *Guidelines for Good Business Practice by South African Companies Operating in the Rest of Africa*.[27] Although the latter is only a voluntary set of codes drawing on international best practices, it suggests some discomfort in government circles about the private sector's record of good corporate citizenship in the rest of Africa, as well as enduring sensitivity to criticisms of a "big brother" role on the continent, despite Tshwane's solid development partnership credentials to the contrary.[28]

Towards a Third Phase of Corporate Expansion: An "SA Inc." Approach for Africa?

Following corporate South Africa's exuberant economic expansion into Africa's frontier markets during the first decade of democracy, there is now intensifying competition for access to Africa's abundant resources and consumer markets. The growing presence of public and private operators from outside the continent, the success of other home-grown African multinational enterprises and companies in sectors from resources to manufacturing[29] and an emerging entrepreneurial class in many African countries means that the continent is no longer a captive market for South African capital. While some companies are struggling to maintain or expand their market presence, or have even clashed with local regulators (for example, MTN in Nigeria – see Adebajo in this volume), most South African firms still retain a strong foothold in many sectors.

Set against these dynamics, the African continent has become a far more complex, challenging and competitive marketplace in which to do business, even for South African corporations that have an established commercial presence or possess firm-specific advantages from years of operating in these frontier markets. Today, these companies must compete increasingly with public and private operators from other industrialised and emerging economies, but are frequently at a strategic disadvantage given the latter's often state-led and government-supported commercial approach to the continent. Major governments around the world have announced significant spending commitments to support the continent's development agenda, shifting from the more traditional (and much-maligned) aid packages to specific trade and investment vehicles for individual countries and projects. In August 2014, for example, the inaugural US-Africa Leaders' Summit, hosted in Washington, DC, by then president Barack Obama, concluded with the US making an investment commitment of $33 billion spanning infrastructure, energy, financial services and technology. While Africa may benefit from these projects, including "Trade Africa" and "Power Africa", many of these US-led initiatives are likely to benefit American companies and assist them to compete more effectively against Chinese operators in Africa.

Other "country-to-continent" summits, including the Forum on China-Africa Cooperation (FOCAC), the India-Africa Forum Summit (IAFS) and the Tokyo International Conference on African Development (TICAD), have produced similar financial pledges and approaches based on the declaratory principle of an "equal partnership" with African countries. China's state-led and state-sponsored approach to engaging with Africa through trade and investment, aid, credit lines and infrastructure projects leveraged through the China-Africa Development Fund is the prime example of the state as the benefactor of Chinese businesses in Africa, even though Beijing's opaque infrastructure-for-minerals aid packages remain a matter of concern (see Liu in this volume). Extra-continental regional trade agreements among subsets of African countries, such as the economic partnership agreements (EPAs) with the EU, could potentially also place South African business at a competitive disadvantage to traders from outside the continent and undermine potential opportunities to grow intra-African trade and investment.[30]

State-business relations in South Africa's democratic era remain fragile and highly fragmented, impaired by mistrust.[31] Nonetheless, there is scope for greater cooperation and alignment of interests and strategies between the state and business to boost South Africa's competitiveness and operate more effectively in African markets. In the post-apartheid era, for example, South Africa has played an instrumental role in providing critical public goods for the rest of Africa, including peace, stability and development, ultimately rendering renascent Africa "safe for business" (see Curtis in this volume). However, there is a pragmatic concern within some government and policy circles that South Africa's role as a development partner in Africa, which involves substantial aid spending, is not delivering any commercial returns for the country, especially in situations where South Africa has underwritten the extensive costs of peace, stability and post-conflict reconstruction. In several African crises such as Burundi and Darfur, South Africa's peace diplomacy has paved the way for external operators to enter these markets and reap the rewards through mining concessions, public investment projects and trade offerings. Succinctly put:

> While South Africa has expended a huge amount of resources and effort on building political relations and providing much needed assistance across the continent, there is a growing perception that this

has not been fully compensated by tangible commercial benefits. It is possible that other countries have benefited more on the back of South Africa's peacebuilding and post-conflict reconstruction efforts.[32]

There may be numerous opportunities for South African businesses to invest in post-conflict African countries. In the case of the Democratic Republic of the Congo (DRC), companies such as Vodacom, MTN, Standard Bank and Shoprite are already visible and invested in development corridors (Bas Congo), hydro-power facilities (Inga Dam) and mining (see Nzongola-Ntalaja in this volume). One assessment of South Africa's post-conflict role in the DRC recommends "ethics for the conduct of business" and managing perceptions that South Africa's intentions in post-conflict development and peacebuilding are purely profit-driven.[33] The South African government's *Guidelines for Good Business Practice*, released in 2016, partly addresses this concern.

This changing African landscape presents a compelling case for the South African government to improve the coordination of the country's trade, investment and development cooperation activities in the rest of Africa through an "SA Inc." approach, drawing lessons from competitor nations like Brazil, China and India, or even European countries like France. There are many South African actors operating on the continent, ranging from the private sector to public entities such as state-owned companies and development finance institutions.[34] Without proper coordination, there is a real risk that these actors will pursue disparate objectives and strategies in Africa, or even unwittingly compete against each other. Although these challenges are not new, reflected in long-standing debates in government about the need for more coordinated "economic diplomacy",[35] the South African government is a late entrant to this game. Only in 2014, for example, did the country's Department of Public Enterprises – working with private sector consultants – draft an "Africa Strategy" that provides guidelines for a market entry strategy for South African state-owned companies into the rest of Africa.[36] Given the vast extent and scale of parastatal investments in the rest of the continent, it is alarming that the department did not undertake such an exercise until two decades into democratic rule. South Africa's Department of Trade and Industry (DTI) has undergone some organisational restructuring to provide greater focus, direction and coordination to trade and investment initiatives in the rest of Africa. "Trade Invest Africa" (formerly known as the "Africa Export Council") was launched in June 2016 to coordinate and implement South Africa's continental economic strategy.[37] The agency aims to facilitate exports of value-added goods and services to the rest of Africa, while creating sourcing relationships for imports from the rest of the continent. While this is a promising initiative, a major shortcoming is the absence of a coherent economic strategy and action plan for engaging the rest of the continent (beyond the nominal priorities outlined in the National Development Plan (NDP), the Industrial Policy Action Plan (IPAP), and the National Export Strategy), hence our call for a more coordinated "SA Inc." approach.

Concluding Reflections: Putting "SA Inc." into Action

South Africa's corporate expansion into the rest of Africa has largely been driven by the private sector, with limited direct facilitation from the government in Tshwane. Evidence and trends indicate that outward foreign direct investment from South Africa into the rest of the continent is growing substantially, but that this landscape is rapidly becoming more complex and challenging with intensifying competition from other home-grown African multinational enterprises and companies, as well as public and private operators from industrialised and emerging economies. Set against these dynamics, we propose three recommendations to implement the idea of "SA Inc." during the third decade of democracy: first, to create a "super fund" to promote trade and investment across Africa; second, to articulate a clear value proposition for South Africa in emerging African markets; and third, to create a formal body to coordinate a strategy involving government and business. We will examine each in turn.

Create a "Super Fund" to Promote Trade and Investment Across Africa

First, it is important to note that many state-owned South African companies and private enterprises are competing on the continent against well-funded and coordinated governments and their public and private operators from countries such as China and Brazil. However, government support for outward foreign direct investment has been limited to fostering enabling conditions through trade and investment agreements, tax and exchange control rules (such as the South African treasury's "HoldCo" and "International Headquarter Company" regimes, which seek to establish the country as a jurisdiction of choice for investments into Africa),[38] under-funded incentive schemes (such as the DTI's Export Marketing and Investment Assistance (EMIA) initiative and the Capital Projects Feasibility Fund) and investment facilitation and market intelligence by dedicated foreign economic representatives working in targeted African markets.[39] Furthermore, from anecdotal evidence, South African multi-nationals intent on expansion are often unaware of these services, however limited, and they see only a limited role for the state as their potential benefactor or partner in doing business in the rest of Africa.

The South African government should therefore create an audited "super fund" of at least R10 billion in order to promote South Africa's trade and investment interests, competitiveness and coordination of activities across the continent. This fund could be leveraged for various purposes, including for credit lines and export insurance, export marketing and promotion and infrastructure and industrial project tenders. Although there are competing demands on the fiscus, the size and scale of this fund would send a strong positive signal to business that the state is a serious partner, and that responsible outward foreign direct investment and sustainable trade partnerships may be a means to advance and achieve the developmental objectives of both the NDP and the African Union's *Agenda 2063*.

Articulate a Clear Value Proposition for South Africa in Developing Africa's Markets

Second, South Africa must clarify and refresh its value proposition as a committed "development partner" in Africa. The growing critiques of the Chinese model of investment in Africa offer a public relations opportunity for "SA Inc." to reaffirm South Africa's partnership credentials. The role and activities of the South African Development Partnership Agency (SADPA) and the Partnership Fund for Development, once established, should also be aligned to support this agenda. SADPA should focus strongly on supporting regional economic integration and infrastructure development to increase intra-African trade and investment.

The South African state, business and civil society will need carefully to consider how to build sustainable trade, investment and development partnerships with the rest of the continent. The continental free trade agreement (proposed to be created by 2028), once launched, provides an opportunity for South Africa to exercise leadership by opening up its own market to help promote trade-led economic growth and development in Africa. By one estimate, this continental free trade area could increase intra-African trade by as much as $35 billion a year.[40] Since most of these gains will be captured by a few countries with stronger supply capacity and export competitiveness, South African multinational enterprises should be encouraged to integrate smaller economies into their regional value chains to boost their productive capacity and participation in intra-African trade.

Establish a Formal Body to Coordinate Government and Business Activity

Finally, an "SA Inc." approach will require stronger institutional coordination and a catalytic role for the state in aligning many of the government's current dispersed and ad hoc programmes into one coherent economic strategy, action plan and coordinating structure for engaging the rest of Africa. Various proposals have already been floated, such as strengthening relations between the Department of International Relations and Cooperation (DIRCO) and the DTI to manage the country's economic diplomacy agenda, or even a public-private government-business advisory council on Africa and emerging markets.[41] An "SA Inc." approach, however, requires bolder thinking. The government should establish a formal structure, chaired by the country's deputy president, with the objectives of coordinating, aligning and signalling the public and private strategies of the major South African players in the rest of Africa. This body should focus on coordinating state-business partnerships for major goods, services and capital projects in the rest of the continent (such as the North-South Corridor or projects put to tender by the World Bank; the New Development Bank (NDB) led by the BRICS bloc (Brazil, Russia, India, China and South Africa); or the International Finance Corporation). It should also ensure stronger alignment with domestic, regional and continental development priorities, and encourage South African firms to think innovatively about ways to collaborate in cross-border value chains, rather than to compete directly with each other.

Notes

1. Francis Fukuyama, *The End of History and the Last Man* (New York: Free Press, 1992).
2. Thomas L. Friedman, *The Lexus and the Olive Tree* (New York: Anchor, 1999).

3. Kingsley Moghalu, *Emerging Africa: How the Global Economy's "Last Frontier" Can Prosper and Matter* (Ibadan: Bookcraft, 2013). *See also* Liam Halligan, "Global Africa? The Last Investment Frontier?", in Adekeye Adebajo and Kaye Whiteman (eds), *The EU and Africa: From Eurafrique to Afro-Europa* (New York: Columbia University Press; London: Hurst; and Johannesburg: Wits University Press, 2012), pp. 171–196.
4. Yadong Luo, Qiuzhi Xue and Binjie Han, "How Emerging Market Governments Promote Outward FDI: Experience from China", *Journal of World Business* 45, no. 1 (2010), pp. 68–79.
5. United Nations Conference on Trade and Development (UNCTAD), *World Investment Report 2016* (Geneva, 2016).
6. *See* Fred Ahwireng-Obeng and Patrick J. McGowan, "Partner or Hegemon? South Africa in Africa", pt. 1, *Journal of Contemporary African Studies* 16, no. 2 (1998), pp. 11–38; Patrick J. McGowan and Fred Ahwireng-Obeng, "Partner or Hegemon? South Africa in Africa", pt. 2, *Journal of Contemporary African Studies* 16, no. 2 (1998), pp. 1–31; John Daniel, Jessica Lutchman and Sanusha Naidu, "The South Africans Have Arrived: Post-Apartheid Corporate Expansion into Africa", in John Daniel, Adam Habib and Roger Southall (eds), *State of the Nation: South Africa 2003–2004* (Pretoria: Human Sciences Research Council (HSRC), 2004), pp. 368–390; Judi Hudson, "South Africa's Economic Expansion into Africa: Neo-Colonialism or Development?", in Adekeye Adebajo, Adebayo Adedeji and Chris Landsberg (eds), *South Africa in Africa: The Post-Apartheid Era* (Scottsville: University of KwaZulu-Natal Press, 2007), pp. 128–149.
7. *See, for example*, Centre for Conflict Resolution (CCR), *South Africa and the BRICS: Progress, Problems, and Prospects*, Seminar Report no. 50 (Cape Town, November 2014), http://www.ccr.org.za (accessed 6 July 2017).
8. Saul Klein and Albert Wöcke, "Emerging Global Contenders: The South African Experience", *Journal of International Management* 13, no. 4 (2007), pp. 319–338.
9. Shawn Hattingh, "BHP Billiton and SAB: Outward Capital Movement and the International Expansion of South African Corporate Giants", unpublished paper, 2007, www.taxjustice.net/cms/upload/.../Ilrig_0809_South_African_giants.pdf (accessed 12 December 2014).
10. Klein and Wöcke, "Emerging Global Contenders".
11. Klein and Wöcke, "Emerging Global Contenders".
12. SABMiller "Who We Are", http://www.sabmiller.com/about-us/who-we-are (accessed 12 December 2014).
13. We are grateful to Stephen Gelb, who introduced us to the term "émigré corporations".
14. Hattingh, "BHP Billiton and SAB", p. 11.
15. Hattingh, "BHP Billiton and SAB", p. 16.
16. Trade data from South African Revenue Service (SARS) trade database, http://www.sars.gov.za/ClientSegments/Customs-Excise/Trade-Statistics/Pages/default.aspx (accessed 6 July 2017).
17. The Southern African Development Community (SADC) free trade agreement was launched in 2008 with twelve member states. Seychelles formally acceded to the accord in May 2015.

18. *See, for example,* Adebayo Adedeji, "South Africa and Africa's Political Economy: Looking Inside from the Outside", in Adebajo, Adedeji and Landsberg, *South Africa in Africa*, pp. 40–62.

19. South African Department of Trade and Industry (DTI), *South Africa's Trade Policy and Strategy Framework* (Tshwane, 2010).

20. South African Institute of Race Relations, "South African Investment in Africa Increasing Four Times Faster Than Overall Foreign Investment", media release, 7 February 2012, http://www.sairr.org.za/media/media-releases/07Feb12.Investm ent_in_Africa.pdf/view?searchterm=investment (accessed 12 December 2014).

21. Standard Bank, "EM10 and Africa: South Africa in Africa – A Steady, Yet Narrow, Ascent", research report (Johannesburg, 12 June 2013), pp. 3–4.

22. Peter Draper and Sören Scholvin, "The Economic Gateway to Africa? Geography, Strategy and South Africa's Regional Economic Relations", Occasional Paper no. 121 (Johannesburg: South African Institute of International Affairs (SAIIA), 2012).

23. Standard Bank, "EM10 and Africa", p. 7.

24. Adekeye Adebajo, "South Africa in Africa: Messiah or Mercantilist?", *South African Journal of International Affairs* 14, no. 1 (2007), p. 40.

25. *See, for example,* Bench Marks Foundation, *Shoprite in Malawi, Swaziland, and Zambia* (Johannesburg, 2009).

26. Peter Draper, Phil Alves and Mmatlou Kalaba, *South Africa's International Trade Diplomacy: Implications for Regional Integration* (Gaborone: Friedrich Ebert Foundation, Botswana Office, 2006), http://library.fes.de/pdf-files/bueros/ botswana/04119.pdf (accessed 12 December 2014).

27. South African Department of Trade and Industry, *Guidelines for Good Business Practice by South African Companies Operating in the Rest of Africa* (Tshwane, 2016).

28. Brendan Vickers, "Towards a New Aid Paradigm: South Africa as African Development Partner", *Cambridge Review of International Affairs* 25, no. 4 (2012), pp. 535–556.

29. The African continent has 400 companies with revenue of more than $1 billion per year, and these companies are growing faster, and are more profitable in general than their global peers. McKinsey Global Institute, *Lions on the Move II: Realizing the Potential of Africa's Economies*, September 2016.

30. *See, for example,* Mareike Meyn, "An Anatomy of the Economic Partnership Agreements", pp. 197–216, and Gilbert M. Khadiagala, "Africa and Europe: Ending a Dialogue of the Deaf?", pp. 217–235, both in Adebajo and Whiteman, *The EU and Africa*.

31. Antoinette Handley, *Business and the State in Africa: Economic Policy-Making in the Neo-Liberal Era* (New York: Cambridge University Press, 2008); Nicoli Nattrass and Jeremy Seekings, "State, Business, and Growth in Post-Apartheid South Africa", Discussion Paper no. 34 (Manchester: Institutions and Pro-Poor Growth (IPPG) Programme, 2010), http://www.ippg.org.uk/papers/dp34a.pdf (accessed 22 September 2014).

32. South African Department of International Relations and Cooperation (DIRCO), *Economic Diplomacy Strategy Framework* (Tshwane, 2013), p. 9.

33. Cheryl Hendricks and Amanda Lucey, "South Africa's Post-Conflict Development and Peacebuilding Experiences in the DRC: Lessons Learnt", Policy Brief no. 47 (Tshwane: Institute for Security Studies (ISS), October 2013).
34. David Monyae, "South Africa's Development Finance Institutions", in Chris Saunders, Gwinyayi A. Dzinesa and Dawn Nagar (eds), *Region-Building in Southern Africa: Progress, Problems and Prospects* (London: Zed; and Johannesburg: Wits University Press, 2012), pp. 164–177.
35. DIRCO, *Building a Better World: The Diplomacy of Ubuntu – White Paper on South Africa's Foreign Policy* (Tshwane, 2011).
36. South African Department of Public Enterprises (DPE), *Africa Strategy: A Market Entry Strategy for State Owned Companies – A Guide for SOC Africa Projects* (Tshwane, 2014).
37. South African Department of Trade and Industry, *Trade Invest Africa: An Initiative of the DTI* (Tshwane, 2016).
38. South African National Treasury, "Gateway to Africa and Other Reforms: Website Annexure to the 2013 Budget Review" (Tshwane, 2013), http://www.treasury.gov.za/documents/national%20budget/2013/review/Annexure%20W3.pdf (accessed 12 December 2014).
39. These markets include Angola, the Democratic Republic of the Congo, Egypt, Ethiopia, Ghana, Kenya, Mozambique, Nigeria, Senegal and Zimbabwe.
40. United Nations Economic Commission for Africa (UNECA), *Industrializing through Trade* (Addis Ababa: UNECA, 2015).
41. DIRCO, *Economic Diplomacy Strategy Framework*.

PART II

SOUTH AFRICA'S KEY BILATERAL RELATIONS IN AFRICA

CHAPTER 6

SOUTH AFRICA IN SOUTHERN AFRICA: ANGOLA, MOZAMBIQUE AND ZIMBABWE

Lloyd M. Sachikonye

South Africa's bilateral relations with its neighbours – Mozambique and Zimbabwe – and its regional ally, Angola, form a substantial block of its post-apartheid foreign policy architecture. This essay explores these relations paying special attention to how their political and economic dimensions have been crafted since 1994. I begin by setting out the wider regional context in which historical factors – particularly the solidarity politics of liberation struggles – have conditioned perspectives towards South Africa, and how the cumulative gains from growth in trade and investment have, on the whole, strengthened bilateral economic and political cooperation in Southern Africa. However, the chapter argues that South Africa's bilateral relations with Angola, Mozambique and Zimbabwe have not necessarily followed the same trajectory. While relations with Maputo have been relatively close and smooth, those with Luanda blossomed only with the end of its civil war in 2002. Meanwhile, ties with Harare have been ambivalent and cool in the context of Zimbabwe's protracted transition to democratic politics. I conclude by highlighting the changing competitive environment of these bilateral relations with the emergence of China as a major investor and player in all three countries.

Regional Context of Bilateral Relations

During the first two decades of the post-apartheid era, South Africa's foreign relations with Angola, Mozambique and Zimbabwe have not been entirely smooth despite the four countries' shared history of liberation struggle. It is noteworthy that Angola and Mozambique share a common lusophone heritage of Portuguese colonialism, while Zimbabwe's relations with South Africa have historically been ambivalent ever since the former Southern Rhodesia voted against joining the Union of South Africa in a referendum in 1923. The shared experience of liberation struggle and overthrow of Portuguese colonialism in 1975 in Angola and Mozambique, and of white settlers in Zimbabwe in 1980, made ruling parties in all three countries proud and prickly about their independence and sovereignty. This has often been manifested in dealings between Tshwane (Pretoria) and both Luanda and Harare, but perhaps less so in South Africa's dealings with Maputo.

Although the past two decades have resulted in new forms of cooperation including increased trade and investment, memories of the role and effects of the apartheid state's destabilisation of Angola, Mozambique and Zimbabwe have not entirely faded. For their solidarity and support of the South African liberation movements, these countries sustained substantial economic destruction estimated at between $60 billion and $90 billion.[1] South Africa's fuelling of civil war through surrogates such as the Mozambican National Resistance (Renamo) and the National Union for the Total Independence of Angola (UNITA) in Mozambique and Angola respectively, and of dissidents in Zimbabwe, caused untold suffering and casualties. This delayed the advent of stability, peace and economic recovery in all three countries. In the specific case of Angola, the battle of Cuito Cuanavale in 1988 was a watershed event in the sub-region's liberation struggle, and the catalyst of negotiations that eventually loosened the grip of the apartheid state over Southern Africa. As British scholar, Stephen Chan, has graphically explained the significance of the battle of Cuito Cuanavale:

> [T]his was the last battle of the Cold War – because this war was also ending. Washington sent a message in answer to Pretoria's anguished pleas. It would not help. The Cuban commander, as his predecessor twelve years earlier had done, sent a message to Pretoria: withdraw your forces while they can still walk, or they will come home in

body bags. Pretoria asked that they be allowed to walk. It was a crucial blow for the securocrats of apartheid.[2]

This historical and regional context of bilateral relations between South Africa and its three neighbours is crucial to an understanding of their evolution since 1994. Some of the rivalries and misunderstandings in the Southern African Development Community's (SADC) institutions such as the Organ on Politics, Defence and Security (OPDS) (see Saunders and Nagar in this volume) and cool relations between leaders (for example, between South Africa's Nelson Mandela and Zimbabwe's Robert Mugabe; and between Angola's Eduardo Dos Santos and South Africa's Thabo Mbeki), stemmed from sensitivities associated with hierarchy and ambition relating to the history of the liberation struggle and of the pursuit of regional leadership. These tensions also related to initial expectations about South Africa's acknowledgement of the effects of apartheid-era destabilisation on the region, and the commitment of the post-apartheid government to the region's reconstruction and integration.

The issue of South Africa's status in the region and continent ever since the transition from apartheid has continued to excite scholarly interest. While some ascribe to it the role of a "hegemon", others argue that South Africa does not meet conditions that would qualify it for this status.[3] On the face of it, the massive size of its economy – in regional terms – makes South Africa a large locomotive of investment and trading power. It is the most sophisticated economy on the African continent, and dominates SADC in which it controls about 60 per cent of the sub-regional economy.[4] With a population of about 55 million, South Africa also possesses a significant domestic market. In addition, Tshwane commands a significant army, and sent about 3,000 peacekeepers to Burundi, the Democratic Republic of the Congo (DRC) and Sudan's Darfur region in the early 2000s (see Naidoo in this volume). South Africa has also played a catalytic mediatory role, with some modicum of success, in various conflicts such as Zimbabwe, Lesotho and Madagascar. (See Curtis in this volume.)

This is the broad regional background and conceptual issues against which we must explore South Africa's bilateral relations with Angola, Mozambique and Zimbabwe. To what extent have these relations included "hegemonic" or "partnership thrusts" or a mix of the two, and what have been the outcomes of these interactions? To what degree have South Africa's initial core principles relating to the centrality of human rights and promotion of democracy been upheld or eclipsed by other priorities such as trade and investment?

South Africa – Angola Relations

By 2013, bilateral relations between South Africa and Angola had improved tremendously. Luanda had by then become Tshwane's second largest trading partner on the continent after Nigeria and a key strategic ally. Indeed, if the ties between both countries can transcend their current reliance on the personal chemistry between their two presidents – South Africa's Jacob Zuma and Angola's Eduardo Dos Santos – this strategic partnership between the strongest powers in Southern Africa could potentially revive SADC; and provide a powerful ally for South Africa in both sub-regional and continental diplomacy.[5] Yet, these relations were not always smooth. The ties between Tshwane and Luanda were frosty, particularly before the end of the Angolan civil war in 2002. Surveying the history of tensions between the two states, Italian scholar Augusta Conchiglia identified two key factors. The first related to disappointed expectations about South Africa's development cooperation and assistance in the post-destabilisation era:

> [A]fter 1994, Angolan leaders complained that the ANC [African National Congress] was not doing enough to reward Luanda for its support in their struggle against apartheid. At the same time, the much-awaited investments in Angola failed to arrive. Given South Africa's relative economic superiority, Angola, like many states in the region, initially expected the post-apartheid government to assume the role of a donor country and development cooperation partner, providing aid and investment capital. These hopes were quickly dashed, at least in the initial years.[6]

There was often a lack of finesse and sensitivity by South Africa's new rulers towards the economic challenges that Angola experienced in the context of a civil war in which one of the key protagonists – Jonas Savimbi's UNITA – had historically received assistance from the apartheid state. Suspicions remained after 1994 that UNITA had – at the very least – a sympathetic ear in Tshwane, especially in light of South Africa's attempts to broker a deal between it and the MPLA (Popular Movement for the Liberation of Angola) government in 1999. In particular, Angolan leaders believed that by insisting on negotiations between UNITA and the MPLA, South Africa might have been rigidly promoting its own model of achieving compromise through negotiations: an approach viewed as paternalistic by Luanda.[7] In addition, the marketing of "conflict diamonds" from zones of conflict by the South African-based De Beers company, poisoned the atmosphere of bilateral relations. This resulted in the exclusion of De Beers from the official diamond market in Angola in 2001, although this decision was later rescinded in 2005. Rightly or wrongly, the South African state was associated with the misdemeanours of its commercial and mining interests. Finally, South Africa's insistence on negotiations while troops from Rwanda and Uganda mobilised to unseat Laurent Kabila in the DRC in 1997–1998 (see Nzongola-Ntalaja in this volume), was another source of irritation in Luanda. Together with fellow SADC members Zimbabwe and Namibia, Angola's armed forces were instrumental in pushing back the invading forces before a peace process was launched.

Several factors conspired to remove the chill in bilateral relations in the second post-apartheid decade. The first was the assassination of Jonas Savimbi by Angolan government forces in February 2002, which led to a rapid conclusion of the civil war. It also resulted in the peaceful participation of UNITA in electoral politics, although the playing field has remained uneven ever since. These developments removed the civil war as a poisonous element in Angola's bilateral relationships.

The second factor was the more assiduous courting of Luanda by South Africa after 2008. The personal chemistry between Jacob Zuma and Eduardo Dos Santos was much warmer than under Zuma's predecessor, Thabo Mbeki. Three months after assuming the presidency in May 2009, Zuma proved his determination to transform the bilateral relationship into a strategic one by making Luanda his first presidential state visit.[8] This was reciprocated by Dos Santos' first visit to Tshwane where he was conferred with South Africa's highest honour for a foreign citizen: the Order of the Supreme Companion of O.R. Tambo.

The third factor that has buttressed the relationship between South Africa and Angola has been the exponential increase in trade and investment between the two countries on a continent where intra-regional trade is generally about 12 per cent. By 2002, South Africa had become Angola's largest source of imports, and the boom in trade was consolidated with the launch in 2003 of the South Africa-Angola Chamber of

Commerce. Angolan imports from South Africa increased by 500 per cent between 2007 and 2008, while Luanda became the second-largest source of oil imports for South Africa after Nigeria. South African parastatals such as Eskom and the Development Bank of Southern Africa (DBSA) became active in Angola's energy sector. In 2009, a new era in economic cooperation was inaugurated with the creation of a strategic partnership. This was symbolised by President Zuma's visit to Luanda in which he was accompanied by 11 cabinet ministers and more than 150 business leaders, making it one of the largest delegations sent outside the country since 1994. During that visit a decision was made to set up a bi-national commission to coordinate economic and political relations between the two countries.

In 2012, trade between Tshwane and Luanda amounted to about R31.2 billion: the largest bilateral trade in SADC. Total imports from Angola amounted to R23 billion, while exports were valued at R8.2 billion.[9] By 2016, bilateral trade had increased to R43 billion.[10] The South African Minister for International Relations and Cooperation, Maite Nkoana-Mashabane, stated in October 2013 that the two countries had signed 22 bilateral agreements and memoranda of understanding spanning a wide range of sectors including trade and industry, mining, energy, science and technology, as well as defence.[11] Quite clearly, the warming of political relations between the two countries in the second post-apartheid decade has energised a significant blossoming of commercial and trade interactions.

However, despite strong growth in trade and investment relations between Angola and South Africa, one should not lose sight of their lop-sided character and overwhelming mono-cultural dependence on oil exports from Angola. Oil accounts for 46 per cent of Luanda's gross domestic product (GDP) and 96 per cent of its exports. Clearly, Angola's reliance on oil revenues and imports leaves the country highly vulnerable to external shocks.[12] Simulation analysis suggests that a shock to global oil prices would significantly reduce Angola's GDP growth, and hence its capacity to absorb imports such as those from South Africa. In addition, Luanda's reliance on both strategic and consumer-good imports – particularly food – means that any substantial increase in international food prices would translate into rapidly rising inflation and food price shocks that would adversely affect the country's poor.[13] Growth in commercial and trade ties between Luanda and Tshwane will therefore partly depend on the degree to which Angola diversifies its economic base, especially the beneficiation of its natural resources and the development of a stronger agricultural sector. Transparency and accountability in the utilisation of revenues from oil, diamonds, and other natural resources will also be crucial to more efficient national budgeting in Angola and its efforts to act as a regional hegemon.

With a well-equipped and battle-hardened military, Angola has wielded considerable clout in the DRC and Congo-Brazzaville. It played a key role in the restoration to power of Daniel Sassou-Ngueso in Congo-Brazzaville in 1997. Luanda's ambitions thus extend beyond its immediate Southern African sub-region. This was exemplified by its moral and material support for Côte d'Ivoire's incumbent leader, Laurent Gbagbo – and its influence on South Africa not to recognise the electoral result – despite his electoral loss in the 2010 presidential election to Alassane Ouattara. This support, however, failed to prevent the restoration of Outtara's presidential mandate (see Adebajo in this volume). Angola also sent troops to support the military in Guinea-Bissau with which it shares a lusophone background. In the exertion of its power and influence in both Central and West Africa, Angola demonstrated that it has ambitions to become a regional power. The Ivorian case, however, underscored the limits of the Tshwane–Luanda axis in a foray beyond the Southern African sub-region.

South Africa–Mozambique Relations

While relations between South Africa, on the one hand, and Angola and Zimbabwe, on the other, have undergone periods of conflict and rivalry, those with Mozambique have been largely smooth. The factors that have contributed to close and mutually beneficial bilateral relations between Mozambique and South Africa relate to history, geography and the solidarity politics of the liberation struggle. Labour flows from colonial Mozambique into South Africa ensured remittance flows that the colonial state, and its successor post-colonial state, received and taxed. Prior to independence in 1975, an average of 100,000 migrant workers were employed in any given year in South Africa, mostly in the mining sector. Although this declined to about 55,000 in the post-1975 period, the civil war from 1976 till its cessation in 1992 led to increased inflows of Mozambican refugees into South Africa.

The proximity of Mozambique's ports, especially Maputo, to the industrial heartland of Gauteng is a major boon to South Africa. Finally, until the Nkomati Accord of 1984 that was signed with the apartheid regime, the ANC used Mozambique as a springboard for infiltration into South Africa. Close ties were developed in the process between the ruling Frelimo (Mozambique Liberation Front) party and the ANC. Although the apartheid regime's destabilisation exacted a huge economic toll on Mozambique, bilateral relations solidified quickly after the 1992 peace agreement with Renamo and South Africa's own transition in 1994.

The affinity between the two liberation movements, Frelimo and the ANC respectively, has expanded into the policy realm and found expression in the foreign policies of the two countries with both prioritising historical bonds and the peaceful settlement of disputes. The significance of these fraternal bonds cannot be overstated with the language of official dialogue even advancing notions of "brotherhood".[14] The relationship between Thabo Mbeki and Joaquim Chissano, former presidents respectively, was warm and close. In addition, the marriage between former president, Nelson Mandela, and former Mozambican first lady, Graça Machel, also came to symbolise the two countries role as political "in-laws". Close relations between the two countries have further been expressed in Mozambique's consistent support for South Africa's positions in SADC, the AU and Tshwane's facilitative role over Zimbabwe. By 2016, bilateral trade had increased to R43 billion.[15] Mozambique also contributed troops to the South African-led AU peacekeeping mission in Burundi between 2003 and 2004. Based on the need to police cross-border crime and long porous borders, security cooperation is another strong feature of the bilateral relationship.

Trade and investment relations between the two countries grew fairly rapidly after 1994. In 2002, Mozambique overtook Zimbabwe – despite its more sophisticated economy – as South Africa's second largest trading partner in Southern Africa. An estimated 27 per cent of Maputo's imports were sourced from South Africa. In 2012, bilateral trade stood at about R29.7 billion:[16] just a little less than that between South Africa and Angola. Tshwane became the leading investor in Mozambique, well ahead of Portugal, the former colonial power.

Undoubtedly, the post-1992 stability achieved in Mozambique with the deployment of a United Nations (UN) peacekeeping force provided a favourable context for both increased trade and investment. The Mozambican leadership did not feel threatened when it allowed foreign capital from South Africa and other countries to initiate a number of mega projects. One of these large projects was the $2.3 billion Mozal aluminium smelter project concluded in 2000. This was the biggest single investment project since Mozambique's independence. Notably, Mozal is owned by an international consortium led by BHP Billiton (47 per cent) and South Africa's Industrial Development Corporation (IDC), which has a 24 per cent stake in it.[17]

Another major project involving both countries has been the collaborative venture between Sasol and both governments in gas production in Temane. Costing $1.2 billion and concluded in 2004, it involved the construction of a 865-kilometre long gas pipeline between Temane in Mozambique and Secunda in South Africa. Further cooperation in the energy field involved significant import of electricity by the South African utility corporation, Eskom, from Mozambique's Cabora Bassa dam from 1997. The insatiable demand of South Africa's industries has therefore relied greatly on these gas and electricity supplies from Mozambique.

The prospects for further investment and cooperation in Mozambique's diverse energy sector look bright. With its plentiful resources of coal, gas, as well as hydro, wind, solar and geothermal power, Mozambique has the potential to generate 15,000 megawatts of electricity annually.[18] Currently, it only generates 2,300 megawatts from Cabora Bassa, which it exports to both South Africa and Zimbabwe. The gas sector has the potential to become a new frontier of enhanced energy development in the aftermath of major gas discoveries off the Rovuma basin in Cabo Delgado province. Estimates in two of Rovuma's five concession areas put the reserves at about 100 trillion cubic feet; and this extremely high potential yield, coupled with projections from other blocks, places these discoveries among the highest in the world.[19] The sheer scale of the resources is likely to bring with it increased access to energy for the population at large, and the economy in general; and depending on how it is managed, it could increase export revenues, encourage foreign direct investment (FDI) and contribute to the development of domestic energy industries. For South Africa, these gas supplies could also substantially replenish its growing power deficit.

In another development, a South African corporation, PetroSA, signed a strategic partnership with its Mozambican counterpart, Petromac, in the field of downstream industries in the hydrocarbons sector in 2011. The two entities have explored the possibility of developing a gas-to-liquids (GTL) venture in Mozambique. For its part, Sasol has been investigating the feasibility of developing gas fields near the Beira coast in Sofala province. There are further opportunities for South African companies to enter the Mozambican hydrocarbons sector in mutually beneficial deals.[20] While Maputo would reap considerable revenues from the joint exploitation of these resources, Tshwane would reduce its exposure to energy insecurity.

Finally, another bilateral development initiative relates to investment in the Maputo corridor as an industrial hub well served with transport communications to South Africa's industrial heartland of Gauteng. Conceived by the two governments, the corridor has attracted investments by companies such as Mozal to take advantage of the proximity to Maputo's port, as well as to industrial and consumer markets in South Africa. Revenues and exports that are generated by the corridor have also resulted in a considerable reduction of Mozambique's deficit; for example, export of goods and services improved from 12.2 per cent of GDP in 1998 to 33 per cent of GDP in 2008.[21]

It needs to be emphasised that these remarkable advances in bilateral trade and investment have been facilitated by several factors. The first relates to the bilateral institutional framework for cooperation established in the 1990s. An Economic Bilateral Forum set up in 1997 by heads of state of the two countries provided a very effective institutional framework. Chaired by both countries' presidents, the forum has provided the necessary clout and decisiveness in trade and investment promotion. In 2011, Jacob Zuma and Armando Guebuza, the South African and Mozambican presidents respectively, committed themselves to accelerating cooperation through the establishment of a bi-national commission in December 2011 to deepen bilateral engagement and cooperation. This development reflects the high level of political commitment by the leadership of the two countries to the promotion of trade, bilateral projects and deeper investment. The second factor relates to realism on the part of the economically weaker partner, Mozambique, which places more premium on cooperation than on competition with its stronger and wealthier neighbour.

Nevertheless, it should not be overlooked that the overall effects of bilateral trade and investment links have not had an even impact on all of Mozambique's provinces. The major beneficiary of South African investments along the Maputo corridor as well as of transport and port upgrading has been Southern Mozambique where the ruling Frelimo party enjoys its largest support. Uneven economic and social development therefore remains a major challenge for Mozambique. If not systematically addressed, this situation could lead to political polarisation as resurgent threats by Renamo in central and northern Mozambique from 2013 suggest. It is thus imperative that investments in mining of coal in Tete in the central province and the development of gas fields in the country's northern provinces should provide economic benefits for populations in these peripheral regions.

To underscore the deep bilateral relations between the two countries, President Zuma visited Maputo in October 2016. With over 300 South African companies operating in Mozambique, South African exports amounted to about R33.3 billion compared to R10.2 billion from Mozambique in 2016,[22] giving rise to concerns about the trade imbalance. Zuma's visit sought to calm these perceptions, as well as complaints about the slow South African government response to xenophobic violence against Mozambican workers, shop-owners and small businesses in 2015.

South Africa–Zimbabwe Relations

Of South Africa's three bilateral partners in Southern Africa, perhaps the most ambivalent and prickly relations have been those with Zimbabwe since 1994. Yet the common historical, cultural and linguistic ties between Tshwane and Harare are much closer as evidenced by considerable migration flows. Historically, the Ndebele-speaking people, who constitute about 20 per cent of Zimbabwe's population, originally migrated from the KwaZulu-Natal region of South Africa in the nineteenth century. The two countries also have a shared history of liberation struggle and solidarity dating back to the 1960s, when ZAPU (the Zimbabwe African People's Union) and ANC cadres fought Rhodesian and South African counter-insurgency forces together on Zimbabwe's northern flank. The integration between the settler economies of Rhodesia and South Africa was also deeper, with the latter's corporations quite formidable in Zimbabwe's mining, industry and agro-business sectors. Although commercial and trade ties remained without significant restructuring after 1994, they did not blossom. Despite a relatively sophisticated and diversified economic base and infrastructure, bilateral economic relations between South Africa and Zimbabwe have not witnessed a comparable upsurge as has been the case with Angola and Mozambique. Nor have political relations between the leadership in Harare and Tshwane been as warm in the post-apartheid era.[23]

So, what explains the lacklustre partnership between South Africa and Zimbabwe? Part of the explanation lies in the wariness with which the leadership in Harare viewed the profile and ambitions of its neighbouring "big brother" under the tutelage of the late Nelson Mandela, a Nobel peace laureate and leader not only of regional, but also of global, stature. Mandela threatened an equally ambitious but autocratic leader, Zimbabwe's Robert Mugabe, who aspired to regional leadership by virtue of seniority in the liberation struggle. It was scarcely surprising that the first skirmishes between Mugabe and Mandela were over the leadership of SADC, specifically the chair of the organisation's Organ on Politics, Defence and Security in the period 1996 to 1999. (See Saunders and Nagar in this volume.) It was Mandela who was reported to have stated that "Mugabe's problem is that he was the star – and then the sun came up".[24] Further differences between the two leaders were sharpened over military intervention in the DRC by Zimbabwe, Angola and Namibia in 1998, with South Africa preferring a diplomatic rather than a military approach. In addition, in the 1990s, Tshwane could have been more sensitive to Harare's needs, such as lower tariffs for some of its industrial exports, as growing trade imbalances in favour of South Africa negatively affected closer economic relations between the two industrialising countries.

Although there was a shift in tone in the relationship after 1999 with the inauguration of Thabo Mbeki as South African president, the international context had become more demanding on the Mugabe administration to institute political reforms and to curb human rights abuses by its security forces. Electoral malpractices and violence in 2000, 2002 and 2005 put the spotlight on Zimbabwe and provoked targeted sanctions from Western countries and the European Union (EU). Development aid and foreign investment dried up. Zimbabwe's economy contracted by 40 to 50 per cent between 2000 and 2008. An ill-planned land reform process dislocated the domestic economy and contributed to hyper-inflationary tendencies that caused considerable distress and shock among the working and middle classes.[25] By 2008, an estimated 3 million Zimbabweans (about a quarter of the population) had migrated for mostly economic and political reasons.[26]

Unlike the situation in Angola from 2002 and in Mozambique from 1992, Zimbabwe underwent a deep political and economic crisis that resulted in a shrinkage not only of its economic base, but also of foreign investment and trade. A constellation of factors – internal economic mismanagement and punitive sanctions in the form of reduced development aid and an investment embargo – weakened growth and development during the "lost decade" of 2000 to 2010.[27] South Africa did not have sufficient economic weight to lift Zimbabwe out of these doldrums.

Tshwane's relations with Harare cannot be sensitively and holistically assessed without placing them in a wider regional context in the post-2000 period. As observed above, Zimbabwe's political crisis was compounded by an economic decline that persisted until 2009. Although SADC had no institutional mechanisms for intervening directly in the domestic affairs of a member state, the deteriorating situation in Zimbabwe warranted the special attention of a series of SADC summit meetings during this period.[28] The SADC heads of state took a broadly supportive position on land reform, but a mildly critical one on human rights and political issues. However, the dilemma of SADC states, including South Africa, was how to admonish the Mugabe government on these issues without appearing to side with the West against it. This partly explained the muted tone of their criticisms of the Mugabe government, and partly the divisions between them over a collective approach.

This was the background against which South Africa adopted a cautious and sometimes contradictory approach towards Zimbabwe between 2000 and 2008. First, it had to contend with the issue of regional solidarity vis-à-vis the wider international community; second, with the need to ensure that the political and economic situation did not become more unstable within Zimbabwe; and third, that it could still play a catalytic leadership role despite the political divisions within SADC.

Thus faced with the challenge of maintaining regional solidarity over the Zimbabwe question, it was difficult for South Africa to adopt a more forthright position on the Mugabe government even if it wanted to. Tshwane would have risked isolation in SADC, and perhaps further afield in the AU – such tags as "regional big brother" would have been derisively used against it. The dilemma of the Mbeki government, and later the Zuma administration, was how to balance the sensitivities in SADC, the AU as well as domestic public opinion against the need to pressure Harare until the formation of the Government of National Unity (GNU) in 2009.

Tshwane's major contribution was its "quiet diplomacy" under the auspices of SADC, especially between 2007 and 2008, to encourage the main parties, ZANU-PF (Zimbabwe African National Union – Patriotic Front) and MDC-T (Movement for Democratic Change – Tsvangirai), to enter into political negotiations. Thabo Mbeki's facilitative skills yielded tangible results only after a disputed and violent election in 2008 in which ZANU-PF lost its parliamentary majority to the MDC for the first time since independence in 1980.

Facilitating or mediating in the Zimbabwe crisis earned South Africa mistrust and suspicion both within Zimbabwe and SADC, but also in the West and the wider international community. Mugabe's deft use of the rhetoric of anti-imperialism and pan-African solidarity made it difficult to condemn his own domestic repression, corruption and mismanagement. By so doing, the regime was able to represent fundamental human and civic rights questions placed on the Zimbabwean political agenda as marginal, elite-focused issues driven by Western interests and having little relation to urgent problems of economic redistribution.[29] This posed dilemmas for South African mediators.

However, the dilemmas were defused when South Africa pursued a multilateral approach towards the Zimbabwe crisis. This opportunity was fortuitously provided in 2007 when SADC entrusted it to act as its mediator in the crisis. In 2009, the facilitation reaped fruit through the formation of a Government of National Unity. This was on the back of a disputed election outcome in which Robert Mugabe had trailed Morgan Tsvangirai in the first round of the presidential election by 43.4 per cent to the latter's 47.9 per cent. Both SADC and the African Union were designated the guarantors of this agreement. The following five years after 2008 witnessed tortuous attempts to implement the provisions of the accord: these ranged from basic political reforms to media and security reform provisions. Under a GNU that was often fractious, with different parties seeking short-term advantage, reforms were painstakingly negotiated. Some reforms such as those involving the security services and equal access to the media had not been implemented when the election season began in June 2013.

Although South African president Jacob Zuma's mediation team often received strong criticism especially from the ZANU-PF, it focused on its brief with consistent support from SADC. Consisting of seasoned ANC negotiators like Mac Maharaj and Charles Nqakula, in a team led by Lindiwe Zulu, the mediating team deftly steered the negotiations and exerted pressure for compromise on meaningful electoral reforms before the 2013 poll. The poll result showed strong gains by ZANU-PF, which won more than 70 per cent of parliamentary seats and the presidential vote by 61 per cent. Although this outcome was disputed by the main opposition MDC-T party and local election monitoring bodies which cited irregularities during the voter registration process and on the voting day itself, this represented a major recovery by ZANU-PF from the 2008 poll. For its part, a SADC Electoral Observer Mission concluded that the electoral process was characterised by an atmosphere of peace and political tolerance, and that the elections themselves had been "free and peaceful".[30]

The period between 2008 and 2013 provided some valuable space for a revival of trade and investment ties between South Africa and Zimbabwe. Bilateral trade amounted to about R23 billion in 2012,[31] although this was skewed since Harare ran a large deficit as a result of its weak agricultural and manufacturing sectors. By 2016, bilateral trade had increased to R35 billion.[32] While South Africa remained the largest investor in Zimbabwe, the uncertainty created by legislation on economic indigenisation may have slowed more investment. A number of roundtable conferences were held bringing together Zimbabwean and South African business firms and government officials on how to increase bilateral trade and investment. One such roundtable in 2011 recommended that South Africa could do more to encourage its private sector to step up investment in Zimbabwe, take an empathetic view to the application of SADC tariff reductions to allow Harare to grow its infant industries and strategic sectors, and facilitate skills development and movement within Southern Africa to further economic development in the sub-region.[33]

The signing of a bi-national commission agreement together with four other agreements, including on trade, customs administration and water resources management in 2015 signalled a deepening of bilateral economic relations. This was followed by a bi-national commission summit in Harare in November 2016 that noted progress in strengthened bilateral cooperation in sectors such as trade, investment, mining, transport, and tourism, among others. Cooperation on defence and security issues was also underscored by the summit.

Finally, an examination of Zimbabwe–South Africa relations would be incomplete without reference to the sensitive issue of migration. Part of the fall-out from the above-mentioned decade of political and economic crisis has been a large flow of economic and political migrants from Zimbabwe. Although estimates vary, it is believed that there are over one million Zimbabwean migrants in South Africa on short-term and long-term residence visas.[34] Sometimes derogatorily termed *amakwerekwere* by some South Africans, the presence of Zimbabwean migrants has provided sources of tension and bursts of xenophobia as witnessed in 2008 against African migrants (particularly those from Zimbabwe and Mozambique), in which 62 people were killed and 100,000 displaced. Frequent deportations of Zimbabweans who are not legal residents have also created a great deal of human suffering and dislocation. It has further been observed that, although the impact of Zimbabwean human or intellectual capital on South Africa's economy (in fields such as academia, journalism and business) is not well documented, it is believed to be substantial.[35] The long-term solution to migration would be stability, peace and accelerated economic development within Zimbabwe itself. At the same time, by virtue of its larger size and shortage of professional and skilled personnel, South Africa will continue to be partly dependent on foreign skilled workers from countries such as Zimbabwe.

Concluding Reflections

This essay has argued that South Africa's relations with Angola, Mozambique and Zimbabwe have followed different trajectories. While relations with Maputo have historically been relatively close and warm, those with Luanda were initially prickly, blossoming only with the end of the Angolan civil war in 2002. Ties with Harare have been ambivalent and cool in the context of the autocratic tendencies of the Zimbabwean leader, Robert Mugabe, and the country's protracted democratic transition.

As post-civil war growth flourished, the environment of Angola–South African relations warmed considerably, as symbolised by the creation of a strategic relationship and a bi-national commission. Although trade patterns are heavily influenced by significant oil imports by South Africa, diversification and further growth can be expected. Already SADC's largest bilateral economic partnership, political and security partnership between Luanda and Tshwane will as well continue to grow in a regional context in which the challenges of peace in countries such as the DRC and Lesotho will be of utmost concern to both countries.

More diversification in economic and trade links between Mozambique and South Africa are in prospect. Although one of the poorer states in SADC, Mozambique has striven to create a more favourable investment climate as well as to take advantage of the discovery of new mineral and energy sources, such as coal and gas, to create new export markets. Although bilateral trade will remain skewed in South Africa's favour for the foreseeable future, cooperation in infrastructure development, as in transport corridors, will likely present dividends to both countries.

Bilateral relations between South Africa and Zimbabwe entered a new phase in the aftermath of the 2013 election in the latter country. As observed above, considerable opportunities exist in investment, trade, tourism and infrastructure development. However, to exploit them will require strong political will and cooperation between the leadership of the two states and their business elites. The establishment of a bi-national commission and subsequent summits are a step in the right direction.

Finally, in all the three states – Angola, Mozambique and Zimbabwe – new players such as China, India and, to some extent, Brazil, are becoming significant investors in direct competition with South Africa itself (see Virk, and Liu in this volume). For the foreseeable future, however, this competition will not likely undermine the foundations of the existing bilateral economic, political and security cooperation between South Africa and its three neighbours.

Acknowledgements

I would like to thank Tawanda Sachikonye for his research assistance in developing this chapter.

Notes

1. *See* Action for Southern Africa and World Development, *Paying for Apartheid Twice: The Cost of Apartheid for the People of Southern Africa* (London, 1998); and Adebayo Adedeji (ed.), *South Africa and Africa: Within or Apart?* (London: Zed Books, 1996). While Adedeji estimated damages at $60 billion for the period 1980–1988, the former publication puts the figure at up to $90 billion for the period 1975–1988.

2. Stephen Chan, *Old Treacheries, New Deceits: Insights into Southern African Politics* (Johannesburg: Jonathan Ball, 2011), p. 44.

3. *See, for example*, Adekeye Adebajo, *The Curse of Berlin: Africa after the Cold War* (Scottsville, South Africa: University of KwaZulu-Natal Press, 2010), p. 102; Maxi Schoeman, "South Africa in Africa: Behemoth, Hegemon, Partner or 'Just Another Kid on the Block'?", in Adekeye Adebajo, Adebayo Adedeji and Chris Landsberg (eds), *South Africa in Africa: The Post-apartheid Era* (Scottsville, South Africa: University of KwaZulu-Natal Press, 2007), pp. 92–104; and John Daniel, Jessica Lutchman and Sanusha Naidu, "South Africa and Nigeria: Two Unequal Centres in a Periphery", in John Daniel, Roger Southall and Jessica Lutchman (eds), *State of the Nation: South Africa 2004–05* (Cape Town: Human Sciences Research Council (HSRC) Press, 2005), p. 565.

4. Centre for Conflict Resolution (CCR) and Friedrich Ebert Stiftung (FES) Botswana, *Region-Building and Peacebuilding in Southern Africa*, Seminar Report no. 52 (Gaborone, Botswana, February 2016), p. 24, http://www.ccr.org.za (accessed 6 July 2017).

5. Adekeye Adebajo, "South Africa and Angola: Southern Africa's Pragmatic Hegemons", *Regional Integration Observer* 6, no. 1 (2012), http://www.ccr.org.za/

index.php/media-release/in-the-media/newspaper-articles/item/181-south-africa-and-angola-southern-africas-pragmatic-hegemons (accessed 6 July 2017).

6. *See* Augusta Conchiglia, "South Africa and Its Lusophone Neighbours: Angola and Mozambique", in Adebajo, Adedeji and Landsberg, *South Africa in Africa*, p. 238.

7. Conchiglia, "South Africa and its Lusophone Neighbours", p. 241. *See also* Devon Curtis, "South Africa: 'Exporting Peace to the Great Lakes Region?'", in Adebajo, Adedeji and Landsberg, *South Africa in Africa*, pp. 253–273.

8. Adebajo, "South and Angola: Southern Africa's Pragmatic Hegemons".

9. Data from South African Revenue Service (SARS) bilateral trade reports by country, http://www.sars.gov.za/ClientSegments/Customs-Excise/Trade-Statistics/Pages/Merchandise-Trade-Statistics.aspx (accessed 6 July 2017).

10. Figures from the South African Revenue Service (SARS), *see* http://www.sars.gov.za.

11. Angola-South Africa Joint Commission for Cooperation: Views from Luanda, Pretoria, http://www.gov.za/speeches/view.php?sid=40735 (accessed 5 February 2014).

12. *See, for example*, World Bank, *Angola: Economic Update* (Washington, DC: World Bank, 2013), p. 10.

13. World Bank, *Angola*, p. 10.

14. Aditi Lalbahadur and Lisa Otto, "Mozambique's Foreign Policy: Pragmatic Non-Alignment as a Tool for Development", Occasional Paper no. 160 (Johannesburg: South African Institute of International Affairs (SAIIA), November 2013). *See also* Chris Landsberg, *The Quiet Diplomacy of Liberation: International Politics and South Africa's Transition* (Johannesburg: Jacana, 2004).

15. Figures from the South African Revenue Service (SARS), *see* http://www.sars.gov.za.

16. Data from SARS bilateral trade reports by country.

17. Conchiglia, "South Africa and Its Lusophone Neighbours", p.248.

18. Ichumele Gqada, "Mozambique's Gas: An Opportunity for South Africa", Policy Briefing no. 53 (Johannesburg: SAIIA), August 2012), p. 1.

19. Gqada, "Mozambique's Gas", p. 2.

20. Gqada, "'Mozambique's Gas", p. 3.

21. United Nations Development Programme (UNDP) Mozambique, Economic and Policy Analysis Unit, "Mozambique Quick Facts", March 2011, http://cebem.org/cmsfiles/publicaciones/Mozambique_Quick_Facts.pdf (accessed 6 July 2017).

22. Data from SARS bilateral trade reports by country.

23. *See, for example*, Merle Lipton, "Understanding South Africa's Foreign Policy: The Perplexing Case of Zimbabwe," *South African Journal of International Affairs*, 16, no. 3 (December 2009), pp. 331–345.

24. As quoted in Alistair Sparks, *Beyond the Miracle* (Johannesburg: Jonathan Ball, 2003), p. 269.

25. *See, for example*, David Harold-Barry (ed.), *Zimbabwe: The Past Is the Future* (Harare: Weaver Press, 2004); Amanda Hammar, Brian Raftopoulos and Stig Jensen (eds), *Zimbabwe's Unfinished Business: Rethinking Land, State and Nation in the Context of Crisis* (Harare: Weaver Press, 2003); and Eldred V. Masunungure (ed.), *Defying the Winds of Change: Zimbabwe's 2008 Elections* (Harare: Weaver Press, 2009).

26. *See* Jonathan Crush and Daniel Tevera (eds), *Zimbabwe's Exodus: Crisis, Migration, Survival* (Cape Town: Southern African Migration Programme (SAMP); and Ottawa: International Development Research Centre (IDRC), 2010).

27. *See, for example*, Lloyd Sachikonye, *Zimbabwe's Lost Decade: Politics, Development & Society* (Harare: Weaver Press, 2012).

28. This part of the chapter partly draws from Lloyd Sachikonye, "South Africa's Quiet Diplomacy: The Case of Zimbabwe", in Daniel, Southall and Lutchman, *State of the Nation*, pp. 569–585.

29. Ian Phimister and Brian Raftopoulos, "Mugabe, Mbeki and the Politics of Anti-Imperialism", *Review of African Political Economy*, no. 101 (2004), p. 399.

30. Statement by SADC Electoral Observer Mission (SEOM), August 2013, p. 17.

31. Data from SARS bilateral trade reports by country.

32. Figures from the South African Revenue Service (SARS), *see* http://www.sars.gov.za.

33. South African Institute of International Affairs, "Zimbabwe-South Africa Business Roundtable: Rapporteur's Report", 2011, p. 9.

34. *See* Southern African Liaison Office (SALO), *South Africa-Zimbabwe Relations, Vol. 1* (Cape Town: SALO 2013), p. 32.

35. SALO, *South Africa-Zimbabwe Relations*, p. 35.

CHAPTER 7

SOUTH AFRICA IN THE GREAT LAKES: THE DEMOCRATIC REPUBLIC OF THE CONGO, BURUNDI AND RWANDA

Georges Nzongola-Ntalaja

The elections marking the transformation of South Africa from a racist apartheid state to a multi-racial democracy took place in April 1994, in the midst of genocide in Rwanda, civil war in Burundi and state-sponsored violence against the democratisation process in Zaire (now the Democratic Republic of the Congo (DRC)). The latter events were interrelated and manifestations of a crisis of national construction in these three countries of the Great Lakes region, which had shared a common Belgian colonial administration for 40 years. Having benefited from African and worldwide solidarity in its struggle against apartheid in South Africa, the ruling African National Congress (ANC) accepted the moral responsibility for, and had the means with which to play a critical role in, seeking an end to the crises in the Great Lakes region. While events occurred too quickly for the newly liberated South Africa to have been involved in the Rwandan tragedy, which resulted in the death of about 800,000 people, Tshwane (Pretoria) would eventually succeed in brokering a power-sharing agreement to end the civil war in Burundi by 2003, and play a major role in a two-decade effort to bring peace and stability to the DRC.

This chapter focuses mostly on South Africa's involvement in the Burundian and DRC crises, while examining Tshwane's relationship with

Rwanda as part of Kigali's entanglement in the Congo's affairs, on the one hand, and the granting of asylum to Rwandan dissidents in South Africa, on the other. Burundi appeared at first to be a success story, at least with respect to the relative peace established since 2003. However, the undermining of democracy by Burundian president Pierre Nkurunziza after a constitutionally questionable election in July 2015 that won him a third presidential term led to growing repression and an unsuccessful coup attempt in the same year, pointing to the limits of the South African "model" of power-sharing[1] as a panacea for ending political conflicts in developing countries (see Curtis in this volume). In the case of the DRC, South Africa hosted the Inter-Congolese Dialogue (ICD) in 2002 and participated in robust peace enforcement efforts through the United Nations (UN) Force Intervention Brigade (FIB), which routed the March 23 Movement (M23) rebels – a proxy armed group for both Rwanda and Uganda – in November 2013. Given South Africa's economic interests in the Congo, questions have been raised as to whether Tshwane is involved in these three countries out of a pan-African ideology (see Maloka in this volume), or in pursuit of its more narrow national interests.[2]

South Africa in the DRC

Unlike Burundi and Rwanda, the Congo has, since 1906, been an integral part of the Southern African economic complex, in which South Africa has been the hegemonic power. This complex is a relatively interdependent region of global capitalism, with a highly developed industrial structure in South Africa and an abundance of mineral wealth throughout the region. When the giant Mining Union of Upper Katanga (UHMK) was established in 1906, Tanganyika Concessions Ltd (Tanks or TCL), a South African corporation, was the second major private shareholder in it after Belgium's largest trans-national, the General Society of Belgium (SGB). The TCL was also the founder and majority owner of the Benguela railway, which connected Katanga's mines to the Atlantic Ocean ports of Benguela and Lobito in Angola. This economic interdependence in mining and transport eventually resulted in an alliance of white settlers, mining companies and their right-wing supporters in the West, which waged a "counter-revolution" against African nationalism and liberation struggles in Central and Southern Africa between 1960 and 1990.

In the post-liberation era, the Congo's economic weight explains why South Africa sought and succeeded in convincing its 13 fellow members in the Southern African Development Community (SADC) to bring the newly resurrected DRC into the organisation. This was done in September 1997, less than four months after the fall of Mobutu Sese Seko and the coming to power of Laurent-Désiré Kabila. Geographically the largest country in Central and Southern Africa, the DRC added a market of more than 60 million consumers to the SADC region, in addition to its mineral wealth and an enormous hydroelectric potential that was already providing electricity to Zambia and Zimbabwe.

Thus, of the three Great Lakes countries examined here, the DRC is by far the most important for South African foreign policy in the region. Tshwane's involvement in the DRC is analysed here with reference to five key issues: first, President Nelson Mandela's failed attempt to mediate a peaceful end to the First Congo War (1996–1997); second, South Africa's ambiguous position in dealing with the Second Congo War (1998–2003); third, President Thabo Mbeki's success in hosting the Inter-Congolese Dialogue; fourth, South Africa's electoral assistance and observation of the DRC elections in 2006 and 2011; and fifth, economic cooperation policy, particularly in the areas of mining, energy, commerce and immigration.

What became known as the First Congo War broke out in October 1996, with the Rwandan invasion of Hutu refugee camps in North and South Kivu. The organisers of what was, in fact, a regionally conceived drive to overthrow the Mobutu regime found a Congolese figurehead for this purpose in the person of Laurent Kabila, a former guerrilla leader turned business operator. As the newest emancipated country in Africa with a globally revered leader in Nobel peace laureate Nelson Mandela, South Africa took on the challenge of mediating a peaceful end to the war between Mobutu and Kabila. Following several meetings with emissaries of both camps in South Africa, it was decided to hold talks between the two principals aboard the South African naval ship *Outeniqua*, off Congo-Brazzaville's port of Pointe-Noire. After delaying tactics, Kabila showed up a day late for the meeting, which was chaired by Mandela, in May 1997. The second meeting, planned ten days later, was boycotted by Kabila, once again showing his "lack of political culture and respect for heads of state and elders", according to Mandela.[3]

While Laurent Kabila's undiplomatic behaviour was due to his obsession with "real or imaginary attempts on his life",[4] it is evident that the negotiations on the *Outeniqua* were a waste of time, as Kabila had nothing to gain from negotiating peace when Rwandan-led rebels were already within striking distance of the Congolese capital of Kinshasa. Furthermore, South Africa – joined by the United Nations and the United States (US) at Pointe-Noire – was powerless in the face of a new troika that had replaced the US, France and Belgium by then as the new "masters" of the DRC: Angola, Rwanda and Uganda.[5]

Despite having failed to bring about a peaceful settlement of the dispute, South Africans welcomed the new regime of Laurent Kabila. Thabo Mbeki, then South Africa's deputy president, was the first African leader to fly into Kinshasa, in May 1997 – a day after the fall of the Mobutu regime – to congratulate Kabila on his triumph.[6] However, having pushed for the DRC's accession to SADC, South Africa opposed military intervention in support of a member state facing foreign aggression, following the outbreak of the Second Congo War with the invasion of the DRC by Rwanda and Uganda in August 1998. Angola, Namibia and Zimbabwe had agreed to intervene in the DRC in accordance, according to them, with the SADC Organ on Politics, Defence and Security Cooperation (OPDS) – a position challenged by South Africa.[7] Other SADC states, including Botswana and Zambia, also challenged the position taken by the three interventionists, and this created an internal crisis in the organisation, particularly between Nelson Mandela as SADC chair, and Zimbabwean leader Robert Mugabe as chair of the OPDS (see Saunders and Nagar, and Sachikonye in this volume). For the Congolese, reports that South Africa was selling arms to Kigali and receiving delegations of Rwandan-supported rebels in Tshwane, suggested that Mandela's government was on the Rwandan side of the armed conflict. If true, this was a position similar to that of the United States.[8] (See Weissman in this volume.)

However, this is not the impression I was given by then deputy president Thabo Mbeki, who, following a conference in South Africa's industrial heartland of Johannesburg on the African Renaissance in September 1998, requested that I provide him a 30-minute briefing on the political situation in the Congo. Given South Africa's limited knowledge of Congolese realities at the time, misunderstandings and policy blunders were to be expected. However, even if Tshwane had a low opinion of President Laurent Kabila, this did not mean that it was willing to accept the takeover of the Congo by Rwanda and Uganda through Congolese intermediaries. Mandela's opposition to military intervention in support of the DRC against its aggressors apparently ended at a SADC meeting held on the sidelines of the Non-Aligned Movement (NAM) summit in South Africa's port city of Durban in September 1998 attended by UN Secretary-General, Ghana's Kofi Annan and Secretary-General of the Organisation of African Unity (OAU), Tanzania's Salim Ahmed Salim.[9] The SADC support for the military intervention by Angola, Namibia and Zimbabwe was confirmed at the subsequent SADC summit held in Grande Baie, Mauritius, in September 1998.[10]

South Africa's desire to see a quick end to the war manifested itself in the ANC government's support of the SADC-led OAU mediation efforts, which culminated in the Lusaka ceasefire agreement of July 1999. Two major resolutions were part of this peace accord. The first involved the deployment of a UN peacekeeping force to police the ceasefire, protect civilians and disarm and dismantle armed militia groups, including rebels from Rwanda and Uganda, who were designated as "negative forces". The world body deployed the United Nations Organisation Mission in the Democratic Republic of the Congo (MONUC) in December 1999, and South Africa was among the first countries to contribute troops to this operation (resulting in a 1,400-strong contingent), which would eventually come to number about 20,000 peacekeepers.

The second major resolution was the requirement for an Inter-Congolese Dialogue among representatives of all political tendencies to restart the democratisation process that had been derailed by Mobutu and stopped altogether by Kabila's takeover of the country. After several false starts and much confusion, the Thabo Mbeki government decided to host the dialogue in South Africa and, with UN and international support, managed the process in Sun City from February to December 2002. While Ketumile Masire, the former president of Botswana, was the officially designated facilitator of the OAU, President Mbeki was the de facto facilitator of the ICD. The Global and Inclusive Agreement (GIA) for the transition was adopted in December 2002, and the provisional constitution agreed in Tshwane in March 2003, with both documents finally ratified in Sun City a month later. Most of the Congolese participants in the ICD were so comfortable in the luxurious hotels of this apartheid-era "sin city" of casinos, and so happy with their lucrative per diems, that they had no problem taking over an entire year to resolve issues that could have been dealt with in a couple of months. Another South African achievement was the signing by Rwanda and the DRC of the Pretoria Agreement in July 2002, putting an end – at least officially – to the Rwandan military presence in the DRC.

As a follow-up to the ICD and the GIA, South Africa provided electoral assistance and participated in electoral observation for the Congolese elections in 2006 and 2011. The South African Independent Electoral Commission (SA-IEC) provided technical assistance to its Congolese counterpart during both elections, including 160 SA-IEC personnel and a contribution of $50 million in 2006. The printing of ballots was done in South Africa, and the South African army ensured their transportation and distribution throughout the Congo (see Naidoo in this volume). With respect to electoral observation, Tshwane participated both times as a member of the SADC delegation, with Nosiviwe Mapisa-Nqakula, then minister of correctional services, serving as chair of the delegation in 2011. Like nearly all official African delegations, the SADC delegation declared both elections peaceful, credible, transparent and well-managed. This was contrary to what was reported in 2011 by nearly all African non-governmental observer groups, including the most respected human rights non-governmental organisation (NGO) in the DRC, La Voix de Sans Voix,[11] as well as the Catholic Church, and nearly all external groups, according to whom the elections were marred by numerous irregularities, fraud and state-sponsored violence. These groups declared the electoral results as not credible.

Finally, economic cooperation is a major issue in the DRC's bilateral relations with South Africa. To the old economic interests of colonial-era corporations such as Anglo-American, De Beers, Tanganyika Concessions Ltd, and their subsidiaries or successors, have been added the mining, energy and commercial interests of BHP Billiton, Eskom, Vodacom and many others. With the establishment of a joint bi-national commission in 2004 under the Thabo Mbeki presidency, the South African government led several trade and investment missions to the DRC, with the aim of promoting collaboration in all areas of economic and social development. Under President Jacob Zuma, Tshwane mobilised internal and external investment for the Grand Inga Dam, designed to provide 15,000 megawatts of electricity to South Africa to help meet its ever-growing power-generation needs. With support from both the World Bank and the African Development Bank (AfDB), Grand Inga is the world's largest proposed hydroelectric dam, designed to generate 40,000 megawatts of electricity. It is to be built in six phases, starting in 2016.

In addition to natural resources and commerce, there is also a human dimension to DRC–South Africa relations. A large number of Congolese have migrated to South Africa in search of a better life.

They include not only young people in various educational institutions, but also many in the informal sector working as traders, service providers and "car-guards", in addition to a significant number of medical doctors, mining engineers and other professional cadres. Bilateral trade between both countries stood at R12.9 billion in 2016.[12]

South Africa in Burundi

In view of the deteriorating situation, and even before President Pierre Buyoya's comeback through a military coup in July 1996, the states of the Great Lakes region had decided to help find a solution to the Burundi crisis that began in October 1993, and had selected "Mwalimu" (the Teacher) Julius Nyerere, the former president of Tanzania, to act as the chief international mediator for the conflict in Burundi. Nyerere tried his best to stop the fighting between the predominantly Tutsi army and armed Hutu rebels, but failed to resolve the conflict before his death in October 1999. Nonetheless, his tough stance towards Buyoya and his determined efforts to move the Arusha peace process forward laid the ground for the peace accord that was eventually signed in August 2000 in the presence of Nelson Mandela, the new mediator, and then US president Bill Clinton.

Like Nyerere, Mandela had a difficult time mediating between 19 political parties. But he used his personal prestige, negotiating skills, elder status and international connections to push through, in eight months of work, a framework agreement that eventually served as a basis for a new constitution and political order for Burundi. Once he accepted the mediation role in December 1999, Mandela announced his intention to include the armed rebel movements that had been excluded from the Arusha talks. When the latter refused to join, he went ahead with the negotiations without them.[13] The two elder statesmen – Nyerere and Mandela – were both criticised for taking a rather autocratic and less diplomatic approach to the negotiations, acting towards the belligerents like schoolmasters facing unruly pupils. Mandela was also accused of viewing Burundi through a South African prism, in which the Hutu represented the oppressed black majority while the Tutsi were comparable to the country's white minority. However imperfect this reading of the situation might have been, it did compel the Tutsi negotiators to behave in a constructive manner.[14]

Bringing the rebel groups into the Arusha peace process turned out to be the major impediment to resolving the Burundian conflict. The South Africans found a solution to it by entrusting the mediation effort to their country's deputy president, Jacob Zuma. Much of the credit for bringing the long, drawn-out negotiations to fruition, culminating in the signing of the Global Ceasefire Agreement of November 2003, must go to Zuma, working with a team of Tanzanian and Ugandan diplomats.[15] The Arusha Accord of 2000 formed the basis on which the ceasefire agreement of 2003 was adopted, and this allowed for the establishment of an all-inclusive transitional process with power-sharing. Unlike his two illustrious predecessors in the Burundi negotiations, the wily former ANC guerrilla was credited with a canny ability to carry the belligerents along throughout the process. The task of bringing the last major armed group into the peace process was achieved by the last South African mediator, former safety and security minister Charles Nqakula, who succeeded in negotiating a ceasefire between the government and the Party for the Liberation of the Hutu People – National Forces of Liberation (Palipehutu-FNL) in 2006.

In the final analysis, the power and diplomatic assets of South Africa as a state were undoubtedly a major factor in Tshwane's decisive role in resolving the Burundian crisis. Already under Mandela's mediation, President Thabo Mbeki had sent soldiers of the South African National Defence Force (SANDF) to provide protection for Burundi's politicians in November 2001. There was general agreement that ensuring the personal safety of the leaders involved in negotiations was essential to the success of the peace talks. Eventually, the SANDF troops became a contingent of the African Union's (AU) first ever peace support operation, the AU Mission in Burundi (AMIB), in February 2003. The South African contingent in AMIB was the largest, with 1,600 troops, while Ethiopia and Mozambique contributed 980 and 280 soldiers respectively. By the end of 2003, the total cost of South Africa's involvement in Burundi – undoubtedly its most successful mediation intervention – was estimated at around R800 million.[16] (See Naidoo in this volume.) When AMIB was transformed into a much larger peacekeeping mission – the United Nations Operation in Burundi (ONUB) – South Africa's General Derrick Mbuyiselo Mgwebi served as the UN force commander between June 2004 and December 2006.

Within the African context, the Burundi peace process could not have succeeded without the financial and military resources that South Africa was able to muster. As a late-comer to continental diplomacy, post-apartheid South Africa led the way in implementing the AU's commitment to promoting continental peace. However, it remains to be seen whether the power-sharing formula that is now part and parcel of Burundi's constitutional framework will endure and provide durable peace and stability. Divisions between the three main parties – the National Council for the Defence of Democracy-Forces for the Defence of Democracy (CNDD-FDD), the Front for Democracy in Burundi (FRODEBU) and the National Forces of Liberation (FNL) – along with Nkurunziza's constitutionally questionable third presidential term secured in July 2015, have demonstrated the limits of a South African-inspired power-sharing formula, with over 200,000 refugees spilling into neighbouring countries since the crisis over the matter started in April 2015.[17]

The crisis began when the ruling party, the CNDD-FDD, announced that President Nkurunziza would stand for a third presidential term. While agreeing that the Burundian constitution does limit the president to two terms of office of five years each, the president and his supporters in the ruling party argued that since the 2005 election had taken place in parliament and not by popular vote, the incumbent was entitled to a second popular vote in 2015. This position was eventually endorsed by Burundi's Constitutional Court, but only after four of its seven members had resigned.

Protest demonstrations by the opposition and civil society began immediately following the announcement of a third term, and an attempted coup was staged in May 2015. Using its control of the armed forces and the police, and emboldened by the African Union's denunciation of the attempted coup, President Nkurunziza went ahead and held the election in July 2015. He did not heed South Africa's request that the election be postponed indefinitely until stability had returned to the country. This very mild rebuke, which was the strongest criticism of Nkurunziza's illegal action in Africa, was the clearest manifestation of a lack of concern by African countries for respect of the 2007 African Charter on Elections, Democracy and Governance, in the midst of a violent repression of protesters, including the killing of unarmed demonstrators.

There is no doubt, however, that South Africa's position has nothing to do with its economic interests in Burundi, since these are very modest, indeed. According to Tshwane's trade statistics, South Africa's exports to Burundi were valued at R74 million in 2014, while imports for the same year were a paltry sum of R2.6 million.[18] Bilateral trade fell to R45 million in 2016.[19]

South Africa and Rwanda

It appears that one of the reasons for the French request to the UN Security Council in June 1994 for authorisation to intervene in Rwanda during the country's genocide was the threat of a South African intervention by the newly established black-majority government. French scholar Gérard Prunier argues that, from a moral point of view, the French action was all the more cynical, given Paris's unabashed support of the Juvénal Habyarimana regime and its Hutu extremists, to whom they had provided weapons until April 1994.[20] South Africa did not intervene, but it did change its arms clients from the old regime to Paul Kagame's Rwandan Patriotic Front (RPF).

Thus, just as the white regime of apartheid South Africa maintained good relations with the "Hutu Power" regime in Rwanda,[21] the ANC and RPF governments got along well. South Africa provided support to Rwanda's reconstruction efforts in a number of sectors including health, education, civil aviation, defence and intelligence. Hundreds of Rwandan students have been admitted to South African universities, and allowed to pay the same fees as South African nationals and students from SADC member countries. In addition to this, Rwanda's economy is growing so fast that Kigali has a much higher volume of trade with South Africa than its debts with Burundi. According to South African trade statistics, in 2014, imports to South Africa were valued at R8 million, while exports to Rwanda totalled R358 million.[22] Bilateral trade increased to R439 million in 2016.[23] Despite these excellent bilateral relations, South African policy since 1998 has been tested by the negative actions of the Kagame regime in the DRC and on South African soil.

In the first case, South Africa and Rwanda confronted each other in the Congo through Kigali's armed militias working for Rwanda's interests in the DRC, such as the National Congress for the Defence of the People (CNDP) and its successor group, the M23. These groups were established to make up for the failure of Rwanda's 1998 invasion to achieve Kigali's strategic objectives of setting up "another Bizimungu in Kinshasa": a puppet government in the DRC.[24] As already indicated, South Africa was at first reluctant to condemn Rwanda for this invasion and was opposed to joining SADC members Angola, Namibia and Zimbabwe in challenging it militarily. Later, however, Tshwane came to see the stark realities of Rwanda's destabilisation and plunder of the DRC, as documented in numerous UN reports.[25]

In March 2013, the United Nations Security Council established within the UN Organisation Stabilisation Mission in the DRC (MONUSCO, successor to MONUC) a Force Intervention Brigade with a mandate to fight and destroy "negative forces" such as the M23.

The brigade is made up of contingents from South Africa, Tanzania and Malawi. The FIB routed the M23 in November 2013, but politics has once again intervened to give the rebel group legitimacy as a political force. An internationally sanctioned agreement between the DRC government and the M23 allows the latter to organise itself as a Congolese political party, and some of its members, whose numbers continue to grow in Rwanda and Uganda, are eligible for amnesty and enrolment into the Armed Forces of the Democratic Republic of the Congo (FARDC).

In the second case, the confrontation is direct, as Rwanda has almost certainly violated South Africa's sovereignty and international law in allegedly carrying out assassination plots against two prominent dissidents who had been granted asylum in South Africa. The first is General Faustin Kayumba Nyamwasa, a former army chief of staff. He fled to South Africa in February 2010, and was granted political asylum and police protection there. He survived an assassination attempt by suspected Rwandan operatives in June 2010, with a bullet to his stomach. Jean-Leonard Rugambage, a Rwandan journalist who undertook to investigate this assassination attempt, was murdered a few days later in Kigali.[26] General Kayumba has faced two further attempts on his life in South Africa: when he was hospitalised following the first assassination attempt, and again in March 2014. The second prominent Rwandan exile to be targeted for assassination was Colonel Patrick Karegeya, former chief of external intelligence in the Rwandan Defence Forces (RDF). Stripped of his rank and later accused of working for South Africa's military intelligence, Karegeya had left Kigali for exile in South Africa in 2007. He was eventually murdered by a suspected Rwandan-backed death squad at a hotel in Johannesburg's plush Sandton suburb in January 2014.[27]

These incidents have damaged the bilateral relations between the two countries. Following Karegeya's assassination and the second attempt on Kayumba's life, South Africa expelled all the diplomats from the Rwandan high commission in Tshwane except the high commissioner, Vincent Karega. Rwanda retaliated, expelling South Africa's high commissioner in Kigali, George Twala. Relations could eventually improve, given the diplomatic arenas in which both countries are currently involved, such as the framework agreement on peace, security and cooperation for the DRC and the region in general, signed by 11 countries and four organisations in Addis Ababa in February 2013.[28]

Concluding Reflections

South Africa's peacemaking efforts in the Great Lakes region have had encouraging outcomes in Burundi and the DRC. However, they need to be focused more on what is good for Africa, and not on what is expected of South Africa by the international community or the great powers in the UN Security Council. South Africa has gone along with the cynical approach of the international community – though one that also accords with its own domestic experience – in imposing power-sharing solutions on most armed conflict situations in Africa, regardless of the political actors involved, including those who have committed heinous crimes against humanity and war crimes (see Curtis in this volume). The Inter-Congolese Dialogue was an excellent example of this, as people who had been recruited by Rwanda and Uganda to wage war against their own citizens and who were accused of killing innocent civilians were deemed suitable for holding high office, including that of vice-president, as well as senior military ranks. The presence of these individuals in the nation's governmental institutions has greatly contributed to the erosion of the values of patriotism, responsibility and public service, which are being superseded by those of selfishness and kleptocracy inherited from the Mobutu era.

In Burundi, South Africa's mediation succeeded in finding a peaceful solution to a deep-seated conflict. However, too much emphasis on power-sharing, and not enough attention to democratic consolidation, threatens this fragile stability. Burundi's current political system is more focused on access to power for elites, instead of the responsibilities of power and of how such institutions should be used to promote peace, security, national cohesion and development.

Rwanda presents an even greater challenge for South Africa. How much knowledge is there in the government, the ruling ANC, the political class as a whole and the intelligentsia about the political dynamics in Rwanda, its shared expansionist aims with Uganda towards the DRC, and the extent of the crimes that the Paul Kagame regime has committed either directly or by proxy in the Congo?

The people of the Great Lakes region will forever remain deeply grateful to South Africa's Navi Pillay, the former president of the International Criminal Tribunal for Rwanda (ICTR) and former UN High Commissioner for Human Rights, for her courage in publishing in October 2010 a mapping report documenting the most serious violations of human rights and international humanitarian law committed in the DRC in the decade from 1993 to 2003.[29] The South African government should follow her example in promoting across Africa and, particularly in the Great Lakes region, the fight against a culture of impunity, which "has encouraged the creation and evolution of armed groups and the use of violence to resolve disputes and gain control over natural resources".[30] This is the major challenge facing Africa's Great Lakes region today.

Notes

1. *See* Devon Curtis, "South Africa: 'Exporting Peace' to the Great Lakes Region", in Adekeye Adebajo, Adebayo Adedeji and Chris Landsberg (eds), *South Africa in Africa: The Post-Apartheid Era* (Scottsville: University of KwaZulu-Natal Press, 2007), pp. 253–273.

2. *See* Centre for Conflict Resolution (CCR), *Security and Governance in the Great Lakes Region*, Seminar Report no. 51 (Franschhoek, South Africa, August 2015), pp. 28–30.

3. Nelson Mandela, quoted by Mobutu Sese Seko's national security adviser, Honoré N'Gbanda, in his book *Ainsi Sonne le Glas! Les Derniers Jours du Maréchal Mobutu* (Paris: Gideppe, 1998), p. 320.

4. Filip Reyntjens, *The Great African War: Congo and Regional Geopolitics, 1996–2006* (New York: Cambridge University Press, 2009), p. 130.

5. Lynne Duke, *Mandela, Mobutu, and Me: A Newswoman's African Journey* (New York: Doubleday, 2003), p. 163.

6. Gérard Prunier, *Africa's World War: Congo, the Rwandan Genocide, and the Making of a Continental Catastrophe* (Oxford and New York: Oxford University Press, 2009), p. 155.

7. CCR, *Security and Governance in the Great Lakes Region*, p. 29.

8. According to Gérard Prunier, Rwanda had ordered South African arms with a $100 million letter of credit countersigned by Uganda on 17 August 1995. This was publicly admitted by South African defence minister Joe Modise on 30 October 1996, before the supply was officially "suspended" on 6 November 1996. American opposition to the Southern African Development Community (SADC) intervention is clearly outlined in a statement by United States (US) assistant secretary of state Susan Rice to the subcommittee on Africa of the US Congress on 15 September 1999. Prunier, *Africa's World War*, p. 385, n. 141.

9. United Nations (UN) Integrated Regional Information Network (IRIN) for Central and Eastern Africa, *Update* 494 (3 September 1998).

10. Reyntjens, *The Great African War*, p. 247.

11. La Voix de Sans Voix (Voice of the Voiceless) is without doubt the best-known non-governmental organisation (NGO) in the Democratic Republic of the Congo (DRC). Its founder, Frederic Chebeya, was murdered while he was arbitrarily held in police custody during the night of 1–2 June 2010 in Kinshasa.

12. Figures from the South African Revenue Service (SARS), *see* http://www.sars.gov.za.

13. Augusta Conchiglia, "L'Afrique du Sud Piégée au Burundi", *Le Monde Diplomatique*, June 2000; René Lemarchand, "Burundi at a Crossroads", in Gilbert

Khadiagala (ed.), *Security Dynamics in Africa's Great Lakes Region* (Boulder, CO, and London: Lynne Rienner, 2006), pp. 52–53.

14. René Lemarchand, *The Dynamics of Violence in Central Africa* (Philadelphia: University of Pennsylvania Press, 2009), pp. 151–152.

15. Lemarchand, *The Dynamics of Violence*, pp. 152, 164.

16. Personal communication from Claude Kabemba, Tshwane (Pretoria), 6 May 2015.

17. According to the United Nations High Commissioner for Refugees (UNHCR), Inter-Agency Informal Sharing Portal of 15 November 2015, 216,455 refugees had left Burundi by this date: 110,977 for Tanzania, 71,108 for Rwanda, 18,382 for the DRC, and 15,988 for Uganda.

18. South African Department of Trade and Industry (DTI), http://tradestats.thedti. gov.za.aspx (accessed 23 October 2015).

19. Figures from the South African Revenue Service (SARS), *see* http://www.sars.gov.za.

20. Prunier, *Africa's World War*, p. 27 and p. 376, n. 109.

21. Prunier, *Africa's World War*, p. 27 and p. 376, n. 109.

22. South African DTI, http://tradestats.thedti.gov.za.aspx (accessed 23 October 2015).

23. Figures from the South African Revenue Service (SARS), *see* http://www.sars.gov.za.

24. That is how President Laurent Kabila explained the intentions of Rwanda and Uganda in the DRC at the special summit of the Organisation of African Unity's (OAU) Central Organ on armed conflicts in Africa held in Ouagadougou, Burkina Faso, on 17–18 December 1998. I was present at the Ouagadougou II conference hall as an observer. The allusion to "another Bizimungu" refers to the powerless role that Pasteur Bizimungu played as Rwanda's president, while real power remained in the hands of General Paul Kagame, the country's vice-president, between 1994 and 2000.

25. All the reports of the UN Panel of Experts on the Illegal Exploitation of Natural Resources and Other Forms of Wealth of the Democratic Republic of the Congo are available at http://www.un.org.

26. On the killing of Jean Léonard Rugambage, acting editor of the newspaper *Umuvugizi*, *see* "Rwanda 'Assasins' Kill Reporter Jean Leonard Rugambage", *BBC News*, 25 June 2010, http://www.bbc.com/news/10413793 (accessed 6 July 2017).

27. News of Karegeya's assassination was carried in all leading South African newspapers on 2 January 2014, and in all major world news bulletins.

28. The 11 countries are the DRC, all nine countries around it (Angola, Burundi, the Central African Republic (CAR), Congo-Brazzaville, Rwanda, South Sudan, Tanzania, Uganda and Zambia) and South Africa. The four organisations are the United Nations, the African Union (AU), the Southern African Development Community and the International Conference on the Great Lakes Region (ICGLR).

29. UNHCR, *Report of the Mapping Exercise Documenting the Most Serious Violations of Human Rights and International Humanitarian Law Committed Within the Territory of the Democratic Republic of the Congo Between March 1993 and June 2003* (Geneva, 2010).

30. Statement of High Commissioner for Human Rights Navi Pillay upon release of her mapping report, Geneva, 1 October 2010.

CHAPTER 8

SOUTH AFRICA IN WEST AFRICA: NIGERIA, GHANA AND CÔTE D'IVOIRE

Adekeye Adebajo

From the nineteenth century, Western imperialism involved God, gold and glory,[1] with missionaries seeking to convert Africans from their "pagan" ancestor worship; with private business interests seeking mineral and agricultural resources; and with empire-builders justifying the whole enterprise as a *mission civilisatrice* of "savage barbarians".[2] In the contemporary case of *Pax South Africana*, could the expansion of mostly white-led businessmen and civil society activists across the continent represent a modern-day equivalent of a bygone era? Could a post-apartheid South Africa be forced to protect the activities of its own trade pioneers, such as Mobile Telephone Networks (MTN) in Nigeria, Ashanti Goldfields in Ghana and Randgold in Côte d'Ivoire? Could South Africa's peacemaking efforts become linked to interventions in strategically important countries such as Côte d'Ivoire in which it has economic interests?

This chapter assesses South Africa's relations with three strategic countries in West Africa over the past two and a half post-apartheid decades: Nigeria, Ghana and Côte d'Ivoire. These oil-rich states are West Africa's three largest economies and have also been South Africa's biggest trading partners in West Africa during this period. Côte d'Ivoire is still the richest and most important country in francophone Africa despite its civil war between 2002 and 2011. This remains the case even despite

Senegalese leader Abdoulaye Wade's (2000–2012) prickly *folie de grandeur* that sought to frustrate South Africa's efforts in creating the New Partnership for Africa's Development (NEPAD) in 2001.[3] Nigeria had a gross domestic product (GDP) of about $415 billion in 2016 and a population of about 180 million; Ghana's GDP was about $43 billion in the same year and its population about 27 million; while Côte d'Ivoire's GDP was about $35 billion in 2016 with a population of about 23 million. In contrast, Senegal's GDP was about $15 billion in the same year, and its population of 15 million[4] was around half of the size of the Ghanaian population and one-twelfth of Nigeria's.[5]

The three *leitmotifs* of God, gold and glory will be used to assess these three bilateral relationships. "God" represents South Africa's missionary zeal in pursuing human rights (most notably in General Sani Abacha's Nigeria in 1995–1996) and peacemaking in Côte d'Ivoire between 2004 and 2006 and in 2010–2011. "Gold" represents the activities of South Africa's corporate sector in expanding into West African markets in all three countries (see also Vickers and Cawood in this volume on the role of South African companies on the continent). "Glory" is represented by South Africa's quest to be recognised as a regional leader through its foreign policy activities, for example leading it to become the only African member of the Group of 20 (G-20) and the Brazil, Russia, India, China and South Africa (BRICS) groupings (see Virk in this volume on BRICS). In a broader sense, each of these three *leitmotifs* could also represent Tshwane's relationship with these three West African countries: "glory" represents South Africa's rivalry with Nigeria for leadership in Africa; "gold" represents Tshwane's relationship with fellow gold producer Ghana; while "God" represents South Africa's efforts to promote peace and reconciliation in Côte d'Ivoire.

South Africa and Nigeria: A Shakespearean Drama[6]

Our location [Nigeria and South Africa], our destiny and the contemporary forces of globalisation have thrust upon us the burden of turning around the fortunes of our continent. We must not and cannot shy away from this responsibility.[7]

– Olusegun Obasanjo, Nigerian president, 1999–2007

South Africa and Nigeria collectively account for about 30 per cent of Africa's economic might. Former Nigerian president Goodluck Jonathan (2010–2015) paid his first state visit to South Africa in May 2013, where he addressed a joint sitting of the South African parliament in Cape Town. With six Nigerian ministers present, agreements were signed in the areas of defence, immigration, oil, gas, geology, mining, mineral processing, metallurgy and power generation. During the visit, Jonathan called for a greater opening of the South African market to Nigerian investors. South African president Jacob Zuma noted that about 73,000 Nigerian tourists had visited South Africa in 2012, spending R720 million in the country.[8] South Africa's trade minister, Rob Davies, pledged to assist Nigeria to develop its automotive sector. The state visit followed a trip by Zuma to Abuja in April 2013 (with Zuma having earlier visited in December 2011). Despite recent spats between both countries, Tshwane's military debacle in the Central African Republic (CAR) in March 2013, when 13 of its soldiers were killed (see Marchal in this volume); its deployment of troops to the Democratic Republic of the Congo (DRC) under the banner of the Southern African Development Community (SADC) by June 2013 (along with Tanzania and Malawi; see Curtis, and Nzongola-Ntalaja in this volume); and its increasing antipathy towards the interventionist French role in African countries such as Côte d'Ivoire and the CAR, appeared to be forcing a rekindling of the previous close relationship between Africa's two giants.

This bilateral relationship – potentially the most strategic in Africa – has always represented a mix of cooperation and competition.[9] The continued dominance of whites in South Africa's economy (over 80 per cent of the Johannesburg Stock Exchange in 2017)[10] and academic institutions, and continuing uncertainties about an African identity, have led to widespread questioning of its legitimacy as an African power by policymakers in Abuja. In July 2012, Nigeria unsuccessfully sought to prevent South Africa's minister of home affairs, Nkosazana Dlamini-Zuma, from assuming the chair of the African Union (AU) Commission, despite Abuja's principled position that no representative of a large African power should occupy the post (see Maloka in this volume). South Africa had, however, supported Nigerian finance minister Ngozi Okonjo-Iweala's unsuccessful bid for the presidency of the World Bank a month earlier.

This rivalry has even extended to sports, with Nigeria's "Super Eagles" victory in the Africa Cup of Nations soccer contest in Johannesburg in February 2013 being greeted with a mixed reaction by the hosts, many of whom supported the less-fancied Burkina Faso team in the final. Nigeria's economy overtook South Africa's as the largest in Africa in 2013, a prospect that had rendered many jingoistic South African analysts apoplectic. However, despite reports South Africa overtook Nigeria again in August 2016, within two months an International Monetary Fund (IMF) report had put Nigeria back in the lead with a GDP of $415 billion, compared to South Africa's $280 billion.[11]

The relationship between South Africa and Nigeria in the post-apartheid era has in fact been akin to a Shakespearean drama in three acts: the first is set during the rule of Nelson Mandela and Nigeria's General Sani Abacha, from 1994 to 1998; the second act occurred during the presidencies of Thabo Mbeki and Olusegun Obasanjo from 1999 to 2007; while the third act is in the period between 2008 and 2017, under the presidencies of Jacob Zuma in South Africa and Umaru Yar' Adua, Goodluck Jonathan and Muhammadu Buhari in Nigeria.

Since South Africa was diplomatically isolated during the apartheid era and forced to bear the brunt of international sanctions, Nigeria was the prophet, South Africa the pariah. Nigeria established the Southern African Relief Fund (SARF) in 1976 to provide South Africans with scholarships (400 black South African students arrived in the country a year later). Nigerian civil servants also had a "Mandela tax" deducted directly from their monthly salaries to support South Africa's liberation struggle. Lagos attended meetings of the Frontline States (FLS) of Southern Africa, and chaired the United Nations (UN) Special Committee Against Apartheid. Following Nelson Mandela's release from jail in February 1990, he visited Nigeria, and received a $10 million campaign contribution for the African National Congress (ANC).[12] There were great expectations that these developments would mark the birth of a strong alliance between Africa's two powerhouses.

The Avuncular Saint and King Baabu, 1994–1998

In Dickensian fashion, these great expectations, however, soon became dashed by hard times following the unexpected souring of relations between Abuja and Tshwane. It is important to understand the two protagonists in the first act of this drama: General Sani Abacha and Nelson Mandela. In his 2002 play *King Baabu*, Nigerian Nobel literature laureate Wole Soyinka depicts Baabu as a brainless, brutish buffoon and greedily corrupt military general who exchanges his military attire for a monarchical robe.[13] The play is a thinly disguised satire of the Macbethian General Abacha's debauched rule between November 1993 and his death in June 1998.[14] In power, Abacha was ruthless and reclusive, but hardly as inept as the caricature depicted by Soyinka and Nigeria's political opposition, who greatly underestimated him. Abacha proved to be a political survivor who understood how to control Nigeria's army and buy off its political class.

Nelson Mandela, with the noble bearing of a Julius Caesar, is the starkest contrast one can imagine to Abacha. An educated, middle-class lawyer and a cosmopolitan anglophile, this Nobel peace laureate spent 27 years as a political prisoner and embodied his people's aspirations for a democratic future.[15] Under Abacha's autocratic rule, it was Nigeria, and not South Africa, that was now facing mounting criticism over its human rights record. Having abandoned its apartheid past, South Africa was widely acknowledged to be the most likely political and economic success story in Africa. It had become the prophet, and Nigeria the pariah.

The nadir of relations between the two countries was reached after the hanging by the Abacha regime of Nigerian environmental activist Ken Saro-Wiwa and eight of his fellow Ogoni campaigners, during the Commonwealth summit in New Zealand in November 1995. Mandela believed he had received personal assurances from Abacha of clemency for the "Ogoni nine". Feeling deeply betrayed and adopting the "God" typology, he condemned the killings and called for oil sanctions against Abacha's regime as well as for Nigeria's expulsion from the Commonwealth. Even Mandela's status, however, failed to rally regional support against Nigeria, with not a single SADC state backing Mandela's call to punish Nigeria at a December 1995 meeting. It took a *deus ex machina* event – Abacha's sudden death of an apparent heart attack in June 1998 – to transform this tale of the prophet and the pariah into a tale of two prophets.

The Philosopher-King and Soldier-Farmer, 1999–2007

Thabo Mbeki and Olusegun Obasanjo assumed the presidencies of their respective countries in 1999. Mbeki greatly admired Coriolanus and suffered a similar politically tragic end to his hero due to his arrogant aloofness. A Sussex University-trained economist, Mbeki often wrote his own speeches and fancied himself as a Philosopher-King.[16] Obasanjo, a Falstaffian figure and soldier-engineer who later became a farmer, was

Nigeria's military head of state between 1976 and 1979, before returning as civilian leader 20 years later.[17] He had visited Mandela in jail in 1986 as a member of the Commonwealth Eminent Persons Group (EPG). From his first-hand experience as head of the ANC office in Lagos in 1977–1978, Mbeki had developed much respect for Nigeria's fierce sense of independence. As president from 1999, both he and Obasanjo worked closely at managing African crises in Liberia, Zimbabwe, the DRC and Burundi; at promoting norms of democratic governance through the AU; and establishing NEPAD as an economic blueprint for the continent's socio-economic development efforts.

Bilateral trade increased, with Nigeria becoming South Africa's largest trading partner in Africa, a relationship worth R36 billion a year by 2013. The Nigerian market of 180 million consumers is over three times larger than South Africa's 55 million, and South Africa has only six big cities, compared to Nigeria's 27.[18] There have been tensions in this relationship, which many Nigerians regard as having one-sidedly benefited South African firms while its markets have remained largely closed to Nigerian companies. South African telecommunications giant, MTN, for example, has been dubbed "Money Thieving Networks" by critics, despite its philanthropic support of social development and sports in Nigeria. After 1994, South Africa's corporate community began to view Nigeria with great interest, helped by its long-serving and energetic high commissioner in Abuja, former trade unionist Bangumzi "Sticks" Sifingo.[19] The South African firms, MTN and M-Net/SuperSport, blazed the trail, with MTN spending $340 million launching its mobile telephone network in Nigeria in August 2001.[20] Already in 2003–2004, MTN Nigeria's post-tax profit of R2.36 billion surpassed MTN South Africa's R2.24 billion profit.[21] By June 2004, MTN had 1.65 million subscribers in Nigeria,[22] which increased tenfold to 16.5 million by December 2007, representing a staggering 29 per cent of all its African subscribers in 16 countries, and more than its 14.8 million South African subscribers.[23] It was MTN's success that convinced many other South African firms that Nigeria was worth investing in. As a senior executive of South African beer and beverages multinational SABMiller – which belatedly entered the Nigerian market in 2008 – noted, if South African firms do not have a Nigeria strategy, they do not really have an Africa strategy.[24]

Other South African "blue chip" commercial giants that followed MTN included Stanbic, Rand Merchant Bank, and more recently retirement fund administrator Alexander Forbes. Within a year of operations, Stanbic's Nigerian affiliate was contributing 13 per cent of its Africa-wide revenues (R1.26 billion). In 2008, Alexander Forbes bought a 40 per cent stake in Nigeria's pension sector, comprising 8 million potential state employees.[25] Sasol, the world's largest producer of petrol from coal, made a $1.2 billion investment in Nigeria to export natural gas. South Africa's government-funded Industrial Development Corporation (IDC) invested in Nigerian oil, gas, infrastructure, tourism and telecommunications. South Africa's Spoornet worked with the Nigerian Railway Corporation to revive Nigeria's railways. Protea has established hotels across Nigeria.[26] Fast-food chains Chicken Licken and Debonairs Pizzas established franchises in Nigeria. Shoprite Checkers opened an outlet in Lagos in 2006 that became profitable within a year, and two large South African-dominated malls had been built in Lagos by 2012.

A Nigeria–South Africa chamber of commerce was also established in 2001, while a joint business investment forum met in South Africa three times between 2004 and 2008. By 2003, Nigeria had already become South Africa's third-largest continental trading partner, after Zimbabwe and Mozambique, and its largest continental importer. Three years later, Nigeria became South Africa's largest trading partner on the continent, and bilateral trade reached R22.8 billion (about $3 billion) by 2008.[27] Businesspeople from South Africa and Nigeria now frequently cross each other's borders, with about 120 South African firms working in Nigeria in 2017, up from 55 in 2003.[28]

Of Nigeria's exports to South Africa in 2003, 98.3 per cent consisted of oil, though Nigeria's Union Bank and First Bank established representative offices in South Africa. In 2005, Nigerian oil company Oando set up shop in Johannesburg.[29] Three years later, the Dangote Group, Nigeria's largest industrial conglomerate, bought 45 per cent of South Africa's Sephaka Cement, at a cost of R3 billion. Many Nigerian professionals also work in South Africa, in fields like academia, medicine, accounting, human resources and property. In turn, South Africa sells Nigeria a more diverse range of goods, including machinery, electrical equipment, wood, paper, foodstuff, beverages, spirits, tobacco, sugar, plastics and rubber.

Six bi-national meetings were held during the period 1999–2007, with Nigeria and South Africa alternating as host. The fourth meeting, in 2002, initiated the idea of a South Africa–Nigeria free trade area (which still had not occurred in 2017), while the fifth meeting, in 2003, called for a joint business investment forum. By the time of the sixth meeting, the focus was on eight working groups: trade, industry and finance; mineral and energy; agriculture, water resources and environment; foreign affairs and cooperation; defence; immigration, justice and crime; social and technical issues; and public enterprises and infrastructure. At the sixth meeting, held in the South African port city of Durban in 2004, officials discussed how to increase trade, with the Nigerians urging the South Africans to accelerate discussions with their Southern African Customs Union (SACU) partners – Botswana, Swaziland, Lesotho and Namibia – in order to establish the proposed free trade area (see Gibb in this volume). The meeting further urged the establishment of a special implementation committee to ensure an effective monitoring mechanism of commission decisions, as well as to develop a concrete programme of action with clear time frames. Continuity of officials was also encouraged, as well as participation of legislators and chief executives of South African provinces and Nigerian states in future bi-national sessions.[30]

There were some strains in relations between Tshwane and Abuja that the bi-national meetings sought to address. In response to difficulties experienced by Nigerians in obtaining visas to South Africa, Abuja imposed stricter visa requirements on South African citizens visiting Nigeria. Nigerian diplomats often complained about negative press reports and xenophobic stereotypes of Nigerians, as drug-traffickers and criminals, in the South African media and popular imagination.[31] A Johannesburg radio station, 94.7 Highveld, was forced by South Africa's Broadcasting Complaints Commission to apologise after it claimed that Nigerian president Olusegun Obasanjo was carrying cocaine in his bag when he attended Mbeki's inauguration in June 2004.[32]

A notorious Hollywood movie that reinforced South African stereotypes of Nigerians was the 2009 science fiction film *District 9*, directed by South African-born Canadian, Neill Blomkamp. Nigerian immigrants are particularly singled out by Blomkamp for xenophobic stereotyping. The cannibalistic crime boss of the aliens is named Obesandjo: a crude and tactless reference to the country's president between 1999 and 2007. Blomkamp is too lazy even to research any Nigerian names, and appears to take a former head of state's surname as representative of the archetypal Nigerian criminal. Nigerians are depicted throughout the movie as involved in drug and arms trafficking, business scams, car-theft, prostitution and cannibalism.[33]

A Decade of Troubles, 2008–2017

The seventh South Africa–Nigeria bi-national meeting did not take place until May 2008. It was held in Nigeria, following Obasanjo's departure from power and the election of President Umaru Yar'Adua the previous year. A month later, Yar'Adua led a 300-strong business delegation to South Africa for a meeting of the joint business investment forum. He also addressed the South African parliament in Cape Town. In October 2008, Mohamed Marwa, a former military administrator turned politician, became Nigeria's high commissioner to South Africa, replacing Olugbenga Ashiru (later foreign minister between 2011 and 2013), who had assumed office in October 2005. On the tenth anniversary of the creation of the bi-national commission, an eighth meeting was held in Abuja in February 2009 that discussed the state of bilateral activities, how to strengthen the structures of the commission, as well as African and global issues. Activities were also held in South Africa and Nigeria in October and November 2009 to commemorate the tenth anniversary of the commission: a business roundtable, civil society and parliamentary meetings and cultural events.

Khalifa is the term used in northern Nigeria for kings-in-waiting, a position sometimes disparagingly referred to in Nigerian popular parlance as that of a "spare tyre". Two such *khalifas* – both former deputy presidents – became presidents of South Africa and Nigeria: Jacob Zuma and Goodluck Jonathan. Both were accused of weak and indecisive leadership. After Zuma's election as South Africa's president in 2009, Tshwane cooperated closely with Angola, having identified it as a key strategic ally. This created tensions with Nigeria by appearing to downgrade the "special relationship" between Tshwane and Abuja. The fact that South Africa is the only African representative in the Group of 20 and BRICS groupings, and the only African strategic partner of the European Union (EU) out of 11 globally, further exacerbated these tensions.

There were also disagreements between Tshwane and Abuja over differing approaches to tackling the conflicts in Côte d'Ivoire and Libya in 2011. During the post-election crisis in Côte d'Ivoire, Nigeria adopted a belligerent stance towards Laurent Gbagbo, who refused to stand down after losing presidential elections in November 2010. South Africa provocatively sent a warship, the *SAS Drakensberg*, to the Gulf of Guinea in Nigeria's traditional West African "sphere of influence". Tshwane, however, argued that the ship was a supply vessel on a routine training operation.[34]

Though Tshwane and Abuja both voted in the UN Security Council to support intervention in Libya in 2011, Nigeria became one of the first African countries to recognise the country's National Transitional Council (NTC). South Africa delayed recognition of the NTC and accused the North Atlantic Treaty Organisation (NATO) of having abused its mandate in Libya. There was another diplomatic clash reported between Jonathan and Zuma at the AU summit in January/February 2013 over readmission into the organisation of the government in Guinea-Bissau, which Abuja was supporting, in a West African country to which Nigeria had deployed about 500 peacekeepers under the auspices of the Economic Community of West African States (ECOWAS) in May 2012. Abuja failed to gain the readmission of the suspended Bissau government back into the AU.

One of the most damaging rifts in this bilateral relationship occurred when South Africa expelled 125 visiting Nigerians (including legislators) in March 2012, claiming that they were carrying fake "yellow fever" certificates. Abuja retaliated by expelling 78 South Africans who were trying to enter Nigeria, forcing Tshwane to apologise. Further tensions occurred when South African officials seized $9 million that had reportedly been smuggled illegally into the country by Nigerian officials in September 2014 to buy arms. The death of 85 South Africans at Pastor T.B. Joshua's Synagogue Church of All Nations in Lagos in September 2014, and the five-month delay in repatriating the final 11 bodies to South Africa, led to further friction.

It will be important for South Africa and Nigeria to re-establish a common strategic approach if Africa's voice is to carry weight on the global stage. Encouragingly, the first meeting of the bi-national commission in four years took place in May 2012, with both sides agreeing to relax visa requirements, particularly for businesspeople. Both countries also agreed to strengthen African regional bodies, establish a tripartite group with Angola on African issues and push for the proposed reform of the UN Security Council. Importantly, an implementation committee was to meet after six months to review progress.[35] But lingering bilateral tensions were again evident when Abuja snubbed Tshwane's invitation to join part of the BRICS summit in Durban in March 2013. South African firms also suffered some reversals in Nigeria. Tiger Brands, the country's biggest food producer, divested its three-year-old 65.7 per cent stake in Tiger Brands Consumer Goods in Nigeria – the former Dangote Flour Mills – in December 2015. Tiger Brands settled a R400 million debt in the process.

The state visit by Jacob Zuma to Nigeria in March 2016 was significant, as it was the first under the new Nigerian administration of Muhammadu Buhari, which had assumed office in May 2015. Both countries agreed to upgrade the bi-national commission from the vice-presidential to presidential level. Zuma's addressing of a joint session of Nigeria's National Assembly in Abuja was a rare privilege that was given disappointingly scant coverage in the South African media. His speech covered three key areas. First, he went out of his way to heal a historical wound that many Nigerian diplomats and citizens have consistently complained about: South Africa's perceived ingratitude for Nigeria's substantial contributions to the anti-apartheid struggle. The second key area of Zuma's speech involved economic and trade relations, at a time when about 120 South African companies were operating in Nigeria. He also addressed the South Africa–Nigeria Business Forum to underline the importance of this key area. Zuma called for a diversification of both countries' economies, with bilateral trade having increased from R17 billion in 2008 to R55 billion in 2016 (down from R62 billion in 2015).[36] South Africa also offered to assist Nigeria's efforts at increasing its electricity supply, building an auto industry, exploring its solid minerals and providing military hardware for Abuja's fight against Boko Haram militants.

The third area of Zuma's speech was building people-to-people relations that implicitly could help improve understanding between the citizens of the two countries. About 48,000 Nigerians travelled to South Africa in 2015, and both countries were looking to increase tourism. The Nigeria Union in South Africa (NUSA), however, lobbied the Nigerian government to address what they complained was widespread xenophobic harassment of Nigerian citizens by South African security and immigration officials.[37] Relations between Nigeria and South Africa had recently been soured by the fine of $3.9 billion (from an initial $5.2 billion) imposed on MTN by Nigerian regulators for failing to disconnect 5.1 million irregularly registered cell-phone subscribers. In his first public comment on the issue and in one of the few discordant notes of this finely orchestrated diplomatic symphony, President Buhari angrily accused the South African company of having contributed to the deaths of thousands of Nigerian victims of Boko Haram through its inaction. The final MTN fine was negotiated down to $1.7 billion.

Tensions again erupted in bilateral relations in March 2017 when hundreds of South African vigilantes burned and looted scores of homes and businesses of Nigerians in Rosettenville, Mamelodi and Atteridgeville that they alleged were drug dens and brothels. The response from Abuja was forceful, calling on South African authorities to stop the violence and protect its citizens, and threatening to go to the African Union to protest. Nigeria claimed that 116 of its citizens had been killed over the preceding two years, figures that Tshwane disputed. Many Nigerians at home were also appalled by these xenophobic acts, which resulted in the vandalism of the offices of South Africa's MTN in Abuja.

This concludes the final act of this Shakespearean drama that has represented "God", "gold" and "glory". In the immortal words of the Bard, the hope for this vital relationship is that: all's well that ends well.

South Africa and Ghana: A Tale of Two Gold Diggers

We go where the gold is and where we think we can generate a return for shareholders.[38]

– Richard Duffy, Vice-President of Continental Africa,
AngloGold Ashanti

During the colonial era, Ghana was known as the "Gold Coast", an African El Dorado in the grasping imagination of avaricious European imperialists. Gold still remained an important export earner in 2017, though increasing oil exports were now key to the country's economy. Ghana is among the world's largest cocoa producers and also exports bauxite, diamonds and manganese. Its legendary founding leader, Kwame Nkrumah (1957–1966), led efforts to liberate Africa from colonial rule from the 1940s, and was a forceful and eloquent advocate for the liberation of apartheid South Africa. Nkrumah sought to promote pan-Africanism through regional integration, a common currency and a continental military command.[39] South Africa's second post-apartheid leader, Thabo Mbeki (1999–2008), similarly sought to act as a Philosopher-King, promoting an "African Renaissance" and improved political and economic governance.[40] Ghana was the second-largest contributor, after Nigeria, to sub-regional peacekeeping efforts in Liberia and Sierra Leone between 1990 and 1999. Since 1960, it has provided 80,000 peacekeepers to more than 30 UN and other multilateral peacekeeping missions, and was in the top 20 global contributors to UN peacekeeping between 2000 and 2010.[41] The country is increasingly evolving into a stable democracy following three changes of government between 2000 and 2017, though many socio-economic challenges remain.

While South Africa's relationship with Nigeria has been both political and economic, its relations with Ghana have tended to focus on economics over the past two and a half decades. "Gold" has tended to overshadow "God" and "glory" in this particular relationship between Africa's two largest gold producers. British, French and German interests historically dominated Ghana's trade and investment market until 1994. Nigeria has also established a large presence in Ghanaian sectors such as banking (Zenith bank) and telecommunications (Glo), taking advantage of ECOWAS, a bloc to which both countries belong.

Large-scale trade and investment relations between South Africa and Ghana began in 1996, with a 36-strong Ghanaian government and business delegation visiting South Africa in September of that year. A South African trade mission reciprocated by visiting Ghana in 1998, and an accord was reached on the promotion and protection of investments between both countries. Ghana's president, Jerry Rawlings, paid a five-day state visit to South Africa in July 1998. During a state banquet in his honour, South African president Nelson Mandela urged the South African business community to ensure that its investments in Ghana transfer technology and skills to the West African country in a sustainable manner, and highlighted increasing investments in the gold mining and brewing sectors.[42] During this visit, Rawlings also met with South Africa's Chamber of Mines and visited the Johannesburg Stock Exchange. Along with his business delegation, he pushed for increased trade and tourism from South Africa to Ghana.[43]

Officials from South Africa's Department of Trade and Industry (DTI) visited Accra in 1999, and a scheme of risk insurance for South African companies operating in Ghana was established. This was the same year in which Eskom launched the Self-Help Electricity Project in Ghana, which helped to boost the provision of electricity to rural areas. President Thabo Mbeki also embarked on a state visit to Ghana in October 2000.[44] He addressed the country's parliament; launched the Ghana–South Africa Business Chamber; laid a wreath at the Kwame Nkrumah Mausoleum; visited Cape Coast and Elmina castles; and delivered a public lecture in Accra on "African Renaissance: The Challenge of Our Time". Mbeki and his Ghanaian counterpart, Jerry Rawlings, discussed how to deepen bilateral trade between Tshwane and Accra; highlighted the cooperation between their individual parliaments and defence forces; and shared views on international issues.[45]

South African exports to Ghana increased from $61 million in 1998 to $231 million (R1.6 billion) in 2003,[46] reaching over R3 billion in 2008.[47] South African imports from Ghana stood at R52 million ($7.5 million) in 2003, and reached R81.7 million by 2006. While Ghana imported mostly processed and manufactured goods from South Africa like alloy products, chemicals, tobacco, plastics, electrical equipment, aircraft, rubber, cars, machinery, vinegar and base metals, it exported agricultural and semi-processed commodities to South Africa such as vegetable products, wood, basketware, textiles, wickerwork, glycerine, cocoa and mineral products. South African firms are major players in Ghana's mining, telecommunications, construction, tourism and general trade sectors. The country's Department of Trade and Industry appointed a representative to South Africa's high commission in Accra to promote opportunities for South African businesses in Ghana and to strengthen bilateral trade and investment ties. In November 2004, then South African foreign minister Nkosazana Dlamini-Zuma visited Accra to establish a joint commission to promote economic cooperation between the two countries. A Ghana–South Africa expo in Accra coincided with this visit.[48]

By 2003, Ghana had established itself as South Africa's second-largest trading partner in West Africa after Nigeria in sectors such as mining, multimedia communication, beverages and franchising. In one of the most successful pan-African commercial ventures, South Africa's AngloGold acquired a 50 per cent share in a $1.4 billion merger with Ghana's largest mining company, Ashanti Goldfields, in 2004 to become AngloGold Ashanti. The company – the jewel in South Africa's West African crown – operates mines in South Africa, Ghana, the DRC, Namibia, Tanzania, Guinea and Mali, contributing to government revenues and even sometimes rehabilitating roads and running malaria prevention programmes.[49] In 2017, the Johannesburg-based multinational company was among the world's largest gold producers, with 20 operations on four continents generating $6.4 billion in 2012.[50] There were some tensions between the government of Ghana's president John Mahama and AngloGold Ashanti in 2016 when *galamsey* – illegal small-scale miners – invaded the Obuasi gold mine, before the dispute was later arbitrated.

South Africa's SABMiller also bought a 69 per cent stake in Accra Brewery in 1997, turning a debt-ridden company into a profitable venture.[51] By 2004, the firm had increased turnover by 60 per cent and doubled its operating profits.[52] In the telecommunications sector, Mulitichoice had signed up over 6,000 subscribers by 2005. South African brand names such as Stanbic, Engen, Sherwood, Protea hotels, Steers, Nando's, Game, Mr Price, Shoprite Checkers and Woolworths, as well as Hytec Engineering, Afripa Telcom and Alliance Media, were all operating profitably in Ghana. Many of these companies could be found in a large South African-dominated mall opened in Accra in 2008, and attracting 138,000 shoppers a week by 2012. MTN, the largest player in the Ghanaian cell-phone market, had 11 million subscribers by 2012, nearly half of its South African subscribers.[53] South African Airways (SAA) started flights between Johannesburg and Accra in April 1996 and, in 2017, had four weekly flights: a sign of the increasing business and tourist interest between the two countries.

By 2004, South Africa had become Ghana's fourteenth-largest external investor; its investment accounted for 60 per cent of Ghana's mining sector; it controlled 90 per cent of the market share in Ghana's multimedia communications sector; Steeledale, 3M South Africa and African Explosives accounted for 30 per cent of Ghana's manufacturing sector; and 35 South African multinational companies had set up shop in Ghana between 1994 and 2003 (this increased to over 80 companies by 2017), investing $36 million (excluding the mining and energy sectors).[54] A bilateral accord on cooperation in mining and minerals beneficiation was signed in 2005. South Africa's investments in Ghana, as elsewhere in Africa, tended to be fairly integrated, with firms providing services to each other; and banks like Stanbic, First Rand and Rand Merchant Bank lending to South African companies; while South African-built malls sold South African products.

Many South African companies regard Ghana as the gateway to the West African market. They have often noted its well-run harbours of Takoradi and Tema, political stability and well-educated workforce. Small and medium-sized South African firms, though, have complained about the cost of, and access to, borrowing. Other criticisms have involved Ghana's slowly functioning legal system, a concern somewhat eased by the establishment of "fast-track" courts to decide cases involving foreign firms. Regulatory uncertainty; an inefficient customs service; corruption; contested property rights; poor port, road and railway infrastructure; and a small market with limited consumers were other complaints expressed by South African firms doing business in Ghana. Under the presidency of John Kufuor between 2001 and 2008, Accra introduced several investor-friendly policies such as lower corporate taxes; 5- to 10-year tax holidays; tax rebates for manufacturing companies; and customs duties exemptions for importing machinery and plant equipment. The Ghana Investment Promotion Centre (GIPC) also sought to assist foreign investors and to create a business-friendly environment in the country.[55]

More recently, a South African and Ghanaian Permanent Joint Commission for Cooperation (PJCC) was agreed in Accra in November 2004 as a way of ensuring a more strategic approach to the bilateral relationship, similar to South Africa's bi-national commission with Nigeria. The PJCC was tasked with convening every two years and to provide a framework for implementing decisions and agreements between Tshwane and Accra. Both countries' ministries of foreign affairs, defence, agriculture, trade, energy, communications, science and technology and arts and culture form part of these meetings.[56] The commission's first ministerial meeting took place in Tshwane in May 2007.[57] Its second meeting was held in Accra in March 2010. Both countries signed accords to cooperate in foreign affairs, including meeting once a year to discuss bilateral and multilateral issues (2010); oil and gas (2011); and defence training (2011). Ghana's president, John Atta Mills, paid a state visit to South Africa in August 2011 in a bid to strengthen bilateral ties further. Along with a call to continue the work of the joint commission, Mills and his counterpart, Jacob Zuma, discussed regional issues and the reform and strengthening of the AU and the UN.

Following the start of Ghana's commercial oil exports in December 2010, the country was expected to produce 120,000 barrels of oil a day. As the United States (US) and EU governments threatened sanctions against countries importing oil from Iran, South Africa lost 29 per cent of its oil imports by 2012. Its deputy president, Kgalema Motlanthe, thus embarked on a working visit to Accra in April 2012 in a bid to have PetroSA buy a stake in the state-owned Ghana National Petroleum Corporation. Tshwane promised, in turn, to help Ghana develop its hydro-electric power station in Akosombo through Eskom.[58] Bilateral trade between South Africa and Ghana increased from $32 million in 2008 to $61 million by 2013.

In July 2013, a South African trade delegation of 29 businesspeople visited Ghana, led by deputy trade minister Elizabeth Thabethe, in an effort to accelerate implementation of a 2011 memorandum of understanding on economic and technical cooperation that sought to increase trade, promote industrial development capacity-building and develop infrastructure. During this visit, Thabethe committed South Africa to participate in the Ghana International Trade Fair in 2014. Tshwane also encouraged Accra to take advantage of its Saldanha Bay Industrial Development Zone for servicing its oil and gas rigs.[59] President Jacob Zuma visited his counterpart John Mahama with a ministerial delegation for two days in November 2013 to sign agreements on energy and transport cooperation.

Bilateral relations were further strengthened by trade and government actions. In September 2014, South Africa's Transnet signed an agreement with the Ghana Ports and Harbours Authority to enhance greater cooperation in this important area. In June 2015, a group of 25 South African companies in the service sector and creative industries based in the Western Cape embarked on a trade mission to Accra, with commerce with these firms worth over R606 million at the time. Total South African exports to Ghana in 2016 were worth R4.9 billion, compared to R192 million in imports.[60] In May 2016, South Africa's foreign minister, Maite Nkoana-Mashabane, led a delegation to Accra for the fourth South Africa–Ghana Permanent Joint Commission for Cooperation at which both countries' mutual interests were discussed.

This relationship has thus represented more "gold" than "God" or "glory".

South Africa and Côte d'Ivoire: The Missionary Position[61]

Africa has a right and a duty to intervene to root out tyranny.... [W]e must all accept that we cannot abuse the concept of national sovereignty to deny the rest of the continent the right and duty to intervene when behind those sovereign boundaries, people are being slaughtered to protect tyranny.[62]
        – Nelson Mandela, president of South Africa, 1994–1999

Just as Ghana was known as the Gold Coast in the colonial era, another important West African country was similarly named the Ivory Coast and, unlike Ghana, has retained its colonial name in French. Cocoa and oil-rich Côte d'Ivoire remains francophone West Africa's largest economy despite its civil conflict between 2002 and 2011. The one sub-regional country in which South Africa has played an important peacemaking role is Côte d'Ivoire, with this relationship largely reflecting a "missionary" role in which the *leitmotif* of "God" has dominated those of "glory" and "gold" that were characteristic of the relationship with Nigeria and Ghana respectively.

Even before the post-apartheid era, Abidjan had already approached the outgoing apartheid government of F.W. de Klerk in Pretoria to help it build the Abokouamekro Game Park, and an agreement was signed in July 1990. Diplomatic relations were established two years later. After 1994, South Africa identified Côte d'Ivoire as one of its strategic economic partners due largely to its strong economy and hosting of the African Development Bank (which was moved to Tunis in 2003 due to instability in Côte d'Ivoire, but moved back to Abidjan in 2013). The country was also regarded as a gateway for South African goods to francophone West African markets in Mali, Guinea and Burkina Faso.

Ivorian president Henri Konan Bédié paid an official state visit to South Africa in September 1998 in order to strengthen bilateral trade and economic relations. During the visit, Bédié and South African president Nelson Mandela discussed concluding a promotion and protection of investment accord between the two countries, which was signed a year later. South Africa encouraged exports rather than direct investment to Côte d'Ivoire. A military coup by General Robert Guei in Abidjan in December 1999 soon led to a thaw in growing bilateral relations. Adopting a moralistic pro-human rights posture and acting as a regional "Mother Teresa", South Africa denounced the military coup in Abidjan and withdrew its DTI representative from the country, refusing to conclude more trade deals and investments until democratic governance had been restored.[63]

Despite these developments, Côte d'Ivoire became South Africa's third-largest bilateral trade partner in West Africa after Nigeria and Ghana by 2001. Tshwane has exported insecticides, polymers and paper-related products to Côte d'Ivoire, while largely importing cocoa and wood. South African companies like Randgold and MTN (among the five largest cell-phone providers in the country) have also invested in Côte d'Ivoire, and Thabo Mbeki was the chief mediator of the country's peace process between 2004 and 2006.

Part of the complication of peacemaking in Côte d'Ivoire lay in the proliferation of external mediators, which raised obvious questions about too many cooks spoiling the broth. Presidents John Kufuor of Ghana, Nigeria's Olusegun Obasanjo, Gabon's Omar Bongo, Sierra Leone's Ahmed Kabbah, Togo's Gnassingbé Eyadéma and Niger's Mamadou Tandja were all involved in peacemaking efforts between 2002 and 2004. South Africa,

ECOWAS, the AU, the UN and the Francophonie also all nominated their own special envoys to Côte d'Ivoire. As AU chair, Obasanjo appointed South Africa's Thabo Mbeki as the organisation's mediator in November 2004, bringing some focus to the peacemaking process.[64] After his appointment, Mbeki visited Abidjan and called the parties to Tshwane to discuss their differences. With continuing delays in the implementation of these accords, the UN Security Council imposed an arms embargo on all the factions in November 2004[65] (followed a year later by an embargo on the trade of diamonds),[66] and threatened travel sanctions and a freezing of the financial assets of individuals obstructing the peace process.[67]

Mbeki successfully urged the UN Security Council to hold off individual sanctions to give his mediation efforts time to bear fruit. A tripartite monitoring group of ECOWAS, the AU and the UN started submitting fortnightly monitoring reports. A major problem, however, was that Ivorian president Laurent Gbagbo refused to empower his prime minister, Seydou Diarra, with decision-making powers, and dragged his feet on amending laws that would have allowed his rival, Alassane Ouattara, to participate in national elections. Rebel leader Guillaume Soro, backed by the Coalition des Marcoussistes opposition parties, refused to disarm until these laws had been passed. Along with other opposition politicians, Soro frequently walked out of his ministerial post in Abidjan to protest what he and his rebel group saw as Gbagbo's recalcitrance in implementing the South African-brokered peace accords.

Between 2002 and 2011, Côte d'Ivoire remained divided between North and South, separated by a 6,240-strong UN operation in the country (UNOCI) established in February 2004 and backed up by 4,600 French troops (later reduced to about 900). The country's volatile Western region saw ethnic and community-based militias continue to clash violently, while the "zone of confidence" separating the belligerents continued to be violated, mainly by the rebel Forces Nouvelles. A peace conference was held under Thabo Mbeki's mediation in Tshwane in April 2005 to prevent a return to full-scale conflict. The host insisted that the parties would not leave the venue until an agreement had been reached. After four days of intense negotiations, the belligerents again committed themselves to implementing their earlier agreements on disarmament and elections signed in Linas-Marcoussis (France) and Accra (Ghana) between 2003 and 2004.[68]

The government of Laurent Gbagbo, Henri Konan Bédié's Democratic Party of Côte d'Ivoire (PDCI), Alassane Ouattara's Rally of Republicans

(RPR), and Guillaume Soro's Forces Nouvelles, however, continued to squabble over the Pretoria agreement. Mbeki was forced to reconvene the parties to talks again in South Africa in June 2005 to agree on the implementation of the accord. He set strict timetables for implementing the agreement: disarmament by August 2005, and elections two months later.

Consistent with the Pretoria accord, Mbeki urged Gbagbo to use his exceptional powers to amend discriminatory laws (on nationality, identification, the Human Rights Commission and the print media) in July 2005 when it became clear that the government-dominated Ivorian parliament would not amend them. After Gbagbo adopted these laws by decree, Soro and the Group of Seven opposition parties challenged these measures, as did Ouattara and Bédié. These politicians argued that certain groups in Côte d'Ivoire were still deprived of their rights under the nationality law and that the country's Independent Electoral Commission (IEC) needed to have clear primacy over the National Institute of Statistics in organising elections. Gbagbo further amended the laws on the IEC, the nationality code and the naturalisation law – again by decree – in August 2005, but this still did not completely break the deadlock.

Aside from recalcitrant politicians and warlords, friction between some of the key mediators further complicated the resolution of the Ivorian crisis. French sensitivities about South Africa's lead role in its *chasse gardée* (private hunting ground) erupted into the open when then president Jacques Chirac, during a visit to Senegal in February 2005, complained that the peace process in Côte d'Ivoire was too slow because the South Africans did not understand "the soul and psychology of West Africans". Regional actors, not least Mbeki, were taken aback by the cultural arrogance and political insensitivity of this statement, which underlined the continuing paternalism with which many Gallic policymakers still regarded their former colonies. The South Africans quipped that they had achieved more in three months than Paris had in two years of mediation (see Marchal in this volume on Franco-South African relations).

Then came the straw that broke the proverbial camel's back. During an address at the UN Security Council in New York in July 2005 by the South African defence minister, Mosiuoa Lekota, to report on his country's mediation efforts, he noted the distrust of the parties for each other and the powerlessness of the Ivorian prime minister. Lekota, however, urged the Security Council to delay imposing sanctions on the parties, controversially noting that international criticisms of Gbagbo were misplaced as he was cooperating with the peace process. The Ivorian opposition interpreted Lekota's UN address as a breach of impartiality in which they were being fingered for a failure to implement the Pretoria accord, while Gbagbo was being absolved of any blame. They thus urged the AU chair, Olusegun Obasanjo, to establish a political transition that would by implication subvert Mbeki's mediation process.[69] After a South African statement specifically blaming Soro for blocking the peace process, the Forces Nouvelles withdrew support from Mbeki's mediation efforts, publicly accusing him of bias toward Gbagbo. The rebel group then also urged Obasanjo to find an alternative way of resolving the impasse.

These events unfortunately coincided with tensions between South Africa and Nigeria over regional diplomatic issues and the acrimonious battle for a proposed African seat on a reformed UN Security Council. At a meeting of the AU's 15-member Peace and Security Council (PSC) on the margins of the UN General Assembly in September 2005, ECOWAS was tasked with overcoming this impasse: a clear attempt to shift the locus of peacemaking from South Africa to Nigeria.[70] Nigerian foreign minister Olu Adeniji became more involved with mediation efforts. Mbeki and Obasanjo jointly visited Côte d'Ivoire in November and December 2005 to meet with all the parties, and were eventually able to convince them to agree on a new prime minister, technocrat Charles Konan Banny, to replace the hapless Diarra.

However, the stalemate over implementing disarmament and the amended laws continued, and the holding of elections continued to be delayed. The distrust between the Ivorian parties remained strong, and divisions between the regional mediators did not help. After UN and AU representatives called for the Ivorian parliament (whose term had expired) to be dissolved, violent demonstrations by the Young Patriots in Abidjan and the West of the country targeted UN and French interests in January 2006. South Africa, which had earlier backed this position, reversed itself to support a parliamentary extension, again raising questions among rebel and opposition groups about Mbeki's bias towards Gbagbo.[71] In February 2006, a UN Security Council committee slapped targeted sanctions on two leaders of the Young Patriots, Charles Blé Goudé and Eugene Djué, as well as a Forces Nouvelles commander, Fofié Kouakou.[72] Contrary to Mbeki's advice, it seemed that the Council had chosen to continue to use sticks rather than carrots.

With both Obasanjo (privately) and Senegal's Abdoulaye Wade (publicly) increasingly critical of Mbeki's mediation, the South African president stepped down from his role at an AU meeting in October 2006. Though Mbeki argued that he was stepping down because South Africa needed to prepare for its role as a non-permanent member of the UN Security Council from January 2007 to December 2008,[73] it was clear that his mediation no longer enjoyed the confidence of key domestic and regional actors.

Mbeki would later become involved in another brief mediation effort in Côte d'Ivoire in December 2010 after the disputed presidential election involving Laurent Gbagbo and Alassane Ouattara. The AU appointed the former South African president (who had been removed from power in September 2008) to resolve the dispute. ECOWAS, the AU and much of the UN was backing Ouattara's election victory and urging Gbagbo to step down. After meeting with domestic and international parties in Abidjan, Mbeki cautioned the AU not to reduce the dispute to a stalemate between "good people and bad people" that would make resolution of the conflict more complicated. He then submitted a report to the AU suggesting a power-sharing deal between both parties.

ECOWAS promptly ignored Mbeki's plea, suspending Gbagbo's government from its institutions a day after the South African envoy left Abidjan in December 2010, with Nigeria threatening to use military force to remove Gbagbo from power. The UN Security Council would also soon recognise Ouattara's electoral victory and impose economic and legal sanctions on Gbagbo and his allies. As earlier noted, President Jacob Zuma – who was part of an AU presidential mediation team that visited Abidjan – also hesitated before belatedly recognising Ouattara's electoral victory in March 2011. This was not the finest hour of South African diplomacy, and Tshwane has had to make strenuous efforts to rebuild its relationship with President Ouattara.[74]

Côte d'Ivoire remains politically unstable following parliamentary elections in December 2011, which Laurent Gbagbo's party boycotted, even as the former president was sent to the International Criminal Court (ICC) in the Hague on charges of war crimes. There have been widespread allegations of "victor's justice" since crimes by troops supporting Ouattara were not investigated and punished. Despite the country's fragility, Côte d'Ivoire still remains the largest economy in francophone West Africa, the third-largest market in the sub-region after Nigeria and Ghana, and has gold mines, oil and other economic prospects in sectors that South African companies would like to invest in.

The government of Côte d'Ivoire opened a trade office in South Africa in September 2013 at a time when bilateral trade was about R1 billion annually, with a five-to-one balance in favour of South Africa. The three large South African companies in the country at this time were Randgold, MTN and SAA. By December 2015, the two countries had signed an agreement to establish a joint commission during a visit to Johannesburg by Alasanne Ouattara, which marked something of a rapprochement. Total South African exports to Côte d'Ivoire in 2016 were worth R1.6 billion, compared to R364 million in imports.[75]

"God" and unfulfilled "glory" have largely defined this relationship, but the allure of "gold" remains visible just over the horizon.

Concluding Reflections

This chapter has examined South Africa's relations, over the last two and a half decades, with three strategic countries in West Africa – Nigeria, Ghana and Côte d'Ivoire – as representing a quest for God, gold and glory. The relationship with Nigeria has been by far the most strategic, and is potentially the most important bilateral diplomatic partnership on the continent. Nigeria remains among South Africa's largest trading partners in Africa, and Tshwane and Abuja have cooperated in the fields of peacemaking and building the institutions of the AU and NEPAD. Both countries have sought to give Africa a stronger global voice, but have also competed as rivals on issues such as peacemaking in Côte d'Ivoire, Libya and Guinea-Bissau. A spat over human rights between Tshwane and Abuja in 1995 badly damaged bilateral relations, and the decade after Mbeki and Obasanjo left power by 2008 has been particularly fractious as the close personal relationship between the two leaders was not institutionalised. God, gold and glory have all been prominent in this relationship.

South Africa's relationship with Ghana has the potential to develop a political dimension, with growing political and military interactions through the bilateral joint commission. However, economic issues have mostly dominated this relationship between Africa's two largest gold producers. Where Ghana actively lobbied the South African government and companies to invest in its country, Nigeria simply sat back and waited for South African companies to "discover" Africa's largest market. Relations with Ghana have thus focused mainly on gold rather than God or glory.

Finally, South Africa's ties with Côte d'Ivoire started with great interest in the francophone country's investment and trade sectors before becoming suffused with human rights concerns following a military coup in Abidjan in 1999. Mbeki's controversial peacemaking role in the country between 2004 and 2006 ended in spectacular failure, and eventually lost the support of key domestic and regional actors. More recently, South Africa found itself on the wrong side of history as it failed to support unambiguously the winner of the 2010 election: Alassane Ouattara. This relationship has thus involved God and gold, but not much glory.

Notes

1. I have borrowed this expression from Ali A. Mazrui, *Cultural Forces in World Politics* (London: Currey, 1990), p. 30.

2. *See, for example*, Niall Ferguson, *Empire: How Britain Made the Modern World* (London: Penguin, 2003); Mazrui, *Cultural Forces in World Politics*; James Morris, *Pax Britannica* (London: Harvest, 1968).

3. *See* Chris Landsberg, "South Africa and the Making of the African Union and NEPAD: Mbeki's 'Progressive African Agenda'", in Adekeye Adebajo, Adebayo Adedeji and Chris Landsberg (eds), *South Africa in Africa: The Post-Apartheid Era* (Scottsville: University of KwaZulu-Natal Press, 2007), pp. 195–212.

4. All data gleaned from "Country Profiles", *Africa Report* no. 86 (December 2016–January 2017), pp. 183–195.

5. These data raise serious questions about the validity of Nomfundo Ngwenya's call for Senegal to act as an anchor state for South Africa in West Africa. *See* Nomfundo Xenia Ngwenya, "South Africa's Relations with African Anchor States", in Chris Landsberg and Jo-Ansie van Wyk (eds), *South African Foreign Policy Review*, vol. 1 (Tshwane: Africa Institute of South Africa and Institute for Global Dialogue, 2012), pp. 165–166.

6. This section builds on Adekeye Adebajo, "An Axis of Virtue? South Africa and Nigeria in Africa", in Adekeye Adebajo, *The Curse of Berlin: Africa After the Cold War* (New York: Columbia University Press; London: Hurst; Scottsville: University of KwaZulu Natal Press, 2010), pp. 143–161.

7. U. Joy Ogwu and W.O. Alli (eds), *Years of Reconstruction: Selected Foreign Policy Speeches of Olusegun Obasanjo* (Lagos: Nigerian Institute of International Affairs, 2007), p. 296.

8. "Nigeria, South Africa Sign Agreements on Various Sectors", *Premium Times* (Nigeria), 7 May 2013, http://premiumtimesng.com.

9. *See, for example,* Gilbert M. Khadiagala, "South Africa and Nigeria in The Liberal International Order," in Trine Flockhart, Charles A. Kupchan, Christiana Lin, Bartlomiej E. Nowak, Patrick W. Quirk and Lanxin Xiang (eds), *Liberal Order In A Post-Western World* (Washington, DC, Transatlantic Academy, 2014), pp. 95–108; Tola Odubajo and Solomon Akinboye, "Nigeria and South Africa: Collaboration or Competition?" *South African Journal of International Affairs* 24, no. 1 (2017), pp. 61–77.

10. Cited in Carl Niehaus, "Leaders Must Rethink Their Stance", *Sunday Independent* (South Africa), 2 July 2017, p. 13.

11. "Nigeria Overtakes South Africa As Africa's Biggest Economy", *BusinessTech* 19 October 2016, http://www.businesstech.co.za.

12. James Barber, *Mandela's World: The International Dimension of South Africa's Political Revolution, 1990–99* (Cape Town: David Philip, 2004), p. 110.

13. Wole Soyinka, *King Baabu* (London: Methuen, 2004).

14. *See* Ifeanyi Ezeugo, *Abacha: Another Evil Genius?* (Lagos: El-Rophekah International, 1998); Chuks Illoegbunam, "A Stubborn Dictator", *Guardian* (London), 9 June 1998, p. 16; Eghosa E. Osaghae, *Nigeria Since Independence: Crippled Giant* (Bloomington: Indiana University Press, 1998), pp. 273–310.

15. *See* Tom Lodge, *Mandela: A Critical Life* (Oxford: Oxford University Press, 2006); Nelson Mandela, *Long Walk to Freedom* (New York: Little, Brown, 1994); Anthony Sampson, *Mandela: The Authorised Biography* (London: HarperCollins, 1999).

16. *See* Adekeye Adebajo, *Thabo Mbeki: Africa's Philosopher-King* (Johannesburg: Jacana, 2016); Mark Gevisser, *Thabo Mbeki: The Dream Deferred* (Johannesburg: Jonathan Ball, 2007); Daryl Glaser (ed.), *Mbeki and After: Reflections on the Legacy of Thabo Mbeki* (Johannesburg: Wits University Press, 2010); Sean Jacobs and Richard Calland (eds), *Thabo Mbeki's World: The Politics and Ideology of the South African President* (Pietermaritzburg: University of Natal Press, 2002); Ronald Suresh Roberts, *Fit to Govern: The Native Intelligence of Thabo Mbeki* (Johannesburg: STE, 2007).

17. *See* Reuben Abati, "Obasanjo: A Psychoanalysis", *Guardian* (Lagos), 8 July 2001, p. 57; John Iliffe, *Obasanjo, Nigeria, and the World* (Suffolk, England, and Rochester, NY: Currey, and Boydell and Brewer, 2011); Olusegun Obasanjo, *My Command* (London: Heinemann, 1980); Oluremi Obasanjo, *Bitter-Sweet: My Life with Obasanjo* (Lagos: Diamond, 2008); Onukaba Adinoyi Ojo, *Olusegun Obasanjo: In the Eyes of Time* (Lagos: Africana Legacy, 1997).

18. Dianna Games, "An Oil Giant Reforms: The Experience of South African Firms Doing Business in Nigeria", *Business in Africa Report* no. 3 (Johannesburg: South African Institute of International Affairs, 2004), p. 66.

19. *See* interview with Bangumzi Sifingo, South Africa's High Commissioner to Nigeria, in *Traders* 13 (February/May 2003), pp. 18–19.

20. *See* James Lamont, "Mobile Phone Network Opens in Nigeria", *Financial Times*, 10 August 2001, p. 7.

21. Games, "An Oil Giant Reforms", p. 57.

22. John Daniel, Jessica Lutchman and Sanusha Naidu, "South Africa and Nigeria: Two Unequal Centres in a Periphery", in John Daniel, Roger Southall and Jessica Lutchman (eds), *State of the Nation: South Africa 2004–2005* (Cape Town: Human Sciences Research Council, 2005), pp. 559–560.

23. John Daniel and Nompumelelo Bhengu, "South Africa in Africa: Still a Formidable Player", in Roger Southall and Henning Melber (eds), *A New Scramble for Africa? Imperialism, Investment, and Development* (Scottsville: University of KwaZulu-Natal Press, 2009), p. 148.

24. Cited in Dianna Games, "Decade of Success and Missed Chances Between SA and Nigeria", *Business Day* (South Africa), 23 November 2009, p. 11.

25. Daniel and Bhengu, "South Africa in Africa", pp. 149–150, 158.

26. Daniel and Bhengu, "South Africa in Africa", p. 149. *See also* William M. Gumede, Vincent Nwanma and Patrick Smith, "South Africa/Nigeria: The Giants Tussle for Influence", *Africa Report* no. 3 (July 2006), p. 16.

27. Cited in Games, "Decade of Success and Missed Chances", p. 11.

28. Daniel and Bhengu, "South Africa in Africa", p. 149.

29. Daniel and Bhengu, "South Africa in Africa", p. 156.

30. "Agreed Minutes of the 6th Session of the Binational Commission Between the Republic of South Africa and the Federal Republic of Nigeria", Durban, 6–10 September 2004.

31. Confidential interview.

32. I am indebted for these points to Games, "An Oil Giant Reforms".

33. *See* the insightful essay by Kimberly Nichele Brown, "'Every Brother Ain't a Brother': Cultural Dissonance and Nigerian Malaise in *District 9's* New South Africa", in Maryellen Higgins (ed.), *Hollywood's Africa After 1994* (Ohio: Ohio University Press, 2012), pp. 193–206.

34. Vasco Martins, "The Côte d'Ivoire Crisis in Retrospect", *Portuguese Journal of International Affairs* (Spring/Summer 2011), p. 82.

35. *See* Centre for Conflict Resolution (CCR),"The Eagle and the Springbok: Strengthening the Nigeria/South Africa Relationship", Seminar Report no. 39 (Lagos, 9–10 June 2012), http://www.ccr.org.za.

36. Cited in "Nigeria, South Africa Trade Volume Fell to N1.3 Trillion in 2016", *Premium Times* (Nigeria), 9 February 2017, http://www.premiumtimesng.com.

37. *See, for example,* Damilola Oyedele, "Nigeria/South Africa Relations – Beyond the Rhetoric", *This Day* (Lagos), 13 March 2016; Sam Mkokeli, "Will Zuma's Visit to Nigeria Bolster Trade?", *Business Day* (South Africa), 14 March 2016.

38. Richard Duffy, "Mining: AngloGold Ashanti", in Dianna Games (ed.), *Business in Africa: Corporate Insights* (Johannesburg: Penguin, 2012), p. 99.

39. *See* Dennis Austin, *Politics in Ghana, 1946–1960* (Oxford: Oxford University Press, 1964); Ali A. Mazrui, "Nkrumah: The Leninist Czar", in Ali A. Mazrui, *On Heroes and Uhuru-Worship* (London: Longman, 1967), pp. 113–134; June Milne, *Kwame Nkrumah: A Biography* (London: Panaf, 2006); Kwame Nkrumah, *Africa Must Unite* (London: Panaf, 1963).

40. *See* Adebajo, *The Curse of Berlin*, pp. 233–259.

41. *See, for example,* Kwesi Aning and Festus K. Aubyn, "Ghana", in Alex J. Bellamy and Paul D. Williams (eds), *Providing Peacekeepers: The Politics, Challenges, and Future of United Nations Peacekeeping Contributions* (Oxford: Oxford University Press, 2013), pp. 267–290.

42. "SA Pledges Investment to Ghana", *The Star* (Johannesburg), 10 July 1998, http://www.iol.co.za.

43. Pamela Dube, "SA-Ghana Trade Links Set to Grow", *Sowetan* (Johannesburg), 8 July 1998, http://www.sowetanlive.co.za.

44. Carin Voges and Lerato Mataboge, "South Africa's Bilateral Relations with West Africa", in *South Africa Yearbook of International Affairs, 2001/02* (Johannesburg: South African Institute of International Affairs, 2001), pp. 332–333.

45. "Joint Communiqué on the Occasion of the State Visit to Ghana of His Excellency, Mr Thabo Mbeki, President of the Republic of South Africa from 4–7 October 2000".

46. Hany Besada, "Glimpse of Hope in West Africa: The Experience of South African Firms Doing Business in Ghana", *Business in Africa Report* no. 4 (Johannesburg: South African Institute of International Affairs, 2005), p. 37.

47. South African Government Information, "Minister Maite Nkoana-Mashabane to Co-Chair South Africa and Ghana Permanent Joint Commission for Cooperation to Be Held in Accra" (Tshwane: South African Department of International Relations and Cooperation, 5 March 2010).

48. Besada, "Glimpse of Hope in West Africa", pp. 37–38.

49. Duffy, "Mining", pp. 99–100.

50. Daniel, Lutchman and Naidu, "South Africa and Nigeria", p. 553.

51. Judi Hudson, "South Africa's Economic Expansion into Africa", in Adebajo, Adedeji and Landsberg, *South Africa in Africa*, p. 136.

52. Besada, "Glimpse of Hope in West Africa", p. 51.

53. Ciaran Ryan, "Ghana Leads Business Boom", *Mail and Guardian* (Johannesburg), 30 November 2012, http://www.mg.co.za.

54. Besada, "Glimpse of Hope in West Africa", pp. 45–52.

55. Besada, "Glimpse of Hope in West Africa", pp. 41–70.

56. *See* Agreement on the Establishment of a Permanent Joint Cooperation Between the Government of the Republic of South Africa and the Government of the Republic of Ghana", Accra, 2 November 2004.

57. South African Government Information, "Minister Maite Nkoana-Mashabane to Co-Chair".

58. "PetroSA to Buy Stake in Ghana's State Owned Oil Company", *SABC News*, 21 April 2012, http://www.sabc.co.za.

59. South Africa Department of Trade and Industry, "South Africa and Ghana to Intensify the Implementation of the Economic and Technical Cooperation Mou" (Tshwane, 28 June 2013).

60. Figures from the South African Revenue Service (SARS), *see* http://www.sars.gov.za.

61. This title is borrowed from Christopher Hitchens, *The Missionary Position: Mother Teresa in Theory and Practice* (London: Verso, 1995).

62. Quoted in Eboe Hutchful, "Understanding the African Security Crisis", in Abdel-Fatau Musah and J. Kayode Fayemi (eds), *Mercenaries: An African Security Dilemma* (London: Pluto, 2000), p. 218.

63. Voges and Mataboge, "South Africa's Bilateral Relations with West Africa", pp. 334–335.

64. This section on South Africa's peacemaking efforts in Côte d'Ivoire builds on Adekeye Adebajo, *UN Peacekeeping in Africa: From the Suez Crisis to the Sudan Conflicts* (Boulder, CO, and London: Rienner, 2011), pp. 152–161.

65. United Nations (UN) Security Council Resolution 1572, 15 November 2004.

66. UN Security Council Resolution 1643, 15 December 2005.

67. Security Council Report, "Monthly Forecast January 2006", 22 December 2005, p. 14; Security Council Report, "Monthly Forecast April 2006", 30 March 2006, p. 8. Both available at http://www.securitycouncilreport.org.

68. Chris Maroleng, "Côte d'Ivoire: Perils and Prospects", in *South Africa Yearbook of International Affairs, 2005* (Johannesburg: South African Institute of International Affairs, 2006), p. 29.

69. Maroleng, "Côte d'Ivoire", pp. 33–34.

70. This information on Côte d'Ivoire draws on two UN Secretary-General's Reports to the Security Council on Côte d'Ivoire, UN Doc. S/2005/398, 17 June 2005, and UN Doc. S/2005/604, 26 September 2005.

71. Francis Ikome, "Côte d'Ivoire Follow-Up Dialogue", unpublished report of the Institute for Global Dialogue from a seminar held in Gauteng, South Africa, on 21 June 2006, p. 4.

72. UN Secretary-General's Report to the Security Council on Côte d'Ivoire, UN Doc. S/2006/222, 11 April 2006, p. 5.

73. Abdul Lamin, "South Africa's Diplomatic Intervention in Côte d'Ivoire, 2004–2006: Lessons for Future Peace Diplomacy in Africa", *South African Yearbook of International Affairs 2006/7* (Johannesburg: South African Institute of International Affairs, 2007), p. 295.

74. Some of the information in this paragraph is from Martins, "The Côte d'Ivoire Crisis in Retrospect", pp. 72–84.

75. Figures from the South African Revenue Service, *see* http://www.sars.gov.za.

CHAPTER 9

SOUTH AFRICA IN EASTERN AFRICA: KENYA, TANZANIA, UGANDA AND SUDAN/SOUTH SUDAN

Gilbert M. Khadiagala

Post-apartheid South Africa's foreign policy towards Eastern Africa has mainly been characterised by the building of bilateral political and economic ties with Kenya, Tanzania, Uganda and Sudan/South Sudan. Tanzania and Uganda, owing to their proximity to conflict-affected Burundi and the Democratic Republic of the Congo (DRC), have also served as entry points for South Africa's conflict resolution efforts in the wider Great Lakes region. Moreover, the tenor and depth of post-apartheid South Africa's bilateral engagements in Eastern Africa have primarily been shaped by pre-existing historical ties between the African National Congress (ANC) and the ruling parties in the sub-region, and by its burgeoning corporate interests in Eastern Africa. Although Kenya, Tanzania and Uganda – three key sub-regional actors – coalesced with Burundi and Rwanda into a resuscitated East African Community (EAC) in 1999, South Africa's multilateral engagement with the EAC is a far more recent phenomenon. It is only since October 2008 that Tshwane (Pretoria) has tried to take a multilateral approach to the East African sub-region through a proposed tripartite arrangement involving the EAC, the Common Market for Eastern and Southern Africa (COMESA) and the Southern African Development Community (SADC), which was initiated at a meeting in Kampala in October 2008.

This chapter analyses the evolution of South Africa's policy in Eastern Africa since 1994. In so doing, it focuses őn the nature and extent of Tshwane's bilateral political and economic relations with its five key partners in the sub-region: Kenya, Tanzania, Uganda and Sudan/ South Sudan. I argue that while South Africa's economic interests and conflict resolution efforts have enhanced its ties with Eastern Africa, the sub-region remains – compared to Southern Africa – politically marginal to the country's foreign policy. I conclude with the recommendation that, given the rich multiplicity of states in Eastern Africa, South Africa's long-term policies towards the sub-region should instead focus more on the building of multilateral institutions that strengthen existing political, economic and security relationships.

Eastern Africa in South Africa's Foreign Policy: Bilateralism or Multilateralism?

A dominant theme in post-apartheid South Africa's foreign policy over the past two and a half decades has been the narrow engagement with the wider African continent. After 1994, beyond its own Southern African sub-region, Tshwane did not regard policies as germane to its interests, unless they were tied to the projection of its broad continental image; the reconstruction of African continental institutions; and the building of alliances with key African leaders for the achievement of these two objectives.[1] This was somewhat understandable given the political and economic links that South Africa had already established in Southern Africa by the end of apartheid in 1994 (see Sachikonye in this volume). Even so, in the immediate post-apartheid period, there was intense debate within the South African foreign policy establishment about the need to set priorities in Africa. In the initial phase of its post-liberation engagement with the continent, Tshwane's focus came to be on the establishment of diplomatic missions across Africa to underscore South Africa's resurgence as an African power. This approach, though, generated a bilateral bent in South Africa's foreign policy that has subsequently dominated its posture towards Eastern Africa.

Providing leadership for the construction of African institutions – particularly the African Union (AU) (see Maloka in this volume) – inevitably injected a modicum of multilateralism into South Africa's policies towards the continent. President Thabo Mbeki's (1999–2008) twin stratagems of an "African Renaissance" and a role in conflict resolution for South Africa compelled the country to scramble to multiple actors and constituencies across Africa (see Curtis in this volume). In Eastern Africa, Tshwane's concern with conflict resolution led it to engage with Tanzania and Uganda in multilateral stabilisation efforts in the Great Lakes region. While these stabilisation efforts became the most visible and publicised role of South Africa's foreign policy in Eastern Africa, at the same time its bilateral relations with individual countries in the sub-region also flourished with the expansion of South African corporate and commercial engagements in individual East African countries. (See Vickers and Cawood in this volume.)

Yet the primacy of bilateralism has persisted in South Africa's relations with Eastern Africa, due at least in part to the absence of a dominant power with which Tshwane could engage to anchor its relations in the sub-region. The symmetry of power in Eastern Africa means that Kenya, Tanzania and Uganda have each been able to play gateway and bridge-building roles in the sub-region without any of them assuming a dominant position. Tanzania, as a member of both the EAC and SADC, initially had a unique advantage that could have helped it become an interlocutor for South Africa's foreign policy in Eastern Africa, and to serve as Tshwane's gateway to the sub-region. However, Tanzania's dual membership generated ambiguity around its identity within Eastern Africa and complicated the emergence of a strong regional community around the EAC. While for Tanzania its double role has since constrained coherent policymaking around sub-regional economic and security integration, for South Africa, this has deepened the bilateralism that undergirds its posture towards Eastern Africa. With the exception of Dar es Salaam's role in contributing to peacemaking efforts in the Great Lakes region, South Africa has been inclined to view Tanzania as a Southern African, rather than an East African, country. As discussed in greater detail later in this chapter, Tanzania's participation in the 2013 SADC intervention force to stabilise the eastern Congo has reinforced the country's Southern African identity and caused further rifts between countries in Eastern Africa such as Burundi, Rwanda and Uganda that harbour suspicious about South Africa's intervention in the Great Lakes region. I will next assess South Africa's key bilateral ties with Kenya, Tanzania, Uganda and Sudan/South Sudan.

South Africa's Key Bilateral Relations in Eastern Africa

Kenya

After its inauguration in 1994, South Africa's ANC-led government had lukewarm relations with the Kenyan government due to Nairobi's long years of collaboration with the previous apartheid regime. In the 1960s and 1970s, Kenya's president, Jomo Kenyatta (1963–1978), paid lip service to the anti-apartheid struggle, while permitting the growth of economic and commercial ties with Pretoria. During the presidency of Daniel arap Moi (1978–2002), Nairobi supported African and international resolutions that prohibited cooperation with apartheid South Africa, but breached these proscriptions by discretely continuing to maintain trade relations with the white minority-led government in Pretoria.[2] Kenya's close ties with Western countries (such as the United States (US) and Britain) that maintained formal relations with the apartheid regime also severely compromised its ability to participate in economic sanctions against South Africa. Thus, for example, Kenya permitted European airlines, including British Airways, flying to South Africa to refuel en route in Nairobi. As one Kenyan newspaper analyst noted: "Pretoria's perception of former presidents Jomo Kenyatta, Moi and Kibaki is that that their governments dined with the perpetrators of apartheid. At the time [the] ANC was waging a guerrilla war against the white supremacist National Party, Nairobi had flourishing economic and diplomatic relations with conservative political parties in the West that propped up apartheid."[3] In June 1990, Kenya defied the Organisation of African Unity (OAU) by making official contact with the apartheid government in South Africa. Furthermore, as Joseph Kipkoech has noted: "[A]fter the release of Nelson Mandela, Kenya allowed South African Airways to land in Nairobi despite the African National Congress (ANC's) call for maintaining the economic boycott until the structure of apartheid was dismantled. Even before the conclusion of reforms, Kenya invited President Frederik de Klerk in June 1991."[4]

Given this pattern of defiance by Kenya of African voices on apartheid South Africa, relations between the ANC-led government in Tshwane and Nairobi were frosty after 1994. Compared to its neighbours, Kenya was accorded a low profile in South Africa's engagements in Eastern Africa. This led Nairobi, which regards itself as the major power in Eastern Africa, to feel ignored and slighted by South Africa's post-apartheid leaders.

Two well-publicised events symbolised the state of play. While transiting through Kenya en route to Egypt in October 1997, President Nelson Mandela (1994–1999) declined to meet a Kenyan ministerial delegation that had come to welcome him at Nairobi's Jomo Kenyatta International Airport.[5] In 1999, President Thabo Mbeki did the same, claiming that he was too tired to disembark from his aircraft to meet Kenyan officials at the airport. In a country in which the government often deploys massive crowds at the airport to greet visiting heads of state, the two incidents remain etched in Kenya's collective memory, and subsequently affected Nairobi's attitude toward post-apartheid South Africa's leadership. Although Mandela briefly visited Kenya in 1990 as part of his African tour after he was released from prison, neither Mandela nor Mbeki made any state visits to Kenya while in office, and instead skirted around Nairobi while visiting Tanzania, Uganda, Rwanda and Ethiopia. After Mandela's death in December 2013, various Kenyan newspapers highlighted theirs as the only "African country that has not erected a monument or named an institution in Mandela's honour".[6]

Although Kenya and South Africa signed various cooperation agreements in the late 1990s and early 2000s, it was not until President Jacob Zuma's historic state visit to Nairobi in October 2016 that the two countries signed formal agreements in various fields including: visa waiver for diplomatic and official passport holders; military training, visits and technical assistance; mutual assistance between customs administrations; police cooperation; bio-diversity conservation and management, and collaboration on the Lamu–Port Southern Sudan–Ethiopia Transport (LAPSSET) Corridor. The visit was, however, overshadowed by Kenyan complaints about South Africa's restrictive visa regime for Kenyan citizens travelling to South Africa, and criticisms of non-tariff barriers imposed on Kenyan exports to South Africa.[7]

Economic tensions further contributed to the deterioration of bilateral relations between Tshwane and Nairobi after the apartheid era. Although South Africa made references to Kenya's significance as the gateway to the larger Eastern African market, there was resentment in Kenya about the encroachment of South African businesses into the sub-region. In Kenya as elsewhere, South Africa's multinational companies made aggressive forays after 1994, with expectations of capturing vast untapped markets in Eastern Africa. (See Vickers and Cawood in this volume.) However, these South African businesses were not received enthusiastically by their Kenyan counterparts, leading to the much-publicised "Beer Wars" of the mid-1990s.[8] South African Breweries (SAB) entered the Kenyan market in 1996, but faced stiff resistance over market shares from East African Breweries. In 2000, SAB withdrew following an acrimonious spate of accusations. SAB's precipitous withdrawal from the country set the pace for investment failures by other South African companies in Kenya, including Metro Cash and Carry, Shoprite Checkers and the telecoms giant Mobile Telephone Networks (MTN), in the early 2000s. The reasons that were identified for these initial failures included, among others, the reluctance of South African companies to build partnerships with their Kenyan counterparts, and the arrogance and condescending attitudes of South African companies toward their local Kenyan partners.[9] (See also Adebajo, and Nzongola-Ntalaja in this volume.)

However, since 2012–2013, South African businesses have re-entered Kenya through mergers and acquisitions, particularly in the banking, capital markets, insurance, accountancy, pharmaceuticals, retail, tourism and engineering sectors, with mixed results.[10] These businesses include Massmart, MTN Business Kenya, Hoggers, Telkom (which has re-gained a strong local presence through a series of direct and indirect acquisitions of local firms), Tiger Brands, Dimension Data, Stanlib and FirstRand Bank. This new wave of South African investments has benefited from a growing understanding about the Kenyan market, as well as a greater appreciation for Kenyan sensitivities. In December 2012, Kenya and South Africa created a joint trade committee to address tariff and non-tariff barriers and to move towards a binding trade and investment pact, in order to smooth their fractious bilateral relations. At a key Kenya–South Africa Business Forum meeting in Nairobi in January 2013, delegates deliberated on ways to reduce Kenya's trade deficit with South Africa. While there were about 35 South African companies operating in Kenya in 2014, the country's imports from South Africa amounted to R7.8 billion, with exports to South Africa totalling only about R243 million in 2013.[11] Bilateral trade between the two countries rose to R8.4 billion by 2016.[12]

President Zuma's visit to Nairobi in October 2016 signalled a new phase in Kenya–South Africa relations, starting the slow process of ending the historical "Cold War" over Nairobi's flirtations with the apartheid regime. The broadening of trade relations and the increasing numbers of Kenyan professionals working in South Africa has also eased tensions in the relationship and created a potentially sound foundation for resolving lingering problems around trade and migration.

Tanzania

As the ANC's home during the liberation struggle, Tanzania holds a special place in South Africa's foreign policy. For many years, Tanzania was an active participant in Southern African affairs through the Frontline States (FLS) and the Southern African Development Coordination Conference (SADCC), the predecessor to SADC.[13] Tanzania was one of the few African countries that Mandela visited after his release from prison in February 1990, underscoring the unique place that Dar es Salaam occupies in South Africa's foreign policy. During Mandela's funeral in December 2013, Tanzania's president, Jakaya Kikwete, spoke of the abiding ties between the two countries, dating back to the early 1960s when Dar es Salaam granted travel documents to leading South African nationalists.[14]

Throughout the 1970s, Tanzania concentrated on building its relations with Southern African countries, partly because of the deterioration in its relationships with its East African neighbours – specifically Kenya and Uganda. Thus, following the break-up of the first East African Community in 1977, Tanzania opted to be a Southern African country in political, security, and economic terms by joining the FLS and SADCC. Then, the revival of sub-regional institutions in Eastern Africa in the 1990s, at the same time as the political transformation of Southern Africa with the end of apartheid, raised profound questions about Tanzania's sub-regional status and membership. Faced with the conundrum of whether to "return" to Eastern Africa or to strengthen its ties with the Southern African Development Community (which replaced SADCC in 1992), Tanzania opted to do both. (On SADC, see Saunders and Nagar in this volume.) However, this duality put Dar es Salaam in an anomalous and problematic position that was reinforced by its decision to withdraw from the Common Market for Eastern and Southern Africa in July 1999. Both Kenya and Uganda remained in COMESA.

Tanzania's SADC membership has consolidated its economic and political relations with South Africa. Warm relations between the ANC and Tanzania's dominant ruling party, Chama Cha Mapinduzi (CCM), as well as close government-to-government relations, have helped solidify economic relationships. Furthermore, membership obligations within SADC have forced Tanzania to develop stronger economic relations with South Africa than with the rest of Eastern Africa. Unlike Kenya, Tanzania actively encouraged South African businesses to invest in its economy after the dismantling of apartheid. Consequently, South Africa's corporate incursion has been central to post-socialist liberalisation and privatisation processes in Tanzania. Thus, compared to Kenya, which hosts about 35 South African companies, there are more than 150 South African companies in Tanzania, in the areas of mining, agriculture and tourism.[15] As South African analyst Judi Hudson notes: "Many Kenyans refer to neighbouring Tanzania as 'little Joburg' because of the predominance of South African companies there."[16] More poignantly, a Tanzanian pastoralist community activist summed up South Africa's growing influx thus: "We now live in the United States of South Africa."[17] Both Mbeki and Zuma led high-level South African delegations to Dar es Salaam, in September 1999 and December 2012 respectively, under the framework of the South Africa–Tanzania Heads of State Economic Commission. The Presidential Economic Commission was established in September 2005 by both countries to encourage regular talks on economic issues, trade, diplomacy, tourism, as well as social and political issues.

Between 1994 and 2005, South Africa was the third-largest source of foreign direct investment (FDI) in Tanzania, injecting nearly R3.9 billion into the Tanzanian economy.[18] By 2011, South Africa had taken the lead from Britain and Canada in terms of FDI inflows. According to a Tanzanian government report, in 2011 South Africa was the leading source of FDI in Tanzania, with investments worth over $2.1 billion; followed by Britain, with investments valued at $1.3 billion; and Canada taking third place, at $1 billion.[19] During Tanzanian president Kikwete's state visit to South Africa in July 2011, the two countries signed agreements on the creation of a bi-national commission and cooperation in arts and culture.[20] However, it is also worth noting that the expansion of South African capital has generated resentment among some Tanzanians. As US scholar Richard Schroeder observed:

> Many Tanzanians, whose political consciousness was shaped under the socialist government of the country's first president, Julius Nyerere, have objected to the rapid privatization of nearly 400 parastatal concerns, including some of the country's most prized economic assets. Others have bemoaned the dumping of cheap goods on national markets, and the extraction of valuable natural resources on concessionary terms by foreign nationals. In each of these areas, the insult added to injury has been the leading role of South African companies – many of them white-owned and managed, and banned

from Tanzania during the long struggle against apartheid in which Tanzania played a leading and costly role. In the eyes of many Tanzanians, the fact that South African companies have now become so centrally involved in their economy effectively de-legitimizes the Tanzanian reform process itself.[21]

Beyond strengthening economic engagement, South Africa's policymakers have also looked to Tanzania as the gateway to conflict resolution in the wider region. Tanzania was first cast into this role when Nelson Mandela became the principal mediator in the Burundi peace process following the death of Julius Nyerere in October 1999. Mandela used Tanzania's mediation infrastructure to bring the warring Burundian parties together to sign the Arusha peace agreement of August 2000, which paved the way for the stabilisation of Burundi. Following the deployment of a South African military protection force in 2001 to assist in the implementation of the Arusha agreement, South Africa's then deputy president, Jacob Zuma, mediated comprehensive ceasefire agreements between the transitional government and Burundian rebels.[22] South Africa and Tanzania also broadened the diplomatic engagement around the Burundi peace process through the establishment of a multilateral framework – the Great Lakes Regional Peace Initiative on Burundi – with Tanzania and Uganda as its anchor states. According to Adonia Ayebare, a Ugandan diplomat and key participant in the initiative: "Zuma formed a technical committee of intelligence officials from Uganda, Tanzania, and South Africa to provide him with strategic information on the motivation of the parties and the regional dynamics that impacted on the talks. This committee could fulfil an early warning role within the mediator's team."[23]

After elections in Burundi in 2005, South Africa – under the leadership of its minister of safety and security, Charles Nqakula – led efforts through the aforementioned Great Lakes regional peace initiative, together with the Joint Verification and Monitoring Mechanism (JVMM), to secure a ceasefire agreement between the Burundian government and the remaining rebel group of Agathon Rwasa. Over a four-year period, Nqakula's tireless diplomatic efforts managed to convince Rwasa to join the electoral process in 2010 (though they never made it to the ballot claiming fraud and intimidation). As one of South Africa's major success stories in the Great Lakes region, the stabilisation of Burundi drew on the collaboration with Tanzania and Uganda. Tshwane gradually strengthened its multilateral engagement from 2005, by subsequently participating in the International

Conference on the Great Lakes Region (ICGLR), a much larger organisation of regional and international actors created in the early 2000s that has since sought to bring peace to the region. (See also Curtis, and Nzongola-Ntalaja in this volume.)

However, the weaknesses of the ICGLR in dealing with the obstacles to peace and security in the DRC forced South Africa and Tanzania to adopt a more aggressive posture that changed the dynamics of the Congolese conflict and reshaped the nature of South African engagement in the sub-region. Notably, Tanzania – as a fellow SADC member – emerged as a key partner for South Africa in the Eastern African sub-region beyond Burundi. The context was provided by the destabilisation of the eastern Congo by a rebel movement, the March 23 Movement (M23), that articulated Tutsi grievances and was linked to Rwanda and Uganda. After elections in the DRC in December 2006, the National Congress for the Defence of the People (CNDP) and M23 emerged as the major militias fighting the Congolese army and other armed groups in the sub-region. Despite efforts by Belgium, Britain, France, the United States, the United Nations Organisation Stabilisation Mission in the DRC (MONUSCO) and the ICGLR, the situation in the eastern Congo deteriorated in November 2012, when M23 rebels captured Kisangani, threatened to overrun MONUSCO and triggered a severe humanitarian crisis.[24]

The M23 offensive led to new diplomatic efforts centred on negotiations between the government of Joseph Kabila and the M23 in Uganda, and on a new military initiative to confront the rebels in the eastern DRC. An ICGLR summit in Kampala in November 2012 proposed the "operationalization of the international neutral force, with a view of deploying it within a period of three months", into the eastern Congo.[25] This idea was transformed into reality during a SADC summit held in Tanzania in December 2012, where the sub-regional body committed to creating a standby force of Tanzanian, South African and Malawian battalions.[26] Then, at a joint summit in Addis Ababa in February 2013, the ICGLR and SADC signed a peace, security and cooperation framework for the DRC and the region that authorised this Force Intervention Brigade (FIB), acting under the auspices of MONUSCO, to assist the Congolese army in forcibly disarming rebels in the eastern DRC. Following intensive negotiations between SADC and the United Nations (UN), in March 2013, the UN Security Council adopted Resolution 2098, authorising deployment of the 3,069-strong intervention brigade. In October 2013, the SADC-led force routed the M23, scattering its forces into Rwanda and Uganda.[27] To signal this victory over the M23 rebels, President Jacob Zuma paid a high-profile visit to Kinshasa in October 2013 and subsequently hosted a joint ICGLR-SADC summit in Tshwane in November 2013. The meeting directed the secretariats of the two organisations to harmonise their work in implementing, monitoring and evaluating the framework on peace, security and cooperation, and agreed to establish a mechanism for their ministers of defence and foreign affairs to meet every six months to review progress, leading to an annual joint ICGLR-SADC summit at the level of heads of state and government.[28] (On the Great Lakes, see Nzongola-Ntalaja in this volume.)

The collaboration between Tanzania and South Africa in the eastern Congo not only strengthened SADC's hand in the Great Lakes, but also led to growing tensions with Rwanda and Uganda. In September and October 2013, a war of words between Tanzanian president Jakaya Kikwete and his Rwandan counterpart, Paul Kagame, was exacerbated when Dar es Salaam expelled 7,000 Rwandan nationals in September 2013 terming them illegal immigrants.[29] Furthermore, Kikwete irked Rwanda by suggesting a dialogue between Kigali and Democratic Forces for the Liberation of Rwanda (FDLR) rebels implicated in the 1994 Rwandan genocide.[30] Furthermore, this deterioration in relations came amid claims that Rwanda had convinced Kenya and Uganda to sideline Tanzania in negotiations on sub-regional infrastructure, immigration and a proposed EAC political federation from which Dar es Salaam was excluded.[31] Confronted with this situation, President Kikwete asked the Tanzanian parliament in September 2013: "Is there a conspiracy to push Tanzania out of the EAC? Is it that my counterparts from Kenya, Rwanda, Uganda hate me personally? We met on April 28 [2013] at a summit in Arusha. Two months later, they met to discuss how to implement the same issues we discussed in April without inviting me. This is a signal of their intent to isolate me. How can we integrate via isolation?"[32] It eventually took the intervention of Kenya to calm the growing diplomatic rift between Dar es Salaam and Kigali. Under the Tanzanian president, John Magufuli, elected in October 2015, relations between Tshwane and Dar es Salaam remained strong. Bilateral trade between the two countries was R1.8 billion in 2016.[33]

Uganda

During the apartheid era, Uganda's ties with the ANC were not as extensive as in the case of Tanzania. Yet, Ugandan president Yoweri Museveni welcomed ANC cadres into his country at a critical moment in 1988, when the UN Security Council mandated the relocation of the ANC from military training camps in Angola. Hosted at the O.R. Tambo School of Leadership on the outskirts of Kampala, the ANC soldiers in Uganda grew in number from 154 in 1989 to 3,000 in 1994, when the Ugandan government arranged for their repatriation to South Africa to participate in the country's first democratic election. In appreciation of President Museveni's support, Nelson Mandela visited Uganda in July 1990 after his release from prison. Following his inauguration as South Africa's first democratically elected president, Mandela visited Uganda two more times, in 1998 and 1999, during the negotiations to end Burundi's civil war. Later, both Thabo Mbeki and Jacob Zuma also made state visits to Uganda, in 2005 and 2010 respectively, to underscore Kampala's contribution to the fight against apartheid.[34]

The bonds between Uganda and South Africa have been enshrined in a number of bilateral economic and political accords, including an agreement establishing a joint commission on cooperation in 2012; a convention on avoidance of double taxation and prevention of fiscal evasion with respect to income taxes in May 1997; an agreement on promotion and protection of investments in March 2010; a bilateral trade agreement in March 2010; and an agreement establishing a joint permanent economic commission in December 2005.[35] In addition, the Uganda–South Africa Business Forum plays an important role in encouraging bilateral trade and investment. South Africa is among the largest investors in Uganda, accounting for net FDI inflows of over $500 million in 2012. According to Kampala's estimates, this accounted for about 10 per cent of total FDI in Uganda.[36] The South African investments are mainly in telecommunications (MTN Uganda); breweries (SABMiller); finance (Stanbic Bank); wholesale and retail (Shoprite Checkers, Metro Cash and Carry, Woolworths and Game); poultry (Bokomo); insurance (Sanlam); energy (Eskom); and tourism (hotels). In 2013 South African exports to Uganda amounted to R1.8 billion and imports from Uganda to R51.2 million.[37] On a state visit to South Africa in March 2012, Museveni hailed South African investments for having created jobs in Uganda, and encouraged more businesses to tap into the opportunities provided by East Africa's common market, with Ugandan products able to enter duty-free into Kenya, Tanzania, Rwanda and Burundi.

Beyond the economic sphere and, as previously mentioned, South Africa acknowledged Uganda's importance in the Great Lakes region by including it in the Burundi peace processes from the late 1990s onwards. The success of the various South African initiatives on Burundi led by

Mandela, Zuma and Nqakula depended considerably on President Museveni's knowledge of, and influence over, the Burundian parties. Although disagreements have emerged over Uganda's role in the DRC in recent years, Museveni and Zuma have forged long-lasting cordial relations.[38] Bilateral trade between the two countries was R1.8 billion in 2016.[39] Museveni, for example, was one of the earliest supporters of the African Capacity for Immediate Response to Crises (ACIRC), an interim measure proposed by South Africa in the aftermath of French interventions in Mali and the Central African Republic (CAR) in 2013, pending the establishment of the African Standby Force (ASF).[40] On a visit to Tswhane in November 2016, Museveni reiterated the significance of South Africa–Uganda relations.

Sudan/South Sudan

The end of apartheid in 1994 coincided with a raging north-south civil war in Sudan that consumed the diplomatic energies of regional as well as international actors. Although South Africa established diplomatic relations with Khartoum in 1994, it adopted a low profile towards the conflict, preferring to work with continental institutions to provide moral support to regional initiatives under the auspices of the Intergovernmental Authority on Development (IGAD). However, after South Sudan gained its independence in July 2011, South Africa played a more prominent role in post-conflict reconstruction efforts in Juba, owing largely to the ANC's pre-existing links with the Sudan People's Liberation Movement (SPLM). Furthermore, through the high-profile role of its former president, Thabo Mbeki, in mediating the continuing bilateral conflict between Sudan and South Sudan, South Africa has retained a significant presence in Khartoum as well.

Beginning in the mid-1990s, the IGAD mediation framework on Sudan was for long the main initiative for resolving the Sudanese conflict. With the exception of those making up the Friends of IGAD group,[41] there were few other external actors from beyond the sub-region involved in the conflict. Preoccupied with domestic reconciliation and reconstruction, as well as issues in Southern Africa and the Great Lakes region, South Africa's policymakers did not pay much attention to the conflict in Sudan during this period. However, a shift occurred in July 2003 when, at a decisive moment in negotiations, Khartoum tried to scuttle Kenya's mediation by inviting South Africa to take over the mediation process. The Sudanese overture to South Africa did not receive a positive reception from the

Kenyan mediators, who viewed it as an attempt to undermine the IGAD framework. South Africa initially embraced the invitation, finding an opportunity to exert its muscle in the Horn of Africa. In the face of opposition from Kenya and other IGAD states, however, Tshwane declined to lead the process.[42]

South Africa's post-conflict reconstruction and development roles in South Sudan have followed primarily from the strengthening of relations between the two countries' ruling parties: the Sudan People's Liberation Movement and the ANC. The SPLM, since its formation in 1983, has forged close ties with the African National Congress. In the Zimbabwean capital of Harare, the ANC and SPLM shared offices; after 1994, the ANC gave up these offices for the SPLM.[43] In the period leading up to the referendum on, and independence of, South Sudan in 2011, South Africa launched numerous training programmes for South Sudanese leaders to prepare them for the tasks of governing. By July 2011, when South Sudan emerged into statehood, Tshwane had trained more than 1,600 South Sudanese civil servants and diplomats as part of its capacity-building programme.[44] Complementing the strengthening of party-to-party relations between the ANC and the SPLM, Tshwane and Juba signed an agreement establishing formal diplomatic relations between the two countries that laid the basis for political, military, and economic agreements following South Sudan's independence. Notably, South Africa's military presence in South Sudan dates back to 2004, when South Africa's Mechem, a subsidiary of Denel (an arms parastatal), started de-mining operations in the then Southern Sudan.[45] There have since been reports of weapons purchases from Denel by South Sudan and of the training of South Sudanese security personnel by the South African National Defence Force (SANDF).[46]

On the economic front, South Africa vigorously pursued trade and investment opportunities in South Sudan, even before the latter gained its independence. For example, in February 2009, South Africa's then Department of Foreign Affairs (DFA) – now the Department of International Relations and Cooperation (DIRCO) – hosted a meeting with key South Sudanese figures to explore economic opportunities for South African firms. Similarly, in July 2009, South Africa's Department of Trade and Industry (DTI) organised a trade and investment mission to South Sudan, comprising representatives from the public and private sectors including telecommunications, agriculture, forestry, water purification, timber, financial services, infrastructure development, energy and minerals.

Following the independence of South Sudan, South Africa's Department of Trade and Industry led another multi-sector delegation on a visit to Juba in October 2011.[47] Through the South African–Sudanese Business Council, leading South African investors have entered South Sudan, including SABMiller, which has invested over $70 million in South Sudan Beverages Limited since 2009; New Kush Exploration Company (registered in South Africa and Britain), which has been awarded several exploration rights for gold and uranium; Joint Aid Management (JAM), which was granted a 32-year lease in 2012 for some 24,300 hectares in Western Equatoria state for agribusiness; and MTN, which acquired a majority shareholding in a local mobile operator, ZTE, in 2011.[48]

Despite deepening relations with South Sudan, South Africa has been careful to maintain its political and economic ties with Sudan to the north. During celebrations marking the independence of South Sudan, President Zuma reiterated that South Africa was ready to "serve as a bridge between the neighbours to ensure that mutual trust and peace prevail ... Sudan (both north and south) needs to serve as an example and a beacon of hope not only to the African continent but to the world at large".[49] As part of its efforts to promote an even-handed approach towards Sudan and South Sudan, South Africa has supported the initiatives of the AU High-Level Implementation Panel for Sudan (AUHIP), chaired by its former president, Thabo Mbeki. Established in 2011, the AUHIP is the successor to the AU High-Level Panel on Darfur (AUHPD) and was tasked by the 15-member AU Peace and Security Council to mediate unresolved issues between the two neighbours, in particular border demarcation, the status of Abyei, oil transit fees, citizenship, security and assets. Bilateral talks between Sudan and South Sudan have been interspersed by brinksmanship, border clashes and outright war, as highlighted by the fighting after South Sudan's military seizure of Sudan's Heglig oil field in April 2012. Tensions also emanated from South Sudan's support of government rebels in Darfur, Blue Nile and Southern Kordofan, and the unresolved issue of the status of Abyei. Despite such skirmishes, Mbeki succeeded in getting the parties to sign a joint cooperation agreement in September 2012 that led to the reduction of hostilities and the resumption of oil production. Even though full implementation of the agreement remained elusive by 2017, the AUHIP has persisted in keeping the two sides at the negotiating table. Throughout these Mbeki-led efforts, the South African government has continually expressed support for the AUHIP framework as the most credible mechanism to resolving the bilateral impasse between Juba and Khartoum.[50] Following the outbreak of violence between competing factions in the SPLM in December 2013, Mbeki signalled his determination to continue the AUHIP-led talks. Meanwhile, in February 2014, the ANC appointed its deputy president, Cyril Ramaphosa, to mediate between South Sudanese president Salva Kiir and the latter's former vice-president, Riek Machar, and to help to resolve the SPLM's internal conflict.[51]

Alongside Tanzania's ruling party, Chama Cha Mapinduzi, Ramaphosa was instrumental in the release of political detainees allied to Machar prior to the commencement of the intra-SPLM political dialogue in Arusha, Tanzania, in January 2014. Billed as supplementing the IGAD negotiations on the South Sudan conflict, the intra-party talks sought reconciliation between Machar and Kiir as a preliminary step to ending the war. Following these talks, both factions of the SPLM committed to rebuilding and democratising the movement internally in order to promote national harmony and end the conflict. The dialogue also recognised the collective responsibility within the SPLM for resolving the conflict in South Sudan. The ANC and CCM became the co-guarantors of the agreement.[52] As a member of the IGAD Plus mechanism comprising regional and international actors, South Africa also continued to push for a negotiated settlement that culminated in a major agreement in August 2015.[53] But due to the deep mistrust between the South Sudanese parties, this agreement collapsed in July 2016 after Machar was removed from the transitional government.[54] Bilateral trade between South Africa and South Sudan was R22 million in 2016, and between South Africa and Sudan R328 million in the same year.[55]

Concluding Reflections: Towards Multilateralism?

The multilateral impulses unleashed by negotiations for a SADC-COMESA-EAC free trade agreement constitute the foundation for more stable future relations between South Africa and Eastern Africa. Furthermore, they could lead potentially to the restructuring of African regionalism in the direction of rationalisation and harmonisation, thus contributing to the incremental realisation of the dream of an African Economic Community (AEC) by 2028. At the first Tripartite Summit, held in Kampala in October 2008, the heads of state and government of SADC, COMESA, and the EAC agreed to establish a grand free trade area, referred to as the Tripartite FTA (T-FTA). They further directed the start of negotiations for the expeditious establishment of the T-FTA.[56] The second

Tripartite Summit, held in Johannesburg, South Africa, in June 2011, launched formal negotiations by adopting negotiating principles and structures, as well as a roadmap for the establishment of the T-FTA. More importantly, 23 out of 26 countries signed the declaration launching the negotiations: Angola, Botswana, Burundi, Comoros, the DRC, Djibouti, Egypt, Kenya, Lesotho, Libya, Malawi, Mauritius, Mozambique, Namibia, Rwanda, Seychelles, South Africa, Sudan, Swaziland, Tanzania, Uganda, Zambia and Zimbabwe. Only Madagascar, Eritrea and Ethiopia did not sign the document, but pledged to join the effort later. Facing an internal political conflict and suspension from SADC, Madagascar was not invited to the deliberations. Eritrea and Ethiopia were not ready to sign the document pending wider consultations at home.

Following the Johannesburg meeting, the Tripartite Task Force, led by the sub-committee on trade, prepared a draft FTA roadmap and a draft agreement establishing the T-FTA, including annexes on non-tariff barriers, rules of origin, customs cooperation, transit trade and transit facilities, trade remedies, competition policy and law, standards, sanitary and phytosanitary (SPS) measures, movement of business persons, intellectual property rights, services negotiations, dispute settlement and institutional arrangements. Building on the FTAs that are already in place in SADC, COMESA and the EAC, the negotiators for the T-FTA sought among other things to: eliminate all tariff and non-tariff barriers to trade in goods, liberalise trade in services, facilitate cross-border investment and movement of businesspeople and harmonise customs procedures and trade facilitation measures. The COMESA-EAC-SADC T-FTA was launched in Sharm el-Sheikh, Egypt, in June 2015 by 26 member states. Stretching from the Cape to Cairo, the T-FTA aims to create an integrated market with a combined population of almost 600 million people and total gross domestic product (GDP) of about $1 trillion.[57]

Although implementation will take several years to come to fruition, the signing of the T-FTA indicates that the member states of these three regional economic communities (RECs) – SADC, COMESA and the EAC – are prepared to broaden economic integration by building on existing structures and institutions. Should these efforts succeed, they could begin to resolve the questions of competitive and overlapping memberships that have dogged regional integration efforts in Africa. With the end of conflicting trade regimes, the three RECs could forge more harmonised economic and social policies that could potentially form the basis for a better-integrated and more coherent regional institutional framework. For Eastern Africa, in particular, the T-FTA could help to resolve the dilemma of Tanzania's dual membership in the EAC and SADC, as well as Burundi, Kenya, Rwanda and Uganda's memberships in both COMESA and the EAC. Similarly, the multilateral economic initiatives could also help to propel regional security cooperation further along the lines envisaged by the November 2013 declaration on the holding of annual ICGLR-SADC summits. In addition to an economic framework anchored on SADC, COMESA, and the EAC, a security umbrella that involves Eastern and Southern Africa would be a momentous step in broadening the contours of regional integration in Africa.

Notes

1. For some of the analyses of South Africa in Africa, *see* Garth le Pere and Chris Alden, "South Africa in Africa: Bound to Lead?", *Politikon* 36, no. 1 (2009), pp. 145–169; Chris Landsberg, "Thabo Mbeki's Legacy of Transformational Diplomacy", in Daryl Glaser (ed.), *Mbeki and After: Reflections on the Legacy of Thabo Mbeki* (Johannesburg: Wits University Press, 2010), pp. 209–241.

2. Godrefy Okoth, "US Foreign Policy Impact on Kenya's Foreign and Domestic Policies, *Journal of West and East Studies* 18, no. 1 (1989), pp. 153–177.

3. Juma Kwayera, "Madiba's Death Offers a Moment of Reflection on Kenya–South Africa Relations", *The Standard*, 29 December 2013, http://www.standardmedia. co.ke/?articleID=2000101034&story_title = Kenya-madiba-s-death-offers-a-moment-of-reflection-on-kenya-south-africa-relations (accessed 13 June 2014).

4. Joseph Kipkoech, "National Interests Paramount in Kenya-South Africa Relations", *Al Shahid*, 26 June 2010, http://english.alshahid.net/archives/8137 (accessed 15 June 2014).

5. Carlos Mureithi, "When Mandela Snubbed Kenyan Delegation", *Daily Nation*, 12 December 2013, http://mobile.nation.co.ke/news/When-Mandela-snubbed-Kenyan-delegation/-/1950946/2108648/-/format/xhtml/-/5e9xsqz/-/index.html (accessed 15 June 2014).

6. Kwayera, "Madiba's Death". *See also* Mwangi Githahu, "Kenya: Mandela and the Visit That Embarrassed Moi", *The Star*, 14 December 2013, http://allafrica.com/stories/201312150040.html (accessed 14 June 2014); Kwametchi Makokha, "When Kenya Rejected Plea to Host the ANC", *Daily Nation*, 7 December 2013, http://mobile.nation.co.ke/news/ANC-Kenya-Tom-Mboya-Joseph-Murumbi-/-/1950946/2102426/-/format/xhtml/-/w1g4av/-/index.html (accessed 14 June 2014).

7. "Zuma Trip: Kenyans Left with "Bitter Taste in Mouth,'" *News 24*, 13 October 2016, http://www.news24.com/Africa/News/zuma-trip-kenyans-left-with-bitter-taste-in-mouth-20161013-2 (accessed 1 December 2016).

8. Judi Hudson, "East Africa's Hub: The Experience of South African Firms Doing Business in Kenya", *Business in Africa Report* no. 9 (Johannesburg: South African Institute of International Affairs (SAIIA), 2007), p. 1.

9. Muthoki Mumo, "Jitters As South African Giants Stage a Comeback", *Daily Nation*, 16 July 2013, http://www.nation.co.ke/Features/smartcompany/Jitters-as-SA-giants-stage-a-comeback/-/1226/1915448/-/fcayb0z/-/index.html (accessed 10 May 2014); Steve Mbogo, "SA Business Shows Renewed Interest in Kenya", *Financial Mail*, 6 February 2014, http://www.financialmail.co.za/coverstory/2014/02/06/sa-business-shows-renewed-interest-in-kenya (accessed 10 May 2014).

10. George Omondi, "Kenya Moves Closer to Striking Trade Deal with South Africa", *The East African*, 22 January 2013, http://www.businessdailyafrica.com/Kenya-moves-closer-to-striking-trade-deal-with-South-Africa/-/539546/1672738/-/pb0ut8z/-/index.html (accessed 14 June 2014); Mumo, "Jitters As South African Giants Stage a Comeback".

11. Mbogo, "SA Business Shows Renewed Interest in Kenya"; Charles Gichane, "Kenya to Host Singular South Africa Trade Delegation", *Daily Nation*, 18 January 2013, http://www.capitalfm.co.ke/business/2013/01/kenya-to-host-singular-sa-trade-delegation/South (accessed 10 May 2014); South African Department of Trade and Industry (DTI), "SA Export Value HS8 (Yearly)" and "SA Import Value HS8 (Yearly)", http://tradestats.thedti.gov.za/ReportFolders/reportFolders.aspx (accessed 21 May 2014).

12. Figures from the South African Revenue Service (SARS), *see* http://www.sars.gov.za.

13. *See* Gilbert Khadiagala, "The SADCC and Its Approaches to African Regionalism", in Chris Saunders, Gwinyayi A. Dzinesa and Dawn Nagar (eds), *Region-Building in Southern Africa: Progress, Problems and Prospects* (London and New York: Zed, 2012), pp. 25–38.

14. "Your Grief Is Tanzania's As Well", *The Star*, 15 December 2013, http://www.iol.co.za/news/south-africa/eastern-cape/your-grief-is-tanzania-s-as-well-1.1622841#.U5l9TnaJlpQ (accessed 14 June 2014).

15. "South Africa and Tanzania Take Relations to New Heights", *Bua News*, 20 July 2011, http://wavuti.weebly.com/news-blog/south-africa-and-tanzania-take-relations-to-new-heights#ixzz34QvNsMZY (accessed 15 June 2014).

16. Hudson, "East Africa's Hub", p. 67.

17. Quoted in Richard A. Schroeder, "South African Capital in the Land of Ujamaa: Contested Terrain in Tanzania", *Africa Files*, http://www.africafiles.org/article.asp?ID=19013 (accessed 14 February 2014).

18. "SA, Tanzania to Strengthen Ties", 4 April 2007, http://www.southafrica.info/news/international/tanzania-040407.htm (accessed 7 May 2014); "Address by President Jacob Zuma at the South Africa–Tanzania Business Forum Meeting", 11 July 2011, http://www.anc.org.za/show.php?id=8828 (accessed 15 June 2014).

19. Cited in "South Africa Tops in Foreign Investment Flows to Tanzania", *Guardian* (Dar es Salaam), 30 November 2013, http://www.ippmedia.com/frontend/?l=62120 (accessed 10 May 2014).

20. "South Africa, Tanzania Strengthen Ties", *Bua News*, 20 July 2011, http://www.southafrica.info/news/international/tanzania-200711.htm#.U57KxXbhvTo (accessed 16 June 2014).

21. Schroeder, "South African Capital in the Land of Ujamaa".

22. Gilbert M. Khadiagala, "Burundi", in Jane Boulden (ed.), *Dealing with Conflict in Africa: The United Nations and Regional Organizations* (New York: Palgrave, 2003), pp. 238–242.

23. Adonia Ayebare, "Peacemaking in Burundi: A Case of Regional Diplomacy Backed by International Peacekeeping and Peacebuilding", briefing paper (New York: International Peace Institute (IPI), n.d.), p. 83.

24. Sadiki Koko, "Peace at Last? Appraisal of the Addis Ababa Peace and Security Cooperation Framework and the United Nations Security Council Resolution 2098 for the Democratic Republic of the Congo", *African Journal on Conflict Resolution* 13, no. 2 (2013), pp. 59–86.

25. Charles Mwanguhya and Risdel Kasasira, "Kabila Told to Resolve M23 Grievances at ICGLR Summit", *Africa Review*, 24 November 2012, http://www.africareview. com/News/Kabila-told-to-talk-to-rebels/-/979180/1628380/-/jc0u76z/-/index. html (accessed 15 June 2014).

26. Jinty Jackson, "SADC Brigade Can 'Impose Peace by Force'", *Business Day*, 13 February 2013, http://www.bdlive.co.za/world/africa/2013/02/11/sadc-brigade-can-impose-peace-by-force (accessed 15 June 2014).

27. "MONUSCO Vows to Target Other Rebels in DR Congo After Routing Out M23", *Xinhua News*, 14 November 2013, http://news.xinhuanet.com/english/ africa/2013-11/14/c_132888390.htm (accessed 8 May 2014); Alice Gatebuke, "The Hard Truths We Must Swallow: Rwanda Is Wreaking Havoc in Congo", *Pambazuka News*, 14 August 2013, http://www.pambazuka.org/en/category/comment/ 88649 (accessed 8 May 2014).

28. SADC-ICGLR, "Joint Summit of the Southern African Development Community (SADC) and the International Conference on the Great Lakes Region (ICGLR)", Tshwane (Pretoria), 4 November 2013; Nick Long, "Congo-Kinshasa: Expanded Role for UN Troops in DRC", *Voice of America*, 14 November 2013, http://allafrica. com/stories/201311150381.html (accessed 8 May 2014).

29. "Humanitarian Crisis Looms for Migrants Expelled by Tanzania", *IRIN News*, 19 September 2013, http://www.irinnews.org/report/98789/humanitarian-crisis-looms-for-migrants-expelled-by-tanzania (accessed 8 May 2014).

30. Steven Ruhanamilindi, "Rwanda: War Mongers in Tanzania Media – Rwanda Supports Peace, Not War", *New Times* (Kigali), 26 August 2013, http://www. newtimes.co.rw/news/index.php?a=69869&i=15462 (accessed 16 June 2014); "Congo-Kinshasa: The Objectives of the Unholy Alliances Operating in DRC", *Rwanda Focus* (Kigali), 29 July 2013, http://allafrica.com/stories/201307301443. html (accessed 16 June 2014); Frederick Golooba-Mutebi, "Rwanda: Kikwete in Trouble over FDLR, but Does He Really Understand Who They Are?", 11 June 2013, http://africanarguments.org/2013/06/11/kikwete-in-trouble-over-fdlr-but-does-he-really-understand-who-they-are-%E2%80%93-by-frederick-golooba-mutebi (accessed 16 June 2014).

31. "Kikwete, Kagame Come Face to Face in Kampala", *The Citizen* (Kampala), 4 September 2013, http://www.thecitizen.co.tz/News/Kikwete–Kagame-come-face-to-face-in-Kampala/-/1840392/1980278/-/p3twoyz/-/index.html (accessed 16 June 2014); Muthoki Mumo, "Fears over EAC's Future As Tanzania Is Sidelined Again", *Daily Nation*, 12 September 2013, http://mobile.nation.co.

ke/business/Fears+over + EACs + future + as + Tanzania + is + sidelined + again + /-/1950106/1975004/-/format/xhtml/-/ (accessed 16 June 2014).

32. "President Kikwete's Landmark Speech on the EAC", *Daily News* (Dar es Salaam), 15 November 2013, http://archive.dailynews.co.tz/index.php/columnists/colum nists/makwaia-wa-kuhenga/24709-president-kikwete-s-landmark-speech-on-eac (accessed 16 June 2014).

33. Figures from the South African Revenue Service (SARS), *see* http://www.sars.gov.za.

34. "President Mbeki Addresses Ugandan Parliament", 13 December 2005, http://www.sahistory.org.za/archive/president-mbeki-address-parliament-uganda (accessed 10 May 2014); Benon Herbert Oluka, "Uganda's Special Ties with South Africa's Leaders and ANC", *The East African*, 7 December 2013, http://www.theeastafrican.co.ke/news/Uganda-s-special-ties-with-South-Africa-s-leaders-and-ANC/-/2558/2103104/-/y4llsm/-/index.html (accessed 16 June 2014); Robert Kabushenga; "Uganda's Role in Liberating South Africa", *New Vision*, 9 December 2013, http://www.newvision.co.ug/news/650310-uganda-s-role-in-liberating-south-africa.html (accessed 16 June 2014).

35. Jacob Zuma, "Uganda, South Africa Are Determined to Trade", *New Vision*, 29 March 2010, http://www.newvision.co.ug/D/8/459/714533 (accessed 10 May 2014).

36. Government of Uganda, "Foreign Direct Investment Inflow", 15 June 2014, http://focusafrica.gov.in/Uganda_foreign_direct_investment.html (accessed 15 June 2014); "Uganda in Top 10 FDI Recipients in Africa", *New Vision*, 1 June 2014, http://www.newvision.co.ug/news/656181-uganda-in-top-10-fdi-recipients-in-africa.html (accessed 15 June 2014).

37. "South African Companies Flourish in Uganda", *AfricanGlobe*, 6 May 2012, http://www.africanglobe.net/business/south-african-companies-flourish-uganda (accessed 15 June 2014).

38. Tabu Butagira, "Museveni Holds Talks with Zuma, to Address Pan African Parliament", *The Monitor* (Kampala), 18 March 2014, http://www.monitor.co.ug/News/National/Museveni-holds-talks-with-Zuma/-/688334/2248576/-/ej1ga3/-/index.html (accessed 15 June 2014); "Zuma, Museveni Meet over Continent's Issues", 3 August 2011, http://www.sanews.gov.za/south-africa/zuma-museveni-meet-over-continents-issues (accessed 15 June 2014).

39. Figures from the South African Revenue Service (SARS), *see* http://www.sars.gov.za.

40. Chris Bathembu, "Zuma, African Leaders Discuss Standby Force", 11 May 2013, http://www.sanews.gov.za/africa/zuma-african-leaders-discuss-standby-force (accessed 20 February 2014).

41. The Friends of IGAD (also known as the IGAD Partners Forum (IPF)) were: Austria, Belgium, Britain, Canada, Denmark, France, Germany, Greece, Ireland, Italy, Japan, Netherlands, Norway, Sweden, Switzerland, the United States, the European Commission, the International Organisation for Migration, the United Nations Development Programme and the World Bank.

42. Waihenya Waithaka, *The Mediator: General Lazaro Sumbeiywo and the Southern Sudan Peace Process* (Nairobi: East African Educational Publishers, 2006).

43. African National Congress, "Media Briefing Statement by ANC National Chairperson, Comrade Baleka Mbete, Following the Occasion of the Republic

of South Sudan's 9th July Independence Day Celebrations", Luthuli House, Johannesburg, 10 July 2011.

44. "South Africa to Lend Helping Hand to South Sudan", *Bua News*, 8 July 2011, http://www.sanews.gov.za/south-africa/sa-lend-helping-hand-south-sudan (accessed 15 June 2014); "SA 'Ready to Welcome South Sudan'", *Bua News*, 10 February 2011, http://www.southafrica.info/africa/sudan-100211.htm?TB_iframe= true&height = 500&width = 500#.U5225HaJlpQ (accessed 15 June 2014); "South Africa, South Sudan Establish Ties", *Bua News*, 27 September 2011, http://www. southafrica.info/news/international/southsudan-270911.htm#.U57QqXbhvTo (accessed 16 June 2014).

45. Wanjohi Kabukuru, "Clearing South Sudan of Its Deadly Landmines", *Africa Renewal*, 16 January 2012, http://www.un.org/africarenewal/web-features/ clearing-south-sudan-its-deadly-landmines (accessed 7 May 2014).

46. Kabukuru, "Clearing South Sudan of Its Deadly Landmines"; Cheryl Hendricks and Amanda Lucey, "South Africa and South Sudan: Lessons for Post-Conflict Development in Peacebuilding Partnerships," Policy Brief no. 49 (Tshwane: Institute for Security Studies (ISS), December 2013).

47. Richard Polack and Kevin Bloom, "Feeding Frenzy in Sudan", *Mail and Guardian*, 21 December 21, 2012, http://mg.co.za/article/2012-12-21-feeding-frenzy-in-south-sudan (accessed 15 June 2014).

48. "The Scramble for the Southern Sudan", *African Business Magazine*, 17 October 2011, http://africanbusinessmagazine.com/special-reports/country-reports/south-sudan-wide-open-for-business/the-scramble-for-the-southern-sudan (accessed 7 May 2014); "Business Suits Replace Fatigues", *African Business Magazine*, 17 October 2011, http://africanbusinessmagazine.com/country-reports/business-suits-replace-fatigues (accessed 7 May 2014); Polack and Bloom, "Feeding Frenzy in Sudan".; "South Sudan: MTN Unveils US \$76 million Expansion Project for South Sudan", *CIO East Africa*, 16 May 2014, http://allafrica.com/stories/201405161151. html (accessed 15 June 2014).

49. "South Africa to Lend Helping Hand to South Sudan", *Bua News*, 8 July 2011.

50. "South Africa Expresses Concern About the Deterioration in Relations Between Sudan and South Sudan", *Bua News*, 13 June 2013, http://www.dfa.gov.za/docs/ 2013/suda0614.html (accessed 15 June 2014).

51. "South Sudan: Mbeki Says Sudan Mediation Continues Amid Conflict", 13 February 2014, http://allafrica.com/stories/201402120049.html (accessed 15 June 2014); "Ramaphosa to Mediate in South Sudan", *Mail and Guardian*, 6 February 2014, http://mg.co.za/article/2014-02-06-anc-ramaphosa-to-mediate-in-s-sudan-to-strengthen-relations (accessed 15 June 2014).

52. "Hope for Peace in South Sudan after Arusha Talks Unite Belligerents," *The East African*, 26 January 2015, 2016).

53. Intergovernmental Authority on Development (IGAD), "Agreement on the Resolution of the Conflict in South Sudan," Addis Ababa, Ethiopia, August 15, 2015.

54. "Machar in South Africa, But Not Under House Arrest, DIRCO," *The Citizen*, 14 December 2016, http://citizen.co.za/news/news-africa/1376383/machar-still-in-sa-but-not-under-house-arrest-dirco/ (accessed 19 December 2016).

55. Figures from the South African Revenue Service (SARS), *see* http://www.sars.gov.za.
56. Trudi Hartzenberg (ed.), *Cape to Cairo: Exploring the Tripartite Free Trade Agenda* (Johannesburg: Tralac, November 2013), http://www.tralac.org/publications/article/5548-cape-to-cairo-exploring-the-tripartite-fta-agenda.html (accessed 16 June 2014).
57. SADC, "Toward a Common Future," June 15, 2015, https://www.sadc.int/news-events/news/comesa-eac-sadc-tripartite-free-trade-area-launched (accessed December 3, 2016); COMESA-EAC-SADC, *Draft Agreement Establishing the COMESA, EAC, and SADC Free Trade Area* (Lusaka: COMESA Secretariat, December 2010); Wolfe Braude, "SADC, COMESA, and the EAC: Conflicting Regional and Trade Agendas", Occasional Paper no. 57 (Tshwane: Institute for Global Dialogue (IGD), October 2008); "COMESA-EAC-SADC Tripartite: Greater Regional Harmonization and Cooperation", http://www.comesa-eac-sadc-tripartite.org/intervention/focal_areas/tripartite_fta (accessed 16 June 2014).

CHAPTER 10

SOUTH AFRICA IN NORTH AFRICA: EGYPT, ALGERIA, LIBYA AND TUNISIA

Rawia Tawfik

North Africa's political landscape has witnessed significant transformation since the popular Arab uprisings that started in Tunisia in December 2010 and led to the ouster of Zine al-Abidine Ben Ali after two decades in power. The wave of political protests spread and gained momentum with the "25 January Revolution" in Egypt, which toppled Hosni Mubarak's three-decade rule. In March 2011, an external intervention in Libya by the North Atlantic Treaty Organisation (NATO) forced a "regime change" in Tripoli by October of that year that resulted in the assassination of Muammar Qaddafi, who had been in power since 1969. These upheavals have produced new political and social realities, with other countries in the sub-region, such as Algeria and Morocco, confronting similar challenges. Algeria – South Africa's main strategic partner in North Africa – is facing a period of uncertainty and unrest under its ailing fourth-term president, Abdelaziz Bouteflika (since 1999): official sources reported more than 9,000 protests in the country in 2013 alone. In Morocco, King Mohammed VI pre-empted mass protests by introducing cosmetic political reforms, including the adoption of a new constitution in July 2011 that introduced fresh limits on the king's powers. However, with youth unemployment at about 22 per cent, increasing inequalities may yet produce greater pressures for reform.[1]

This chapter asks whether, and how, South Africa has been able to reformulate its foreign policy towards North Africa in response to the political and social upheavals that have gripped the sub-region. The discussion opens by examining how post-apartheid South Africa defined its relationship with North Africa between 1994 and 2010, and then assesses Tshwane's (Pretoria) response to the political changes that have since swept Tunisia, Egypt and Libya. In particular, I focus on how South Africa's foreign policy principles – especially the tension between supporting democracy and rejecting "regime change" by force – and its tendency to "export" the country's domestic "model" of transition (see Curtis in this volume), have affected Tshwane's approach to the political unrest in North Africa. The chapter also outlines the potential areas of cooperation between South Africa and North Africa, while highlighting the challenges that Tshwane faces in pursuing an active foreign policy in this turbulent sub-region.

Furthermore, the analysis is not confined to government actions alone, but also considers the role of business and civil society in shaping South Africa's engagement with North Africa. Since 1994, South Africa's multinational companies have emerged as active players in expanding its economic reach across Africa. Although the overall level of South African investments in North Africa has thus far been low, recent developments have opened new business opportunities in the sub-region and improved its prospects for increasing economic integration in the long term. Equally important, South African civil society, with its long history of struggle for political freedom and economic and social rights, has a wealth of experience that it could share with its counterparts in North Africa.

North Africa in South Africa's Post-Apartheid Foreign Policy, 1994–2010

After 1994, post-apartheid South Africa's foreign policy viewed North African countries through different, even contradictory, lenses. First, newly democratic South Africa valued Algeria, Libya and Egypt, in particular, as countries that had supported its long fight against apartheid. During the liberation struggle, these North African countries hosted leaders of the African National Congress (ANC) as well as the Pan-Africanist Congress (PAC), and provided training to cadres of both movements. It is against this background that Nelson Mandela, as South Africa's first democratically elected president (1994–1999), rejected Western sanctions against Muammar Qaddafi's regime in Libya and mediated between it and the West to end the Lockerbie crisis by 1999. South African leaders also continued to express appreciation for the role played by Algeria, as president of the United Nations (UN) General Assembly in 1974, to isolate the apartheid government and for its hosting of members of South Africa's liberation struggle.[2]

Second, in keeping with the emphasis on multilateralism in its diplomacy, post-apartheid South Africa partnered with North African sub-regional powers in key continental initiatives. In 1999, Algeria's Abdelaziz Bouteflika joined South Africa's Thabo Mbeki and Nigeria's Olusegun Obasanjo to help to develop the Millennium Africa Recovery Plan (MAP), which became the basis for the New Partnership for Africa's Development (NEPAD) in 2001. Notably, NEPAD reflected Mbeki's idea of an "African Renaissance", a notion that sought to inspire Africa's socio-economic renewal and bridge the geographical and political divide between North Africa and sub-Saharan Africa. In his famous "I am an African" speech, delivered to members of South Africa's Constitutional Assembly in May 1996, Mbeki talked about an African identity based on the struggle for liberation on the entire continent, not just in sub-Saharan Africa. He proudly claimed: "I am an African. I am born of the peoples of the continent of Africa. The pain of the violent conflict that the peoples of Liberia, Somalia, the Sudan, Burundi and Algeria [bear] is a pain I also bear."[3]

Third, while accepting North Africa's sub-regional powers as partners in fulfilling the dream of an African Renaissance, South Africa also came to view them as competitors for the mantle of continental leadership. Qaddafi's Libya played an instrumental leadership role in the creation of the African Union (AU). In 1999, the Libyan city of Sirte hosted the Organisation of African Unity's (OAU) extraordinary summit that agreed on the transformation of the continental body into the AU. Moreover, Tripoli paid the debts of a number of African states to the OAU to enable them to vote for the creation of the AU. South African scholar-diplomat Iqbal Jhazbhay characterised relations between Mbeki and Qaddafi at the Sirte summit as a "struggle for the soul of the AU". Mbeki, among other African leaders, rejected Qaddafi's impractical proposals for setting up a single army and currency: a revival of ideas propounded by Ghana's Kwame Nkrumah from the 1950s.[4] In his turn, Qaddafi criticised NEPAD, which became the socio-economic programme of the AU and was integrated into the structures of the continental body by 2003, as a colonial plan, wondering: "[H]ow can [Africa] seriously expect [its] economic salvation to be guaranteed by [its] former slavers, colonisers and oppressors?"[5] However, in 2002, a year after the official launching of NEPAD in the Nigerian capital of Abuja, Tripoli became a member of the initiative's enlarged steering committee responsible for the coordination and administration of its activities.

Similarly, Egypt has occasionally competed with South Africa to represent the continent on the regional and international stages, such as when both countries applied to host the 2010 Football World Cup, and when Cairo considered vying with Tshwane to host the AU's Pan-African Parliament (PAP) in 2004. If the United Nations were to respond to the African proposal – as contained in the Ezulwini Consensus of 2005 – for enlarging its 15-member Security Council, such as to include two permanent members with veto power from the continent, Egypt and South Africa (along with Nigeria) would be the forerunners in the race to secure one of the seats (see Mashabane in this volume).[6]

Furthermore, South Africa's strong political relations with the three sub-regional powers in North Africa have not translated into more active economic engagement, despite the fact that South Africa has set up bi-national commissions with all the countries of the sub-region, except Morocco. Official sources admit, for example, that a key challenge in South Africa's relationship with its main strategic North African partner, Algeria, is how to "translate the excellent political relations, as characterised by the common vision [shared] on continental and global matters, into concrete [economic] programmes that benefit ... peoples [of the two countries]".[7] Algeria is South Africa's top trade partner in North Africa, but trade with Algiers represented only 0.2 per cent of Tshwane's total trade in 2012. Economic ties with Egypt have been slowly expanding, and as a destination for South Africa's exports, the country improved in ranking from 61st in 2005 to 47th in 2012. Even so, trade with Egypt – €124 million in 2012 – represented only 0.1 per cent of South Africa's total trade.[8]

South Africa's business presence in North Africa has similarly lagged behind, even though the investment climate in the sub-region – in terms of the availability of developed infrastructure, human resources, level of political stability and market size – was much better than in most other parts of the continent. South African companies in Egypt have previously cited strong competition from European, American and Middle Eastern companies; nepotism and lack of transparency in the awarding of government contracts; and an unfavourable legal system, as impediments to greater investment in the country.[9] According to Egypt's State Information Services, South African investments in Egypt amounted to $20.6 million in 2007, with most of these investments directed to the oil, services, communications and agricultural sectors.[10] In an effort to boost economic ties, during a state visit to Cairo in October 2010, South Africa's president Jacob Zuma signed a number of memorandums of understanding (MOUs) with the Egyptian government in the information technology, energy and tourism sectors. The two regional powers also discussed progress towards establishing the tripartite free trade area (FTA) that seeks to connect the Common Market for Eastern and Southern Africa (COMESA), the East African Community (EAC) and the Southern African Development Community (SADC). The envisaged FTA encompasses the 26 member states of the three regional organisations, including Egypt (a member of COMESA) and South Africa (a member of SADC), and aims at harmonising trade arrangements, improving joint planning of infrastructural projects and enhancing the free movement of businesspeople within the tripartite region (see Saunders and Nagar in this volume). An Egyptian–South African business forum was also convened on the margins of the October 2010 presidential visit to Cairo.

South Africa and the Arab Uprisings: Between State Ambivalence and Societal Solidarity

In managing its relationships with its partners and rivals in North Africa until the recent upheavals, South Africa was restrained in its criticism of human rights abuses and lack of democracy in the sub-region. This may be attributed to Tshwane's attempt to strike a balance between promoting an agenda based on democratic governance, on the one hand, and adhering to the principles of African solidarity and non-intervention, on the other hand.[11] This restraint, in turn, garnered criticism from several quarters, given the oft-stated centrality of human rights to post-apartheid South Africa's foreign policy (see Fritz in this volume). Responding to this criticism, South Africa would have been expected by many to see in North Africa's recent democratic uprisings an opportunity to promote its reformist agenda. However, Tshwane took an ambivalent, if not conservative, position towards the upheavals in the sub-region.

Egypt and Tunisia: Welcoming Reform, But Not Revolution

The South African government remained silent on the protests that started in Tunisia in December 2010 that forced President Zine al-Abidine Ben Ali to flee to Saudi Arabia after 23 years in power. This may be attributed to the low-profile relations between Tunis and Tshwane. The bilateral commission between Tunisia and South Africa, which was established in 1996, had met only three times by 2006. Trade and business links were limited. South Africa admired Ben Ali's poverty alleviation programmes, but declined to comment on his regime's poor human rights record.[12]

Tshwane's first statement on the "25 January [2011] Revolution" in Egypt, issued six days later, was fairly conservative, describing the situation as a "crisis" and inviting "the government and the people of Egypt to seek a speedy and peaceful resolution to [it]".[13] While acknowledging the right of citizens to exercise their political and civil rights, the ANC's first statement on the political turmoil enveloping North Africa highlighted the negative impacts of instability in the sub-region on consolidating South Africa's African agenda (see Maloka in this volume).[14] Like many other countries, South Africa was taken by surprise by the quick spill-over of protests from Tunisia to Egypt, and adopted a cautious approach. It took Tshwane three days after Egyptian president Hosni Mubarak's resignation in February 2011 to issue a statement welcoming his decision, calling it "a victory of the will of the people" and a "dawn of a new era of democracy in Egypt".[15] Even then, South Africa continued to avoid describing the political developments in North Africa as "revolutions" or "uprisings", referring to them instead as "unrest" or "political changes".[16]

Two factors can help to explain South Africa's seemingly lukewarm attitude towards political developments in Tunisia and Egypt. First, South Africa's own experience of internal political transformation made it more tolerant towards negotiated, rather than revolutionary, change. Although the country's black majority had waged a long revolutionary campaign against white minority rule, this struggle finally came to fruition with elections in 1994 as the result of a negotiated settlement. In other words, South Africa's domestic experience showed it that a political compromise achieved through dialogue between different parties – as opposed to radical change introduced by a single party – was key to securing long-term stability. This has since translated into a tendency by Tshwane to propose the country's "model" of transition as a way out of political crises in other parts of the continent. However, it is uncertain that the South African solution, based on a pacted transition and the introduction of a government of national unity, is suitable for solving political conflicts in other African countries (see Curtis in this volume).

Second, South Africa may have feared a potential spill-over of the popular revolts in North Africa into other African countries, including those with democratically elected but poorly performing governments. Since 1996, South Africa itself has witnessed a rise in popular dissatisfaction with its neo-liberal economic policies and poor service delivery that has led to workers' demonstrations and protests in the country's black townships. In the wake of the Arab uprisings, a number of South African scholars noted how South African citizens and civil society were beginning to follow in the footsteps of their Tunisian and Egyptian counterparts in mobilising against government policies.[17] Protesters in a marginalised area such as the small South African town of Ermelo in 2011, for example, referred to the site of their protests as "Tahrir Square".[18] There was concern in some quarters that South Africa could face upheavals similar to those taking place in North Africa, if the government continued to fail to address the triple challenges of poverty, unemployment and inequality (see Landsberg in this volume). This led President Jacob Zuma to declare, in March 2011, that South Africa would never witness similar uprisings as those in North Africa, because it had sound and functioning democratic institutions.

Tshwane was swifter, however, to oppose the so called "unconstitutional change" of government that removed from office Mohamed Morsi, Egypt's first democratically elected president in July 2013, and strongly condemned the subsequent use of violence against demonstrators calling for the return of Morsi to power.[19] In line with South African ambivalence, this opposing position did not last long, as Tshwane started to deal with the post-3 July arrangements in Egypt as a fait accompli. In February 2014, South Africa sent a delegation led by then state security minister Siyabonga Cwele to Cairo to express South Africa's solidarity with Egypt in its "war on terrorism".

This practical approach continued after the election of President Abdel Fattah el-Sisi in June 2014. In his interview with Nile TV during his visit to Cairo in April 2015, President Jacob Zuma claimed that South Africa had misunderstood what happened in Egypt and recognised that the army had to intervene in response to popular dissatisfaction with the Muslim Brotherhood's regime to prevent further divisions within Egyptian society. He further hailed Egypt's strategic role in the region and the continent, and stressed that the restoration of stability to Egypt could revive and strengthen economic relations between Cairo and Tshwane. Trade figures indicate a gradual growth of bilateral trade from around R1.6 billion in 2014 to R3.9 billion in 2016.[20]

Libya: An Exceptional Foreign Policy Dilemma?

Elaborating a position on the revolution in Libya was more challenging for South Africa. Unlike the Tunisian and Egyptian forms of peaceful revolutionary change in December 2010 and January/February 2011 respectively, the situation in Libya quickly developed into a series of military confrontations between the Qaddafi regime and an armed opposition. Similar to its initial response to the Egyptian 25 January Revolution, South Africa's first official statement on Qaddafi's brutal reaction to the protests that started in February 2011 called upon the involved parties to "exercise restraint" and to "seek a peaceful resolution to the crisis".[21] With the escalation of atrocities and bloodshed, Tshwane condemned the "indiscriminate use of force" and the "killing of innocent people", and called upon the Libyan authorities to "end the carnage against its people".[22] At the same time, South Africa remained committed to a political solution to the crisis, and declared its rejection of "regime change" by force. President Zuma led the AU's High-Level Ad Hoc Committee on Libya, established in March 2011 by the African Union's 15-member Peace and Security Council, to help resolve the crisis peacefully through a dialogue on political reforms between the Libyan parties.

Yet in March 2011, as an elected, non-permanent member of the UN Security Council, South Africa voted for Resolution 1973, imposing a "no-fly zone" over Libya – although Tshwane also made clear that it "supported the Resolution with the necessary caveats to preserve the sovereignty and territorial integrity of Libya" and rejected "any foreign occupation or unilateral military intervention under the pretext of protection of civilians".[23] Later, when the intervening Anglo-French-led NATO powers went beyond the UN Security Council's mandate and sought to enforce a policy of "regime change" in Tripoli, Tshwane called for an immediate end to the military intervention in Libya. For South Africa, the continuation of the loss of lives and the deterioration of the humanitarian situation in Libya also meant that NATO's intervention contradicted the letter and spirit of the UN Security Council resolution.

South Africa remained hopeful of reaching a political solution to the Libyan crisis even after the launching of NATO's operation in March 2011. As a member of the AU Peace and Security Council's High-Level Ad Hoc Committee, President Zuma visited Libya in April and May 2011 to encourage dialogue between Qaddafi, whom South Africa continued to regard as the legitimate leader of Libya, and the Benghazi-based National Transitional Council (NTC), which was recognised by Western governments as the representative of the Libyan people. Indeed, Tshwane only recognised the NTC in September 2011, continuing to argue until then for a more inclusive political settlement in Libya, even though Nigeria and Ethiopia had led many African countries to recognise the National Transitional Council.

South African officials explained Tshwane's position by reference to its foreign policy principles, viewing the Libyan crisis as a test of South Africa's defence of "African solutions to African problems". In September 2011, South Africa's deputy minister for international relations and cooperation, Ebrahim Ebrahim, condemned the NATO military intervention to enforce "regime change" under the pretext of defending human rights as a facet of the "structural inequalities and abuses of power in the global system" and a reflection of a militaristic approach that engenders, rather than resolves, war and conflicts. Ebrahim openly criticised the way in which the AU and its efforts to find a sustainable political solution to the Libyan crisis were completely sidelined by the West.[24] South Africa's former president Thabo Mbeki went even further, suggesting that the popular uprising in Libya and the subsequent NATO military intervention might "mark the moment of the asphyxiation of the dream of an African Renaissance".[25] (See also Mashabane in this volume.)

However, the Libyan crisis equally revealed key tensions and dilemmas in South Africa's own foreign policy. First, it exposed the tension between supporting democracy and human rights on the one hand, and rejecting "regime change" by force on the other. The caveats identified by South Africa when explaining its vote on UN Security Council Resolution 1973 indicated awareness that the mandate was vulnerable to abuse. Some critics, including several Western governments, such as the United States (US), viewed Tshwane's later rejection of the intervention's aim of "regime change" and its initial refusal to recognise Libya's National Transitional Council as a pro-Qaddafi posture. Yet others, more critical of the NATO intervention as an act of Western "neo-imperialism", regarded South

Africa's vote for UN Security Council Resolution 1973 as contradictory to the political solution proposed by the African Union.[26]

Second, the Libyan crisis reflected the limitations of South Africa's foreign policy principle of "African solutions to African problems" when Western strategic interests were at stake. Even if the Libyan parties to the conflict had welcomed the African Union's roadmap to resolve the crisis, it is highly doubtful that powerful Western actors such as Washington, Paris and London would have left the situation to African mediators. In 2012, more than 70 per cent of Libya's oil exports were sent to Europe. In 2016, Libya had the largest oil reserves (more than 40 billion barrels) and ranked fourth in terms of proven gas reserves in Africa (after Nigeria, Algeria and Egypt). Several French, British, Dutch, Spanish, Italian and Austrian oil companies have signed agreements with Libya for oil and gas exploration since 2004.[27] There can be little doubt that these state and corporate interests would have been factored into the NATO decision to intervene in Libya. The question that this case raised then, and which remains relevant, is: What actual sources of leverage do South Africa and other African regional powers have to prevent a military intervention by the West when its core interests are affected on the continent?

Third, the crisis again indicated that the South African "model" might not be relevant to resolving all conflict situations in Africa. The South African government itself admitted that the Libyan authorities continued to kill and displace thousands of civilians even after the UN Security Council adopted Resolution 1970 in February 2011, demanding the end of human rights violations in the country, and despite the start of AU-sponsored mediation in March 2011. There is also some evidence to suggest that South Africa believed that Qaddafi should not be part of a post-crisis Libyan government, and may have been able to convince him to accept that.[28]

Engaging New Regimes
Since the fall of Hosni Mubarak's 30-year autocracy in Egypt in 2011, South Africa has established contacts with various Egyptian political parties from across the political spectrum, including the Islamist Muslim Brotherhood-affiliated Freedom and Justice Party (FJP), the Salafi Al-Nour Party and the Liberal Al-Wafd Party, and has sought to share its experience of democratic transition with them.[29] However, the ANC's more systematic method of party-to-party cooperation and regular

consultation has remained largely focused on Southern Africa and, more specifically, on former liberation movements, to the neglect of new and emerging political forces in North Africa.

Egypt's president Mohamed Morsi attended the BRICS summit (Brazil, Russia, India, China and South Africa) in South Africa's port city of Durban in March 2013, expressing the hope that his country might join the BRICS group (see Virk in this volume) once "it gets its economy back on track".[30] Although the implementation of previously agreed bilateral economic cooperation between Tshwane and Cairo was negatively affected by Egypt's institutional instability, the two countries continued to work together for the establishment of the COMESA-EAC-SADC tripartite free trade area (see Saunders and Nagar in this volume). In June 2011, Egyptian prime minister Essam Sharaf attended the second tripartite summit, held in Johannesburg, South Africa, at which the negotiating principles and roadmap for establishing the tripartite FTA were adopted, seeking to promote market integration, infrastructure development and industrial development. Egypt hosted the third tripartite summit in Sharm el-Sheikh in June 2015, which officially launched the tripartite FTA and gave member states 12 months from the launch of the area to conclude outstanding negotiations on rules of origin, trade remedies and tariff offers.

In the case of Libya, South Africa pledged to contribute to the process of reconstruction and development, and urged the transitional government to launch an inclusive political dialogue after the assassination of Qaddafi in October 2011. Following months of rejecting the unfreezing of Libyan assets in South Africa, Tshwane declared in June 2013 that it would release them. Even so, this issue has since remained a matter for dispute between the South African government and the Libyan transitional authorities. Tripoli claimed that Qaddafi had transferred billions of dollars to South Africa, while Tshwane has continued to insist that the only Libyan shareholdings in South Africa were limited to hotels and real estate.[31]

Notwithstanding the recent turbulence in the sub-region, Algeria remains South Africa's main strategic partner in North Africa. In April 2013, President Jacob Zuma paid a state visit to Algiers to strengthen bilateral ties and discuss continental challenges.[32] The two countries agreed to foster economic relations by establishing a trade and investment committee. During his visit to Algeria in March/April 2015, President Zuma was accompanied by a South African business delegation that engaged with their Algerian counterparts to try to increase business links.

Bilateral trade, however, remained limited, declining between 2013 and 2016, when it stood at R583 million: less than 0.5 per cent of South Africa's global trade.[33] Also, there is little to no evidence of bilateral initiatives between the two regional powers to address the growing political and security challenges in North Africa.

Societal Responses: Civil Society Solidarity and Business Reluctance

While the South African government's position towards the North African uprisings was hesitant and conservative, societal responses were less ambivalent and more consistent. The two leftist partners in South Africa's governing tripartite alliance were more vocal than the ANC in expressing their support for the popular movements in Tunisia and Egypt. The Congress of South African Trade Unions (COSATU) and the South African Communist Party (SACP) welcomed the political revolts in Egypt and Tunisia, viewing them as a backlash against the neo-liberal policies adopted by dictatorships in the two countries.[34] Local trade unionists called for demonstrations at the Egyptian embassy in Tshwane in support of the uprising. However, both COSATU and the SACP backed the South African government's later position on the NATO intervention in Libya, regarding the military action as an attack against the people of Libya by "neo-imperialist" forces seeking to secure their narrow political and economic interests. Both also supported the African Union's roadmap for Libya and the South African-led mediation to the country.[35]

Similarly, a number of South African scholars and civil society activists welcomed the popular revolutions in North Africa, but also warned of setbacks and of the consequences of Western intervention to influence the march of democracy in the sub-region.[36] For example, an International Solidarity Conference, convened in Tshwane in October 2012, commended the calls for democracy and social justice by North Africa's masses, while highlighting the negative role of "external players and reactionary forces".[37]

Meanwhile, South African companies have been hesitant, if not reluctant, to extend their limited activities in North Africa in the wake of the uprisings. Exceptions include Coronation Fund Managers, a fund management company, which indicated in March 2011 that it may direct "meaningful amounts" of its funds to buy assets in North Africa. However, Prescient Investment Management, another South African company, which extended its equity fund activities in the telecommunications and financial sectors to Egypt, Tunisia and Morocco, reported producing negative or marginal returns on its investments in all three countries.[38] Although North African countries, especially Libya and Algeria, offer good opportunities for investment in the energy sector, South African businesses face stiff competition from European, and more recently Chinese, companies that have already established a strong presence in the sub-region. For example, South African oil companies have failed in recent years to secure exploration contracts in Algeria, although PetroSA signed a nuclear cooperation agreement with its Algerian counterpart in 2010.[39] Additionally, a lack of stable institutions and deteriorating security conditions pose political risks that have further hindered the expansion of foreign investments into the North African sub-region.

South Africa in North Africa: A Policy Agenda

Since the popular uprisings began in 2010, uncertainty has remained the central characteristic of politics in North Africa. Many challenges still lie ahead for the march towards democracy and economic renewal in the sub-region. During this transition, three issues will be particularly pertinent for South Africa's foreign policy towards North Africa. The first concerns the sharing of experiences of reconciliation and institutional reform, as already proposed by Tshwane, to assist its North African peers in their transitions to democracy. Tunisia, for example, in drafting its law for transitional justice that established a Truth and Dignity Commission, and was finally adopted by its Constituent Assembly in December 2013, has been particularly interested in South Africa's Truth and Reconciliation Commission. In April 2013, a Tunisian delegation led by the minister of human rights and transitional justice, Samir Dilou, visited South Africa in order to learn lessons from the country's experience.[40]

However, Tshwane's position on Libya and the dispute with the transitional authorities over Qaddafi's assets in South Africa may impede cooperation with Tripoli in the short term, as with Egypt. Following the removal of Mohamed Morsi and the ensuing diplomatic spat with South Africa, Cairo criticised what it considered to be Tshwane's attempt "to export its model of national reconciliation" to other countries. Egypt further raised doubts about the success of the "model", pointing to the challenges of "creating genuine coexistence among the spectra of its people" and of "providing the basic needs of the people who suffer from one of the highest rates worldwide in violence, crime, corruption, poverty, unemployment, and the outbreak of epidemic diseases".[41] Thus, in the case of Egypt, cooperation between South African and Egyptian civil society, including trade unions and think tanks, may be more relevant in terms of sharing experiences of reconciliation and transition, at least in the short term.

In this context, if South Africa is to formulate well-informed policies towards the new regimes in North Africa, it must develop a better understanding of the particularities of the countries in the sub-region and the character of the major political forces in them. In particular, Tshwane needs to elaborate a nuanced position on Islamist movements in the sub-region, one that differentiates between moderate movements that engage in the political process, and violent groups who opt for non-peaceful means of political struggle. This is especially important in post-revolutionary North Africa, where competing forces are tarring Islamist parties who won majorities in democratic elections with the "terrorist" brush in order to distort their image internationally and eliminate their popularity domestically.

In the past, South Africa has generally adopted a cautious approach towards the threat of "terrorism" in North Africa, refusing to subscribe to the Western politicised use of the term to justify military interventions in strategic regions. Tshwane's diplomacy towards Islamist groups in Algeria at the beginning of the 1990s revealed "South Africa's naiveté in dealing with the phenomenon of 'Islamism'".[42] Mandela considered armed Islamist groups as victims of Algerian repression and received their leaders, an approach that caused a diplomatic crisis between the two countries. Since then, Tshwane has shown solidarity with the government in Algiers in its fight against "terrorist" groups. South Africa similarly received the exiled leader of Tunisia's an-Nahda movement, Rachid Ghannouchi, in 1994, but this turned out to be less problematic. Good relations with Ghannouchi and an-Nahda, which formed the largest Islamist movement in Tunisia after the fall of Ben Ali in 2011, facilitated cooperation between Tunis and Tshwane. Given the current crisis that faces emerging Islamist movements, South Africa needs continuously to review and develop its position on these forces in North Africa, based on an understanding of the agenda of different Islamist groups and parties, as well as the drivers of violence, in the sub-region.

The second issue on South Africa's foreign policy agenda must focus on providing assistance to the new regimes in North Africa in the area of institutional capacity-building. Libya, in particular, is confronted with a legacy of decades of dysfunctional state institutions, including its security and military apparatus. Assassinations and rising instability prompted a renegade ex-general, Khalifa Haftar, backed by militias and "tribal" forces, to launch an armed campaign against the fragile government and parliament since May 2014, increasing uncertainty over the country's political future. Since then, Libya has fallen prey to contestation between an Islamist government installed in Tripoli by the elected, but expired, General National Council (GNC) and another internationally recognised administration in Tobruk appointed by a parliament elected in June 2014. Mediation efforts by the United Nations led to the signing of a political agreement in December 2015 and the formation of a Government of National Accord (GNA) in March 2016. But the new government hardly represents all the country's political groups and factions and the fighting on the ground between different militias continued in 2017. In this context, establishing a professional national army and a functional security apparatus will remain an urgent priority for Libya.

The third, and related, issue that should be a focus of South Africa's foreign policy agenda in North Africa is to support the process of restoring sub-regional peace and security. In September 2011, the AU Peace and Security Council's High-Level Ad Hoc Committee noted that the situation in Libya since the fall of Qaddafi had undermined regional security and increased the threats of terrorism and weapons proliferation, not only in North Africa itself, but also in the Sahel region and beyond. The subsequent conflict in northern Mali that started with a Tuareg rebellion in January 2012 was, to a large extent, a consequence of the proliferation of small arms from post-Qaddafi Libya. South African support for the consolidation of peace and security in the North African sub-region could thus take the form of advice and mediation to help to revitalise the largely moribund Arab Maghreb Union (AMU). Building a strong regional economic community in North Africa is an essential way of addressing common political and security challenges in the sub-region.

An active South African foreign policy based on the three priorities identified here needs to be supported by rigorous, policy-oriented research by South African think tanks, and to be implemented by a capable diplomatic corps. With the exception of the Johannesburg-based Afro-Middle East Centre (AMEC), South African think tanks have thus far shown little interest in North African politics. Developing expertise and fostering systematic exchange between research centres are important tools for facilitating cooperation between South Africa and North Africa. Selecting competent officials with the necessary linguistic skills, and sufficient knowledge and experience in the sub-region, to serve in South Africa's diplomatic missions in North Africa is equally important.

Concluding Reflections

Political developments in North Africa since the Tunisian uprising of December 2010 have challenged South Africa's foreign policy in the sub-region. While civil society in South Africa was forthright in expressing its support for the mass democratic movements in North Africa, the government in Tshwane took a more ambivalent and cautious approach, thereby forsaking an opportunity to consolidate its reformist, democracy and human rights-focused African agenda. The situation in Libya, in particular, and its aftermath, have posed a number of key questions that South Africa's foreign policymakers and scholars must address: Under what conditions can, and should, South Africa support armed intervention in Africa? What leverage does Tshwane have, and what policies can it pursue, when confronted with Western determination to intervene under the guise of "humanitarian intervention" in Africa's conflicts in pursuit of more parochial interests? How can South Africa, working alongside Africa's other sub-regional powers, more effectively implement the principle of "African solutions to African problems"? Under what conditions can the South African "model" of transition be suitable for resolving political conflicts and crises on the continent?

Finally, it must be asked: Have the setbacks faced by Egypt, Libya and Tunisia since the popular revolts vindicated South Africa's cautious approach towards these three countries? Continuing instability in the sub-region; the closed political space in Egypt; economic and security challenges in Tunisia; and the continuing fragmentation of state and society in anarchic Libya, all point to the high costs that the revolutions in the three countries have exacted. However, given the deeply entrenched nature of authoritarianism and its institutions in North Africa, the instalment of democratic regimes is bound to be a long and fragile process vulnerable to setbacks and resistance. To help North African countries sail through their democratic transitions, South Africa must share its own historical experiences with them while remaining sensitive to the particularities of individual countries; assist in building the capacity of their emerging institutions; and support the maintenance of regional peace and security in this turbulent sub-region.

Notes

1. Hisham Yezza, "Algeria: Has the Post-Bouteflika Era Already Begun?",
   3 June 2013, http://www.opendemocracy.net/hicham-yezza/algeria-has-post-
   bouteflika-era-already-begun-0 (accessed 1 August 2013); Marina Ottaway and
   Marwan Muasher, "Arab Monarchies: Chances for Reform, Yet Unmet",
   The Carnegie Papers (Washington, DC: Carnegie Endowment for International
   Peace, 2011), pp. 3–6.

2. Iqbal Jhazbhay, "South Africa–North Africa Relations: Bridging a
   Continent", *South African Journal of International Affairs* 11, no. 2 (2004),
   pp. 158–159.

3. Thabo Mbeki, "Statement on the Occasion of the Adoption by the Constitutional
   Assembly of the Republic of South Africa Constitutional Bill", Cape Town,
   8 May 1996.

4. Iqbal Jhazbhay, "South Africa's Relations with North Africa and the Horn", in
   Adekeye Adebajo, Adebayo Adedeji and Chris Landsberg (eds), *South Africa in
   Africa: The Post-Apartheid Era* (Scottsville: University of KwaZulu-Natal Press,
   2007), p. 283.

5. Muammar Qaddafi, quoted in Gamal Nkrumah, "A Tall Order", *Al-Ahram
   Weekly* no. 549, 11–17 July 2002, http://weekly.ahram.org.eg/2002/594/fr1.htm
   (accessed 5 August 2013).

6. Jhazbhay, "South Africa's Relations with North Africa and the Horn", p. 285.

7. South African Department of Foreign Affairs (DFA), *Strategic Plan: 2005–2008*,
   2005, p. 29, http://www.dfa.gov.za/department/stratplan05-08.pdf (accessed
   8 May 2014).

8. Hany Besada, *Meeting the Sphinx: The Experience of South African Firms Doing Business
   in Egypt* (Johannesburg: South African Institute of International Affairs (SAIIA),
   2006), p. 4; European Union (EU), "South Africa: EU Bilateral Trade and Trade
   with the World", 5 July 2013, http://trade.ec.europa.eu/doclib/docs/2006/september/
   tradoc_113447.pdf (accessed 5 August 2013).

9. Besada, *Meeting the Sphinx*, pp. 1–7.

10. Egyptian State Information Service, "Egypt and South Africa", 2013, http://www.
    sis.gov.eg/En/Templates/Articles/tmpArticles.aspx?CatID=116 (accessed 5
    August 2013).

11. This tension between promoting human rights and pursuing a non-interventionist
    approach has turned South Africa into a "reluctant leader" or a "hegemon without
    hegemony". For more information about this discussion, *see, for example*, Adam
    Habib and Nthakeng Selinyane, "South Africa's Foreign Policy and a Realistic Vision
    of an African Century", in Elizabeth Sidiropoulos (ed.), *Apartheid Past, Renaissance
    Future: South Africa's Foreign Policy, 1994–2004* (Johannesburg: SAIIA, 2004);
    Chris Landsberg, "Promoting Democracy: The Mandela-Mbeki Doctrine", *Journal of
    Democracy* 11, no. 3 (2000), pp. 114–115.

12. Jhazbhay, "South Africa–North Africa Relations", pp. 247–248.

13. South African Department of International Relations and Cooperation (DIRCO),
    "Media Statement on the Situation in Egypt", 31 January 2011.

14. African National Congress (ANC), "ANC statement on North Africa", 2 February 2011.

15. DIRCO, "Media Statement on the Resignation of President Mubarak", 14 February 2011.

16. DIRCO, *Annual Report 2010–2011*, 2011, p. 16; and *Annual Report 2011–2012*, 2012, p. 45.

17. Patrick Bond, "The South African Government's 'Talk Left Walk Right' Climate Policy" (Durban: South African Civil Society Information Service, Centre for Civil Society, 2 February 2011); Na'eem Jeenah, "From North to South Africa: Echoes of the Uprisings" (Johannesburg: Afro-Middle East Centre, 27 August 2011); Narnia Bohler-Muller and Charl van der Merwe, "The Potential of Social Media to Influence Socio-Political Change on the African Continent", Briefing no. 46 (Tshwane: Africa Institute of South Africa, March 2011), pp. 7–8.

18. Na'eem Jeenah, "From North to South Africa"; Moeletsi Mbeki, "ANC Blunder Pushing South Africa Towards Uprising", *SABC News*, 19 October 2011, http://www.sabc.co.za/news/a/f78d400048bf9a87973a9fbfc112ae94/anc-blunders-pushing-sa-towa (accessed 15 August 2013).

19. DIRCO, "South Africa Calls on Egyptians to Refrain from Violence", 30 June 2013; and "South Africa Condemns Acts of Violence in Egypt", 15 August 2013.

20. Data from South African Revenue Service (SARS) bilateral trade reports by country, http://www.sars.gov.za/ClientSegments/Customs-Excise/Trade-Statistics/Pages/Merchandise-Trade-Statistics.aspx (accessed 6–7 July 2017).

21. DIRCO, "Media Statement on the Situation in Libya", 21 February 2011.

22. DIRCO, "South Africa Welcomes and Supports the UNSC Resolution on Libya", 27 February 2011.

23. DIRCO, "South Africa Welcomes and Supports the UN Security Council's Resolution on No Fly Zone in Libya", 18 March 2011.

24. Ebrahim Ebrahim, "Libya, the United Nations, the African Union and South Africa: Wrong Moves? Wrong Moves?", public lecture, University of Pretoria, 15 September 2011; Ebrahim Ebrahim, "South Africa's Position vis-à-vis Recent UNSC Resolutions on Libya and the Libyan Crisis as a Test of South Africa's Leadership Role on 'African Solutions to African Problems'", lecture, University of Venda, Limpopo, South Africa, 2 August 2011.

25. Thabo Mbeki, "West Has Hijacked Africa's Concerns", *Cape Times*, 5 April 2011, p. 9.

26. *See, for example*, Hillary Clinton, "Africa Must Abandon Gaddafi, Support Democracy in Libya", 14 June 2011, http://www.globalresearch.ca/clinton-africa-must-abandon-gaddafi-support-democracy-in-libya/25265 (accessed 6 August 2013); Yoweri Museveni, "Libya Needs Dialogue", *ANC Today* no. 11, 1–7 April 2011; Yusuf Ali, "Libya: Nigeria, South Africa in Cold War over Gaddafi's Fate", *The Nation*, 4 September 2011.

27. For more information on Western interests in Libya's energy resources, *see* Gawdat Bahgat, "The Geo-Politics of Energy: Europe and North Africa", *Journal of North African Studies* 15, no. 1 (2010), pp. 39–49. *See also* Horace Campbell, *Global NATO and the Catastrophic Failure in Libya* (New York: Monthly Review Press, 2013), pp. 85–113.

28. Eusebius McKaiser, "Looking an International Relations Gift Horse in the Mouth: SA's Response to the Libyan Crisis", 2011 Ruth First Memorial Lecture, Johannesburg, 17 August 2011, http://www.politicsweb.co.za/politicsweb/view/politicsweb/en/page71619?oid=251952&sn=Detail%3c (accessed 15August 2013); Alex de Waal, "African Roles in the Libyan Conflict", *International Affairs* 89, no. 2 (2013), pp. 373–374.

29. DIRCO, *Annual Report 2011–2012*, p. 45.

30. "Egypt Could Join BRICS Countries to Form E-BRICS: President Morsi", *Ahram Online*, 26 March 2013, http://english.ahram.org.eg/NewsContent/3/12/67158/Business/Economy/Egypt-could-join-BRICS-countries-to-form-EBRICS-Pr.aspx (accessed 15 August 2013).

31. "Hand Evidence of Libyan Assets to UN: Gordhan", *Times Live*, 20 June 2013.

32. Presidency of South Africa, "President Zuma Concludes Working Visit to Algeria", 15 April 2013.

33. Data from SARS bilateral trade reports by country.

34. Congress of South African Trade Unions (COSATU), "Press Statement on COSATU Central Committee Meeting", 24 February 2011; National Education Health and Allied Workers Union (NEHAWU), "NEHAWU Supports the Egyptian Revolution", 1 February 2011; South African Communist Party (SACP), "SACP Supports Popular Uprisings in Tunisia, Egypt", 2 February 2011.

35. COSATU and SACP, "COSATU-SACP Joint Statement on Fighting Corruption and Tenderpreneurship", 7 April 2011; COSATU, "COSATU Supports March by Our Affiliate NUMSA to Demand End to NATO Bombings in Libya", 5 July 2011.

36. Patrick Bond, "Egyptian Revolution Thrills Civil Society but There Is a Danger of Getting Drunk on Our Own Rhetoric", *Pambazuka Newsletter* no. 517, 17 February 2011, http://pambazuka.org/en/category/features/70958 (accessed 15 August 2011); Khadija Sharife, "After Mubarak? What's Next for Egypt?", *Pambazuka Newsletter* no. 516, 10 February 2011, http://www.pambazuka.org/en/category/features/70774 (accessed 15 August 2011); Na'eem Jeenah, "Uprising in the Middle East: Making a New World Possible" (Tshwane: Afro-Middle East Centre, 5 May 2011); Richard Pithouse, "The World Remade", *Pambazuka Newsletter* no. 518, 24 February 2011, http://pambazuka.org/en/category/features/71171 (accessed 15 august 2011).

37. ANC, "Tshwane Declaration: 3rd International Solidarity Conference", 25–28 October 2012.

38. "Coronation May Chase Bargains in North Africa", *Reuters*, 9 March 2011, http://www.reuters.com/article/2011/03/09/us-africainvest-summit-fundmanagers-idUSTRE7284KF20110309 (accessed 17 August 2013); Prescient Holdings, "Opportunity Knocks: The African Frontier" (Cape Town: Prescient House, 2011), http://www.prescient.co.za/holdings/index_page.php?PageID=Press_African Markets&SubMenuItemID=&mainMenuID=&SubMenuID= (accessed 17 August 2013).

39. South African Department of Energy, "Minister Peters and PetroSA Signs Agreement with Algeria", 16 May 2010.

40. South African Department of Justice and Constitutional Development, "SA, Tunisia, Strengthen Bilateral Relations", 3 April 2013, http://www.justice.gov.za/events/2013events/20130403-tunisia.html (accessed 23 August 2013).

41. Egyptian Ministry of Foreign Affairs, "Statement from the Ministry", 17 August 2013.

42. Jhazbhay, "South Africa's Relations with North Africa and the Horn", p. 280.

PART III

SOUTH AFRICA'S KEY MULTILATERAL RELATIONS IN AFRICA

CHAPTER 11

SOUTH AFRICA AND THE SOUTHERN AFRICAN DEVELOPMENT COMMUNITY

Chris Saunders and Dawn Nagar

The ways in which the relationship between South Africa and the Southern African Development Community (SADC) has evolved over the two decades since the country joined SADC in August 1994 remains a surprisingly neglected topic.[1] What role has SADC played in South Africa's foreign policy since 1994? How has South Africa's membership shaped the Community? In beginning to answer such questions, this chapter will first consider political aspects, then economic ones. Both aspects need to be explored if the country's relationship with the sub-regional organisation is to be understood fully. The chapter begins with some historical background, though, for it is also only possible to understand the relationship between post-apartheid South Africa and SADC by relating it to aspects of their past. In so doing, it also seeks to show how South Africa's involvement in the Community has changed over time.

Since 1994, although South Africa's presidency has been the main driver of foreign policy, rather than its Department of International Relations and Cooperation (DIRCO), other departments, including the Department of Trade and Industry (DTI) and National Treasury, have interacted separately with SADC, thus contributing to incoherence in South Africa's involvement with the sub-regional organisation. The chapter further suggests that on the whole, South Africa has not, in its first two decades as a democracy, given sufficient attention to SADC and has sometimes acted as if the regional body does not exist. Yet, a closer relationship in the future would be in the interests of both.

South Africa in Southern Africa: A Brief History

When the Union of South Africa was founded in 1910, it brought together four British colonies: the Cape, Natal, the Orange Free State and the Transvaal.[2] The new rulers of the Union – all men of European descent – envisaged that, in time, neighbouring countries would be incorporated into a much larger, white-ruled South Africa. In the same year that the Union came into being, a Southern African Customs Union (SACU) was created that included, besides South Africa – which has always been the dominant country in SACU – three African territories then ruled by Britain: present-day Botswana, Lesotho and Swaziland. Because of Pretoria's segregationist racial policies, these territories were never incorporated into South Africa. Neither was neighbouring Rhodesia (now Zimbabwe), because the white settlers there did not want to become part of a South Africa dominated by Afrikaner nationalists. And although the former German territory of South West Africa (now Namibia) was ruled by Pretoria for 75 years, it never became part of South Africa. Namibia, when it eventually freed itself from South African rule in March 1990, joined SACU, which was by then the oldest customs union in the world (see Gibb in this volume). White South Africa did not incorporate other territories in the sub-region. Rather, with the end of apartheid and the advent of democracy, it was a new, multi-racial South Africa that joined a pre-existing sub-regional institution – the Southern African Development Community – in 1994.[3]

SADC was only two years old then, having come into existence in August 1992 at a conference held in Windhoek, Namibia, of what until then was known as the Southern African Development Coordination Conference (SADCC). SADCC had been born in April 1980 as the successor to the Frontline States (FLS), an informal organisation of the leaders of Angola, Botswana, Mozambique, Tanzania and Zambia. These five countries worked together from the mid-1970s to decrease their economic and other dependence on white minority-ruled South Africa, whose policy of apartheid was anathema to the leaders of the newly independent Southern African states.[4] As Zimbabwe became independent, and with the addition of Lesotho, Malawi and Swaziland, the FLS became SADCC in April 1980.

By then, Pretoria had embarked on a policy of destabilising its neighbours, to prevent them organising against it and, in particular, to try to ensure that they did not allow guerrillas of the African National Congress (ANC), which was engaged in an armed struggle against the apartheid regime, to move into South Africa. In the early and middle 1980s, South Africa's war against its neighbours intensified, and involved major raids by the South African Defence Force (SADF) into southern Angola (see Naidoo in this volume). With the winding down of the Cold War in the late 1980s, however, an agreement was reached between South Africa, Cuba and Angola for the withdrawal of both the SADF and Cuban forces from Angola and for the independence of Namibia.

In 1990, apartheid leader Frederik Willem de Klerk conceded to the internal and external pressures mounting on his country and announced the abandonment of apartheid and his willingness to negotiate a democratic constitution. The negotiated settlement reached in November 1993 enabled the first democratic election to take place in South Africa in April 1994. That, in turn, made it possible for South Africa to become a member of SADC at the annual meeting of heads of state held in Gaborone, Botswana, in August that year.[5]

Political Aspects of the Relationship between South Africa and SADC

In becoming a part of SADC, South Africa joined an organisation comprising territories of vastly different geographies and economies, including Namibia, a large territory with a very small population; tiny Lesotho, entirely surrounded by South Africa; and countries that were not close neighbours of South Africa, such as Tanzania and Malawi. In 1997, SADC was enlarged further when the Democratic Republic of the Congo (DRC) became a member. Although most of those who lived in the SADC countries spoke one or another Bantu language, their very different colonial experiences had left their governments operating under different European languages, including two (Angola and Mozambique) with Portuguese as their official language and one (the DRC) with French. While movement of people across Southern Africa had a long history, and the diamond and later gold mines in South Africa had attracted labour from as far north as what is now Malawi, as well as from Mozambique, Lesotho, Swaziland and Botswana, no common set of values bound this very diverse sub-region together.

South Africa not only dominated the Southern African sub-region economically, but also had by far the largest minority populations, who had been attracted there by relatively favourable climatic conditions and then, from the late nineteenth century onwards, by the discovery of vast mineral riches. With its relatively large and diverse economy, and a significant manufacturing sector that had developed on the back of mineral exploitation, South Africa immediately became SADC's most important member. The country's iconic transition to democracy under the revered Nelson Mandela, moreover, gave it a role on the world stage out of proportion to its size and economic strength.

Nelson Mandela and SADC

Concern about South Africa's dominance, along with suspicions of its intentions, limited the role that the country might otherwise have played in Southern Africa following the end of apartheid. The headquarters of SADC remained in Gaborone, and Pretoria's apartheid-era aggression in the sub-region was not forgotten by those who had suffered from it. This destabilisation had resulted in much damage and loss of life estimated at $60 billion of damages and one million deaths in the 1980s alone.[6] After 1994, the new South African government was sensitive to the need not to appear as an overbearing hegemon, or to play a "big brother" role in SADC, when asserting its influence in the sub-region. It therefore sought consensus, and worked especially closely with other governments that had come to power after having taken up arms to fight for liberation. President Robert Mugabe of Zimbabwe, however, who had been active in SADCC/SADC since 1980 and was the leading figure in the organisation at the time South Africa joined it, was particularly concerned that Mandela, South Africa's president from 1994 to 1999, was usurping his role. From the beginning of this complex relationship, then, there were tensions within SADC between South Africa and some of the other members, given that Pretoria/Tshwane's relations with its Southern African peers differed from country to country (see Sachikonye in this volume).

On coming to power in 1994, the new government in South Africa, led by Mandela, had enormous problems to deal with, including threats from right-wing elements unhappy with the country's abandonment of apartheid, as well as significant socio-economic issues having arisen from the poverty of much of the population (see Landsberg in this volume). Mandela himself, the former prisoner who had become president, strode the global stage like a colossus and did not give particular attention to the Southern African sub-region. Though his government stated that Southern Africa was the most important priority in its foreign policy, there were those who believed that the country's priorities should lie at home, not in the sub-region, and others who argued that its foreign relations should focus on the country's immediate neighbours, rather than the much larger SADC. On the other hand, the ANC had close ties with most other countries in SADC, many of which had hosted it in exile or supported its struggle in other ways.[7] These ties encouraged the idea that South Africa should engage with the broad Southern African sub-region.

However, under Mandela, the attempts to prioritise SADC were half-hearted. Though South Africa assumed its responsibilities in SADC by hosting a summit meeting for the first time as SADC chair in August 1996 and by signing most of the many SADC protocols, Mandela tried unsuccessfully to broker a power-sharing arrangement in the DRC in 1998 and his government did not support the armed intervention in that country in that year by Angola, Namibia and Zimbabwe (see Curtis, and Nzongola-Ntalaja in this volume). Ironically, however, in the same year – 1998 – South African forces, along with some from Botswana, moved into Lesotho in a controversial and botched operation to restore stability there – an intervention that was only post facto declared to be on behalf of SADC. (See Curtis, and Naidoo in this volume.)

Thabo Mbeki and SADC

Thabo Mbeki, an active deputy president of South Africa after 1994, took over from Mandela as president of the country in 1999. He believed that South Africa should be involved in the continent as a whole, to promote peace and development and to give content to what he described as the "African Renaissance".[8] Although this sometimes worked against a focus on South Africa's relations with the Southern African sub-region, Mbeki played a major role in working for the inclusion of the DRC – Africa's geographically third-largest country, far from South Africa and long embroiled in conflict – into SADC in 1997. When, in 1998, three SADC countries (Angola, Namibia and Zimbabwe) sent armies into the DRC in what was said to be a SADC operation to bring stability there, Tshwane did not regard the intervention as a SADC one.[9] The major struggle within SADC over the status of its Organ on Politics, Defence and Security (OPDS) that began under Mandela continued after Mbeki became

South Africa's president. While Zimbabwe's Mugabe sought to make the SADC security organ autonomous under his leadership, South Africa believed the organ should report to the annual SADC summit. It was only at the Windhoek summit of SADC heads of state in August 2001 that the issue was resolved, with the SADC security organ brought under the authority of SADC's main body.[10] From then on, relations between South Africa and other members of the Community became less conflictual.

Between 2001 and 2003, South Africa, under Mbeki's leadership, played a vital role in bringing peace to the DRC. Tshwane has since continued to play an important role as mediator and peace-enforcer for SADC. South Africa, under Thabo Mbeki's direct leadership, was the main facilitator in the internal conflict in Zimbabwe. Notably, in September 2008, Mbeki helped bring about the Global Political Agreement (GPA) between the ruling Zimbabwe African National Union – Patriotic Front (ZANU-PF) and the two factions of the opposition Movement for Democratic Change (MDC).[11] (See Sachikonye, and Curtis in this volume.)

Jacob Zuma and SADC

When Jacob Zuma became South Africa's president in May 2009, he took over from Mbeki as chief SADC "facilitator" on Zimbabwe, and sought to get the opposing parties to agree to a new constitution as a prelude to the holding of a free, fair and credible election. Based on its own domestic experience of a peaceful and negotiated settlement, South Africa saw itself as well-placed to work to bring together the parties in conflicts elsewhere (see Curtis in this volume). However, in the case of Zimbabwe, the Mbeki-negotiated GPA was not effectively enforced: though it brought a measure of stability to Zimbabwe, this did not mean a return to the rule of law. When elections were held in Zimbabwe in July 2013, the polls were controversial, with the voter roll not being available until the very day of the election. However, SADC accepted the ZANU-PF victory as the outcome of a credible election, and South Africa's president Zuma hastened to extend his congratulations to Mugabe on his re-election.

Following a military coup in Madagascar in 2009, SADC similarly set in place a mediation process in which Mozambique took the leading role, but because the ousted president had fled to South Africa, Tshwane was necessarily involved. Zuma played a major role in persuading the two leading opposing figures, Marc Ravalomanana and Andry Rajoelina, to agree that neither would contest the first post-coup election, which finally took place in December 2013 (see Curtis in this volume).

Generally speaking, Zuma has been more concerned than Mbeki with cementing relations with other former liberation movements that have become ruling parties in Southern Africa.[12] Since 2008, South Africa has taken the lead in pushing for SADC to join with the East African Community (EAC) and the Common Market for Eastern and Southern Africa (COMESA) in a tripartite agreement (discussed later in more detail). Although SADC regularly meets at the level of heads of state summits – sometimes held twice a year – South Africa's bilateral relations with individual member states often appear to trump those it has with the sub-regional body.[13] And South Africa has had to accept that SADC does not always speak with one voice: witness, for example, the opposition expressed by Botswana's president, Ian Khama, to the SADC position on the contested poll results in Zimbabwe in 2008 and again in 2013.

The view that SADC is little more than a club to protect the Community's ruling interests appeared to be validated when its heads of state agreed in August 2010 to disband the tribunal they themselves had set up to adjudicate on disputes in the sub-region, after that tribunal had ruled against the Zimbabwean government in a case involving the country's white farmers' confiscated land. The chief judge of the SADC tribunal, Ariranga Pillay of Mauritius, was at the time extremely critical of South Africa, in particular, for not using "its power as the SADC's largest state and its 'moral authority' to prevent the tribunal being emasculated".[14] (See Fritz, and Sachikonye in this volume.)

Along with other states in SADC, South Africa has remained opposed to the transfer of national sovereignty to the sub-regional body, presumably based on a lack of confidence in the Community as much as on a wish to ensure that its national interests continue to be paramount at all times. South African analyst Laurie Nathan has argued that South Africa, as well as other SADC member countries, have been reluctant to transfer any sovereignty to the sub-regional organisation in part because their sovereignty – itself acquired relatively recently – remains so fragile.[15] Tshwane's engagement with SADC has continued to appear half-hearted in many respects. For example, South Africa has done very little to ensure that ordinary citizens in the 281 million-strong bloc play an active role in SADC, which in turn has made little attempt to inform the wider public of its activities. The SADC website remains poor, while its newsletter has a very limited circulation. Membership in SADC, on the other hand, brings South Africa clear benefits. It was only because Nkosazana Dlamini-Zuma was put forward as the SADC candidate, and received the support of most of its 15 members, that South Africa was successful in getting her elected Chair of the African Union (AU) Commission in July 2012 (see Maloka in this volume).

Economic Aspects of the Relationship between South Africa and SADC

Before South Africa joined SADC in 1994, the country was already an economic giant in Southern Africa, a region rich in mineral resources, with gold, platinum and other precious metals found in South Africa; diamonds in Botswana, Angola and the DRC; copper in Zambia; and oil in Angola. South African multinational corporations (MNCs), such as Anglo-American and De Beers (diamond marketing), have long been a driving force in exploiting these mineral resources, while others such as Mobile Telephone Networks (MTN) and Vodacom (mobile phones), and Shoprite Checkers (retail), have developed new markets in the sub-region since 1994 (see Vickers and Cawood in this volume).[16] From an economic perspective, key external actors such as the United States (US) and the European Union (EU) have also long viewed South Africa as a vital geo-strategic interest and, with the end of apartheid, as an ideal entry point into Southern Africa and Africa at large.[17] Both Western powers have pushed for market liberalisation in Southern Africa, with the US seeking to do so through its African Growth and Opportunity Act (AGOA) of 1998,[18] to which South Africa became a signatory in 2000 (see Weissman in this volume). Meanwhile, the EU signed the Trade, Development and Cooperation Agreement (TDCA) with South Africa in 1999,[19] and has sought to enlarge its agricultural market for exports in the sub-region more widely through the EU-SADC economic partnership agreement (EPA) finalised in 2016 with Botswana, Namibia, Lesotho, Mozambique, South Africa and Swaziland.[20] (See Nkosi in this volume.) Though with Britain poised to extract itself from the EU by 2019, following a June 2016 referendum, new trading arrangements between SADC countries and both London and Brussels will now need to be negotiated (see Large in this volume).

Following the advent of democracy in 1994, successive South African governments have employed a range of economic policy instruments to try to deliver on their promise of social development (see Landsberg in this volume). With the apparent failure of the Growth, Employment and Redistribution (GEAR) policy – introduced in 1996 – to address the post-apartheid economy's structural weaknesses and tackle its persistent poverty, Tshwane has increasingly looked towards Southern Africa to help accelerate its economic development.[21] Notably, both the New Growth Path (NGP) of 2010 and the National Development Plan (NDP) of 2011 set out economic growth policies that emphasised cross-border infrastructure projects in Southern Africa.

SADC's market integration efforts have been relatively unsuccessful to date. Despite initiatives to strengthen Southern Africa's weaker economies, about 83 per cent of South Africa's trade was still conducted outside the sub-region in 2013.[22] In 2003, SADC launched its 15-year Regional Indicative Strategic Development Plan (RISDP), intended to be the Community's key economic instrument and blueprint for increasing and developing trade among its 15 member states. The plan's ambitious goals included the establishment of a free trade area (FTA) by 2008, a customs union by 2010, a common market by 2015, a monetary union by 2016 and a common currency by 2018.[23] Due to the unequal economies of SADC member states, these goals remain unmet, and to make progress, SADC member states will have to deal effectively with such issues as trade in services; free movement of businesses, people and goods; removal of non-tariff barriers; and harmonisation of rules of origin. The mid-term review of the RISDP in 2013 provided an opportunity for SADC's 15 member states to develop a regional integration agenda that could enhance trade in both goods and services; generate growth and employment opportunities; and develop migration policies allowing for the freer movement of people across Southern Africa. The key objective of the post-2018 period, when the RISDP of 2003 comes to an end, will be the setting of various regional targets and programmes to deepen SADC's regional integration plans and work towards finalising its tripartite agreement with COMESA and the EAC.

Given the enormity of South Africa's domestic socio-economic development challenges, it may be too much to demand consistency from the country's region-building efforts in Southern Africa. As a developing country itself, South Africa has a national interest in building its own economy and addressing the socio-economic inequalities inherited from the apartheid regime, an effort that remains of paramount importance.[24] Inevitably, as Tshwane's foreign economic policy tries to meet regional and domestic objectives, there are bound to be times when the balance will tip in favour of its internal priorities. In this respect, South Africa's contradictory behaviour towards region-building efforts in Southern Africa can be explained, at least in part, by the fact that it has to balance its relationship with SADC and its domestic efforts to address inequality and poverty, as well as its relationship with SACU.

Although South Africa's membership and role in SACU (see Gibb in this volume) demonstrate a commitment to support smaller and weaker economies in the sub-region, this has also complicated larger region-building efforts in SADC. A year after South Africa joined the Community, South Africa's regional exports in 1995 already totalled $2.8 billion, while its regional imports totalled merely $0.4 billion. The country accounted for about 60 per cent of the Southern African economy in 2017. The huge economic disparities among SACU's five member states, in particular, all of which are also members of SADC – Botswana, Lesotho, Swaziland and Namibia (the BLNS states), and South Africa – have led to strained relations between the smaller BLNS economies and South Africa, which disproportionately dominates intra-SACU trade. As SADC has moved towards an FTA, South Africa has had great difficulty balancing SADC and SACU in its foreign policy. For example, while SADC was concentrating on a framework to liberalise tariffs among its member states, Swaziland, a vibrant sugar producer, had to compete against other sugar-producing SADC states, especially South Africa, which had the most developed sugar industry in the region. This caused much resentment within SACU.[25]

At SADC's August 2014 Summit, South Africa was not in a position to sign the SADC Trade Protocol Services Agreement, and Namibia similarly refused, while Zimbabwe's Robert Mugabe, who was in the chair, expressed his disappointment at South Africa's one-sided trade practices.[26] In retaliation at South Africa's stringent trade policies, Zimbabwe went on to sign a $533 million power project with China and a further $3 billion deal with Russia jointly to mine platinum in Zimbabwe, with Moscow providing the investment funds and not South Africa. This was a counter-move by Mugabe to South Africa's excluding Zimbabwe from a platinum deal.[27] This illustrates again the tensions within SADC, and the reality that South Africa does not always have the same economic interests as the organisation's 14 other member states.

Concluding Reflections

Since 1994, South Africa has sought to play a role on the global stage, and SADC has not been one of its main priorities. SADC remains a weak institution, heavily dependent on donor funding, much of which comes from the EU Commission in Brussels. While the EU, which sees itself as a successful example of regional integration, is sometimes seen as a model for SADC,[28] the Southern African sub-region's historical and economic positions are very different from those of Europe, where regional integration was undertaken largely to avoid recurrence of the devastation of World War II (1939–1945), which ended in the defeat of Germany, a country that subsequently went on to become the region's economic powerhouse. In Southern Africa, while violence and conflict marred relations between apartheid South Africa – the sub-region's largest economy – and other states, the collapse of apartheid brought those conflicts to an end. But, the memory of the apartheid-era wars remained and negatively affected the pursuit of regional integration. This was the case despite the evident benefits of regionalism in particular areas, such as in promoting economic growth and development, tackling the spread of HIV/AIDS, and dealing with illegal immigration and refugees, as well as narcotics and arms smuggling.

Regional integration in Southern Africa thus remains very much a work in progress. South Africa's relations with SADC are complex, and have shifted over time, while coming to form a part of its broader interactions with other sub-regional organisations such as SACU, COMESA and the EAC, as well as the AU. Summits of governments have continued to be held in August each year, at great cost especially to the poorer countries, such as Swaziland, which hosted SADC's August 2016 summit. South Africa has also protected its markets and productive firms through implementing high domestic entry barriers in various sectors. For example, at the SADC summit in August 2014, Zimbabwe's president Robert Mugabe noted: "[W]e appeal to South Africa, which is highly industrialised, to lead us in this [industrialisation] and work with us, and cooperate with us and not just regard the whole continent as an open market for products from South Africa. We want a reciprocal relationship where we sell to each other [and] not just receiving products from one source."[29]

Extraordinary summits have also been held, such as that in Zimbabwe in April 2015 to adopt a regional industrialisation strategy and road-map. South Africa played a leading role as a member of the troika made up of past, present and future chairs. In June 2016, an extraordinary double summit of the troikas of both the heads of state and of the Organ met in Gaborone to discuss the instability in Lesotho. Meanwhile, South Africa's deputy president Cyril Ramaphosa has continued to be SADC's chief mediator in the crisis in the kingdom of Lesotho, while the presence of South African troops in the UN mission in the DRC has given South Africa a special role in SADC's efforts to resolve ongoing conflict there. In 2017 South Africa again took over as chair of SADC and hosted its annual meeting.[30]

While the rhetoric emanating from South Africa's foreign ministry has continued to suggest that the Southern African sub-region is South Africa's main priority in its foreign policy, in reality SADC has often not been accorded prime attention by the country's policymakers. Similarly, although DIRCO has often asserted that South Africa is a "gateway" into the rest of the continent, other countries – notably Nigeria in West Africa and Kenya in East Africa – are increasingly being seen as "gateways" into Africa. Given the unwillingness of the sub-region's countries to surrender their sovereignty, it remains unclear how far they will take regionalism in Southern Africa. Even so, SADC is a key building block of Africa's broader region-building and regional integration project and, as such, is a bridge between the national and continental levels. Bearing this in mind, it is likely that South Africa – in view of its economic resources and dominance – will continue to drive the ongoing region-building project in Southern Africa.

Notes

1. The leading study of the Southern African Development Community (SADC) as an organisation concerned with peace and security is Laurie Nathan, *Community of Insecurity: SADC's Struggle for Peace and Security in Southern Africa* (Aldershot: Ashgate, 2012). An earlier, more general study with greater focus on South Africa's role is Peter Vale, *Security and Politics in South Africa: The Regional Dimension* (Cape Town: University of Cape Town Press, 2003). *See also* Maxi Schoeman, "The Limits of Regionalisation in Southern Africa", in Nana Poku (ed.), *Security and Development in Southern Africa* (Westport, CT: Praeger, 2001), pp. 139–156; and Chris Landsberg and Jo-Ansie van Wyk (eds), *South African Foreign Policy Review*, vol. 1 (Tshwane: Africa Institute of South Africa; and Midrand: Institute for Global Dialogue (IGD), 2012). The most recent relevant works are Chris Saunders, "South Africa and Africa", in Robert I. Rotberg (ed.), "Strengthening Governance in

South Africa: Building on Mandela's Legacy", *Annals of the American Academy of Political and Social Science* 652 (2014), pp. 221–137; and Gilbert M. Khadiagala, "South Africa in Africa: Groping for Leadership and Muddling Through", in Gilbert M. Khadiagala, Prishani Naidoo, Devan Pillay and Roger Southall (eds), *New South Africa Review 4* (Johannesburg: Wits University Press, 2014), pp. 275–289.

2. *See, for example*, Martin Meredith, *Diamonds, Gold, and War: The British, the Boers, and the Making of South Africa* (Johannesburg: Jonathan Ball, 2007); and compare to Martin Chanock, *Unconsummated Union: Britain, Rhodesia, and South Africa, 1900–45* (Manchester: Manchester University Press, 1977).

3. On the early 1990s, *see especially* Chris Landsberg, *The Quiet Diplomacy of Liberation: International Politics and South Africa's Transition* (Johannesburg: Jacana, 2004). On SADC generally, *see* Gabriel H. Oosthuizen, *The Southern African Development Community: The Organisation, Its Policies, and Prospects* (Johannesburg: IGD, 2006); South African Department of Foreign Affairs (DFA), "Southern African Development Community (SADC): History and Present Status", last updated 12 February 2004, http://www.dfa.gov.za/foreign/Multilateral/africa/sadc.htm (accessed 21 June 2014).

4. *See especially* Gilbert M. Khadiagala, *Allies in Adversity: The Frontline States in Southern African Security, 1975–1993* (Athens: Ohio University Press, 1994).

5. *See* DFA, "Southern African Development Community".

6. Adebayo Adedeji, "Within or Apart?", in Adebayo Adedeji (ed.), *South Africa in Africa: Within or Apart?* (London: Zed, 1996), p. 9.

7. *See especially* South African Democracy Education Trust, *The Road to Democracy in South Africa*, vol. 5, pt. 1 (Pretoria: Unisa, 2013); and Stephen Ellis, *External Mission: The ANC in Exile* (Johannesburg: Jonathan Ball, 2013).

8. Thabo Mbeki, *Africa: The Time Has Come: Selected Speeches* (Cape Town: Tafelberg, 1998).

9. Gilbert M. Khadiagala, "South Africa's Role in Conflict Resolution in the Democratic Republic of Congo", in Kurt Shillinger (ed.), *Africa's Peacemaker? Lessons from South African Conflict Mediation* (Auckland Park: Jacana, 2009), pp. 67–80.

10. Nathan, *Community of Insecurity*, pp. 35–62.

11. Siphamandla Zondi and Zandile Bhengu, *The SADC Facilitation and Democratic Transition in Zimbabwe* (Midrand: IGD, 2011). On the background to the signing of the Global Political Agreement (GPA), *see* Southern African Liaison Office (SALO), *South Africa–Zimbabwe Relations*, vol. 1 (Johannesburg: Jacana, 2013).

12. These movements, besides the Zimbabwe African National Union – Patriotic Front (ZANU-PF) in Zimbabwe, include the Popular Movement for the Liberation of Angola (MPLA), the Front for the Liberation of Mozambique (Frelimo) and the South West Africa People's Organisation (SWAPO) in Namibia. On the African National Congress (ANC), ZANU-PF and SWAPO, *see* Roger Southall, *Liberation Movements in Power* (Pietermaritzburg: University of KwaZulu-Natal Press, 2013).

13. *See* Centre for Conflict Resolution (CCR), *Governance and Security Challenges in Post-Apartheid Southern Africa*, Seminar Report no. 43 (Cape Town, South Africa, September 2013), http://www.ccr.org.za/index.php/media-release/reports/seminar-

reports/item/869-governance-and-security-challenges-in-post-apartheid-southern-africa (accessed 25 August 2014).

14. Peter Fabricius, "Selfish JZ Allowed Mugabe to Kill SADC Tribunal", South African Foreign Policy Initiative (SAFPI), 4 March 2013, http://www.safpi.org/news/article/2013/selfish-jz-allowed-mugabe-kill-sadc-tribunal (accessed 12 October 2013).

15. Nathan, *Community of Insecurity*.

16. Dawn Nagar, "Regional Economic Integration", in Chris Saunders, Gwinyayi A. Dzinesa and Dawn Nagar (eds), *Region-Building in Southern Africa: Progress, Problems and Prospects* (London: Zed; and Johannesburg: Wits University Press, 2012), pp. 131–147.

17. Dawn Nagar, "The Politics and Economics of Regional Integration in Africa: A Comparative Study of COMESA and SADC, 1980–2015", PhD thesis, University of the Witwatersrand (Wits), Johannesburg.

18. Nomfundo Xenia Ngwenya, "The United States", in Saunders, Dzinesa and Nagar, *Region-Building in Southern Africa*, pp. 264–281.

19. Margaret C. Lee, *The Political Economy of Regionalism in Southern Africa* (Boulder, CO: Rienner; and Cape Town: University of Cape Town Press, 2003), p. 212.

20. Nagar, "The Politics of Regional Integration in Africa".

21. Landsberg and van Wyk, *South African Foreign Policy Review*, vol. 1, p. 117.

22. Jorge Iván Canales-Kriljenko, Farayi Gwenhamo and Saji Thomas, "Inward and Outward Spillovers in the SACU Area", International Monetary Fund (IMF) Working Paper no. WP/13/31 (January 2013), https://www.imf.org/external/pubs/ft/wp/2013/wp1331.pdf (accessed 7 July 2017). Data available from the South African Department of Trade and Industry (DTI), http://tradestats.thedti.gov.za/ReportFolders/reportFolders.aspx?sCS_referer=&sCS_ChosenLang = en.

23. SADC, "Desk Assessment of the RISDP 2005–2010 Plan", November 2011, http://www.sadc.int/index.php?cID=201 (accessed 8 September 2014); SADC, "1966 Trade Protocol on Integration", http://www.sadcstan.co.za/Secure/downloads/protocol.pdf (accessed 8 September 2014).

24. Nagar, "The Politics of Regional Integration in Africa". *See also* Neissan Alessandro Besharati, "South African Development Partnership Agency (SADPA): Strategic Aid or Development Packages for Africa?", Research Report no. 12 (Johannesburg: South African Institute of International Affairs (SAIIA), Economic Diplomacy Programme, August 2013), http://www.saiia.org.za/research-reports/347-south-african-development-partnership-agency-sadpa-strategic-aid-or-development-packages-for-africa/file (accessed 31 August 2013).

25. Lee, *The Political Economy of Regionalism*, p. 122.

26. Dawn Nagar, personal interview conducted at COMESA Secretariat, 22 August 2014. *See also* Everson Mushava and Owen Gagare, "Red Faces as South Africa, Namibia Refuse to Sign SADC Trade Protocol", *News Day*, 19 August 2014, https://www.newsday.co.zw/2014/08/19/red-faces-sa-namibia-refuse-sign-sadc-trade-protocol/ (accessed 31 August 2014).

27. *See* "Zimbabwe, Russia Sign $3bn Platinum Deal", *Fin24*, 16 September 2014, http://www.fin24.com/Economy/Zimbabwe-Russia-sign-3bn-platinum-deal-20140916 (accessed 31 August 2014). Dawn Nagar, confidential interview, 2014.

28. Amos Saurombe, "The European Union as a Model for Regional Integration in the Southern African Development Community: A Selective Institutional Comparative Analysis", *Law Democracy and Development* 17 (2013), pp. 457–476.

29. Dawn Nagar, personal interview conducted in Zambia, August 2014, with key COMESA officials who attended the 34th SADC Summit. *See also* Mushava and Gagare, "Red Faces as SA, Namibia, Refuse to Sign SADC Trade Protocol".

30. *See also* CCR and Friedrich Ebert Stiftung (FES) Botswana, *Region-Building and Peacebuilding in Southern Africa*, Seminar Report no. 52 (Gaborone, Botswana, February 2016), http://www.ccr.org.za (accessed 7 July 2017).

CHAPTER 12

SOUTH AFRICA IN THE SOUTHERN AFRICAN CUSTOMS UNION

Richard Gibb

The Southern African Customs Union (SACU) is a remarkable regional institution. As well as being the most effectively functioning and sophisticated example of customs-led integration in Africa, it is also the oldest customs union in the world, predating the European Union (EU) by almost 50 years.[1] In addition, SACU has a specific and unique historical trajectory that, thus far, has been influenced more by international relations and geo-politics than economic integration or development imperatives. One of SACU's most pronounced character-istics is the variation in size of its member states and the sharply contrasting levels of development among them. The existence of considerable absolute and relative inequalities between Botswana, Lesotho, Namibia and Swaziland (the BLNS states) and South Africa has influenced significantly the nature and evolution of this customs union. The high levels of economic dependence that the BLNS states have on South Africa and SACU-generated income underpins an asymmetric power relationship among the organisation's five member states. Within SACU, South Africa is the undisputed hegemonic power. Thus, any examination of SACU in the two decades after apartheid must necessarily be contextualised in terms of South Africa's dominance; the organisation's longevity, sophistication, structural inequalities and dependence; as well as its regional and international geo-politics.

I contend in this chapter that South Africa's interests have determined – almost without exception – the nature, evolution and character of SACU. These interests were mediated through London in the colonial era; through Pretoria during the white-minority apartheid regime; and through Tshwane in post-apartheid South Africa. SACU can therefore be interpreted as a barometer of the principles, policies and priorities guiding post-apartheid South Africa's foreign policy towards Africa in general, and towards regional integration in particular. As observed by Rob Davies, South Africa's minister of trade and industry, in August 2011: "The government is deeply committed to fostering mutually beneficial regional integration in Southern Africa, particularly in the Union ... African development remains the priority of our economic foreign policy and has become more compelling as the prospects for growth and development in Africa have vastly improved."[2]

In exploring the moral and geo-economic compass guiding the direction of South Africa's foreign policy in the post-apartheid era, SACU is an excellent place to begin. It is important to remember that SACU is, first and foremost, a customs union based on a free trade area (FTA) protected by a common external tariff. Common to the 1910, 1969 and 2002 SACU agreements is the free movement of goods.[3] As Article 18 of the 2002 agreement states: "Goods grown, produced or manufactured in the Common Customs Area, on importation from the area of one Member State to the area of another Member State, shall be free of customs duties and quantitative restrictions."[4] SACU can effectively be categorised into three distinct time periods associated with the three different SACU agreements: first, the colonial era, 1910–1969; second, the apartheid-dominated era, 1969–2002; and third, the post-apartheid era, from 2002 onwards. The focus here is on understanding the nature, evolution and development of SACU in the post-apartheid era and what this reveals about South Africa's foreign policy. Tshwane's current policies related to sovereignty, inter-governmentalism, multilateralism, international redistribution, regional integration and how the African power manages "hegemony" can all be explored using SACU as a case study.

A Post-Apartheid Geo-Political Realignment

The democratic transition in South Africa inevitably changed Tshwane's geo-political priorities and provided an opportunity to renegotiate and restructure all the regional economic communities (RECs) in Southern Africa. The extent to which regional integration in Southern Africa has consequently been transformed following the end of apartheid should not be underestimated. Southern Africa's three most important sub-regional institutions – SACU, the Southern African Development Community (SADC) (see Saunders and Nagar in this volume) and the Common Market for Eastern and Southern Africa (COMESA) – have all changed their institutional structures and integrative ambitions in order to respond and adapt to the changes resulting from the end of apartheid.

Until 1994, regional integration throughout Southern Africa was defined and often rationalised in the context of apartheid, which divided both South and Southern Africa. The sub-region's political economy was dominated and divided by apartheid-related policies. Thus, apartheid South Africa's policy of regional détente and the promotion of a Constellation of Southern African States (CONSAS) were sub-regional policies designed primarily to defend the white-minority regime.[5] The most extreme and destructive sub-regional policy embraced by South Africa – destabilisation – was an attempt to subjugate Southern Africa militarily when its economic and diplomatic policies had failed to do so (see Naidoo in this volume).

For most of the majority-ruled states in Southern Africa, CONSAS and destabilisation aimed to "turn the free states of Southern Africa into little more than sub-regional bantustans".[6] CONSAS, they observed, was "simply apartheid as a foreign policy".[7] In this context, the Frontline States' (FLS) efforts to resist white-minority rule and the formation of the Southern African Development Coordination Conference (SADCC) – the precursor to SADC – in 1980, were attempts to promote regional integration and cooperation outside Pretoria's sphere of influence and to defend Southern Africa against sub-regional apartheid.[8]

A polarisation of political attitudes, focused on the issue of apartheid, resulted in Southern Africa being geo-politically divided. Notwithstanding a high degree of economic interdependence, Southern African regionalism during the late apartheid era was thus characterised by political divisions, hostility and conflict. Paradoxically, while Southern Africa was well integrated geo-economically,[9] it was fragmented between competing camps geo-politically, each supporting their own sub-regional strategies. Both SADCC and CONSAS were, first and foremost, politically motivated and prioritised geo-political concerns over sub-regional trade objectives.

In the apartheid era, compared to SADCC, SACU remained largely "under the wire" of critical and contentious scrutiny. Whereas SADCC and destabilisation generated a vast literature of academic and policy reports,[10] SACU received very limited attention and was promoted by all member states as a functionally pragmatic solution to managing high levels of economic integration that existed between the BLNS states and apartheid South Africa. Nonetheless, SACU lent the apartheid regime both political legitimacy and a strong anti-sanctions argument. SACU's existence and evolution in the apartheid era can be explained, in part, by the BLS states (Botswana, Lesotho and Swaziland) also being members of SADCC and, in addition, the longevity and importance of SACU to the economic well-being of the BLS.

If destabilisation is taken as a starting point, regional integration among the countries of Southern Africa has indeed experienced a fundamental transformation in the post-apartheid era. Four months after its first democratic election, South Africa joined SADC in August 1994. Since 1990, all the regional institutions of Southern Africa have changed their institutional structures and integrative ambitions, with SADCC and the Preferential Trade Area (PTA) being transformed into SADC and COMESA respectively, while SACU adopted a new agreement in 2002.

SACU has its origins in the fundamentally unstable colonial and apartheid regimes that governed and dominated this sub-region up to 1994. Nonetheless, and somewhat paradoxically, SACU has been instrumental in the promotion of economic stability among its member states, especially the BLNS states. There is thus a significant and structural paradox running through SACU: created and supported by unstable regimes, the organisation has nonetheless successfully promoted economic integration and regional development, and enhanced stability among its five member states. Furthermore, for the majority of its existence, SACU has been a profoundly undemocratic institution structurally challenged by South Africa's hegemony and inequalities among its member states. SACU, 100 years old in 2010, is an institution that should logically have collapsed.

In the post-apartheid era, two key issues dominate SACU, and both focus on the South Africa–BLNS division: first, the democratisation of SACU with "common" institutions and an agreed collective framework for unified engagement in trade negotiations with third countries/parties; and second, the fiscal and budgetary governance of SACU, especially the Common Revenue Pool (CRP) and associated Revenue Sharing Formula (RSF).

Democratising SACU

Negotiations leading to the 2002 SACU agreement began in 1994, immediately after South Africa's first democratic election. The new African National Congress (ANC) government defined SACU as reflecting the "colonial oppressor's mentality",[11] and rejected the power relations underpinned and sustained by SACU institutions under the colonial and apartheid eras. Despite the apparent enthusiasm to restructure the organisation, negotiations took eight years to complete: testimony to the difficulties of democratising an institution with such extreme inequalities while at the same time maintaining stability of development, income for the BLNS states and trade opportunities for South African businesses.

Given SACU's association with colonialism, apartheid, overbearing South African hegemony and the fundamentally undemocratic institutional structures associated with both the 1910 and 1969 agreements, democratising the organisation was a key priority for South Africa's post-apartheid foreign policy. While democracy is a universally recognised ideal and one of the core values of the United Nations (UN), defining and measuring "democracy" at the state level is often problematic. Several variants of democracy exist, and it can take many different forms. There is no consensus on what constitutes a democratic state, but at its most basic and ideal form, it is when all eligible citizens participate equally in the creation of law.[12] Translating this problematic definition of democracy to an international institution – whether inter-governmental or multilateral – is both contentious and hugely problematic, and not that useful. International relations theory has devoted a great deal of attention to the so-called democratic deficit of international organisations, both global and regional. As American scholar Robert Keohane has observed, international institutions are more often than not "managed by technocrats and supervised by high governmental officials. That is, they are run by elites".[13] However, Keohane also argues that international institutions may not need to be fully democratic in order to function effectively, citing the case of the International Monetary Fund (IMF) as an institution that "can only be effective if it is insulated from direct democratic control".[14] Indeed, Keohane makes a strong case that international institutions, in order to function well, should not be *fully* democratic.

Thus, South Africa's post-apartheid goal of democratising SACU is ambitious, challenging and problematic. Understanding what democracy means, what form it should take, and how it can be represented and measured in a sub-regional institution with five nation states, is not straightforward. Furthermore, democratising an international organisation with such vast inequalities in population size, gross domestic product (GDP), per capita income and "capacity" is contentious. For example, if democratic representation in SACU were linked to population size, as opposed to state structure, then South Africa would have over 80 per cent of the vote. Given South Africa's hegemonic status, using economic, demographic or other socio-economic indicators to distribute power would, inevitably, result in a very skewed voting distribution in South Aftrica's favour.

Structurally, the new institutional infrastructure resulting from the 2002 SACU agreement is indicative of a very different power-sharing arrangement compared to the 1910 and 1969 agreements. Article 2 of the new agreement sets out eight objectives for the new SACU, including a desire "to create effective, transparent and democratic institutions that will ensure equitable trade benefits to Member States".[15] Rather than the South African Department of Trade and Industry being unilaterally in control of policymaking in SACU, as was the case in the 1910 and 1969 SACU agreements, the new model operates, de jure, by "consensus" decision-making. This requires all countries to agree to policy changes and, in theory, gives all member states the power of veto.[16] In international organisations, the ability to exercise a power of veto is both influential and significant. Clearly, the new 2002 SACU agreement aimed to establish a democratic rules-based structure to govern the sub-regional trading bloc.[17]

Provision was created for a number of formal institutions to preside over various functions of SACU and to provide checks and balances. Articles 7 to 17 of the new agreement provide for the establishment of six new SACU institutions: a Council of Ministers; a Customs Union Commission; a Secretariat in Windhoek, Namibia; a Tariff Board; Technical Liaison Committees; and a Tribunal. In addition, each member state was directed to create a "National Body" to make trade recommendations based on its national interest and perspectives. The Tariff Board, containing delegates from each member state, was tasked with submitting policy options to the Council of Ministers, which is composed of ministers from all five member states and is the ultimate decision-making body. These key decision-making bodies are deemed to gain administrative support from the Customs Union Commission and the Secretariat, with technical expertise provided by a range of Technical Assistance Committees. For the first time in a century, SACU has a dedicated set of permanent institutions that are inter-governmental in nature and are – at least in theory – independent of South African national institutions and ministries.

Also for the first time in the organisation's history, the BLNS states have a de jure right of veto over all SACU legislation, including the setting of tariffs and rebates. In sharp contrast to the 1910 and 1969 SACU agreements, under the 2002 agreement, each BLNS state now participates on an equal basis with South Africa. Individual SACU member states have equal power to determine, and at the very least veto, policy proposals in the Council of Ministers and Tariff Board. Under the 2002 SACU structure, member states also share sovereignty over tariff matters.

As a consequence, SACU should be involved intimately in all trade negotiations with third parties. Article 31 of its revised 2002 treaty states: "No Member State shall negotiate and enter into new preferential trade agreements with third parties or amend existing agreements without the consent of other Member States"[18] and "Member States shall establish a common negotiating mechanism in accordance with the terms of reference to be determined by the Council".[19]

This is neither the time nor the place to discuss in detail the economic partnership agreements (EPAs) promoted by the 28-member EU to govern trade relations between Europe and the 79-member African, Caribbean and Pacific (ACP) group of states.[20] (See Nkosi in this volume.) However, the impact of these negotiations on SACU is noteworthy. The EPA negotiations have tested not only EU-ACP relations, but also intra-SACU relations. South Africa, denied access to Lomé in 1994, negotiated the Trade, Development and Cooperation Agreement (TDCA) with the EU as a bilateral trade and aid agreement by 1999.[21] However, being part of the SACU agreement, the TDCA would inevitably have impacted significantly on the BLNS states, whose trade with Brussels at the time was governed by Lomé. The BLNS states, although consulted by South Africa during the TDCA negotiations, were not formally part of the discussions. For example, BLNS agricultural exports to the EU were governed largely by special protocols under Lomé, covering beef and sugar, whereas South Africa's agricultural access to Europe under the TDCA was based on reciprocity. Governing these two different regimes from the perspective of a SACU customs union was a challenge, negotiated primarily by Tshwane and Brussels (see Nkosi in this volume).

Equally, in the negotiations to establish a SADC economic partnership agreement including the BLNS states, South Africa was originally not included, despite being the economic hegemon in both SACU and SADC.

Furthermore, Tshwane perceived its economic interests to be threatened by the character of the EPAs, which included "new generation" issues, including services. The EPA negotiations exposed the fragility of the 2002 SACU agreement and the sub-regional body's lack of cohesiveness in negotiating third-party trade agreements. The process fundamentally exposed the divergent economic interests of the BLNS states and South Africa. For South Africa and the BLNS states, the EPA negotiations raised serious issues about pooling sovereignty within SACU over trade issues, and how effective a "democratic" SACU can be in defending simultaneously both South African and BLNS economic interests. An EPA between the SADC group[22] and the EU was finally signed in June 2016.

Has a Democratic SACU Been Achieved?

The incomplete implementation of the 2002 agreement and failure to establish all the proposed SACU institutions have limited the effectiveness of the organisation. By 2013, the only parts of the institutional framework to have been established were the Council of Ministers and the administrative bodies: the SACU Commission, Secretariat and Technical Liaison Committees. Only South Africa had established a functioning National Body – the International Trade Administration Commission (ITAC) – which performs the tasks attributed to the Tariff Board. Potentially the most influential institution – the supra-national Tribunal – charged with the promotion of regional over national interests, has not yet materialised. The lack of progress associated with fulfilling the democratic reforms embedded in the 2002 SACU agreement is arguably a direct consequence of the underlying power relations and tensions between SACU members.

More importantly, the inequality in the size and levels of development among SACU members raises important concerns about the meaning of democracy in a regional organisation characterised by one overwhelmingly dominant partner. South Africa accounts for over 80 per cent of SACU's population, gross domestic product (GDP), manufacturing output, merchandise exports and electricity generation (see Table 12.1). Is it therefore "democratic" for South Africa to share power equally with Swaziland, with just 2 per cent of SACU's population, or Lesotho with 0.7 per cent of its GDP? Is it democratic for BLNS states individually to have a veto power? Probably not.

Table 12.1 Selected Socio-Economic Indicators, SACU Member States

	Population (millions) / % of SACU Total Population, 2016	Gross Domestic Product ($ millions) / % of SACU Total GDP, 2016	Gross National Income per Capita,* 2015	Human Development Index Ranking, 2014	Merchandise Exports ($ millions) / % of SACU Total Merchandise Exports, 2016	Energy Production (million metric tons of oil equivalent), 2013
Botswana	2.3 (3.6)	15,275 (4.7)	14,663	107	7,321 (8.2)	1.4
Lesotho	2.2 (3.4)	2,200 (0.7)	3,319	161	897 (1.1)	N/A
Namibia	2.5 (3.9)	10,267 (3.1)	9,770	126	4,816 (5.4)	0.4
South Africa	55.9 (87.1)	294,840 (90.4)	12,087	119	74,111 (83.5)	165.7
Swaziland	1.3 (2.0)	3,727 (1.1)	7,522	149	1,612 (1.8)	N/A
SACU Total	64.2	326,309	9,472 (average)	132 (average)	88,757	–

Source: United Nations Development Programme (UNDP), *Human Development Report 2016: Human Development for Everyone* (New York, 2016); World Bank Open Data, http://data.worldbank.org/; and World Bank Development Indicators, http://wdi.worldbank.org/tables (both accessed 11 July 2017).

*adjusted for purchasing power parity (PPP), in constant 2011 $.

The Customs Union Task Force, set up in 1994 to negotiate the new SACU agreement, was tasked with the objective of designing institutions and decision-making procedures in order to "democratise" SACU. During the course of negotiations, the choice of an appropriate decision-making procedure developed into a highly contentious issue. Initially South Africa, although recognising the need to share "tariff sovereignty", proposed a system based on qualified majority voting, and opposed the idea of each member state being allocated equal powers of decision-making authority. During the course of the negotiations, several alternative decision-making models were explored, most with an emphasis on qualified majority voting. Any form of proportional representation, with votes based on either population or gross national product, would serve to reinforce South Africa's dominance of SACU. In 1998–2000, the model being proposed was based on a form of qualified majority voting, with South Africa allocated three votes, while Botswana, Lesotho, Namibia and Swaziland each had one vote. For a policy to be adopted, a qualified majority of five votes, out of a maximum of seven, would be required. The rationale behind this system was that it protected the smaller BLNS states from South African dominance (Tshwane would have to gain the support of at least two partners) while, at the same time, giving South Africa an effective veto (any decision would still effectively need Tshwane's support). Although several alternative qualified majority voting systems were explored, in the end, and to the surprise of several officials in South Africa, Alec Erwin, South African minister of trade and industry at the time, agreed to decision-making through "consensus".

The self-conscious need within post-apartheid South African to break symbolically with the previous colonial and apartheid regimes had prompted Tshwane to seek a more even-handed SACU agreement. Nonetheless, the democratic character of the new SACU institutions, and their actual operations and decisions are, and should be, constrained by the geo-political realities of continued South African hegemony, as measured by population size, GDP and manufacturing output.

Revenue Distribution Formula

Not only has SACU been an effectively functioning customs union for over 100 years, but it has also, since 1969, supported a significant and sophisticated redistributive allocation of its "own resources". The Revenue Distribution Formula (RDF) – sometimes referred to as the Revenue Sharing Formula – is used to allocate SACU's Common Revenue Pool among its five member states. The 1969 SACU agreement contained a powerful and positive redistributive mechanism aimed at compensating the BLNS states for being in a customs union dominated, both economically and politically, by South Africa. For the BLNS states up to 2002, three adverse consequences of belonging to SACU are often cited as the basis for the compensation: first, the detrimental economic impact of trade diversion; second, the loss of fiscal discretion and sovereignty; and third, the polarisation of economic development towards South Africa. It was also in apartheid South Africa's national interests to support links with immediate neighbouring states. The pronounced longevity of SACU is largely a product of this redistributive mechanism, and the new 2002 SACU agreement maintains a significant redistributive mechanism in favour of the BLNS states.

The Revenue Distribution Formula has consistently been one of the most contentious and divisive policies among SACU members. The formula highlights the sharp divide between South African interests – which focus primarily on tariff and trade policy in terms of development – and BLNS interests – which although far from homogeneous, focus more on the fiscal implications of revenue generated through the Common Revenue Pool. This is not the place to review either the 1910 or 1969 RDF agreements. Attention here is focused exclusively on the 2002 agreement, which substantially changed the way revenue is distributed within SACU. Under the 2002 agreement, the total Common Revenue Pool is disaggregated and distributed according to three basic components, each with a different set of distribution criteria:

Customs revenues: The customs component consists of all duties and surcharges collected by SACU's Common External Tariff (CET). Although this income is derived from duties and surcharges applied to imports into SACU, the criterion used for distribution is intra-SACU imports. As a result, the distribution of the customs component bears no relation to contributions made to the Common Revenue Pool. This component therefore represents the most distorting element of the Revenue Distribution Formula. In short, this formula discriminates positively in favour of the BLNS states, whose trade profiles, especially imports, are heavily distorted in favour of intra-SACU trade, specifically imports from South Africa. Tshwane, on the other hand, imports very little from the BLNS states. Because South African imports are largely from the rest of the world, while its imports from the BLNS are relatively insignificant, it finds itself generating income for the Common Revenue Pool far in excess of what it gets back.

Excise duties: The excise component consists of all excise duties, less 15 per cent that is directed towards a development fund (see below). Thus, 85 per cent of excise is distributed in relation to each member state's share of SACU GDP. South Africa therefore generates and attracts the largest share of the excise component.

Development fund: This consists of the 15 per cent share of the excise component (above), allocated to member states according to the inverse of each country's GDP per capita. Thus the poorest states obtain a disproportionately larger share of the development fund.

Individually and collectively, the BLNS states receive a significant proportion of their total government revenue from this source, and there is a considerable fiscal redistribution from South Africa to the BLNS states. Importantly, the Revenue Distribution Formula has resulted in Tshwane receiving approximately 90 per cent of its SACU revenue from the excise component, whereas the BLNS states receive almost 80 per cent of their income from the customs component.[23] Hence, BLNS countries have a dependence – indeed over-dependence – on the revenue generated through SACU tariffs. Lesotho and Swaziland, for example, depended for about 70 per cent of their national budget on SACU revenue in 2012.

South Africa, which essentially drove the negotiations that led to the Revenue Distribution Formula of 2002, had a flawed assumption underpinning its negotiating strategy. Tshwane erroneously believed that the income generated through the Common External Tariff would reduce sharply as a result of multilateral trade liberalisation and bilateral trade agreements, such as the Trade, Development and Cooperation Agreement with the EU, centred on a free trade area (see Nkosi in this volume). Under the 2002 agreement, South Africa is now a beneficiary of the Revenue Distribution Formula and no longer a recipient of residual income, as was the case in the 1969 RDF. Tshwane therefore negotiated the 2002 agreement on the basis that the Common Revenue Pool would fall dramatically, and that it would no longer be liable to sustain RDF payments "unconnected" to the Common Revenue Pool. However, the absolute opposite has happened. The size of the Common Revenue Pool has experienced considerable and sustained growth, driven by strong consumer-led consumption of imported goods from outside SACU.[24]

This has resulted in a significant increase in Common Revenue Pool payments to poor BLNS countries – for example, Lesotho, whose relative percentage share of the Common Revenue Pool rose almost 20 per cent, from 7.9 to 9.4 per cent, in the period 2005/2006–2009/2010, experienced a dramatic increase in its absolute revenue, from R1,983 billion to R4,918 billion, representing a 250 per cent increase over the four-year period.[25] However, in 2012/2013, Lesotho's SACU revenue dropped to 7.8 per cent.[26] For many of the BLNS states, SACU payments are a critical source of income, underpinning government revenue and finance. Based on SACU's Common Revenue Pool and Revenue Distribution Formula for 2011/2012, Botswana received R9.7 billion, Namibia R8.1 billion, South Africa R4.5 billion, Swaziland R3.3 billion and Lesotho R3.1 billion.[27] How is it that a country like South Africa, which accounts for more than 90 per cent of SACU's GDP, received only 15.6 per cent of customs revenue, whereas Botswana, which accounts for about 5 per cent of the customs union's GDP, but has a higher gross national income (GNI) per capita, obtained 34 per cent? (See Table 12.1.)

South Africa has since been determined to renegotiate the Revenue Distribution Formula. In June 2010, the SACU Secretariat in Windhoek issued a tender for a study into alternative formulas to manage the Common Revenue Pool. The resulting consultancy report recommended a Common Revenue Pool based essentially on the "destination principle", whereby member states receive what they put into the pool.[28] In July 2012, SACU member states rejected the destination principle, and in February 2017, the issue of the Revenue Distribution Formula remained unresolved and contested. Estimates of the size of South Africa's net redistribution through the RDF vary, ranging from at least R13 billion[29] to R28 billion.[30] For Swaziland and Lesotho, the destination principle would be catastrophic, with Lesotho's share of the revenue dropping from 9 per cent to 3 per cent, and Swaziland's falling from R3.3 billion to just R1.1 billion (as projected in 2011/2012).

Concluding Reflections: SACU 100 Not Out?

The ethical integrity of South Africa's SACU policy in the immediate post-apartheid era has been pronounced. The objectives of democratising SACU and creating a new revenue agreement that would see the BLNS states gradually remove their dependence on the Common Revenue Pool were politically and economically justified. However, the policies, institutions and revenue agreements adopted to enact and fulfil these policy objectives were, as detailed here, inadequate. The institutional infrastructure and decision-making processes adopted to promote democracy within SACU have also been problematic. Moreover, the nature and character of what a democratic SACU should look like – given the strength of the inequalities between its member states – are contentious, particularly in the negotiation of trade agreements with third parties. Equally, the 2002 Revenue Sharing Formula was based on false assumptions about the impact of multilateralism in reducing the absolute size of the Common Revenue Pool, resulting in the direct opposite of what was intended.

For South Africa, the skilful management of these tensions within SACU remains crucial. The key question moving forward is how South Africa can balance a respect for its neighbours' economic sovereignty with its desire that a greater share of the SACU revenue should go to regional economic integration and development. Key to promoting this regional agenda, and managing the tensions that will inevitably develop when the revenue agreement is restructured, is the prioritisation of new regional policies designed to promote "deeper" integration and more coordinated regional development within the group. SACU, while effectively functioning as a merchandise customs union, should expand its integrative strategy to include five key pegs: first, regional industrial policy; second, trade facilitation policy; third, a framework for unified trade negotiations; fourth, services and other "new generation" issues such as public procurement and intellectual property; and fifth, common policies to address shared constraints (for example, infrastructure, agriculture and energy).

SACU has evolved remarkably little. With the exception of the 1969 Revenue Distribution Formula and the 2002 democratisation strategy, little of significance has changed for over a century. This organisation remains basically a customs union. South Africa's minister of trade and industry, Rob Davies, commented in August 2011 that "[t]he government is deeply committed to fostering mutually beneficial regional integration in Southern Africa, particularly in the union … [W]e have forged a common vision and work programme to consolidate the customs union, so that it remains relevant, effective and benefits all".[31] Extending SACU's longevity by deepening and widening its policy competence, and making it fit for the twenty-first century, should be the priority of both South Africa and its BLNS partners.

Notes

1. *See* Richard Gibb and Karen Treasure, "SACU at Centenary: Theory and Practice of Democratising Regionalism", *South African Journal of International Affairs* 18, no. 1 (2011), pp. 1–21.

2. Rob Davies, "Customs Union Gives Added Economic Clout", *Mail and Guardian*, 15 August 2011.

3. Richard Gibb, "The New Southern African Customs Union Agreement: Dependence with Democracy", *Journal of Southern African Studies* 32, no. 3 (2006), pp. 583–603.

4. Southern African Customs Union (SACU), *Southern African Customs Union Agreement 2002* (Windhoek: SACU Secretariat, 2002).

5. Joseph Hanlon, *Beggar Your Neighbours: Apartheid Power in Southern Africa* (Oxford: James Currey, 1986).

6. Hanlon, *Beggar Your Neighbours*, p. 32.

7. Aloysius Kgarebe, *SADCC 2 Maputo: The Proceedings of the Second Southern African Development Co-ordination Conference*, 27–28 November 1980, p. 12.

8. Gilbert Khadiagala, "The SADCC and Its Approaches to African regionalism", in Chris Saunders, Gwinyayi A. Dzinesa and Dawn Nagar (eds), *Region-Building in Southern Africa: Progress, Problems and Prospects* (London: Zed, 2012), pp. 25–38; Kaire Mbuende, "The SADC: Between Cooperation and Development – An Insider Perspective", in Saunders, Dzinesa and Nagar, *Region-Building in Southern Africa*, pp. 29–60.

9. Peter Vale and Khabele Motlasa, "Beyond the Nation State: Rebuilding Southern Africa from Below", *Harvard International Review* 17, no. 4 (1995).

10. *See, for example*, Hanlon, *Beggar Your Neighbours*; Samir Amin, Derrick Chitala and Ibbo Mandaza (eds), *SADCC: Prospects for Disengagement and Development in Southern Africa* (London: Zed, 1987).

11. Patrick McGowan and Ahwireng-Obeng, "Partner or Hegemon? South Africa in Africa", *Journal of Contemporary African studies* 36, no. 4 (1998), pp. 669–692.

12. Dennis Thompson, *The Democratic Citizen: Social Science and Democratic Theory in the 20th Century* (Cambridge: Cambridge University Press, 1970); Larry Diamond and Marc Plattner, *Electoral Systems and Democracy* (Baltimore, MD: Johns Hopkins University Press, 2006); R. Alan Dahl, I. Shapiro and J. A. Cheibub, *The Democracy Sourcebook* (Cambridge: Massachusetts Institute of Technology Press, 2003).

13. Robert Keohane, "International Institutions: Can Interdependence Work?", *Foreign Policy* 110 (Spring 1998), p. 82.

14. Robert Keohane, "International Institutions", p. 87.

15. SACU, *Southern African Customs Union Agreement 2002*.

16. Colin McCarthy, "The Southern African Customs Union in Transition", *African Affairs* 102 (2003), pp. 605–630.

17. Gerhard Erasmus, "New SACU Institutions: Prospects for Regional Integration", working paper (Stellenbosch: Trade Law Centre for Southern Africa, 2004).

18. SACU, *Southern African Customs Union Agreement 2002*, art. 31.3.

19. SACU, *Southern African Customs Union Agreement 2002*, art. 31.2.

20. Gilbert Khadiagala, "Africa and Europe: Ending a Dialogue of the Deaf?", in Adekeye Adebajo and Kaye Whiteman (eds), *The EU and Africa: From Eurafrique to Afro-Europa* (London: Hurst; New York: Columbia University Press; and Johannesburg: Wits University Press, 2012), pp. 217–235; Mareike Meyn,

"An Anatomy of the Economic Partnership Agreements", in Adebajo and Whiteman, *The EU and Africa*, pp. 197–216.

21. Talitha Bertelsmann-Scott, "South Africa and the EU: Where Lies the Strategic Partnership?", in Adebajo and Whiteman, *The EU and Africa*, pp. 121–135.

22. This group comprises seven Southern African Development Community (SADC) member states – South Africa; Botswana, Lesotho, Namibia and Swaziland (the BLNS states); Mozambique; and Angola – though Angola did not sign the agreement in June 2016. *See* Xavier Carim, "South Africa, the EU, and the SADC Group Economic Partnership Agreement: Through the Negotiating Lens", in Annita Montoute and Kudrat Virk (eds), *The ACP Group and the EU Development Partnership: Beyond the North-South Debate* (New York: Palgrave, 2017), pp. 161–179.

23. Frank Flatters and Matthew Stern, *Implementing the SACU Revenue-Sharing Formula: Customs Revenues* (Tshwane: South African National Treasury, 2005).

24. These data are relevant to all five SACU states, though dominated by South Africa.

25. Roman Grynberg and Masedi Motswapong, "The SACU Revenue Sharing Formula: The History of an Equation", 2011, http://www.bidpa.bw/documents/TheSACURevenueFormula-TheHistoryofAnEquation.pdf (accessed 7 January 2014).

26. Central Bank of Lesotho, "An Increase in the Southern African Customs Union Revenue in 2012/13: Case for Lesotho", *Economic Review* no. 132 (June 2012), pp. 1–8, http://www.centralbank.org.ls/publications/MonthlyEconomicReviews/2012/June%202012%20Economic%20Review.pdf (accessed 16 September 2016).

27. Roman Grynberg, "New Way to Cut the SACU Cake", *Mail and Guardian*, 31 January 2011; "Swaziland's SACU Share May Drop to 3%", *Times of Swaziland*, 14 February 2011.

28. Grynberg and Motswapong, *The SACU Revenue Sharing Formula*.

29. Grynberg and Motswapong, *The SACU Revenue Sharing Formula*.

30. Mike Schussler, "SACU Is a Waste of Money", *The Namibian*, 11 March 2010.

31. Davies, "Customs Union Gives Added Economic Clout".

CHAPTER 13

SOUTH AFRICA AND
THE AFRICAN UNION

Eddy Maloka

In a famous 1993 article in the American establishment journal *Foreign Affairs*, Nelson Mandela, South Africa's first post-apartheid president, described the Africa policy that his party, the African National Congress (ANC), was going to pursue on assuming political power after the end of apartheid in 1994. As Mandela noted:

> South Africa cannot escape its African destiny. If we do not devote our energies to this continent, we too could fall victim to the forces that have brought ruin to its various parts. Like the United Nations [UN], the Organisation of African Unity (OAU) needs to be attuned to the changes at work throughout the world. A democratic South Africa will bring to an end an important chapter in Africa's efforts to achieve unity and closer cooperation, but it will not close the book.[1]

Indeed, the foreign policy of post-apartheid South Africa is determined in the structures of the ruling ANC. As such, an examination of South Africa's relationship with, and policy on, the OAU/African Union (AU) must necessarily begin with an understanding of the ANC's thinking and approach on the subject. This chapter assesses the historical relationship of the ANC to the OAU in their common battle against apartheid between 1963 and 1994; traces the evolution of

South Africa's "African Agenda" within the context of the OAU between 1994 and 2000; examines South Africa's efforts to build an effective African Union and related institutions between 2000 and 2008; and analyses Tshwane's (Pretoria) efforts to consolidate the African Agenda since 2009.

The ANC and the OAU, 1963–1994

South Africa's encounter with the Organisation of African Unity was, until 1994, conducted through its two main liberation movements: the ANC and the Pan-Africanist Congress (PAC). The OAU had been created in 1963 without South Africa's participation, and the racist policy of apartheid kept the country on the agenda of the continental body for three decades. The ANC's engagement with the OAU dates back at least to the days of the Conference of Independent African States and the All-African People's Conference, both of which convened for the first time in Accra, Ghana, in 1958. Albert Luthuli, then president of the ANC, recorded in his 1962 autobiography, *Let My People Go*, how his organisation had responded to the call for the celebration of Africa Day:

> We lost no time after the Accra Conference [of 1958] in giving effect here to the decision to observe ... Africa Day. All over the country we organised meetings ... Africa Day became a new big event on our calendar, and the meetings were well attended in all the larger centres. It has lately become a feature of such meetings that there are as many people unable to gain access as there are inside the places of meeting.[2]

The ANC was among the participants at the All-African People's Conference of December 1958, effectively represented by a former Treason Trialist, Alfred "Tough" Hutchinson, who was resident in Ghana, where he was working as a teacher at the time. With the founding of the OAU in 1963, both the ANC and the PAC participated in the continental body as recognised South African liberation movements. The OAU was not only instrumental in giving international legitimacy to the struggle against apartheid, but also played a critical role in leading the international community towards the negotiations for, and the subsequent transition to, democracy in South Africa between 1990 and 1994. Mandela highlighted the continental organisation's importance in one of his first international engagements after his release from prison in February 1990, when he addressed the OAU summit in Addis Ababa, Ethiopia, five months later:

> Earlier in the year, in the aftermath of the unbanning of the ANC and other organisations, we addressed an urgent request through the OAU ad hoc committee and the Secretary-General of the OAU for financial assistance to help us re-establish the legal structures of the ANC after 30 years of illegality ... I would like to take this opportunity to report on the truly excellent response by a number of African countries to these appeals. We thank these dear brothers and sisters most sincerely and are deeply moved by the confidence they have shown in our organisation.[3]

Since its period in exile from the 1960s, the ANC developed a post-apartheid foreign policy that set out its position on the OAU. The organisation defined this position in its "Strategy and Tactics" framework, the first iteration of which was adopted in 1969 at the organisation's conference in Morogoro, Tanzania; through resolutions adopted at the party's national and policy conferences; and through a programme of action developed by its executive organs.[4]

However, since 1994 the context on the African continent and globally has not been static, and the ANC's foreign policy has had to evolve and adapt to changing conditions. From 1990 to the immediate post-apartheid era after 1994, the ANC focused on developing a broad foreign policy framework and integrating South Africa into the international community, including prioritising its membership of the OAU.

This approach was articulated in the ANC's "Ready to Govern" policy guidelines of May 1992, the purpose of which was to unveil the party's plans for a democratic post-apartheid South Africa. On foreign policy, the document set out four modest and practical goals for the transformation of the country's international political and economic relations for the pursuit of peace and friendship; the integration of South Africa into the world after decades of diplomatic and economic isolation; the development of a foreign policy informed by the promotion of regional cooperation, peace and security; and the establishment of a professional foreign service based on the principles of equity and affirmative action.[5]

Following the 1994 election, the ANC put forward as one of the principles of post-apartheid South Africa's foreign policy a "belief that our foreign policy should reflect the interests of the continent of Africa".[6] In anticipation of the "African Renaissance" vision of Thabo Mbeki, deputy president at the time, which would capture the imagination of the country and continent two years later (see Introduction in this volume), the ANC acknowledged that "with fellow Africans we share a vision to transform our continent into an entity that is free, peaceful and vibrant – a continent which is capable, given the opportunity, to make an abiding contribution in all fields of human endeavour – particularly in the sphere of international relations".[7] This perspective informed South Africa's accession to the OAU: "Accordingly we joined the Organisation of African Unity ... with the prime objective to help the organisation in realising its goals of deepening the unity of Africa's diverse peoples and cultures and advancing their common well-being."[8]

By the end of the Mandela presidency in 1999, a more elaborate Africa policy was in the making, based on Thabo Mbeki's vision of an African Renaissance following his famous "I Am an African" speech to the South African parliament in May 1996. In the course of Mbeki's first term as president between 1999 and 2004, the African Renaissance vision was encapsulated into a programme of government that became known as the "African Agenda". This concept continues to direct South Africa's policy towards the African Union. In the meantime, over the years, the OAU was transformed into the AU, with the New Partnership for Africa's Development (NEPAD) and the African Peer Review Mechanism (APRM) – which I head in 2017 – emerging in the process as the continent's socio-economic and democratic governance programmes, respectively.[9]

The ANC's current pillar of international work, as detailed in the party's "Strategy and Tactics" document adopted at its 53rd national conference in December 2012,[10] has been developed further into a programme of action built around six key themes: contributing to building a better Africa and a better world; continental and international solidarity; party-to-party, intra-lateral and multilateral relations; transformation of global governance institutions; policy development issues; and campaigns.

From Calabashes to the African Agenda, 1994–2000

Since 1994, South Africa's policy towards the OAU/AU has been framed under the rubric of the African Agenda, which is central to the country's foreign policy in three ways. First, this approach is one of the key pillars of the policy; second, the agenda is overarching and crosscutting over other pillars that seek to promote South-South and North-South cooperation, bilateral political and economic relations with other countries and participation in institutions of global governance; third, Africa, beginning with the Southern African Development Community (SADC) neighbourhood (see Sachikonye, and Saunders and Nagar in this volume), is considered the centrepiece of the country's foreign policy.

The Mandela presidency (1994–1999) represented somewhat of a transition within a transition because, at least until 1996, the country was under a government of national unity, while a new constitution was drafted by the Constituent Assembly during these two years. The country's Department of Foreign Affairs (DFA) – now the Department of International Relations and Cooperation (DIRCO) – was also in transition in terms of administrative personnel at the helm of the department and the development of a new foreign policy on the basis of which the country would accede to multilateral entities such as the OAU.

By the time Thabo Mbeki became South Africa's president in 1999, the country was in a better position to develop a more elaborate foreign policy approach and programme. The ANC's foreign policy pledge in its 1994 election manifesto was simply about South Africa taking its "rightful place in the world" – with respect to a "destiny ... intertwined with that of Southern Africa" – and becoming a full member of the OAU. By contrast, the ruling party's 1999 election manifesto had a much grander vision: "The time has come for Africa's Renaissance", was the opening line of the manifesto's section dedicated to "building a better Africa and a better world". The party outlined its foreign policy plans with four key goals for the next five years: act more decisively to promote peace in the Southern African sub-region and Africa as a whole; campaign for a better-managed global economy, including the restructuring of international financial and trade institutions to make them more sensitive to the needs of developing countries, especially in Africa; advocate strongly for relieving the debt burden on the poorest countries of the world, many of them in Africa; and promote equitable trade, investment and development plans for Southern Africa, while also promoting a common set of democratic values, including fair labour and environmental standards.[11] There was no specific reference in the 1999 manifesto to the OAU as an organisation, but this was to change with the transition from the OAU to the AU between 1999 and 2002.

In this context, the process of developing a more elaborate Africa policy and programme began in earnest during the Mbeki presidency (1999–2008), drawing its ideological inspiration from the African Renaissance. The 2002/2003 annual report of South Africa's Department of Foreign Affairs explained that the country's "role within the vision of Africa's rebirth is aimed at promoting peace, prosperity, democracy, sustainable development, progressive leadership and good governance".[12] As for the African Renaissance, it was defined in the same report thus:

> The African Renaissance vision is an all-embracing concept that draws its inspiration from the rich and diverse history and cultures of Africa. It acknowledges Africa as a cradle of humanity, whilst providing a framework for the modern Africa to re-emerge as a significant partner in the New World Order. This framework touches all human endeavour; political, economic, social, technological, environmental and cultural. The concept of the African Renaissance has been transformed into a tangible reality through the development and the adoption of the African Union's principal agenda for development (NEPAD).[13]

From this perspective, an "African Century" was imminent; a "better Africa" and thus a "better world" were in the making. This foreign policy objective interfaced with identified domestic priorities of developing human resources; building the economy and creating jobs; combating crime and corruption; and transforming the state (see Landsberg in this volume).

Before the advent of the African Agenda, South Africa's Africa policy had been conceptualised through the prism of the outcomes of the Conference on Security, Stability, Development and Cooperation in Africa (CSSDCA), which had met in the Ugandan capital of Kampala in 1991 under the stewardship of the former Nigerian military ruler General Olusegun Obasanjo's Africa Leadership Forum.[14] The CSSDCA concept was built on the notion of security, stability, development and cooperation as four dialectically linked "calabashes". This became OAU policy when it was adopted at the Lomé summit in Togo in July 2000 through a Solemn Declaration.[15]

Once the CSSDCA concept had become OAU policy, South Africa set out to integrate it into its own Africa policy, even seconding a staff member to the CSSDCA unit created at the OAU headquarters in Addis Ababa. In the course of 2000, using the calabashes model, a strategic approach was developed in South Africa's foreign ministry based on four high-level objectives (the calabashes), each with their thematic sub-elements, which in total amounted to eighteen. The OAU's work cut across the four calabashes. Although this approach was meant to inform the work of South Africa's foreign ministry over the period 2002–2005, this did not occur, as from the 2003/2004 financial year the department adopted the African Agenda to replace the calabashes model. The calabashes model and the African Agenda discourse emerged as South Africa was expanding its diplomatic missions on the continent, and in the context of the transition to the AU and the founding of NEPAD (in 2001) and the APRM (in 2003).

The African Union and Implementation of the African Agenda, 2000–2008

The African Union was born in South Africa's port city of Durban in 2002 following a three-year transition from the OAU that had began in 1999. South Africa, as host of the inaugural summit, became the first chair of the African Union. NEPAD was born outside the OAU. This was Thabo Mbeki's initiative, and he had raised the need for such a programme with the ANC's National Working Committee at one of its meetings in 2000. A brainstorming process then began in the ANC under the stewardship of Kgalema Motlanthe in his capacity as secretary-general of the party. In South Africa's presidency, a small task team of five officials was subsequently established, chaired by Wiseman Nkuhlu, Mbeki's trusted economic adviser. Other members included officials from the Department of Foreign Affairs, the Department of Trade and Industry (DTI) and the National Treasury (finance ministry). I was also a member of the team. Once the initial draft of what would become NEPAD had been completed, with Mfundo Nkuhlu from the DTI as lead drafter for the task team, consultations with other African countries began, mainly with Nigeria and Algeria. This continued until the programme was unveiled as the Millennium Africa Recovery Plan (MAP) by Mbeki at the January 2001 World Economic Forum in Davos, Switzerland. The programme was adopted by the OAU in July 2001, a decision endorsed by the AU at its inaugural summit the following year. At its second summit, in the Mozambican capital of Maputo in July 2003, the AU decided to integrate NEPAD into the structures and processes of the AU. South Africa became the host of the Midrand-based NEPAD secretariat and seconded Wiseman Nkuhlu to serve as its first chief executive officer.

Within the OAU, whose future was uncertain at the time, the unveiling of the MAP by Mbeki was viewed with suspicion by some key actors, with a rumour even circulating that some member states were creating a parallel continental body. This fear was allayed partially when the plan was adopted as a programme of the OAU. The integration of NEPAD into the AU was, however, a painful and divisive process due to competing interpretations of the Maputo decision, with some at the AU even suggesting that the NEPAD secretariat be moved from Midrand to Addis Ababa. Today, NEPAD is fully integrated at the level of both its governance structure, which includes country representation from Africa's five sub-regions, and the secretariat, which has adopted AU administrative rules and procedures. In the integration process, NEPAD lost its initial goals of creating an exclusive club of countries that accepted binding, governance-related conditions for membership. Credit for the operationalisation of the APRM should go to Smunda Mokoena, who was seconded by South Africa to the NEPAD secretariat as the chief operations officer in November 2001.

In practice, the African Agenda was about South Africa's role in the AU, NEPAD and SADC. In the South African foreign ministry's strategic plan for 2006–2009, engagement with Africa was to rest on three key pillars: strengthening Africa's multilateral institutions, particularly the AU and SADC; supporting implementation of NEPAD, Africa's socio-economic development programme; and strengthening bilateral political and socio-economic relations through effective structures for dialogue and cooperation.[16]

The programmatic elements under the AU component of this strategy contained a comprehensive list of actions for strengthening the governance and institutional capacity of the AU, and operationalising the AU's financial institutions, the African Court of Justice, the African Court on Human and Peoples' Rights,[17] as well as the Specialised Technical Committees of the AU. In this action list, South Africa was to carry out all its obligations to the AU within an identified timeframe. Implementation of summit decisions and the AU Gender Declaration of 2004 (which introduced the principle of gender parity, among others) was to be ensured. AU organs that had been established already, notably the Pan-African Parliament (PAP) and the AU's Economic, Social and Cultural Council (ECOSOCC), were to be supported by Tshwane.[18] The African Diaspora was also to be engaged, and the AU–European Union (EU) partnership launched in the Egyptian capital of Cairo in 2000 was to be strengthened (see Nkosi in this volume). Furthermore, support was to be mobilised for harmonisation and rationalisation of Africa's regional economic communities (RECs) in order to curb their proliferation and discourage the practice of multiple REC membership by African governments.[19]

The action areas around NEPAD in the 2006–2009 strategic plan were equally comprehensive. They ranged from implementation of decisions of the NEPAD policy organs and NEPAD programmes and projects in infrastructure, agriculture, environment, tourism, information and communications technology (ICT), health, human resources and science and technology, to supporting the AU/NEPAD integration process and establishment of continental development funds for NEPAD projects. As the APRM was, at this stage, a component of the NEPAD process, its operationalisation in the country and on the continent represented another action area for South Africa's foreign ministry.[20]

In the South African cabinet's cluster on international cooperation, trade and security, an African Renaissance committee was created to ensure the country's high-level focus on the AU, NEPAD, SADC and the Southern African Customs Union (SACU) (see Gibb in this volume on SACU). The then foreign minister, Nkosazana Dlamini-Zuma, supported by her trade counterpart, Alec Erwin, was tasked by the cabinet to lead the country's NEPAD processes, backed by a technical team of directors-general. While during the calabashes phase OAU/AU matters had been under the rubric of "cooperation" and "multilateralism" in South Africa's foreign ministry, with the shift to the African Agenda a stand-alone "multilateral" departmental branch was created. South Africa's bilateral and multilateral programmes in Africa were thereafter implemented by two separate branches. This moved the AU from simply being a crosscutting issue to being a special departmental focus area.

As the first chair of the AU in 2002–2003, South Africa under Thabo Mbeki put its diplomatic energy and financial resources into the operationalisation of the continental organisation, particularly its evolving organs. For example, negotiations for the Pan-African Parliament protocol were driven by South Africa's national parliament through its speaker, Frene Ginwala. Tshwane became host to the secretariats of NEPAD and the APRM, as well as the headquarters of the PAP. When the 15-member AU Peace and Security Council (PSC) was operationalised by 2004, South Africa was among the five countries with a three-year membership tenure. Following the launch of ECOSOCC in 2005 as the AU organ for civil society participation, a national chapter was established in the country.

South Africa was tasked in 2005 with chairing the AU's ministerial sub-committee on its budgetary scale of assessment, whose work developed a formula whereby 75 per cent of the operating budget of the AU was covered by five countries: South Africa, Nigeria, Algeria, Libya and Egypt. Tshwane was tasked with other responsibilities such as chairing the sub-committee of the Permanent Representative Committee on Multilateral Cooperation, and the Ministerial Committee of Post-Conflict Reconstruction and Development on Sudan.

It was during this period that South Africa intensified its activism on the peace and security front, including making troop contributions to international peacekeeping operations on the continent (see Curtis, and Naidoo in this volume). The 2001/2002 annual report of South Africa's foreign ministry reported a modest beginning:

> South Africa's commitment to peace, stability and security in the continent was evidenced by, amongst others, its hosting of the Inter Congolese Dialogue (ICD), its facilitation of the Burundi peace process and, broadly, the promotion of peace in the Great Lakes region [see Nzongola-Ntalaja in this volume]. As part of the countries of the region South Africa participated in efforts to bring about stability in the Comoros.[21]

The foreign ministry's 2003/2004 annual report noted South Africa's commitment to initiatives in Angola, Burundi, the Central African Republic (CAR), Côte d'Ivoire, the Democratic Republic of the Congo (DRC), Eritrea, Ethiopia, Liberia, Rwanda, São Tomé and Príncipe, Sudan and Western Sahara, as well as to the Palestinian–Israeli conflict.[22] This exponential growth of South Africa's activism on the continent has continued to encompass preventive diplomacy through mediation, peacekeeping and humanitarian support – mostly under the mandate of SADC or the AU.

The South African business sector was also mobilised behind the African Agenda, at two levels: first through the NEPAD Business Group, chaired by Ruel Khoza; and second through South Africa's parastatals and financial institutions such as Eskom, the Development Bank of Southern Africa (DBSA), Transnet, the Industrial Development Corporation (IDC)[23] and Telkom, which were urged to support NEPAD. A continental private sector African Renaissance fund was also established at the behest of South Africa for infrastructure development.

South Africa can also take credit for giving momentum to the AU's African Diaspora programme. In March 2005, when celebrating the tenth anniversary of the end of apartheid, and in collaboration with the AU and the Caribbean Community (CARICOM), South Africa hosted an African Diaspora conference in Jamaica whose outcomes set in motion a process that would result in the AU's African Diaspora Summit held in Johannesburg in May 2012. At the AU, South Africa is a recognised champion of the Diaspora programme.

In addition, and in line with the ANC's strong stance on international solidarity, South Africa became one of the leading advocates of the self-determination of the people of Western Sahara (fighting unsuccessfully to keep Morocco out of the AU in February 2017) and South Sudan (supporting its January 2011 independence referendum) within the AU. Tshwane has also been vocal in debates at the AU in support of the Palestinian struggle for the right to self-determination as well as Cuba's campaign for the lifting of its three-decade economic embargo imposed by the United States (US).

When South Africa became a non-permanent member of the UN Security Council for the first time in 2007–2008, it used its position not only to articulate AU positions, but also to promote cooperation between the UN Security Council and the AU Peace and Security Council. Tshwane, under its long-serving permanent representative to the UN, Dumisani Kumalo, co-led the Security Council mission to AU headquarters in Addis Ababa and other African countries in 2007. South Africa also chaired the Somalia sanctions committee as well as the ad hoc Working Group on Conflict Prevention and Resolution in Africa on the UN Security Council. Tshwane further contributed to revitalisation of the debate on the relationship between the UN and regional organisations during its tenure, and focused attention on this important issue, during its presidencies of the UN Security Council in March 2007 and April 2008.[24] The same approach would be repeated during the country's second tenure on the Security

Council in 2011–2012, resulting during its presidency of the Council in the adoption of Resolution 2033, which aimed at enhancing the relationship and effective cooperation between the Council and African regional organisations. (See Mashabane in this volume.)

By the end of the Mbeki presidency in September 2008, a much clearer and more coherent AU policy and approach had been achieved. South Africa had completed its transition from being a member of the OAU/AU through its liberation movements, to being a full state member. It was left to the Jacob Zuma administration to take the baton of the African Agenda forward after the 2009 elections.

The African Union and Consolidation of the African Agenda Since 2009

The AU agenda of the Jacob Zuma administration (since 2009) was captured in the ANC's 2009 election manifesto, which sought to:

> Work together with people of our continent and its Diaspora for cohesion, unity, democracy and prosperity of the Southern African Development Community and African Union and strengthening our capabilities to respond to the challenges we face.
>
> Continue to work towards regional economic integration in Southern Africa on a fair, equitable and developmental basis, promoting SADC integration based on a developmental model that includes infrastructure development, cooperation in the real economy and development of regional supply-chains . . .
>
> Spare no energy in our efforts to find urgent, democratic and lasting solutions to the situation in Zimbabwe, Swaziland, Sudan, Democratic Republic of the Congo, Western Sahara, Somalia and other countries.[25]

This programme informed the 2009–2012 strategic plan of South Africa's foreign ministry, whose priorities included consolidation of the African Agenda; strengthening South-South and North-South cooperation; participation in the global system of governance; and intensification of South Africa's political and economic relations with other countries. These priorities had been confirmed by the January 2008 cabinet *lekgotla* (retreat) when Mbeki was still the country's president. Their adoption by the Zuma administration thus signalled continuity in the broad thrust of the government's foreign policy. Even though a strategic plan for the 2010–2013 period was developed soon afterwards, and the "consolidation" of the African Agenda was reframed as "continued prioritisation of the African continent", the core actions under this priority remained essentially unchanged, still focused on the AU, NEPAD and SADC and thematic areas such as peace and security.

With the introduction by the Zuma administration of the monitoring and evaluation system based on a set of high-level outcomes in 2004, foreign policy was put under the outcome of "creating a better South Africa and contributing to a better and safer Africa in a better world", with "enhanced African Agenda and sustainable development" replacing the "continued prioritisation of the African continent" as a priority area. The core elements of this outcome-based priority are still consistent with the African Agenda. However, in the 2013–2018 strategic plan of South Africa's foreign ministry, there are new elements under "enhanced African Agenda and sustainable development" such as contributing through deployment of personnel and annual financial contributions to strengthening mechanisms and structures of the AU and SADC; and advancing implementation of NEPAD programmes related to priority sectors and supporting the Presidential Infrastructure Championing Initiative (PICI).[26]

These two new areas – deployment of South African personnel to AU and SADC structures, and the presidential focus on infrastructure – are among the innovations introduced by the Zuma administration to the African Agenda programme. The first area resulted in the election of South Africa's former foreign minister, Nkosazana Dlamini-Zuma, to the position of chair of the AU Commission in July 2012. She was in the position until February 2017, when she was replaced by Chad's foreign minister, Moussa Faki Mahamat. During the early phases of the African Agenda, very few South Africans worked in the AU and SADC secretariats as employees, partly as government policy, but also because of the unattractiveness of the remuneration packages in these organisations. Besides the few who were seconded by the South African government to the NEPAD secretariat in its early years, there were only two South Africans at the AU Commission in Addis Ababa in 2012 – one seconded to the CSSDCA unit, and the other as a director in the science and technology section of the Commission. The decision to field Dlamini-Zuma as chair of the AU Commission was the result of a shift that saw the country develop a secondment policy to encourage South Africans to apply for positions in African regional institutions and the United Nations.

Jacob Zuma, once he became president of South Africa, became concerned that the "union government" debate – for greater political federation and a common African currency and army – led by Libya's Muammar Qaddafi, was diverting the AU's attention from key challenges, and was focusing instead, summit after summit, on the divisions among its member states. He thus proposed to Qaddafi that Tshwane and Tripoli work together on infrastructure projects to connect their two countries. Zuma's hope was that this would give Qaddafi a new focus. However, Libya's self-styled "Brother Leader" was assassinated during the crisis of 2011 (see Tawfik, and Mashabane in this volume). Nevertheless, the idea of a continental infrastructure initiative survived as Zuma took it to his NEPAD colleagues and the entire AU, thus resulting in the Presidential Infrastructure Championing Initiative of July 2010, in which a group of heads of state each champion a specific infrastructure project on the continent. South Africa champions the North-South Corridor connecting Southern, Central and East Africa through railways and roads. It should be noted, however, that the NEPAD Infrastructure Short-Term Action Plan (STAP) and the AU's Programme for Infrastructure Development in Africa (PIDA) both predate the PICI. The latter's uniqueness lies in being championed by presidents instead of being left solely in the hands of technocrats and government officials whose well-laid plans often suffer as a result of a lack of political enthusiasm from their political masters.

South Africa's peace and security role in Africa has continued under the Zuma presidency, with the country joining the AU Peace and Security Council in January 2014. Tshwane's focus expanded to prioritise what the AU should do to curb the increasing scourge of unconstitutional changes of government in Africa in spite of the existence of an AU policy against this, replete with a sanctions regime applied since 2000. A related issue is a trend towards "regime change" at the instigation of non-African actors, as was witnessed in the Libyan conflict in 2011, when France and Britain led the ousting of Qaddafi through the North Atlantic Treaty Organisation (NATO). Out of this concern, Zuma has been campaigning for the establishment of an African rapid response force – the African Capacity for Immediate Response to Crises (ACIRC) – as proposed by the AU Commission at its May 2013 summit. The ACIRC is to be an interim measure while processes towards full operationalisation of the African Standby Force (ASF) – whose deployment was postponed – are finalised. The Mali crisis of 2013, in which a French intervention recaptured the northern part of the country from Tuareg and Islamist fighters, has been cited as another example of why the ACIRC is urgently needed. French military influence in the Central African Republic in the same year provided another catalyst (see Introduction, and Marchal in this volume).

South Africa's journey in the OAU/AU since 1994 has not been a smooth and easy ride. The cost of AU membership stood at over R200 million in the South African foreign ministry's financial year ended in March 2009, and stabilised to about R125 million in the financial year that ended in March 2012. Tshwane was still assessed at 15 per cent of the organisation's operational budget in 2017. If membership fees and other financial obligations to SADC, NEPAD, APRM and the PAP are added to what South Africa pays annually to the AU, it becomes clear that the African Agenda has not been a cheap exercise for a developing country that has its own development challenges as one of the most unequal societies in the world.

Financial issues aside, the difficulties of implementing an African Agenda in the AU – an organisation of 55 members each with its own geo-political dynamics – is another complication that every African country encounters in its diplomacy on the continent. The interests and activities of non-African actors on the continent are an additional factor that can hamper progress towards the intended objectives of the African Agenda. At the domestic level, coordination challenges will always arise when several actors, such as different government departments, are involved as focal points for various AU programmes. In the case of South Africa, for example, while its foreign ministry is the overall coordinator, its departments of trade and industry; defence; and public service and administration; as well as its national treasury, are all among government departments with a specific mandate on AU matters.

Concluding Reflections

South Africa has come of age diplomatically since its low starting base of seven diplomatic and consular missions in Africa in 1994, expanding its diplomatic presence across the continent to 45 embassies in 2017. The South African foreign ministry's annual budget in 2017/2018 was

R6.5 billion (up from about R5 billion in 2013). The OAU/AU has also changed since South Africa joined the organisation in 1994. It is no longer perceived as a "club of dictators", having adopted "shared values" within the framework of a continental governance architecture. But what has been South Africa's impact on the OAU and the AU? One thing is for certain: the end of apartheid created a new environment within the OAU, making it possible for the AU to emerge. There was a sense in OAU circles that South Africa's freedom had brought to an end the era of the struggle for decolonisation. It is very unlikely that the OAU would have been transformed into a new organisation if South Africa were still under apartheid rule.

South Africa has been effective as a member of the OAU and the AU, politically and in terms of deploying its diplomatic and financial resources behind both organisations. It hosted the summit in Durban in July 2002 at which the OAU was transformed into the AU. It also hosted the AU summit in Johannesburg in June 2015. South Africa further hosted three AU institutions: the Pan-African Parliament; NEPAD; and the APRM. However, this influence has not been one-way. The country has contributed to shaping the AU and its agenda in the same way that its Africa policy and programmes were also shaped by developments in the OAU and the AU and more broadly on the continent. Tshwane's three-pronged AU strategy has entailed a combination of taking initiative and leadership in some cases; working with and through other countries in other cases; while lending its weight to back general programmes of the AU in others. The country has become an important advocate of the African Common Positions, developed by the AU, on a number of global issues including conflict and sanctions.

The African Agenda has undergone some mutation since its evolution from the CSSDCA's four-calabash model. Its core elements, however, remain focused on the AU and SADC, including their institutions, programmes and activities. This will certainly change with the passage of time. South Africa's African Agenda will have to respond to the new direction articulated in the AU's 50th Anniversary Solemn Declaration and driven by its then South African commission chair, Nkosazana Dlamini-Zuma, which was adopted at its May 2013 summit,[27] and in *Agenda 2063*, which the AU Commission has since developed as the continent's Africa programme for the next five decades. The strength of the African Agenda as South Africa's Africa strategy lies in its alignment with successive strategic plans of the AU Commission since the era of its first chair, Mali's Alpha Konare (2003–2008). The international environment is also changing. If the current trends are sustained, the world of the next two decades could be dominated by countries from the global South such as China, Brazil and India, with which South Africa is cooperating in the BRICS bloc (Brazil, Russia, India, China and South Africa) (see Virk in this volume). Such a world will be in Africa's interest. South Africa, in its public pronouncements and diplomatic manoeuvres in multilateral forums such as the AU and the UN, is positioning itself to emerge as one of the key players in the world of the future.

At the domestic level, South Africa's AU engagements in the immediate future will be impacted by implementation of the country's 2011 national development plan[28] and its foreign ministry's 2011 white paper on "building a better world".[29] One conclusion to be drawn from the foregoing is that since 1994, South Africa was able to take its seat in the OAU and the AU to play a continental role that was expected of a country of its size and capacity. In the process, Tshwane has become more and more dedicated to reaching its African destiny.

Notes

1. Nelson Mandela, "South Africa's Future Foreign Policy", *Foreign Affairs* 72, no. 5 (November/December 1993), pp. 86–94.

2. Albert Luthuli, *Let My People Go: An Autobiography* (Johannesburg: Collins, 1962; new ed., Cape Town: Tafelberg, 2006), p. 208.

3. Speech by African National Congress (ANC) deputy president Nelson Mandela at the 26th Assembly of the OAU (Organisation of African Unity) Heads of State and Government, Addis Ababa, 9 July 1990.

4. United Nations (UN) General Assembly Resolution, *The Policies of Apartheid of the Government of the Republic of South Africa*, 6 November 1962; and Conference of Independent African States Resolution, *Resolution Adopted by the Second Conference of Independent African States*, 24 June 1960.

5. ANC, "Ready to Govern: ANC Policy Guidelines for a Democratic South Africa", Economic Policy, *Regional Cooperation in Africa and Southern Africa*, http://www.anc.org.za/show.php?id=227 (accessed 2 July 2014).

6. ANC, "Foreign Policy Perspective in a Democratic South Africa", 1 December 1994, http://www.anc.org.za/content/foreign-policy-perspective-democratic-south-africa (accessed 7 July 2017).

7. ANC, "Foreign Policy Perspective".

8. ANC, "Foreign Policy Perspective".

9. *See, for example*, Chris Landsberg, "South Africa and the Making of the African Union and NEPAD: Mbeki's 'Progressive African Agenda'", in Adekeye Adebajo, Adebayo Adedeji and Chris Landsberg (eds), *South Africa in Africa: The Post-Apartheid Era* (Scottsville: University of KwaZulu-Natal Press, 2007), pp. 195–212; Adebayo Adedeji, "NEPAD's African Peer Review Mechanism: Progress and Prospects", in John Akokpari, Angela Ndinga-Muvumba, and Tim Murithi (eds), *The African Union and Its Institutions* (Johannesburg: Jacana, 2008), pp. 241–269.

10. ANC, "Decisive and Sustained Action to Build a National Democratic Society", preface to the 2007 "Strategy and Tactics", adopted by the 53rd ANC National Conference, 16–20 December 2012.

11. For the ANC's 1994 and 1999 election manifestos, *see* http://www.anc.org.za/list. php?t=Manifesto (accessed 2 July 2014).

12. South African Department of Foreign Affairs (DFA), *Annual Report 2002/2003*, p. 106.

13. DFA, *Annual Report 2002/2003*, p. 107.

14. *See* Africa Leadership Forum, jointly with the Secretariats of the OAU and the United Nations Economic Commission for Africa (UNECA), *The Kampala Document: Towards a Conference on Security, Stability, Development, and Cooperation in Africa*, Kampala, 19–22 May 1991.

15. Declarations and Decisions adopted by the 36th Ordinary Session of the OAU Assembly of Heads of State and Government, Lomé, 10–12 July 2000.

16. DFA, *Strategic Plan 2006–2009*, p. 6.

17. *See, for example*, John Akokpari and Daniel Shea Zimbler (eds), *Africa's Human Rights Architecture* (Johannesburg: Jacana, 2008).

18. *See, for example*, Jakkie Cilliers and Prince Mashele, "The Pan-African Parliament: A Plenary of Parliamentarians", *African Security Review* 13, no. 4 (2004), pp. 73–83; Charles Mutasa, "A Critical Appraisal of the African Union–ECOSOCC Civil Society Interface", in Akokpari, Ndinga-Muvumba and Murithi, *The African Union and Its Institutions*, pp. 291–306.

19. *See* DFA, *Strategic Plan 2006–2009*.

20. DFA, *Strategic Plan 2006–2009*.

21. DFA, *Annual Report 2001/2002*, p. 1.

22. DFA, *Annual Report 2003/2004*, p. 72.

23. *See, for example*, David Monyae, "South Africa's Development Finance Institutions", in Chris Saunders, Gwinyayi A. Dzinesa and Dawn Nagar (eds), *Region-Building in Southern Africa: Progress, Problems and Prospects* (London: Zed; and Johannesburg: Wits University Press, 2012), pp. 164–177.

24. DFA, *South Africa in the United Nations Security Council (2007–2008)*, p. 10.

25. ANC, "2009 Manifesto: Working Together We Can Do More", p. 15, http://www. anc.org.za/docs/manifesto/2009/manifesto.pdf (accessed 2 July 2014).

26. South African Department of International Relations and Cooperation (DIRCO), *Strategic Plan 2013–2018*, p. 22.

27. African Union, *50th Anniversary Solemn Declaration*, May 2013, http://www.un. org/en/africa/osaa/pdf/au/50anniv_declaration_2013.pdf (accessed 16 September 2016).

28. Government of South Africa, *National Development Plan: Vision for 2030*, November 2011, http://www.gov.za/sites/www.gov.za/files/devplan_2.pdf (accessed 16 September 2016).

29. Government of South Africa, *Building a Better World: The Diplomacy of Ubuntu*, White Paper on South Africa's foreign policy, May 2011, http://www.gov.za/sites/www.gov.za/files/foreignpolicy_0.pdf (accessed 16 September 2016).

PART IV

SOUTH AFRICA'S KEY EXTERNAL BILATERAL RELATIONS

CHAPTER 14

SOUTH AFRICA AND THE UNITED STATES: A PRAGMATIC FRIENDSHIP

Stephen R. Weissman

To unpack the complicated post-apartheid political relationship between the United States (US) and South Africa, one should begin by recognising that there has been a major difference between the two parties' *feelings* about their association and what actually happens on the ground. In interviews conducted for this chapter, former US officials and other close American observers repeatedly called attention to this paradox: "The US and South Africa have a more productive relationship than the overall tone"; "Relations have been benign, by which I mean what's going on beyond feelings"; and "George W. Bush and [Bill] Clinton glamorised the relationship as warmer than it has ever been". A former American ambassador to South Africa initially portrayed the relations by making a series of up and down waves with his hands, but later described the relations as "generally strong". A well-placed South African diplomat suggested that the two countries have been on an emotional roller coaster that was at last slowing down: "Twenty years ago there was a sentimental relationship. The next decade or so was very complicated ... The [Barack] Obama era is more normal in the sense that there is neither exhilaration nor standoffishness".[1]

Much of the gap between these oscillating perceptions and hard realities appears to be a legacy of the two countries' relations at different moments during the apartheid era. On the one hand, both American and South

African leaders have held unreasonably high expectations that were inevitably dashed; on the other, the South Africans have retained an abiding distrust that sometimes appears to have been vindicated. Amid this welter of emotions, the relatively even course of the objective relationship may be hard to discern.

"Constructive Engagement" and Beyond

For almost the entire four decades of apartheid (1948–1990), America's foreign policy was governed by its Cold War with the erstwhile Soviet Union and China. During that conflict, Washington generally prioritised areas of the world that it considered more strategic than Africa. In South Africa, US policymakers focused on protecting military, scientific and economic interests that were useful for anti-Communist campaigns elsewhere.[2] Even as the anti-apartheid struggle intensified in the 1960s and 1970s, America took only modest steps to adjust its stance. It was only when formally Marxist liberation movements began to succeed in Southern African countries such as Mozambique and Angola that Washington developed new policies towards the sub-region.

In 1981, US president Ronald Reagan inaugurated the policy of "constructive engagement." This boiled down to supporting "pro-Western" apartheid South African president Pieter Willem Botha's attempt to create a "modernising autocracy" without major political change, as well as his military and diplomatic campaign against Cuban troops in Angola.

However, a burgeoning American anti-apartheid movement soon challenged the intellectual credibility and moral integrity of "constructive engagement". Within just a few years, it succeeded in resetting American policy. Television coverage of the "rolling mass action" in South Africa's black townships reminded ordinary Americans of their own wrenching civil rights struggles in the 1960s. A low-profile black American foreign policy lobby led an innovative campaign of civil disobedience at the South African embassy in Washington, DC, and consulates across the US, attracting thousands of activists including representatives of church, labour, civil rights groups, politicians and celebrities. With crucial leadership from a bipartisan cadre of Representatives and Senators, the American Congress overrode Ronald Reagan's veto to pass meaningful economic sanctions in October 1986 in a bid to force political negotiations between the apartheid regime and representatives of the black majority. South African and American leaders subsequently acknowledged that US and Western sanctions had contributed significantly to the birth of a new South Africa.[3]

Having ridden into the post-apartheid era on a wave of moral triumph, the South African and American governments had high expectations of each other. These hopes help account for the recurrent expressions of disappointment emanating from officials of both countries. Thus, President Nelson Mandela publicly dismissed President Bill Clinton's post-apartheid three-year $600 million aid programme as "peanuts",[4] while diplomats from the George W. Bush administration complained that President Thabo Mbeki resisted international economic sanctions against the oppressive Zimbabwean government of Robert Mugabe despite the fact that the African National Congress (ANC) had called for, and benefited from, sanctions against apartheid's tyranny.[5]

At the same time, bitter recollections of American policies before sanctions nourished Tshwane's (Pretoria) suspicions of Washington, exacerbating contemporary differences between both countries. As one US official with recent experience of South Africa policy observed: "It was striking how the ANC had long memories of where we had been in the struggle".[6] Former president Thabo Mbeki expressed this residual distrust in February 2012 following the US-led overthrow of the Muammar Qaddafi regime in Libya and French military intervention in Côte d'Ivoire (see Tawfik, and Adebajo in this volume): "Recent events, as in Libya and Côte d'Ivoire, have confirmed that the major Western powers remain interested and determined to attach Africa to themselves as their appendage, at all costs, ready to use all means to achieve this objective".[7]

Yet when one looks beyond such rhetoric and examines the actual encounters between the two countries, giving appropriate weight to their higher-priority concerns with each other, their overall relationship appears to be surprisingly positive. Naturally the leaders of a rich Western superpower and a "progressive" developing nation emerging from a long struggle against "imperialism" would have different perspectives on international affairs. Nevertheless, both countries have found ways to cooperate closely around several core concerns of their foreign policies, compromise or "work around" other significant issues, and – with a few outstanding exceptions – "agree to disagree" on matters of less immediate consequence.

To begin with, South Africa and the US are relatively stable, "rule of law" democracies. Therefore they start off with a basic ease about each other

At a June 2005 press conference with Mbeki, George W. Bush called South Africa "a stalwart when it comes to democratic institutions".[8] More than that, both Republican and Democratic administrations in the United States have supported South Africa's multiracial democracy as a model for other countries to emulate, especially those recovering from violent conflicts. One former US policymaker drew a contrast with America's relations with sub-Saharan Africa's other major regional power: Nigeria. While the latter's positions on some key international issues are closer to America's than those of South Africa, Nigeria/US relations have been complicated by the West African power's chequered history of coups and rigged elections, corruption and Islamic extremism (see Adebajo in this volume).

When it comes to their foreign policies, both the US and South Africa have, for different reasons, prioritised conflict resolution in Africa (see Curtis in this volume), with a special focus on the explosive Great Lakes region (see Nzongola-Ntalaja in this volume). This has led to productive cooperation in lengthy peacemaking processes in Burundi and the Democratic Republic of the Congo (DRC). In recent years, South Africa has been associated with American efforts to head off conflict between Sudan and the new state of South Sudan.

Although frequently overlooked, South Africa and the US have also worked together closely for two decades on one of the world's most important problems: the proliferation of nuclear weapons. Proceeding bilaterally and through various multilateral channels, both countries have racked up major achievements. Where they have disagreed, they have often been able to compromise over their differences.

Strains have sometimes arisen over US programmes in, or affecting, South Africa. However, these have been relatively quickly resolved or mitigated. This was the case during the Clinton administration (1993–2000) when President Mandela reacted coolly to a unilateral US initiative to lower trade barriers for certain African imports, and during the George W. Bush administration (2001–2008), when President Mbeki's resistance to accepted methods of AIDS prevention and treatment challenged Bush's signature anti-AIDS programme, the President's Emergency Programme for AIDS Relief (PEPFAR). Similar tensions were evident when South Africa led opposition to the establishment of a US military command on the continent in 2007.

Probably the most important disagreements have occurred over responses to repression in Zimbabwe (2002–2008) and military intervention in Libya (2011). The heart of the dispute over Zimbabwe was not so much that Washington and Tshwane had different visions for a successful democratic political transition, but that South Africa rejected the somewhat half-hearted American appeal for Tshwane to use its economic and political leverage to force political change in Zimbabwe. By contrast, the US and South Africa had major differences over Libya in 2011 regarding both the substance of a democratic transition, and the forcefulness of the international response. Libya's fate was also very important to both countries. South Africa considered this case a major litmus test of the African Union's (AU) ability to resolve the continent's civil wars. For the US, Libya represented a major test of the West's ability to reposition itself in the Middle East in the course of the "Afro-Arab Spring".

The rest of the chapter examines the approaches of both countries to conflict resolution; nuclear non-proliferation; key US programmes on trade, health and security; and political transitions in Zimbabwe and Libya, before offering some concluding reflections.

Cooperating to Resolve African Conflicts

Burundi

Burdened by its failure to prevent or halt the 1994 genocide by Hutu extremists that killed about 800,000 mostly Tutsi victims in Rwanda, the US moved to avoid a similar outcome in Rwanda's imploding ethnic twin of Burundi. However, the Clinton administration excluded preventive international military intervention, fearing that Washington would be dragged into a politically unsustainable quagmire, as it had been in Somalia between 1992 and 1993. Instead, Clinton appointed former Congressman Howard Wolpe – who had led the battle in the US House of Representatives for sanctions against apartheid in the 1980s – as the US presidential special envoy to the Great Lakes region. Wolpe's principal mandate involved working with East and Central African leaders and their designated "facilitators" – former Tanzanian president Julius Nyerere and, after 1999, former South African president Nelson Mandela – to resolve the Burundian civil war through diplomatic means. By 1998, Nyerere had succeeded in launching all-party negotiations. In August 2000, Mandela rammed through the Arusha peace agreement for a democratic political transition based on power-sharing between the majority Hutu and minority Tutsi.

The US contributed significantly to these African-led advances. At a critical moment in 1996, Wolpe marshalled American support for regional economic sanctions against Burundi's Tutsi-dominated military regime led by Pierre Buyoya. He shared political intelligence with, and counselled, Nyerere and Mandela. Wolpe also worked with regional leaders, Catholic Church intermediaries and the parties to the conflict to narrow differences and clear up misunderstandings. The American diplomatic involvement, along with that of the European Union (EU), strengthened the facilitators' positions with Burundi's parties. On the eve of the Arusha accord in August 1998, Mandela invited President Clinton to witness the signing ceremony. When a number of Tutsi parties balked, Mandela asked Clinton to use his speech to press for their signatures. "That speech was pivotal in persuading some of the most resistant Tutsi delegations to sign the accord", Wolpe later recounted.[9]

Although Mandela was an ex-president who had been "hired" by the regional leaders, his mediation was also an expression of developing South African policy towards the Great Lakes region. It was certainly viewed as such by many of the Burundian and regional actors.[10] In 2004, President Mbeki explained the basis for South Africa's by now full-blown involvement in the region:

> We have sent troops to countries like Burundi and the DRC because we know that we will never develop and be happy forever all by ourselves while wars and poverty are prevalent in our neighbouring states ... It helps South Africa to work for peace so that we increase the number of countries we can trade with while developing the economy of our country and of Africa as a whole.[11]

In fact, even before Mandela grasped the Burundi nettle, he and Mbeki, then his deputy president, had engaged in diplomatic efforts to end the ruinous conflict in Burundi's giant neighbour, the DRC, in which Burundi's largest rebel movement, the Hutu-dominated National Council for the Defence of Democracy – Forces for the Defence of Democracy (CNDD-FDD), had major bases. Furthermore, South Africa had hosted several secret meetings between the rebels and the Buyoya government in an unsuccessful effort to lure the former into Nyerere's negotiations.[12] President Mandela had also seconded his chief legal and constitutional adviser, Nicholas "Fink" Haysom, and one of his generals, Andrew Masondo, to assist Nyerere's efforts.[13]

When Mandela effectively withdrew as the facilitator in Burundi after the Arusha accord, he was succeeded by South Africa's deputy president, Jacob Zuma. From 2001 to 2009, no outside government was more important to sustaining Burundi's transition than that of South Africa. Zuma and President Mbeki personally negotiated the incorporation of the two major armed rebel movements, the CNDD-FDD and the Forces of National Liberation (FNL), into the Arusha settlement of August 2000. South Africa also furnished about 750 protection personnel to guard members of the Burundian transition government returning from exile, as well as other opposition politicians. Tshwane contributed about 1,600 troops to African Union and United Nations (UN) peacekeeping operations between 2003 and 2006. These international military missions in Burundi were commanded by South Africans.[14] Other assistance provided by Tshwane focused on elections and security sector reform (SSR).[15]

At critical junctures in the peace process, the US maintained its support for South African diplomacy. Washington participated in an international appeal to the Burundian government to abide by the timetable for installation of a Hutu president, Domitien Ndayizeye; backed Zuma's recommendation for converting the AU force into an expanded UN operation by 2004; and joined with South Africa and Tanzania in insisting that Burundi's government maintain its consensual electoral process for the 2010 election.[16]

The Democratic Republic of the Congo

In 1999, Thabo Mbeki began to take major responsibility in the Southern African Development Community (SADC)-sponsored negotiations to bring "Africa's First World War" in the Congo – which had started three years earlier – to an end. In support of the Zambian mediation, the South African president helped to persuade six countries (Angola, the DRC, Namibia, Rwanda, Uganda and Zimbabwe) and two major rebel movements (the Liberation Movement of the Congo and the Congolese Union for Democracy) to sign the Lusaka agreement in July 1999. In addition to the ceasefire, this accord provided for withdrawal of foreign forces, deployment of UN peacekeepers and establishment of an inclusive "Inter-Congolese Dialogue" to establish a new political dispensation. Many of these ideas were derived from Mbeki's own peace plan.[17]

Mbeki subsequently played "the lead role"[18] in mediating the Inter-Congolese Dialogue, which culminated in the 2002 Sun City and Pretoria agreements. These accords created a temporary government under President Joseph Kabila and four vice-presidents from different political parties and civil society, envisioned integration of the various armed forces and looked forward to a new constitution and the holding of democratic elections. Working alongside official mediators from the Organisation of African Unity (OAU) – now the African Union – and the UN, Mbeki produced what French scholar Gerard Prunier described as "a triumph of South African diplomacy".[19]

As in Burundi, the US provided significant support for the South African-led peacemaking effort. For more than 40 years, the Congo had been the centrepiece of American policy towards Africa. Propelled by exaggerated fears of a Communist takeover of this immense, mineral-rich and strategically located country at the heart of the continent, the US Central Intelligence Agency (CIA) and other US government agencies made long-term investments in the incompetent and corrupt three-decade Mobutu Sese Seko dictatorship, which finally collapsed in 1997. Ironically, the ruinous inter-African war that ensued underlined the Congo's continuing importance for American policy towards Africa. Deciding to work closely with South Africa at Sun City, the George W. Bush administration dispatched its top representative in the DRC, Ambassador Aubrey Hooks, to the talks.

According to his oral history of the period, Ambassador Hooks met with South African foreign minister Nkosazana Dlamini-Zuma and told her: "I have known all the Congolese parties for some time and I am here to encourage them to work with you on finding a solution". Hooks was also "frequently in touch" with two close advisers sent by Congolese president Joseph Kabila. He further noted: "I called President Kabila almost every day to brief him on my take of events and encourage him to show more flexibility in his position". Once, at the request of the South African foreign minister, Hooks telephoned Kabila to persuade him to accept "a proposal the South Africans had put on the table". At another point he "told various [Congolese] parties trying to hold out that if they didn't come together, we would support a partial agreement and leave them aside". Wielding the prestige of a superpower with a long engagement in the Congo, Hooks played "the role of intermediary in a close collaboration with South Africa". As he later noted: "It was interesting how we were able to play an important role in communications in Sun City in helping to bring about an agreement".[20]

During the ensuing four-year political transition, the US and South Africa were among five or six principal countries providing political guidance and support as well as economic assistance to the DRC.[21] A major vehicle for these efforts was the International Committee to Accompany the Transition (CIAT). Between CIAT and a major US-backed 20,000-strong UN peacekeeping operation in the Congo (including 1,400 South African soldiers), "[t]he DRC was put under a *de facto* international trusteeship which on several occasions prevented the process from collapsing".[22]

Although CIAT died a natural death after the climatic 2006 elections, the US and South Africa have continued to pursue complementary policies towards the DRC. Both have been major aid donors specialising in the areas of security, governance and elections. Both accepted President Joseph Kabila's 2011 "victory" in what was widely considered a non-credible election, demonstrating their shared preference for short-term political stability. And both were in the forefront of the UN's 2013 decision to authorise a new, more offensive-minded 3,000-strong Force Intervention Brigade to confront Rwandan-supported insurgents and other armed groups. This SADC-authorised force included troops from South Africa, Tanzania and Malawi.

Sudan and South Sudan

Encouraged by an active Evangelical Christian constituency, the George W. Bush administration – led by Senator John Darnforth – worked with Kenya and other regional mediators to end Sudan's three-decade civil war between Muslim-led Northerners and Christian-led Southerners. Following the 2005 Comprehensive Peace Agreement (CPA) – which provided for wealth and power-sharing, regional autonomy and a future referendum on independence for South Sudan – the US launched a major economic assistance programme for the disadvantaged South.

Consistent with its emphasis on conflict resolution in Africa, the Mbeki administration strongly backed the CPA. Tshwane also provided governance training to South Sudan, whose Sudan People's Liberation Movement (SPLM) had long-standing ties with the ANC.[23] (See Khadiagala in this volume.)

A few months after resigning from the presidency in September 2008, Thabo Mbeki became the chair of the AU High-Level Implementation Panel for Sudan. In this capacity, he facilitated implementation of the North-South accord, culminating in the 2011 referendum in which the

South overwhelmingly voted for its independence (see Khadiagala in this volume). Since then, Mbeki has conducted negotiations that have produced agreements between the two countries on such critical issues as oil revenues, security arrangements, trade, banking and borders. At the same time, US special envoys to Sudan and South Sudan, Princeton Lyman and Donald Booth, have worked closely with Mbeki. The US has "played a critical supporting role" in Mbeki's deal-brokering, envoy Donald Booth wrote in October 2014.[24] The US State Department prohibits American diplomats from contacting Sudanese president Omar al-Bashir, due to his indictment by the International Criminal Court (ICC) for alleged war crimes in Darfur. The AU, which has opposed Bashir's arrest in the interest of peacemaking, has no such restriction. So, the special envoys have to communicate indirectly with Bashir through Mbeki.[25]

Although Mbeki represents the AU (where South Africa has substantial influence; see Maloka in this volume), he is also plausibly implementing a well-established South African foreign policy towards northern and South Sudan that he himself authored. According to a former US policymaker in the region, South Africa's own special envoy in Sudan until 2012, longtime Mbeki cabinet minister Charles Nqakula, was not active because "he did not want to cut across Mbeki", while President Zuma "has followed Mbeki's lead including in the UN Security Council".[26]

Building Bridges for Nuclear Non-Proliferation

Operating the sole commercial nuclear reactor on the African continent, holding the only effectively permanent African seat on the International Atomic Energy Agency (IAEA) board and imbued with the moral authority of a nation that relinquished its own nuclear weapons programme during the early 1990s, post-apartheid South Africa has been an important player in the international nuclear non-proliferation regime. Within this system, Tshwane shares the same general goals as Washington, which helped author the regime. However, like many other non-weapons states, South Africa has criticised the slow progress of the nuclear powers towards nuclear disarmament, their restrictiveness on access to nuclear energy and America's differential treatment of its friends, Israel and India.[27]

Since Mandela's presidency, South Africa has collaborated with the US in multilateral fora to narrow differences and formulate compromises on these issues, and sell the results to fellow members of the Non-Aligned Movement (NAM). While these deals have not eliminated the underlying differences, they have helped to preserve the non-proliferation system, and enabled it to move forward:

- At the 1995 Non-Proliferation Treaty (NPT) Review Conference, there was considerable resistance to the American proposal for an indefinite extension of the treaty because its provisions for nuclear disarmament had not been implemented. South Africa negotiated new guidelines for implementation and strengthened review processes with the US, and lobbied the Non-Aligned Movement to adopt them. The treaty was extended by a unanimous vote.[28]

- In 1996, South Africa and the US "worked through" the latter's concerns that the Africa Nuclear Weapons Free Zone Treaty could lead to new restrictions on the movement of nuclear materials through the southern Indian and Atlantic Oceans. America's awareness of the value of South Africa's non-proliferation policies helped secure its support for a popular African proposal.[29]

- In March 2007, despite its dissatisfaction with the George W. Bush administration's non-proliferation policies, South Africa joined the US in voting for targeted sanctions against Iran in the UN Security Council, thereby modifying its previous preference for diplomatic "carrots" over economic "sticks".[30]

- Under the Barack Obama administration (2009–2016), South Africa and the US drafted a compromise in the Nuclear Suppliers Group (NSG) on recipients of sensitive nuclear materials and recipients adhering to the "additional protocol" requiring increased IAEA inspections. They successfully marketed the product to the NAM.[31]

A good sense of the closeness of this relationship was conveyed in an August 2009 cable from a US diplomat summarising his discussion with South African IAEA governor Abdul Minty:

> Minty commented on US priority issues for the upcoming IAEA Board of Governors and General Conference meetings, arguing that an objective for both sides should be healing the rift between developed and developing countries that surfaced in the course of the long IAEA Director-General election. On Iran, Minty expressed concern about how the new NAM troika of Cuba, Iran and Egypt could feed into the Iranian misperception that they might normalize

their status at the IAEA without coming clean on their past nuclear activities. He pledged continued tough South African statements in the Board room and said he had reached out to newly appointed AEOI [Atomic Energy Organisation of Iran] head Ali Akbar Salehi to urge an early constructive response to the renewed P5 + 1 offer. On fuel assurances, Minty counseled a further cooling off period to dispel developing country concerns about a "Western group" rush to push through a fuel bank arrangement that could be used to deny NPT rights. Recalling his previous role in brokering an IAEA General Conference compromise on the Middle East resolutions, Minty welcomed our commitment to working for a consensus formula, but underlined that Egypt's position (and even its agenda) remain unclear, despite private Egyptian statements of concern about Iran's nuclear activities.[32]

Furthermore, South Africa and the US have a long history of bilateral cooperation on nuclear issues. Its fruits have included the conversion of South Africa's SAFARI 1 reactor to low-enriched uranium, and repatriation to the US of its highly enriched uranium. Collaboration also involved early investigation and prosecution of South African members of Pakistani nuclear scientist Abdul Qadeer (A.Q.) Khan's network, which aided nuclear weapons programmes in Libya, North Korea, Iran and perhaps other countries.[33]

Resolving Controversies Over US Programmes

The African Growth and Opportunity Act

As the American Congress was considering the African Growth and Opportunity Act (AGOA) in March 1998, President Mandela denounced it as "not acceptable" during a press conference with President Bill Clinton in Cape Town. Enacted in May 2000, AGOA has become a cornerstone of US policy towards Africa. It provides duty-free access to American markets for certain imports from sub-Saharan African countries, and envisions that this benefit will spur economic growth, trade and investment on the continent. AGOA also includes technical and other assistance to achieve these goals.

The Mandela government objected to AGOA on the grounds that it was a unilateral foreign initiative requiring African governments to meet a number of vague and potentially inappropriate conditions to receive its benefits. "South Africa bristled at the conditions, which it saw as neocolonialist" (these included respect for the rule of law, elimination of barriers to trade and investment, protection of worker rights and non-interference with US national security and foreign policy efforts). But by the time the bill passed, South Africa had changed its position. President Mbeki described AGOA as "a very good signal … an important step". Tshwane had pragmatically adjusted to other African countries' strong support for AGOA as well as the priority placed by the Clinton administration on the measure.[34]

But AGOA has hardly been a panacea. While Africa's share of total American imports has risen sharply since the legislation was enacted, it has remained at under 2 per cent and fell back to 1.1 per cent in 2014 largely due to declining petroleum imports. The overwhelming majority of AGOA's financial rewards, 68 per cent in 2014, have gone to a handful of energy exporters: Angola, Nigeria, Gabon, Chad and Congo-Brazzaville. South Africa was the major beneficiary of the non-energy component of the programme, accounting for 70 per cent of such imports in 2014, valued at $3.1 billion. Of this amount, about half represented luxury vehicles such as BMWs and Mercedes. Also, the conditionality that initially concerned South Africa has not proved to be onerous. A threatened suspension of eligibility over restrictions on imports of American poultry, pork and beef was resolved through a settlement in 2016.[35] Countries suspended temporarily from AGOA benefits have mainly been those undergoing anti-democratic military coups that South Africa and the AU also oppose or, more recently, those slipping away from democracy towards violence such as Burundi, the DRC and South Sudan.[36] A veteran South African diplomat noted: "Today AGOA is perceived as a success".[37] Certainly AGOA imports have played a role in the increase in US–South Africa bilateral trade in goods from $7.3 billion in 2000 to $14.7 billion in 2014 and $12.8 billion in 2015 (without adjusting for inflation).[38]

President's Emergency Programme for AIDS Relief

As early as the Clinton and Mandela administrations, the US and South Africa clashed over policies related to the HIV/AIDS epidemic. In December 1997, President Mandela approved legislation aimed at lowering the prices of "essential drugs" in the government's new health entitlements. The new Medicines Act permitted "parallel importing" of patented drugs from cheaper foreign suppliers and "compulsory licensing", whereby copies of patented drugs could be produced in South Africa with some compensation for the patent holder. However, the Pharmaceutical

Manufacturers Association of South Africa tied the law up in the country's High Court, contending that it was an unconstitutional override of both South African patent law and the international Agreement on Trade-Related Aspects of Intellectual Property Rights (TRIPS).

Under political pressure from the US pharmaceutical industry (subsidiaries of which controlled 27 per cent of the South African market) and Congress, the Clinton administration attempted to coerce South Africa into repealing or amending the law. In 1998–1999, Washington placed South Africa on a "watch list" for violations of intellectual property rights meriting bilateral attention. It also withheld previously approved trade preferences for four key imports. Furthermore, the Clinton administration persuaded some European governments to express their opposition to the Medicines Act. The issue quickly became a major focus of discussion in the US–South Africa Bi-National Commission, chaired by US vice-president Al Gore and South African deputy president Thabo Mbeki.

Crucially, the controversy became entwined with the widely recognised need to provide inexpensive drug treatment for the 16 per cent of South Africans estimated to be infected with HIV. Influenced by that imperative as well as international and domestic pressures, the Clinton administration gradually changed course. South Africa mobilised support for its position in the World Health Organisation (WHO) and the Non-Aligned Movement. It also benefited from campaigns by non-governmental organisations (NGOs) such as Doctors Without Borders and Health Action International. Perhaps most important, Vice-President Gore – who officially launched his campaign for the US presidency in mid-1999 – was pushed hard by the Congressional Black Caucus (a key Democratic constituency) and by anti-AIDS activists, who dogged his campaign with signs proclaiming "Gore's Greed Kills" and "No Medical Apartheid". By September 1999 the two governments declared the dispute settled, essentially on South African terms, with a genuflection to the ambiguous language of TRIPS, and US sanctions quickly disappeared. In April 2001, the drug companies subsequently dropped their suit against the South African government.[39]

If there was one policy that vindicated President George W. Bush's domestic political brand as a "compassionate conservative", it was his $15 billion, five-year global anti-AIDS initiative. With one-sixth of the world's HIV infections, South Africa became one of the legislation's 15 "focus countries" in Africa, Asia and the Caribbean. But President Mbeki questioned the link between HIV and AIDS and doubted the safety of Western anti-retroviral treatments. Mbeki's stance, which was criticised in both the US and South Africa, might have posed a major obstacle to Bush's programme.

But it did not. As soon as the legislation passed the US Congress in 2003, the American embassy began to roll out its programme. As a subsequent US Agency for International Development (USAID) evaluation explained: "Due to the political environment non-governmental organisations ... became key implementing partners and interventions were developed with little, if any, engagement with government structures".[40] Despite this obstacle, the effort was extremely well funded from the beginning.[41] By 2008, when Mbeki left office, the President's Emergency Programme for AIDS Relief was supporting anti-retroviral treatment for 549,000 South Africans: 32 per cent of those eligible for treatment. Although the average treatment rate for the 15 focus countries was somewhat higher at 38 per cent, South Africa had much larger numbers of infections than any other country.[42]

Notwithstanding its own recalcitrance, the Mbeki government accommodated the massive American health intervention. According to two US officials in Tshwane during this period, Mbeki "quieted down, let us move". He regularly met with the American ambassador, Cameron Hume, to exchange views on AIDS issues, and agreed to make helpful statements "a couple of times".[43]

Even before the birth of PEPFAR, Ambassador Hume had negotiated an anti-retroviral treatment programme with the South African military in 2002–2003. It was run as a "clinical trial" by the US National Institutes of Health (NIH), and included management training. A prevention component drew on US defence department health unit laboratories.

Mbeki's stance on AIDS, which changed slowly, was undoubtedly an irritant to both the US government and concerned Americans. Even so, former American officials insisted that his views did not significantly affect US–South Africa relations. With Jacob Zuma's assumption of the presidency in May 2009, and his subsequent acceleration of South Africa's department of health anti-AIDS programmes, tensions between Washington and Tshwane over the issue dissipated.

The US Africa Command

In February 2007, the George W. Bush administration unveiled its plan to create a new Africa Command (AFRICOM) to rationalise US military responsibility for Africa, which was shared at the time by three different existing commands. AFRICOM'S headquarters and subsidiary offices were to be located on the continent. In a changing series of public statements, administration officials elaborated various objectives for the new command, but failed to define any order of priorities. Invoking a panoply of rising threats to US interests from terrorism, failed states and China, they suggested that AFRICOM might respond with a range of options, from combat forces, to programmes to strengthen African security forces, to "soft power" initiatives coordinated with the US State Department. What was clear to Africans was that Washington wanted to build upon its growing "counter-terrorism" and peacekeeping missions in Africa by establishing a new military footprint on the continent.[44]

Against the background of the Iraq war of 2003 (conducted without a clear UN Security Council mandate) and other perceived excesses of the Bush administration's "War on Terror," African governments – including such close US friends as Nigeria and Kenya – overwhelmingly refused to host AFRICOM. Leading Southern Africa's opposition, South Africa's defence minister, Mosiuoa Lekota, declared: "Africa has to avoid the presence of foreign forces on [its] soil. There's a certain sense in the countries of our region that if there was to be an influx of armed forces into one or other of the African countries, that might affect the relations between the sister countries, and not encourage an atmosphere ... of security".[45]

The US quickly dropped its plan to establish an African outpost. AFRICOM was located in Stuttgart, Germany, where it remained in 2017. Although the issue would seem settled, it has merely subsided. Media reports and interviews confirmed in 2013 and 2014 that some South African political leaders and government officials suspected the US of attempting, by stealth, to establish elements of AFRICOM in Botswana.[46]

Differences over Political Transitions in Zimbabwe and Libya

Zimbabwe

Beginning in 2000, the then 20-year rule of Robert Mugabe and his Zimbabwe African National Union – Patriotic Front (ZANU-PF) was increasingly challenged by Morgan Tsvangirai's opposition Movement for Democratic Change (MDC). In response, Mugabe encouraged his supporters to seize white-owned commercial farms, and embarked on a campaign of political repression. An estimated one million refugees fled to South Africa (see Sachikonye in this volume).

During most of its nine years in office, the Mbeki administration sought a political solution to this impending conflict through diplomatic means. As in Burundi and the DRC, its model was based on the successful South African political transition: dialogue between the opposing political forces, creation of a national unity government and constitutional reform, followed by democratic elections (see Curtis in this volume). A November 2006 cable from the American embassy in Tshwane gave a sense of the kind of change that Mbeki was seeking and the tactics he was employing:

> Senior South African officials are increasingly frustrated by president Mugabe's erratic rule, and we believe president Mbeki would like to see new leadership in Zimbabwe. South Africa has tried a number of behind-the-scenes initiatives to spur change, including a proposed loan, negotiations on a compromise constitution, encouraging Mugabe's timely retirement, and intelligence operations. Yet, Pretoria has refused to criticise publicly the Mugabe regime, believing that "quiet diplomacy" and internal negotiations are the best ways to effect change.[47]

Looking at Zimbabwe, a country whose leaders often thumbed their noses at the West, through a human rights prism, the George W. Bush administration had a vision of its political future that was not very different from Mbeki's. In a June 2003 newspaper editorial, US secretary of state Colin Powell proposed that "ZANU-PF and the opposition party ... together legislate the constitutional changes to allow for a transition. With the president gone, with a transitional government in place and with a date fixed for new elections, Zimbabweans ... would ... come together".[48] While Powell's recipe put more emphasis than Mbeki's upon Mugabe's early retirement, a former US official indicated that Washington could have countenanced a short-term role for Mugabe in a transitional government. Indeed, it eventually did more than that. In September 2008, according to the same official, the Bush administration "accepted" a Mbeki-mediated agreement establishing a five-year unity government including Mugabe to lead a democratic transition.[49]

The main disagreement between the US and South Africa was over the latter's refusal to escalate pressure on Mugabe by publicly criticising his rigged elections in 2002, supporting a UN Security Council arms embargo and targeted sanctions and, most important, wielding its economic leverage including control over Zimbabwe's power and water supplies. Mbeki was reluctant to take this path for several reasons, including his preference for African national self-determination, fear of the domestic consequences of disruption in Zimbabwe and widespread sympathy for Mugabe and distrust of the MDC within both the ANC and SADC. Yet the division between Washington and Tshwane over this issue was not as intense as it sometimes appeared. Visiting Mbeki in South Africa in July 2003, George W. Bush told a joint press conference: "The president is the point man on this subject ... He is working very hard. He believes he's making good progress. I think Mr. Mbeki can be an honest broker".[50] This was just two weeks after Colin Powell's opinion editorial had declared that South Africa "can and should play a more sustained role that fully reflects the urgency of Zimbabwe's crisis".[51] According to a former administration official, Powell's article had never been cleared by the White House: "There is substance to the fact that the White House was not as strong on Zimbabwe as the State Department".[52] Another former official dryly commented: "We had opinions about Zimbabwe but did nothing".[53]

Although the 2008 agreement was imperfectly implemented and the subsequent 2013 election (in which the ZANU-PF trounced a weakened and divided MDC) was not fully free and fair, Zimbabwe – despite its continuing problems – largely disappeared as a point of friction between the Obama and Zuma administrations.

Libya

In Libya's chapter of the "Afro-Arab Spring", Muammar Qaddafi's brutal repression of widespread peaceful demonstrations in February 2011 quickly morphed into a raging civil war.[54] (See Tawfik in this volume.) The US, Britain and France, which had all cozied up to dictatorships in North Africa and the Arab world for decades, had been caught by surprise by the wave of popular unrest sweeping through the region. Seeking to reposition themselves as supporters of political change, they decided to embrace the Libyan revolution led by the Transitional National Council (TNC) against longtime autocrat Muammar Qaddafi. In March 2011, the three Western allies backed UN Security Council Resolution 1973, authorising a no-fly zone and the use of force "to protect civilians ... threatened with attack".[55]

Following a telephone appeal from Barack Obama to Jacob Zuma that – according to two former US officials – emphasised an imminent threat to civilians in the eastern city of Benghazi, and the Security Council resolution's incorporation of a South African-drafted paragraph high-lighting the African Union's role in "facilitating dialogue to lead to the political reforms necessary to find a peaceful and sustainable solution", Tshwane signed on to the Security Council resolution. In contrast to South Africa, the other members of the BRICS group – Brazil, India, Russia and China – attempted to create some distance from the resolution by abstaining (see Virk in this volume).

It was only seven months later that President Obama publicly acknowledged that the North Atlantic Treaty Organisation's (NATO) open-ended military campaign was also designed "to make sure that Muammar Qaddafi didn't stay there".[56] Obama had misled not only Zuma, but also the American people, whom he had assured: "Broadening our military mission to include regime change would be a mistake".[57]

South African diplomacy was heavily engaged by the Libyan conflict. Zuma was the leading member of the AU's five-president High-Level Ad Hoc Committee on Libya, which sought a mediated political solution to the crisis. With the UN resolution and NATO bombing providing political leverage, in April 2011 the AU committee obtained Qaddafi's agreement to its "roadmap", which envisaged that Libya's self-styled "Guide" step down within months, and an inclusive transitional government oversee democratic elections. Consulting with both sides of the conflict, the AU prepared a Framework Agreement in July 2011 to be the basis for negotiations. This was a recipe for consensual "regime change" under the protection of UN peacekeepers.

However, the US and NATO preferred to use force to oust Qaddafi and to replace him with the supposedly pro-democratic Transitional National Council. Western powers discouraged the rebels from negotiating with the AU, and declared that the only mediator that they would recognise was the UN special envoy, Abdel-Elah Al-Khatib, who had never met Qaddafi nor even presented a full proposal to the parties. After the rebellion prevailed militarily in August 2011, Zuma complained that NATO had "deliberately undermined" the African peace initiative.[58]

In October 2011, South Africa abstained (along with Brazil, India and Lebanon) from a US-sponsored UN Security Council resolution threatening sanctions against the Syrian government of Bashar al-Assad. In explanation, the South African permanent representative to the UN, Baso Sangqu, expressed his "deep concern" about violations of human rights during the civil war in Syria, but indicated that Tshwane's vote had been influenced by events in Libya (see Mashabane in this volume). According to a summary of his remarks, Sangqu charged that "[Security] Council texts had been abused and implementation had gone far beyond mandates. South Africa was concerned about the imposition of punitive measures on Syria believing that they had been designed as a prelude to other actions. The Council should not be part of any hidden agenda for regime change".[59]

Concluding Reflections

The US and South Africa have disagreed on several important foreign policy issues beyond Zimbabwe and Libya. Most notably, Tshwane opposed Washington's invasion of Iraq in 2003; has been more supportive of the Palestinian struggle (though it favours a two-state solution); and has been unwilling to take as strong a stance as the US in international fora on human rights violations in places such as Cuba, Iran, Syria and Myanmar.

Nevertheless, one should not exaggerate the significance of these differences for the overall bilateral relationship. In the first place, South Africa does not seem to fall very much below the international norm for dissent from American positions. For example, in non-unanimous votes in the 2012 UN General Assembly, the average country agreed with the US only 42 per cent of the time. South Africa's agreement was 36 per cent, almost the same as Nigeria's and higher than Kenya's. On eight mainly Middle Eastern issues that Washington deemed "very important", the coincidence of South African and American voting was zero per cent. But the average coincidence rate for the entire Africa Group was only 26 per cent.[60]

Moreover, these differences between the US and South Africa have not attracted the same level of diplomatic energy and investment as have the issues explored in this chapter. This is because these issues have not negatively affected what the two countries have, in practice, defined as the core issues in their bilateral relationship. Also, South Africa's critical positions on issues such as the 2003 Iraq war or the Middle East peace process have not obstructed the American superpower's pursuit of its own international priorities.

What about South Africa's heavy investment in efforts to enhance the power of the global South in relation to the US and other industrialised countries in the World Trade Organisation (WTO) (see Ismail in this volume), the International Monetary Fund (IMF), the World Bank and the

UN Security Council? And what about South Africa's related commitment to the BRICS? Thus far, there is no evidence that these initiatives have achieved sufficient critical mass to affect the diplomatic conversation between Tshwane and Washington. If and when they do, their impact will depend in part on how accommodating the US becomes.[61]

Looking back over the past two and a half decades, the continuity of US–South Africa relations since the end of apartheid is impressive. Major areas of partnership have persisted through three presidencies on each side since 1994. While issues, circumstances and presidential styles have changed, it is difficult to conclude that the core relationship has been significantly better under one administration than another. Clinton and Mandela came together on nuclear non-proliferation and Burundi, but came into conflict over US aid levels and AGOA. Bush and Mbeki worked together on the DRC and PEPFAR, but differed over Zimbabwe and AFRICOM. Obama and Zuma have cooperated on the DRC and Sudan, but broken apart over Libya.

What then is the best short description of the relationship that South Africa has developed with the United States, one in which a superpower and a regional power depend upon each other across a broad range of issues and argue about others? Terms like "ally", "client", "close friend", "enemy" and "adversary" do not really fit this complex bilateral relationship. However reluctant they may be to admit it, these two proud countries – still carrying the emotional burdens of their pasts – might best be characterised as "independent-minded friends".

It is impossible to conclude this essay without noting that a certain shadow began to fall over this friendship in 2015–2016. President Zuma's highly publicised corruption scandals and instances of disrespect for the law tarnished South Africa's political reputation in the US. More important, a gap opened between Tshwane's and Washington's policies towards conflicts in the Great Lakes region. As Burundi's president, Pierre Nkurunziza, and the DRC's president, Joseph Kabila, offered dubious legal arguments to obliterate their term limits, South Africa seemed to abandon its past championing of democratic constitutionalism in these violence-prone countries. In contrast, the Obama administration belatedly and haltingly mobilised international pressure, including targeted economic sanctions, on both regimes to preserve their political settlements. In these cases, an important pillar of the broad US–South African relationship – joint action to resolve African conflicts – appeared to be weakening.

Finally, the election in November 2016 of Donald Trump – a strong nationalist determined to "put America first" – as US president raised the question of how highly the new administration would value its partnership with South Africa in world politics. Nevertheless, the very existence of this relationship across a wide array of issues is likely to act as a brake upon any abrupt changes.

Notes

1. I conducted ten interviews, seven with former United States (US) officials in the Bill Clinton, George W. Bush and Barack Obama administrations, two with knowledgeable American observers and one with a veteran South African diplomat. To encourage candour, the conversations took place on a confidential basis.

2. US Department of State, *Foreign Relations of the United States, 1969–1976*, vol. 28, *Southern Africa*, Document no. 17 (Washington, DC, December 1969), https://history.state.gov/historicaldocuments/frus1969-76v28/d17 (accessed 13 December 2014).

3. Stephen R. Weissman, *A Culture of Deference: Congress's Failure of Leadership in Foreign Policy* (New York: Basic, 1995), pp. 165–176.

4. Princeton N. Lyman, *Partner to History: The U.S. Role in South Africa's Transition to Democracy* (Washington, DC: US Institute of Peace Press, 2002), pp. 231–235.

5. Confidential interviews; and US Embassy Pretoria (Tshwane) to Secretary of State 001467, "Pahad Outlines SAG Concern About UNSC Resolution," 8 July 2008, https://search.wikileaks.org/plusd/cables/08PRETORIA1467_a.html (accessed 13 December 2014).

6. Confidential interview.

7. Thabo Mbeki, "Reflections on Peacemaking, State Sovereignty, and Democratic Governance in Africa", lecture, Community Law Centre, University of the Western Cape, Bellville, 12 February 2012, p. 13.

8. US White House, "President and South African President Mbeki Discuss Bilateral Relations", news release, 1 June 2005, http://www.whitehouse.gov/news/releases/2005/06/print/20050601.html (accessed 13 December 2014).

9. Howard Wolpe, "Making Peace After Genocide: Anatomy of the Burundi Process", *Peaceworks* 70 (March 2011), p. 58.

10. Wolpe, "Making Peace", p. 52.

11. Thomas Mandrup, "Africa: Salvation or Despair?", PhD dissertation, Institute of Politics, University of Copenhagen, May 2007, p. 249.

12. Wolpe, "Making Peace", p. 49.

13. Kristina A. Bentley and Roger Southall, *An African Peace Process: Mandela, South Africa, and Burundi* (Cape Town: Human Sciences Research Council (HSRC) Press, 2005), pp. 65–66.

14. Devon Curtis, "The International Peacebuilding Paradox: Power Sharing and Post-Conflict Governance in Burundi", *African Affairs* 112, no. 446 (2012), p. 83, including n. 27; Mandrup, "Africa: Salvation or Despair?", pp. 239–244; Wolpe, "Making Peace", pp. 58–60; Bentley and Southall, *An African Peace Process*, pp. 85–124; US Embassy Pretoria to Secretary of State 004790, "South Africa's UN

Security Council Priorities", 21 November 2006, https://cablegatesearch.wikileaks. org/cable.php?id=06PRETORIA4790&q = south-africa (accessed 14 December 2014); US Embassy Pretoria to Secretary of State 000827, "South Africa Concerned About CNDD-FDD Split", 6 March 2007, https://search.wikileaks.org/plusd/ cables/07PRETORIA827_a.html (accessed 14 December 2014).

15. Centre for Conflict Resolution (CCR), *Post-Apartheid South Africa's Foreign Policy After Apartheid*, Seminar Report no. 47 (Cape Town, June 2014), pp. 13, 21, http:// www.ccr.org.za (accessed 16 December 2014).

16. Wolpe, "Making Peace", p. 60; International Crisis Group (ICG), *Burundi: Ensuring Credible Elections*, Africa Report no. 155, 12 February 2010, p. 5, including n. 23.

17. Filip Reyntjens, *The Great African War: Congo and Regional Geopolitics, 1996–2006* (Cambridge: Cambridge University Press, 2009), pp. 247–252; Chris Landsberg, "The Impossible Neutrality? South Africa's Policy in the Congo War", in John Clark (ed.), *The African Stakes of the Congo War* (New York: Palgrave, 2002), p. 178.

18. Reyntjens, *The Great African War*, p. 256.

19. Gérard Prunier, *Africa's World War: Congo, The Rwandan Genocide, and The Making of a Continental Catastrophe* (New York: Oxford University Press, 2009), p. 269 (*see also* p. 277); Reyntjens, *The Great African War*, pp. 256–261.

20. Association of Diplomatic Studies and Training, Oral History Interviews, "Ambassador Aubrey Hooks", September 2009, pp. 128–130, http://adst.org/wp-content/uploads/2012/09/Hooks-Aubrey.pdf (accessed 13 December 2014).

21. *See, for example*, US Embassy Kinshasa to Secretary of State 002047, "The Congolese Transition, Current and Future, and the U.S. Role", 5 November 2004, https:// search.wikileaks.org/plusd/cables/04KINSHASA2047_a.html (accessed 13 December 2014); Maud Dlomo, "South Africa's Post-Conflict and Transitional Diplomatic Efforts in the DRC: Lessons Learnt", unpublished essay, University of Pretoria, Department of Political Science, May 2010, http://upetd.up.ac.za/ thesis/available/etd-09232010-181518/unrestricted/dissertation.pdf (accessed 14 December 2014).

22. Reyntjens, *The Great African War*, p. 262.

23. Laurie Nathan, "Explaining South Africa's Position on Sudan and Darfur", transcript, Chatham House, 12 February 2008, http://www.cmi.no/sudan/doc/? id=934 (accessed 13 December 2014).

24. Donald E. Booth, "US Policy in Sudan and South Sudan: The Way Forward", speech, Atlantic Council, Washington, DC, 9 October 2014, p. 10. http://www.atlanti ccouncil.org/images/publications/Speech_US_Policy_on_Sudan_and_South_ Sudan_Donald_Booth.pdf (accessed 13 December 2014).

25. US Institute of Peace, "A Conversation with Special Envoy Princeton Lyman", pt. 2, 30 April 2014, http://www.usip.org/olivebranch/sudan-conversation-former-s pecial-envoy-princeton-lyman-part-2 (accessed 13 December 2014).

26. Confidential interview.

27. Jessica Piombo, *Perspectives on Security, Disarmament, and Nonproliferation: Views from the United States and South Africa, PASCC*, March 2014, http://www.nps.edu/ Academics/Centers/CCC/PASCC/Publications/2014/2014%20001%20South% 20Africa%20Dialogue.pdf (accessed 13 December 2014).

28. Lyman, *Partnership to History*, pp. 238–239.

29. Lyman, *Partnership to History*, pp. 241–242; and Helen E. Purkitt and Stephen F. Burgess, *South Africa's Weapons of Mass Destruction* (Bloomington and Indianapolis: Indiana University Press, 2005), pp. 190–191.

30. United Nations (UN), "Security Council Toughens Sanctions Against Iran, Adds Arms Embargo", press release, 24 March 2007, http://www.un.org/press/en/2007/s c8980.doc.htm (accessed 13 December 2014). Compare with South Africa's earlier position in US Embassy Pretoria to Secretary of State, "South Africa's UN Security Council Priorities".

31. Piombo, *Perspectives on Security, Disarmament, and Nonproliferation*, p. 32.

32. US Mission to Vienna to Secretary of State 000371, "Abdul Minty Sketches Agenda for Cooperation", 4 August 2009, https://search.wikileaks.org/plusd/ cables/09UNVIEVIENNA371_a.html (accessed 13 December 2014).

33. Piombo, *Perspectives on Security, Disarmament, and Nonproliferation*, pp. 7, 32; US Embassy Pretoria to Secretary of State 000234, "AQ Khan Trial, Daniel Gerges Pleads Guilty", 5 February 2008, https://search.wikileaks.org/plusd/ cables/08PRETORIA234_a.html (accessed 13 December 2014).

34. Lyman, *Partnership to History*, p. 249.

35. Office of the United States Trade Representative, "2016 Biennial Report on the Implementation of the African Growth and Opportunity Act", pp. 51–52, https:// agoa.info/downloads/reports/6178.html (accessed 24 November 2016).

36. Brock R. Williams, *African Growth and Opportunity Act (AGOA): Background and Reauthorization* (Washington, DC: Congressional Research Service, 22 April 2015) and earlier version of same titled report, 24 July 2014; and Office of the United States Trade Representative, "2016 Biennial Report on the Implementation of the African Growth and Opportunity Act", pp. 16–17, 24–25, 53–54.

37. Confidential interview.

38. US Census Bureau, "Trade in Goods with South Africa", https://www.census.gov/ foreign-trade/balance/c7910.html#2000 (accessed 1 May 2015 and 24 November 2016).

39. Discussion of this case is based on Patrick Bond, "Globalization, Pharmaceutical Pricing, and South African Health Policy: Managing Confrontations with U.S. Firms and Politicians", *International Journal of Health Services* 29, no. 4 (1999), pp. 765–792; Charan Deveraux, Robert Z. Lawrence and Michael D. Watkins, *Case Studies in U.S. Trade Negotiations*, vol. 1, *Making the Rules* (Washington, DC: Institute of International Economics, 2006), pp. 78–94; and William W. Fisher III and Cyril P. Rigamonti, "The South Africa AIDS Controversy: A Case Study in Patent Law and Policy", 10 February 2005, http://cyber.law.harvard.edu/people/ tfisher/South%20Africa.pdf (accessed 1 May 2015).

40. Global Health Technical Assistance Project, *USAID South Africa PEPFAR Treatment Programme: Final Evaluation September 2011*, p. xiv.

41. Derived from an examination of annual reports on the programme to the US Congress, 2005 to 2007, http://www.pepfar.gov/reports/progress/index.htm (accessed 13 December 2014).

42. *Celebrating Life: The US President's Emergency Plan for AIDS Relief – 2009 Annual Report to Congress*, pp. 13–14, 46, http://www.pepfar.gov/documents/organization/ 113827.pdf (accessed 13 December 2014).

43. Confidential interview.

44. Stephen F. Burgess, *US Africa Command, Changing Security Dynamics, and Perceptions of US Policy* (Colorado Spring, CO: US Air Force Academy Institute for National Security Studies, 2008), http://www.usafa.edu/df/inss/Research%20Papers/ 2008/US%20AFRICA%20COMMAND,%20CHANGING%20SECURITY% 20DYNAMICS.pdf (accessed 13 December 2014); Carl LeVan, "The Political Economy of African Responses to the US Africa Command", *Africa Today* 57, no. 1 (Fall 2010), pp. 2–23.

45. "Lekota: AFRICOM Should Stay Off the Continent", *Mail and Guardian*, 29 August 2007, http://mg.co.za/article/2007-08-29-lekota-africom-should-stay-off-the-continent (accessed 13 December 2014).

46. Confidential interviews; Queen Mosarwe, "No Plans to Move AFRICOM to Africa", *Botswana Gazette*, 29 November 2014, http://www.gazettebw.com/? p=9919 (accessed 13 December 2014); and Mtokozis Dube, "Botswana, US Brush Off Fresh AFRICOM Speculation," *The Nation*, 14 October 2013, http://mobile. nation.co.ke/News/Botswana–US-brush-off-fresh-AFRICOM-speculation/-/ 1950946/2031924/-/format/xhtml/-/11il3ktz/-/index.html (accessed 13 December 2014).

47. US Embassy Pretoria to Secretary of State, "South Africa's UN Security Council Priorities." For more on Mbeki's view, *see* US Embassy Harare to Department of State 21233, "South African Take on Dialogue", 28 October 2003, https://search. wikileaks.org/plusd/cables/03HARARE2141_a.html (accessed 14 December 2014); US Embassy Pretoria to Department of State 004632, "IDASA's Masamvu Says South Africa Pushing Mugabe to Retire in 2008", 8 November 2006, https:// search.wikileaks.org/plusd/cables/03HARARE2141_a.html (accessed 14 December 2014); and US Embassy Pretoria to Secretary of State 000957, "South Africa Expresses 'Concern' About Zimbabwe Crackdown", 16 March 2007, https://search. wikileaks.org/plusd/cables/07PRETORIA957_a.html (accessed 14 December 2014).

48. Colin L. Powell, "Freeing a Nation from a Tyrant's Grip", *New York Times*, 24 June 2003, http://www.nytimes.com/2003/06/24/opinion/24POWE.html (accessed 14 December 2014).

49. In January 2009, two and a half weeks before the George W. Bush administration relinquished power, the US State Department at least had second thoughts and urged Southern African leaders to insist on Mugabe's resignation. US Embassy Pretoria to Secretary of State 000005, "South Africa: A/S Frazer's Consultations on Zimbabwe: Prospects for Change", 2 January 2009, https://search.wikileaks.org/ plusd/cables/09PRETORIA5_a.html (accessed 14 December 2014); and US Embassy Maputo to Secretary of State 000010, "A/S Frazer in Maputo, Message Zimbabwe Delivered", 6 January 2009, https://search.wikileaks.org/plusd/ cables/09MAPUTO10_a.html (accessed 14 December 2014).

50. Rory Carroll, "Bush Backs Mbeki on Zimbabwe", *Guardian* (London), 10 July 2003, http://www.theguardian.com/world/2003/jul/10/zimbabwe.rorycarroll (accessed 14 December 2014).

51. Powell, "Freeing a Nation".

52. Confidential interview.

53. Confidential interview.

54. The following section on Libya is based on Stephen R. Weissman, "In Syria, Unlearned Lessons from Libya", *In These Times*, 19 April 2013, http://inthesetimes. com/article/14898/in_syria_unlearned_lessons_from_libya (accessed 14 December 2014).

55. UN Security Council SC/10200, Meeting Coverage, "Security Council Approves 'No-Fly Zone' over Libya, Authorizing 'All Necessary Measures' to Protect Civilians, by Vote of 10 in Favour with 5 Abstentions", 17 March 2011, http://www.un.org/ press/en/2011/sc10200.doc.htm#Resolution (accessed 27 April 2015).

56. Commission on Presidential Debates, Debate Transcript, "President Barack Obama and Former Gov. Mitt Romney, R-Mass., Candidates Debate", Lynn University, Boca Raton, Fla., 22 October 2012, http://www.debates.org/index.php? page=october-22-2012-the-third-obama-romney-presidential-debate (accessed 27 April 2015).

57. Barack Obama, "President Obama's Speech on Libya", National Defense University, Washington, DC, 28 March 2011, https://www.whitehouse.gov/ photos-and-video/video/2011/03/28/president-obama-s-speech-libya#transcript (accessed 27 April 2015).

58. *See* UN Security Council S/PV.6621, 22 September 2011, http://www.un.org/en/ ga/search/view_doc.asp?symbol=S/PV.6621, pp. 5–6; and South African Press Association (SAPA), "Zuma: West Undermined AU on Libya", *Times Live*, 24 August 2011, http://www.timeslive.co.za/local/2011/08/24/zuma-west-undermi ned-au-on-libya (accessed 27 April 2015).

59. UN Security Council SC/10403, Meeting Coverage, "Security Council Fails to Adopt Draft Resolution Condemning Syria's Crackdown", 4 October 2011.

60. US Department of State, *Voting Practices in the United Nations 2012*, Report to Congress Submitted Pursuant to Public Laws 101-246 and 108-447, April 2013, pp. 17–20, 35–36, http://www.state.gov/documents/organization/208072.pdf (accessed 14 December 2014).

61. Sevasti-Eleni Vezirgianndou, "The United States and Rising Powers in a Post-Hegemonic Global Order", *International Affairs* 89, no. 3 (2013), pp. 635–651.

CHAPTER 15

SOUTH AFRICA AND BRITAIN: "AN EMERGING POWER AND AN OLD FRIEND"

Daniel Large

Following talk of a "twenty-first-century partnership", April 2013 was a watershed month in South Africa's relations with Britain. History was made, but in a symbolic, slightly shambolic fashion. The British secretary for international development, Justine Greening, announced at *The Times* CEO Africa Summit at the Savoy Hotel in London that British aid to South Africa would end in 2015. Attending the same event, South Africa's finance minister, Pravin Gordhan, later insisted that the announcement had not been agreed, and a diplomatic spat erupted between Tshwane (Pretoria) and London.

South Africa's relations with Britain have always had an uneasy quality.[1] A violent colonial past was superseded by difficult post-imperial relations, after which the politics of apartheid from 1948 made bilateral ties controversial. Then, in the post-apartheid era, the rejuvenated moralism about international development projected in the New Labour government's foreign policy after 1997 to some extent complemented democratic South Africa's foreign policy.[2] Despite tensions arising primarily out of differences concerning Zimbabwe, there remained a sense of common purpose, and London kept looking to Tshwane as its key continental ally. However, as a result of changing domestic politics and shifting patterns of international relations that have seen the apparent elevation of South Africa in world affairs amid a wider narrative of "Africa rising" and Chinese prominence (see Liu in this volume), the period between 2010 and 2013 saw a recalibrated relationship characterised by efforts to evolve the nature and purpose of British–South African links. The argument about the end of British aid to South Africa was a barometer of this change.

This chapter examines the context and nature of contemporary South African–British relations in the post-apartheid era. It first considers the deeper, still controversial history of relations in which the apartheid era continues to cast a long shadow. I then examine South Africa's post-apartheid relations with Tony Blair's Labour government, which swept to power in May 1997 and forged notable changes in bilateral relations. Finally, the chapter explores more recent efforts by the British coalition governments led by David Cameron (2010–2016) and Theresa May (since July 2016) to "reset" relations between the two countries through balancing faith in the market and trade, with a continuing moralism regarding international development and "humanitarian intervention". This signals a transitional phase in bilateral relations, indicative of South Africa's own efforts to become a more influential international actor, including as a development force of its own.

Background: A Special History

South Africa's long history of relations with Britain is important and unavoidable when it comes to contemporary relations, much though these may have changed and continue to change. South Africa was a British "super-colony", ensuring a "colonial special bond" between both countries.[3] This informed the evolution of relations over the twentieth century, in tandem with domestic South African politics and Britain's changing political trajectory from former world imperial power to protracted post-imperial decline. Following the turbulent colonial era, connections were maintained through a large British population in South Africa, through Pretoria's support for London during both World Wars (1914–1918 and 1939–1945), and through significant trade and investment links.

The apartheid regime's ties with London were especially significant. Opposition to apartheid gained momentum in Britain after its prime minister, Harold Macmillan (1957–1963), addressed the parliament of South Africa in Cape Town in February 1960, signaling differences with Pretoria concerning his "deep convictions about the political destinies of free men".[4] South Africa withdrew from the Commonwealth in March 1961.

The most controversial period of British–South African relations came after 1979, when Britain was governed by the Conservative Party. The disjuncture between Prime Minister Margaret Thatcher's (1979–1990) "constructive engagement" policy and wide, mounting opposition to apartheid among the wider British public was such that it became a fiercely contested political issue. Already in 1979, in the context of Rhodesia/Zimbabwe Lancaster House negotiations, Thatcher had spoken of the prospects for "progress towards an ending of the isolation of South Africa in world affairs".[5] At this point, Britain had strong economic relations with South Africa, a favourite destination for overseas British trade missions and businesses in Africa until – and even after – the anti-apartheid sanctions and disinvestment campaigns mobilised more effectively from 1984. Views in Britain about South Africa were mixed, but marked in many quarters by strong solidarity with the African National Congress (ANC). Opposition to apartheid and the unholy London–Pretoria "special relationship"[6] grew. The British government was denounced for its continuing efforts to "defend the apartheid regime from the impact of effective economic sanctions".[7] Later, Thatcher sought to vindicate and reaffirm her view that "the worst approach was to isolate South Africa further".[8]

The way in which domestic politics fed into bilateral relations, and also assumed a global dimension, was a notable dynamic of this period in relations between London and Pretoria, just as it has been more recently. Always indicative of domestic British political divisions, the politics of South Africa also played out in a number of related areas including the Commonwealth; London's regional relations with Southern Africa; and Britain's relations with the United States (US) and its role in the Cold War's Southern African theatre, in which apartheid South Africa was very involved. (See Weissman in this volume.)

By the time of South Africa's historic transition from apartheid to constitutional democracy in 1994, Britain had mixed interests in the country. In addition to economic ties, there was a sizeable British population in South Africa of about 350,000 passport holders.[9] Yet, by the time that London welcomed the return of South Africa to the Commonwealth in July 1994, there was also "a formidable legacy of mistrust" between the ANC and the ruling Conservative Party.[10]

More than being merely a colourful backdrop, the history of British–South African relations has been a continuing influence in myriad ways. Apartheid impacted on British politics in notable ways that would later actively feed into foreign policy. This was seen not just in terms of the links forged between the Labour Party and the ANC (or, indeed, involving exiled South Africans like Peter Hain who entered British politics), but also in shaping the party's views on how foreign policy should be conducted. This signals an enduring influence of South Africa in British foreign policy towards Africa and, in certain respects, beyond the continent. The rejection of the Conservative Party's preference for privileging material national interests over all else became instrumental in shaping the foreign policy of the New Labour government from 1997. For Labour foreign secretary Robin Cook; the secretary of state of the Department for International Development (DFID), Clare Short; and later Prime Minister Tony Blair and his Chancellor of the Exchequer (finance minister), Gordon Brown, the Tory government's rejection of sanctions in the 1980s on South Africa "represented one of the clearest cases of national self-interest trumping wider ethics".[11] This fed into New Labour efforts to pursue an "ethical dimension" in British foreign policy.[12] Flawed though this may have been in practice, it set the tone for the combination of moralism and material economic interest that the coalition government that assumed power from the Labour Party in 2010 sought thereafter to pursue in its relations with South Africa.[13]

New Labour and South Africa: The Elusive Third Way

The South African transition continues be held up as an inspirational model and political point of reference for a host of British politicians. As one Foreign and Commonwealth Office (FCO) minister, Brian Wilson, noted during former president Nelson Mandela's visit to London in April 2001: "South Africa continues to offer inspiration and hope to many in the world".[14] In certain respects, it was South Africa's "exertion of moral leadership on the continent"[15] that combined with the Labour government's foreign policy to usher in a period during which there were notable common aims, even when these were rocked, at times, by political disagreements, most notably over Zimbabwe. As testament to the desire to be associated with the iconic figure of former South African president, Nelson Mandela, Tony Blair's final tour of Africa as prime minister in 2007 featured a South African leg and mandatory photo-op with Mandela.

Moralism: Ethical Foreign Policy for a Change?
From May 1997, the New Labour government claimed that it was no longer driven by a narrow conception of national interest, but would pay

serious attention to the ethical dimensions of Britain's foreign policy. This new agenda linked domestic renewal with a reinvigorated sense of actively engaged internationalism, elevating human rights into a far more prominent formal concern. Prime Minister Tony Blair's "third way" that Labour claimed to be undertaking at home and abroad was loudly trumpeted as new, superior and imbued with an efficacy that had been previously lacking in British Africa policy. Always rooted in and reflecting the politics of New Labour's domestic project, Blair nonetheless later claimed that his views on Africa "had always been essential third-way stuff" featuring "a partnership between the developed and undeveloped world", addressing governance, corruption and conflict resolution.[16]

Tony Blair saw an ally in President Thabo Mbeki's government between 1999 and 2008 insofar as "third way" politics were concerned. This was partly a reflection of the Labour Party's own modernisation and ANC links before and after 1994. It also reflected the pursuit of like-minded allies and potential supporters. While visiting South Africa as prime minister for the first time in January 1999, Blair praised the country's 1996 Growth, Employment and Redistribution (GEAR) macro-economic programme as "the 'third way', South Africa style".[17] Mbeki subscribed to the "third way" and, together with the likes of US president Bill Clinton and German chancellor Gerhard Schroeder, as well as Blair, participated in a number of meetings starting with a summit in Berlin in 2000. Blair's "third way" diplomacy thus dovetailed with Mbeki's efforts to play the role of a continental norms-builder through initiatives at the African Union (AU), and particularly the New Partnership for Africa's Development (NEPAD), which assumed a more global significance through South African diplomacy and the mobilisation of its moral capital.[18] A number of interlinked themes stood out in bilateral relations at this time that highlight some of the efforts behind pursuing the more ambitious, moralistic nature of this attempted "third way".

The first major area was New Labour's pursuit of development as foreign policy.[19] Foreign secretary Robin Cook declared that Britain had "a moral obligation to fight poverty abroad".[20] It was the new Department for International Development under Clare Short, however, that spearheaded an energetic reform and expansion of development diplomacy. After the release of a white paper on international development declaring DFID's overall aim to be "the elimination of poverty in poorer countries", which became the International Development Act in 2002, this approach enshrined DFID's commitments into law. This super-ministry – to the chagrin of the British foreign office – became an influential part of government. Under DFID, British development assistance was untied from the promotion of strategic or commercial interests, and the use of overseas development to promote domestic political objectives was taken to new levels in coalition with supportive non-governmental organisations (NGOs).

A further area of British engagement was governance and democracy promotion. From 2001, NEPAD became a key part of London's regional and continental engagement. While touring four West African states in February 2002, Blair even claimed that Britain had "a 'discreet' hand in drafting it, working closely with South Africa".[21] NEPAD was regarded as an ambitious but comprehensive framework, with the advantage of being African-led. It came to be seen by London as a core vehicle for achieving the United Nations (UN) Millennium Development Goals (MDGs), which aimed to halve poverty by 2015.[22] As well as areas of complementarity, there were policy divergences and political disagreements in which Zimbabwe was the most outstanding example during the Blair–Mbeki era.[23] The afterlife of this affair was ignited in November 2013 when Mbeki and Blair clashed over whether or not Britain had planned to overthrow Zimbabwe's president Robert Mugabe through military action. Mbeki alleged that Blair had tried to pressure him into joining a "regime change scheme", but Blair denied having planned to intervene in South Africa's neighbouring state.[24]

A third, related aspect was a peace and conflict resolution agenda, which saw British and South African efforts overlap. Peace and conflict resolution became a priority area of London's engagement in the later years of Blair's government. During his first term in office (1997–2001), Tony Blair provided little material assistance to, and was content to let South Africa and several other African states lead in external mediation efforts in, the Democratic Republic of the Congo (DRC), even while London was providing much financial support to Rwanda and Uganda. The Labour government became more engaged with conflict management efforts when the Africa Conflict Prevention Pool was implemented from 2001, with a pooled £50 million fund drawn from the FCO, the Ministry of Defence (MOD) and DFID. In 2003, four regional conflict adviser posts were created, with one operating out of Tshwane covering Southern Africa (the others operating out of Addis Ababa, Nairobi and Abuja). London also played a role in related conflict initiatives, notably the Kimberly Process.[25]

It was only in his second term as prime minister (2001–2005), and in the aftermath of the terrorist attacks on the United States in September 2001, that Blair's evangelical African mission took off. A profusion of initiatives were designed to address what he branded "a scar on the conscience of the world",[26] a term that many in Africa found offensive. This upgraded the British role in seeking to forge new international partnerships designed to further Africa's cause. In this, Thabo Mbeki's South Africa played a key role. In February 2004, Blair launched the Commission for Africa, which fed into the 2005 Group of Eight (G-8) industrialised countries' Gleneagles Summit.[27]

While Blair's quest for an "ethical" foreign policy appeared to signal a change in Britain's relations with South Africa and beyond, at the same time economics and the pursuit of prosperity were integral to the "third way". These remained a core part of British–South African relations. Beneath and amid the well-spun and not entirely instrumental "ethical" foreign policy agenda, in other words, the relationship represented business as usual.

Mercantilism: Business As Usual

Britain's economic relations with Africa were traditionally concentrated upon South Africa, long its most significant partner on the continent. Although this began to change under the Labour government, South Africa retained its status as the only African country among Britain's top 20 countries for imports, even as other countries were increasing their economic ties with the latter – Europe's third-largest economy after Germany and France. South Africa topped the list of the five biggest African states exporting goods to Britain by 2001, and also the list of the largest importers of British goods.[28]

South Africa's "gateway" economy status continued to be compelling. The high-profile development diplomacy and humanitarian thrust of New Labour's relations with Africa might have suggested otherwise. But the reality of Africa's comparatively marginal status to Britain in narrow economic terms in the decade from 1997 was apparent. South Africa was an exception: an important economic partner with a mixed profile of extractive, manufacturing and other investment links. Efforts were made to enhance economic ties, and to build links between companies in both countries.

Beyond this bilateral business context, one new departure involved different forms of economic competition in the context of post-apartheid

South Africa's business expansion and its growing footprint on the continent. (See Vickers and Cawood in this volume.) At times, and in places, this competitive South African corporate thrust came partly at the expense of British business, notably in East African countries such as Kenya (see Khadiagala in this volume). In part to respond to this more competitive situation, as well as growing business competition from China, India and other actors (see Liu, and Virk in this volume), British firms began to explore new markets in francophone West Africa.

For all its carefully spun presentation of self-ascribed high "ethical" credentials and foreign policy intent, Blair's Labour government followed a decidedly mercantilist approach to arms exports. In part, this reflected divisions within the government, such as contending interests between DFID and the Ministry of Defence. However, alongside New Labour's moralism was a much more familiar aspect of British foreign policy: military relations and the arms trade. Between 1997 and 2004, Britain was the world's second-largest exporter of military equipment (its arms deliveries totalling $4.7 billion) behind the US.[29] Concurrent with its efforts to, and claims about, promoting peace and security in Africa, Britain simultaneously lobbied for British arms exports.

Tony Blair's government, like its predecessors, pursued very active efforts to court and win South African arms contracts.[30] In December 1999, the ANC government entered into five major arms purchase transactions. These featured the purchase of nine Swedish/British advanced light Gripen fighter aircraft and 12 BAE Systems Hawk fighter trainer aircraft (with options in both cases to order more later). This, and other contacts, exposed the connections between British arms companies, notably BAE, and South African politicians; various BAE-sponsored trips for South African cabinet ministers, parliamentarians and government officials; and other gestures designed to curry favour.[31]

London persuaded Tshwane to make a deal that diverted resources away from the country's huge domestic challenges and did little to enhance its security amid a relative absence of serious military threats. The arms deals also made a few individuals rich and have since been a source of corruption allegations.[32] These continue, amid a protracted saga of official enquiry into the BAE deal and other arms deals, revived in 2013 in the form of a new commission of enquiry. A striking theme raised by this issue from the British side, however, was the stark incongruence between the efforts of those parts of the British government that were trying to win arms contracts at the same time as other parts of the British government were trying to persuade Thabo Mbeki's government to play a bigger part in peacekeeping, crisis management and conflict resolution in Africa.

Overall, in South Africa and Africa more generally, New Labour pursued what British scholar Paul Williams describes as "multiple and contradictory roles. None of them were set in stone. Instead, Blair's government chose to live with its contradictions".[33] Despite frequent statements about the virtues of international free trade, London rarely practiced what it preached. Unsurprisingly, this attracted persistent criticism, including from Nelson Mandela, who argued in favour of fairer – rather than freer – trade.[34] The tensions between seeking concurrently to promote social justice and economic neo-liberalism were evident in British policy, as well as South Africa's domestic policy. For British diplomacy towards South Africa, any aspiration towards having ethical content in foreign policy was thus undermined by London's commitment to economic liberalism and enhanced economic globalisation. The "third way" thus represented "little new".[35]

Reinvigorating British–South African Relations

The coalition Conservative–Liberal Democratic government that came to power under David Cameron in the British general election of 2010 inherited an active portfolio of development policy engagements and foreign policy commitments. The coalition also had to contend with a new domestic political context. Such was the prominence of Labour's overseas aid that it was deemed necessary to "ring-fence" DFID's budget, even amid an economic downturn, and to stick to Labour's aid commitments while increasing aid to 0.7 per cent of gross national income.[36] At first, British policy continued in much the same vein. Gradually, policy was revised according to the new government's priorities, which had prepared for office by consulting widely on options for British aid.

One area of continuity concerned Prime Minister David Cameron's commitment not just to engage "the challenge of a starving Africa", but also, as he told President Jacob Zuma during his first visit to South Africa as prime minister in July 2011, "the opportunity of a booming Africa" that South Africa was thought to exemplify. Cameron wanted Britain to be seen to engage both versions of Africa and, in particular, rebalance a market engagement with the inherited moralism of New Labour's Africa foreign policy.[37]

South Africa has long been a highly favoured destination for British politicians. From 2010, the country received a steady stream of visitors.[38] The United Kingdom (UK)–South Africa Bilateral Forum was enhanced.[39] On top of this, and in contrast to previous Thatcher-led political relations, the Conservative-led government sent a message of congratulations to President Jacob Zuma on the ANC's centenary in 2012 that affirmed: "[W]e will stand with you in the ongoing struggle for equality, democracy and prosperity for the people of South Africa, and for justice and freedom from tyranny around the world".[40]

From the British perspective, the visit to South Africa by foreign secretary William Hague in February 2012 best expressed the change of tack in bilateral relations. Officially touted as part of efforts to "reinvigorate the UK–South Africa relationship",[41] this visit attempted to inject a new coziness, bordering on an amorous intent, into bilateral relations. Hague declared Britain to be "a warm friend and close partner for the twenty-first century ... Today in Britain we are looking at our relationship with South Africa with fresh eyes and we are investing in that relationship too".[42]

Economic Stimulus

There has been renewed interest from British companies in doing business in Africa, and particularly in South Africa. This has been accompanied by initiatives to regulate and enhance trade, including political engagement to promote business. The tone was set in July 2011 by Prime Minister David Cameron's trip to South Africa, when he was accompanied not only by the then development secretary, Andrew Mitchell, but also the trade and investment minister, Lord Green, and a delegation consisting of 25 representatives from a range of blue-chip companies, private equity firms and small businesses.[43] During his visit, Cameron declared that it was "time to make African free trade the common purpose of the continent and the world".[44]

Britain remains one of South Africa's major trading partners, although this relationship declined between 2004 and 2013. The country had been South Africa's third-largest source of imports between 1998 and 2003, but fell to sixth in 2008 in the context of the global financial crisis of 2008–2009. Similarly, Britain had been the leading recipient of goods from South Africa in 2001 and 2002, but dropped to fourth position in 2008. Compared to 1998, Britain was overtaken by Germany, China, the US, Saudi Arabia and Japan as South Africa's biggest sources of imports. It was also overtaken by Japan, the US and Germany over the same period in terms of South Africa's export trade. Nevertheless, South Africa remains one of the top 20 exporters to Britain. The European power also remains one of the top two largest foreign investors in South Africa, while more than 200 South African companies operate in Britain.

Furthermore, South Africa remains the leading country for British exporters in Africa, accounting for about 60 per cent of such exports.[45] Overall trade dropped by some 37 per cent from 2008 to 2009 amid the global financial crisis, but recovered somewhat thereafter. Trade performance has since remained mixed: in 2014, trade totalled just over R73 billion, and in 2015 it ran at R76.8 billion.[46]

While not reflected in trade figures, both London and Tshwane sought to enhance economic links, which by June 2016 faced the challenges caused by the British referendum vote in favour of leaving the EU. This featured efforts to brand South Africa as a well-regulated, expanding economy with regional potential, as "the easiest BRICS [Brazil, Russia, India, China and South Africa] nation to do business in".[47] A special British trade envoy to South Africa, Baroness Scotland of Asthal, was appointed in 2012 to assist Britain's expansion into South Africa. In September 2013, a new South Africa–United Kingdom Business Partnership was launched, followed in April 2014 by a new British Chamber of Commerce. Amidst such bilateral efforts to strength economic ties, the question of South Africa's relations with Britain and the EU became topical following the country's vote to leave the EU in June 2016. In 2015, South Africa's trade with the 28 members of the EU totaled $38.3 billion, representing about 26 per cent of South Africa's total merchandise trade. Britain represented about 15 per cent of South Africa's total trade with the EU, and 3.7 per cent of South Africa's global trade.[48] (See Nkosi in this volume.) The vote in favour of "Brexit" triggered efforts by the British government, including a visit to South Africa by the British Chancellor of the Exchequer, Philip Hammond, in December 2016, to attempt to look ahead to future economic relations outside of the EU–Africa trade framework.

South Africa as a Rising BRICS Power

That a new part of marketing South Africa to British business is its BRICS membership is notable insofar as it signals how Britain's relations with South Africa are evolving amid wider geo-political shifts. In some senses, London has been looking at, and seeking to engage, South Africa in new ways that reflect changing trends in Africa's international relations, especially those involving China, India and other emerging powers (see Liu, and Virk in this volume).

Allied to sometimes inflated perceptions of South Africa's economic performance, and often overly high expectations about what it can or should do in African and world affairs, the apparent changes under way led by emerging powers and involving South Africa constituted an important reason why the British foreign secretary, William Hague, described the country as "a growing force in world affairs ... that is shaping a new global role for itself". As the foreign secretary told his South African audience at the University of the Western Cape in February 2012: "You are an emerging power and an old friend".[49] Such a view can be seen in the 2011 Joint Strategy for a Modern Partnership between South Africa and Britain, which set out ambitious goals for bilateral relations covering sustainable development, security, governance and society. The British government has sought to reposition itself in a changing world, regarded as being formatively shaped by rising powers, and in which a "rising Africa" has become more prominent.[50]

While the thrust of bilateral South African–British relations is invariably presented in positive, synergistic terms, the external projection of shared goals has not always involved underlying substantive shared opinion. In a certain sense, British politics has tended to project a version of its own values onto South African foreign policy, and then defined what it would like this to be. Using the still resonant example of Nelson Mandela, the post-New Labour British government initially combined the interventionism of Tony Blair with efforts to revive commerce for David Cameron's "austerity" Britain. This points to a number of tensions in a relationship that continues to be constantly revised. Perhaps exemplifying this perpetual motion in bilateral relations has been the issue of "humanitarian intervention". As William Hague put it, Britain and South Africa have "a difference of opinion over how we protect human rights in other countries".[51] This highlights the important differences centred around contending attitudes to state sovereignty that were revealed over Syria in 2011, and previously Myanmar in 2007 and Libya in 2011. Furthermore, London claims to support an expansion of the current 15-member UN Security Council, but has neither fully nor explicitly backed South Africa's ambitions to become a member of an expanded future Council. (See Mashabane in this volume.)

Development Aid: *"Redefining a Relationship"*

In addition to recognition of South Africa's progress since 1994, the changing geo-politics of development aid has been another factor in changing relations between Tshwane and London. South African analysts had recognised the growing importance of China in South Africa and Africa more generally long before it became a media story and policy challenge in the West.[52] (See Liu in this volume on China–South Africa relations.) Not long after the Commission for Africa's myopic 2005 report that almost entirely overlooked Beijing, DFID began to address more systematically the nature and implications of China for its programme of international development. From 2007, and led by DFID's office in Beijing, this became a programme called Working with China on International Development Issues. During the late Labour period, the opposition Conservative Party undertook research of its own about the future of British aid in a changing world. By the time that Andrew Mitchell became the new secretary for international development in 2010, it was clear that he was determined to reform DFID. Together with a newly branded "UKaid" logo, this was emboldened by a government pledge to make aid equal to 0.7 per cent of gross domestic income, which passed into law in 2015. As part of a review initiated by the new government, DFID emphasised value for taxpayer money in "combating poverty, disaster and conflict", and further noted that "[a]id is not an end in itself".[53] London had originally aimed to end aid to such countries as Angola, China and Russia, but South Africa was one of the 27 countries to which British aid would continue. However, this policy subsequently changed.

As earlier noted, this issue dramatically came to a head in April 2013, when the South African finance minister, Pravin Gordhan, participated in *The Times* CEO Africa Summit in London. Prefigured in an article *The Times* (of London) ran in April 2013, headlined "End of Funding Shows South Africa's Coming of Age",[54] the British announcement ending aid to South Africa in 2015 appeared to be unwelcome news to Gordhan. He revealed that he had been informed of the British government's new aid strategy in July 2012 by the former secretary for international development, Andrew Mitchell, and had then affirmed the need for further debate about the implications of this for British aid to South Africa. According to the DFID press release of the same day, Justine Greening, the new secretary of state for international development, stated: "I have agreed with my South African counterparts that South Africa is now in a position to fund its own development".[55] When he read news reports on the morning in April 2013 about what she was due to say, Gordhan reported that he "was surprised to read the statement ... There was no such agreement".[56] One of Gordhan's main complaints appears to have been that "British aid was seen as an important demonstration of solidarity".[57] South Africa's foreign ministry further noted that the "unilateral announcement" was "tantamount to redefining our relationship".[58]

Underneath what was a "communications fiasco" was a shift in relations with South Africa.[59] As a DFID official explained, there would be no "cliff edge" in 2015, but the end of the government spending round. The official noted that there had been consultations such that from the British perspective this was not a unilateral decision. Bilateral aid would continue to decline and be based not on aid transfer, but on technical assistance to South Africa's National Development Plan (NDP). In this way, the process marked "the ending of the conventional aid model and the start of a different way of working".[60] With a bilateral aid programme of £19 million (roughly R341 million) in 2013, down from a peak of over £40 million (roughly R719 million) in 2003, DFID's position was that this reflected South Africa's progress and a move to a "new relationship based on sharing skills and knowledge, not on development funding".[61] South Africa is Africa's most industrialised country and Britain's largest trading partner in Africa. DFID's plan for its own post-2015 relationship with South Africa focused on "technical assistance, sharing skills and knowledge to accelerate poverty reduction and tackle inequality there, providing access to international best practice in areas like health and economic growth" and "a regional and global development partnership beyond South Africa's borders, working to reduce poverty and drive economic growth across Africa by supporting the country's growing role as a development partner in its own right, as well as its position as the region's major trading hub".[62]

Concluding Reflections

Overlaid onto a colonial and post-colonial history in which the apartheid period during the 1980s figured most prominently, the relations cultivated between post-1994 South Africa and post-1997 Britain set the tone for more recent bilateral relations. These continue to be redefined and developed in changing circumstances. If there are changes to contemporary relations, the future of the past of South Africa's relations with Britain is another area of uncertainty and likely change. This can be seen most obviously in recent revelations about the recent past.[63] More important, declassified documents from the early Margaret Thatcher government promise to shed more light on the controversial links of British government and business with apartheid South Africa.

The dispute concerning the end of British aid to South Africa by 2015, and London's efforts to reposition itself towards Tshwane, reflected how much has changed in bilateral relations, and South Africa's own evolution, as well as Britain's political and economic trajectory. In certain respects, this speaks to a transitional phase in relations indicative of South Africa's own efforts to become a more influential international actor, including as a development force of its own, and Britain's response to these actions. At the same time, and outside the narrow parameters of development aid, when DFID's aid to South Africa is compared against overall trade levels, a better sense of where the main energy in relations lies can be gleaned. To these remain attendant the matters of foreign policy coordination and efforts to pursue a genuine partnership. As the case of India demonstrates, South Africa is not the only country that Britain has been seeking to reposition itself towards. Similarly, South Africa too has been seeking to rebalance its economic strategy to reflect changes in the global economy and what its government identifies as a shift to a multipolar world.

The implications of Brexit for future Anglo–South African relations remained highly uncertain on multiple fronts, which was in turn indicative of broader uncertainty about most aspects of Brexit. While it seemed that a new South African–British trade agreement to replace existing EU agreements was going to be required, wide uncertainty concerning the impact of Brexit on the British economy, and economic relations with South Africa, prevailed after June 2016. Opinion about the impact of Brexit on South Africa ranged from pessimistic projections about negative effects, to arguments that any disruptions would be minimal.[64] This meant that how Tshwane and a Britain outside the EU would continue the process of revising relations was hard to discern. At the time, the symbolic month of April 2013, and efforts by London to revise its aid to South Africa, represented something of a watershed. However, the June 2016 Brexit referendum vote in favour of leaving the EU represented a historic departure that appeared likely to most influence the next phase of the Anglo-South African "twenty-first-century partnership".

Notes

1. James Barber, *The Uneasy Relationship: Britain and South Africa* (London: Heinemann, 1983).

2. Paul Williams, "Britain, the EU, and Africa", in Adekeye Adebajo and Kaye Whiteman (eds), *The EU and Africa: From Eurafrique to Afro-Europa* (London: Hurst; New York: Columbia University Press; and Johannesburg: Wits University Press, 2012), pp. 343–364; Kaye Whiteman and Douglas Yates, "France, Britain, and the United States", in Adekeye Adebajo and Ismail Rashid (eds), *West Africa's Security Challenges: Building Peace in a Troubled Region* (Boulder, CO, and London: Rienner, 2004).

3. Christopher Landsberg, *The Quiet Diplomacy of Liberation: International Politics and South Africa's Transition* (Johannesburg: Jacana, 2004), p. 25.

4. Harold Macmillan, transcript of speech made to South African Parliament, Cape Town, 3 February 1960.

5. Margaret Thatcher, "The West in the World Today", speech to the Foreign Policy Association, New York, 18 December 1979.

6. Labour Research Department, *Profiting from Apartheid: Britain's Links with South Africa* (Rochdale, 1986), p. 2.

7. Anti-Apartheid Movement, *Selling Out to Apartheid: British Government Support for Trade with South Africa* (London, 1989), p. 13.

8. Margaret Thatcher, *The Downing Street Years* (London: HarperCollins, 1995), p. 313.

9. Simon Baynham, "Through the Looking Glass: Britain, South Africa, and the Sub-Continent", in Greg Mills (ed.), *From Pariah to Participant: South Africa's Evolving Foreign Relations, 1990–1994* (Johannesburg: South African Institute of International Affairs (SAIIA), 1994), p. 115.

10. Ronald Hyam and Peter Henshaw, *The Lion and the Springbok: Britain and South Africa Since the Boer War* (Cambridge: Cambridge University Press, 2003), p. 347.

11. Julia Gallagher, *Britain and Africa Under Blair: In Pursuit of the Good State* (Manchester: Manchester University Press, 2011), p. 129.

12. Robin Cook, "Foreign Policy Mission Statement: Speech at the Foreign and Commonwealth Office, London, 12 May 1997", *Guardian*, https://www.theguardian.com/world/1997/may/12/indonesia.ethicalforeignpolicy (accessed 12 August 2013).

13. Williams, "Britain, the EU, and Africa".

14. British Foreign and Commonwealth Office (FCO), "Statement by Brian Wilson", press release, 29 April 2001.

15. Peter Kagwanja, "An Encumbered Regional Power? The Capacity Gap in South Africa's Peace Diplomacy in Africa", Democracy and Governance Research Programme Occasional Paper no. 6 (Cape Town: Human Sciences Research Council (HSRC) Press, 2009), p. 4.

16. Tony Blair, *A Journey* (London: Hutchinson, 2010), p. 555.

17. Tony Blair, "Facing the Modern Challenge: The 'Third Way' in Britain and South Africa", speech at South African Parliament, Cape Town, 8 January 1999.

18. *See* Chris Landsberg, *The Diplomacy of Transformation: South African Foreign Policy and Statecraft* (Johannesburg: Macmillan, 2010).

19. Tom Porteous, *Britain in Africa* (London: Zed, 2008).

20. Robin Cook, "Promoting Peace and Prosperity in Africa", speech to the United Nations (UN) Security Council, 24 September 1998.

21. Richard Dowden, "Blair Throws a Lifeline to Africa", *The Tablet*, 16 February 2002.

22. *See, for example*, Centre for Conflict Resolution (CCR), *Achieving the Millennium Development Goals in Africa*, Seminar Report no. 44 (Cape Town, November 2013), http://www.ccr.org.za (accessed 8 July 2017).

23. *See* Stephen Chan, *Southern Africa: Old Treacheries and New Deceits* (New Haven: Yale University Press, 2011).

24. David Smith, "Mbeki: Blair Plotted Military Intervention to Remove Mugabe", *Mail & Guardian*, 28 November 2013; and David Blair, "Tony Blair Denies Asking South Africa to Help Overthrow Robert Mugabe", *The Telegraph*, 27 November 2013.

25. The non-governmental organisation Global Witness played a catalytic role in this process, which began in May 2000 in Kimberly, South Africa. In 2002, the British Foreign Office established a Government Diamond Office to ensure that all diamond imports and exports were conflict-free.

26. Tony Blair, full text of speech to Labour Party conference, 2 October 2001, from the *Guardian*, https://www.theguardian.com/politics/2001/oct/02/labourconference. labour6 (accessed 12 August 2013).

27. Other initiatives included the Group of Eight (G-8) Africa Action Plan of 2002; the G-8 Plus Outreach Five Initiative Heiligendamm Process; Group of Twenty (G-20) initiatives; and parts of the EU–South Africa Strategic Partnership.

28. Markus Weimer and Alex Vines, "UK–South Africa Relations and the Bilateral Forum", Chatham House, June 2011.

29. International Institute for Strategic Studies (IISS), *The Military Balance* (London: Routledge, 2004), p. 359.

30. For example, Defence Systems and Equipment International Fairs. Part of British aid was directed to reorganising South Africa's armed forces, including a British military advisory and training team.

31. These included a reported R5 million BAE donation to the African National Congress (ANC) MK Veterans Military Association. *See* Paul Kirk, "South Africa: Millions for MK Veterans Go Astray", *Mail and Guardian*, 2 March 2001.

32. Paul D. Williams, *British Foreign Policy Under New Labour, 1997–2005* (Houndmills: Palgrave Macmillan, 2005), p. 139.

33. Williams, *British Foreign Policy Under New Labour*, p. 212.

34. Remarks at Commonwealth Summit, Edinburgh, 24–27 October 1997.

35. Rita Abrahamsen and Paul D. Williams, "Britain and Southern Africa: A Third Way or Business as Usual?", in Korwa Gombe Adar and Rok Ajulu (eds), *Globalization and Emerging Trends in African States' Foreign Policy-Making Process: A Comparative Perspective of Southern Africa* (Aldershot: Ashgate, 2002), pp. 307–328.

36. Projected as £11.3 billion in 2013.

37. Press conference with British prime minister David Cameron, and South African president Jacob Zuma, Tshwane, 18 July 2011. Cameron had visited South Africa in 1989.

38. The Lord Mayor of London, Michael Bear, visited in August 2011; the Prince of Wales visited in November 2011; minister for Africa, Henry Bellingham, in July 2012; and international development minister, Lynne Featherstone, in July 2013.

39. The Britain–South Africa Bilateral Forum was set up in 1997 to enhance political and economic relations.

40. Letter to President of South Africa, Prime Minister's Office, London, 8 January 2012.

41. "Foreign Secretary Visits South Africa", FCO announcement, 12 February 2012, https://www.gov.uk/government/news/foreign-secretary-visits-south-africa (accessed 12 August 2013).

42. William Hague, "Britain and South Africa: A 21st Century Partnership", speech delivered at the University of the Western Cape, 14 February 2012.

43. Notably this group included: Barclays chief executive Bob Diamond; Premier League communications director Bill Bush; and senior executives from Waitrose, Vodafone, Diageo and G4S.

44. David Cameron, "Free Trade in Africa Shows a Way out of Poverty", *Business Day*, 18 July 2011.

45. *See* Barclays, "Africa: The UK's Emerging Trade Partner", 2013.

46. Data from the South African Revenue Service, http://www.sars.gov.za/Client Segments/Customs-Excise/Trade-Statistics/Pages/Merchandise-Trade-Statistics.aspx. (accessed 28 December 2016).

47. Confederation of British Industry, "CBI Members Discuss Business Prospects with High Commissioner to South Africa", press release, 17 May 2013.

48. Richard Gibb, "The Impact of Brexit on South Africa", Brenthurst Foundation Discussion Paper, December 2016, p. 7.

49. Hague, "Britain and South Africa".

50. This was a theme of David Cameron's speech to the 2012 Conservative Party conference, where, interestingly, he cited Nigeria, not South Africa, as an example of a rising African power and key British ally. "Conservative Conference: David Cameron's Speech, Full Text", *The Spectator*, 10 October 2012, http://blogs.spectator.co.uk/2012/10/conservative-conference-david-camerons-speech-in-full/ (accessed 12 August 2013).

51. Hague, "Britain and South Africa".

52. *See* Greg Mills, "Editors Introduction", in Mills, *From Pariah to Participant*, p. 7; and Peter Draper and Garth le Pere (eds), *Enter the Dragon: Towards a Free Trade Agreement Between China and the Southern African Customs Union* (Midrand: Institute for Global Dialogue/SAIIA, 2006).

53. "We will work to see more countries standing on their own two feet, graduating from UK aid and enjoying long-term economic growth. By creating more jobs, business opportunities and trade, we will give people the chance to lift themselves out of poverty and get on the path to prosperity." Britain's Department for International Development (DFID), "UK Aid: Changing Lives, Delivering Results" (London, 2011).

54. Jerome Starkey and Lucy Bannerman, "End of Funding Shows South Africa's Coming of Age", *The Times* (London), 30 April 2013.

55. DFID, "UK to End Direct Financial Support to South Africa", press release, 30 April 2013.

56. Pravin Gordhan, "Statement on British Government's Decision to Cut Aid to South Africa", South African Ministry of Finance, 2 May 2013.

57. Patrick Smith, "South Africa's Growth Must Engender Social Cohesion – Gordhan", *Africa Report*, 2 July 2013.

58. South African Department of International Relations and Cooperation (DIRCO), "UK Unilateral Decision to Terminate Official Development Aid to South Africa", press release, 30 April 2013.

59. Interview at the South African Institute of International Affairs, Johannesburg, 31 July 2013.

60. Confidential interview with DFID official, Tshwane, 1 August 2013.

61. DFID, "UK to End Direct Financial Support to South Africa", press release, 30 April 2013, https://www.gov.uk/government/news/uk-to-end-direct-financial-support-to-south-africa (accessed 12 August 2013).

62. DFID, "UK to End Direct Financial Support".

63. For example, it appeared that Britain spied on key allies, including South Africa, at two G-20 summits in London in 2009. Part of this took the form of a campaign to penetrate South African computers and access communications, including delegate briefings for South African observer representatives to G-20 and G-8 meetings; Ewen MacAskill, Nick Davies, Nick Hopkins, Julian Borger and James Ball, "GCHQ Intercepted Foreign Politicians' Communications at G20 Summits", *Guardian*, 17 June 2013. The South African ministry of foreign affairs, a target of a British Government Communications Headquarters (GCHQ) hacking operation launched in 2005, voiced concerns; DIRCO, "SA Response to Spy Allegations", 17 June 2013.

64. Gibb, "The Impact of Brexit on South Africa".

CHAPTER 16

SOUTH AFRICA AND FRANCE: A RISING VERSUS A DECLINING POWER?

Roland Marchal

South Africa and France enjoy a somewhat paradoxical relationship. Both share strong and sometimes conflicting views of the African continent. Paris – willingly or unwillingly – has to articulate diplomatic views on Africa and African crises because of its particular history on the continent, which is based not only on its colonial legacy, but also on previous engagements and perceived global responsibilities. Tshwane (Pretoria), after years of apartheid-era isolation, is seeking to gain diplomatic and economic weight on the continent while it is still the most industrialised economy in Africa and the most widely acknowledged African interlocutor beyond the continent. (See Virk in this volume on the BRICS bloc.)

The weaknesses of both France and South Africa's Africa policies are well-known. French political elites have been losing interest in Africa since the early 1980s if measured by the French government's development aid policies. At the same time, economic interests are no longer substantial enough to build a powerful lobby within the business community: Gallic policies have therefore been dictated more by opportunistic factors such as country-specific bilateral relations and the character, as well as policy priorities, of incumbent French presidents, rather than on a systemic appraisal of the country's long-term interests in Africa.

Meanwhile, South Africa is seeking to speak on behalf of the continent at a time when sub-regions are becoming stronger, and are contesting the idea of a continental hegemon. Tshwane failed dramatically, for example, to secure a seat on the United Nations (UN) Security Council in 2004–2005, and it had to push hard in a bruising and costly campaign for its candidate, Nkosazana Dlamini-Zuma, to secure the chair of the African Union (AU) Commission in 2012 (see Maloka in this volume). South Africa also adopted positions on African crises such as Libya in 2011 and the Central African Republic (CAR) in 2013 that either isolated it politically or demonstrated that its continental ambitions were not that different from those of non-African actors.

Yet these developments in South African and French policies towards Africa have not shaped the nature of bilateral relations between Tshwane and Paris in its entirety. One needs also to consider the depth of the economic ties and the frequent convergence of both countries' diplomatic interests. While this chapter emphasises the leadership rivalry and policy differences between the two countries, it is indeed important to note that South Africa and France also cooperate on many issues, and do so despite the high-profile incendiary statements occasionally made by politicians and leaders on both sides.

France and the Apartheid Regime

France, like many other countries such as the United States (US), Britain and Japan, shared a vision of the apartheid regime that was distorted by the Cold War (see Weissman, and Large in this volume). During the apartheid era, Pretoria was viewed as a regional hegemon that protected and consolidated Western interests, while weakening Cuban–Soviet attempts to extend communist influence into Southern Africa. Pretoria kept the Cape of Good Hope route safe, and had the largest volume of strategic minerals outside the Soviet Union. Similarly, Angola's liberation struggle – more than any other in Southern Africa – was seen in Paris as strategically important for France, even before Luanda gained formal independence in November 1975. Relations with Angolan rebel leader Jonas Savimbi developed in that context and lasted somewhat beyond 1992, at least for several right-wing French politicians such as François Léotard.

At the same time, this French Africa policy was not a purely internal outcome of Gallic decision-making. French policies, although their influence varied considerably over the years and depended on the issues at stake, were also supported and advocated by many francophone African leaders who had their own concerns over the possible emergence of a radical opposition at home or in their neighbourhood: Côte d'Ivoire's Félix

Houphouët-Boigny and, later, Gabon's Omar Bongo and Burkina Faso's Blaise Compaoré were prominent in pushing for a French commitment to endorse anti-communist regimes from Rabat to Pretoria, as well as to defend friendly regimes.

The fact that French presidents were right-wing politicians in the 1960s and 1970s sheds further light on the country's pro-apartheid posture. Jacques Chirac, for example, called Nelson Mandela a "Xhosa tribal leader",[1] and his political friends were equally uncharitable. Mandela, when not described as a "terrorist",[2] was seen as a puppet in the hands of the South African Communist Party (SACP). In contrast, Mangosuthu Buthelezi, leader of the Inkatha Freedom Party (IFP) and a *Bantustan* (homeland) leader, was praised for his "responsible" approach,[3] as well as his anti-communism and moderation in opposing the apartheid regime.

Furthermore, from 1961 to 1977, France was the first country to export military equipment to Pretoria, making Paris reluctant to endorse international sanctions against the apartheid regime. Charles de Gaulle (1958–1969), Georges Pompidou (1969–1974) and Valéry Giscard d'Estaing (1974–1981) were closely aligned to Washington in the Cold War,[4] and were also backed in France by large corporations, particularly in the military-industrial sector, through companies such as Dassault, Matra and Panhart. When the implementation of sanctions could no longer be avoided,[5] qualified French staff (engineers and skilled technicians) were asked to stay in South Africa to keep these businesses going.

This intimacy between France and South Africa's military-industrial complex stretched beyond the export of French technologies and the trade of military hardware. French theories of counter-insurgency were taught in South African military institutions, and used by the South African Defence Force (SADF) in its operations in Angola, Namibia and elsewhere in Southern Africa (see Naidoo in this volume). In particular, General André Beaufre – one of the most well-known French theoreticians of counter-insurgency – had very close friends in the senior levels of the apartheid regime, including apartheid leader Pieter Willem Botha (1984–1989). The destructive "total strategy" military policy pursued by the apartheid regime from the 1980s was clearly inspired by the French general's thinking.[6]

The electoral victory in May 1981 of French left-wing politician François Mitterrand was expected by many to bring about a dramatic reversal of right-wing Gallic support for the apartheid regime. Both the African National Congress (ANC) and the South West Africa People's Organisation (SWAPO) were allowed to open offices in Paris in 1981 and 1985 respectively, and sanctions were imposed on apartheid South Africa after 1984. There was also a ban on coal imports and new investments. However, ambiguities persisted, with Mitterrand reluctant to challenge the overall economic relationship. He further believed that he had to honour the commitments made by his predecessor, Valéry Giscard d'Estaing, to the apartheid regime. Paris, therefore, often adopted an equivocal stance towards Pretoria, even as the ruling Socialist Party – led by Mitterrand between 1981 and 1995 – was clear in its denunciation of apartheid.[7] Notably, South Africa's Koeberg nuclear power plant – later the target of several ANC attacks – was completed in 1982 under Mitterrand's presidency.

The French anti-apartheid movement was also unique compared to its counterparts in other European countries. While elsewhere the movement was able to recruit massively among diverse sections of the population – including church leaders, trade unions, civic groups and various political parties – in France the anti-apartheid movement's backbone consisted of the Communist Party and an associated trade union (the General Confederation of Labour). Despite the involvement of many activists with no formal links to these organisations, the control of the Communist Parties in both France and South Africa resulted in significant limitations in developing the social roots of the anti-apartheid movement. Especially in the 1980s, when the struggle inside South Africa reached a climax, the French Communist Party continued to be a major component of the anti-apartheid movement at a time when the party's relations with other social and political sectors of French society had deteriorated badly.

These developments had a strong impact on ANC perceptions of France, despite some increased support for it from the Socialist Party and the France-Libertés Foundation, chaired by François Mitterrand's wife, Danielle Mitterrand. The perception was that the anti-apartheid movement did not have strong support in France at a time when the French people were being mobilised against racism amidst the growth of extreme right-wing politics in their country. A further problem was that many French aid projects were organised through Winnie Mandela's football club, which already had a controversial reputation among the ANC's core leadership.

Changing Faces in France and South Africa

To assess the contemporary relationship between France and South Africa, one has to take into account the different dynamics of change in both countries. History is prominent in many ways that are not easy to understand, even for French analysts.[8] The term *Françafrique* was coined in 1953 by an African politician – Ivorian leader Félix Houphouët-Boigny – and meant something quite different from its current understanding: a social group consisting of French and African politicians, high-ranking civil servants and businesspeople who shared a strong belief that France and its former African colonies had a common future. This original meaning has little to do with its current one as a term for shadow business networks that operate between Paris and Africa, and seek to make money based on collusion between private and public interests.

Furthermore, while South African observers have tended to see a permanent set of patterns in French policies towards Africa, the view from Paris has been far less systematic and been shaped by the roles of key individuals in the policymaking process, often including ministers, political advisers and the president himself. Public opinion shifts and dynamics within the European Union (EU) have also had some impact on issues related to Africa. In particular, the importance of European integration should not be downplayed in French foreign policy-making. While in some periods (for example, 1995–1997 and 2007–2012) French bilateral relations with African countries were of paramount importance, in others (typically between 1997 and 2002) Paris sought to collaborate more closely with the European Union and to avoid making unilateral decisions. In those years, influenced by the much criticised French role during the Rwandan genocide of 1994,[9] Gallic interventions in Africa had a stronger international legal basis, though criticisms continued and were sometimes well founded, as in the Franco–British-led North Atlantic Treaty Organisation (NATO) intervention in Libya in 2011.[10]

François Mitterrand lost interest in Africa after his first term (1981–1988). The overly hyped speech he made in La Baule, France, in 1990, in which he defended democratisation, was more a swansong than the beginning of a new era. The Balkan wars of the early 1990s had a much greater impact on French political elites than did the genocide in Rwanda in 1994.[11] Developments created by the collapse of the Soviet Union and the lack of clear democratic progress on the continent reinforced a negative perception of the continent ("if you are interested in Africa, sooner or later you will be accused of being part of the Françafrique corruption networks", to put it simplistically). This trend was also reflected in the decrease of French aid to Africa in the 1990s.[12]

Even Jacques Chirac was not consistent in addressing African issues over the 12 years he spent in the Elysée Palace (1995–2007). Between 1995 and

1997, Chirac had two different sets of presidential advisers on Africa, illustrating his inability to choose between the older guard (Jacques Foccart) and a more reformist group (Michel Dupuch). He became slightly more coherent only after 1997, as he had to appoint the opposition Socialist Party leader, Lionel Jospin, as prime minister in a "cohabitation" government.[13] The overhaul of the cooperation ministry and the defence ministry, undertaken between 1996 and 1999, also had important consequences for the French presence in Africa. It basically ended the possibility of closed-door agreements that contradicted the general framework of French foreign policy. However, their impacts were neither immediate nor did they reshape policies in a predetermined direction.[14] Willingly or unwillingly, France has a history in Africa, and decisions were not made on a simple definition of what its interests were.[15]

After 2002, French policy towards the continent became increasingly ad hoc, although European integration limited Paris's ability to set its own policies unilaterally. For example, French military intervention had to be discussed at a European level and an international mandate secured. French presidents could still play hardball, but the political costs of such an approach had to be carefully considered. This trend, already apparent in the second term of Jacques Chirac's presidency (2002–2007), became dominant under Nicolas Sarkozy's term in the Elysée Palace (2007–2012). Among the many examples, one should consider the drastic differences between Sarkozy's Dakar speech in July 2007 – largely a collection of quotes from nineteenth-century philosophers tainted with racism and paternalism – and his Cape Town speech in February 2008, which asserted a strong sense of urgency in reforming French views of Africa. Libya, assessed in detail later, is another important illustration of this lack of consistency. At the same time, it would be wrong to assume that Sarkozy was just a reactionary: he carried out a number of reforms, especially in restructuring defence agreements with African countries such as the Central African Republic, that later constrained Paris's foreign policy.[16]

French policymakers were also influenced by the differences that they perceived between South Africa's presidents. After the end of apartheid in 1994, Paris was eager to establish a strategic partnership with Tshwane. Like other external actors such as the US, China and Britain (see Weissman, Liu and Large in this volume), France was happy to acknowledge South Africa's self-defined role of representing the African continent, although Paris took note that African countries such as Nigeria and Angola were not as eager to endorse this mandate. As a key actor on the continent, Paris also had to take a position on South African policies towards Africa beyond empty rhetorical statements.

For many in France, Nelson Mandela was the global statesman who promoted a unique brand of conflict resolution and elevated the moral stature of the continent in the process. In that sense, South Africa still enjoys an exceptional status and "soft power"[17] in Paris that are deeply rooted in the personality and ethics of Mandela. As South Africa's first black president (1994–1999), Mandela achieved much, most importantly the rehabilitation of his country on the continent as one that was now – in the post-apartheid era – committed to a special role and supportive of democratic and universal values. This made South Africa a rare case among African countries. There were never the same expectations of Nigeria and Angola when these countries were considered as regional hegemons. (See Adebajo on Nigeria and Sachikonye on Angola in this volume.) Paradoxically, Mandela's presidency occurred at a time when civil war erupted in several African countries, such as Rwanda, Burundi and the Democratic Republic of the Congo (DRC), and international interest towards the continent (as reflected in aid flows) was steadily declining. His message of peace and political accommodation was scarcely heeded on the continent.

South Africa's president Thabo Mbeki (1999–2008) was quite different in character from his predecessor and, from the start, was not seen as having the same ethical persona as Mandela. Mbeki's "Africanist" assertiveness did not convince many in France, because the narrative was not really new to them; rather it seemed to be a throwback to the continent's pre-independence era (whose outcomes are well-known), while echoing the "Africanist" stance of some of the worst post-independence regimes in Africa, such as that of Zaire's French-backed Mobutu Sese Seko, with his *authenticité*. Some French policymakers also found Mbeki's rhetoric unconvincing when weighed against concrete issues such as his neo-liberal economic policies, the aggressive expansion of South African firms into the rest of the continent, and his more controversial policies, especially on Zimbabwe and HIV/AIDS.[18]

Yet Thabo Mbeki, though often a difficult partner for most of his years as South African president, was considered a consequential leader in France – one with a clear vision of how Africa should transform and the role that his own country needed to play in this transformation. Mbeki was perceived as the smart newcomer in global politics, sometimes overusing cheap rhetoric, but always for a purpose that had a meaning beyond South Africa's crude interests or those of its corporate firms. Mbeki was also seen to be part of the dynamic that gave a new impetus to the Non-Aligned Movement (NAM) and challenged the existing international order.

Jacob Zuma, South Africa's president since 2009, has a quite different image among French politicians and observers. Seen sometimes as purely opportunistic, sometimes as a talented pragmatist, he – not unlike the two French presidents Jacques Chirac and Nicolas Sarkozy – has not articulated a real project for the African continent, but has been, in the French view, eager to promote South African interests at all costs without thinking twice about the unintended consequences of such an approach. Zuma's image in France has also suffered from the many allegations of corruption and, sometimes, of sexual misconduct levelled against him. He also leads an ANC that is no longer seen as the same great political movement that implemented a complex and inclusive political deal for South Africa's peaceful transition to democracy between 1990 and 1994. "Crony capitalism", corruption and embezzlement of public money, admittedly, do not make the headlines in the French media. However, those who follow South Africa increasingly see a country affected by the same weaknesses afflicting many other African countries, although South Africa still has a vibrant media, judiciary and civil society who have not been shy to challenge its leaders.

The stark picture depicted here could be qualified in several ways. Over the years, a strategic dialogue has successfully taken place between Paris and Tshwane. Economic cooperation and, from time to time, coordinated actions to cool down conflicts, are two important outcomes. Relations between the two countries are also not dictated by pure political and ethical differences, but by shared interests in economic growth. Two key issues have distorted this relationship: the recurrence of significant disagreements on African crises that has made the construction of caricatures much easier in Paris and Tshwane; and the more complex issue of the extent to which economic interests have sometimes been fed by rivalry and competition.

Crises, What Crises?

While Paris's interest in Africa – as viewed from France – has diminished, it still has the means and influence to act in crises, though much less decisively than it could during the Cold War era. The French intervention in Mali in January 2013 is a good example of Paris's ability to deploy troops to an ongoing crisis and to make a difference. However, these military involvements have been viewed very differently in Europe and South Africa. While the latter has denounced French "neo-colonial" interventions, European observers have tended to assess each intervention individually and to stress the differences between them.

Between 2005 and 2009, Paris intervened militarily in Chad to save the autocratic regime of Idriss Déby. Analysts have been much more cautious about saying the same with regard to Mali and the Central African Republic. This again reflects an aspect often missed by South African observers: France and French politicians do not decide on interventions lightly. This was the case even under the presidency of Nicolas Sarkozy between 2007 and 2012. Gallic politicians often have a quite rational – though arguably debatable – assessment of the political and diplomatic costs of such interventions. Moreover, despite the fact that all of these countries are officially French-speaking, Senegal, Côte d'Ivoire, the CAR and Chad are all different as far as French politicians are concerned. It would be wrong to imagine that French president François Hollande's decision to intervene in Mali in January 2013 was taken without first discussing the situation with West African leaders who were extremely supportive of Gallic actions.[19]

In that sense, criticising French interventionism can at times be more of a Pavlovian reaction than the outcome of rigorous political analysis. As the CAR crisis illustrates, such criticisms are often used to focus attention on a rival without asking basic questions about Tshwane's policy (or lack of it) in specific crises. The same way that France believes that it has a special responsibility to act in certain African crises (but not all), South Africa assumes that it speaks on behalf of an African continent that is often deeply divided on the issues at stake.

Several crises have recently put the two countries at loggerheads. Not all of these cases had clear political implications for the continental order, but Paris's policy challenged basic assumptions made by Tshwane. In the same way, South Africa's policy on other conflicts often put France in a difficult position. Among these crises, I focus here on five: Zaïre/DRC, Côte d'Ivoire, Libya, the Central African Republic and the contest for chair of the AU commission.

Zaïre/DRC

The Zaïre/DRC conflict has a long history that reflects deep polarisation in the Great Lakes region. This was more a regional confrontation than an internal war, and produced strange alliances. After August 1998, the conflict placed South Africa in a difficult position, as its former friends were not all its current allies. Zimbabwe and Angola played their own game with a military intervention to protect Laurent Kabila (a policy opposed by Tshwane), at a time when Harare and Luanda's own relations with Tshwane were not exactly flourishing. France and Belgium also sealed an alliance that was at loggerheads with an anglophone cluster of countries including Britain, the United States, Rwanda and Uganda. South Africa played a major role in bringing all stakeholders to the negotiating table, and was able to secure the Sun City agreement in May 2002 (see Nzongola-Ntalaja in this volume). To a large extent, despite France's initial reactive goals in this conflict (restoring influence in Central Africa a decade after the Rwandan genocide of 1994), Paris and Tshwane were eventually able to work together in the Congo and to narrow their differences.

Côte d'Ivoire

While accommodation prevailed in the DRC conflict, nothing similar happened in the Ivorian situation after South African president Thabo Mbeki became the AU mediator in this crisis in 2005 (see Adebajo in this volume). From the start, it was difficult to narrow the differences between Paris and Tshwane. Both Jacques Chirac and Nicolas Sarkozy had personal relationships with opposition leader Alassane Ouattara and Burkinabè leader Blaise Compaoré, who had also cultivated his connections with their party, the Rally for the Republic, and later the Union for a Popular Movement, for years. France, whatever neutrality it claimed, had its own candidate, and was eager to rid West Africa of President Laurent Gbagbo at all costs. Gbagbo was articulating a narrative of a "second independence" from France that resonated profoundly with the "Africanist" vision of Thabo Mbeki. Ouattara's image in Tshwane was also tarnished by the pragmatism of Ivorian leader Houphouët-Boigny towards the apartheid regime (Ouattara had served as Houphouët's prime minister between 1990 and 1993).

It was therefore not surprising that France, under Chirac and Sarkozy between 1995 and 2007, did not pursue a common agenda with South Africa towards the Ivorian crisis. The ideological divisions also reflected diverse economic interests, and became the paradigmatic contradiction between the old "neo-colonial" power and a "new" South Africa that has pushed for a radical reorganisation in the relations of African countries with former European colonial powers. Yet, what South Africa was unwilling to acknowledge was that Paris was not as isolated as Thabo Mbeki had thought. A recurrent problem in South Africa's policy towards the continent was a tendency to bypass sub-regional organisations – in this case the Economic Community of West African States (ECOWAS) – to obtain the endorsement of the African Union for its policies. Eventually, South Africa had to retreat, and join ECOWAS in its approach, as Nigeria and Senegal pushed for Mbeki's ouster as the AU mediator.[20] (See Adebajo in this volume.) In the 2011 electoral crisis in Côte d'Ivoire, Nigeria, as the chair of ECOWAS, supported the French stance to the despair of Tshwane. Most francophone African leaders often align with Paris, as they have convergent interests, or have sometimes actually convinced Paris to move in their direction. This bargaining dimension of relations between France and francophone African countries is often misunderstood by South African diplomats, especially at a time when the ANC as a party seems more in control of South Africa's foreign policy than do its professional diplomats.

Libya

The year 2011 was indeed an *annus horribilis* for relations between Paris and Tshwane. With the crisis in Côte d'Ivoire barely concluded, a militarised protest movement began challenging the Libyan regime of Muammar Qaddafi, who had been a longtime friend of the ANC and other liberation movements. South Africa, then a non-permanent member of the UN Security Council, cast its vote in favour of Security Council Resolution 1973, which backed strong measures against Qaddafi's regime. Tshwane understood too late that Western powers (France, Britain and the US) were pursuing a "regime change" agenda. (See Mashabane, and Tawfik in this volume.)

In this respect, South Africa showed some naiveté in its assessment of the aims of Western powers in Libya. The idea of an internal liberalisation of the Libyan regime had long disappeared, and from 2009 to 2011 Western chancelleries were increasingly hostile to Tripoli.[21] The media and the propaganda in Paris, London and Washington were moving in the direction of a direct intervention.[22] To have any impact, the diplomatic debate should have been handled in quite a different manner by the African

Union, but this was not possible because Africa (more than the African Union) was also divided on the future of Qaddafi.

South Africa can console itself over this failure by pointing to the unresolved consolidation of the new regime in Libya, the growth of jihadist groups in many parts of the country and the current creeping destabilisation of the Western Sahel as a result of illicit arms flows from Libya. France and its Western allies are paying a heavy price for having been unable to avoid the looting of Libya's military arsenal, and the collapse of the regional order. However, as always, the price has been highest for the local populations.

It is worth noting that many observers, such as Vincent Darracq and others,[23] believe that the control exercised by the ANC on South African foreign policy grew out of these two failures of Côte d'Ivoire and Libya. Yet a more politicised and ideologically confrontational foreign service was not the best tool with which to assess French policy on the continent, especially at a time when such policy also lacked consistency.

Central African Republic

The election of a new socialist president, François Hollande, in France in May 2012, was also a moment when assumptions about French "neo-imperialism" in Africa simply missed the point. Arguably, only African ideologues or politicians backed into a corner by their own mistakes could mobilise such rhetoric, as illustrated by the CAR crisis in 2013 and the deep humiliation and misstep of Tshwane in its botched military intervention in the country. French diplomats are clear on this issue, and these views were confirmed by leading politicians in the CAR, including ANC International Socialist members. For Paris, there were two key moments in this crisis. The first took place in 2007 when, at France's initiative, talks started with South Africa on providing training for the Central African Armed Forces (FACA), and especially the Presidential Guard. An agreement was eventually reached between Bangui and Tshwane, though the text of the accord was not made public. Following this episode, a small contingent (comprising about a couple dozen personnel) of the South African National Defence Force (SANDF) was deployed in Bouar and Bangui. CAR politicians add that mining contracts were also signed with Tshwane, but French diplomats could not confirm this allegation.[24]

The second event took place when France was renegotiating its defence agreement with the CAR between 2009 and 2010. This was based on a commitment by Nicolas Sarkozy during his Cape Town visit in February 2008 and represented a major achievement for his presidency. A major change in the defence agreement was that France no longer wanted to guarantee the survival of regimes, even when confronted with an internal insurgency. Unlike in the past, such an intervention now required a UN Security Council resolution or at least a multilateral decision.

Throughout the time of the re-negotiation of the military agreement, Bangui undertook a parallel dialogue with Tshwane. The key negotiator on the CAR side was not the minister of defence (François Bozizé himself), nor his deputy, Jean-Francis Bozizé, but the minister of mining and energy, Sylvain Ndoutingai: the potential heir apparent. French diplomats confirm that a further agreement between Bangui and Tshwane was reached, but again say that they never saw the text.[25] Nevertheless, new contracts were signed in the same period that could be interpreted as offering an economic counterpart to that deal. One can be cynical about this outcome, as France had followed the same approach many times in the past, only to end up with failures.

A final episode – denied by the South African presidency – was the visit, in October 2012, of Jean-Francis Bozizé to Tshwane to obtain a new consignment of weapons from Jacob Zuma, as Séléka rebels threatened to march on the capital of Bangui. CAR politicians confirm the visit and the role of Didier Pereira, who often played the middle-man between the regime in Bangui and the South African presidency.[26]

What happened in the CAR from December 2012 to March 2013 says much about the inability of South African diplomacy fully to grasp a crisis such as CAR's with its complex regional politics. The South African military and its special forces also failed spectacularly to collect vital intelligence on the situation in the country. For any independent observer, the SANDF contingent of about 200 personnel[27] was too big and had too many heavy weapons to be there just for training.[28] It was also clearly unrealistic, and frankly unprofessional, to deploy soldiers to a conflict situation without a proper understanding of whom they were supposed to fight against or for, and the purpose for which they had been deployed to the country.

Interviews in the South African media and a small booklet based on these testimonies do not leave any doubt about the political naiveté of the South African contingent and its political leaders. In March 2013 – when the new Séléka rebel offensive started – it was clear to everyone that Chad had given the green light to the rebels to advance, and that Séléka had much better equipment and skilled fighters. South Africa, however, still behaved as if it believed Bozizé's propaganda that the Séléka rebels were just a bunch of disorganised bandits.[29]

The disturbing aspect of this incident, beyond two days of bloody confrontations, was that the South African presidency did not provide any explanation to the country's parliament and citizens on this military misadventure. The intervention had been undertaken without any international mandate, been based only on a secret agreement, and reportedly involved business deals provided to ANC securocrats and associates of President Zuma.[30]

Railing against French "neo-colonialism" was the easiest damage-control strategy that Tshwane could employ. However, the French army on the ground that was controlling Bangui airport protected South African soldiers after they had been attacked by the Séléka rebels on 22 and 23 March 2014. They also protected the airport against Séléka fighters who tried to attack this location while South African troops were there. That said, France was in the CAR largely to provide support to the Mission for the Consolidation of Peace in the Central African Republic/Multinational Force in the Central African Republic (MICOPAX/FOMUC), endorsed by the AU and the Economic Community of Central African States (ECCAS), and not in pursuit of a "neo-colonial" strategy.[31]

There is no doubt that what happened to the South African military contingent in Bangui was humiliating for Tshwane, in both military and economic terms. The CAR certainly needs foreign investors, and South African firms may enjoy better success than French firms, which have for the most part failed to sustain their investments in the country. South Africa's military role in Africa also continues to be important, as its deployment of a 3,000-strong force to the DRC, with Tanzania and Malawi, by June 2013 demonstrated (see Nzongola-Ntalaja in this volume). However, lessons must be learned, and those who live in glass houses should not throw stones.

The AU Commission Chair

A final case of friction in Franco–South African relations involved the election of Nkosazana Dlamini-Zuma as chair of the African Union Commission in July 2012. (See Maloka in this volume.) French diplomats argued that Paris had little interest in the outcome of this election. By claiming the AU leadership, South Africa had broken a "gentleman's agreement" that no big country should claim the position.

Tshwane's detractors were therefore not only or always francophone countries (Chad, for example, voted for Dlamini-Zuma). Countries that viewed Tshwane's ambition with suspicion included Rwanda, Ethiopia and Nigeria. Smaller countries (including francophone ones) resented the new AU leadership, arguing that South Africa's influence had gone too far, with claims that Dlamini-Zuma had too many South African advisers (paid for by Tshwane) in her office.

In this regard, South Africa's leaders may have a distorted and mostly anachronistic view of francophone African leaders based on a belief that France is still able to give orders that francophone African leaders simply obey. Many observers in Europe would argue that the opposite is true, in the sense that the influence of African leaders on French policy towards the continent is often more palpable than the inverse. There is still a "special relationship" between France and its former colonies, but this should not be overestimated. This relationship is also based on long-term history and short-term benefits: France, not the AU or South Africa, took the lead in launching an international force into the CAR by December 2013. This is widely acknowledged among African leaders.

Economic Relations: A Win/Win Situation?

Economic relations between France and South Africa reflect, to a large extent, these inherently contradictory dynamics, but they are less subject to ideological disputes and labelling. As earlier mentioned, Paris had developed good economic relations with the apartheid state, and as a result was ostracised in the early period of the post-apartheid era. However, this does not fully explain the marginal role initially played by French companies in South Africa compared to other Western partners such as Germany, Britain and the US, not to mention China. This relative weakness may be related to two different features of the French economic presence in Africa.

The first is that it took several years for French firms to enter non-francophone African countries, and those that did were, in any case, international companies with extensive experience of working across the globe. Nowadays though, France has more investments in lusophone Angola than in any francophone country.[32] Anglophone countries such as South Africa, Kenya and Nigeria are also considered to be more lucrative than francophone Senegal. It could be further argued that French companies that had operated in South Africa under apartheid were already accustomed to "affirmative action" policies (at that time benefiting Afrikaners), and adapted quickly to the new post-apartheid rules.

A second reason is more difficult to grasp and is related to the structure of French companies and their own reluctance to work in a competitive foreign market without major diplomatic support. French firms willing to work abroad assume that the French government will support them. French foreign direct investment in South Africa is not impressive (about 1 per cent of an estimated total €1.4 billion by 2015).[33]

That being said, the number of French firms establishing businesses in South Africa has increased significantly since 2007, reaching 326 and employing more than 23,000 people in 2015. The biggest French firms in South Africa are there as part of a long-term policy. French companies in South Africa are operating in key sectors including electricity (Alstom); pharmaceuticals (Sanofi-Aventis, Ceva, Yirbac); mining (Imerys, Total Coal, Areva); oil and chemical products (Total, Air Liquide); aeronautics (Thales, Turbomeca, Eurocopter); electrical equipment (Schneider Electric, Tenesol, Solaire Direct); building materials (Saint Gobain, Lafarge, Colas); automobiles (Renault, Faurecia, Valeo, Inergy, Plastic Omnium); water and environment (Veolia, Suez); consumer goods (L'Oréal, Essilor, Bic); and food processing (Danone, Union Invivo). French firms are also well represented in financial services (BNP Paribas, Société Générale, Coracle); hotels (Accor, Sodexho); engineering (Interpol, Areva, EDF, Air Liquide Engineering, Coteba, Technip); urban transportation (RATP); and logistics (Bolloré, AGS, Geopost). Beyond the controversial apartheid-era nuclear plant of Koeberg, French firms also contributed to the building of major infrastructure such as mega power-plants in Medupi and Kusile (Alstom); and more recently the express train (Gautrain) connecting Johannesburg, Tshwane and the O.R. Tambo international airport (Bouygues TP, Thales, RATP).

Furthermore, South Africa is France's leading trade partner in sub-Saharan Africa, with a trade volume in 2015 worth more than €2.6 billion. The trade balance is currently skewed in favour of France; €963 million in 2015. This indicates that South Africa is a profitable market for French companies. South Africa's commercial presence in France has also grown significantly.[34]

Concluding Reflections

South Africa's use of its economic and diplomatic potential has made it an indispensable partner for most emerging economies and the African continent – a reality that French policymakers sometimes undervalue. On the other hand, as a former European colonial power in Africa, France is an easy target for criticism by South Africa. "Neo-colonialism" is, however, an oversimplified explanation for the French presence and interest in Africa, and in single-mindedly focusing on it, South African politicians may be missing a key point: African sub-regions have developed their own, often divided views on what is best for the continent, and frequently prefer to negotiate pragmatically with all external powers, including France.

South Africa's own success also should not be overstated. The country faces significant internal problems and economic bottlenecks that may even increase in future. In light of the enormous domestic socio-economic challenges that South Africa faces (see Landsberg in this volume), it is important not to overstate Tshwane's foreign policy successes. South Africa may yet face a "new" challenge in its foreign policy: to prove that it can compare favourably with regional powers such as Nigeria (which overtook South Africa as Africa's largest economy in 2013), Kenya and Ethiopia. Against this backdrop, a strategic dialogue may thus be useful between South Africa and France, which also faces its own domestic socio-economic challenges. The question that both countries have to answer is how to maintain international influence amidst diminishing economic power.

Notes

1. Quoted in interview of Antoine Bouillon on *Radio France Internationale*, 28 July 2013, http://www.rfi.fr/afrique/20130728-bouillon-mandela-apartheid-communis te-chirac-buthelezi-deklerk (accessed 7 December 2016).
2. "Quand le FN Traitait Mandela de Terroriste", *Slate*, 27 June 2013, http://www.s late.fr/monde/74497/fn-mandela-terroriste (accessed 7 December 2016).
3. Mangosuthu Buthelezi was received in Paris in 1985 by Jacques Chirac, then mayor of Paris. In 1987, Buthelezi again met with Chirac, then prime minister. Buthelezi also met with influential right-wing politicians such as François Léotard, Claude Maluret, Jaques Chaban-Delmas and Alain Poher. For more information, *see* http://www.humanite.fr/node/78139#sthash.9X24388k.dpuf (accessed 7 December 2016).
4. The French Intelligence Service (SDECE) under Alexandre de Marenches (1970– 1981) was rabidly anti-communist.
5. United Nations (UN) Security Council Resolution 418, adopted in November 1977, imposed an arms embargo on South Africa.
6. Philip Frankel, *Pretoria's Pretorians: Civil-Military Relations in South Africa* (New York: Cambridge University Press, 1985).

7. Christophe Champin and Francis Kpatindé, "Antoine Bouillon: 'Il a Fallu le Combat des Associations de Lutte Contre l'Apartheid pour Amener les Etats à Dénoncer le Régime'", *Libération*, 8 August 2013.

8. *See, for example*, Jean-François Bayart, *La Politique Africaine de la France* (Paris: Karthala, 1984), or more recently Jean-Pierre Dozon, *Frères et Sujets: La France et l'Afrique en Perspective* (Paris: Flammarion, 2003). My own views are expressed in a short review in *La Revue Internationale et Stratégique* no. 52 (Autumn 2003), pp. 161–162.

9. André Guichaoua, *Rwanda: De la Guerre au Génocide – Les Politiques Criminelles (1990–1994)* (Paris: La Découverte, 2013).

10. Roland Marchal, "France and Africa: The Emergence of Essential Reforms", *International Affairs* 74, no. 2 (1998), pp. 355–372.

11. The parliamentary commission that tried to shed light on the alleged French responsibility in the genocide was never granted full powers of investigation. The French government traditionally does not like transparency in its foreign policy, which remains a *domaine réservé*.

12. For figures, *see* http://www.oecd.org/dac/stats/idsonline.htm (accessed 7 December 2016); and for comments, *see* the special issue on "France-Afrique: Sortir du Pacte Colonial", *Politique Africaine* no. 105 (March 2007).

13. Richard Banegas and Roland Marchal, "La Politique Africaine de Jacques Chirac", in Christian Lequesne and Maurice Vaisse, *La Politique Étrangère de Jacques Chirac* (Paris: Riveneuve Editions, 2012), pp. 179–198.

14. Julien Meimon, "En Quête de Légitimité: Le Ministère de la Coopération (1959–1999)", PhD dissertation, University of Lille, 2005.

15. Roland Marchal, "The French Policy Toward Africa Under Jacques Chirac", in *South African Yearbook of International Affairs 2006/7* (Johannesburg: South African Institute of International Affairs (SAIIA), 2008), pp. 335–347.

16. Richard Moncrieff, "French Relations with Sub-Saharan Africa Under President Sarkozy", Occasional Paper no. 107 (Johannesburg: SAIIA, 2012), pp. 20–24.

17. Joseph Nye, *Soft Power: The Means to Success in World Politics* (New York: PublicAffairs, 2004).

18. *See, for example*, Adekeye Adebajo, *The Curse of Berlin: Africa After the Cold War* (Scottsville: University of KwaZulu-Natal Press; and London: Hurst, 2010), pp. 233–259.

19. Roland Marchal, "Military (Mis)Adventures in Mali", *African Affairs* 12, no. 448 (2013), pp. 486–497.

20. Vincent Darracq, "Jeux de Puissance en Afrique: Le Nigeria et l'Afrique du Sud Face à la Crise Ivoirienne", *Politique Étrangère* no. 2 (2012), pp. 361–374.

21. Ethan Chorin, *Exit the Colonel: The Hidden History of the Libyan Revolution* (New York: PublicAffairs, 2012).

22. Hugh Roberts, "Who Said Gaddafi Had to Go?", *London Review of Books* 33, no. 22 (November 2011), pp. 8–18.

23. *See* Darracq, "Jeux de Puissance en Afrique".

24. Author interviews, Bangui and Paris, January 2013.

25. This is based on off-the-record interviews with leading Central African Republic (CAR) politicians and French diplomats who had to oversee the CAR file through those years.

26. Author interviews with CAR politicians, May 2013. *See also* the journal *La Lettre du Continent* no. 647, 22 November 2012; or Amabhungane Reporters, "Central African Republic: Is That What Our Soldiers Died For?", *Mail and Guardian*, 28 March 2013, http://mg.co.za/article/2013-03-28-00-central-african-republic-is -this-what-our-soldiers-died-for (accessed 12 March 2014).

27. Number quoted by President Jacob Zuma. *See* http://mg.co.za/article/2013-03-26-sandf-releases-names-of-sa-soldiers-killed-in-car (accessed 7 December 2016).

28. As illustrated by Zuma's letters related to the South African National Defence Force (SANDF) deployment in the CAR, contradictions in the mandate were expressed at the highest level. For further analysis, *see* http://mg.co.za/article/2013-04-08-zuma-constitution-car-deployment-sandf (accessed 7 December 2016). The letters can be found at http://mg.co.za/article/2013-04-08-zuma-constitution-car-deployment-sandf (accessed 7 December 2016).

29. Helmoed Heitman, *The Battle of Bangui: The Untold Inside Story* (Johannesburg: Parktown, 2013).

30. Amabhungane Reporters, "Central African Republic". The South African presidency reacted very strongly, but did not provide any evidence challenging the business deals. For this chapter, other newspapers were also consulted, such as the *Sunday Independent* (notably Helmoe Römer Heitman, "How Deadly CAR Battle Unfolded", 31 March 2013) and *Business Day* (such as David Meunier, "The President Misled the Parliament", 4 April 2013; and Palesa Morudu, "Bangui Falls Off National Key Points Wish List", 9 April 2013).

31. *See* French Ministry of Defence, "L'Opération Boali", http://www.defense.gouv.fr/operations/autres-operations/operation-boali-rca/dossier/les-forces-francaises-en-republique-centrafricaine (accessed 12 March 2014).

32. Banque de France, "Stock des Investissements Directs Français à l'Étranger au 31 Décembre 2011", https://www.banque-france.fr/fileadmin/user_upload/banque_de_france/Economie_et_Statistiques/SID13-35z_Stocks_IDFE.pdf (accessed 7 December 2016).

33. France Diplomatie, "Les Chiffres Clés des Échanges Bilatéraux et Dispositif de Soutien aux Entreprises Françaises en Afrique du Sud", http://www.diplomatie.gouv.fr/fr/politique-etrangere-de-la-france/diplomatie-economique-et-commerce-exterieur/la-france-et-ses-partenaires-economiques-pays-par-pays/afrique/article/afrique-du-sud (accessed 7 December 2016).

34. Vincent Darracq, "L'Un Plus Égal Que l'Autre? Les Relations Économiques Entre l'Afrique du Sud et la Chine Depuis 1994" (Paris: Institut Français des Relations Internationales (IFRI), June 2013).

CHAPTER 17

SOUTH AFRICA AND CHINA: SOLIDARITY AND BEYOND

Liu Haifang

China is not South Africa's sole strategic partner. Formal diplomatic ties between the two countries were only established in 1998.[1] In contrast, Tshwane's (Pretoria) relations with the European Union (EU) and Russia,[2] for example, date further back, to the end of apartheid and 1992 respectively. Soon enough, however, even with irritants such as the Taiwan issue, the South Africa–China bilateral relationship was upgraded to the level of a comprehensive strategic partnership in 2010. Yet, as South African analyst Sanusha Naidu has pointed out, while "China ... established institutional mechanisms – in particular, the Forum on China-Africa Cooperation (FOCAC) in 2000", the South African government did not have a clear instrument to achieve its aims or an explicit definition of its "strategic partnership" with Beijing.[3] This has contributed to several South African scholars' suspicions of Beijing's intentions.[4] Chinese analysts, in contrast, have tended to view the China–South Africa strategic relationship in terms of its potential to contribute to economic globalisation and the reform of institutions of global governance, and as a progressive partnership.[5] In order to understand the nature of bilateral relations, it is important to trace how this "comprehensive strategic partnership" was formalised, before assessing its possible impacts, positive or negative.

The Establishment of the Comprehensive Strategic Partnership

The year 1992 has been widely regarded as a turning point in the development of Beijing's foreign direct investment (FDI) policy, with an exponential increase in Chinese outward FDI from 1993 onwards. Significantly, South African FDI had already started to flow into China in 1992, indicating that economic demand for such investments was strong and that South African business elites had seen the need to engage China, ahead of the adjustment of Beijing's official policy to attract FDI globally from 1993.[6]

However, this "early bird" trend did not lead immediately to the establishment of formal diplomatic relations between South Africa and mainland China, mostly due to the Taiwan issue, dating back to 1962, when the white apartheid regime was isolated by the international community due to its suppression of the black majority. By 1976, after Taiwan and South Africa had been effectively expelled from the United Nations (UN) General Assembly, their bilateral consular relationship was upgraded to an ambassador-level diplomatic relationship, following which hundreds of Taiwanese factories were lured with special initiatives to set up shop in South Africa, which had been facing increasing international sanctions since the mid-1970s. Taiwan continued its generosity towards South Africa during the country's transition period between 1990 and 1994. Economic cooperation between South Africa and both mainland China and Taiwan increased rapidly, and the concept of "dual recognition" of both Taipei and Beijing was employed from 1995.

China's foreign minister during the 1990–1994 period, Qian Qichen, revealed later in his memoirs that Pik Botha, the reformist-minded foreign minister in South Africa's apartheid government, had secretly visited China in October 1991, ahead of Nelson Mandela's visit in October 1992. Qian, however, did not think that South Africa's white minority regime would develop further ties with Beijing as, according to him, Pretoria was "only keen to establish economic relations".[7] The switch in diplomatic ties from Taipei to Beijing would have to await the ascent to power of the African National Congress (ANC).[8]

Yet, because of limited understanding of mainland China, and Taiwan's special diplomatic efforts to support the ANC's election campaign and development-related investments (including cultural and educational programmes), the ANC did not *automatically* switch diplomatic ties from

Taiwan to mainland China. The proverbial last straw, according to Qian, turned out to be an offer of $5 billion by Xu Lide, Deputy Executive of the Taiwanese government, to help to build a chemical industry park during a visit to the country in August 1996.[9] Meanwhile, a "new" Chinese community was growing in South Africa, which had contributed to an increase in bilateral trade, officially restarted only in 1993. This commerce increased from $658 million in 1993 to $1.5 billion in 1995, making South Africa Beijing's largest trading partner on the continent. As South Africa's investments in China also increased, the largely white apartheid-era business elite emerged as a serious pressure group in favour of a shift away from Tshwane's "dual recognition" policy.[10]

Diplomatic ties between South Africa and China were formally established in January 1998, following which Mandela made his second visit to China, in May 1999. Serious strategic consideration was given to deepening cooperation in April 2000 with the signing of the Pretoria Declaration, which highlighted potential areas for a more comprehensive partnership. Importantly, the declaration sought to establish a joint South Africa–China Bi-National Commission (BNC). The commission was established in Beijing in December 2001 by President Thabo Mbeki and his Chinese counterpart, Jiang Zemin, marking the institutionalisation of the partnership, with BNC sub-commissions covering diplomacy, economics and trade, science and technology, military and defence, education and energy.[11]

In June 2004, during a visit to South Africa by Chinese deputy president Zeng Qinghong, the South African government acknowledged Beijing's status as a market economy, and the two sides jointly announced the launch of negotiations for a free trade agreement between China and the Southern African Customs Union (SACU) (see Gibbs in this volume on SACU). The bilateral relationship reached a peak in 2006–2007, with several high-level state visits by the two countries' leaders. Chinese premier Wen Jiabao visited South Africa in June 2006, witnessing the signing of an important document establishing a programme to deepen the bilateral strategic partnership between the two countries. With South Africa set to commence its first two-year term as a non-permanent member of the UN Security Council in January 2007, the programmatic document identified areas of coordination between Tshwane and Beijing on priorities such as UN Security Council reform. In November 2006, South African president Thabo Mbeki attended the Forum on China–Africa Cooperation summit in Beijing. This was followed by a visit to South Africa by President Hu

Jintao in February 2007. Formal communication channels between the two countries have further multiplied since the launch of the China–South Africa Strategic Dialogue in April 2008.

In the late 2000s, South Africa was confronted with the waning of its post-apartheid position as an "international darling" for aid, investment and other forms of cooperation. With the World Bank classifying it as an upper-middle-income country in 2007, aid programmes to South Africa began to be phased out by several donor countries. Against the backdrop of the global financial crisis of 2008–2009, South Africa also faced a slowdown in economic growth. Building its relationships with emerging market economies, in particular China, became a priority for South Africa's foreign policy, as indicated by President Jacob Zuma's trips to all four of the BRIC countries (Brazil, Russia, India and China) in 2010 (see Virk in this volume). The Beijing Declaration on establishing a comprehensive China–South Africa strategic partnership, along with 13 new cooperation agreements and protocols between the two countries, constituted a key outcome of Zuma's visit.[12]

By 2011, Chinese foreign direct investment to South Africa stood at $830 million. Meanwhile, South African companies in China were earning significant profits. For example, SABMiller, partnering with Chinese Resource Enterprises Limited, enjoyed a 23 per cent share of the Chinese beer market in 2013, with an estimated further 2 per cent increase in 2014.[13] South Africa's Naspers, which purchased shares in the Chinese media company Tencent in 2001, has been relying on its stake in the Chinese company for its growth since 2009.[14] Building on this momentum, in July 2012, South African president Zuma – during a visit to Beijing for the fifth FOCAC meeting – acknowledged the importance of the strategic partnership with China as well as expressing his hopes to expand South Africa's export volume to China and enhance Chinese investment in South African infrastructure – including the industrial, park and mining sectors.[15]

South Africa's Evolving Expectations

The rapid increase in bilateral cooperation between South Africa and China has been boosted by both special efforts and growing high expectations from the two sides. In 2004, the relationship was upgraded to a "strategic partnership". This diplomatic momentum strengthened business confidence, helping to drive South African FDI in China from $491 million in 2004 to $770 million by the end of 2005, with large companies such as Anglo-American, Sasol and SABMiller all making substantial investments in the country. Meanwhile, Chinese foreign direct investment in South Africa, which was initially slower, increased from $130 million in 2004 to $580 million in 2006. Bilateral trade volumes similarly increased, from $7.3 billion in 2005 to $8.9 billion in 2006 – an increase of 40 per cent over the previous year.

However, there was an imbalance in this burgeoning trade relationship, with South Africa recording a deficit of $4.78 billion in 2006.[16] The resulting concern among policymakers in Tshwane translated into an agreement crafted during Chinese premier Wen Jiabao's visit in June 2006. Through this accord, 31 tariff lines of textile and apparel products to South Africa were targeted for quotas.[17] According to Mandisi Mpahlwa, South Africa's minister of trade and industry in 2007, Tshwane expected that the measure would encourage stakeholders to communicate better and work well with each other, encouraging Chinese entrepreneurs, in particular, to invest in South Africa's textile sector, given the country's impressive infrastructure, the low costs of electricity and labour and connectivity with other markets.[18]

However, the quota measure was controversial and had faced criticism from various groups within South Africa even before it was unveiled. South Africa's National Union of Textile Workers (NUTW) had demanded the policy. However, six big South African retail chains, including Woolworths and Edcon Holdings, issued a joint declaration criticising the measure as seriously harming the interests of consumers by creating a shortage of supply, worsening inflation and encouraging corruption. Meanwhile, Phumzile Mlambo-Ngcuka, then deputy president of South Africa, went so far as to charge retailers with "treason" for seeking to buy cheap clothing from third countries in an effort to circumvent quotas on imports from China.[19] A memorandum of understanding for the quota was signed in August 2006, which the Chinese government requested its corporate sector to observe beginning in September of that year.[20] Following the lapse of the two-year quota period, many South African analysts "highlighted the fact that importers simply developed new strategies to circumvent the restrictions." As Mike Morris and Lyn Reed commented, based on their research, the quota-setting measure was pursued "only because [the] South African government had a tunnelled perspective on the clothing sector crisis, bowing to the narrow political agendas of sectoral interest groups".[21] Rescuing its textile sector is thus certain to be a long battle for the South African government.

Tshwane and Beijing's expectations of each other were closer in February 2007 at the time of Chinese president Hu Jintao's visit to South Africa. While Tshwane identified infrastructure, agriculture, mining and job training as key priority areas for greater cooperation, Beijing expressed an interest and willingness to work together in the building of infrastructure, poverty alleviation, job creation, rural development, skills training, capacity-building and Chinese-language teaching. At the Sino–South African Economic and Trade Symposium held in Beijing in September 2007, South Africa's deputy president, Phumzile Mlambo-Ngucka, noted that the bilateral relationship between the two countries was moving from political cooperation towards greater economic cooperation. South Africa's expectations of China were clearly demonstrated by the theme of the South African pavilion at the World Expo in Shanghai, from May to October 2010: "Ke Nako ["it is time"] for [South Africa] to rise as a modern economic power!"[22]

Since the global financial crisis of 2008–2009, the need for South Africa to diversify its economic partners – to generate economic growth and employment – has become urgent. In July 2009, Tshwane created the Economic Development Department (EDD) to respond to the financial crisis and to the rise of China, India and Brazil.[23] This indicated a significant shift in priorities from the mid-1990s, when Tshwane had prioritised engagement with African countries, Europe and the United States (US) over other rich and emerging economies.[24] The unprecedented size of the business delegation (representing 300 businesses) that accompanied South African president Jacob Zuma on his visit to the World Expo in Shanghai in August 2010 clearly demonstrated Tshwane's need for, and expectation of, a shift towards more deeply embedded economic cooperation between the two countries.

Tourism, which generated one in every 12 jobs in South Africa and contributed to 5 per cent of its gross domestic product (GDP) in 2011,[25] provides a good example of this expectation. By 2012, the number of foreign visitors to South Africa had grown by 300 per cent annually, to 13.5 million, compared with a mere 3.4 million in 1993, of which 9.2 million were tourists, indicating the value of this industry in generating ever-increasing numbers of jobs. China had traditionally not been a large contributor to South African tourism, due to geographical constraints and a lack of knowledge. Among the 6.4 million tourists who travelled to South Africa in 2002, Asians numbered barely 37,000, with the majority of these being from China.[26] According to Statistics South

Africa, among all foreign travellers to the country, arrivals from China have more than tripled since 2009.[27] In May 2010, the South Africa Tourist Bureau officially opened an office in Beijing, reflecting a dramatic increase in the number of Chinese tourists to South Africa by 12.4 per cent over the previous year, at about 45,000. South Africa's tourism promotion in Beijing, as well as two other big cities – Shanghai and Guangzhou – has been energetic, especially since the simplification of visa procedures in 2011, with the South African visa service centre in Beijing expanded and localised to meet Chinese needs. Since the end of 2011, South African Airways (SAA), the country's national carrier, has supported these efforts through frequent promotions for travellers from China.[28] With all these efforts, in 2013, China – after Britain, the US and France – became the fourth-biggest overseas tourism market for South Africa, representing about 132,000 tourists (an increase of 56 per cent over 2011) among a total of 9.2 million international tourist arrivals in South Africa.[29]

Bilateral trade between South Africa and China increased from $1.3 billion in 1995 to $25 billion by 2013.[30] China has become the biggest gold consumer in the world since 2013. Beijing has not only imported gold from South Africa, but also invested in the country's gold mines. The mining sector has been another key area for Tshwane in terms of increasing its bilateral cooperation with China, as indicated by the series of mining promotion events that South Africa has hosted in major Chinese cities (such as through Expo and the South Africa–China Mining Cooperation Forum, held respectively in Shanghai and Tianjin) since 2009.[31]

Inspired by China's success in reducing poverty and promoting economic growth, South Africa has also looked to Beijing for policy ideas in its own efforts to achieve growth and development.[32] In September 2008, officials of Johannesburg's Emergency Services, as part of their own preparations for the 2010 Football World Cup, visited Qingdao in Shandong province, exchanging expertise with the Firehouse Branch of the province's Public Security Department about the latter's safety and security work undertaken for the 2008 Olympic Games.[33] The first training programme of the National Executive Committee of the African National Congress was hosted in November 2009 by the Chinese Communist Party's Department of International Liaison, to exchange governance experience. Several groups comprising ANC National Executive Committee members have attended this training programme.[34] In 2013, there were 102 South African officials from various sectors being trained in China under a FOCAC platform, with two specific programmes – held at the request of the South African government – focused on textiles and apparel technology, as well as special economic zones.[35]

In sum, South Africa's expectations from its partnership with China have grown incrementally. The global financial crisis of 2008–2009 was a watershed in this regard. While business elites were quicker to identify their interests in China, South Africa's politicians – only since the global financial crisis – have gradually moved to focus on a comprehensive economic partnership with China (as well as with other new and emerging markets).

Interestingly, as earlier mentioned, South Africa's president Thabo Mbeki hoped to harness Sino–African cooperation to meet the demand for socio-economic development across the African continent. Zuma's ascent to power has not really changed this tendency, and very often South Africa's expectations of China have increased the awkwardness of this partnership, given South Africa's obvious need for external financing to realise its large continental ambitions. This mixing of South Africa's "China agenda" with its "African agenda" has been criticised for being too idealistic and for lacking in specificity as a practical roadmap.[36] However, realities on the ground have shown that there may not necessarily be a dilemma here. Beijing could, in fact, be pulled into deepening engagement with African institutions, including the Southern African Development Community (SADC) and the African Union (AU) (see Saunders and Nagar, and Maloka in this volume), as well as the New Partnership for Africa's Development (NEPAD). In June 2011, for example, China and SADC jointly hosted an economic and trade forum in Beijing, which was attended by Chinese vice-premier Wang Qishan.[37] According to Premier Wang, China's 12th five-year plan, starting from 2011, would provide support to SADC's South-North Economic Corridor plan, which aims to unlock the economic potential of landlocked countries in Southern and Eastern Africa by linking the port of Durban to the copperbelt in the Democratic Republic of the Congo (DRC) and Zambia, extending to the port of Dar es Salaam. The latest data from the United Nations Conference on Trade and Development (UNCTAD) show that China has become the largest investor in SADC, with $9.9 billion of a total of $13 billion in FDI coming from China in 2014.[38]

China's Evolving Expectations

The disappointment, or rather shock, that the post-apartheid South African government did not act immediately and decisively to recognise Beijing's "One China" policy, and switch diplomatic recognition from Taipei to

Beijing, has been written about extensively in Chinese scholarship. This shows that Chinese scholars may have failed to understand the complexity of South Africa's domestic social dynamics. Notwithstanding Tshwane's desire to present a moral persona in its foreign policy, the country's diplomatic relationships have been grounded in the pursuit of concrete national interests. Tshwane's "two-China dilemma" was not just a problem of finding a balance between moral image and pragmatism, but also a process full of delicate calculations about the extent to which Beijing and Taiwan could help to meet South Africa's immediate development needs.[39] The complexity of foreign policymaking in South Africa and of differences in the agendas pursued by various social groups, including the country's political and business elites, has been rather underestimated by Chinese scholars, who had forecast an immediate shift in South Africa's diplomatic recognition to Beijing from Taipei, based on the ANC's revolutionary history and historical ties with Beijing. For China, the establishment of formal diplomatic ties with the post-apartheid government was very important symbolically, with Beijing viewing it as a matter of political correctness rather than a pragmatic calculation.[40]

It is useful to trace the evolution of Chinese perceptions towards South Africa. Overall, even though South Africa holds a much larger share of Chinese trade than does the rest of the continent, Chinese scholarship on the country remains limited.[41] Data from the Chinese Network of Knowledge Infrastructure (CNKI)[42] – a comprehensive national digital library of journals and newspapers since the late 1980s – shows that there has been an upward trend in the total number of Chinese publications on, or about, South Africa since 1994. The birth of the "new" South Africa in that year was clearly a key moment in China, with the number of publications suddenly rising to 221 in 1994 compared to 112 in the previous year (see Table 17.1). There was another peak in interest in 2010, as Beijing sought to diversify its own markets in the aftermath of the global financial crisis of 2008–2009. This came at a time of numerous academic discussions and debates on the value of South Africa to China as a "gateway to Africa", although Chinese businesses on the ground were already expanding directly into other African countries. South Africa's political evolution has continued to be a primary focus in Chinese media and publications, although there has been a surge in interest in economic issues since the late 1990s. It is worth noting that there was no debate in either the mass media or academic publications on the controversial issue of South Africa joining the BRIC bloc, given that

Table 17.1   Numbers of Publications on South Africa in China, 1989–2014

1989	1990	1991	1992	1993	1994	1995	1996	1997	1998	1999	2000	2001
25	53	73	66	112	221	122	136	132	114	251	205	210
2002	2003	2004	2005	2006	2007	2008	2009	2010	2011	2012	2013	2014
304	324	332	387	472	461	331	457	913	540	451	504	360

Source: China National Knowledge Initiative (CNKI), http://epub.cnki.net/kns/brief/ default_result.aspx (accessed 3 January 2015).

South Africa's economic strength and capacity lagged far behind that of the other four members (see Virk in this volume).

Meanwhile, there were an estimated 300,000 to 400,000 Chinese citizens living in South Africa in 2014. The Chinese community in South Africa dates back to the late nineteenth century, with a fresh wave of Chinese immigrants arriving in South Africa beginning in the late 1980s – from the mainland, but also from other African countries such as Lesotho – forming the "new" Chinese community. As an immigration destination, South Africa had historically been a fourth choice, after Europe, the United States and Japan.[43] It was common for this first wave of Chinese immigrants to regard South Africa as a stepping stone to the US, which demanded greater skills and more financial resources as an emigration destination. However, as apartheid gave way to a multi-racial democracy in South Africa and the country opened up to the outside world, these Chinese immigrants increasingly found more business opportunities, as well as a more comfortable climate compared to their homeland. More Chinese chose to stay in South Africa, claiming either citizenship or permanent residence status.[44] Tshwane thereafter attracted an increasing number of individual Chinese traders, especially following the formalisation of the bilateral relationship in 1998. Since then, the unique market that these Chinese traders have identified has been the majority black population in order to take advantage of the low price of "made-in-China" everyday consumer goods, given that the traditional South African market had historically targeted mainly the minority white population. In the early 2000s, due to a lack of domestic industry, and as the South African economy continued to grow, the Chinese business community in the country also increased. While South African markets continued to dominate in urban areas, Chinese wholesale and retail traders flourished in the country's townships and rural areas, notwithstanding language and cultural barriers. In 2014, an estimated 30 per cent of the bilateral trade between South Africa and China was attributable to these private Chinese businesspeople, though this contribution has not been acknowledged by either government.[45]

While the South African government finally made the decision around 2008 to "look east" – to China in particular – for economic cooperation beyond trade, Chinese investors – drawing lessons from elsewhere in the world – were entering the African continent through mergers and looking to acquire more mines, gold mines specifically.[46] For Chinese companies, the South African market economy is more advanced than China's own in many respects, for it offers much value, such as an important export base, a regional headquarters, a model to learn from and a training ground for becoming globalised.[47] In various publications providing information about the South African market to the Chinese business sector, this value has been emphasised, including the mature international experiences of South African companies (see Vickers and Cawood in this volume). For example, in a publication from Chinese Food Business Net, South African supermarket chains – Shoprite, Pick n Pay, Spar and Woolworths – have been highly praised as successful models for Chinese businesses to adopt, while Chinese food companies have also been encouraged to use the established supermarket chains in South Africa to expand further into the country.[48] South Africa, with a more mature business environment compared to China, often becomes the latter's first choice destination in Africa, and training ground of how to do business in Africa. For example, Gold One International Limited, a gold mine located in Benoni, a small town in the eastern suburb of Johannesburg, and listed on the Australian and South African stock markets, was purchased by the Chinese in 2011, though it is operated at all levels by South Africans.[49]

Since 2008, many Chinese scholars, most prominently Justin Yifu Lin, former vice-president of the World Bank, have called for a shift in the focus of Chinese investment, with growing economic fatigue with Beijing's traditional partners (the US, Japan and the Europe Union), and argued that China needs to find new markets and new space to transfer labour-intensive manufactures for sustained growth. In July 2014, Lin led a group of entrepreneurs to visit several African countries and confidently confirmed that "African economic development is low on a global scale", making the continent "the ideal base" for this transfer.[50] However, long before this new movement, companies like Hisense – a leading Chinese household appliance industry – had already set up factories in Africa (in the case of Hisense, in South Africa's North-West province, in 1996).[51] Since 2003, when Chinese enterprises entered a new round of becoming internatio-nalised, South Africa, together with Singapore and Brazil, has been regarded as among the most important destinations for China to increase its investments.[52] The experience of First Chinese Automobile Works (FAW), for example, has encouraged more Chinese automobile companies to assemble first and then to manufacture in South Africa, taking advantage of Tshwane's trade agreements with the US and Europe to access those markets.[53]

Although South Africa experienced an economic slowdown between 2009 and 2017, Chinese businesses have continued to rate the country highly for its infrastructure and remained keen to invest in the country (compared with other African countries). In addition, more private Chinese businesses have turned to South Africa as labour costs in China have increased. Some Chinese businesses – such as Apollo Solar Water Heater – have also benefited from South Africa's policy shift to a green economy. South Africa's National Development Plan (NDP) of 2013 has also been widely regarded as an opportunity for Chinese businesses to expand into the country, due to South Africa's emphasis on infrastructure construction and diversifying its mining-dominant economy, which matches exactly the knowledge and skills that Chinese companies have to offer.[54]

The Chinese presence in South Africa is still relatively new, and South African stakeholders have expressed controversial opinions about this presence. The Chinese government, however, has reacted calmly to criticism of its presence. One example is the area of anti-dumping measures. By the end of 2009, South Africa had initiated 43 cases of anti-dumping investigations against Chinese products, the largest number of investigations undertaken by any African country.[55] With China a newcomer to the international market, Chinese businesses view anti-dumping measures as an irritant and hindrance, and some are not even aware of the problem, let alone responsive to charges of dumping. However, through the websites of both the Chinese embassy in South Africa and its trade ministry in Beijing, other than presenting basic information about regulations in South Africa and international norms against dumping, the Chinese government has been encouraging its companies to accept South Africa's anti-dumping measures as part-and-parcel of the experience of going global, and part of an unavoidable learning curve, especially in export-dependent sectors.

In 2007, the Chinese Ministry of Commerce (MOFCOM) published a country report on South Africa that identified a number of concerns for

Chinese business prospects in, and with, the country, including a lack of transparency in government procurement processes; an emphasis on added value so as to limit the export of some expensive and raw materials; violations related to intellectual property; business ownership require-ments under the Black Economic Empowerment (BEE) Act; the slow speed of visa processes; and security concerns. Some of these barriers are due to a lack of knowledge and inefficient communication and are being addressed, but personal security has been a growing concern that may divert further Chinese investment away from South Africa.[56] Guidance on overcoming these barriers, though imprecise and superficial, has been published publicly through the MOFCOM website, and widely used by the Chinese business sector.

Concluding Reflections: Whither South Africa–China Relations?

All too often, China's cooperation with African countries – including its "comprehensive strategic partnership" with South Africa – has been perceived cynically as an asymmetrical game. As far back as the 1960s, when China began building the Tan–Zam Railway (linking Tanzania and Zambia),[57] Tanzania's Julius Nyerere called it "a friendship between the most unequal equals". As new and emerging powers such as China rise in the global South, what will South-South cooperation mean? Will China and the other "new" powers forge relations with developing countries that are different from those with the existing great powers? To answer these questions, especially with regard to South Africa–China relations, more comprehensive and historically grounded knowledge will be needed to understand the nuance and true nature of these new types of South-South cooperation.

Notwithstanding differences in expectations and mutual misunder-standing of their respective contexts, cooperation between South Africa and China has expanded quickly, both bilaterally and multilaterally. The history of solidarity between the ANC and China played a key role in laying the foundation for the gradual blossoming of the increasingly comprehensive bilateral cooperation. The Pretoria Declaration of 2007 identified mutual trust and strategic consultation as the most important basis for the bilateral relationship[58] – a widely held Chinese perception already in evidence based on Chinese scholarship. While China seemingly has made every effort to nurture this partnership based on a sense of historical South-South solidarity, and to forge a different world order jointly (such as helping South Africa join the BRIC bloc in April 2011), it has been rather dependent on the weaker side of the partnership to harness it. The case of Libya in 2011, when South Africa broke ranks from the rest of the BRICS in voting in favour of UN Security Council Resolution 1973 sanctioning military intervention in the country, showed the extent to which the partnership is still new and vulnerable to influences from powerful Western countries (US president Barack Obama had reportedly called President Jacob Zuma to support the resolution; see Weissman in this volume).[59] For both China and South Africa, learning how to balance between considerations of *realpolitik* and their long-term visions of their own positions in the world remains a major challenge that scholars and think tanks in both countries can help to address through active debates.

Notes

1. *See* Sanusha Naidu, "Balancing a Strategic Partnership? South Africa–China Relations", in Kweku Ampiah and Sanusha Naidu (eds), *Crouching Tiger, Hidden Dragon? Africa and China* (Scottsville: University of KwaZulu-Natal (UKZN) Press, 2008), pp. 167–191.

2. *See* Talitha Bertelsmann-Scott, "South Africa and the EU: Where Lies the Strategic Partnership?", in Adekeye Adebajo and Kaye Whiteman (eds), *The EU and Africa: From Eurafrique to Afro-Europa* (London: Hurst; and Johannesburg: Wits University Press, 2012), pp. 121–135; Vladimir G. Shubin, *The Hot "Cold War"* (London: Pluto; and Scottsville: UKZN Press, 2008).

3. Naidu, "Balancing a Strategic Partnership?", p. 186.

4. Adam Habib showed a balanced attitude of cautious optimism towards Chinese engagement with South Africa, which the Chinese thought different from the American approach yet also conditioned by the game decided by the United States (US) on the world stage, therefore threatening South African interests in the long term; *see* Naidu, "Balancing a Strategic Partnership?"; and Adam Habib, "Western Hegemony, Asian Ascendancy and the New Scramble for Africa", in Ampiah and Naidu, *Crouching Tiger, Hidden Dragon?*, pp. 259–227. On the other hand, a more critical perspective about China's engagement with South Africa does exist, and the latest trend of this school has been about Chinese traders, focusing on their distrust, fear and alienation with local society, and pointing out that in the long term, their presence could result in an unpredictable future for the bilateral relationship; *see* Terence McNamee (with Greg Mills, Sebabatso Manoeli, Masana Mulaudzi, Stuart Doran and Emma Chen), "Africa in Their Words: A Study of Chinese Traders in South Africa, Lesotho, Botswana, Zambia, and Angola", discussion paper (Johannesburg: Brenthurst Foundation, March 2012), http://www.thebrenthurstfoundation.org/a_sndmsg/news_view.asp?I=124294&PG = 288 (accessed 2 January 2015).

5. Yang Lihua, "China's Strategic Choice for Establishing Diplomatic Relations with South Africa", pt. 2, *West Asia and Africa* no. 10 (2007), pp. 51–55.

6. Data from China's Ministry of Commerce (MOFCOM), http://en.cnki.com.cn/Article_en/CJFDTOTAL-XYFZ199905006.htm (accessed 19 September 2016).

7. Qian Qichen, *Waijiao Shi Ji (Ten Diplomatic Episodes)* (Beijing: Shijie Zhishi Xhubanshe, 2003), pp. 267–268.

8. Qian, *Waijiao Shi Ji*, p. 268.

9. Qian, *Waijiao Shi Ji*, p. 277.

10. Yang, "China's Strategic Choice", pt. 1., p. 16.

11. "Jiang Zemin and Mbeki Jointly Opened the First Meeting of BNC", *Xinhua*, 10 December 2001, http://news.xinhuanet.com/news/2001-12/10/content_156128.htm (accessed 30 December 2014).

12. Feng Difan, "Zuma Visits China with an Unprecedented Big Business Delegation", *China Business News*, 25 August 2010, http://finance.jrj.com.cn/2010/08/2502418016364.shtml (accessed 16 October 2014); "Chinese Ambassador Said, to Address the Imbalanced Trade Is the Most Important Task of Zuma's Visit", *People's Network*, 14 September 2014.

13. Economic Observation, "Snow Beer Estimates to Reach 25 per cent Market Share by the End of 2014", *Guangming Daily*, http://9.gmw.cn/2014-09/17/content_13261026.htm (accessed 20 December 2014).

14. Faeeza Ballim, "South Africa and China in Awkward Embrace", *Mail and Guardian*, 20 July 2012, http://mg.co.za/article/2012-07-19-south-africa-and-china-in-awkward-embrace (accessed 2 August 2014).

15. "Hu Jintao Held Meeting with Zuma", *Xinhua*, 18 July 2012, http://news.xinhuanet.com/politics/2012-07/18/c_112471371.htm (accessed 16 October 2014).

16. MOFCOM, *South Africa Country Report* no. 1 (2007). *See also* Yun Sun, "Africa in China's Foreign Policy" (Washington, DC: Brookings Institution, April 2014), p. 14, https://www.brookings.edu/wp-content/uploads/2016/06/Africa-in-China-web_CMG7.pdf (accessed 19 September 2016).

17. Johann van Eeden and Taku Fundira, "South African Quotas on Chinese Clothing and Textiles: 18 Month Economic Review", Working Paper no. 8 (Cape Town: Trade Law Centre (Tralac), 2008). http://www.tralac.org/cause_data/images/1694/WP200808VEedenClothingTextile18mnth20081111.pdf (accessed 31 December 2014).

18. China Textile Net, "Setting Quota to Chinese Textile Import Has Promoted Domestic Stakeholder Cooperation", 1 June 2007, http://info.texnet.com.cn/content/2007-06-01/108765.html (accessed 31 August 2014).

19. "South Africa Retailers Hit by 'Imports Treason' Claim", *Financial Times*, 12 September 2006, http://www.ftchinese.com/story/001006762/ce (accessed 2 September 2014).

20. For the MOFCOM announcement, *see* "Announcement of 2006 (on Item Names of Related Textile Products, Tax Numbers of South Africa, Management Duration, and Related Regulations)", http://www.customs.gov.cn/publish/portal0/tab2752/info34899.htm (accessed 16 October 2014). *See also* "South Africa Delays Imposing Quota on Chinese Textiles", 15 September 2006, http://www.china.org.cn/english/international/181219.htm (accessed 16 October 2014).

21. Mike Morris and Lyn Reed, "Review of the Impact of the China Restraint Agreement on the Clothing and Textile Industry in South Africa", research report (Cape Town: School of Economics, University of Cape Town, November 2008), http://www.cssr.uct.ac.za/publications/research-report/2008/review-impact-china-restraint-agreement (accessed 1 August 2014).

22. Shen Zejin, "South Africa Launched South Africa–China Trade and Investment Promotion Month Activity", 6 July 2010, http://district.ce.cn/zg/201007/06/t20100706_21585489.shtml (accessed 16 October 2014).

23. Government of South Africa, Economic Development Department, *Economic Development Department Annual Report 2009/10*, 2010, p. 39, http://www.economic.gov.za/communications/annual-reports (accessed 3 October 2014).

24. Yang Lihua, *Guide to the World States: South Africa* (Beijing: Social Sciences Academic Press, 2010), pp. 510–513.

25. Organisation for Economic Cooperation and Development (OECD), "South Africa", in *OECD Tourism Trends and Policies 2014*, http://dx.doi.org/10.1787/tour-2014-55-en (accessed 31 December 2014).

26. South African Department of Communication, "Tourism", *South African Yearbook 2002–03*, p. 581.

27. South African Department of Communication, "Tourism", *South African Yearbook 2013–14*, p. 582, http://www.gcis.gov.za/content/resource-centre/sa-info/yearbook/2013-14 (accessed 31 December 2014).

28. In July 2014, I was invited to speak about China–Africa relations on a large scale at South African Airways' (SAA) promotion activity in Beijing. Airline tickets between South Africa and China, and South African wines, were given to Chinese customers through lucky draws, and the number of participants was huge. *See also* Jing Shengxian, "Chinese Tourists Market in South African Eyes", *Review of China Development* no. 7 (2005), pp. 49–52.

29. South African Department of Communication, "Tourism", *South African Yearbook 2013–14*, p. 381.

30. "South Africa's Trade with China Surges by 32 pct in 2013", *China Daily*, 13 March 2014, http://www.chinadaily.com.cn/business/2014-03/13/content_17343780.htm (accessed 30 December 2014).

31. Lswfm, "South African Mining Projects Coming to China to Attract Investment", 22 November 2010, http://original.10s1.com/ArticleShow.aspx?ID=159111 (accessed 30 December 2014).

32. Ballim, "South Africa and China in Awkward Embrace".

33. "South African Officials Came to Seek for Safety and Security Experiences", 18 September 2008, http://119.china.com.cn/ywxf/txt/2008-09/28/content_2500128.htm (accessed 2 August 2014).

34. "Li Yuanchao Met with South African Guests", *People's Daily*, 24 November 2009, http://paper.people.com.cn/rmrb/html/2009-11/24/nw.D110000renmrb_20091124_6-03.htm?div=-1 (accessed 4 November 2014); Xu Can, "Meng Jianzhu Met with ANC National Executive Committee Training Programme", 13 July 2013, http://www.mps.gov.cn/n16/n1237/n1357/3842108.html (accessed 16 October 2014).

35. Economic and Commercial Counsellor's Office, Embassy of China in South Africa, "Reception for South African Participants in China's 2013 Training Programs", 26 November 2013, http://za.mofcom.gov.cn/article/h/201311/20131100403659.shtml (accessed 16 October 2014).

36. Naidu, "Balancing a Strategic Partnership?".

37. "China-SADC Herald Year of Dragon", *International Business Daily*, 19 March 2012, http://www.shangbao.net.cn/zuhe/special/d/87236.html (accessed 16 October 2014).

38. Yu Shuaishuai, Li Xiaopeng and Wang Yue, "Africa Looks East, and Chinese Capitals Join in 'South-North Economic Corridor' Program", *Jingji Cankao Bao* (Economic Information), 19 August 2014, http://www.jjckb.cn/2014-08/19/content_517488.htm (accessed 28 December 2014).

39. Garth le Pere, "The Geo-Strategic Dimensions of the Sino-African Relationship", in Ampiah and Naidu, *Crouching Tiger, Hidden Dragon?*, pp. 20–38; Naidu, "Balancing a Strategic Partnership?".

40. Greg Mills, "The Case for Exclusive Recognition", in South African Institute of International Affairs (SAIIA) Research Group (ed.), *South Africa and the Two Chinas Dilemma* (Johannesburg: SAIIA, 1995).

41. For example, searching the China National Knowledge Initiative (CNKI) database for "United States" and "Europe", in 1994, reveals total numbers of 13,930 and 2,408, respectively, of combined journal articles, PhD and MA theses, conference papers and articles from core newspapers; in 2010, the total numbers are 60,131 and 10,807. In contrast, searching for "South Africa" reveals numbers of only 221 and 913 in 1994 and 2010 respectively. *See* the CNKI website, http://www.cnki.net (accessed 3 January 2015).

42. The CNKI database includes the following sub-databases: "China Academic Journals", 1994 onwards, "China Doctoral Dissertations"; 1984, "China Masters' Theses", 1984; "China Proceedings of Conference", 1953 onwards; "International Proceedings of Conference", 1981 onwards; "China Core Newspapers", 2000 onwards; "China Yearbooks", 1949 onwards. *See* http://oversea.cnki.net/kns55 (accessed 31 December 2014).

43. Personal interviews with the first batch of Chinese immigrants from mainland China – Gao Guoqiang, Si Hai, Han Fang and Wang Guoqing – Johannesburg, 31 August–4 September 2014.

44. Personal interviews with the first batch of Chinese immigrants, Johannesburg, 31 August–12 September 2014.

45. Personal interview with Yang Peidong, China's vice-consul-general in Johannesburg, 6 September 2014.

46. Wang Lin, "South African Mining Thieves Disclosed the Map Showing How Many That Chinese Enterprises Have Acquired", 18 February 2014, http://www.yicai.com/news/2014/02/3475513.html (accessed 30 December 2014).

47. Ren Peiqiang, "South Africa: Gateway to Invest in Sub-Sahara Africa – A Field Investigation to the Chinese Companies Investing in South Africa", *Journal of International Economic Cooperation*, 20 April 2013.

48. Ma Xiaochun and Li Xiande, "Country Report on Opportunities of Chinese Agricultural Products: South Africa", 7 February 2007, http://www.21food.cn/html/news/12/107341.htm (accessed 16 October 2014).

49. I visited the mine in 2012. The South African staff had not yet seen, or met, the new owners. This shows that the Chinese – given their lack of expertise in local mining operations – prefer to invest only money, while leaving all the technological and managerial tasks to South Africans. It is possible that miners and lower-level managers were not even aware of the change in ownership. The buyers are China International Trust and Investment Corporation Group (CITIC), China African Development Fund (CADF) and Long March Capital Group.

50. "Justin Yifu Lin Leads Chinese Business Delegation to Examine Africa's Investment Environment", 2 September 2014, http://english.pku.edu.cn/News_Events/News/Global/11570.htm (accessed 3 December 2014).

51. "Made-in-China Helps African Industrialization: Chinese Manufactories Enter Africa", *People's Daily*, 27 December 2011, http://www.fmprc.gov.cn/zflt/chn/zxxx/t891210.htm (accessed 6 October 2014).

52. Li Zhongmin, "Chinese Enterprises Steered at the Fast Track of Internationaliza-tion", *China First Financial Daily*, 25 October 2011.

53. Economic and Commercial Counsellor's Office, Embassy of China in South Africa, "Status Quo of Automobile Industry in South Africa", 1 February 2007, http://www.csc.mofcom.gov.cn/article/csacsbdt/200702/62013_1.html (accessed 6 October 2014).

54. Cheng Hui, "Sino–South African Cooperation Enters New Channel", *China Economic Herald*, 28 March 2013.

55. Tong Shenghua, "What Should Be Done to Export to South Africa?", http://www.tbtmap.cn/portal/Contents/Channel_2125/2010/0723/107291/content_107291.jsf?ztid=2169 (accessed 6 October 2014).

56. MOFCOM, "Report on Environment of Trade and Investment in South Africa", 26 September 2007, http://win.mofcom.gov.cn/alert/2007ch.pdf (accessed 16 October 2014).

57. *See* Muna Ndulo, "Chinese Investments in Africa: A Case Study of Zambia", pp. 138–151; and Mwesiga Baregu, "The Three Faces of the Dragon: Tanzania-China Relations in Historical Perspective", pp. 152–166, both in Ampiah and Naidu, *Crouching Tiger, Hidden Dragon?*

58. Joint Communiqué Between the People's Republic of China and the Republic of South Africa, Tshwane, 6 February 2007, http://durban.china-consulate.org/eng/zt/zfgx/t387485.htm (accessed 16 October 2014).

59. At the BRICS (Brazil, Russia, India, China and South Africa) Sanya summit in April 2011, for example, South African president Jacob Zuma expressed appreciation for the alignment of China's policy with the African Union's position on the Libya issue. *See* "Hu Jintao Met with Zuma", 13 April 2011, http://politics.people.com.cn/GB/1024/14384660.html (accessed 2 January 2015).

PART V

SOUTH AFRICA'S KEY EXTERNAL MULTILATERAL RELATIONS

CHAPTER 18

SOUTH AFRICA AND THE UNITED NATIONS

Doctor Mashabane

Since its readmission to the United Nations (UN) in 1994, South Africa has been an active, reliable and responsible member of the world body. The country's foreign policy reaffirms the centrality of the UN in multilateralism and global governance, and places multilateralism at the centre of Tshwane's (Pretoria) relationship and cooperation with other states. South Africa's return to the United Nations was celebrated by the general membership as the institution's victory over the system of racial discrimination and apartheid.[1] The UN itself had been seized with the situation of South Africa and its policy of apartheid between 1948 and 1994. It was therefore natural that the world body would be at the centre of the promotion of a democratic South Africa's foreign policy after 1994.

South Africa joined the UN at a critical juncture in world history, with the Cold War having just ended. There were great expectations that with South Africa having been a product of international solidarity and the UN having been the centre of gravity in the struggle against apartheid, the country would lead efforts against violations of human rights around the world. The UN is founded on three pillars: peace and security, human rights, and development. The related pillars will be discussed in this chapter and cannot exist in isolation of each other. South Africa, with its capacity as a middle-income country, took up various leadership roles in these areas at the UN after 1994.[2]

South Africa and the UN's Peace and Security Mandate

The mandate to deal with matters of international peace and security is vested in the 15-member United Nations Security Council, which is the principal UN organ in this area. The Security Council is the only UN body whose decisions are legally binding on all its 193 member states. In the past few decades, many of the conflicts that the UN Security Council has dealt with have occurred in Africa. The outbreak of a civil war in the Democratic Republic of the Congo (DRC) by 1996 attracted the attention of the Council. South Africa was involved in regional efforts to resolve the conflict and subsequently deployed troops there as part of a UN peacekeeping mission from 2000. It also led an African Union (AU) peacekeeping mission to Burundi in 2003, which the UN took over – "re-hatting" the regional peacekeepers – a year later. The conflict and war in Sudan, particularly in Darfur (where South Africa deployed troops in 2004 under an AU mission), has continued to be a major item on the Security Council's agenda in the past two decades. (See Curtis, and Naidoo in this volume on South Africa's peacekeeping efforts.) The situation in Somalia has similarly remained on the agenda of the Security Council, though the Council was unwilling to deploy a United Nations peacekeeping mission there to replace the AU mission. The situations in Côte d'Ivoire, Sierra Leone and Liberia were also part of the Council's agenda.[3]

In 2006, for the first time ever since 1945, South Africa was elected by members of the UN General Assembly to serve as a non-permanent member of the Security Council for a two-year term from 2007 to 2008. By this time, Tshwane had earned its stripes in the United Nations for its peacemaking role in conflicts in Lesotho, the DRC and Burundi. South Africa's non-permanent membership in the Security Council was motivated by its desire to contribute to the peaceful resolution of conflicts in Africa and the world. This was also an opportunity to advance one of Tshwane's foreign policy pillars: the promotion of the African Agenda (see Maloka in this volume). No doubt membership of the Council was further meant to strengthen the case for South Africa's capacity, readiness and willingness to serve as a permanent member in a reformed UN Security Council should the continent decide to nominate South Africa. Membership in the Security Council by its nature puts any country with leadership ambitions in pole position. But this comes with heavy responsibilities and demands that place a toll on a country's resources and test its independence of great powers, given the complex decisions that have to be taken. Some of the decisions may also not be popular with different constituencies nationally. With South Africa's experience of a peaceful transition from white minority apartheid rule to a majority-ruled constitutional democracy, there were widespread expectations in 1994 of the country contributing to the resolution of global conflicts. However, the current configuration of the UN Security Council – dominated by the veto-wielding permanent five (P-5) members: the United States (US), Russia, China, France and Britain – makes it extremely difficult for the ten non-permanent members to have a great impact on decision-making during their two-year terms.[4] Even so, with about 60 per cent of the Security Council's agenda typically focusing on Africa, South Africa felt that it had to be at the forefront of efforts to champion African positions on peace and security issues.

One of the most important legacies of South Africa's membership in the Security Council is the strengthening of the relationship between the United Nations and the African Union. Chapter VIII of the UN Charter of 1945 provides for cooperation between the UN Security Council and regional organisations like the AU when dealing with issues relating to the maintenance of international peace and security.[5] The African Union is one of few regional organisations around the world with a comprehensive peace and security architecture. It also deals with almost all the African issues on the agenda of the Security Council, making it logical for the Council to cooperate and collaborate with the AU. In 2008, South Africa organised a Security Council open debate on Chapter VIII of the UN Charter, on dealing with cooperation between the UN and regional organisations – and in this case the African Union – which was presided over by South African president Thabo Mbeki. The debate led to the Council's adoption of Resolution 1809, a groundbreaking decision that – for the first time in its history – institutionalised the relationship between the UN and the AU on the maintenance of international peace and security.[6] Additionally, Resolution 1809 introduced annual consultations between the 15-member African Union Peace and Security Council and the 15-member UN Security Council, with meetings rotating between Addis Ababa and New York. These meetings now occur annually.

In October 2010, after a two-year hiatus, South Africa was re-elected to the Security Council by an overwhelming number of members of the UN General Assembly, obtaining 184 out of 193 votes. South Africa's re-election within two years of leaving the Security Council was a strong affirmation of the international community's confidence in the country.

This vote was also perceived by Tshwane as a form of appreciation of South Africa's contributions to the Council during its first tenure, in 2007–2008, particularly on issues affecting the global South in general and Africa in particular. South Africa sought in its second term to continue to focus on resolving African conflicts and on reforming the working methods of the Security Council.[7] Although the reform of the Council was not discussed within the body itself – except for its working methods – the presence of countries like South Africa in the Security Council in 2011–2012 alongside Brazil, India and Nigeria challenged the unsustainability of the Council's current anachronistic configuration (I was fortunate to have served as South Africa's deputy permanent representative at the UN during this second stint). There was an expectation of possible collaboration between South Africa and Nigeria, as both sought to project their commitment and abilities to promote African interests on the Council.[8] In the end, this collaboration was selective. South Africa and Nigeria held the same position on the question of Western Sahara, strengthening the African Union Mission in Somalia (AMISOM) and support to the United Nations/African Union Mission in Darfur (UNAMID), but had sharp differences on the approach to the situation in Côte d'Ivoire after the 2010 disputed elections. (See Adebajo in this volume.)

In January 2012, in order to advance its African Agenda during its UN Security Council presidency, South Africa organised another open debate on cooperation between the African Union and the UN Security Council. The debate was presided over by South Africa's president, Jacob Zuma, and the Council adopted Resolution 2033 following the discussions.[9] The adoption of this resolution followed the Security Council-authorised North Atlantic Treaty Organisation (NATO) intervention in Libya in 2011, which had ignored the efforts of the African Union and its roadmap for the peaceful resolution of the conflict.[10] Resolution 2033, which was built on and deepened the foundation laid earlier by Resolution 1809, called for closer collaboration between the AU Peace and Security Council and the UN Security Council on African issues. The resolution also addressed the funding and logistical challenges of African peacekeeping operations. South Africa stressed the importance for the UN Security Council to take into account the views of the African Union when dealing with the maintenance of international peace and security issues in Africa. Resolution 2033 further called on the UN Security Council to take into account African perspectives and to exchange views on conflicts on the continent.

The impact and the significance of UN Security Council Resolution 2033 was confirmed in May 2012 when the Council adopted Resolution 2046, on the situation between Sudan and South Sudan, endorsing the recommendations of the AU Peace and Security Council.[11] This was a major break from the past practices of the Security Council, in particular the practices of its veto-wielding permanent members who otherwise continued to insist that the Security Council was independent from regional organisations and had the primary responsibility for the maintenance of international peace and security. The reality, however, was that the UN Security Council had little or no role at all to play in the situation between Sudan and South Sudan, other than passing presidential statements and issuing press releases. Later, in December 2012, the UN Security Council similarly adopted a resolution on the African-led International Support Mission in Mali (AFISMA) – Resolution 2085 – at the request of the AU Peace and Security Council following the recommendation of the Economic Community of West African States (ECOWAS).[12] Throughout both of its Security Council tenures, in 2007–2008 and 2011–2012, South Africa sought to be guided by the positions and decisions of the African Union and its Peace and Security Council, where such decisions and positions existed. In 2012, all the African countries on the UN Security Council at the time – Nigeria, Gabon and South Africa – voted in favour of Resolution 1973, regarding the issue of Libya as presented to the Council by the League of Arab States as an Arab regional matter. Libya is a member of both the African Union and the League of Arab States, and the primary challenge with Resolution 1973 was not mainly its adoption but its implementation and the motives behind its main sponsors, mainly NATO countries, led by France and Britain.

One of the principles guiding South Africa's foreign policy at the United Nations is respect for, and observation of, international law and the rule of law. When NATO forces in Libya started abusing the mandate of Resolution 1973, pursuing an agenda of "regime change" beyond the ambit of the UN Security Council's authorisation, South Africa was at the forefront of challenging NATO's actions and calling for a peaceful resolution to the conflict. NATO hijacked the implementation of the resolution, and went beyond its provisions in furtherance of its parochial political agenda. Tshwane had included a paragraph in Resolution 1973 calling for a political process to resolve the conflict peacefully and to take into account the African Union roadmap for ending the crisis.[13] South

Africa consistently challenged what it considered to be NATO's violation of international law. The Anglo-French-led actions in Libya were also a violation of the rule of law at the international level, since these actions went beyond the authorisation of Resolution 1973. When France – one of the five permanent members of the Security Council – started supplying arms to civilians and rebels in Libya in direct contradiction of the Security Council resolution it had approved, South Africa warned of the adverse consequences of the flow of arms into the volatile Sahel region. Under the presidency of South Africa in January 2012, the Council adopted a presidential statement on the rule of law.[14] While permanent members – the US, France and Britain – were concerned about the rule of law only at the national level, South Africa insisted that the rule of law should also be observed at the international level.

When the UN Security Council started dealing with the situation in Syria in March 2012, South Africa advocated a political solution to the conflict rather than a military one. Due to the experience with Resolution 1973 on Libya, there was, and continued to be, gridlock in the Security Council in 2013. Western members of the Council – Washington, London and Paris – pushed for action and called for Syrian leader Bashar al-Assad to step down. Tshwane called for a peaceful resolution of the conflict and, together with India and Brazil, sent a deputation of envoys – South Africa's deputy minister for international relations and cooperation, Ebrahim Ebrahim; Brazil's sub-secretary for Middle East issues, Paula Cordeiro; and India's foreign ministry additional secretary Dillip Sinha – to Damascus in August 2011 to impress on the al-Assad government the need for political reforms and for the cessation of violence and military action against civilians. South Africa also opposed attempts by the Security Council to usurp the mandates of the other principal organs and bodies of the United Nations such as the General Assembly and the Economic and Social Council (ECOSOC).

UN Peacekeeping

South Africa is not among the larger United Nations troop-contributing countries. As of September 2016, it was among the top 20 peacekeepers globally and the top 13 in Africa, with 2,226 troops deployed to UN peacekeeping missions.[15] However, Tshwane plays a strategic role in UN peacekeeping. South Africa is an active member of the UN Special Committee on Peacekeeping Operations, which is responsible for developing policies and doctrines for UN peacekeeping operations. South Africa's participation in UN peacekeeping operations has been informed by the country's experience in conflict resolution.[16] (See Curtis in this volume.) Tshwane has consistently advocated supporting, strengthening and enhancing the African Union's peacekeeping operations, as well as the UN's missions in Africa. Of the world body's $8.3 billion peacekeeping budget in 2015/2016, about $6 billion was spent in Africa. The major challenge facing AU peacekeeping operations is a lack of resources, both financial and logistical. As a member of the UN Security Council in 2007–2008 and 2011–2012, South Africa sought to address the issue of funding of African peacekeeping operations. Tshwane consistently argued that UN peacekeeping has an important role to play in creating an environment conducive for political processes, and that this represents a means to an end and not an end in itself. Peacekeeping must thus complement political efforts towards the peaceful resolution of conflicts. Given the high number of incidents of violence and rape of civilians in areas where the UN has deployed peacekeeping missions, Tshwane has supported the inclusion of the protection of civilians as part of the mandate of UN peacekeeping missions.

South Africa believes in an active role for UN peacekeeping missions based on a holistic approach, rather than a passive one that narrowly focuses only on keeping peace without regard for the broader context. This is why Tshwane, together with members of the Southern African Development Community (SADC), called for a more active and enhanced role for the United Nations Organisation Stabilisation Mission in the Democratic Republic of the Congo (MONUSCO) in 2013 to deal with the challenges posed by armed militia groups in the eastern Congo. The 21,219-strong UN peacekeeping mission in the DRC was at the time the world's largest UN peacekeeping operation, yet there have been widespread violations of human rights and international humanitarian law by armed groups and militias that have resulted in the massive displacement of civilians, while over three million people have died since 1997. The actions of March 23 Movement (M23) rebels prompted an active effort by South Africa and SADC to change MONUSCO's mandate to include peace enforcement. This led to the UN Security Council creating a 3,000-strong Force Intervention Brigade (FIB) within MONUSCO in March 2013. South Africa demonstrated its commitment to the force by contributing a battalion, with Tanzania and Malawi also deploying troops to the intervention force. While Tshwane acknowledged the role of the UN

Security Council in crafting mandates for UN peacekeeping operations, it also insisted on the need for consultation between the UN Security Council and troop-contributing countries when renewing and adding new mandates to peacekeeping operations. As a clear vote of confidence on South Africa's leadership role in conflict prevention, resolution and management and in peace operations in general, South Africa's General Derrick Mgwebi was appointed the Force Commander of MONUSCO in December 2015.

Reform of the UN Security Council

In a 1993 article in *Foreign Affairs* outlining the future of South Africa's foreign policy, Nelson Mandela emphasised the pivotal role of the United Nations in fostering global security and order.[17] South Africa's first post-apartheid president further noted that serious attention must be paid to reforming the organisation, and committed South Africa to playing a vigorous role in this effort. True to this commitment, President Mandela pushed consistently for UN reform, particularly of its Security Council.[18] The current configuration of the 15-member UN Security Council is undemocratic and unrepresentative, and still reflects the global realities at the end of World War II in 1945.

South Africa has supported the Common African Position, as contained in the 2005 Ezulwini Consensus and the 2006 Sirte Declaration.[19] The Ezulwini Consensus was a strategic negotiating framework informed by conditions and developments at the time of its adoption, but not meant to be rigid. It is clear that developments of the past decade require that tactics be developed to strengthen the Ezulwini Consensus in order to move the reform debate forward and deliver on some tangible outcomes. The idea of a common African position on reform of the UN Security Council remains noble to the extent that it does not itself become a stumbling block to progress due to an insistence on two veto-wielding permanent seats for Africa to add to its existing three rotating seats. All the different blocs from other regions that are sympathetic to Africa always note that there are complex geo-political realties that make it impossible to support the African approach. Washington has made it clear that it supports modest reform of the UN Security Council but would not like to see the current veto configuration tampered with. The reality is that the majority of P-5 members all subscribe to the US position. This means that, as long as Africa – in terms of the Ezulwini Consensus – continues to insist that the veto should be extended to new permanent members, there will be no movement on the reform debate in the next three decades. Many African states, including South Africa and Nigeria, are aware of this reality – that the Ezulwini Consensus presents challenges that Africans themselves must confront in an open and frank manner. The biggest question will be whether Africa is better off not having permanent representation that lacks veto privileges. Given the mandate of the UN Security Council to safeguard international peace and security, the body must reflect the global realities of the twenty-first century. As earlier noted, about 60 per cent of the discussions of the Security Council focus on African issues, yet Africa has no permanent representation on the body, and the Council takes critical decisions on behalf of Africa and on African issues as if Africans have no capacity to contribute to these decisions.

The debate surrounding reform of the UN Security Council has continued for more than two decades, and clearly the Council's five permanent veto-wielding members (the US, Russia, China, Britain and France) are not keen on reforming the Council, regardless of their public utterances. The Security Council, however, must be reformed so as not to lose its legitimacy. The UN is over seven decades old, and its membership has quadrupled since 1945. Yet its most powerful organ has remained largely unchanged.[20] If two permanent seats in a reformed Security Council were to be allocated to Africa (to add to its three rotating non-permanent seats), the continent's record and commitment to the maintenance of international peace and security would be a primary consideration. The primary focus of Africa should therefore be to push for reform of the Security Council, rather than squabbling over which country should represent Africa in the permanent category. Serving in the UN Security Council entails great responsibility, and comes with certain obligations and attached political costs. Both times that South Africa served on the Security Council (2007–2008 and 2011–2012), Tshwane established its credentials and proved its ability to advance and defend Africa's interests and those of the developing world. The country acted independently, without bowing to the pressure and dictates of the great powers on the Council.

Development

South Africa has emphasised the importance of development to the work of the United Nations, particularly given the nexus between development and security. Even though the UN was created in the aftermath of World War II (1939–1945), its Charter clearly recognises the significance of economic and social development.[21] In the past two decades, South Africa has been elected twice to serve as a member of the UN's Economic and Social Council, first from 2004 to 2006 and then from 2013 to 2015. Tshwane has used its ECOSOC membership to advance Africa's interests and those of the developing world, continuing to call for the reform of the two main international financial institutions – the World Bank and the International Monetary Fund (IMF). South Africa has also called for closer cooperation between these institutions and ECOSOC. After the adoption of the New Partnership for Africa's Development (NEPAD) in 2001, as the economic and social development blueprint of the African Union (see Maloka in this volume), South Africa, with other African founding members Nigeria, Egypt, Algeria and Senegal, introduced a resolution on NEPAD at the UN General Assembly in August 2012.[22] NEPAD is now streamlined into the United Nations as a basic framework to guide the world body's work on development issues in Africa. The UN General Assembly is required to meet annually for a debate to review implementation of NEPAD (the influence of the South Africa-based NEPAD has, however, declined in recent years, as donors have failed to deliver on their commitments to fund its development programmes). Morocco is a member of the UN's 54-strong African Group and rejoined the African Union in February 2017. Western Sahara's Polisario Front is a member of the AU but not of the UN's African Group. The newly created state of South Sudan joined both the AU and the UN's African Group. Tshwane has continued to argue that Africa should be at the centre of the UN's development programmes, given its special development needs.[23] Out of the 47 UN member states classified as least developed countries (LDCs) in 2017, more than 30 are from Africa. This constitutes a more than two-thirds majority of all African states. South and Central America as a region has only Haiti classified as an LDC, while the Asia and the Pacific region has 13 LDCs.[24]

South Africa hosted the UN Conference on Sustainable Development in Johannesburg in September 2002. One of the key outcomes of the summit was integration of the three pillars of sustainable development: economic, social and environmental. Tshwane argued that poverty eradication should be at the centre of sustainable development, as opposed to being solely preoccupied with the environment. The adoption of an action plan at the Johannesburg summit – agreeing to integration of the three pillars of sustainable development – remains one of the major contributions of South Africa to the UN's development discourse and programmes.

The Johannesburg summit took place after the Millennium Summit in 2002, which resulted in the adoption of the Millennium Declaration, from which the Millennium Development Goals (MDGs) were extrapolated, with poverty eradication at their centre.[25] In 2006, South Africa was elected by the members of the Group of 77 (G-77) and China to chair the group under its permanent representative, Dumisani Kumalo. He forcefully challenged US efforts to diminish the development proposals in the 2005 World Summit Outcome Document. South Africa was again elected as Chair of the Group of 77 in 2015, under its permanent representative, Kingsley Mamabolo, at the height of the negotiations of the Post-2015 Development Agenda containing the 17 Sustainable Development Goals (SDGs), known as the 2030 Agenda for Sustainable Development. Tshwane was central to ensuring that the outcome was adopted by consensus of all UN member states. This further confirmed South Africa's status as a leader of the global development agenda. Tshwane has also been at the forefront of promoting South-South cooperation within the context of the UN development framework. Through the IBSA (India, Brazil and South Africa) Poverty Alleviation Fund Facility, South Africa, together with New Delhi and Brasilia, has identified and supported development-related projects in poor and developing countries as a reflection of its commitment to South-South solidarity (see Virk in this volume).

South Africa has also played a critical role in the UN's efforts to address the challenge of climate change. Despite having attended the first Conference of the Parties (COP) as only a non-member observer in 1995, South Africa hosted the Conference of the Parties (COP 17) to the United Nations Framework Convention on Climate Change (UNFCCC) in its port city of Durban in November/December 2011. As president of the conference, South Africa played a significant role in the adoption of the conference outcome – the Durban Platform for Enhanced Action – which sought to craft a legally binding instrument for climate change by 2015. Much work has been done since COP 17, and the November 2015 COP conference adopted a legally binding instrument known as the Paris Agreement. South Africa also provided strategic leadership during the negotiations of the Paris Agreement as Chair of the Group of 77, the largest caucus group in the climate change negotiations process, and that the Paris Agreement was adopted by consensus was in no small measure due to the role played by the G-77 and South Africa as its Chair.

Human Rights

The South African struggle for liberation against apartheid was a human rights struggle, since apartheid had been declared by the UN General Assembly as a "crime against humanity" and a gross violation of human rights and human dignity. Apartheid constituted an affront to the principles and values of the UN Charter of 1945 and the world body's Universal Declaration of Human Rights of 1948. Nelson Mandela noted in 1993 that South Africa's future foreign policy would be based on the "belief that human rights should form the core concern of international relations".[26] Since human rights constitute one of the three intertwined pillars of the United Nations, along with peace and security, and development, Tshwane has played a significant role in this area. Guided by the Bill of Rights of its 1996 constitution, South Africa has acceded to and ratified all the major UN human rights instruments. In recognition of South Africa's role on human rights issues at the United Nations, it was elected chair of the UN Commission on Human Rights in 1998. South Africa also played an important role in the reform of this commission (replaced by the Human Rights Council in 2006),[27] which was plagued by accusations of double standards, politicisation of human rights and squabbles over its role as a subsidiary body of the UN General Assembly. South Africa was elected as one of the founding members of the newly created Human Rights Council in 2006. In the Council, South Africa consistently pushed for an equal focus on socio-economic rights as opposed to the rich countries' one-sided prioritising of civil and political rights.

As part of its human rights agenda in the United Nations, South Africa has sought to highlight the challenge of racism that still persists across the world. In August and September 2001, the country hosted the World Conference Against Racism, Xenophobia and Other Intolerances, which agreed on the Durban Declaration and an action plan – for the first time representing a common course of action. One of the key outcomes of the Durban conference was an acknowledgement that racism and racial discrimination remained a major challenge in the twenty-first century, though with different manifestations. South Africa sought to streamline the outcomes of the conference within the United Nations, and has since been at the forefront of passing an annual General Assembly resolution on global efforts to eliminate racial discrimination on behalf of the Group of 77 and China. South Africa's Navi Pillay also served as UN High Commissioner for Human Rights between 2008 and 2014.

Going against the African grain, but guided by its Bill of Rights, South Africa has consistently supported efforts – including initiatives and resolutions at the United Nations – to highlight the plight of vulnerable groups and minorities, including the lesbian, gay, bisexual and trans-sexual (LGBT) communities, who continue to suffer discrimination and are subjected to violence and arbitrary and extra-judicial killings. In June 2011, South Africa piloted a landmark resolution at the Human Rights Council calling for the High Commissioner for Human Rights to compile a report on incidents worldwide of violence and discrimination against members of LGBT communities.[28] South Africa has also been a staunch supporter of efforts at the United Nations aimed at the empowerment of women and gender equality. In 2013, South Africa was re-elected to serve in the Human Rights Council for a three-year renewable term, starting January 2014 and ending December 2016. (For a critique of South Africa's human rights record at the UN, see Fritz in this volume.)

Concluding Reflections

South Africa's foreign policy as a middle power in the United Nations over the past two decades has had to contend with the realities of a changing world order. Tshwane has used the UN to influence global discourses on issues on the international community's agenda. It has promoted respect for human rights and fundamental freedoms, as well as observance of international law and the rule of law at the international level. South Africa has also used its memberships in the G-77 and African Group to influence many UN decisions in the field of development. By the end of its first decade of membership in the United Nations – including two terms on the Security Council – South Africa had emerged as one of the most respected advocates and defenders of the global South, alongside India, Brazil, Nigeria, Indonesia and others. Tshwane has consistently promoted its African Agenda in the resolution and prevention of conflicts on the continent. Membership in the UN Security Council has provided South Africa with an opportunity to contribute significantly to global peace and security challenges. The country has used its peaceful transition to democratic rule to leverage influence in debates at the UN and to bolster its role in international affairs. The promotion of multilateralism and a rules-based approach to global challenges has thus been at the centre of Tshwane's role at the UN. In two and a half decades,

South Africa has distinguished itself as a reliable and principled player in multilateral affairs and global governance.

The struggle for reform of institutions of global governance, particularly the United Nations and its Security Council specifically, will continue to remain a major challenge facing South Africa in the next decade, as will implementation of the 2030 Agenda for Sustainable Development, the Paris Agreement on Climate Change of 2015, and the consolidation of the role of the UN in Africa's development efforts. The strengthening and revitalisation of the organisations of the South such as the Non-Aligned Movement (NAM), as well as the G-77 plus China, and the African Group at the UN, will become increasingly dynamic and complicated given the divergent and complex economic and political relationships between countries of the South and the rich states of the North. Though the advancement and championing of the African Agenda on the basis of the African Union's *Agenda 2063* will continue to guide South Africa's foreign policy in the next decades, a delicate balance between alliances such as the BRICS (Brazil, Russia, India, China and South Africa), loose formations like the Group of 20 (G-20), and strategic partnerships with the European Union (see Nkosi in this volume) will be critical in ensuring that South Africa remains a bridge-builder in efforts to strengthen global multilateralism.

Notes

1. *See* Adekeye Adebajo (ed.), *From Global Apartheid to Global Village: Africa and the United Nations* (Scottsville: University of KwaZulu Natal Press, 2009); Adekeye Adebajo and Helen Scanlon (eds), *A Dialogue of the Deaf: Essays on Africa and the United Nations* (Johannesburg: Jacana, 2006).

2. *See, for example*, Suzanne Graham, *Democratic South Africa's Foreign Policy: Voting Behaviour in the United Nations* (London: Palgrave Macmillan, 2016).

3. Adekeye Adebajo, *UN Peacekeeping in Africa: From the Suez Crisis to the Sudan Conflicts* (Boulder, CO, and London: Rienner; and Johannesburg: Jacana, 2011).

4. Jakkie Cilliers, Francis Ikome, Anton du Plessis, Noel Stott, Guy Lamb and Cheryl Hendriks, "South Africa's Second Term at the UN Security Council: Managing Expectations", Situation Report (Pretoria: Institute for Security Studies (ISS), 2010), p. 3.

5. Margaret Vogt, "The UN and Africa's Regional Organisations", in Adebajo, *From Global Apartheid to Global Village*, pp. 251–268; Musifiky Mwanasali, "The African Union, the United Nations, and the Responsibility to Protect: Towards an African Intervention Doctrine", *Global Responsibility to Protect* 2, no. 4 (2010), pp. 388–413.

6. United Nations (UN) Security Council Resolution 1809 on peace and security in Africa, UN Doc. S/RES/1809, adopted at its 5868th meeting, 18 April 2008.

7. Maite Nkoana-Mashabane, "A Vision for South Africa's Foreign Policy: Now and Beyond", public lecture, University of Pretoria, 11 September 2012, http://www. dirco.gov.za/docs/speeches/2012/mash0911.html (accessed 15 July 2013).

8. *See* Centre for Conflict Resolution (CCR), *The Eagle and the Springbok: Strengthening the Nigeria/South Africa Relationship*, Policy Brief no. 12 and Seminar Report no. 39 (Lagos, 9–10 June 2012), http://www.ccr.org.za (accessed 9 July 2017).

9. UN Security Council Resolution 2033 on cooperation between the United Nations and regional and sub-regional organisations in maintaining international peace and security, UN Doc. S/RES/2033, adopted at its 6702nd meeting, 12 January 2012.

10. Horace Campbell, *Global NATO and the Catastrophic Failure in Libya* (New York: Monthly Review Press, 2013), p. 135.

11. African Union (AU) Peace and Security Council, 319th ministerial meeting, communiqué, 24 April 2012.

12. AU Peace and Security Council, 339th ministerial meeting, communiqué, 24 October 2012.

13. UN Security Council Resolution 1973 on Libya, UN Doc. S/RES/1973, adopted at its 6498th meeting, 17 March 2011, operational para. 2.

14. UN Security Council, Statement by the President, "The Promotion and Strengthening of the Rule of Law in the Maintenance of International Peace and Security", UN Doc. S/PRST/2012/1, adopted at its 6705th meeting, 19 January 2012.

15. "United Nations Peacekeeping, Troop, and Police Contributors", http://www.un. org/en/peacekeeping/resources/statistics/contributors.shtml (accessed 9 September 2016).

16. Paul D. Williams, "Pragmatic Multilateralism? South Africa and Peace Operations", in Donna Lee, Ian Taylor and Paul D. Williams (eds), *The New Multilateralism in South African Diplomacy* (Basingstoke: Palgrave, 2006).

17. Nelson Mandela, "The New South Africa's Future Foreign Policy", *Foreign Affairs* 72, no. 5 (1993), pp. 86–97.

18. Speech by Nelson Mandela at a special meeting of the UN Special Committee Against Apartheid, 22 June 1990.

19. AU Executive Council, "The Common African Position on the Proposed Reform of the United Nations: 'The Ezulwini Consensus'", Doc. EX.CL/2 (VII), adopted at its 7th extraordinary session, Addis Ababa, 7–8 March 2005.

20. David Bosco, *Five to Rule Them All: The UN Security Council and the Making of the Modern World* (Oxford: Oxford University Press, 2009).

21. Preamble of the Charter of the United Nations. *See also* Adebajo, *From Global Apartheid to Global Village*.

22. UN General Assembly Resolution 286 on the New Partnership for Africa's Development: Progress in Implementation and International Support, UN Doc. A/RES/66/286, adopted at its 122nd plenary meeting, 23 July 2012.

23. Scarlett Cornelissen, "Displaced Multilateralism? South Africa's Participation at the United Nations: Disjunctures, Continuities, and Contrasts", in Taylor and Williams, *The New Multilateralism in South African Diplomacy*, p. 34.

24. UN Department of Economic and Social Affairs, "List of Least Developed Countries (as of June 2017)", https://www.un.org/development/desa/dpad/wp-content/uploads/sites/45/publication/ldc_list.pdf (accessed 9 July 2017).

25. UN General Assembly, *Millennium Summit Declaration*, UN Doc. A/RES/55/2, 8 September 2000. *See also* CCR, *Achieving the Millennium Development Goals (MDGs) in Africa*, Policy Brief no. 19 and Seminar Report no. 44 (Cape Town, October/November 2013), http://www.ccr.org.za (accessed 9 July 2017).

26. Mandela, "The New South Africa's Future Foreign Policy".

27. Kader Asmal, "South Africa, the UN, and Human Rights", in Adebajo and Scanlon, *A Dialogue of the Deaf*, pp. 227–241.

28. UN Human Rights Council Resolution on human rights, sexual orientation, and gender identity, UN Doc. A/HRC/RES/17/19, adopted at its 17th session, 14 July 2011.

CHAPTER 19

SOUTH AFRICA AND THE WORLD TRADE ORGANISATION

Faizel Ismail[1]

This chapter discusses South Africa's role in the multilateral trading system since the country's transition to democracy in 1994, focusing in particular on the World Trade Organisation's (WTO) Doha Round of trade negotiations – a historic process that has witnessed the emergence of a stronger and more assertive voice among developing countries in which I was closely involved as South Africa's ambassador to the WTO at the time. Tshwane (Pretoria) actively contributed to this process, its participation helping to shape the debates and the demands of the global South for a fairer, more equitable, development-friendly and inclusive multilateral trading system.

In this chapter, I argue that South Africa's participation in the WTO – both before and after the launch of the Doha Round in 2001 – was informed by its domestic development challenges, and based on values derived from its long struggle against apartheid and subsequent transition to democracy in 1994 (see Landsberg in this volume). These values, as articulated by the country's first post-apartheid president, Nelson Mandela, reflected a deep commitment to multilateralism, consensus-building, fairness, justice and inclusiveness, as well as an abiding desire to support and promote development in South Africa and the developing countries of the global South, especially in Africa.[2] South Africa's political leadership in the Doha Round also drew strength from the country's deep democratic institutions and consultative processes. I further suggest that the principles and approaches that have guided South Africa's negotiators in the WTO since 1994 have contributed to building its credibility and influence internationally, helping to make the country eligible for joining a major emerging power grouping such as the BRIC bloc (Brazil, Russia, India and China), now the BRICS. (See Virk in this volume.)

Towards that end, this chapter assesses South Africa's role in the Doha Development Agenda negotiations in five areas: first, the launch of the Doha Round; second, the negotiations on trade-related aspects of intellectual property rights (TRIPS) and public health; third, the creation of the Group of 20 (G-20) alliance of developing countries on agriculture; fourth, the negotiations on special and differential treatment for developing countries; and, fifth, the establishment of the Non-Agricultural Market Access (NAMA-11) group of developing countries. The chapter also considers South Africa's role at the ninth WTO ministerial conference, held in Bali, Indonesia, in December 2013. The chapter illustrates how South Africa has been at one and the same time part of a group of major emerging developing countries, and a crucial bridge between these emerging powers and a smaller group of developing countries – particularly in Africa – in the multilateral trading system.

South Africa's Guiding Principles and Approaches in the Multilateral Trading System

As Nelson Mandela noted in the Swiss city of Geneva in May 1998, South Africa had been a member of the General Agreement on Tariffs and Trade (GATT) – replaced by the Geneva-based WTO in 1995 – since its inception in 1947, when "the vast majority of South Africans had no vote". Even so, Tshwane was committed to "vastly improve on the management of the world trading system to the mutual benefit of all nations and people",[3] and to work towards a rules-based multilateral trading system that was just and inclusive, and addressed the needs of developing countries. In an earlier article in *Foreign Affairs* in 1993, Mandela had also clarified that post-apartheid South Africa's foreign policy would be driven by the need to address its deep-seated economic development challenges, in particular the country's "severe poverty, and extreme inequality in living standards, income and opportunity".[4] (See Landsberg in this volume.) These principles would guide South Africa's negotiators in the multilateral trading system from 1994 onwards.

In the course of WTO negotiations over the past two decades, South Africa sought to adhere to its principles in striving to build and strengthen a fairer multilateral trading system, one with a focus on the problems and prospects of development in the world's poorer countries. This approach reflected the "idealist and aspirational" values that emerged from South Africa's own struggle for democracy, freedom and human dignity, though it also pursued its own interests in order to promote socio-economic development in South Africa and the developing world. At the same time, South African negotiators adopted different strategies and tactics at different stages of the negotiations on key issues as the situation changed.

South Africa's Role in the Doha Round

The Launching of the Doha Development Agenda

South Africa was a founding member of GATT in 1947. However, the apartheid regime after 1948 considered South Africa to be an industrialised country. The government mainly represented the interests of the country's small white minority, and did not argue for development issues to be addressed in the negotiated liberalisation of world trade that followed under GATT. In the Uruguay Round (1986–1993) – the eighth and final round of talks under GATT before the creation of the WTO – South Africa thus had to undertake rich-country commitments in key market access areas such as agriculture, industrial tariffs and services.[5] These commitments have since become a major burden for South Africa in the present-day Doha Round of negotiations, as Tshwane's legal commitments in each of these areas are vastly higher than those of its fellow developing countries in the WTO.

In March 1999, South Africa's minister of trade and industry, Alec Erwin, set out the country's approach to the next round of negotiations in a speech at a high-level symposium on trade and development in Geneva.[6] Erwin argued that mainly rich countries should be required to undergo reforms in the new round, in order to allow for a structural shift of resources to developing countries. He repeated this argument in another speech in the Swedish capital of Stockholm in April 1999,[7] calling for the structural impediments on the trade of developing countries to be removed by the opening up to them of agricultural markets and other so-called grandfather industries, which are commonly known by trade negotiators as the highly protected sectors in rich countries such as sugar, cotton, textiles and steel. Erwin noted that "the challenge of development remains fundamental and will have to be a top priority for the coming deliberations in the WTO". While acknowledging that the existence of the rules-based multilateral trading system was "an essential achievement and starting point", he argued that "it [was] imperative that the rules are designed to achieve clear and equitable objectives".[8]

South Africa subsequently played a key role in supporting the launch of a new round of negotiations in Doha in November 2001.[9] Erwin, together with five other ministers – Singapore's trade and industry minister, Brigadier-General George Yeo; Swiss economic affairs minister, Pascal Couchepin; Chile's external relations vice-minister, Heraldo Muñoz Valenzuela; Canada's international trade minister, Pierre Pettigrew; and Mexico's economics secretary, Luis Ernesto Derbez Bautista – was appointed as a friend of the conference chair, Youssef Hussain Kamal, Qatar's finance, economy and trade minister. Erwin was entrusted with the responsibility of assisting the chair to broker a consensus on the objectives and mandates of the Doha Round. Furthermore, South Africa was instrumental in ensuring that the final text of the Doha Declaration (later called the Doha Development Agenda) of November 2001 contained various commitments in support of the interests of developing countries.

Intellectual Property Rights and Public Health

Over the course of the Doha Round, between 2002 and 2003, a key issue area in which South Africa played an active role related to intellectual property rights and public health. The TRIPS agreement of 1994 – an outcome of the Uruguay Round – was controversial from the outset. Policymakers in both rich and developing countries continued to debate how to create an optimum balance between the health interests of society; the use of patents (market exclusivity) to incentivise pharmaceutical companies to invest in research and development of new drugs to combat diseases; and the need to ensure that this exclusivity did not make the drugs unaffordable for a majority of people, particularly in poorer, developing countries. The TRIPS agreement contained some flexibility (use of compulsory licenses and parallel imports) to prevent abuse by patent owners. However, this flexibility was contested by the pharmaceutical industry in the United States (US). In 1998, 39 pharmaceutical companies launched a case against South Africa in the country's Supreme Court after failing to persuade the South African government to withdraw or modify the provisions of Article 15(c) of the South African Medicines and Related Substances Act of 1965. This provision allowed South Africa to import affordable generic drugs for public health purposes from suppliers in any country. The US pharmaceutical companies alleged that this practice was not allowed under the TRIPS agreement and that South Africa would have to purchase more expensive patented drugs from mainly US pharmaceutical companies. The US government and pharmaceutical companies held that this provision was "inconsistent with South Africa's obligations and commitments under the WTO TRIPS Agreement".[10] (See Weissman in this volume.)

There was increased public pressure on the WTO in Doha from developing countries and non-governmental organisations (NGOs) in the US and Europe to reaffirm the right of governments to act in the interests of public health. In addition, there was recognition that many developing countries were unable to use the compulsory license mechanism provided by the TRIPS agreement to access affordable drugs, as they did not have the capacity to manufacture pharmaceuticals. In Doha in November 2001, trade ministers thus instructed the WTO – in the sixth paragraph of the Doha Declaration – to develop a legal mechanism, by December 2002, that could enable countries without sufficient manufacturing capacity to produce and/or import such life-saving drugs.

South Africa made a significant contribution on this issue at each stage of the subsequent WTO negotiations. First, Tshwane helped to build agreement between the two major developing country groups that had a deep interest in the proposed solution: the Africa Group (which had no or limited capacity to produce pharmaceutical drugs), and another group of developing countries (with some capacity to manufacture the drugs) led by Brazil and India. Second, South Africa played a leading role in forging consensus on a range of complex issues for negotiation including the scope of diseases; the range of products; the eligible beneficiary members and eligible exporting countries; and the need for additional safeguards for inclusion in the new mechanism. Third, South Africa was instrumental in building agreement and support for the chair's text of December 2002 – which provided the flexibility required by developing countries to access more affordable drugs – with the European Union (EU) and other industrialised countries such as Canada, Australia and Switzerland. Fourth, in the first half of 2003, South Africa continued to engage the US and its pharmaceutical industry to break the impasse on the sixth paragraph of the

Doha Declaration on Public Health, which had instructed the members of the WTO to negotiate a detailed agreement that would allow developing countries to both produce and import generic drugs for public health purposes. This included the meetings in January 2003 in Davos, Switzerland, where South Africa's trade minister, Alec Erwin, warned the leaders of several pharmaceutical companies (such as Pfizer, Merck and GlaxoSmithKline) that their intransigence threatened the entire system of intellectual property rights.[11] Fifth, South Africa worked with the US ambassador to the WTO, Linnet Deily, as part of a small team of ambassadors that also included Brazil, India and Kenya, to reach a compromise and draft a chair's statement that could enable Washington to join the December 2002 consensus. This statement, together with the December 2002 chair's text on the sixth paragraph, was finally adopted by the WTO General Council by consensus in August 2003.[12]

The G-20 Alliance of Developing Countries on Agriculture

Soon thereafter, at the next WTO ministerial conference, in Cancún, Mexico, in September 2003, South Africa helped to establish one of the most important developing-country alliances in the World Trade Organisation – the G-20 alliance of developing countries on agriculture. The Doha Declaration envisaged agreement on the modalities for negotiations on agriculture by March 2003. In the lead-up to Cancún, however, the EU failed to table any proposals that would meaningfully meet its Doha commitment to agree to a methodology to reduce agricultural tariffs by March 2003. This deadline for the establishment of a methodology for agriculture negotiations was thus missed.

As the Cancún ministerial conference drew closer, Washington and Brussels shifted to a strategy of bilateral engagement, and reached an accommodation on each other's trade-distorting farm support policies. In return for the protection of payments to its farmers (of approximately $19.1 billion under the US Farm Bill of 2002), the United States reduced its ambition to open the European Union's markets and to eliminate fully the EU's destructive export subsidies on agricultural products of over €50 billion a year. Agricultural subsidies in the United States are estimated at between $10 billion and $30 billion annually.[13] In the WTO, the two Western powers tabled a joint text on agriculture in August 2003, which galvanised developing countries, in particular, into action to prevent another "Blair House"-type agreement (a deal that was struck between the US and the EU on agriculture in November 1992 during the Uruguay

Round) that would accommodate the interests of Washington and Brussels, and reduce the ambition of the round.[14] The US–EU text was strongly challenged by a diverse group of countries that included not only Brazil, Argentina and South Africa, but also Australia and several former US allies (such as Columbia, Costa Rica and Panama), which coalesced around the common objective of securing freer global agriculture markets.[15] The developing countries – led by Brazil, India, China, South Africa and Argentina, among others – established a broad-based alliance driven by their need to advance liberalisation and reform of agriculture in the rich North, and social justice and development in the global South. This group later grew into the present-day WTO G-20 bloc (this G-20 is distinct from the more prominent G-20 major economies group, which includes the US, Germany, Japan, France and other industrialised countries).

It is important to note that South Africa was also a member of the more competitive Cairns Group of rich and developing agricultural exporting countries. However, South Africa's need to secure more policymaking space to support its small emerging farmers, as well as its desire to promote the needs and interests of Africans, made it more sensitive to the concerns of the more protective agricultural exporting countries – a group that included India, China and most African countries (see the Introduction in this volume for another interpretation). South Africa thus gradually became a natural bridge in the ensuing debate on the issue between the various interest groups, and became the third country – after Brazil and India, once they had found balanced positions – to join the then emerging WTO G-20 alliance.

In particular, South Africa was, and remains, an important link between the WTO G-20, the Africa Group and other developing-country groupings such as the African, Caribbean and Pacific (ACP) group of states (see Nkosi in this volume)[16] and the NAMA-11. South Africa's early entry into the WTO G-20 also provided the impetus for other African countries such as Egypt, Nigeria, Zimbabwe and Tanzania to join the group. The WTO G-20 met in Hong Kong in December 2005 at the ministerial level with all the other major developing-country groupings, including the NAMA-11, the Group of 33 (G-33) and the Group of 90 (G-90), with the latter comprising the Africa Group, the ACP group of states and the least-developed countries (LDCs) group of states. These groupings coalesced into a united platform called the Group of 110 (G-110) in Hong Kong in 2005,[17] with South Africa – alongside Brazil and India – playing a significant role in bringing them together.

Treatment of Small and Vulnerable Developing Economies

South Africa brought to bear a similar bridge-building capacity among developing countries on another issue of vital importance to the global South in the Doha Round: negotiations on special and differential treatment for small and vulnerable economies in the WTO. In February 2004, South Africa was nominated by WTO members to serve as the chair of a key Doha Round negotiating group: the Committee on Trade and Development Special Session (CTDSS). In this position, South Africa made three substantial contributions to the evolving architecture of the multilateral trading system. First, it helped to develop the concept of "situational flexibility", which sought to address the particular concerns of small and vulnerable developing country economies. Second, as chair of the CTDSS, it facilitated the negotiating and drafting processes for a compromise text on the concept of "small and vulnerable economies", during talks for a framework agreement in July 2004. Third, South Africa also shepherded the process of evolving a positive outcome for the least-developed countries at the Hong Kong ministerial conference in December 2005.[18] Largely due to this experience, and the positive reputation that South Africa had earned as chair of the CTDSS, the country was entrusted with coordinating the NAMA-11 group in December 2005. This was another important developing-country alliance in the Doha Round negotiations.

Non-Agricultural Market Access and the NAMA-11

In the period leading up to the Hong Kong ministerial conference in December 2005, a group of developing countries began to work closely together on the issue of non-agricultural market access, and produced a critique of the EU and other rich countries' emerging approach to the Doha Round negotiations.[19] The NAMA-11 group, formed shortly before this Hong Kong ministerial conference, comprises Argentina, Brazil, Egypt, India, Indonesia, Namibia, the Philippines, South Africa, Tunisia and Venezuela. (The original membership was constituted by 11 members but has since remained as ten members.)

In a paper submitted to the WTO Committee on Trade and Development in November 2005, this group argued that developing countries "cannot be expected to pay for the much-needed reforms in the agriculture sectors of developed countries ... by overly ambitious requests of them in industrial tariffs that do not take into account the realities of their levels of economic development and their adjustment needs".[20]

South Africa was instrumental in building convergence among the members of the group, and presented a statement on the grouping's behalf to the WTO Committee on Trade and Development, also in November 2005. Calling for the "development content of the [Doha] round to be reclaimed", the group's members were united by their need to defend the flexibilities that developing countries had previously obtained in the July 2004 framework agreement.

South Africa played a key role in consolidating the growing convergence within this developing-country group in Hong Kong, with the grouping's trade ministers presenting joint proposals in the negotiations on non-agricultural market access issues.[21] South Africa was requested to coordinate the efforts of the NAMA-11, and its then deputy minister of trade and industry, Rob Davies, chaired the group's first meeting, in December 2005. With their increased bargaining power in the WTO, the NAMA-11 countries were able to achieve three important victories. First, the coalition successfully resisted attempts by rich countries to force a premature agreement on modalities in NAMA, ahead of any significant agreement on the main issues in agriculture. Second, these developing countries were able to confirm that the principle of "less than full reciprocity" would be adhered to when making industrial tariff reduction commitments, and appropriate flexibilities would be provided to them in order to preserve their domestic policymaking space. Third, the group was also able to establish a strong link in the final text of the Hong Kong ministerial declaration between the level of ambition in NAMA and that in agriculture.[22]

After the failure of WTO ministerial meetings in Potsdam, Germany, in June 2007, Pascal Lamy, the French director-general of the global trade organisation, requested the chairs of the agriculture and NAMA negotiations to draft texts for an agreement in consultations with their members. The chair of NAMA, Canadian ambassador, Don Stephenson, then produced three draft texts, with the first circulated in July 2007.[23] The Group of Seven (G-7) ministers of trade, from the US, the EU, Japan, Australia, India, Brazil and China, deliberated over this first draft, until the collapse of the ministerial meetings convened by Pascal Lamy in July 2008 in Geneva. South Africa again played a significant role in advancing the negotiating positions of the NAMA-11 in each of these processes; in maintaining the cohesion and solidarity of the NAMA-11; and in strengthening the alliances between the NAMA-11 and other developing-country groups. The collapse of the negotiations was due mainly to the breakdown of the discussion on agriculture between the US and India. While Washington appeared to be advancing the interests of its exporters pushing for greater market access into emerging markets, such as India, the real concern of the US was its protectionist agricultural sectors such as cotton, dairy and sugar.

South Africa's Role in the Bali (2013) and Nairobi (2015) Ministerial Conferences

The continuing impasse in the Doha Round after the collapse of the 2008 WTO ministerial meetings led some to declare the round dead.[24] Susan Schwab, the American chief trade representative during the George W. Bush administration (2001–2008), stated emphatically in 2011: "[The] Doha round has failed. It is time for the international community to acknowledge this sad fact and move on".[25] The new US trade representative in the Barack Obama administration (after January 2009), Ron Kirk, offered a consistent narrative for the impasse in the Doha Round after taking office. He noted that the overall package on the table – as contained in the 2008 WTO chairs' texts on NAMA (Ambassador Don Stephenson of Canada) and Agriculture (Ambassador Crawford Falconer of New Zealand) – did not offer any real gains to American stakeholders, and that the US thus required major developing countries to provide additional market access to that already provided in the chairs' texts.[26] By the time of the December 2011 WTO ministerial conference in Geneva, Washington had developed its narrative on the reasons for the failure of the Doha Round and its alternative "new pathways" strategy to "save" the WTO.[27] The new narrative was based on an analysis developed by business interests and think tanks in the US on the changes in the global economy, as reflected in deepening global value chains; the waning support in the US for trade liberalisation; and the need to prioritise trade facilitation at the ninth WTO ministerial conference held in Bali in December 2013. The weaknesses and ideological bias in this approach have been criticised at length elsewhere.[28] Here, it suffices to say that Washington had decided to abandon its commitment to the Doha Round, as its main stakeholders believed that the round was not in its interests and that China and other emerging countries would make more economic gains from the round.

Following his appointment as the new director-general of the WTO in September 2013, Roberto Azevêdo, Brazil's former ambassador to the

WTO, then began his valiant effort to advance negotiations for a package agreement at the controversial Bali ministerial conference, with the various developing-country groups divided on the three main issues to be addressed. First, should the meeting in Bali be a negotiation conference? Second, could the balance represented in the ten existing draft documents that were being negotiated prior to the Bali conference be acceptable to members as the basis for a final Bali package agreement? And finally, should the gathered trade ministers try to develop a declaration in the final outcomes that also addressed the post-Bali work programme?

South Africa took a strong stance against detailed textual negotiations in Bali in the belief that this was unlikely to be practical or fruitful, given the existing imbalance within and between the three different pillars of the Bali package: trade facilitation; agriculture; and development (including four LDC proposals).[29] This scepticism was shared by India, Argentina, Bolivia, Venezuela and Zimbabwe.

South Africa also expressed concern that there was no clear post-Bali work programme, and that the narrative prioritising trade facilitation was most likely to be used to prioritise other issues of interest to rich countries such as services, environmental goods and services, investment, state trading enterprises and local content rules in the post-Bali period.[30] Thus, South Africa argued that a strong effort should be made to have clear declaratory language in the Bali outcomes document that prioritised the issues that were at the time only a "best endeavour" (namely, a mere exhortation rather than a legally binding agreement) in the Bali package, and that also re-affirmed the development mandate of the Doha Round.

Furthermore, in the working session for the ministerial declaration in Bali, South Africa made a strong case for the need to provide political guidance on issues of concern to the poorest countries, including duty-free access for LDCs; elimination of export subsidies in rich countries; reduction of cotton subsidies in the US that undermined the livelihoods of poor cotton farmers in West Africa; and food security for developing countries such as India. These issues were at the time "best endeavour" in nature. South Africa argued that they should be prioritised in a post-Bali package, so that these challenges could be turned into concrete deliverables. As noted by South Africa's minister of trade and industry, Rob Davies, in his formal statement to the Bali plenary in December 2013: "This programme (post-Bali) should prioritise turning the best endeavour undertakings that we have in the draft package on LDC issues and [a]griculture into effective, time-bound programmes of delivery."[31]

Davies further urged the WTO director-general, Roberto Azevêdo, to ensure that any interim measure would allow African countries to benefit from the "peace clause",[32] and that the final agreement to be negotiated would include the concerns of all developing countries.

The revised text of the final outcomes document in Bali included this language.[33] The final declaration on the post-Bali package also included some of the language from South Africa's call in the prior Bali package to prioritise turning "best endeavour" clauses on least-developed country issues, as well as other development issues, into binding commitments through time-bound negotiations in a post-Bali work programme.[34] Thus, South Africa's strategy to rebalance the Bali package, with a view to improving its development content, resulted in some real gains. However, despite South Africa's best efforts, developing country coalitions were divided in Bali, with many, such as the G-20 on agriculture, the ACP group of states, the African Group and G-33, divided on whether trade facilitation should be agreed as a stand-alone agreement even before development and other issues in the Doha negotiations, such as agriculture, were finalised.

The Bali ministerial conference was also marked by the death of Nelson Mandela in December 2013. At the final plenary the next day, South Africa's trade minister, Rob Davies, made a special statement paying tribute to Mandela.[35] In these and many other ways, Tshwane made a deep impression at the Bali conference. Its delegation, comprising representatives from business, trade unions, non-governmental organisations and parliamentarians, carried a unified message to various forums and meetings that sought to remind others of, and imprint into the fabric of the multilateral trading system, the values that Mandela – and South Africa – represented in the Doha Round negotiations: social justice, equity and a commitment to development for all.

At the tenth ministerial conference of the WTO held in Nairobi, Kenya – on African soil for the first time – in December 2015, the South African delegation was led by Rob Davies, and included representatives from all the main stakeholders, including business and labour. South Africa's objectives at the conference were to support an outcome that would preserve the Doha development mandate, and deliver a small package of measures in favour of developing countries.[36] However, just as in the period before the ninth ministerial conference, WTO members were divided once again just months before Nairobi, and could not agree on both the agenda and the way forward post-Nairobi.[37] The most significant decision taken at the conference was to eliminate export subsidies and to discipline export credits in agriculture. A number of other issues of interest to developing countries were also discussed, but as the director-general of the WTO, Roberto Azevêdo, himself stated: "more limited progress was achieved in other areas on the SSM [special safeguard mechanism], public stock-holding, minimizing the negative consequences of food aid, the LDC package and strengthening S&D [special and differential treatment] provisions."[38] On the crucial issue of the future of the Doha Round, WTO members were divided and the final Nairobi declaration stated: "We recognised that many Members reaffirm the Doha Development Agenda". However the declaration went on to note that, "other members ... do not reaffirm the Doha mandates, as they believe new approaches are necessary to achieve meaningful outcomes in multilateral negotiations."[39]

Thus, in the post-Nairobi WTO Geneva negotiating process, the Africa Group as a whole will have to regain its approach of unity and solidarity in the WTO negotiations and develop its own strategy for engagement in the changed circumstances of the WTO negotiations. South Africa will need to continue to play a key role in talks in Geneva and in contributing to the unity of the Africa Group and that of the developing country groupings. Tshwane's leadership role will be tested during the tenure of the ambassador of South Africa to the WTO, Xavier Carim, who became chair of the WTO General Council in January 2017.

Concluding Reflections

All through the protracted and difficult Doha Round of negotiations in the WTO, South Africa sought to maintain a strong commitment to the principles of equity and fairness, with a view to creating and strengthening a balanced, development-oriented, multilateral trading system. At the same time, Tshwane also showed itself to be willing to engage with its trading partners and to search for pragmatic solutions to complex challenges. Its negotiating approach was, in other words, flexible. At the launch of the Doha Round, South Africa was willing to accommodate the interests of rich countries in the negotiating mandate for the talks. In the deliberations on agriculture, when the alliance between the US and the EU threatened to undermine the promise of a development-focused outcome, Tshwane rose to the challenge (on Brazil and India's invitation) of helping to build an alliance of developing countries in response. Similarly, South Africa's WTO delegation played an important leadership role in the negotiations on intellectual property rights and public health, as it did in facilitating a compromise among developing countries in the talks on small and vulnerable economies. Tshwane was also instrumental in the creation of the NAMA-11 group, which countered efforts to impose obligations on developing countries to reduce their industrial tariffs (which would have undermined their industrial policymaking space).

Given its own greater economic capacity, South Africa has demonstrated a commitment to contribute to promoting the interests of other African countries at the WTO. This willingness to recognise its responsibilities vis-à-vis the smaller and more vulnerable economies on its own continent also informed Tshwane's efforts to build consensus within the developing-country groups that it joined (G-20, NAMA-11, Africa Group), as well as between these groupings, in the WTO. Furthermore, South Africa was also thrust into leadership positions, because it showed itself to be independent-minded, while being willing to engage effectively with major industrialised countries on specific issues. The appointment of Xavier Carim, South Africa's ambassador to the WTO, as the Chair of the WTO General Council, represented a reflection of the confidence of the organisation's membership in the leadership role that South Africa has played in the WTO since the birth of its democracy over two decades ago.

Notes

1. I was South Africa's Head of Delegation to the World Trade Organisation (WTO) from 2002 to 2009 and Permanent Representative to the WTO from 2010 to 2014, and am the author of two books on the WTO: *Mainstreaming Development in the WTO: Developing Countries in the Doha Round* (Jaipur: Consumer Unity and Trust Society (CUTS) International; and Geneva: Friedrich Ebert Stiftung (FES), 2007); and *Reforming the World Trade Organisation: Developing Countries in the Doha Round* (Jaipur: CUTS International; and Geneva: FES, 2009). I have written this chapter in my personal capacity, building on my article "Reflections on a New Democratic South Africa's Role in the Multilateral Trading System", *Global Policy* 3, no. 3 (September 2012), pp. 270–280.

2. *See* South African Department of Trade and Industry (DTI), "A South African Trade Policy and Strategy Framework", 2010, http://www.dti.gov.za (accessed 1 September 2014).

3. WTO, "Statement of Nelson Mandela, President of South Africa", 50th Anniversary of the Multilateral Trading System, Geneva, May 1998.

4. Nelson Mandela, "South Africa's Future Foreign Policy", *Foreign Affairs* 72, no. 5 (November/December 1993), pp. 86–97.

5. Alan Hirsh, *Season of Hope: Economic Reform Under Mandela and Mbeki* (Scottsville: University of KwaZulu Natal Press; and Ottawa: International Development Research Centre (IDRC), 2005).

6. Alec Erwin, "The Integration of Developing Countries in the Multilateral Trading System", speech, High-Level Symposium on Trade and Development, WTO, Geneva, 18 March 1999.

7. Alec Erwin, "The Integration of the Developing Countries into the World's Multilateral Trading System", speech at the symposium "The Global Trade Agenda: Challenges and Opportunities", Stockholm, 12 April 1999.

8. Erwin, "The Integration of the Developing Countries into the World's Multilateral Trading System".

9. *See* Stuart Harbinson, "The Doha Round: 'Death-Defying Agenda' or 'Don't Do It Again'?", Working Paper no. 10/2009 (Brussels: European Centre for International Political Economy (ECIPE), 2009).

10. For a detailed discussion of the issue, *see* Carolyn Deere, *The Implementation Game: The TRIPS Agreement and the Global Politics of Intellectual Property Reform in Developing Countries* (Oxford: Oxford University Press, 2009), p. 163.

11. My speech was subsequently published as "The Doha Declaration on TRIPS and Public Health and the Negotiations in the WTO on Paragraph 6: Why PHRMA Needs to Join the Consensus!", *Journal of World Intellectual Property* 6, no. 3 (May 2003), pp. 393–401.

12. *See* WTO General Council, Minutes of Meeting, 25, 26, and 30 August 2003, Doc. WT/GC/M/82 (17 November 2003).

13. Cato Institute, *Cato Handbook for Policymakers*, 7th ed. (Washington, DC, 2009), pp. 625–635, http://object.cato.org/sites/cato.org/files/serials/files/cato-handbook-policymakers/2009/9/hb111-18.pdf (accessed 16 September 2016). *See also* "Should Washington End Agriculture Subsidies?", *Wall Street Journal*, 12 July 2015, http://www.wsj.com/articles/should-washington-end-agriculture-subsidies-1436757020 (accessed 16 September 2016); the *Wall Street Journal* estimates that $20 billion is distributed to farmers annually for agricultural subsidies.

14. *See* Jarrod Wiener, *Making Rules in the Uruguay Round of the GATT* (Aldershot: Dartmouth, 1995), pp. 191–215.

15. Faizel Ismail, "Agricultural Trade Liberalization and the Poor: A Development Perspective on Cancún", *Bridges Weekly* 8, no. 1 (January 2004), pp. 4–5.

16. *See* Centre for Conflict Resolution (CCR), *The African, Caribbean, and Pacific (ACP) Group and the European Union (EU)*, Seminar Report no. 45 (Cape Town, January 2014), http://www.ccr.org.za (accessed 9 July 2017).

17. *See* Faizel Ismail, "The G20 and the NAMA 11: Perspectives Revisited", *Indian Journal of International Economic Law* 1, no. 1 (2008), pp. 80–108.

18. *See* Faizel Ismail, "How Can Least Developed Countries and Other Small, Weak, and Vulnerable Countries Also Gain from the Doha Development Agenda on the Road to Hong Kong?", *Journal of World Trade* 40, no. 1 (2006), pp. 37–68.

19. *See* WTO, "Statement by South Africa to the 55th Session of the Committee on Trade and Development on Behalf of Argentina, Brazil, India, Indonesia, Namibia, the Philippines and Venezuela", 28 November 2005.

20. WTO, "Reclaiming Development in the WTO Doha Development Round", Doc. WT/COMTD/W/145 (1 December 2005), submission by Argentina, Brazil, India, Indonesia, Namibia, Pakistan, the Philippines, South Africa and Venezuela to the Committee on Trade and Development.

21. *See* "Letter from Argentina, Bolivarian Republic of Venezuela, Brazil, China, Egypt, India, Indonesia, Namibia, Pakistan, Philippines, South Africa, and Tunisia, to the Chairman of the Conference and the Director-General of the WTO at the Hong Kong Ministerial Conference", 14 December 2005, available from the South African Mission to the WTO, Geneva.

22. *See* WTO, "Doha Work Programme: Ministerial Declaration", Doc. WT/MIN (05)/DEC (22 December 2005), para. 24.

23. *See* WTO, "Draft NAMA Modalities", Doc. Job (07)/126 (17 July 2007).

24. "Life After Doha", *Financial Times*, 18 April 2011, http://www.ft.com/cms/s/0/f759d08a-69ee-11e0-89db-00144feab49a.html#axzz3197d3035 (accessed 8 May 2014).

25. Susan C. Schwab, "After Doha: Why the Negotiations Are Doomed and What We Should Do About It", *Foreign Affairs* 90, no. 3 (May/June 2011).

26. *Washington Trade Daily*, 29 June 2009.

27. Faizel Ismail, "Narratives and Myths in the WTO Doha Round: The Way Forward?", *Economic and Political Weekly* 47, no. 31 (4 August 2012), pp. 55–67.

28. Faizel Ismail, "Towards an Alternative Narrative for the Multilateral Trading System", *SouthViews* no. 40 (7 November 2012).

29. South African Permanent Mission to the WTO, "South Africa's Statement to the WTO General Council", 26 November 2013.

30. *See* "Trade: EU, US Unveil Post-Bali Assault Plans on Third World", *South-North Development Monitor (SUNS)* no. 7714 (10 December 2013), http://www.sunsonline.org/results.php (accessed 10 September 2014).

31. Rob Davies (South African Minister of Trade and Industry), "South Africa's Statement to the 9th World Trade Organisation Ministerial Conference", Bali, 4 December 2013.

32. The "peace clause" is a provision in Article 13 of the Agriculture Agreement saying agricultural subsidies committed under the agreement cannot be challenged under other WTO agreements, in particular the Subsidies Agreement and GATT. It expired at the end of 2003.

33. *See* WTO, "Bali Ministerial Declaration: Revised Draft", 9th WTO Ministerial Conference, Bali, 3–7 December 2013, Doc. WTO/MIN(13)/DEC/W/1/Rev.1 (7 December 2013).

34. *See* WTO, "Bali Ministerial Declaration".

35. WTO, "Statement by Dr Rob Davies, Minister of Trade and Industry, on the Passing of Mr Nelson Mandela", closing session, 7 December 2013, 9th WTO Ministerial Conference, Bali, 3–7 December 2013, Doc. WTO/MIN(13)/48 (7 December 2013).

36. WTO, "World Trade Organization Tenth Ministerial Conference: South Africa Country Statement, Nairobi, Kenya", 16 December 2015.

37. D. Ravi Kanth, "What Happened at Nairobi and Why: Dismantling of Doha Development Agenda and India's Role", *Economic and Political Weekly* 51, no. 11 (12 March 2016).

38. Roberto Azevêdo, "Speaking Notes for the UCT Seminar on the Future of the WTO Doha Round of Trade Negotiations and The Implications for Africa's Regional Integration", seminar held at the University of Cape Town, 17 March 2016.

39. WTO, "Tenth WTO Ministerial Conference, Nairobi, 2015: Nairobi Ministerial Declaration", 19 December 2015, Doc. WT/MIN (15)/DEC.

CHAPTER 20

SOUTH AFRICA; THE AFRICAN, CARIBBEAN AND PACIFIC GROUP; AND THE EUROPEAN UNION

Mxolisi Nkosi

Both South Africa's membership of the 79-member African, Caribbean and Pacific (ACP) Group of States and its relations with the 28-member European Union (EU)[1] are situated within a framework of progressive internationalism that has been the hallmark of the African National Congress (ANC), the country's former liberation movement and governing party since 1994. (See Maloka in this volume.) Through its active internationalism, the ANC mobilised a wide and diverse international solidarity network that supported its long struggle against apartheid. After 1994, this universalism and diversity of the ANC's informal apartheid-era international relations formed the basis of post-apartheid South Africa's foreign policy.

In 1993, Nelson Mandela – the country's first black president (1994– 1999) – provided an early snapshot of the role that democratic South Africa would seek to play in the global South, and of its key priorities in relations with the North, particularly the European Community (EC): "[We] recognise the importance of the European Community, our largest trade and investment partner, and will actively seek to consolidate our long-standing relationship with the EC ... with a view to gaining preferential access to European markets. ... [At the same time, we] will strive to strengthen our South-South ties to help protect us against economic marginalisation."[2] Ever since this statement, these themes have featured prominently in Tshwane's (Pretoria) foreign policy under successive South African presidents, from Mandela to Thabo Mbeki (1999–2008) and Jacob Zuma (since 2009).

The objective of this chapter – based also on my first-hand experiences as South Africa's ambassador to the EU and the ACP between 2012 and 2016 – is to explain the rationale behind South Africa's decision to join the ACP Group, despite its exclusion from the preferential trade and aid benefits from the EU to ACP states under the Lomé Convention of 1975. The chapter also seeks to assess the strategic relationship between South Africa and the EU.

South Africa and the ACP Group

The ACP Group was established in Georgetown, Guyana, in 1975. Its creation was the culmination of a process of cooperation among delegations from the African, Caribbean and Pacific regions, begun in 1973 and continued during negotiations with the European Economic Community (EEC) – now the EU – for the first Lomé Convention (signed in 1975). Recognising the commonality of their circumstances, the delegations from the three ACP regions coordinated and harmonised their negotiating positions, and used their combined numerical strength to secure favourable terms – including, in particular, non-reciprocal duty- and quota-free market access to the European common market – from the EEC. The link between the ACP Group and the EU was enshrined in Article 1 of the Georgetown Agreement of 1975, which clearly states: "The Members of the ACP Group shall be the African, Caribbean and Pacific States which are signatory to the Convention of Lomé and to this Agreement".[3] The Lomé Convention was revised and renewed three times before being replaced in June 2000 by the 20-year Cotonou Partnership Agreement (CPA), itself due to expire in 2020. Together, these agreements have over time formed the basis of the present-day ACP-EU development partnership.[4]

As Guyana's foreign minister in 1975, Shridath Ramphal, recounted in November 2013: "I began to see the ACP as a group whose genesis was in negotiations with Europe but which had to have an existence outside of those relations".[5] The preamble to the Georgetown Agreement affirms the ACP countries' desire to enhance "the political identity of the ACP Group to enable them to act and speak with a single voice in all international fora and organisations", as well as their resolve to "contribute towards the realisation of a new, fairer and more equitable world order".[6] However, over the four decades since its formation, the group – contrary to the ambitions of its founders – has not been able to gain an independent existence, beyond its paternalistic relationship with the EU. The ACP remains dependent on the patronage of Brussels, with nearly half of the grouping's secretariat budget of €15.3 million for the year 2014, for instance, funded by the EU. As has been the case in previous years, almost all of the group's activities are entirely funded from the EU's European Development Fund (EDF) resources. For 2014, the source of funding for 95.6 per cent of the ACP's activities was the EDF.[7]

South Africa became a member of the ACP Group in April 1997, as part-and-parcel of its re-integration into the international system after the formal end of apartheid in 1994. Tshwane's decision to join the ACP was a concrete manifestation of South Africa's commitment to South-South solidarity and cooperation. In view of the formal relationship between the ACP's founding Georgetown Agreement and its development partnership with the EU, Tshwane also acceded to the Lomé Convention in April 1997; and later ratified its successor, the Cotonou Partnership Agreement, in June 2002. However, given South Africa's level of economic development relative to the rest of the ACP, the country was excluded from the trade and aid provisions of the Cotonou Agreement. Instead, South Africa–EU trade relations were covered under a separate Trade, Development and Cooperation Agreement (TDCA), signed in October 1999. Tshwane has also benefited from an average annual EU aid package of €125 million since 1995 through a separate facility called the Development Cooperation Instrument (DCI).[8]

South Africa's rationale for joining the ACP lay in the country's desire to use the group as a platform to advance the collective development interests of its members. In particular, Tshwane wanted to support the ACP's efforts to strengthen its internal unity and solidarity, and to ensure better coordination and coherence within the grouping, in order to extract more favourable concessions on its behalf from Europe. South Africa also sought to break down the linguistic and geographic divides within the ACP Group by uniting it around common interests and concerns, including intra-ACP cooperation and securing favourable outcomes for the group in multilateral trade negotiations in order to address the development needs of ACP countries (see Ismail in this volume). In this respect, Tshwane had fully embraced Georgetown's spirit of unity and solidarity among ACP countries long before it formally joined the group.

In September 2001, South Africa hosted the first ACP Trade Ministers Committee meeting, in Johannesburg, at which economic partnership agreements (EPAs) with Europe – mandated by the Cotonou Agreement – were vigorously discussed. At this meeting, then South African deputy president Jacob Zuma stressed the importance of the unity of ACP states. In his words:

> [It] is important for the [then] 77 ACP member countries to find this common ground, as failure to do so will render us vulnerable to being played one against the other. While it is important for each country to define its own development objectives it is equally important that these should fit in within a common regional framework. Furthermore, we have a responsibility to guard against disintegration of the ACP Group of States. We may negotiate as regions; individual countries or any other fora that would serve our interests best but these negotiations must not be at the expense of a united African, Caribbean and Pacific Group of States.[9]

In addition to hosting this meeting and various others, South Africa has also participated in expert-level capacity-building programmes for ACP states. For example, South African experts involved in the TDCA negotiations have shared their experiences of the talks with their ACP colleagues at a number of seminars and workshops.

However, even before South Africa acceded to the Lomé Convention in April 1997, the EU had begun reviewing its relations with the ACP Group. The end of the Cold War by 1990 and the establishment of the World Trade Organisation (WTO) in 1995, among other factors, helped to trigger a major policy shift in the EU away from the ACP, casting doubt on the 79-member group's existence beyond the expiry of the Cotonou Agreement in 2020. The collapse of the "Iron Curtain" created favourable conditions for an eastward expansion of the EU, and contributed to diminishing the geo-political significance to Brussels of the ACP as a group. At the same time, post-Cold War international trade liberalisation compelled a reconsideration of the preferential trade provisions of the Lomé Convention, specifically the non-reciprocal duty-free entry enjoyed by ACP products into the European market, which became incompatible with the most-favoured-nation (MFN) principle of the newly established WTO.[10]

The EU initially obtained a waiver from the WTO in November 2001 for its granting of non-reciprocal trade preferences to the ACP. Upon the expiry of this waiver in 2007, however, the EU proposed that mutual reciprocity through economic partnership agreements – launched in 2002 under Cotonou – with regional zones within the ACP Group, were the most appropriate basis to rearrange its economic relations with the grouping and ensure their compatibility with the new WTO framework. Although non-reciprocity for the ACP's least-developed countries (LDCs) was retained through the "Everything But Arms" (EBA) initiative, which grants duty- and quota-free access to the EU market for almost all imports, except arms and armaments, from LDCs.[11]

Negotiations for the economic partnership agreements between the EU and ACP countries began in September 2002. The ACP's 79 member states were grouped into seven (initially six) EPA configurations: the Southern African Development Community (SADC) EPA group; Eastern and Southern Africa; the East African Community (EAC); West Africa; Central Africa; the Caribbean; and the Pacific. The African EPA groupings, particularly those covering Southern and East African countries, are a complex web – a virtual "spaghetti bowl" – of arrangements. The SADC EPA group, for example, comprises Botswana, Lesotho, Swaziland, Namibia, South Africa (which only joined in 2004), Angola and Mozambique.[12] The remaining eight SADC states formed part of other regional EPA negotiating processes: Madagascar, Malawi, Mauritius, Seychelles, Zimbabwe and Zambia joined the Eastern and Southern Africa EPA group; while Tanzania and the Democratic Republic of the Congo (DRC) are part of the East African Community and Central Africa EPA groups respectively. This has only added complexity, to the already existing and overlapping regional economic integration landscape on the continent.[13]

South Africa and the SADC Economic Partnership Agreement
Although South Africa already had a stand-alone free trade agreement (FTA) with the EU in the form of the Trade, Development and Cooperation Agreement, it decided to join the SADC EPA negotiations in 2004.[14] In this, Tshwane was motivated by a desire to strengthen regional integration in Southern Africa, as well as to preserve the integrity of the Southern African Customs Union's (SACU) common external tariff. (See Gibb in this volume.) Through the EPA process, South Africa also sought to consolidate the sub-region's various trading arrangements vis-à-vis the EU, and to align its own TDCA more closely with the SADC EPA.

Faced with the threat of losing preferential market access to the EU market, Botswana, Lesotho and Swaziland (BLS), along with Mozambique, agreed an interim EPA with Brussels in December 2007, while Namibia only initialled the agreement. The pragmatism that informed the three BLS countries' decision to conclude the interim EPA was evident in a statement made by Botswana's then trade minister, Daniel Neo Moroka, that "[t]he decision to get into an interim EPA was simply to ensure that there would be uninterrupted flows from the ACP countries into the European market".[15] South Africa and Angola, however, opted not to sign the agreement. Tshwane did not sign because of the serious challenge the EPA posed to regional integration in Southern Africa.

In December 2007, the EU adopted a temporary measure extending duty- and quota-free market access to ACP countries that had concluded EPA negotiations but not yet ratified the agreement. This was intended to avoid a disruption in their trade flows to the EU following the lapse of the WTO waiver, which had until then allowed ACP countries non-reciprocal market access under Cotonou. A bridging solution, it also provided space for outstanding issues in the EPA negotiations to be finalised, namely tariff negotiations on agriculture, export taxes, rules of origin, the most-favoured-nation clause and safeguards.

However, in May 2013, the EU decided to withdraw market access to ACP countries that had not taken the necessary steps towards ratifying their EPA by October 2014. This meant that countries which had not signed, or ratified, an EPA by the deadline would be removed from the list of beneficiaries of duty- and quota-free market access to the EU market, with the exception of the least-developed countries, which would be covered under the "Everything But Arms" initiative. This would not have had any impact on South Africa. The short deadline, however, put pressure on both sides to conclude an agreement within the set time. With the October deadline looming, a series of intensive negotiating sessions took place within the various EPA configurations, culminating in EU agreements first with some members of the West Africa group and then with the SADC EPA group. There were a series of meetings at the technical and political levels aimed at reaching an amicable settlement on outstanding issues. South Africa participated in all these meetings, under the leadership of Botswana, the coordinator of the SADC EPA group.

The SADC EPA agreement, initialled in July 2014 and signed in June 2016, is a positive development for South Africa and the Southern African sub-region. According to the South African Department of Trade and Industry

(DTI), Tshwane achieved its two strategic objectives of ensuring coherence in Southern Africa's various trade arrangements, and gaining improved market access for South Africa, through the EPA. As the DTI noted: "It preserves SACU's functional coherence, particularly in regard to maintaining the common external tariff, although the EU continues to provide the other Members of the SADC EPA Group better access to its market than it offers South Africa. Nevertheless, the outcome marks an improvement for South Africa over the TDCA in important ways."[16] South Africa will gain improved market access for 32 agricultural products. Furthermore, the EPA rules of origin are an improvement on those of the TDCA. Several other trade rules under the TDCA have also been eased under the EPA.

With the signing of the SADC economic partnership agreement in June 2016, an arduous and seemingly intractable negotiation process had been brought to a satisfactory end, increasing the total number of regional EPAs signed to three, with the other signatories being the West Africa[17] and Caribbean groups. Negotiations for the agreement with the EAC were concluded in October 2014, but only Kenya and Rwanda signed the EPA in September 2016 in the wake of uncertainty generated by the results of the British referendum, held in June 2016, in favour of exiting the EU. In Southern Africa, the EPA process has provided an historical opportunity to consolidate SACU's common external tariff vis-à-vis the EU and, in the other direction of trade, it will help to remove the dichotomy in EU trade policy towards the BLNS states (Botswana, Lesotho, Namibia and Swaziland) on the one hand, and South Africa on the other.

South Africa and the European Union

South Africa's present-day engagement with the European Union is extensive, and goes beyond the framework of the ACP-EU development partnership.[18] During the apartheid era, the European Economic Community did not have any ties with the white-minority regime in Pretoria, although individual EEC members maintained strong commercial ties with it. (See Large on Britain and Marchal on France in this volume.) Brussels's policy towards Pretoria gravitated from apathetic caution to unequivocal opposition only in the dying days of apartheid. The EU's largest members – Britain, France and, to a lesser extent, Germany – adopted a cautious approach, protecting their strong trade and investment ties with the apartheid regime. Ireland, Denmark, Sweden and the Netherlands (occasionally joined by Italy) formed the core of a progressive minority within the EEC in support of sanctioning the apartheid regime and supporting a democratic transition, demonstrating a willingness and an ability to help big powers focus on broader ethical concerns as opposed to their material interests.

Acting through the European Political Cooperation (EPC) mechanism,[19] Brussels's first concrete act against apartheid came in 1977 in the form of a code of conduct for EEC companies with interests in South Africa, which established numerous protections for the black workers of these firms. The Dutch, in particular, argued that sanctions against the apartheid government were meaningless unless implemented by all European member states.[20] In a series of foreign policy debates leading up to and following the collapse of the apartheid regime, a core of EU states argued for collective foreign policy actions to put pressure on Pretoria and pave the way for a democratic transition in South Africa. In addition to the 1977 code, such actions included diplomatic and economic support for non-violent anti-apartheid groups, and sanctions against the white-minority government and its armed forces. These sanctions were, however, implemented more by the European Commission than by individual member states. The most significant of the measures was a ban imposed in 1986 on imports of gold coins, and iron and steel worth approximately $1 billion, which had a crippling effect on the South African economy.

Collective international action, together with domestic political mobilisation in South Africa, eventually forced the apartheid regime to the negotiating table in 1990, with initially reticent European governments succumbing to the *cri de cœur* of anti-apartheid activists at home. The role of the European Parliament in supporting South Africa's liberation struggle is also worth mentioning in this regard. In its clearest act of solidarity with the anti-apartheid struggle, the Parliament awarded its inaugural Sakharov Prize[21] to Nelson Mandela in 1989. A year later, following his release from prison, Mandela was also granted the rare honour of addressing the European Parliament, presaging the implementation of the EU's anti-apartheid Common Foreign and Security Policy (CFSP).

In 1993, the European Union provided political support to South Africa's Transitional Executive Council (TEC), which laid the groundwork for a new democratic state. The EU's Common Foreign and Security Policy placed emphasis on support for democracy, the rule of law, social justice and the promotion of human rights. European support for the "new" South Africa included monitoring the country's first democratic election process in 1994; negotiating a new bilateral economic framework with Tshwane;

and making a long-term commitment to the country through a special programme of development assistance.[22]

The Trade, Development and Cooperation Agreement

The negotiation of a free trade agreement with the EU was an integral part of a broader South African strategy of re-integrating the country into the global economy after the end of apartheid. The FTA was viewed as a key instrument for the attainment of South Africa's development objectives, as set out in its Reconstruction and Development Programme (RDP) of 1994 and later its Growth, Employment and Redistribution (GEAR) strategy of 1996 (see Landsberg in this volume). As Rob Davies, then chair of South Africa's Parliamentary Portfolio Committee on Trade and Industry, noted in 2000, "to stimulate its economic growth and development, South Africa considered it imperative to lock in its relations with the EU, which had traditionally been its main economic partner".[23] In this respect, it was only natural that Tshwane would give priority to striking a deal with the European Union, which accounted for more than 40 per cent of South Africa's exports; 33 per cent of the country's imports; and over 70 per cent of its foreign direct investment (FDI) at the time.[24]

However, Tshwane negotiated with Brussels for a broad development framework, as opposed to a mere free trade agreement with an exclusive focus on trade in goods and services. Signed in October 1999, following four years of tough negotiations, the South Africa–EU Trade, Development and Cooperation Agreement was provisionally implemented in January 2000, and fully implemented from May 2004 onwards following ratification by both sides. The agreement established a free trade area between South Africa and the European Union, with Tshwane required to eliminate tariffs on 86 per cent of traded goods over a transition period of 12 years, and Brussels eliminating tariffs on 95 per cent of goods over the course of 10 years. The trade provisions were further complemented by a comprehensive development assistance package.[25] Although mainly dealing with trade in goods, the TDCA also included non-binding provisions related to services, investment, government procurement, competition policy and intellectual property.

Furthermore, the agreement extended South Africa–EU cooperation to areas as diverse as social development, health (in particular, HIV/AIDS), culture, drugs, money-laundering and the environment. The TDCA is therefore a comprehensive framework that covers a wide and diverse range of relations between Tshwane and Brussels. To drive the agreement's implementation, a Joint Cooperation Council (JCC), made up of expert-level working groups and supervised by the relevant South African ministers and EU commissioners, was established in 2007. The technical working groups have met regularly since their inception and have expanded to include new areas such as human rights. High-level expertise and the efficient management of the JCC have contributed to the effective implementation of projects.

The South Africa–EU Strategic Partnership

In 2007, South Africa and the EU formally elevated their relationship to a strategic partnership, given the interdependence, shared values, intensity and ever-widening scope of their interaction. As part of Brussels's response to changing global dynamics, the establishment of strategic partnerships with countries across traditional North-South and East-West divides was identified as a priority by then EU High Representative for Foreign and Security Policy, Britain's Catherine Ashton, in 2010.[26] By 2014, the EU had established strategic partnerships with only 11 countries globally, grouped into "established" partners (the United States, Canada, Japan and Russia) and "emerging/new industrial powers" (China, India, Brazil, South Africa, Indonesia, South Korea and Mexico).

The idea for a strategic partnership between Brussels and Tshwane was first discussed at a meeting between then South African president Thabo Mbeki (1999–2008) and Louis Michel, then European Commissioner for Development and Humanitarian Aid, in Tshwane in February 2006. At a media briefing after the meeting, Louis Michel remarked:

> I think the time has come to upgrade our political dialogue and move towards a strategic partnership. The European Union has recognised Africa as a geo-strategic priority and is committed, more than ever, to its economic and social development. South Africa has taken on a pivotal role in Southern Africa and throughout the continent, which is reflected in its international profile and its commitment to multilateralism. Therefore, we have a clear common interest in having a broader and deepened dialogue.[27]

The proposed strategic partnership was discussed in greater detail during the annual South Africa–EU ministerial Joint Cooperation Council meeting held in Brussels in November 2005, with both sides agreeing on the need to "strengthen and broaden their existing relationship through a holistic and innovative approach beyond 2006". Brussels and Tshwane further agreed "to broaden the scope of [their] relations and work towards a truly strategic partnership based on political, trade, development and economic co-operation".[28]

In June 2006, the European Commission formally adopted a communication proposing a strategic partnership between the EU and South Africa, and setting out a "comprehensive long-term framework for the EU's relations with South Africa, which takes account of the country's position as an anchor in the region and its important role on the African continent and in international relations".[29]

A month later, the South African government called a briefing – conducted by Aziz Pahad, then deputy minister of foreign affairs – for ambassadors and high commissioners of the ACP countries in Tshwane, to appraise them of developments with regard to the mooted strategic partnership. Pahad's briefing also sought to reassure ACP countries that South Africa would "only enter into a strategic partnership with the EU on condition that the partnership enhances South Africa's national, regional and African responsibilities"; and that this was "one of the issues [to be] discussed at the [their] Ministerial Joint Co-operation Council to be held in November this year [2006]".[30]

In May 2007, following intensive discussions, Tshwane and Brussels signed a joint action plan for implementing the strategic partnership between South Africa and the EU. The plan established the Mogôbagôba Dialogue, which covers existing areas of cooperation (development, trade and science and technology) between the two sides, but also focuses on promoting closer interaction in other fields such as the environment, climate change, regional policy, information and communications technology (ICT), social affairs, education and training, culture and international crime. The cornerstone of the strategic partnership involves strengthened political dialogue. In particular, the two partners agreed to meet twice a year, once at ministerial level and once at the level of heads of state and government.[31]

The first South Africa–EU summit was held in July 2007 in Bordeaux, France, and presided over by South Africa's president, Thabo Mbeki; French president and chair of the EU Council, Nicolas Sarkozy; and European Commission president, Portugal's José Manuel Barroso. Over and above the usual bilateral issues, the summit discussed African security issues, in particular, the situation in Zimbabwe; the economic partnership agreements, focusing on the SADC EPA negotiations; the New Partnership for Africa's Development (NEPAD); and climate change.

Subsequent summits also focused on strengthening cooperation within the framework of the TDCA, the EPAs, climate change, the global economic crisis of 2008–2009, as well as African peace and security issues. Taking place three months ahead of the Copenhagen Climate Change Conference, the second summit, held in Kleinmond, outside Cape Town, in September 2009, was as expected dominated by discussions on climate change. Discussions also focused, among other things, on trade, peace and security, global issues such as the EPAs and the SADC mediation in Zimbabwe. On climate change, the language of the summit declaration reflected a balance between the positions of the two parties, with South Africa emphasising the Rio principle of common but differentiated responsibilities and capacities, and the importance of funding for adaptation and mitigation measures in developing countries. For its part, the EU underscored the importance of low-carbon economy and clean energy as an opportunity to promote economic green growth and sustainable development. On the EPAs, the parties had candid discussions, with South Africa emphasising the need for a fair outcome that complements regional economic integration. Insofar as Zimbabwe is concerned, the parties reaffirmed their support for the Global Political Agreement (GPA) of September 2008 brokered by former South African president, Thabo Mbeki, and urged the inclusive government to fully implement the agreement's provisions.

The third summit, held in September 2010 in Brussels, took place at the height of the global financial and eurozone crises. In this regard, both sides agreed on the need for a global response within the framework of the Group of 20 (G-20) to stem an impending global recession and address multiple crises, including food insecurity and energy scarcity. On developments in Zimbabwe, both sides noted the EU's meeting with a Zimbabwean ministerial delegation and called for the EU–Zimbabwe political dialogue to be intensified with a view to normalising the situation in that country.

The agenda of the fourth summit, held at Kruger National Park in South Africa's Mpumalanga (eastern) province in 2011, was dominated by discussions on the situation in the Middle East and North Africa (MENA) region following the outbreak of the "Afro-Arab Spring". The parties agreed on the centrality of the multilateral system in finding a durable solution to the conflicts afflicting the MENA countries. Due recognition and support was given to the African Union (AU) high-level panel and its roadmap on Libya, as well as the role of the United Nations (UN) Security Council in the resolution of the Syrian crisis.

Held in September 2012 in Brussels, the fifth summit marked the full implementation of South Africa's TDCA with the EU, with the phasing-out of remaining duties under the agreement and a 128 per cent increase in total trade between Tshwane and Brussels since the agreement's entry into force in 2004. South Africa–EU trade in goods stood at €47.1 billion in 2012, topping the pre-financial crisis totals of 2008. Foreign direct investment stock in South Africa grew five-fold, from R44.7 billion in 1994 to R1.38 trillion in 2012,[32] with the EU the largest source of the FDI. Other items on the summit agenda reflected continuity from previous summits, with the two sides exchanging views on issues including the global financial crisis of 2008–2009, climate change and the ongoing EPA processes. The South Africa–EU Business Forum was also inaugurated on the sidelines of the summit, with a view to increasing trade and investment, against a backdrop of low economic growth in both partner economies.

The sixth summit was held in Tshwane in July 2013, against the backdrop of an EU decision to introduce restrictive measures against South African citrus products in the event that a threshold of five interceptions was exceeded. Tshwane is the second-largest citrus exporter in the world, with the European Union the destination for between 45 and 50 per cent of its total citrus exports, worth R8 billion annually. The citrus industry supports about 120,000 jobs, directly and indirectly, in South Africa.[33] To defuse the negative impact of a potential EU ban on South African citrus exports, agreement was reached at the 2013 summit that Tshwane would improve its risk management systems for possible infection, while Brussels agreed to notify South Africa of interceptions of citrus black spot (CBS, a fungal disease) before taking any drastic measures. Both parties also agreed to exchange information on the CBS risk profile, and to assess whether measures taken by the EU were consistent with scientific studies on the risks posed by CBS. This was deemed necessary in order to dispel concerns that Brussels's actions were essentially non-tariff barriers disguised as sanitary and phyto-sanitary measures. Notably, because this agreement was reached at the summit, South African citrus exports to the EU in the year 2013 were not subjected to restrictive measures as earlier contemplated by the European Commission.

The EU's continued provision of development assistance to South Africa was also discussed at the sixth summit. Brussels had provided Tshwane with an average of €125 million annually since 1995 in the areas of health, education and employment creation, in support of the country's key development goals. Between 2007 and 2013, the EU allocated €980 million in aid to South Africa. In addition to the funding that Tshwane receives through the Development Cooperation Instrument, it is worth noting that South Africa has also benefited immensely from the European Investment Bank (EIB), the EU's investment arm. The EIB provided competitive loans of over €2 billion to support infrastructure and development of small, micro and medium enterprises in South Africa between 2007 and 2013.

The discussion on development assistance at the 2013 summit followed proposals by the European Commission for a new policy directive called "Agenda for Change", seeking to adopt a differentiated approach by the EU to its development partnerships. Based on this approach, the European Union would end bilateral programmes with upper-middle-income countries such as South Africa by 2020, and instead focus on low-income countries, fragile states and Europe's southern neighbourhood.[34] Many within the EU had felt for a while that South Africa did not need continued funding under the Development Cooperation Instrument due to Tshwane's level of development; the socio-economic progress it had made since 1994; and its membership in groupings such as the G-20 and the BRICS bloc (Brazil, Russia, India, China and South Africa) (see Virk in this volume). Some also pointed to South Africa's own provision of aid for capacity and institution-building programmes on the continent through the African Renaissance Fund (ARF), to be replaced by the South African Development Partnership Agency (SADPA) – which was still awaiting implementation in 2017 – as a reason why the country did not need aid from the EU.

However, Tshwane put forward a compelling case for the continued provision of development assistance. In an article published in *The New Age* in July 2013, South Africa's foreign minister, Maite Nkoana-Mashabane, argued:

Despite considerable socio-economic development since 1994 South Africa is still grappling with the inherited apartheid economic mould of wealth distribution and high level of inequality, blighted by high unemployment and the stubborn reality of poverty. Given these realities, we are of the firm view that the EU should continue its development programmes in South Africa, which complement the work of government in providing the public good.[35]

As a result of Tshwane's lobbying efforts with the European Commission and Parliament, South Africa was retained on the list of countries that will continue to receive official development assistance (ODA) under the EU's Development Cooperation Instrument, albeit with a significant decrease in the 2014–2020 period. Tshwane's indicative allocation for the period was €241 million: less than a third of its previous allocation of €980 million for the 1997–2013 multi-annual financial framework.

Due to their shared values, South Africa and the EU have emerged from their six summits thus far with common positions on a range of issues, from Africa's peace and security challenges to global issues such as reform of the multilateral system, terrorism, climate change and the Millennium Development Goals (MDGs, since replaced by the Sustainable Development Goals (SDGs)). In the few instances when there have been differences (for example, with respect to the situations in Zimbabwe, Libya and Syria – see Mashabane, and Tawfik in this volume), both sides have shown mutual respect towards the other's position, and have agreed to disagree: a sign of maturity in the relationship, and mutual recognition that the strategic partnership is not defined by its disagreements. By and large, Tshwane and Brussels have agreed on more issues than they have disagreed on. Furthermore, the divergences have often centred on specific issues and on tactics, or strategy, for achieving similar goals, rather than on broad principles. Over time, the distance between the South African and European positions on these issues has also tended to narrow – as in the case of Zimbabwe, with the EU moving to lift remaining sanctions on Harare. (See Sachikonye in this volume.)

After the sixth summit, held in Tshwane in 2013, further summits were delayed between South Africa and the EU. This was largely due to the cyclical elections taking place in the EU and its institutions between May and October 2014, as well as the subsequent transition overflowing into 2015. The EU elections coincided with the fifth democratic elections in South Africa in May 2014. The electoral processes in both South Africa and the EU broke the regular cycle of summit level engagement that had characterised the South Africa–EU relationship. In addition, for the rest of 2015 and 2016, Brussels was preoccupied with intensive negotiations to keep Britain in the EU, responding to new threats, namely, increased terrorist attacks in major

European capitals such as Paris, Brussels and Berlin, and an unprecedented wave of migration from Africa and the Middle East.

In order to give fresh impetus to the strategic partnership, South Africa's foreign minister, Maite Nkoana-Mashabane, and her then newly appointed counterpart, Federica Mogherini, the EU High Representative for Foreign and Security Policy, met in Tshwane in February 2016 and reaffirmed their commitment to enhance the strategic partnership in pursuit of shared values and interests. The meeting provided both parties with an opportunity to review the strategic partnership and exchange views on how future South Africa–EU relations should be configured. Both parties used the occasion to welcome the conclusion of protracted EPA negotiations; reaffirm their commitment to intensify their cooperation to promote peace, security and development in Africa; and work towards the realisation of an equitable and inclusive global order consistent with the Sustainable Development Goals of 2016 and the Paris climate change agreement of 2015.

Finally, an inter-parliamentary dialogue has been an important aspect of the South Africa–EU strategic partnership. The European Parliament has a committee dedicated specifically to relations with South Africa, highlighting the importance of Tshwane to Brussels. Parliament-to-parliament cooperation has enabled both sides to exchange information and share experiences on best practices in order to improve their respective institutional efficiencies. Beyond annual consultations and high-level visits, these interactions have provided a useful platform for reinforcing the strategic partnership.

Concluding Reflections

It is obvious that South Africa's membership in the ACP Group, and its decision to develop a comprehensive framework for relations with the EU, were part of a well-calibrated foreign policy strategy, giving concrete expression to Tshwane's stated objectives of promoting South-South solidarity and North-South cooperation. While relations with the EU will endure, the future of the ACP Group beyond 2020 remains uncertain.

Recent developments in Eastern Europe (Ukraine), growing concerns about migration in Europe, and the multiple conflicts in the Middle East will see the EU's Common Foreign and Security Policy focused more towards the East and its so-called neighbourhood. In this context, the ACP has come to be seen by many within the EU as a post-colonial relic. The relegation of attendance by the EU to the European Commission at joint ACP–EU summit and ministerial meetings since about 2007 is indicative of the loss of interest by EU leaders in the ACP. The absence of high-level representation from the EU at these gatherings has been mirrored by ACP member states, particularly African countries, which have tended to be represented at the ambassadorial level in ministerial and summit meetings.

As part of its response to changing global political dynamics and to the emergence of "new" partners such as China and India for Africa, the EU has sought to renew and prioritise its relations with Africa, rather than the ACP as a grouping. A scenario in which the EU manages relations with ACP countries separately through three key regional bodies – the African Union, CARIFORUM (Forum of the Caribbean Group of ACP States), and the Pacific Islands Forum – cannot be entirely ruled out.

The future and destiny of the ACP Group surely rests squarely in the hands of its 79 members. Beyond finding consensus on a raison d'être and common vision for the group, the ACP countries have to demonstrate their commitment to the future of the organisation beyond 2020.

In November 2010, the ACP Council of Ministers set up a working group on the future perspectives of the ACP Group to find ways in which the grouping can maintain its unity, strength and solidarity, while remaining relevant beyond the Cotonou accord post-2020.[36] In a study commissioned by the ACP secretariat in October 2011,[37] a majority of high-level respondents from African, Caribbean and Pacific countries favoured an independent ACP with multiple sets of relations with new and emerging powers, as well as with the EU. South Africa participates actively in debates about the future of the ACP.

For the aspiration to become a reality, ACP countries will have to assume responsibility for the 37 per cent of their Brussels-based secretariat's budget that is currently funded by the EU through the European Development Fund.[38] As Nigerian scholar Adekeye Adebajo has argued: "If reforms are not urgently undertaken, the ACP could become extinct ... many are asking if this 'trade union of the poor' has outlived its usefulness".[39]

As for South Africa's relations with the EU, these have evolved over time to cover the widest possible scope of bilateral relations that Tshwane has with any other partner. Through the Mandela, Mbeki and Zuma presidencies, between 1994 and 2017, the South Africa–EU relationship has reflected continuity and consistency. During the Mandela period

(1994–1999), the focus was on negotiating a broad trade, development and cooperation framework as part of the process of reintegrating South Africa into the global economy. The Mbeki presidency (1999–2008) enlarged the architecture of South Africa–EU relations to include a political dimension, with a focus on support for African peace and security efforts; the creation of a platform for discussion on global issues; and the promotion of multilateralism. The Zuma era (since 2009), meanwhile, has witnessed an expansion of thematic dialogue areas; the consolidation of the strategic partnership between Tshwane and Brussels; and the introduction of a business forum to stimulate the long-standing economic ties between the two partners.

As the single most integrated region in the world with the highest number of industrialised countries and a concentration of global wealth, the EU is likely to remain an important player in global affairs, and a key strategic partner for South Africa's development for many years to come.

Notes

1. In a national referendum in June 2016, Britain voted to exit the European Union (EU). Negotiations on the terms of the departure – "Brexit" – are set to be concluded by 2019.
2. Nelson Mandela, "South Africa's Future Foreign Policy", *Foreign Affairs* 72, no. 5 (November/December 1993), p. 5.
3. United Nations (UN), Treaties Series, Multilateral, vol. 1247, no. 20345 (1981).
4. *See* Kaye Whiteman, "A History of the ACP-EU Relationship: The Origins and Spirit of Lomé", in Annita Montoute and Kudrat Virk (eds), *The ACP and the EU Development Partnership: Beyond the North-South Debate* (New York: Palgrave, 2017), pp. 33–52.
5. Shridath Ramphal, "ACP Beginnings", speech at ACP Eminent Persons Group (EPG) Caribbean Regional Consultations, Grenada, 1–2 November 2013, http://www.epg.acp.int/documents (accessed 6 July 2014).
6. UN, Treaties Series, Multilateral, vol. 1247, no. 20345 (1981).
7. African, Caribbean, and Pacific (ACP) Council of Ministers, *ACP Programme and Budget for the Financial Year 2014*, ACP/45/012/13 Rev.8, Decision no. 2/XCVIII/13, Brussels, February 2014.
8. Launched in January 2007, the Development Cooperation Instrument (DCI) replaces a wide range of geographic and thematic EU aid instruments; and provides for cooperation programmes in 47 developing countries in Latin America; Asia and Central Asia; the Gulf region (Iran, Iraq and Yemen); and South Africa. *See* European Commission, "Development Cooperation Instrument", http://ec.europa.eu/europeaid/how/finance/dci_en.htm (accessed 4 September 2014).

9. Jacob Zuma, "Closing Remarks by Deputy President Zuma at the ACP Trade Ministers Committee Workshop", Johannesburg, September 2001, http://www.dfa.gov.za/docs/speeches/2001/zuma0411.htm (accessed 6 July 2014).

10. Olufemi Babarinde and Gerrit Faber, "From Lomé to Cotonou: Business as Usual", paper prepared for the 8th biennial conference of the European Union Studies Association (EUSA), Nashville, TN, March 2003, p. 4.

11. Sheila Page and Adrian Hewitt, "The New European Trade Preferences: Does 'Everything But Arms' (EBA) Help the Poor?", *Development Policy Review* 20, no. 1 (2002), p. 91.

12. At the end of negotiations, Angola did not join the rest of the group in signing the final economic partnership agreement (EPA) in June 2016.

13. *See* Gilbert M. Khadiagala, "Africa and Europe: Ending a Dialogue of the Deaf?", in Adekeye Adebajo and Kaye Whiteman (eds), *The EU and Africa: From Eurafrique to Afro-Europa* (New York: Columbia University Press; London: Hurst; and Johannesburg: Wits University Press, 2012), pp. 217–236; Mareike Meyn, "An Anatomy of the Economic Partnership Agreements", in Adebajo and Whiteman, *The EU and Africa*, pp. 197–216. *See also* John Akokpari, "The EU and Africa: The Political Economy of an Asymmetrical Partnership", pp. 55–77; and Peter H. Katjavivi, "The Economic Partnership Agreements: An African Perspective", pp. 135–159, both in Montoute and Virk, *The ACP Group and the EU Development Partnership*.

14. For an account of the negotiations, also from a South African perspective, *see* Xavier Carim, "South Africa, the EU, and the SADC Group Economic Partnership Agreement: Through the Negotiating Lens", in Montoute and Virk, *The ACP Group and the EU Development Partnership*, pp. 161–179.

15. Quoted in Jo-Mara Duddy, "Namibia: Giengob Lays Into EU", *The Namibian*, 1 June 2009, http://allafrica.com/stories/200906010608.html (accessed 6 July 2014).

16. South African Department of Trade and Industry (DTI), "Conclusion of the EPA Negotiations", media release, Cape Town, July 2014, http://www.dti.gov.za/editmedia.jsp?id=3079

17. The West Africa EPA was signed in December 2014 by all members of the Economic Community of West African States (ECOWAS) except Nigeria and Gambia.

18. *See, for example*, Talitha Bertelsmann-Scott, "South Africa and the EU: Where Lies the Strategic Partnership?", in Adebajo and Whiteman, *The EU and Africa*, pp. 121–135.

19. European Political Cooperation (EPC) was a process in which the European Economic Community's (EEC) 12 member states sought to have a single coherent approach in the field of foreign policy in order to maximise their influence in international affairs. With the signing of the Maastricht Treaty of 1992, EPC was replaced by the European Union's Common Foreign and Security Policy (CFSP).

20. Alfred Pijpers, "The Netherlands: How to Keep the Spirit of Fouchet in the Bottle", in Christopher Hill (ed.), *National Foreign Policies and European Political Cooperation* (London: Allen and Unwin, 1983), pp. 175–176.

21. The Sakharov Prize for Freedom of Thought is awarded each year by the European Parliament. The prize was established in 1988 to honour individuals or organisations for their efforts to promote human rights and fundamental freedoms.

22. Lorenzo Fioramonti, "The European Union Promoting Democracy in South Africa: Strengths and Weaknesses", discussion paper (Brussels: European Development Policy Study Group, May 2004), http://www.edpsg.org/Documents/DP30.doc (accessed 6 July 2014).

23. Rob Davies, "Forging a New Relationship with the EU", in Talitha Bertelsman-Scott, Greg Mills and Elizabeth Sidiropoulos (eds), *The EU-SA Agreement: South Africa, Southern Africa, and the European Union* (Johannesburg: South African Institute of International Affairs (SAIIA), 2000).

24. European External Action Service (EEAS), *Cooperation Between the European Union and South Africa*, Joint Country Strategy Paper 2007–2013, Brussels, 2013, http://eeas.europa.eu/south_africa/csp/07_13_en.pdf (accessed 25 September 2014).

25. Talitha Bertelsmann-Scott and Peter Draper, "The TDCA: Perspectives for EU–South and Southern Africa Relations", *Trade Negotiations Insight from Doha to Cotonou* 4, no. 1 (January/February 2005), http://www.ictsd.org/tni/tni/TNI.EN 4.1pdf (accessed 13 July 2014).

26. Catherine Ashton, "Europe and the World", speech at Megaron: Athens Concert Hall, 8 July 2010.

27. European Commission (EC), "President Mbeki and EU Commissioner Louis Michel Discuss Strengthening the EU–South Africa Partnership", press release, Brussels, March 2006, http://europa.eu/rapid/press-release_IP-06-249_en.htm?locale=en (accessed 25 September 2014).

28. South African Department of Foreign Affairs (DFA), *South Africa–European Union Strategic Partnership: Joint Action Plan*, May 2007, http://www.dfa.gov.za/foreign/saeubilateral/docs/jap%20-%20final%20-%20signed%20copy.pdf (accessed 25 September 2014).

29. European Commission, "Towards an EU–South Africa Strategic Partnership", communication from the Commission to the Council and European Parliament, Brussels, June 2006, http://eur-lex.europa.eu/legal-content/EN/TXT/?uri=CELEX:52006DC0347 (accessed 25 September 2014).

30. DFA, "Briefing to AU and ACP Ambassadors on the European Commission's Proposal to Elevate South Africa–European Union Relations to a Strategic Partnership", press statement, Tshwane, 31 July 2006, http://www.dfa.gov.za/docs/speeches/2006/paha0731.htm (accessed 13 July 2014).

31. DFA, *South Africa–European Union Strategic Partnership: Joint Action Plan*.

32. Presidency of South Africa, *Twenty Year Review: South Africa, 1994–2014* (Pretoria, 2014), p. 159.

33. Jacques Classen, "Intense Lobbying to Ensure Citrus Export", *Farmer's Weekly*, 2 June 2014, http://www.farmersweekly.co.za/article.aspx?id=58330&h = intense-lobbying-to-ensure-citrus-exports (accessed 30 September 2014).

34. EC, "Increasing the Impact of EU Development Policy: An Agenda for Change", communication from the European Commission to the European Parliament, the European Council, the European Economic and Social Committee and the Committee of the Regions, http://ec.europa.eu/europeaid/what/development-policies/documents/agenda_for_change_en.pdf (accessed 13 July 2014).

35. Maite Nkoana-Mashabane, "Cementing a Strategic Partnership", *The New Age*, July 2013.

36. *See, for example*, Centre for Conflict Resolution (CCR), *The African, Caribbean, and Pacific (ACP) Group and the European Union (EU)*, Seminar Report no. 45 (Cape Town, January 2014), http://www.ccr.org.za (accessed 25 September 2014).

37. Mirjam van Reisen, "Executive Summary", *Study on the Future Perspectives of the ACP Group*, http://www.acp.int/sites/acpsec.waw.be/files/ACP27017%2012%20ENG %20VanReisen.pdf (accessed 13 July 2014).

38. ACP member states contribute 51 per cent, while the remainder is obtained from rebates on internal taxes from staff salaries (8 per cent) and interest on arrears in assessed contributions (4 per cent).

39. Adekeye Adebajo, "Trade Union of the Poor Versus Club of the Rich", *Business Day*, 30 June 2014, http://www.ccr.org.za/index.php/media-release/in-the-media/news paper-articles/item/1166-acp-and-eu (accessed 13 July 2014).

CHAPTER 21

SOUTH AFRICA AND THE BRICS

Kudrat Virk

In December 2010, after over a year of hard campaigning by President Jacob Zuma's government, South Africa received an invitation – described by the country's minister of international relations and cooperation, Maite Nkoana-Mashabane, as "the best Christmas present ever"[1] – from China, in its capacity as the rotating chair of the BRIC group (Brazil, Russia, India and China), to join the bloc. Africa's then-largest economy, with an estimated gross domestic product (GDP) of $295 billion in 2016,[2] formally acceded to the bloc at Sanya, China, in April 2011, transforming BRIC into BRICS and intensifying South Africa's engagement with four of the world's biggest emerging market economies. Despite some scepticism about the country's inclusion into an elite club of five, of which it was by far the smallest in both demographic and economic size, the expanded BRICS became a reality. In October 2016, the Indian coastal state of Goa hosted the eighth BRICS summit under the theme "Building Responsive, Inclusive and Collective Solutions".[3] Beyond summitry and declarations, the bloc has sought to give concrete shape to its agenda through the establishment of new institutions such as the New Development Bank (NDB), which has an initial authorised capital of $100 billion and signed its first loan agreement in December 2016. Over the years, intra-BRICS cooperation has further grown in a wide range of areas including trade, health, education and agriculture.

While there is evident commitment to widening cooperation among the five BRICS, questions remain over the group's cohesion, resilience and capacity to achieve concrete impact and become more than the sum of its catchy acronym, photo-ops and joint communiqués. A cursory survey of headlining articles about the bloc – including near-obituaries that "bid farewell to the Brics"[4] – is illustrative of the divided opinions that the bloc has generated over a short lifetime. Sceptics include those who variously view the grouping as "BRICS Without Mortar" that are "not likely to become a serious political organisation of like-minded states",[5] but rather as "an artificial bloc founded on a Goldman Sachs's catchphrase";[6] one "at risk of crumbling under [the] weight of individual agendas",[7] and "a concept in search of a common identity and institutionalised cooperation".[8] However, more optimistic views see the grouping as "a useful multilateral instrument" that could become "a 'go-to' institution for setting regional and global agendas"[9] and the New Development Bank, in particular, as "a fine idea whose time has come".[10] This nascent institution-building shows, to some extent, the ability of the grouping to go beyond criticism.[11] Yet beyond the ongoing strengthening of bilateral economic relations, political cooperation among the five BRICS countries has been anything but sturdy, with their failure to agree on a common approach to the escalating crisis in Syria in 2011, for example, serving as a clear illustration of deeper divergences among them. Even favourable assessments rest on the loosely formed bloc's potential as opposed to its actual achievements.

Dovetailing with the cautious to dismissive assessments of the grouping as a whole, there is doubt and uncertainty about the actual benefits for South Africa, as well as for the wider African continent, of the country's participation in the BRICS. In March 2013, the South African port city of Durban hosted the fifth BRICS summit under the theme "BRICS and Africa: Partnership for Development, Integration and Industrialisation". Officially, the African focus of the Durban summit was characterised as "a testimony to the consensus that exists among the BRICS countries on the importance of forging a true and effective partnership with the African continent".[12] Yet while the summit theme reflected South Africa's prioritisation of Africa's need for infrastructure development, regional integration and industrialisation, the degree and nature of the individual BRICS countries' interests on the continent are more complex and driven by individual agendas that may not necessarily converge with Africa's expectations, stoking fears of a new "scramble for Africa" among critics. Beyond the economic sphere, there is further debate about the extent to which the BRICS are genuinely committed to a fundamental transformation of the global order, as well as concern about the negative aspects of the bloc's collective challenge to the West, including the pressure that it has generated against "the progressive development of international norms that strive to protect people against kleptocratic and authoritarian rulers".[13]

Neither Africa as a whole (in the form of the African Union (AU), see Maloka in this volume) nor South Africa in particular seems to have a clear or detailed strategy in place for engaging with the BRICS.[14] South Africa's May 2011 foreign policy white paper includes only a broad intention to use Tshwane's (Pretoria) membership of the bloc "as a strategic opportunity to advance the interests of Africa in global issues such as the reform of global governance, the work of the G20 [Group of 20], [i]nternational trade, development, energy and climate change".[15] Similarly, the ruling African National Congress's (ANC) June 2017 foreign policy discussion document simply describes the New Development Bank as "a tangible way of expanding alternative sources of support to developing countries in need of finance" and identifies South Africa's hosting of its Africa office as part of the country's "efforts to implement the vision of an African Renaissance while deepening south-south cooperation", before noting the need for discussion on the impact of internal election results within the BRICS.[16] Moreover, in the absence of a unified continental approach to the emerging powers – or at least one with buy-in from key regional actors – it is unclear whether South Africa can, or should, claim to be the "gateway to Africa".

The Rise of the BRICS

In recent years, long-term structural changes in the world economy have contributed to an ongoing shift in political influence and economic wealth from North to South and West to East.[17] This rebalancing is historic, and "unprecedented in its speed and scale".[18] Whereas it took 50 years (1820–1870) for the United States (US) to double its GDP per capita during the industrial revolution, it has taken 12 years for China and 16 years for India to do the same over the past two decades.[19] This "rise of the South" – also the title given by the United Nations (UN) to its 2013 *Human Development Report* – became dramatically evident during the 2008–2009 global financial crisis, when Asian and African economies continued to register rapid growth even as those of the United States and European countries came to a virtual standstill. Also, the ability of Western-dominated financial institutions, such as the International Monetary Fund (IMF), to deal with the financial crisis was severely challenged, bringing the Group of 20 – an informal group of 19 advanced and emerging economies and the European Union (EU) – to the fore as a premier forum for coordinated policy action. Perceptions of Western decline were further strengthened by the European sovereign debt crisis, described in September 2011 by then European Commission president José Manuel Barroso as "the greatest challenge" faced by the EU since its creation.[20] In contrast, within the rising South, the rise of new economic powerhouses, in particular China and India, has been striking.

Together, the BRICS countries account for about 22 per cent of world GDP and more than 40 per cent of the world's population. Their growing importance has been reflected in changes in trade and investment flows. For example, outward foreign direct investment (FDI) from the original four BRIC countries – driven in particular by Russia and China – surged from less than $10 billion a year in the late 1990s to $147 billion in 2008, rising from 1–2 per cent to 9 per cent as a share of global total FDI flows.[21] Intra-BRIC trade grew equally rapidly: China's combined trade with Brazil, Russia and India rose from less than $18 billion in 2001 to more than $120 billion by 2009.[22] Indeed, the BRICS countries are expected to be the main engines of world economic growth in the years ahead. According to UN estimates, by 2050 Brazil, India and China will together produce 40 per cent of global economic output – up from 10 per cent in 1950 – outpacing the original Group of Seven (G-7) countries.[23] This will profoundly reshape the international economy. China's share of world GDP, for example, rose from 2 per cent in 1980 to 13 per cent in 2010,[24] with Beijing becoming the world's second-largest economy by the end of that year. This share had further risen to nearly 15 per cent by December 2016.[25] Even if projections prove overly optimistic given internal weaknesses in the BRICS and the risk of contagion from economic crises elsewhere, the structural factors that are pushing these economies up the global economic ladder are such that some, if not all, of these countries will be important players on the world stage, where power will be more diffuse than it is today.

Relations between the BRICS and the rest of the South have burgeoned side by side, with a 2011 IMF study identifying the group's four founding member states as "new growth drivers for low-income countries". According to this study, "LIC [low-income country] growth would have been 0.3 ... to 1.1 percentage points lower during the [recent financial] crisis if BRICs' GDP growth had declined at the same pace as [that of] advanced economies".[26] Neither China, India, Russia nor Brazil are newcomers to Africa. However, their engagement with the continent has greatly expanded over the past decade, with all four emerging economies widely expected to play a prominent role in its economic future. Between 2000 and 2008, Africa's real GDP increased by 4.9 per cent per year – more than double its pace in the 1980s and 1990s – and its collective GDP stood at $1.6 trillion in 2008 – roughly equal to that of Brazil or Russia.[27] It is nearly impossible to establish a direct link between the continent's growth spurt and the role of the BRIC countries. Research from McKinsey and Company indicates that only about one-third of Africa's accelerated growth can be attributed to the commodities boom generated by increased demand from the emerging economies, particularly China and India.[28] Even so, this is not insignificant. Africa's trade with the BRIC countries increased from about $20 billion in 2000 to over $180 billion in 2008, with BRIC–Africa trade accounting for more than 19.2 per cent of Africa's trade with the world (up from 4.6 per cent in 1993).[29] In 2016, bilateral trade between Africa and the BRICS was an estimated $258 billion.[30] Generally speaking, the rise of the BRICS has therefore generated great expectations for the economic prospects of Africa, as well as for the rest of the developing world. Though China's slowdown, combined with the lacklustre economic performance of Brazil, Russia and South Africa, had lowered these expectations somewhat by 2016.

The origins of the BRICS, as a concept, lie in an acronym coined in 2001 by Jim O'Neill of Goldman Sachs in an attempt to capture the economic potential of Brazil, Russia, India and China's fast-growing economies. The concept became a political reality when it was embraced by the four emerging powers at the first BRIC summit, in Yekaterinburg, Russia, in June 2009. At the same time, it would be overly reductionist to accept the idea of the BRICS as an investment strategist's invention, or even as a purely economic label. As Oliver Stuenkel writes, an alternative narrative holds that O'Neill's BRIC concept only "articulated an already existing drive towards a 'rising power identity' and closer cooperation between these countries".[31] For example, in December 1998, Russia's prime minister, Yevgeny Primakov, raised the idea of a strategic triangle comprising Moscow, Beijing and New Delhi to counteract US dominance after the Cold War, with the first official meeting of the three countries' foreign ministers taking place on the sidelines of the UN General Assembly in September 2002.[32] Indeed, for a number of commentators, mainly Russian, this initiative – the RIC forum (Russia, India and China) continues to meet regularly – formed the foundation of the BRICS.[33] Before they formally came together as a bloc, the four future BRIC countries first met – on Moscow's invitation – at the ministerial level on the sidelines of the UN General Assembly in September 2006.

In this context, it is also worth bearing in mind that the BRICS bloc is, to some extent, the most-hyped formation in a field that includes, among others, the G-20; RIC; the IBSA Forum (India, Brazil and South Africa); BASIC (Brazil, South Africa, India and China); the New Asia–Africa Strategic Partnership (NAASP); the Shanghai Cooperation Organisation (SCO); and the Indian Ocean Rim Association (IORA). These groups are in various stages of evolution and, taken together, are symptomatic of a wider trend towards issue-specific coalitions, as traditional and rising powers both seek to navigate a fluid, still evolving international landscape. The emerging power alliances, in particular, and among which the BRICS bloc stands out, are motivated by a powerful shared desire to shape "a more democratic and just multi-polar world order based on the rule of international law, equality, mutual respect, cooperation, coordinated action and collective decision-making of all states".[34] Furthermore, while the BRIC countries may have started their journey by focusing mainly on reform of the international financial and economic architecture (as the opening statement of their inaugural joint communiqué in June 2009 clearly indicates),[35] successive summits have witnessed the BRICS acknowledge an expanding array of common concerns – the 2016 Goa Declaration, for example, touched on peace and security issues including the role of the AU, the situations in Syria and Afghanistan, the Palestinian–Israeli conflict, and the threat posed by international terrorism, not to forget the need for UN Security Council reform.[36]

South Africa in the BRICS

In April 2011, South Africa was formally welcomed into the BRICS to a host of varied reactions, including excitement, introspection, scepticism, incomprehension and even dismay. To start with, as Simon Freemantle observes, "South Africa's size and global relevance is dwarfed by that of the individual BRIC economies, let alone the collective".[37] South Africa's population of about 55 million pales in comparison to that of both China and India, each of which has a population of over 1 billion. While South Africa is one of Africa's two largest economies, it ranked only 38th in the world – behind South Korea (11th), Mexico (15th), Indonesia (16th),

Turkey (17th) and Argentina (21st) – in 2016, not to mention the fact that the rest of the BRICS far outranked it.[38] As a share of the grouping's total GDP, South Africa accounts for a mere 2.5 per cent.[39] In addition, while China and India were among the fastest-growing large economies in the world between 2006 and 2016, South Africa's economy has experienced deceleration, with growth estimated to have been a mere 0.4 per cent in 2016.[40] Between 2001 and 2010, six of the world's fastest-growing economies were in sub-Saharan Africa; South Africa was not one of them.[41] Meanwhile, Nigeria – Africa's "other" powerhouse with the potential to drive growth and development on the continent – grew its economy at an annual average rate of 8.9 per cent during the same period,[42] and in 2014, overtook South Africa as Africa's largest economy.

Looking beyond size, however, South Africa compares far more favourably. In the World Economic Forum's (WEF) Global Competitiveness Index for 2016–2017, the country is the highest-ranked state in sub-Saharan Africa. Placing 47th overall (out of 138 countries surveyed), it is the fourth-most competitive BRICS economy, ahead of Brazil (81st) and only a short distance behind Russia (43rd) and India (39th). In terms of its financial market development, the African BRICS country is a relative heavyweight, ranked 11th; India (38th) comes in next, while Russia (108th) is outclassed completely.[43] South African banks are well-capitalised and well-regulated, "attracting investors who want to access loans, trade finance and other products for African business", while the Johannesburg Stock Exchange (JSE) is the largest on the continent.[44] Particularly impressive is the country's ability to attract broad-based foreign direct investment, which belies its size. In 2010, South Africa had inward FDI stock of $180 billion – only $26 billion less than the figure for India, an economy about four times its size (though this gap had widened significantly to $114 billion in 2014).[45] Against this backdrop, it was not entirely surprising that President Jacob Zuma's government was successful in its then bid to join the elite grouping, while rhetorically claiming to be the "gateway to Africa".

Still, the question as to why South Africa was inducted into the BRICS has continued to generate commentary, particularly among "literal-minded economists".[46] Not only is there not space enough here to delve too deeply into this question, but it is also not particularly relevant – at least for now, given that South Africa (even if seen as a "briquette" relative to the other member states of the BRICS)[47] is now a member of this "big five" group, and in 2017 remained the continent's second largest economy and its foremost financial hub.[48] Similar questions were, and continue to be, asked about the rest of the BRICS. For example, American scholar Graham Allison has pointed out that China, the heavyweight that dwarfs the other four members across a swathe of macro-economic indicators, could easily be a club of one, making the case for the group's transformation into RIBS (Russia, India, Brazil and South Africa).[49] In a similar vein, in December 2011, Indian-American analyst Fareed Zakaria asked if India, with its then struggling economy and paralysed coalition government, was "the broken BRIC", suggesting that "the 'I' in BRIC might stand for Indonesia, not India" one day.[50] Russia, on the other hand, is not, strictly speaking, an emerging power, but rather a re-emerging power; and prior to South Africa's entry into the club, one did not have to reach very far to find an argument for taking the "R" out of BRIC to form BIC (Brazil, India and China). Russia was the smallest economy in the grouping until 2011, when South Africa joined, and questions remain over its capacity to sustain its commodity-driven growth. In this respect, finding the odd BRIC out could easily be a veritable cottage industry. None of this is to say that there are not any genuine questions to be asked about South Africa's BRICS membership. Rather, it should be remembered that the BRICS are still a new grouping, striving to create cohesion – politically and economically; as such, questioning of the "S" in BRICS needs to be placed in a wider context. It is also worth bearing in mind that identities – including group identities – are not a given, but a shared and social construct requiring time and process. The BRICS are only just getting to know each other.

Furthermore, this debate misses the point that the economic dynamism of the BRICS is an important basis for, but does not constitute the entirety of, their existence. The bloc is evolving into a geo-political grouping, and the inclusion of South Africa "completes" its geography. Without South Africa, the BRIC grouping lacked representation from Africa, which weakened the group's claim to global legitimacy, as well as its demand for more representative global governance institutions. Similarly, from a South African point of view, its membership in the bloc bolsters the country's claim to a seat at the "top table" of global governance and creates an opportunity for it to, at least in theory, influence decision-making and exercise leadership on issues of concern to itself, as well as to Africa, in partnership with the world's most significant emerging powers. South Africa's inclusion in the BRICS, as in the case of IBSA, BASIC and others, is an expression of the country's strategic priority of strengthening

South-South relations. Whether its BRICS membership will actually achieve this benefit is another question altogether; as South African scholars Chris Landsberg and Candice Moore have noted, "South Africa is the last to arrive in BRICS, and may therefore be seen as a 'rule-taker'. This, along with its questionable criteria for entry, appears to limit the space that South Africa has for initiative and leadership in BRICS".[51] The political case also rests on the assumption – one that, at the risk of repetition, underlies any BRICS analysis – that the bloc as a whole will be able to articulate a clearer "agenda for reform" and cohere into a genuine countervailing agent with "real" impact.

Opportunities and Challenges

The Economic Aspect

It cannot be denied that South Africa will benefit from strengthening and diversifying its economic engagement with the other BRICS members. Starting from a low base, South Africa's overall trade with the rest of the grouping has grown steadily over the past few years, rising from $10.4 billion in 2005 to $28.9 billion by 2016.[52] The EU, as a whole, is still South Africa's main trading partner (see Nkosi in this volume), but, as South Africa's ambassador to the WTO, Xavier Carim, has noted, its share of the country's trade declined from 44 per cent in the mid-1990s to 23 per cent in 2013, while China has now become the country's largest bilateral commercial partner, accounting for around 14 per cent of its total trade in 2013 (see Liu in this volume).[53] Similarly, trade between India and South Africa has grown very rapidly and amounted to an estimated $6.3 billion in 2016, up from about $616 million in 2001.[54] Commercial engagement has also expanded, as reflected in the purchase of a 20 per cent stake in Standard Bank, South Africa's largest bank, by the Industrial and Commercial Bank of China (ICBC). According to one analysis, the deal – the largest investment by a Chinese bank outside China at the time – "allows the South African bank increased access to the largest and fastest-growing economy in the world", and a number of cooperative projects have since been developed.[55] Several major companies from the BRICS countries have established a significant presence in South Africa over recent years, including India's Tata, which is one of the biggest investors in South Africa, with Johannesburg serving as the headquarters for its continental operations.

However, there are a number of important issues to consider. First, on the one hand, it makes strategic sense for South Africa to formalise its ties with its major developing country partners through BRICS membership. On the other hand, it is difficult to say with any measure of certainty how much of the expansion in trade and investment has accrued from formal membership in the grouping, given that the growth trajectory pre-dates South Africa's joining date.[56] The ICBC–Standard Bank deal, for example, was announced in 2007, while Tata arrived in South Africa as far back as 1994 (with the ending of apartheid). That said, participation in the BRICS – especially with the establishment of the BRICS Business Council in Durban in March 2013 and the promotion of trade expos – offers greater opportunities to enhance commercial ties.

In this context, it is also worth bearing in mind that BRICS membership per se does not come with any preferential trade treatment. Negotiations for a preferential trade agreement (PTA) between India and South Africa (since expanded to the Southern African Customs Union (SACU); see Gibbs in this volume) pre-date the creation of the BRICS, while a PTA with the Southern Common Market (MERCOSUR, which includes Brazil) and SACU, similarly pre-dates the inclusion of South Africa in the BRICS.[57] At some point, it is important to make a distinction between the multilateral and bilateral dimensions of South Africa's engagement with the BRICS – that is, its membership in the bloc versus its relations with individual countries within that bloc.

Second, the current pattern of South Africa–BRIC trade is problematic in a number of ways. In the case of China, it is asymmetrical – or, to quote a recent headline, "[South] Africa isn't a big bull in China's shop".[58] In 2015, while China accounted for 14.1 per cent of South Africa's trade and ranked second (after the EU) as a partner, South Africa accounted for less than 2 per cent of China's trade and did not even rank in its top ten trading partners.[59] In the case of India, bilateral trade shares are still extremely low: South Africa again does not rank in the top ten trading partners, and its share of India's imports and exports remained less than 2 per cent in 2015.[60] Against this background, it remains vital that enthusiasm about the rise of the BRICS does not sweep away South Africa's efforts to maintain a solid footing in its relationship with key traditional partners, such as the EU, the United States (see Weissman in this volume) and Japan – particularly in the current political-economic environment, in which old patterns have been disrupted, while new patterns are still emerging and remain unsettled.[61]

Arguably most worrying, is the unsustainable pattern of trade between South Africa and its two top-ranked BRICS trade partners: China and India. This pattern is heavily weighted in favour of primary product exports from South Africa and manufactured and/or value-added good imports to South Africa. To take the example of India–South Africa trade, the top ten exports to India include coal, briquettes, solid fuels, manganese ores, copper ores, ferrous waste and scrap and scrap of iron; while the top ten imports from India consist of petroleum oils, cars, telephone sets, equipment and transport vehicles.[62] This unbalanced trade is a growing concern, which was highlighted by the establishment of a joint trade study, under South Africa's chair at the 2013 Durban summit, to find ways to promote more value-added exports.

Third, beyond the benefits that may accrue to South Africa itself, it is important, too, to examine the potential gains (or their lack thereof) for the wider continent from the country's BRICS membership – especially given that, as Landsberg and Moore note, Tshwane "has made no secret of its intentions to use the BRICS relationship to further the African agenda".[63] This in turn makes it vital to cut through official BRICS rhetoric – as a whole and on an individual country basis – of South-South cooperation and assess the ground reality of their engagement with Africa.[64] This is a difficult exercise, due in part to the nature of that engagement, in which foreign aid, development finance, trade and FDI are often bound up in complex package deals, and in part due to the lack of availability of robust data. For example, as a study by the European Union points out: "Not all BRICS are publishing respective statistics [on outward FDI to LICs]."[65] That said, the evidence so far is, on balance, somewhat mixed. In terms of trade, there is – as in the case of South Africa, in particular – reason for concern, with the pattern of BRICS–Africa trade "reminiscent of colonial and post-colonial trade relations with the developed world": about 90 per cent of Africa's exports to non-African developing countries consist of primary products.[66] Furthermore, according to the Africa Research Institute, in the case of China, the exponential growth in trade "was not accompanied by significant skills development, technology transfer or productivity improvements in Africa" in the 2000s.[67] In addition, there is genuine concern about "land grabbing" in Africa by a number of countries, including (but not only) the BRICS – India in Ethiopia and Kenya; South Africa in Angola, Benin, the Democratic Republic of the Congo (DRC), Ethiopia, Madagascar and Mozambique; Brazil in Ethiopia and Mozambique; and China in the DRC, Sudan and Zimbabwe, among others.[68] Admittedly, not all of this "grabbing" – land use, as well as commercial activities – is exploitative. While China and India are resource-hungry Asian giants, with their domestic growth imperatives having created a strategic need for oil, minerals and grains that has lured them to resource-abundant Africa, their presence on the continent is becoming diversified. There is commercially driven, private sector-led investment – particularly from India and increasingly from China – over which state imperatives have less control. Investment follows opportunity, and on a continent with a fast-rising middle class, this means that the "new game" in Africa is not reducible to exploitation. Nonetheless, this should not dilute the need for Africa – as well as South Africa, if it truly claims to advance Africa's interests – to have a clearly articulated strategy, or unified approach, towards the emerging economies (though with a caveat – South Africa, itself, is implicated in the activities of the BRICS).

Fourth, South Africa has sought to position itself as a gateway to Africa.[69] Politically and economically, this is a questionable proposition. It rests on the assumption that this role is still necessary. For a number of years, given its relatively sophisticated and developed economy as well as stable political system, post-apartheid South Africa has indeed been seen as a preferred entry point for new businesses on the continent. It remains for the moment the leading destination for foreign direct investment, in terms of the number of projects.[70] However, as the continent's prospects for peace and stability have improved and as the economic growth trajectory of Africa as a whole has risen, this is changing and South Africa may no longer, or not for long, be the continent's obvious "landing slot for investors".[71] According to Deloitte: "The reality is that significant investments are flowing directly into respective African economies, as these markets currently boast higher GDP growth rates than South Africa – off a low base, admittedly."[72] Similarly, a 2012 report by KPMG asserts: "The 'gateway' to Africa idea is a little outdated ... Practically, there is no single 'gateway' to Africa no matter how much Brand South Africa may believe South Africa fulfils this need."[73] Instead, there are multiple business gateways into Africa including Nigeria, Ghana, Kenya and Mauritius. For example, in 2012, General Electric chose to base its operations in sub-Saharan Africa in Nairobi, Kenya, following in the footsteps of Nestlé, Coca-Cola and Heineken.[74] As South African analyst Dianna Games observes, South Africa is increasingly seen as an entry point into the Southern African Development Community (SADC) region, rather than the continent as a whole, by a number of businesses, though even within SADC, Angola is a preferred gateway for Brazilian companies.[75] (See also Vickers and Cawood in this volume.)

The BRICS countries, in particular, have shown a distinct preference for dealing directly with individual African countries and/or sub-regions.[76] For example, while the China–Africa Development Fund (CADFund) – which supports Chinese companies investing in Africa – may have opened its first representative office on the continent in Johannesburg in March 2009, it now also has offices in Addis Ababa, Ethiopia; Lusaka, Zambia; and Accra, Ghana.[77] Furthermore, China, as well as India, have set up alternative channels for their commercial diplomacy that go through neither South Africa nor any BRICS mechanism, befitting their status as competitors on the African continent. The Forum on China–Africa Cooperation (FOCAC), which was established at a ministerial conference in Beijing in October 2000, convenes at a summit-level conference every three years; the sixth FOCAC meeting was held in South Africa's financial capital, Johannesburg, in December 2015, at which China tripled its financial pledges to Africa to $60 billion, up from $20 billion in 2012.[78] While FOCAC meetings have produced joint declarations and action plans that inform the broad contours of Sino–African relations, in practice, China has preferred to sign trade and investment agreements and project contracts bilaterally with individual African governments.[79] Admittedly, Beijing signed a framework agreement with the East African Community (EAC) in November 2011 and "outlined new measures to negotiate infrastructure projects directly with Africa's regional institutions".[80] However, these are not the norm in Sino–African relations. India has followed in China's footsteps, hosting the first India–Africa Forum Summit (IAFS) in New Delhi in April 2008, with the third, also in New Delhi, in October 2015; the second having been held in Addis Ababa in May 2011.

Also, while the BRICS may have accepted South Africa as an interlocutor for Africa "by default", it is highly questionable that the continent has done the same.[81] In the words of Landsberg and Moore, "several countries have questioned South Africa's claim to fairly represent the interests of African states within BRICS and the G20. Many African countries like Nigeria and Senegal also take umbrage at the fact that external powers look to South Africa as Africa's global representative".[82] It is not entirely unreasonable to contend that as these countries "rise" along with the rest of the continent, South Africa will likely face greater competition for the mantle of leadership and as Africa's voice in global forums. Moreover, against the backdrop of its past role as a destabilising force on the continent during the apartheid era (see Introduction in this volume), the country has taken great care not to be seen to wear that mantle too assertively or to be seen to lead by anything other than consensus.[83] In the words of Ebrahim Ebrahim, South Africa's deputy minister of international relations and cooperation, voiced shortly after its first BRICS summit in April 2011: "We wish to state that, we have no mandate nor have we asked for one from the African Union (AU) to represent them within the BRICS Mechanism."[84] Shortly thereafter though, South Africa engaged in a bruising process to secure the chair of the AU Commission for Nkosazana Dlamini-Zuma, a former foreign minister, in 2012, clashing with, among others, Nigeria (see Adebajo in this volume).

The Geo-Political Aspect

A large challenge centres on the ability and willingness of the BRICS to coalesce as a group, and the position of South Africa in particular in this endeavour.[85] On the one hand, there is general consensus among the BRICS that developing countries are under-represented in global governance institutions. However, the bloc does not necessarily agree on how these institutions should be reformed, with the UN Security Council serving as one example. India, Brazil and South Africa are liberal democracies, which certainly neither Russia nor China can claim to be. Brazil and Russia are primarily exporters of commodities, while China and India are in the main importers of natural resources. Furthermore, bilateral relations within the grouping have been fraught with tension, distrust and rivalry. For example, India and China, in addition to their strategic competition in Africa, are rivals for influence in the Indian Ocean, and, in Asia, share a disputed border over which they have previously gone to war in 1962. American scholar Michael Glosny, for example, concludes that "as BRIC commonalities and shared interests are excessively shallow, there has been little evidence of any 'BRICs mentality', and one is unlikely to form given the differences".[86]

In 2011, Brazil, India and South Africa served together on the UN Security Council concurrently, joining veto-wielding permanent members Russia and China in a decision-making capacity.[87] With all five BRICS countries represented at the Council's horseshoe table for the first time since the grouping's inception, this created a unique, shared opportunity for them to identify and work together on issues of common concern, including institutional reform, and give some substance to their desire for greater influence over the international security agenda. For South Africa, this development also afforded an early opportunity to assess the grouping's potential as a means to increase its diplomatic clout and advance the wider African agenda that it could represent, as well as to take stock of the challenges that the alignment presents for its broader foreign policy objectives.[88]

The "Afro-Arab Spring", in particular events in Libya and Syria, was a dominant item on the UN Security Council's agenda during 2011 and into early 2012, when India and South Africa remained on the Council even as Brazil rotated out of it. On Resolution 1973, which formed the basis for the North Atlantic Treaty Organisation (NATO)-led action against Libya, South Africa was at odds with its BRICS partners in voting for it (see Tawfik, and Mashabane in this volume). Along with Germany, the four original BRIC countries abstained on the resolution. While it is possible to see the abstentions as "non-negative" votes that effectively authorised the NATO intervention (though not "regime change") as expressions of solidarity with Afro-Arab interests[89] – India, for example, cited support for the action from the Arab League in its statement – the abstentions also pointed to tension on issues including the threshold criteria for the use of force. The concept of responsibility to protect (R2P) – which was invoked by Resolution 1973 – has been embraced in Africa, where it has been given its most concrete expression in the African Union's Constitutive Act of 2000, which grants African countries the collective right to intervene in a member state to prevent mass atrocities, and of which South Africa is a part. On the other hand, China and India's support for the idea is weak, with both countries extremely reluctant to depart from traditional ideas about sovereignty and non-intervention as the foundation of international order.[90] However, the intervention in Libya did not necessarily enjoy the support of the AU as a whole, which raises questions about not only South Africa's ability to make common cause with the BRICS, but also, to some extent, its ability to represent African interests.

There was greater unity among the BRICS subsequently in terms of criticism of the disproportionate use of force by NATO and the "mission creep" to regime change. In addition, blowback from the experience in Libya initially translated into a shared wariness among the BRICS to act in the Syrian crisis. However, with developments on the ground, differences surfaced, with India and South Africa at odds with the Russian and Chinese exercise of veto power on a draft resolution in February 2012. Unlike Moscow and Beijing, New Delhi and Tshwane are rising democracies with a shared commitment to human rights and members of the IBSA Forum (along with Brazil), raising the question of whether that grouping may not provide a more fruitful avenue for cooperation within the context of a UN Security Council agenda with a similar normative focus.[91]

The question of Security Council reform, which was mostly crowded out by more immediate events in 2011–2012, is an additional source of tension within the BRICS. While the veto power of the two BRICS countries who are among the permanent five (P-5) members of the Security Council lies at the epicentre of the bloc's clout on the Council, it is also what divides them from the rest. One of the main objectives of South Africa's participation in the BRICS is "to partner with key players of the South on issues related to global governance and its reforms".[92] Though there is general consensus among the BRICS on the problem of Southern under-representation in global governance institutions, there are differences on the choice of remedy. The grouping's IBSA members are separated from China and Russia by not only their shared democratic identity, but also their common objective of acquiring permanent membership on the UN Security Council. Despite positive statements, China, in particular, is a status quo power. Though broadly in favour of "necessary and reasonable reform" and greater representation for developing countries (especially African countries),[93] it has not been keen on expansion of the Council's veto-wielding, permanent membership.[94] Notably, India and Brazil, along with Germany and Japan, make up the Group of Four (G-4) interest group in mutual support of their candidature for permanent membership of the Council. South Africa is not a member of the group, though in June 2010 India and South Africa expressed mutual support for each other's candidature.[95] In the broader context of a fluid, international scene characterised by still coalescing alliances, this begs the question of whether the BRICS is the only, or even the "right", game in town, for South Africa to leverage itself at the Security Council in particular or its diplomatic fortunes at the UN more generally.

Concluding Reflections

For South Africa, membership in the BRICS is replete with challenges, not least of which are posed by the grouping's still ongoing attempts to craft a distinct and shared identity for itself on the global stage. Membership of the bloc is also a potential opportunity for the country to raise its own clout, and strengthen its ties across the board with key emerging partners. However, given that South Africa has a less-than-imposing profile (in terms of size) within the BRICS bloc, and given that the country has positioned itself – be it problematically – as a representative for/from Africa, it bears responsibility for articulating a more coherent approach to navigating the tensions between its African agenda, its own ambitions for a leadership role on the continent and its ability to be an equal, contributing BRICS member. In this respect, South Africa is an odd one out within the grouping in more than one way – it cannot escape its region. India, China and Russia are located in parts of the world where regionalism is not as potent or as well-developed a driving force; while Brazil is able to play a role within BRICS "without having to obtain consensus from the region".[96] South Africa, on the other hand, by virtue of its own articulation of its national interests, is inseparable from the continent, and the challenge may lie in determining – and then articulating – the need, as well as viability, of an African agenda for engagement with the emerging powers versus a unified BRICS approach to Africa.

Furthermore, given the weaknesses of the BRICS as a collective, and the emerging trend towards issue-based alliances, as well as an unsettled international landscape, South Africa has to leverage different groups in different forums to advance its interests – as illustrated by its experiences at the UN Security Council in 2011–2012. This, in turn, means that the country's "need for sophisticated analysis of global trends and specific issues almost certainly will increase, particularly in light of its growing prominence in the developing world".[97] In this context, debating BRICS versus IBSA is, to some extent, not a fruitful exercise, not least of all as both bodies serve different purposes (one of which is to provide a forum to discuss concerns about China, especially for India). Rather, the challenge of the early twenty-first century in a plural world, moving towards some form of multipolarity, is for South Africa – as much as any other emerging power – to possess the capacity in terms of resources and knowledge to navigate multiple vectors and even hedge its diplomatic bets.

Acknowledgements

I would like to thank Margaret Struthers, former Librarian of the Centre for Conflict Resolution (CCR) Peace Library, Cape Town, South Africa, for her invaluable time and assistance in finding research resources for the writing of this chapter. This chapter builds and draws, in part and as indicated, on two previous works: Kudrat Virk, "India and South Africa", in David M. Malone, C. Raja Mohan and Srinath Raghavan (eds), *The Oxford*

Handbook of Indian Foreign Policy (Oxford: Oxford University Press, 2015), pp. 552–565; and "The ACP, the EU, and the BRICS: Opportunities on the Horizon or Just a Mirage?", in Annita Montoute and Kudrat Virk (eds), *The ACP Group and the EU Development Partnership: Beyond the North-South Debate* (New York: Palgrave Macmillan, 2017), pp. 317–340.

Notes

1. Nasreen Seria, "South Africa Is Asked to Join As a BRIC Member to Boost Emerging Markets", *Bloomberg*, 24 December 2012, http://www.bloomberg.com/news/2010-12-24/south-africa-asked-to-join-bric-to-boost-cooperation-with-emerging-markets.html (accessed 22 July 2013).
2. World Bank, http://databank.worldbank.org/data/download/GDP.pdf (accessed 11 July 2017).
3. Previous summits were held in Yekaterinburg, Russia, in June 2009; Brasília, Brazil, in April 2010; Sanya, China, in April 2011; New Delhi, India, in March 2012; Durban, South Africa in March 2013; Fortaleza/Brasília, Brazil, in July 2014; and Ufa, Russia, in July 2015.
4. Philip Stephens, "A Story of Brics Without Mortar", *Financial Times*, 24 November 2011, http://www.ft.com/intl/cm/s/0/352e96e8-15f2-11e1-a691-00144feabdc0.html#axzz2zsPDMAj7 (accessed 23 July 2013).
5. Joseph S. Nye, "BRICS Without Mortar", *Project Syndicate*, 3 April 2013, http://www.project-syndicate.org/commentary/why-brics-will-not-work-by-joseph-s–nye (accessed 23 July 2013).
6. Walter Ladwig, "An Artificial Bloc Built on a Catchphrase", *New York Times*, 26 March 2012, http://www.nytimes.com/2012/03/27/opinion/an-artificial-bloc-built-on-a-catchphrase.html?_r=0 (accessed 18 October 2012).
7. Jaswant Singh, "Brics at Risk of Crumbling Under Weight of Individual Agendas", *Business Day* (South Africa), 24 March 2013, http://www.bdlive.co.za/opinion/bdalpha/2013/03/24/brics-at-risk-of-crumbling-under-weight-of-individual-agendas (accessed 23 July 2013).
8. Brahma Chellaney, "The Cracks in the BRICS", *Al Jazeera*, 24 March 2012, http://www.aljazeera.com/indepth/opinion/2012/03/2012324155232689239.html (accessed 18 October 2012).
9. Samir Saran and Vivan Sharan, "Giving BRICS a Non-Western Vision", *The Hindu*, 14 February 2012, http://www.thehindu.com/opinion/op-ed/article2889838.ece (accessed 18 October 2012).
10. Mattia Romani, Nicholas Stern and Joseph Stiglitz, "Brics Bank Is a Fine Idea Whose Time Has Come", *Financial Times*, 5 April 2012, http://www.ft.com/intl/cms/s/0/1770f242-7d88-11e1-81a5-00144feab49a.html#axzz2zsPDMAj7 (accessed 23 July 2013).
11. André de Mello e Souza, "Brick by Brics – Building Institutions", *Livemint*, 2 November 2016, http://www.livemint.com/Opinion/cVRKI9tH9uQdRLsE48iWNK/Brick-by-Bricsbuilding-institutions.html (accessed 25 February 2017).

12. Maite Nkoana-Mashabane, "The Brics Come to Durban", in Patrick Bond (ed.), *BRICS in Africa: Anti-Imperialist, Sub-Imperialist, or In Between? A Reader for the Durban Summit*, March 2013, p. 7.

13. Merle Lipton, "Are the BRICS Reformers, Revolutionaries, or Counter-Revolutionaries?", *South African Journal of International Affairs* 24, no. 1 (2017), p. 55.

14. Memory Dube, "BRICS Summit 2013: Strategies for South Africa's Engagement", Policy Briefing no. 62 (Johannesburg: South African Institute of International Affairs (SAIIA), March 2013), p. 2.

15. *Building a Better World: The Diplomacy of Ubuntu*, White Paper on South Africa's Foreign Policy, 13 May 2011, http://www.info.gov.za (accessed 23 July 2013).

16. African National Congress (ANC), "The ANC in an Unpredictable and Uncertain World That Is Characterised by Increased Insecurity and the Rise of Populism: An ANC NEC International Relations Sub-Committee Discussion Document Towards the 5th National Policy Conference", Midrand, South Africa, 30 June– 5 July 2017, pp. 4–5, 15.

17. National Intelligence Council, *Global Trends 2025: A Transformed World* (Washington, DC, November 2008), p. 7. This paragraph and the next two paragraphs draw on Kudrat Virk, "The ACP, the EU, and the BRICS: Opportunities on the Horizon or Just a Mirage?", in Annita Montoute and Kudrat Virk (eds), *The ACP Group and the EU Development Partnership: Beyond the North-South Debate* (New York: Palgrave Macmillan, 2017), pp. 317–340, especially pp. 318–319.

18. United Nations Development Programme (UNDP), *Human Development Report 2013: The Rise of the South – Human Progress in a Diverse World* (New York, 2013), p. 11.

19. UNDP, *Human Development Report 2013*, p. 11. *See also* Yuvan Atsmon et al., *Winning the $30 Trillion Decathlon: Going for Gold in Emerging Markets* (McKinsey and Company, August 2012), p. 4.

20. "EU 'Faces Its Greatest Challenge' – Jose Manuel Barroso", *BBC News*, 28 September 2011, http://www.bbc.co.uk/news/world-europe-15087683 (accessed 24 July 2012).

21. Montford Mlachila and Misa Takebe, "FDI from BRICs to LICs: Emerging Growth Driver?", International Monetary Fund (IMF) Working Paper (Washington, DC: IMF, African Department, July 2011), p. 5, http://www.imf.org/external/pubs/ft/wp/2011/wp11178.pdf (accessed 25 October 2012).

22. Simon Freemantle, "Perspective: Standard Bank – Is There an IBSA-BRIC Business Future?", in Francis Kornegay and Lesley Masters (eds), *From BRIC to BRICS: Report on the Proceedings of the International Workshop on South Africa's Emerging Power Alliances: IBSA, BRIC, BASIC* (Pretoria: Institute for Global Dialogue (IGD), 2011), pp. 85–86.

23. UNDP, *Human Development Report 2013*, p. 13. *See also* National Intelligence Council, *Global Trends 2025*, p. 7.

24. Ed Dew et al., "China's Changing Growth Pattern", *Bank of England Quarterly Bulletin* 51, no. 1 (2011), p. 49.

25. "China's Growing Contribution to World Economy", *People's Daily*, 14 January 2017, http://english.gov.cn/news/top_news/2017/01/14/content_281475541536155. htm (accessed 26 February 2017).

26. IMF, "New Growth Drivers for Low-Income Countries: The Role of BRICs", 12 January 2011, p. 31, http://www.imf.org/external/np/pp/eng/2011/011211.pdf (accessed 1 October 2012).

27. Acha Leke et al., "What's Driving Africa's Growth", *McKinsey Quarterly*, June 2010, http://www.mckinseyquarterly.com/Whats_driving_Africas_growth_ 2601 (accessed 27 October 2012).

28. Leke et al., "What's Driving Africa's Growth".

29. Freemantle, "Perspective: Standard Bank", p. 87.

30. Data from the International Trade Centre (ITC), Trade Map, http://www.trademap. org (accessed 26 February 2017).

31. Oliver Stuenkel, "Will Brics Change the Course of History?", in Bond, *BRICS in Africa*, p. 59.

32. Harsh Pant, "The Moscow-Beijing-Delhi 'Strategic Triangle': An Idea Whose Time May Never Come", *Security Dialogue* 35, no. 3 (2004), p. 313. *See also* Samir Saran and Nandan Unnikrishnan, "RIC Needs to Work for an Asian Trading Region", 4 November 2011, http://orfonline.org/cms/export/orfonline/html/Brics/ article4.html (accessed 25 July 2013).

33. *See, for example*, Vladimir Shubin, "Brics Viewed Positively from Moscow", in Bond, *BRICS in Africa*, pp. 22–24; and Vladimir Radyuhin, "For a New Order", *Frontline* 25, no. 12 (7–20 June 2008), http://www.hindu.com/ fline/fl2512/stories/20080620251205200.htm (accessed 25 July 2013).

34. "Joint Statement of the BRIC Countries' Leaders", Yekaterinburg, Russia, 16 June 2009, http://archive.kremlin.ru/eng/text/docs/2009/06/217963.shtml (accessed 16 July 2013).

35. "Joint Statement of the BRIC Countries' Leaders".

36. "Goa Declaration", Eighth BRICS Summit, Goa, India, 16 October 2016, http:// brics2016.gov.in/upload/Goa%20Declaration%20and%20Action%20Plan.pdf (accessed 25 February 2017).

37. Freemantle, "Perspective: Standard Bank", p. 91.

38. World Bank, http://databank.worldbank.org/data/download/GDP.pdf (accessed 11 July 2017).

39. Roy Robins, "One of These BRICS Is Not Like the Other", *Foreign Policy*, 26 March 2013, http://www.foreignpolicy.com/articles/2013/03/26/is_ south_africa_really_a_bric?page=full (accessed 25 July 2013).

40. World Bank, *Global Economic Prospects: Weak Investment in Uncertain Times* (Washington, DC, January 2017), p. 4.

41. The six were: Angola, Nigeria, Ethiopia, Chad, Mozambique and Rwanda. "Africa's Impressive Growth", *The Economist*, 6 January 2011, http://www. economist.com/blogs/dailychart/2011/01/daily_chart (accessed 27 February 2017).

42. "Africa's Impressive Growth".

43. Klaus Schwab (ed.), *The Global Competitiveness Report 2016–2017* (Geneva: World Economic Forum, 2016), pp. xiii, 48–49.

44. Dianna Games, "South Africa as Africa's Gateway: A Perspective from Business", Policy Briefing no. 46 (Johannesburg: SAIIA, March 2012), p. 2.

45. Organisation for Economic Cooperation and Development (OECD) Data, FDI Stocks, https://data.oecd.org/fdi/fdi-stocks.htm#indicator-chart (accessed 26 February 2017); Freemantle, "Perspective: Standard Bank", p. 95.

46. Robins, "One of These BRICS Is Not Like the Other".

47. David Smith, "South Africa: More of a Briquette Than a Bric?", *Guardian*, 24 March 2013, http://www.guardian.co.uk/world/2013/mar/24/south-africa-bric-developing-economy (accessed 25 July 2013).

48. *See* Sven Grimm, "South Africa: BRICS Member and Development Partner in Africa", *China Monitor*, Special Edition: "The BRICS Summit 2013: Is the Road from Durban Leading into Africa?" (Stellenbosch: Centre for Chinese Studies, 2013), p. 38.

49. Graham Allison, "China Doesn't Belong in the BRICS", *The Atlantic*, 26 March 2013, https://www.theatlantic.com/china/archive/2013/03/china-doesnt-belong-in-the-brics/274363/ (accessed 24 July 2017).

50. Fareed Zakaria, "Is India the Broken BRIC?", *CNN*, 21 December 2011, http://globalpublicsquare.blogs.cnn.com/2011/12/21/zakaria-india-as-the-broken-bric (accessed 26 July 2013).

51. Chris Landsberg and Candice Moore, "BRICS, South-South Cooperation, and the Durban Summit: What's In It for South Africa?", *Portuguese Journal of International Affairs* no. 7 (Spring/Summer 2013), p. 10.

52. Data from the ITC, Trade Map. It is worth noting that this data can vary significantly by source and that the ITC's Trade Map tool draws largely on the UN Comtrade Database.

53. Xavier Carim, "South Africa, the EU, and the SADC Group Economic Partnership Agreement: Through the Negotiating Lens", in Montoute and Virk, *The ACP Group and the EU Development Partnership*, pp. 163–164.

54. Data from the ITC, Trade Map. Once again, this data can vary significantly by source; the ITC's Trade Map tool draws largely on the UN Comtrade Database. *See* Alex Vines, "India's Africa Engagement: Prospects for the 2011 India-Africa Forum", Programme Paper no. AFP 2010/01 (London: Chatham House, December 2010), p. 6.

55. Hany Besada, Evren Tok and Kristen Winters, "South Africa in the BRICS: Opportunities, Challenges, and Prospects", *Africa Insight* 42, no. 4 (March 2013), p. 5.

56. Besada, Tok and Winters, "South Africa in the BRICS", p. 5.

57. Ernst & Young, "South Africa: Building BRICS in Africa", March 2011, http://tmagazine.ey.com/wp-content/uploads/2011/04/South-Africa-BRICS.pdf (accessed 26 July 2013).

58. Chantelle Benjamin, "Africa Isn't a Big Bull in China's Shop", *Mail and Guardian*, 21 June 2013, http://mg.co.za/article/2013-06-21-00-africa-isnt-a-big-bull-in-chinas-shop (accessed 26 July 2013).

59. European Commission, Directorate-General for Trade, "European Union, Trade in Goods with South Africa", 17 February 2017, http://trade.ec.europa.eu/doclib/docs/2006/september/tradoc_113447.pdf; and "European Union, Trade in Goods

with China", 16 February 2017, http://trade.ec.europa.eu/doclib/docs/2006/september/tradoc_113366.pdf (both accessed 26 February 2017).

60. Based on data from the ITC, Trade Map. *See* European Commission, Directorate-General for Trade, "European Union, Trade in Goods with India", 16 February 2017, http://trade.ec.europa.eu/doclib/docs/2006/september/tradoc_113390.pdf (accessed 26 February 2017).

61. I make a similar argument in Virk, "The ACP, the EU, and the BRICS", pp. 317–340.

62. *See* Kudrat Virk, "India and South Africa", in David M. Malone, C. Raja Mohan and Srinath Raghavan (eds), *The Oxford Handbook of Indian Foreign Policy* (Oxford: Oxford University Press, 2015), pp. 556–557.

63. Landsberg and Moore, "BRICS, South-South Cooperation, and the Durban Summit", p. 10.

64. The rest of this paragraph draws on Virk, "The ACP, the EU, and the BRICS", pp. 317–340, especially pp. 325–326.

65. European Union, "The Role of BRICS in the Developing World", April 2012, p. 20, http://www.ecologic.eu/4738 (accessed 27 October 2012).

66. Maxi Schoeman, "Of BRICs and Mortar: The Growing Relations Between Africa and the Global South", *International Spectator* 46, no. 1 (2011), pp. 38–39.

67. Africa Research Institute, "Between Extremes: China and Africa", Briefing Note no. 1202 (London, October 2012), http://www.africaresearchinstitute.org/ (accessed 24 October 2012).

68. Tomaso Ferrando, "Brics Grab African Land and Sovereignty", in Bond, *BRICS in Africa*, pp. 30–37.

69. This paragraph draws on Virk, "India and South Africa", p. 557.

70. Courtney Fingar, "Foreign Direct Investment in Africa Surges", *Financial Times*, 19 May 2015, https://www.ft.com/content/79ee41b6-fd84-11e4-b824-00144feabdc0 (accessed 27 February 2017).

71. "South Africa: The Gateway to Africa?", *The Economist*, 2 June 2012, http://www.economist.com/node/21556300 (accessed 26 July 2013).

72. Deloitte, "South Africa: Gateway to Africa … or Simply Being Bypassed?", 13 February 2012, http://pressoffice.mg.co.za/deloitte/PressRelease.php?StoryID=226775 (accessed 26 February 2017).

73. KPMG, *African Emergence: The Rise of the Phoenix*, 2012, http://www.kpmg.com/africa/en/issuesandinsights/articles-publications/pages/african-emergence-the-rise-of-the-phoenix.aspx (accessed 26 July 2013).

74. "South Africa: The Gateway to Africa?"

75. Games, "South Africa as Africa's Gateway", p. 3.

76. This paragraph draws on Virk, "The ACP, the EU, and the BRICS", pp. 317–340, especially pp. 331–332.

77. Games, "South Africa as Africa's Gateway", p. 3.

78. Yun Sun, "Xi and the 6th Forum on China-Africa Cooperation: Major Commitments, But with Questions", *Africa in Focus*, 7 December 2015, https://www.brookings.edu/blog/africa-in-focus/2015/12/07/xi-and-the-6th-forum-on-china-africa-cooperation-major-commitments-but-with-questions/ (accessed 26 February 2017).

79. Dot Keet, "South-South Strategic Bases for Africa to Engage China", in Fantu Cheru and Cyril Obi (eds), *The Rise of China and India in Africa: Challenges, Opportunities, and Critical Interventions* (London and New York: Zed, 2010), p. 22.

80. Africa Research Institute, "Between Extremes".

81. Francis Kornegay, "South Africa and Emerging Powers", in Chris Landsberg and Jo-Ansie van Wyk (eds), *South African Foreign Policy Review*, vol. 1 (Pretoria: Africa Institute of South Africa, 2012), pp. 198–214. *See* Chris Alden and Garth Le Pere, "South Africa in Africa: Bound to Lead?", *Politikon* 36, no. 1 (April 2009), pp. 145–169.

82. Landsberg and Moore, "BRICS, South-South Cooperation, and the Durban Summit", p. 10.

83. Kornegay, "South Africa and Emerging Powers", p. 202.

84. Keynote address by Deputy Minister of International Relations and Cooperation, Ebrahim I. Ebrahim, at the BRICS Roundtable Discussion hosted by the International Marketing Council (IMC) of South Africa and the *Financial Times*, 11 May 2011, http://www.dfa.gov.za/docs/speeches/2011/ebra0511.html (accessed 27 October 2012).

85. This paragraph draws on Virk, "The ACP, the EU, and the BRICS", pp. 317–340, especially p. 332.

86. Michael A. Glosny, "China and the BRICs: A Real (But Limited) Partnership in a Unipolar World", *Polity* 42 (2010), p. 126.

87. The rest of this section is from Kudrat Virk, "The Influence of the BRICS on the UN Security Council", unpublished, 18 October 2012, thereafter incorporated into the Centre for Conflict Resolution (CCR), "South Africa, Africa, and the United Nations' Security Architecture", concept note (Cape Town, December 2012), pp. 5–6, part of which was subsequently published in CCR, *Africa, South Africa, and the United Nations' Security Architecture*, Seminar Report no. 42 (Cape Town, June 2013), pp. 12–13.

88. Francis A. Kornegay, "South Africa's Second Tenure in the UN Security Council: A Discussion Paper", in *South Africa in the UN Security Council 2011–2012: Promoting the African Agenda in a Sea of Multiple Identities and Alliances*, research report (Pretoria: IGD, April 2012), pp. 11–13. *See also* Candice Moore, "BRICS Partnership: A Case of South-South Cooperation? Exploring the Roles of South Africa and Africa", *Global Insight* 99 (September 2012), http://www.igd.org.za/publications/global-insight (accessed 18 October 2012).

89. Kornegay, "South Africa's Second Tenure in the UN Security Council", pp. 20–21.

90. *See also* Lipton, "Are the BRICS Reformers, Revolutionaries, or Counter-Revolutionaries?".

91. Ted Piccone and Emily Alinikoff, "Rising Democracies Take on Russia and China", *National Interest*, 17 February 2012, http://nationalinterest.org/commentary/rising-democracies-take-russia-china-6525 (accessed 18 October 2012).

92. Quoted in Moore, "BRICS Partnership".

93. United Nations General Assembly, *Position Paper of the People's Republic of China*, 67th session, 20 September 2012, http://www.china-un.org/eng/hyyfy/t971887.htm (accessed 18 October 2012).

94. Olivier Serrão, "South Africa in the UN Security Council 2011–2012" (Berlin: Friedrich Ebert Stiftung, Global Policy and Development Department, June 2011), p. 3, http://library.fes.de/pdf-files/iez/08166.pdf (accessed 18 October 2012).

95. Security Council Report, "UN Security Council Elections 2010", Special Research Report no. 3 (New York, 17 September 2010), pp. 4–5, http://www.security councilreport.org (accessed 18 October 2012).

96. Kornegay and Masters, *From BRIC to BRICS*, pp. 32–33.

97. John Siko, *Inside South Africa's Foreign Policy: Diplomacy in Africa from Smuts to Mbeki* (London and New York: I.B.Tauris, 2014), p. 256.

PART VI

CONCLUDING REFLECTIONS

CONCLUSION

Kudrat Virk

This book has sought to provide a comprehensive survey of South Africa's foreign policy since its democratic transition in 1990–1994, covering over two decades of the country's diplomacy in Southern Africa, Africa and beyond under the three presidencies of Nelson Mandela, Thabo Mbeki and Jacob Zuma. Cognisant of the weight of expectations that the "new" South Africa carried, as well as of the simultaneous fluidity generated by the end of the Cold War by 1990, Mandela, in an oft-cited article – published in 1993 – in *Foreign Affairs*, laid out the African National Congress's (ANC) broad vision of post-apartheid foreign policy, not only "to take South Africa into the new world order as a responsible global citizen", but also to enable it to address the devastating socio-economic legacies of apartheid at home.[1] This idealistic vision has since been used, variously and at different times, as a source, a marker and a tool for criticism – often without regard for changes in context[2] – of the actual conduct of post-apartheid South Africa's foreign policy under successive ANC-led governments, while providing it with broad identifiable contours.

This is not to say that across-the-board constancy and consistency could, or even should, have been leitmotifs of the country's diplomacy; that Mbeki and Zuma have not placed their own distinctive stamps on it (see Introduction in this volume); or that idealism has not been blunted by greater pragmatism and more parochial national interests. Quite the contrary. Under Mbeki, for example, there was greater emphasis on, and investment in, conceptualising the "African pillar", building institutions, and pursuing multilateralism; while under Zuma, economic diplomacy in its various guises, from development cooperation to trade and investment, has gained prominence and definition. Rather the suggestion is that Mandela's aspirational vision has continued, for the most part, to serve as a point of reference, both at home as well as abroad, to view and assess the narrative arc of the country's post-apartheid diplomacy. As the momentum generated by South Africa's successful democratic transition has seemed to stutter and stall in recent years, though, the narrative has tended towards disappointment and, at times, an overly narrow focus on its human rights diplomacy, even seeming to overlook the larger sweep of its achievements and challenges since 1994, not to forget its continuing potential as a regional hegemon and pivotal African voice in global governance. Without denying disappointments, including at the loss, to some extent, of a sense of purpose in South African foreign policy, this collection of essays has sought to provide a more balanced, yet critical, assessment, mainly by virtue of taking the long view and drawing into the debate diverse South African and non-South African voices.

The evolution of South Africa's diplomacy in the post-apartheid period has, in large part, been defined by a perennial struggle for an elusive balance between competing principles, and between principles and interests, as well as for effectiveness in the pursuit of its goals. Such striving is not exceptional, but rather a challenge faced, in theory, by nearly every state in international society, that in today's changing world has continued to generate age-old, though no less difficult, dilemmas (for example, human rights versus self-interest) for traditional powers, like the United States (US) and the European Union (EU), as well as for new powers, such as Brazil, India and South Africa.[3] It is the particularities that vary. For South Africa, the challenge of pursuing a values-driven foreign policy has been compounded by various factors including its contested regional hegemony, in terms of both capacity and legitimacy; the long shadow cast by its apartheid-era history and democratic transition, which have – as preceding chapters show – generated varying demands, expectations and perceptions; and, more recently, changes in its external environment, such as the emergence of "new" competitors and the increasing complexity of global governance, that have made it harder for its leadership ambitions to stay anchored ideationally.[4]

Revisiting the Concentric Circles of South Africa's Foreign Policy

The overall record of South Africa's foreign policy, viewed through its four overlapping concentric circles (see Introduction in this volume), has been mixed. As South African scholar Chris Landsberg has pointed out in his chapter, overcoming the socio-economic legacy of apartheid – in particular, reducing poverty and inequality – has formed the domestic epicentre of Tshwane's external relations, from Mandela to Mbeki to Zuma. Yet in the absence of a coherent strategy that moves beyond assertions and assumptions, South African policymakers have struggled to demonstrate convincingly the contribution of foreign policy to improving the lived reality of the country's poor and marginalised majority: South Africa remains among the most unequal societies in the world, with an estimated Gini coefficient of 63.4.[5] The problem, though, runs deeper and has a dual aspect: on the one hand, a key purpose of South Africa's foreign policy is – as Landsberg has noted – to help in addressing domestic needs, but on the other hand, the domestic context is as important for South Africa to have the capacity, as well as legitimacy, to project its influence; to play a leadership role in its region and beyond; and to achieve goals ranging from regional integration to greater global leverage.[6] This finds some credence in South African scholars Chris Saunders and Dawn Nagar's account of the weakness of Tshwane's (Pretoria's) efforts to drive regional economic integration in the Southern African Development Community (SADC), which, as Saunders and Nagar reflect in their joint chapter, has struggled to balance the objectives of region-building and those of domestic socio-economic development. More than two decades on from the end of apartheid, a fundamental challenge for South Africa remains, thus, to transform its domestic socio-economic order, while defining "national interest" in a way that more coherently – and, for ordinary South Africans, more persuasively – links the domestic and other three concentric circles of its diplomacy.[7]

Beyond the material, South Africa's anti-apartheid struggle, negotiated democratic transition and liberal constitutional values have provided it with a relatively strong foundation of "soft power"[8] for a hegemonic role in the region (the second and third concentric circles) and, to a significant extent, allowed it to punch above its weight internationally (the fourth concentric circle). This soft power has found expression not only in its human rights activism, but also in its peacemaking diplomacy.

For example, South Africa played an entrepreneurial role, under Mbeki, in crafting the African Union's (AU) "'responsible sovereignty' regime",[9] and was instrumental in the creation of the International Criminal Court (ICC). But as South African legal analyst Nicole Fritz has argued in her chapter, Tshwane's commitment to upholding human rights has been inconsistent, even disappointing in more recent years, as evidenced in, among other cases, its acquiescence in the dismantling of the SADC Tribunal in 2012 and flagrant disregard, in 2015, of its obligation towards the ICC to arrest Sudanese president Omar al-Bashir.[10] Similarly, its own experience of a successful democratic transition has helped South Africa to carve out an important role in conflict resolution in Africa, based on an approach that has, by and large, favoured the peaceful settlement of disputes under the multilateral aegis of SADC and the AU.[11] Its peacemaking efforts have, as Canadian scholar Devon Curtis has argued in her chapter, achieved limited short-term successes, but been unable to address the root causes of instability and conflict. Even so, a sense remains that South Africa should be able to do better, through greater critical self-awareness and bolder thinking; to strike a balance more in favour of universal freedoms, despite the "genuinely hard choices" that it faces (Fritz), and to create space for debate on "alternative ideas for a more equitable peace" (Curtis). Indeed, its intersecting human rights and peacemaking diplomacies form important planks of South Africa's case for leadership (see also Mashabane in this volume), and addressing their weaknesses needs to be a vital priority for sustaining that case.

Southern Africa and the wider continent thus are, as South African scholar Garth le Pere has noted, "the crucible" for the country's ability to act as a regional hegemon, both effectively and with legitimacy. Yet these spaces – the overlapping second and third concentric circles of its foreign policy – are where South African leadership and ambition have tended to generate, arguably, the most discontent.[12] The end of apartheid was a fundamental break in South Africa's foreign policy. But at the same time, this did not create an entirely blank slate for post-apartheid ANC-led governments. In Southern Africa, in particular, apartheid-era mercantilism and destabilisation policies have left behind a legacy of abiding suspicion and distrust of South African motives (see Sachikonye, and Saunders and Nagar in this volume). This has served, in one sense, as an "antidote" to the soft power of Tshwane's human rights and peacemaking enterprises, impelling it to submerge its leadership and, at times, "hegemonic intent" under the multilateral umbrellas of SADC or the AU, and to prioritise abiding with the collective regional consensus (see, for example, Fritz in this volume).[13] Questions have also continued to be raised about South Africa's African identity, despite the gradually deepening emphasis on, and forceful assertion of the centrality of, an "African agenda" and regional solidarity in its foreign policy.[14] This owes to several factors including the lingering white dominance of South Africa's expansionist corporate sector, often perceived – rightly or wrongly (see Vickers and Cawood in this volume) – as the vanguard of a mercantilist, hegemonic thrust; and the persistence of an attitude of South African exceptionalism (see Introduction in this volume).

This does not mean that the challenges to South Africa's hegemony, or even its consensual and ambivalent nature, are specific to its apartheid history; only that this past casts a long shadow and forms part of the dynamics of regional contestation of that hegemony. There are other obstacles. One, there is the matter of its mixed record of success. Though the framing has varied under Zuma,[15] the prioritisation of Africa forms a notable continuity in the country's post-apartheid foreign policy, with its core focus on the AU, its institutions and, closer to home, SADC. The contributions that South Africa has made to continental initiatives cannot be gainsaid (see Maloka in this volume). However, the African institutional architecture that it has helped to create remains weak (see Introduction in this volume); and, in its own immediate neighbourhood, South Africa has struggled to drive regional economic integration and development through not only SADC, but also the smaller Southern African Customs Union (SACU), within which it is – in the words of British scholar Richard Gibb in this volume – "the undisputed hegemonic power". Two, its hegemony rests on relatively weak building blocks, mainly its bilateral relationships,[16] which have been, at best, weakly institutionalised. This includes its ties with Nigeria and Angola, both among its most important strategic partners on the continent, which have seemed, in large part, to rely for their "health" on the priorities of different governments and the personal chemistry (or its lack thereof) between individual leaders (see Sachikonye, and Adebajo in this volume), rather than a shared understanding of the strategic foundation of the relationship between the partners. Three, South Africa has rivals for influence, including African peers – foremost among them Nigeria and, potentially, Angola – as well as external powers, notably France (old) (see Marchal in this volume) and China (new). For Tshwane, how it manages the dynamics of competition and cooperation with, and among, these players, while managing regional discontent with its leadership, remains a major challenge, one that needs to be addressed if it is to consolidate and retain its hegemony on the continent and its influence outside it.[17]

Within the outermost concentric circle of South Africa's foreign policy – the rest of the world beyond Africa – its leadership role on the continent has been more willingly accepted. The reasons are varied and, to some extent, speculative, seeming to rest in two broad sets of ideas: one set relates to its international rehabilitation (see Liu in this volume), and democratic transition and maturity (see Weissman, and Marchal in this volume); and the other to its relative economic sophistication and weight in its regional cohort (see Virk in this volume). South African scholars Chris Alden and Maxi Schoeman have also argued, beyond the pages of this volume, that the country's membership in institutions such as the Group of 20 (G-20) and the BRICS bloc (Brazil, Russia, India, China and South Africa) has less to do with its actual position in Africa, and more to do with the intersection of an international demand for African representation with South African ambition.[18] Be that as it may, there is little to doubt about the country's desire for global influence, reflected in, among other things, its ambitious early human rights diplomacy under Mandela; courtship of partnership with the Group of Eight (G-8) under Mbeki (see Large in this volume);[19] successful campaign for membership of the then BRIC bloc under Zuma (see Virk in this volume); and ongoing pursuit of permanent membership in the United Nations (UN) Security Council (see Mashabane in this volume). Nor is there any doubt about the prominence it has acquired and the leadership role it has played, since 1994, in forums such as the World Trade Organisation (WTO). Its efforts to promote African concerns and interests in these forums have, to be fair, been earnest and notable (see Mashabane, and Ismail in this volume).

South Africa's global role, though, faces several challenges, not the least of which is that it is based on a perceived capacity to deliver leadership in Africa, which – as the preceding discussion has suggested – is open to question. In addition, the mantle of leadership that Tshwane has sought to bear, and the responsibilities it has assumed in multiple spaces, require resources that the country may not have, given its domestic development challenges and critical skills shortages. South African analyst Sagaren Naidoo in his chapter, for example, points to the gap between the capacities of its armed forces, and the range of roles and responsibilites – domestic as well as external – they have been expected to shoulder (see also Marchal in this volume), one that is, in his view, "largely a consequence of the transitional nature of the post-apartheid state". The country's international obligations also require – to borrow the words of South African diplomat Doc Mashabane in this volume – striking "a delicate balance between alliances such as the BRICS . . ., loose formations like the Group of 20 . . ., and strategic partnerships with the European Union" (see also Ismail, Nkosi and Virk in this volume). This again requires knowledge, skills and resources, backed up further by a clear sense of purpose.

Looking Ahead

Since its successful return to the fold of international society, South Africa has sought to forge a leadership role in Southern Africa and Africa, and in projecting African concerns and interests in the wider international arena. Its re-crafted regional hegemony – in stark contrast to apartheid-era exertion of military and economic "hard power", and "apart-ness" from its own continent – is premised, in large part, on its capacity for, and record of, promoting peace, security and socio-economic development through the use of soft power assets, such as "the power of its example",[20] and its human rights and peacemaking diplomacies; the building of institutions; the management of its bilateral and multilateral partnerships; and strategies to leverage them in different spaces. But there are weaknesses in this foundation, as well as doubts about, and discontent with, the effectiveness and legitimacy of its endeavours. Addressing these is vital if the country is meaningfully to claim the niche that it has sought as an African regional power with global influence. The task is formidable, made all the more so by the continual demands of an unsettled and increasingly complex international context; the fragility of the South African economy; the seeming fragility of aspects of the country's democracy; and, amid recent failures of leadership, a sense that moral purpose is giving way to parochial interests and attitudes.

Whether South Africa can rise to the challenge remains an open question. What is more certain is the effort and investment required, first and foremost, in the strengthening of its knowledge base and policy development capacity. Landsberg (in this volume), in particular, identifies this as a "critical gap", noting the need to achieve greater professionalisation of the country's foreign service. Indeed, that there is often insufficient expertise and experience within the South African government and diplomatic corps – especially with regard to the wider African continent, beyond its own

Southern African sub-region – is an issue raised in several chapters of this volume (see, for example, Nzongola-Ntalaja, Tawfik and Marchal). But in a context of scarce resources and competing priorities, this cannot be the only answer. South African universities, research centres and think tanks remain an under-utilised resource in policymaking processes. This has been the case despite their broadening engagement, since 1994, with government, which has provided access but less in terms of impact.[21] Yet these institutions can often offer not only expertise, but also valuable outside-in perspectives that could stimulate the bold, creative and innovative thinking that South Africa's ambitious foreign policy requires. Such openness rests on greater government receptiveness to criticism, and the willingness of an assured leadership to accept this as a short-term "pain" for larger gain.

In a similar vein, there is a need to consider non-state vectors, including the role of business and civil society actors, and political parties, beyond formal policymaking processes in shaping the prospects of South Africa's regional leadership role. The ubiquitous presence of major South African corporations across sub-Saharan Africa reflects the country's economic weight and reach, but has – as noted earlier – tended to court controversy and criticism in Southern, West, Eastern and Central Africa and, in so doing, shaped negative perceptions of South African hegemony. Yet as South African analysts Brendan Vickers and Richard Cawood have noted in their joint chapter, the roles and impact of South African firms remain weakly understood, and there is untapped potential for greater coordination and synergy between South African state and business actors that could help both achieve their objectives more effectively. In the case of North Africa, where South Africa's corporate presence has lagged behind, Egyptian scholar Rawia Tawfik has similarly noted, in her chapter, the potential of cooperation at the level of civil society to contribute to democratisation and peacebuilding efforts in the region in the wake of the Afro-Arab Spring of 2011. Likewise, the potential role of political parties, in particular the ruling ANC, in South Africa's peacebuilding diplomacy, needs greater attention. In South Sudan, for example, the ANC is co-guarantor – along with Tanzania's ruling Chama Cha Mapinduzi – of a dialogue aimed at promoting unity within the warring Sudan People's Liberation Movement (SPLM) (see Khadiagala in this volume). These various non-state actors have tended, though, as American analyst John Siko has observed elsewhere, to operate "within their boxes", allowing "South Africa's foreign policy ... [to] remain an elite preserve".[22]

South Africa's leadership role and the challenges it faces today require a bolder and more collective endeavour than has hitherto been the case. This, in turn, requires not only more knowledge-based and analytically astute foreign policymaking, but also greater investment by the state, and interest beyond the state, in its prospects. Hegemonic ambition demands nothing less.

Notes

1. Nelson Mandela, "South Africa's Future Foreign Policy", *Foreign Affairs* 72, no. 5 (November/December 1993), pp. 86–87.

2. Sanusha Naidu and Faith Mabera, "South Africa's Foreign Policy Has Been at Sixes and Sevens – Here's Why", *Mail and Guardian*, 10 January 2017, https://mg.co.za/article/2017-01-10-south-africas-foreign-policy-has-been-at-sixes-and-sevens-heres-why (accessed 20 July 2017).

3. On the role of ideas and material interests in foreign policy, for example, *see* Judith Goldstein and Robert O. Keohane (eds), *Ideas and Foreign Policy: Beliefs, Institutions, and Political Change* (Ithaca, NY: Cornell University Press, 1993).

4. Naidu and Mabera, "South Africa's Foreign Policy Has Been at Sixes and Sevens".

5. United Nations Development Programme (UNDP), *Human Development Report 2016: Human Development for Everyone* (New York, 2016), tab. 3, p. 207.

6. Adam Habib, "South Africa's Foreign Policy: Hegemonic Aspirations, Neoliberal Orientations, and Global Transformation", *South African Journal of International Affairs* 16, no. 2 (2009), p. 150. *See* Chris Alden and Garth le Pere, "South Africa in Africa: Bound to Lead?", *Politikon: South African Journal of Political Studies* 36, no. 1 (2009), pp. 145–169.

7. Chris Landsberg, "The Concentric Circles of South Africa's Foreign Policy Under Jacob Zuma", *India Quarterly* 70, no. 2 (2014), pp. 1–20. *See also* Habib, "South Africa's Foreign Policy".

8. The term "soft power" was coined by Joseph S. Nye, to describe the changing nature of power in an interdependent and information-based world. *See* Joseph S. Nye, "Soft Power", *Foreign Policy* no. 80 (1990), pp. 153–171. *See also* Joseph S. Nye, *Bound to Lead: The Changing Nature of American Power* (New York: Basic Books, 1990).

9. Chris Landsberg, "*Pax South Africana* and the Responsibility to Protect", *Global Responsibility to Protect* 2, no. 4 (2010), pp. 436–437.

10. In July 2017, a ruling by the Hague-based International Criminal Court (ICC) confirmed that South Africa had failed in its obligations to the ICC by not arresting Sudanese president Omar al-Bashir while he was in the country in June 2015.

11. South Africa's controversial military intervention in Lesotho (1998) and contribution to the United Nations-authorised Force Intervention Brigade in the Democratic Republic of the Congo (since 2013) are notable exceptions.

12. Garth le Pere, "Critical Themes in South Africa's Foreign Policy: An Overview", *Strategic Review for Southern Africa* 36, no. 2 (2014), p. 45.

13. Chris Alden and Maxi Schoeman, "South Africa's Symbolic Hegemony in Africa", *International Politics* 52, no. 2 (2015), p. 241.
14. This is one of several identities that South Africa tries, or has tried, to inhabit. Others might include "human rights champion", "peacemaker", "emerging power" and "bridge-builder", but its "African-ness" has, arguably, been one of the most contentious in its own region.
15. *See* Landsberg, "The Concentric Circles of South Africa's Foreign Policy Under Jacob Zuma", especially pp. 5–7.
16. On this point in relation to the Southern African Development Community, in particular, *see also* Centre for Conflict Resolution (CCR), *Governance and Security Challenges in Post-Apartheid Southern Africa*, research report (Cape Town, September 2013).
17. Alden and Schoeman, "South Africa's Symbolic Hegemony in Africa", especially pp. 251–252.
18. Alden and Schoeman, "South Africa's Symbolic Hegemony in Africa".
19. Alden and Schoeman, "South Africa's Symbolic Hegemony in Africa".
20. *Building a Better World: The Diplomacy of Ubuntu*, White Paper on South Africa's Foreign Policy, 13 May 2011, p. 36.
21. John Siko, *Inside South Africa's Foreign Policy: Diplomacy in Africa from Smuts to Mbeki* (London and New York: I.B.Tauris, 2014), pp. 255–256, 260–261.
22. Siko, *Inside South Africa's Foreign Policy*, p. 262.

EPILOGUE

Jack Spence

This collection of essays on South Africa's foreign policy deserves a wide readership. The editors have assembled a diverse range of scholars who have examined the current pattern of the country's foreign relations in impressive and convincing detail; indeed, the structure of the work covers both the geographical spread of the country's global interests and commitments, together with an analysis of institutional roles in key regional and international organisations. The structure of the country's diplomatic representation abroad is outlined, offering in-depth studies of political accreditation – in large and powerful, small and weak states alike.

The domestic constraints on foreign policy are well explained, together with helpful chapters on, among other things, defence policy, peacemaking in Africa, South Africa's human rights record and its corporate expansion into the rest of Africa.

However, this is far more than a discreet collection of individual contributions. The editor's introduction to this volume, examining the domestic boundaries of South Africa's foreign policy, provides a valuable theoretical context, offering a rubric for understanding South Africa's overall performance in foreign policy and giving form, relevance and substance to the collection as a whole. I know of no work that so successfully examines the scope of the country's diplomatic landscape, the incentives and constraints governing policy and the aspirations of leaders to give their country a significant and productive role in international society.

What follows is in the nature of a friendly critique, taking the argument on some issues a stage further – an indication of the impact that the work has made on one solitary reader. Space will not permit a detailed exegesis on each section or chapter; these remarks are simply reflections on a powerful work of scholarship that – one hopes – will stimulate debate among scholars, the interested public, and diplomatic cadets and their superiors with a sophisticated understanding of how their country has fared in world politics since the emergence of the new South Africa and – more important – its prospects for the future in an uncertain and complex world.

In a famous article in *Foreign Affairs* in 1993, Nelson Mandela – South Africa's then president-in-waiting – claimed that the protection and assertion of human rights would be "the light that guides our foreign policy".[1] In the early years of the new democratic government, expectations were high at home and abroad that South Africa, blessed with the advantage of a "rectitude base" of democratic governance and Mandela's iconic leadership, would become a major player advancing the cause of human rights at the United Nations (UN) and in other international and regional organisations.

The hope was that South Africa might buck the "realist" pressures of global politics and espouse "liberal" causes consistent with the ruling African National Congress (ANC) party's history as a staunch opponent of racism and global inequalities between peoples and states, becoming in the process a fervent supporter of "humanitarian intervention" whenever and wherever this would promote welfare, poverty reduction and the principles and practice of democratic governance.

Another driver of foreign policy was the assumption that maintaining and indeed increasing trade and investment links with Western countries was essential to promoting growth and prosperity, and to help repair the damage that apartheid had inflicted on South Africa's impoverished black majority. Certainly Mandela's aspiration for a "liberal" foreign policy was reflected in the government's engagement in a variety of peacekeeping and peacebuilding initiatives in Angola, Burundi, Mozambique and Sudan and South Sudan, as described in detail in this book.

Running parallel with these policies – most notably during Thabo Mbeki's presidency, between 1999 and 2008 – was a commitment to find "African solutions to African problems" through the country's role in the African Union (AU), the Southern African Development Community (SADC) and the Non-Aligned Movement (NAM). This strategy was – at least in part – motivated by a deeply felt ambition to avoid too heavy a dependence on rich Northern countries for trade and investment. This attitude, in part, arose from a visceral hostility to the perceived excessive influence of Western capitalism – its theory and practice – on the structure and processes of international relations. And in this context, we should also note the role and influence of the South African Communist Party (SACP): a longtime ally of the African National Congress. Appearing to be the West's poodle was therefore unacceptable – certainly to both communists and nationalists within the movement.

As the contributors to this volume indicate, these sometimes conflicting objectives of foreign policy had somehow to be reconciled. Indeed, a complex balancing act was required to satisfy the various constituencies with an interest in foreign policy: liberals, realists, nationalists, communists, the business community, intellectuals, think tanks and a critical media: all had to be placated. This is not always easy, as Mandela himself found, to his cost, when African governments took strong exception to his critical outburst against the Nigerian government's execution of Ken Saro-Wiwa and his eight fellow environmental campaigners in November 1995. South Africa's military intervention in Lesotho in 1998 also ended in disaster, demonstrating yet again the difficulty of reconciling a Western-style concern for human rights and necessitating compromises with the traditional African commitment to the twin principles of domestic jurisdiction and non-interference.

On the other hand, realism surfaced in South Africa's foreign policy, as Mandela and his successors felt obliged to maintain ties of gratitude to, for example, Libya and Algeria, for their help in the anti-apartheid struggle despite their unimpressive human rights record. And this was equally true of decisions to recognise the People's Republic of China in preference to Taiwan in January 1998. In all of these cases, principle clashed with pragmatism, and the latter won resounding victories.

With respect to the human rights issue, a 2016 study by South African scholar Suzanne Graham offers an excellent commentary on South Africa's role at the United Nations and, in particular, its stand on human rights, arms control and the reform of the UN.[2] She demonstrates, with painstaking statistical analysis, how the country's voting record on human rights, for example, between 1994 and 2014, has been mixed. The promotion of human rights is not the priority it once was, despite the South African government's assurances to the contrary. What is most evident is Tshwane's (Pretoria) determination not to be lost in the crowd and to take, in its own words, "principled decisions when voting" – but what principles exactly? South Africa's repeated commitment to the promotion of human rights and democracy meant nothing when it failed to do just that over cases such as Myanmar, Sudan, Zimbabwe, Uzbekistan and Belarus. This reflects inconsistency in South Africa's human rights-driven foreign policy.

This finding should not surprise us: after all, states that profess support for the maintenance – indeed, effective diffusion – of human rights across the globe, inevitably find themselves caught in a clash of "liberal" principles, and "realist" and other pressing claims of national interest that surface, especially with respect to economic benefits (it might be argued that Britain selling arms to Saudi Arabia also represents such an example). In practice, decisions rarely involve a simple choice between good and bad courses of action, but rather choosing between evils – the trick being to choose the lesser one. Or so the realist argues. Thus, as the archetypal American realist Hans Morgenthau opined: during the civil war in the United States (US) in the 1860s, Abraham Lincoln – the great American liberal president – recognised that he had to put "saving the Union" as his first priority above freeing the slaves. In other words, his private wish in favour of freedom for slaves had to take second place to his public commitment as president of the country to save the Union. (Incidentally, what this interesting example demonstrates is that even hard-nosed realism can demonstrate a degree of moral sensitivity.)

Of course, in this context, some states make a virtue out of necessity: the Scandinavian quartet (Sweden, Denmark, Norway and Finland), Canada, Switzerland and the Papacy have all carved out a niche in international society enabling them to enjoy a high degree of legitimacy as mediators, neutral go-betweens using "good offices" to bring warring combatants to the conference table: in effect, "knocking heads together". This role, particularly, has been successful in many cases, not least paradoxically because these governments lacked resources and capability to engage in coercive diplomacy. Indeed, they often had to rely on "soft power" to exert influence on warring parties. These governments are, in effect, agents of conflict resolution, but again, they set themselves limited, achievable goals rather than seek influence in a wider global society. And in this enterprise, they often combine goodwill with neutrality and diplomatic skill. These niche players thus have the advantage of a "rectitude base": a reputation, second to none, for democratic governance, due respect for human rights at home and effective economic performance.

By contrast, the South African government has always had aspirations to be a "mover and shaker" on wider global issues, and to this end – after persistent lobbying – was invited to become a member of the BRIC

(Brazil, Russia, India and China) grouping of states in 2010. This outcome was a "realist" calculation on the part of South African policymakers, but we should note the incisive words of South African academic R.W. Johnson in his 2015 book *How Long Will South Africa Survive?*:

> South Africa thus entered Brics in a state of complete naivety, apparently unaware that each of its members had its own reasons for joining ... which had nothing to do with developing Africa, let alone promoting South Africa's ambitions to act as the midwife of such development, to be Africa's representative on the UN Security Council ... The Alliance is peculiarly ideological. South Africa does little trade with Russia, while the other three Brics members are all major trade competitors.[3]

Again a debatable judgement, but one worth taking seriously.

At best, South Africa is a "middle power" as compared with the great-power claims of its partners. Thus its very presence, influence and resource base seem disproportionate in comparison with the advantages enjoyed by its BRICS colleagues. Indeed, one can only conclude that South Africa regards membership in the grouping as giving its government status and influence in global politics; that association with more powerful BRICS will have a "spill-over" effect, with South Africa basking in the reflected glory of the group's achievements. Yet Mandela's aspiration for his country to be a global human rights standard-bearer looks forlorn, given the very different perceptions that govern the policies of South Africa's partners with respect to human rights and other issues.

And it could be argued that a decisive and continuing impact by the BRICS will not be easily achieved. First, the group lacks the cohesion, as well as the multilateral and mutual commitment, of an orthodox military alliance as a means of providing and maintaining security in the face of "new" global threats such as terrorism, international crime, failing and collapsing states, climate change, nuclear proliferation, "states of concern" and the prevalence of civil war. Several of these threats require, among other things, a highly sophisticated capacity for intelligence-sharing by like-minded states. Is this likely, indeed possible, with a loose grouping such as the BRICS? And what contribution, if any, could South Africa make in this context?

Second, all five BRICS have major domestic preoccupations. All have to cope with population growth, massive job creation and a crucial need to raise living standards in line with popular expectations. These commitments must set limits to what can be done by way of maximising and sustaining international pressure for major institutional reform both at home and abroad. Indeed, could the BRICS countries collaborate to promote a sanctions programme if required to push the case for change in international forums? This – to my mind – would be a Herculean task for governments hard-pressed with multiple policy commitments. And in this context, it will be difficult, if not impossible, to organise a BRICS-wide trading regime governed by diplomatic negotiation through a bureaucratic structure capable of operating across several continents. We should also bear in mind the great variation in the political and social culture of the five BRICS. Some approximation here is surely essential, as the example of the history and development of the European Union (EU) amply demonstrates.

Third, the international system is undergoing profound changes. Much will depend on the way in which China and the United States relate to each other in the coming decades. India and Russia will also seek to increase their influence both within their respective regions and farther abroad. We may well see the emergence of a new balance of power, with the four major BRICS constituting alternative poles in that balance, but requiring subtle diplomacy to maintain a reasonable semblance of international order. Oh, for a Bismarck or a Talleyrand!

What contribution, if any, South Africa will make to this complex structure is open to question. No one doubts its capacity to play a regional hegemonic role. But does it have the capacity to play a role comparable to the global ambitions of its BRICS partners? Indeed, in the event of competing claims for support from rival BRICS states at odds with each other on key global issues, South Africa could find itself with difficult choices to make. Certainly, its electorate may well come to feel that an excessive concern with grandiose foreign policy ambitions is no substitute for a failure to make significant progress on economic and social issues at home.

Electoral losses in South Africa's August 2016 local government elections in three major urban areas – Johannesburg, Tshwane-Pretoria and Port Elizabeth – together with the ANC's total vote falling below 60 per cent, would seem to confirm the priority of domestic concerns over foreign policy achievements for the great bulk of the electorate. Trying to be one of the "big beasts" of the BRICS constellation may well be beyond South Africa's political and diplomatic prowess, hampered as it is by the declining reputation of President Jacob Zuma and clear evidence of corruption in the public sector. It does seem reasonable to conclude that, on wider global issues, South Africa will remain a supplicant for development aid and economic assistance rather than a major player, unlike its weightier BRICS partners. This, I appreciate, is also debatable.

Finally, how will the rest of Africa react to South Africa's grandiose ambitions – with envy, resentment, or in the last analysis, downright hostility? Watch this space. Whatever happens, realism – however misguided – reigns supreme.

Some Personal Observations: Present Indicative, Future Uncertain

These tentative conclusions are offered by way of commentary on the thrust of this impressive volume's argument. South African foreign policy is a scholarly work in progress of continuing interest to both academe and the world of practitioners. It would be a mistake to believe that the new South African government elected in 1994 had the advantage of an entirely "clean slate" in both domestic and international affairs. Clearly, it had an ambivalent but nonetheless equally important inheritance of past practice – notably apartheid in all its forms – profound popular deprivation and discontent, enormous expectation of radical change at home and an honourable and effective role abroad.

That inheritance, at a domestic level, included a tradition of strong statehood; parliamentary government (admittedly racially exclusive in membership); persistent, if precarious, acknowledgement of the rule of law; and a noisy, boisterous civil society. The new government was concerned at the very least to frame a proactive foreign policy, one no longer required to defend apartheid in international forums and states the world over.

To this extent then, a "clean slate" rather than a "mirror" reflected in style and context was achievable. And what this book does well is to demonstrate with skill and conviction the strengths and weaknesses that inevitably attend the making of foreign policy – past and present – and the vital role that leadership plays: for good or for ill.

Notes

1. Nelson Mandela, "The New South Africa's Foreign Policy", *Foreign Affairs* 72, no. 5 (1993), p. 86.
2. Suzanne Graham, *Democratic South Africa's Foreign Policy: Voting Behaviour in the United Nations* (London: Palgrave Macmillan, 2016).
3. R.W. Johnson, *How Long Will South Africa Survive? The Looming Crisis* (Johannesburg and Cape Town: Jonathan Ball, 2015), pp. 199–200.

INDEX

References to tables are in **bold**.